THE CORRESPONDENCE

OF

JONATHAN SWIFT, D.D.

VOL. IV

LONDON : G. BELL AND SONS, LTD.
PORTUGAL STREET, KINGSWAY, W.C.
CAMBRIDGE : DEIGHTON, BELL & CO.
NEW YORK : THE MACMILLAN CO.
BOMBAY: A. H. WHEELER & CO.

THE CORRESPONDENCE

OF

JONATHAN SWIFT, D.D.

EDITED BY

F. ELRINGTON BALL

HONORARY LITT.D., DUBLIN

WITH AN INTRODUCTION BY

THE RIGHT REV. J. H. BERNARD, D.D.

BISHOP OF OSSORY, FERNS AND LEIGHLIN

VOL. IV

LONDON

G. BELL AND SONS, LTD.

1913

CHISWICK PRESS: CHARLES WHITTINGHAM AND CO.
TOOKS COURT, CHANCERY LANE, LONDON.

CONTENTS

LETTERS

CONTENTS

CONTENTS

PAGE

CONTENTS

PAGE

CONTENTS

PAGE

CONTENTS

CONTENTS

CONTENTS

SUPPLEMENTAL LETTERS

APPENDIXES

LIST OF ILLUSTRATIONS

CORRESPONDENCE OF JONATHAN SWIFT

DCLXXXV. [*Sheridan.*]

SWIFT TO LORD CARTERET

January 18, 1727-8.

MY LORD,[1]

I WAS informed that your Excellency having referred to the University here for some regulations of his Majesty's benefaction for Professors, they have, in their answer, insinuated as if they thought it best, that the several professorships should be limited to their Fellows, and to be held only as they continue to be so.[2] I need not inform

---

[1] After a residence in England of eighteen months, Carteret had returned to Ireland in November to open the Irish Parliament. Swift's dissatisfaction with him had not abated in the preceding year, and arose, as has been surmised, from the neglect to provide preferment for Delany (*supra*, vol. iii, p. 321). Shortly before Swift's last visit to England the precentorship of Christ Church Cathedral in Dublin had fallen to the gift of the Crown, but Delany had been again passed over, and a Huguenot, a member of the Saurin family, had been appointed. When calling upon Stratford (*supra*, vol. iii, p. 386, n. 2) Swift had enlarged on the subject and had made a bitter attack upon Carteret. According to his account, Carteret, who had been introduced at his own desire to Delany and frequently visited him at his house, promised Delany any preferment in his gift, but told him, when the one which he most desired fell vacant, that he was ineligible owing to his politics, and promoted a man whose only claim was a recommendation from the Duchess of Kendal (" Portland Manuscripts," vii, 447). But this incident was now forgotten, for two days before this letter was written, Delany had been given the chancellorship of Christ Church Cathedral.

[2] The reference is to the foundation, under the trusts of the will of Erasmus Smith, of professorships of Natural and Experimental Philosophy and Oratory and History in Dublin University. The latter chair

IV   B

your Excellency how contrary such a practice is to that of all the Universities in Europe. Your Excellency well knows how many learned men, of the two last ages, have been invited by Princes to be professors in some art or science for which they were renowned; and that the like rule has been followed in Oxford and Cambridge. I hope your Excellency will show no regard to so narrow and partial an opinion, which can only tend to mend fellowships and spoil professorships; although I should be sorry that any Fellow should be thought incapable on that account, when otherwise qualified, and I should be glad that any person, whose education has been in this University, should be preferred before another upon equal deservings. But that must be left to those who shall be your Excellency's successors, who may not always be great clerks, and I wish you could in some measure provide against having this benefaction made a perquisite of humour or favour. Whoever is preferred to a bishopric, or to such a preferment as shall hinder him from residing within a certain distance of this town, should be obliged to resign his professorship.

As long as you are governor here, I shall always expect the liberty of telling you my thoughts, and I hope you will consider them, until you find I grow impertinent, or have some bias of my own. If I had not been confined to my chamber by the continuance of my unconversable disorder, I would have exchanged your trouble of reading for that of hearing. I am, etc.

I desire to present my most humble respects to my Lady Carteret. Your friend Walpole has lately done one of the cruelest actions that ever I knew, even in a Minister of State, these thirty years past, which if the Queen hath not intelligence of, may my right hand forget its cunning.[1]

was held by Delany, who resigned then his fellowship, and would have lost his professorship if the proposed regulations had come into force.

[1] Swift is alluding to the indignity done Gay in offering him the office of a gentleman-usher, which he attributed to Walpole's misrepresentations of his friend (*supra*, vol. iii, p. 431).

DCLXXXVI. [*Elwin.*[1]]

Alexander Pope to Swift

January, 1727-8.

Dear Sir,

I HAVE a mind to be in the spleen and quarrel with half the accidents of my life, they have so severally and successively hindered me from writing to you.[2] First, a continuation of such very ill-health, that I cared not to give you such an account as from your friendship would have been so uneasy to you, and which almost disabled me, indeed, from giving it by attacking me in that part which only qualifies one to write. Then I was advised to a journey which gave me as sore an ailment at the other end, and was no sooner crawled home, but I found my mother at the gates of death. We did not for two days expect her life, and in that day of trouble I really thought of flying to you, in my anguish, if it had pleased God to have taken her from me. She is still very weak, but we think in a fair way, if there can be such a thing at her age, of recovery. Pray do your utmost to preserve the friend that I shall have left, against that loss arrives, which cannot be far off.[3] Dr. Delany gave me a pleasure, which I hope was not ill-grounded, in saying, since I heard from you, that your deafness was removed.[4] The season here is very sickly, and all honest men will be dead, or in danger, by the meeting of our House.[5] I have not seen Lords Bolingbroke, Bathurst, nor the Doctor,[6] nor Lewis, nor Gay, nor anybody above once since you writ last—Lord Bolingbroke not these three months. Naming Lewis, I should tell you that I have ten times spoken to Gay to give him the note to

[1] By permission of Mr. John Murray. *Supra,* vol. iii, p. 148, n. 1.
[2] This letter is a reply to the one from Swift dated November 23 (*supra,* vol. iii, p. 432).
[3] At that time Swift was also weighed down with anxiety about Stella, which terminated in her death on the 28th of that month. In Appendix I I have collected any information that I have found in the course of my researches with regard to her life.
[4] Delany had been in England in 1726 or 1727 at the same time as Swift, and had then been introduced no doubt by him to Pope.
[5] The British Parliament assembled on the 26th of that month.
[6] *I.e.,* Arbuthnot.

send to Motte,¹ and he was within this week so careless as
not to have done it. I will take it myself at my next going
to town, and see Mr. Lewis write about it. The third
volume of the Miscellanies is coming out post now, in
which I have inserted the treatise περὶ βάθους.² I have entirely
methodized, and in a manner written it all. The Doctor
grew quite indolent in it, for something newer, I know not
what. It will be a very instructive piece. I want to see the
journals of your travels from Holyhead, which Mr. Sheridan
seems highly delighted with.³ And it grieves me to the soul
that I cannot send you my *chef d'œuvre*, the poem of
Dulness, which, after I am dead and gone, will be printed
with a large commentary, and lettered on the back, Pope's
Dulness.⁴ I send you, however, what most nearly relates
to yourself, the inscription to it, which you must consider,
reconsider, criticize, hypercriticize, and consult about with
Sheridan, Delany, and all the *literati* of the kingdom,—I
mean, to render it less unworthy of you.

INCIPIT PROPOSITIO.

Books and the man I sing, &c.

INSCRIPTIO.

And thou! whose sense, whose humour, and whose rage,
At once can teach, delight, and lash the age,
Whether thou choose Cervantes' serious air,
Or laugh and shake in Rab'lais' easy chair,
Praise courts, and monarchs, or extol mankind,
Or thy grieved country's copper chains unbind;

---

¹ Although he was now in direct correspondence with Motte (*supra*,
vol. iii, p. 438) Swift had probably left the financial arrangements in
Lewis's hands.

² *Supra*, vol. iii, p. 440.   ³ *Supra*, vol. iii, p. 425.

⁴ In the opinion of Mr. Courthope ("Works of Pope," v, 212)
the conception of the "Dunciad" had been formed by Pope as far back
as 1720, and it was to an early version of it that he referred when
writing to Swift in the autumn of 1725 (*supra*, vol. iii, p. 281). At that
time Swift was not very enthusiastic about the idea, but, as Mr. Courthope believes, saved the original draft from the flames when he and
Pope were discussing the compilation of the Miscellanies. From statements made by both Swift and Pope it is at least certain that the
"Dunciad" in its final form began to be written in the summer of
1727 when Swift was ill at Twickenham, and from Pope's letter in the
autumn of that year that Swift was aware of the fact before he left
England (*supra*, vol. iii, p. 427).

> Attend whatever title please thine ear,
> Dean, Drapier, Bickerstaff, or Gulliver.
> From thy Boeotia, lo! the fog retires,
> Yet grieve not thou at what our Isle acquires;
> Here dulness reigns, with mighty wings outspread,
> And brings the true Saturnian age of lead, etc.[1]

John Gay's opera is just on the point of delivery.[2] It may be called, considering its subject, a jail-delivery. Mr. Congreve, with whom I have commemorated you, is anxious as to its success, and so am I. Whether it succeeds or not, it will make a great noise, but whether of claps or hisses I know not. At worst, it is in its own nature a thing which he can lose no reputation by, as he lays none upon it.

Mrs. Patty is very grateful for your memory of her, but not a jot the wiser for another winter. It is hard time should wrinkle faces and not ripen heads. But she is a very honest woman, and deserves to be whipped. To make her wise is more than you can do, but it is in your power by writing to her once in your life to make her proud, which is the best supplement for want of wisdom.

Courts I see not, courtiers I know not, Kings I adore not, Queens I compliment not, so am never like to be in fashion nor in dependence. I heartily join with you in pitying our poor lady for her unhappiness,[3] and should only

---

[1] Even after that time the "Dunciad" underwent extensive revision as the final form of these few lines shows:

> "The mighty mother, and her son, who brings
> The Smithfield muses to the ear of Kings,
> I sing.
>
> .　.　.　.　.　.　.
>
> O thou! whatever title please thine ear,
> Dean, Drapier, Bickerstaff, or Gulliver!
> Whether thou choose Cervantes' serious air,
> Or laugh and shake in Rabelais' easy chair,
> Or praise the court, or magnify mankind,
> Or thy grieved country's copper chains unbind;
> From thy Boeotia though her power retires
> Mourn not, my Swift, at aught our realm acquires.
> Here pleased behold her mighty wings outspread
> To hatch a new Saturnian age of lead."

[2] The "Beggar's Opera" was acted for the first time on the 29th of that month.

[3] *I.e.*, Mrs. Howard. It seems possible that there was a reference to her relations with her husband in Swift's letter to Pope which has been omitted (*infra*, p. 15).

pity her more if she had more of what we call Court happiness. I have seen her very seldom. I had lately many compliments to you from Mr. Morice, etc.[1] Pray make mine to all you think worth remembering. But I will not exclude Messrs. Delany, Sheridan, and Stopford, the latter of whom treats me the most kindly by never writing to me, which proves he thinks himself, as he is, secure of my remembrance. I wish I could make Dr. Delany and Mr. Sheridan so uneasy by my not writing to them, as to bring them hither the sooner. As for yourself, you cannot be absent, go where you will. Do you but keep well and live, and if I keep well and live, we must meet. Adieu.

To mortify you, I acquaint you that I am a hundred pounds a year richer than when you was here, and I owe it to no great man; and I believe I am in as good health as you; and my Lord Oxford has given me a great gold cup and salver, which quite eclipses your silver ones:[2]

> micat inter omnes
> *Harlaeum* sidus, velut inter ignes
> Luna minores.[3]

Send me an inscription to grave at the bottom of it. I have also a fine seal of Plato, with which I will not seal this letter.

DCLXXXVII. [*Original.*[4]]

SWIFT TO BENJAMIN MOTTE

Dublin, *February*, 1727-8.

SIR,

MR. JACKSON, who gives you this, goes to London upon some business.[5] He is a perfect stranger, and will have need of those good offices that strangers want; he is an

---

[1] Morice was the son-in-law of Bishop Atterbury, whose compliments are guardedly conveyed in the *et cetera*.

[2] In his acknowledgement of the gift Pope gracefully proposed to inscribe on the cup: "This is the least thing Alexander Pope owed to Edward, Earl of Oxford."

[3] Hor. "Od.," i, 12, 47.

[4] In the Forster Collection. The letter is printed in the "Gentleman's Magazine," xliii, 152.

[5] It was probably Dan Jackson's brother, the vicar of Santry (*supra*, vol. iii, p. 11, n. 1) who was the bearer of this letter.

honest worthy clergyman, and friend of mine; I therefore
desire you will give him what assistance and information
you can.

I have been looking over my papers to s[ee] if anything
could be fo[und in the hou]se fit to add to that volume,[1]
but[great]numbers of my p[oems have] been so [imp]ounded
by certain accidents, that I co[uld only find those I sen]d
here enclosed, two of which Mr. Pope already h[as seen.
He sent back the]se because they were translations, which
indeed they are not, and therefore I suppose he did not
approve them; and in such a case I would by no means
have them printed, because that would be a trick fitter for
those who have no regard but to profit. I wrote to you a
long letter some time ago wherein I fairly told you how that
affair stood, and likewise gave you my opinion as well as I
was able, and as you desired, with relation to Gulliver.[2]

I have been these ten weeks confined by my old disorders of deafness and giddiness by two or three relapses;
though I have got a remedy which cured me twice, but
obliges me to avoid all cold. If I have any confirmed health
I may probably be in London by the end of summer, where
I shall settle matters relating to those papers that I have
formerly spoke to you about, and some of which you have
seen.[3]

Your very humble servant,

J. S.

I send you likewise a little trifle for a prose volume,
which Ben[4] printed, but you could not find a copy. The
enclosed verses must be shown to Mr. Pope and Mr. Gay,
[and] not published without their approbation.

---

[1] *I.e.*, the third volume of the " Miscellanies." It had evidently been
represented to Swift as a reason for the delay in its appearance that
there was not sufficient material, but Mr. Courthope believes that
Pope did not wish the βάθους to be published until the " Dunciad " was
ready to be brought out as retaliation for the attacks which the former
essay was certain to arouse (Pope's " Works," v, 213).

[2] *Supra*, vol. iii, p. 438.

[3] The last sentence is only partly preserved: " I hope you . . . my
service to Mr. . . . and . . ."

[4] *I.e.*, Ben Tooke.

DCLXXXVIII. [*Elwin.*]

VISCOUNT BOLINGBROKE AND ALEXANDER POPE TO SWIFT

February [15], 1727-8.

BOLINGBROKE

POPE charges himself with this letter; he has been here two days, he is now hurrying to London, he will hurry back to Twickenham in two days more, and before the end of the week he will be, for aught I know, at Dublin. In the mean time his Dulness grows and flourishes as if he was there already. It will indeed be a noble work; the many will stare at it, the few will smile, and all his patrons, from Bickerstaff to Gulliver, will rejoice to see themselves adorned in that immortal piece.

I hear that you have had some return of your illness, which carried you so suddenly from us, if indeed it was your own illness which made you in such haste to be at Dublin. Dear Swift, take care of your health, I will give you a receipt for it, *à la Montaigne*, or, which is better, *à la Bruyère. Nourrisser bien vôtre corps, ne le fatiguer jamais: laisser rouiller l'esprit, meuble inutil, voire outil dangereux: laisser sonner vos cloches le matin pour éveiller les chanoines, et pour faire dormir le doyen d'un sommeil doux et profond, quy lui procure de beaux songes: lever vous tard, et aller à l'eglise, pour vous faire payer d'avoir bien dormi et bien dejeune.*[1]

As to myself, a person about whom I concern myself very little, I must say a word or two out of complaisance to you. I am in my farm, and here I shoot strong and tenacious roots: I have caught hold of the earth, to use a gardener's phrase, and neither my enemies nor my friends will find it an easy matter to transplant me again. Adieu, let me hear from you, at least of you. I love you for a thousand things, for none more than for the just esteem and love which you have for all the sons of Adam.

---

[1] It has been suggested that the receipt was inspired by Boileau's "Lutrin."

POPE

According to Lord Bolingbroke's account I shall be at Dublin in three days. I cannot help adding a word, to desire you to expect my soul there with you by that time, but as for the jade of a body that is tacked to it, I fear there will be no dragging it after. I assure you I have few friends here to detain me, and no powerful one at Court absolutely to forbid my journey. I am told the gynocracy [1] are of opinion, that they want no better writers than Cibber,[2] and the British Journalist;[3] so that we may live at quiet, and apply ourselves to our more abstruse studies. The only courtiers I know, or have the honour to call my friends, are John Gay and Mr. Bowry; the former is at present so employed in the elevated airs of his opera, and the latter in the exaltation of his high dignity, that of her Majesty's waterman,[4] that I can scarce obtain a categorical answer from either to anything I say to them. But the opera succeeds extremely, to yours and my extreme satisfaction, of which he promises this post to give you a full account. I have been in a worse condition of health than ever, and think my immortality is very near out of my enjoyment: so it must be in you, and in posterity, to make me what amends you can for dying young. Adieu. While I am, I am yours. Pray love me, and take care of yourself.

---

[1] *I.e.*, Queen Caroline and her ladies-in-waiting.

[2]   " Great Cibber sate: the proud Parnassian sneer,
            The conscious simper, and the jealous leer
            Mix on his look: All eyes direct their rays
            On him, and crowds turn Coxcombs as they gaze."

[3] One of the writers in Walpole's pay, and supposed to have been William Arnall, whom Peter Wentworth describes as "a shamby attorney" of no great courage ("Wentworth Papers," p. 465).

            " No crab more active in the dirty dance,
            Downward to climb and backward to advance."

[4] He was evidently the Queen's waterman as well as Pope's (*supra*, vol. iii, p. 348).

DCLXXXIX. [*Original.*[1]]

JOHN GAY TO SWIFT

Whitehall, *February* 15, 1727-8.

DEAR SIR,

I HAVE deferred writing to you from time to time, till I could give you an account of the Beggar's Opera. It is acted at the playhouse in Lincoln's Inn Fields with such success, that the playhouse hath been crowded every night. To-night is the fifteenth time of acting, and it is thought it will run a fortnight longer. I have ordered Motte to send the play to you the first opportunity. I made no interest either for approbation or money, nor hath anybody been pressed to take tickets for my benefit: notwithstanding which, I think I shall make an addition to my fortune of between six and seven hundred pounds. I know this account will give you pleasure, as I have pushed through this precarious affair without servility or flattery.

As to any favours from great men, I am in the same state you left me; but I am a great deal happier, as I have expectations. The Duchess of Queensberry hath signalized her friendship to me upon this occasion in such a conspicuous manner that I hope, for her sake, you will take care to put your fork to all its proper uses, and suffer nobody for the future to put their knives in their mouths.[2] Lord Cobham says that I should have printed it in Italian over against the English, that the ladies might have understood what they read.[3] The outlandish, as they now call it, opera has been so thin of late that some have called that the Beggar's Opera, and if the run continues, I fear I shall have remonstrances drawn up against me by the Royal

---

[1] In the British Museum. See Preface.

[2] As appears from his reply Swift had known the Duchess of Queensberry, who was a daughter of his friend the fourth Earl of Clarendon, when a child, but had not seen her since her marriage to the Duke of Queensberry, who was the third duke of his line. The fair lady's parentage was a subject of gossip, and her likeness to Lord Carleton did not escape the scandal-mongers of her time ("Complete Peerage," vi, 311). For his lapse of good manners Swift blamed two-pronged forks and want of consistency in the sauce (*infra*, Letters DCCXLVII, DCCLVII).

[3] A sarcasm on the rage which then prevailed in England for the Italian opera.

Academy of Music.[1] As none of us have heard from you of late, every one of us are in concern about your health: I beg we may hear from you soon. By my constant attendance on this affair I have almost worried myself into an ill state of health, but I intend, in five or six days, to go to our country seat at Twickenham for a little air. Mr. Pope is very seldom in town. Mrs. Howard frequently asks after you, and desires her compliments to you. Mr. George Arbuthnot, the Doctor's brother, is married to Mrs. Peggy Robinson.[2] I would write more, but as to-night is for my benefit, I am in a hurry to go out about business. I am, dear Sir,

Your most affectionate and obedient servant,
J. GAY.

My service to Dr. Delany.

Addressed—To the Reverend Dr. Swift, Dean of St. Patrick's in Dublin, Ireland.

DCXC. [*Elwin.*[3]]

SWIFT TO JOHN GAY

February 26, 1727-8.[4]

NOW why does not Mr. Pope publish his Dulness? The rogues he mawls will die of themselves in peace, and so will his friends, and so there will be neither punishment nor reward.[5] Pray inquire how my Lord St. John does? There

---

[1] A society founded to promote the performance of Italian operas, of which Handel was the director.

[2] Arbuthnot's brother George, who was twenty years his junior, figures in the Journal to Stella as the rival of her friend Bernage. He was then an officer in the guards, but after the death of Queen Anne joined his brother Robert as a wine-merchant in France, and was mixed up in Jacobite intrigues. His wife was a sister or half-sister of Lord Peterborough's wife or *chère amie* (Aitken's "Life of Arbuthnot," *passim*).

[3] By permission of Mr. John Murray. *Supra*, vol. iii, p. 148, n. 1.

[4] Although apparently commenced on that day this letter was not completed, as the following one shows, until the 29th of that month.

[5] To Swift's perusal of the inscription (*supra*, p. 4) Mr. Courthope attributes this eagerness for the publication of the "Dunciad" (Pope's "Works," v, 214).

is no man's health in England I am more concerned about than his.[1] I wonder whether you begin to taste the pleasure of independency; or whether you do not sometimes leer upon the Court, *oculo retorto*? Will you now think of an annuity, when you are two years older, and have doubled your purchase money? Have you dedicated your opera, and got the usual dedication fee of twenty guineas? How is the Doctor? Does he not chide that you never called upon him for hints? Is my Lord Bolingbroke, at the moment I am writing, a planter, a philosopher, or a writer? Is Mr. Pulteney in expectation of a son,[2] or my Lord Bathurst of an employment,[3] or my Lord Oxford of a new old manuscript?

Ask Mrs. Howard if she will take the remedy with which I twice perfectly cured my deafness, though I am again relapsed, and I will send her the receipt. I said something of this to Mr. Pope.[4] Does Walpole think you intended an affront to him in your opera? Pray God he may, for he has held the longest hand at hazard that ever fell to any sharper's share, and keeps his run when the dice are charged. Present my most humble service to the deliverer of this letter,[5] for so he must be, and not Dr. Delany, who stole away without it, by an accident.[6] It is probable that I have forgot something of more moment than anything here. My service to Mr. Pope and all friends. Adieu.

I bought your opera to-day for sixpence, a cursed print. I find there is neither dedication nor preface, both which wants I approve; it is in the *grand goût*.

[1] Swift was afraid that the death of Bolingbroke's father (*supra*, vol. ii, p. 313, n. 5) might lead to his removal from Dawley to the family seat (*infra*, Letter DCCLVIII).

[2] In a letter communicated by Sheridan ("Works," xii, 243) Pulteney wrote to Pope that if his wife only brought him a son he would not care one sixpence how long Walpole governed England.

[3] Bathurst, as well as Bolingbroke, would not have refused office on the accession of George II (*supra*, vol. iii, pp. 397, 448).

[4] Probably in a reply, which has been suppressed, to Pope's last letter.

[5] *I.e.*, the post.

[6] It was on the day this letter was written that Delany's resignation of his fellowship took effect (*supra*, p. 1, n. 2). In addition to his chancellorship he was given the College living of Derryvullen in the county of Fermanagh, and as appears from the next letter signalized his appointment to a cure of souls by going on a visit to England.

DCXCI. [*Original.*[1]]

SWIFT TO MISS MARTHA BLOUNT

Dublin, *February* 29, 1727-8.

DEAR PATTY,

I AM told you have a mind to receive a letter from me,[2] which is a very undecent declaration in a young lady, and almost a confession that you have a mind to write to me; for as to the fancy of looking on me as a man *sans consequence*, it is what I will never understand. I am told likewise you grow every day younger, and more a fool, which is directly contrary to me, who grow wiser and older, and at this rate we shall never agree. I long to see you a London lady, where you are forced to wear whole clothes, and visit in a chair, for which you must starve next summer at Petersham,[3] with a manteau out at the sides; and sponge once a week at our house, without ever inviting us in a whole season to a cow-heel at home. I wish you would bring Mr. Pope over with you when you come, but we will leave Mr. Gay to his beggars and his operas till he is able to pay his club. How will you pass this summer for want of a squire to Ham Common and Walpole's Lodge;[4] for as to Richmond Lodge and Marble Hill, they are abandoned as much as Sir Spencer Compton,[5] and Mr. Schutz's[6] coach, that used to give you so many a set-down, is wheeled off to St. James's. You must be forced to get a horse, and gallop with Mrs. Janssen[7] and Miss Bedier.[8]

Your greatest happiness is, that you are out of the chiding of Mrs. Howard and the Dean, but I suppose Mr.

---

[1] British Museum, Stowe MS. 755, f. 47.   [2] *Supra*, p. 5.
[3] Where she lived in the summer with her mother and sister.
[4] In Richmond Park.   [5] *Supra*, vol. iii, p. 402, n. 4.
[6] Augustus Schutz, a great favourite of George II. See Pope's "Works," *passim*, and the "Countess of Suffolk's Letters," i, 233:

" If honest Schutz take scandal at a spark,
That less admires the palace than the park."

[7] A daughter of Sir Theodore Janssen of Wimbledon, who was created a baronet by Queen Anne, and involved, as a director, in the collapse of the South Sea Company.
[8] The use of the word "Miss" indicated an inferiority in rank. Possibly she was "Mrs." Janssen's companion.

Pope is so just as to pay our arrears, and that you edify as much by him as by us, unless you are so happy that he now looks upon you as reprobate and a castaway, of which I think he hath given me some hints. However, I would advise you to pass this summer at Kensington, where you will be near the Court, and out of his jurisdiction, where you will be teased with no lectures of gravity and morality, and where you will have no other trouble than to get into the mercer's books, and take up a hundred pounds of your principal for quadrille. Monstrous, indeed, that a fine lady, in the prime of life and gaiety, must take up with an anti-quated Dean, an old gentlewoman of fourscore,[1] and a sickly poet. I will stand by my dear Patty against the world; if Teresa[2] beats you for your good, I will buy her a fine whip for the purpose. Tell me, have you been confined to your lodging this winter for want of chair-hire? (Do you know that this unlucky Dr. Delany came last night to the Deanery, and being denied, without my knowledge, is gone to England this morning, and so I must send this by the post. I bought your opera to-day for sixpence, so small printed that it will spoil my eyes. I ordered you to send me your edition, but now you may keep it till you get an opportunity.) Patty, I will tell you a blunder: I am writing to Mr. Gay,[3] and had almost finished the letter; but by mistake I took up this instead of it, and so the six lines in a hook are all to him, and therefore you must read them to him, for I will not be at the trouble to write them over again. My greatest concern in the matter is, that I am afraid I continue in love with you, which is hard after near six months' absence. I hope you have done with your rash and other little disorders, and that I shall see you a fine young, healthy, plump lady, and if Mr. Pope chides you, threaten him that you will turn heretic.

Adieu, dear Patty, and believe me to be one of your truest friends and humblest servants; and that, since I can never live in England, my greatest happiness would be to have you and Mr. Pope condemned, during my life, to live in Ireland, he at the Deanery, and you, for reputation sake, just at next door; and I will give you eight dinners a-week, and a whole half dozen of pint bottles of good French wine at your lodgings, a thing you could never expect to arrive

---

[1] Her mother.   [2] Her sister.   [3] *Supra*, p. 11.

at, and every year a suit of fourteen-penny stuff that should not be worn out at the right side; and a chair costs but sixpence a job; and you shall have Catholicity as much as you please, and the Catholic Dean of St. Patrick's, as old again as I, for your confessor. Adieu again, dear Patty.

Addressed—To Patty Blount.

DCXCII. [*Original.*[1]]

SWIFT TO BENJAMIN MOTTE

March 12, 1727-8.

DCXCIII. [*Original.*[2]]

JOHN GAY TO SWIFT

March 20, 1727-8.

DEAR SIR,

I AM extremely sorry that your disorder is returned; but as you have a medicine which has twice removed it, I hope by this time [you] have again found the good effects of it.[3] I have seen Dr. Delany at my lodgings, but, as I have been for a few days with Mr. Pulteney at Cashiobury,[4] I have not yet returned his visit. I went with him to wait upon Lord Bathurst and Lord Bolingbroke; both of whom desire me to make you their compliments. Lady Bolingbroke was very much out of order; and, with my Lord, is now at Dawley; she expects a letter from you. Mrs. Howard would gladly have the receipt you have found so much benefit by; she is happier than I have seen her ever since you left us, for she is free as to her conjugal affairs by articles of agreement.[5] The Beggar's Opera hath now been

---

[1] This letter was a few years ago in the possession of Mr. Sabin of 172, New Bond Street.

[2] In the British Museum. See Preface.   [3] *Supra*, p. 12.

[4] The owner, the third Earl of Essex of the Capel creation, had married as his first wife the Duchess of Queensberry's sister, whom Swift had known as a "mighty pretty girl" and "top-toast" ("Prose Works," ii, 211, 327), but she was then dead.

[5] Her husband, Charles Howard, who became, three years later, Earl of Suffolk, has been described as "wrong-headed, ill-tempered, obstinate, drunken, extravagant, and brutal." But her relations with George II gave him just cause for complaint, and as a solatium an annuity of £1,200 a year was paid to him.

acted thirty-six times, and was as full the last night as the first, and as yet there is not the least probability of a thin audience, though there is a discourse about the town, that the directors of the Royal Academy of Music [1] design to solicit against its being played on the outlandish opera days, as it is now called. On the benefit day of one of the actresses last week, one of the players falling sick, they were obliged to give out another play, or dismiss the audience. A play was given out, but the audience called out for the Beggar's Opera, and they were forced to play it, or the audience would not have stayed.

I have got by all this success, between seven and eight hundred pounds, and Rich,[2] deducting the whole charge of the house, hath cleared already near four thousand pounds. In about a month I am going to the Bath with the Duchess of Marlborough and Mr. Congreve;[3] for I have no expectations of receiving any favours from the Court. The Duchess of Queensberry is in Wiltshire, where she hath had the small-pox in so favourable a way that she had not above seven or eight in her face; she is now perfectly recovered. There is a mezzotinto print published to-day of Polly, the heroine of the Beggar's Opera, who was before unknown, and is now in so high vogue, that I am in doubt, whether her fame does not surpass that of the opera itself.[4] I would not have talked so much upon this subject, or upon anything that regards myself, but to you; but as I know you interest yourself so sincerely in everything that concerns me, I believe you would have blamed me if I had said less.

Your singer owes Dr. Arbuthnot some money, I have forgot the sum, I think it is two guineas: the Doctor desired me to let you know it.[5] I saw him last night with Mr. Lewis at Sir William Wyndham's, who, if he had not the

---

[1] *Supra*, p. 11, n. 1.

[2] The manager of the theatre at Lincoln's Inn Fields who was said on the success of the opera to have become Gay while the author became Rich.

[3] *Supra*, vol. iii, p. 337.

[4] Lavinia Fenton, afterwards Duchess of Bolton, not only secured a husband but also the success of the opera by her acting in the part of Polly Peachum. She had then been only two years on the stage, but is said to have quickly become "the talk of the coffee-houses and the most celebrated toast in town."

[5] As Swift's reply explains, the reference is to William Fox, who was a member of Swift's choir from 1727 until his death in 1734.

gout, would have answered your letter you sent him a year and a half ago.[1] He said this to me a week since, but he is now pretty well again, and so may forget to write, for which reason I ought to do him justice, and tell you, that I think him a sincere well-wisher of yours. I have not seen Mr. Pope lately, but have heard that both he and Mrs. Pope are very well. I intend to see him at Twickenham on Sunday next. I have not drunk out the Goodrich cider yet,[2] but I have not so much as a single pint of port in my cellar. I have bought two pair of sheets against your coming to town, so that we need not send any more to Jervas upon that account.[3] I really miss you every day, and I would be content that you should have a whole window to yourself, and half another, to have you again. I am, dear Sir,

Yours most affectionately.

You have half a year's interest due at Lady-day, and now it is March the 20th, 1727-8.

Addressed—To the Reverend Dr. Swift, Dean of St. Patrick's, in Dublin, Ireland.

DCXCIV. [*Elwin.*]

ALEXANDER POPE TO SWIFT

March 23, 1727-8.

I SEND you a very odd thing, a paper printed in Boston, in New England, wherein you will find a real person, a member of their Parliament, of the name of Jonathan Gulliver. If the fame of that traveller has travelled thither, it has travelled very quick, to have folks christened already by the name of the supposed author. But if you object, that no child so lately christened could be arrived at years of maturity to be elected into Parliament, I reply, to solve the riddle, that the person is an Anabaptist, and not christened till full age, which sets all right. However it

[1] *Supra*, vol. iii, p. 350.   [2] *Supra*, vol. iii, p. 426.
[3] *Supra*, vol. iii, p. 341.

be, the accident is very singular that these two names should be united.

Mr. Gay's opera has been acted near forty days running, and will certainly continue the whole season. So he has more than a fence about his thousand pounds;[1] he will soon be thinking of a fence about his two thousand. Shall no one of us live as we would wish each other to live? Shall he have no sure annuity, you no settlement on this side, and I no prospect of getting to you on the other? This world is made for Caesar, as Cato said,[2] for ambitious, false, or flattering people to domineer in; nay they would not, by their goodwill, leave us our very books, thoughts, or words, in quiet. I despise the world yet, I assure you, more than either Gay or you, and the Court more than all the rest of the world. As for those scribblers for whom you apprehend I would suppress my Dulness, which, by the way, for the future you are to call by a more pompous name, the Dunciad, how much that nest of hornets are my regard will easily appear to you when you read the Treatise of the Bathos.

At all adventures, yours and my name shall stand linked as friends to posterity, both in verse and prose, and, as Tully calls it, in *consuetudine studiorum*.[3] Would to God our persons could but as well and as surely be inseparable! I find my other ties dropping from me; some worn off, some torn off, others relaxing daily. My greatest, both by duty, gratitude, and humanity, time is shaking every moment, and it now hangs but by a thread. I am many years the older for living so much with one so old; much the more helpless for having been so long helped and tendered by her; much the more considerate and tender for a daily commerce with one who required me justly to be both to her; and consequently the more melancholy and thoughtful, and the less fit for others, who want only in a companion or a friend, to be amused or entertained. My constitution too has had its share of decay as well as my spirits, and I am as much in the decline at forty as you at sixty. I believe we should be fit to live together could I get a little more health, which might make me not quite insupportable. Your deafness would agree with my dul-

[1] *Supra*, vol. iii, p. 431.
[2] Addison's "Cato," V, i, 19.
[3] Possibly a slip for *conjunctione studiorum* ("Ep. ad Fam.," ix, 8, 1).

ness; you would not want me to speak when you could not hear. But God forbid you should be as destitute of the social comforts of life as I must when I lose my mother, or that ever you should lose your more useful acquaintance so utterly as to turn your thoughts to such a broken reed as I am, who could so ill supply your wants. I am extremely troubled at the returns of your deafness. You cannot be too particular in the accounts of your health to me; everything you do or say in this kind obliges me, nay delights me, to see the justice you do me in thinking me concerned in all your concerns; so that though the pleasantest thing you can tell me be that you are better or easier, next to that it pleases me that you make me the person you would complain to.

As the obtaining the love of valuable men is the happiest end I know of this life, so the next felicity is to get rid of fools and scoundrels, which I cannot but own to you was one part of my design in falling upon these authors, whose incapacity is not greater than their insincerity, and of whom I have always found, if I may quote myself,

> That each bad author is as bad a friend.

This poem will rid me of those insects:

> Cedite, Romani Scriptores, cedite, Graii;
> Nescio quid majus nascitur Iliade.[1]

I mean than my Iliad, and I call it "nescio quid," which is a degree of modesty; but however if it silence these fellows, it must be something greater than any Iliad in Christendom. Adieu.

DCXCV. [*Elwin.*[2]]

SWIFT TO JOHN GAY

Dublin, *March* 28, 1728.

I HAD yours of the 20th last night. As to the remedy that twice cured my deafness, I would not take it the third time, because it made me so tender that the least cold brought on my disorder again, which went off, however,

---

[1] Propertius, ii [iii], 34, 65-6.
[2] By permission of Mr. John Murray. *Supra*, vol. iii, p. 148, n. I.

without using it any more. This I say on Mrs. Howard's account, yet she shall have it if she pleases. I am now tolerably well, but my fears of relapsing hang over me, and very much take down my mettle. I will write to my Lady Bolingbroke, but I would be glad first that you would know from her whether she will have such usquebaugh as I can get, and how much, and whether the green or the yellow, for there is no such thing as white, or will she leave all but the quantity to my discretion.[1] We have your opera for sixpence, and we are as full of it *pro modulo nostro* as London can be; continually acting, and house crammed, and the Lord Lieutenant several times there laughing his heart out.[2] I wish you had sent me a copy, as I desired, to oblige an honest bookseller. It would have done Motte no hurt, for no English copy has been sold, but the Dublin one has run prodigiously. I did not understand that the scene of Lockit and Peachum's quarrel[3] was an imitation of one between Brutus and Cassius,[4] till I was told it. I wish Macheath, when he was going to be hanged, had imitated Alexander the Great when he was dying. I would have had his fellow-rogues desire his commands about a successor, and he to answer, Let it be the most worthy, etc.[5]

[1] The liquor known then as usquebaugh was a compound of plain spirit with such flavouring matters as saffron, nutmegs, and sugar. "The fault of green usquebaugh," writes Bishop Clayton, "is that it loses its colour if it is kept above a year, and if it is drank before that time it tastes fiery and hot" (Mrs. Thomson's "Memoirs of Viscountess Sundon," ii, 300).

[2] In the "Dublin Intelligence" of 23 March, 1727-8, the following paragraph appears: "The New Opera which is again to be Play'd to Night was on Thursday more Crowded with Spectators than ever, and really it is now so far the Topick of General Conversation here that they who have not seen it are hardly thought worth Speaking to by their Acquaintance, and are only Admitted into Discourse on their Promise of going to see it the first Opportunity, which is so advantageous to our Comedians that we are told Boxes &c. are bespoke for 16 or 18 Nights to come."

[3] "*Peach.* We shall be losers in the dispute, for you know we have it in our power to hang each other. You should not be too passionate. *Lock.* Nor you so provoking. *Peach.* 'Tis our mutual interest, 'tis for the interest of the world we should agree."

[4] Plutarch's "Life of Brutus," c. 34, or Shakespeare's "Julius Caesar," iv, 3.

[5]
> "The crown will find an heir; great Alexander
> Left his to the worthiest; so his successor
> Was like to be the best."
> > "Winter's Tale," v, 1, 47.

We hear a million of stories about the opera, of the encore at the song, "That was levell'd at me,"[1] when two great Ministers were in a box together, and all the world staring at them. I am heartily glad your opera has mended your purse, though perhaps it may spoil your court. I think that rich rogue, Rich, should in conscience make you a present of two or three hundred guineas. I am impatient that such a dog by sitting still should get five times more than the author. You told me a month ago of seven hundred, and have you not quite made up the eight yet? I know not your methods. How many third days are you allowed, and how much is each day worth, and what did you get for copy? Pray give one to Doctor Delany for me.

Will you desire my Lord Bolingbroke, Mr. Pulteney, and Mr. Pope, to command you to buy an annuity with two thousand pounds, that you may laugh at Courts, and bid Ministers "kiss, etc." And ten to one they will be ready to grease you when you are fat. I hope your new Duchess will treat you at the Bath, and that you will be too wise to lose your money at play. Ever preserve some spice of the alderman, and prepare against age and dulness, and sickness, and coldness, or death of friends. A whore has a resource left, that she can turn bawd; but an old decayed poet is a creature abandoned, and at mercy, when he can find none. Get me likewise Polly's mezzotinto. Lord, how the school-boys at Westminster and University lads adore you at this juncture! Have you made as many men laugh, as Ministers can make weep?

I am glad your goddess Duchess has preserved a face which I never saw since it was on the shoulders of a girl. Doctor Arbuthnot lent Fox, the singer, whom he sent me, five guineas, and had his note. This note I took from the Doctor, and paid him five guineas honestly at his house in Cork Street, over against my Lord Hervey's. If he lent the fellow any other money without a note, I know nothing of it. I will excuse Sir William Wyndham the trouble of a letter. When ambassadors came from Troy to condole

[1]
        "When you censure the age
        Be cautious and sage,
  Lest the courtiers offended should be,
      If you mention vice or bribe,
       'Tis so pat to the tribe,
  Each cries: That was levell'd at me."

with Tiberius upon the death of his nephew, after two years, the Emperor answered, that he likewise condoled with them for the untimely death of Hector.[1] I always loved and respected Sir William very much, and do still as much as ever; and it is a return sufficient, if he pleases to accept the offers of my most humble service.

I have twenty dozen of Goodrich cider, as good as yours, which cost me eight pounds, and if you will just cross the water hither from the Bath, I will give you a bottle of it every day. I had a letter from Joe Taylor last post, recommending one Waghorne for my choir. He must be answered, by your means, that I did admit him to a half place, a year ago or more, and have recommended him to the Dean of our other Cathedral to be taken in there. But the man by his indiscretion is got so deep in debt, that I doubt he must run away back to England, as I suppose he did from thence hither for the same reasons.[2] This I would have said to Mr. Taylor without troubling him with a letter, neither do I know his address, unless it be to Bridewell.[3] My most humble service to Mr. Pulteney and Mrs. Howard, and Mr. Pope, etc., and the Doctor. I hope Dr. Delany has shown you the tale, writ by Mrs. Barber, a citizen's wife here, in praise of your Fables. There is something in it hard upon Mr. Congreve, which I sent to her, for I never saw her, to change to Dryden, but she absolutely refused.[4]

[1] " Quin et Iliensium legatis paulo serius consolantibus . . . irridens se quoque respondet vicem dolore quod egregium civem Hectorem amisissent" (Suet., "Tib.," 52).

[2] John Waghorne, who had been appointed to Swift's choir in 1726, remained a member of it until his death in 1733. The interchange of choirmen between the two Dublin cathedrals has been noticed (*supra*, vol. ii, p. 73, n. 5).

[3] Taylor was clerk of Bridewell Hospital. He died in 1759 at the age of eighty.

[4] Mary Barber, whose acquaintance with Swift gave fresh opportunity to his detractors, is frequently mentioned in the succeeding letters. She was the wife of Jonathan Barber, a woollen-draper of Dublin, and was mother of Constantine Barber, who practised medicine in that city and became President of the College of Physicians in Ireland. To her anxiety to secure the advancement of this son and her other children such indiscretions as she committed are clearly traceable, and to the same cause, as she explains in the preface to her "Poems on Several Occasions" (Lond., 1735), are attributable her essays in verse, which she believed to be the best mode of conveying instruction to young maids, and "to give early a proper and graceful manner of speaking." The poem to which Swift alludes is one entitled

I am now descended . . ., but I have not yet descended so low as a halfpenny: that indeed would be an indignity.[1] Tell Dr. Delany that our town is full of speculations about his journey, and they have found out three ladies for him. One is Lady Rawdon, of Ireland;[2] another is a daughter of Sir Constantine Phipps;[3] and the third is a lady who has no name, but six hundred pounds a year estate. These conjectures entertained this town till your opera drove them out, so that I fear at present they are under little concern whether he gets a wife or no.

The Beggar's Opera has knocked down Gulliver; I hope to see Pope's Dulness knock down the Beggar's Opera, but not till it has fully done its job. They have not been told how easy a thing it is to get eight hundred pounds by two or three months' writing. If you were an alderman you could never fail of writing two or three such trifles every year. To expose vice, and to make people laugh with innocence, does more public service than all the Ministers of State from Adam to Walpole, and so adieu.

"A True Tale," and was written ostensibly with the former object, but was no less calculated to recommend her to Swift's circle than to instruct her children. She relates in it how after mentioning Addison and Pope she

> "Told Tully's and the Gracchi's doom,
> The Patriots, and the Pride of Rome,
> Then blessed the Drapier's happier fate,
> Who sav'd, and lives to guard the State."

The reference to Congreve has disappeared, no doubt in obedience to Swift's behest, but one can imagine that comedies forbidden " as poison to the mind" included those of which he was the author:

> "Those authors' wit and sense, said she,
> But heighten their impiety."

[1] The reference is probably to the low value of the Irish coinage. The rate of exchange was then a subject of controversy.

[2] The widow of Sir John Rawdon of Moira, the third baronet of his line. She was a daughter of Chief Justice Levinge, and married soon after this letter was written, as her second husband, Charles Cobbe, then Bishop of Dromore, and afterwards Archbishop of Dublin.

[3] To whom Delany had been chaplain.

DCXCVI. [*Original.*[1]]

JOHN BROWNE TO SWIFT

Dawson Street,[2] *April 4th*, 1728.

REVEREND SIR,[3]

BY a strange fatality, though you were the only person in the world from whom I would conceal my being an author, yet you were unaccountably the only one let into the secret of it. The ignorant poor man who was intrusted by me to deliver out the little books, though he kept the secret from all others, yet from the nature of the subject he concluded that I could have no interest in concealing it from you, who were so universally known to be an indefatigable promoter of the general welfare of Ireland. But though the accident gave me some uneasiness at first, yet when I consider your character I cannot doubt, however slender the foundation of such a hope may be from any merits of my own, but your generosity will oblige you to conceal what chance has revealed to you, and incline you to judge of me, not from the report of my enemies, but from what I appear in the little tracts which have waited on you.

[1] In the Forster Collection, No. 562.

[2] One of the principal streets in Dublin which, as already mentioned, is named after Joshua Dawson (*supra*, vol. i, p. 178, n. 4).

[3] Shortly before the Drapier Letters were published, the writer of this letter, who was the father of the first Lord Kilmaine, and succeeded to the baronetcy now merged in that peerage, had come into conflict with a member of the Irish House of Commons, and had been severely censured by that assembly and ordered to be taken into custody by the Sergeant-at-Arms. From the consequence of that resolution he escaped by going to England, but was induced to give evidence before the English Privy Council in favour of Wood's coinage, and brought upon himself the choler of Swift, who held him up to public odium in the third Drapier's Letter. As soon as he ventured to return to Ireland Browne assumed a patriotic character, and issued a tract appealing for help for his country in the terrible famine by which it was then devastated. Swift replied to this tract in an answer that imputed the misfortunes of the country to its inhabitants, and exposed the author to anyone reading between the lines with great severity. By the present letter Browne sought to assuage Swift's wrath, and not without success, as the reference to him was omitted in a subsequent edition of the Drapier Letters ("Prose Works," vi, 61, 74; vii, 107).

I shall not presume, Sir, to detain you with the narrative of the original and progress of the Parliamentary accusations and votes against me, though would you do me the honour to enquire I could easily convince you from my own particular case, that men have two characters, one which is either good or bad, according to the prevailing number of their friends or enemies, and one which never varies for either; one which has little or no regard to the virtue or vice of the subject, and one which regards that alone, is inherent, if I may say so, in the subject, and describes it what it really is, without regard either to friends or enemies.

All I shall beg of you is to suspend your judgement upon it, since all parties allow that though I had several summonses from the Committee for Monday, and many evidences on the road in obedience to their summons, yet I was tied down by the Committee the preceding Saturday, and deprived of the benefit of all my evidences, notwithstanding anything I could urge to the contrary.[1] This I hope I may say without injury to Mr. Bingham, for sure he may be entirely innocent, and yet a magistrate under the immediate direction of the Lord Chief Justice who takes examinations against him, examinations that do not even contain matter to form an indictment upon, may be innocent also. It shall suffice, therefore, to say I went from Ireland loaded with the severest censures of the House of Commons, injured, as I thought, and oppressed to the greatest degree imaginable, robbed of that character which was dearer to me than life itself, and all that by an overbearing, overpowering interest.

I sought in England for that peace and protection which was denied me at home. My public character followed me: my countrymen avoided me, the nature of man is sociable, I was forced to herd with strangers. A Prime Minister engaged in the success of a scheme wants no emissaries to spy out all that makes for him, and to fly with what they have found to their employer. I was unfortunately set by those sort of creatures. My sentiments on the state of our money matters were industriously sifted

---

[1] This reference is to the proceedings in the Irish House of Commons against Browne, which centred in a charge that he was "a chief promoter and adviser of a conspiracy to take away the life and fortune of John Bingham." In 1730 he tried to induce Bingham to prosecute him without success ("Dublin Intelligence," 28 April, 4 Aug.).

through me, and when that was done before I knew anything of the matter, I was served with his Majesty's summons; in a hurry I ran out of town, and stayed in the
country awhile, but, on my return again, found another
summons at my lodgings, and terrified by the dismal effects
of power at home from risking a second shipwreck abroad,
I yielded to it, and appeared at the Cockpit.

It is true my appearance at the Cockpit to those who
knew me only by the votes of the House of Commons
must have looked like a design of revenge, and I had many
and powerful enemies who gave all my actions the worst
colour. But to take the matter impartially, Sir, is there no
allowance to be made for a mind already broken by the
dismal effects of prevailing power, and filled with the
apprehensions of second dangers? Is there no allowance
for a man young in the knowledge of the world, under all
these fears and misfortunes, if he has yielded to the repeated
summons of the Council of England, in which his Majesty
was present, and if he was there, after a long and strenu-
ous opposition, forced to tell his sentiments, forced, Sir, to
tell his sentiments, not in the manner represented to the
world, but in a manner the most cautious of giving room
for a pretence to oppose the inclinations of our Parliament?

But, alas, the consequence: you, Sir, the defender of
Ireland, were soon engaged against me on that account,
and that fatal genius of yours in an instant ruined my
character; but even ruin-bearing as it was, I blessed it.
The cause which you undertook was dear to me, and
though fame is the last thing which one would sacrifice
even for his country, yet I parted with that with pleasure,
whilst you thought it necessary for the public good so to
do. But now the end is served, dear Sir, may not the man
have his mare again?[1]

Plato being told that certain persons aspersed his character and represented him abroad as a very ill man, instead
of expostulating with his enemies and returning reproach
for reproach, concealed himself saying, " No matter, my
friends, the whole life of Plato shall give his accusers the
lie." Could I set before me a greater example? Under the
general displeasure of my country, under all the censures
which the restless malice of my enemies could devise, and

---

[1] "The man shall have his mare again, and all shall be well " (" Midsummer Night's Dream," iii, 2, 463).

under the keen edge of the Drapier's wit the only revenge
I indulged myself in, was by a steady love for my country,
and by manifest acts of affection thereto, to be a silent reproach to the foul tongues of my enemies.

Permit then, Sir, permit me in peace to take his great
example and no longer give way to the power of my
enemies by continuing to oppress me. They have already
gained their cause by you, but I must say it was not the
sword of Ajax, but the armour of Achilles which he put on,
that won the day. The cause for which you undertook my
ruin, was the cause of my country. It was a good cause
and you shall ever find me of that side you have carried
it, and I know you will no longer be my enemy. But, alas,
Sir, as long as your works subsist, wherever they be read,
even unto the end of time, must I be branded as a villain?
It is a hard sentence, and yet unless the spear of Achilles,
the same instrument which gave the wound, administers
the remedy it must be so.

In short, Sir, you must be a man of honour. It is not
possible that honour should be wanting where all the dis-
tinguishing characteristics of it are found. I cannot doubt
it, and I will therefore let you fully into a secret which
accident has given you a part of, and I am sure you will
keep it. The source of all my misfortunes was the vote of
the House of Commons; but I have laboured, however, as I
always shall to serve my country, and make myself agreeable to them, and though the misfortune of a bad public
character deprived me of the private conversation of my
countrymen, which is the surest and best way to know our
true interest, yet, I flatter myself, that my little essays may
be useful, at least they may be no bad beginning. And
you know it is easy to add to a work once begun. But if
the work is known to be mine the very name will condemn
it and render it useless to my country.

Whatever the faults may be I have publicly applied to
you to amend them before the bearer's mistake made me
determine this private application to you, and I must
here say that I shall reckon it no small degree of honour,
if you take that trouble upon you.[1] In the mean time, I

---

[1] Browne afterwards obtained a seat in the Irish Parliament, and
the recovery of his reputation was probably in some degree due to
Swift, as he erected a monument in Swift's honour at his home in the
County of Mayo. See Appendix II.

shall beg the favour of you to keep a secret which no other person but my printer, my bookseller, and the bearer knows. I am, Reverend Sir,

> Your most obedient servant,
>
> JOHN BROWNE.

DCXCVII. [*Deane Swift.*]

MISS MARTHA BLOUNT TO SWIFT

May 7, 1728.

SIR,

I AM very much pleased with your letter,[1] but I should have thought myself much more obliged, had you been less sincere, and not told me, I did not owe the favour entirely to your inclinations, but to an information that I had a mind to hear from you, and I mistrust you think even that as much as I deserve. If so, you really are not deserving of my repeated inquiries after you, and my constant good wishes and concern for your welfare, which merits some remembrance without the help of another. I cannot say I have a great inclination to write to you, for I have no great vanity that way, at least not enough to support me above the fear of writing ill, but I would fain have you know how truly well I wish you.

I am sorry to hear no good account of your health: mine has been, since Christmas, at which time I had my fever and rash, neither well nor ill enough to be taken notice of, but within these three weeks I have been sick in form, and kept my bed for a week, and my chamber to this day.

This confinement, together with the mourning,[2] has enabled me to be very easy in my chaise-hire, for a dyed black gown, and a scoured white one, have done my business very well, and they are now just fit for Petersham, where we talk of going in three weeks, and I am not without hopes I shall have the same squire I had last year. I am very unwilling to change, and moreover I begin to fear I have no great prospect of getting any new danglers, and therefore, in order to make a tolerable figure, I shall endeavour to behave myself mighty well, that I may keep my old ones.

[1] *Supra*, p. 13.   [2] The Court mourning for George I.

As a proof that I continue to be well received at Court, I will tell you where the royal family design to pass their summer: two months at Richmond Lodge, the same time at Hampton Court, and six weeks at Windsor. Mrs. Howard is well, and happier than ever you saw her; for her whole affair with her husband is ended to her satisfaction.[1] Dr. Arbuthnot I am very angry with; he neglects me for those he thinks finer ladies. Mr. Gay's fame continues, but his riches are in a fair way of diminishing. He is gone to the Bath. I wish you were ordered there, for I believe that would carry Mr. Pope, who is always inclined to do more for his friends than himself. He is much out of order and is told nothing is so likely to do him good.

My illness has prevented my writing to you sooner. If I was a favourite at Court, I would soon convince you that I am very sincerely,

Your faithful friend and very humble servant,

M. B.

DCXCVIII. [*Elwin.*]

SWIFT TO ALEXANDER POPE

Dublin, *May* 10, 1728.

I HAVE with great pleasure shown the New England newspaper with the two names Jonathan Gulliver;[2] and I remember Mr. Fortescue sent you an account from the assizes, of one Lemuel Gulliver who had a cause there, and lost it on his ill reputation of being a liar.[3] These are not the only observations I have made upon odd, strange accidents in trifles, which in things of great importance would have been matter for historians. Mr. Gay's opera has been acted here twenty times, and my Lord Lieutenant tells me it is very well performed; he has seen it often, and approves it much.[4]

You give a most melancholy account of yourself, and which I do not approve. I reckon that a man subject like

---

[1] *Supra*, p. 15.   [2] *Supra*, p. 17.

[3] Swift had probably met, while staying at Twickenham, Pope's friend, William Fortescue, then a barrister, and afterwards Master of the Rolls. Fortescue is included by Churton Collins (" Jonathan Swift," p. 100) amongst the members of the Scriblerus Club, but had not made Swift's acquaintance before 1726 (Pope's " Works," ix, 107).

[4] *Supra*, p. 20.

us to bodily infirmities, should only occasionally converse with great people, notwithstanding all their good qualities, easinesses, and kindnesses. There is another race which I prefer before them, as beef and mutton for constant diet before partridges; I mean a middle kind both for understanding and fortune, who are perfectly easy, never impertinent, complying in everything, ready to do a hundred little offices that you and I may often want, who dine and sit with me five times for once that I go to them, and whom I can tell without offence, that I am otherwise engaged at present. This you cannot expect from any of those that either you or I, or both, are acquainted with on your side; who are only fit for our healthy seasons, and have much business of their own. God forbid I should condemn you to Ireland (*Quanquam O!*), and for England I despair, and indeed a change of affairs would come too late at my season of life, and might probably produce nothing on my behalf.

You have kept Mrs. Pope longer, and have had her care beyond what from nature you could expect; not but her loss will be very sensible whenever it shall happen. I say one thing, that both summers and winters are milder here than with you; all things for life in general better for a middling fortune. You will have an absolute command of your company, with whatever obsequiousness or freedom you may expect or allow. I have an elderly housekeeper, who has been my Walpole above thirty years, whenever I lived in this kingdom.[1] I have the command of one or two villas near this town. You have a warm apartment in this house, and two gardens for amusement.[2] I have said enough, yet not half. Except absence from friends, I

[1] It would appear from this reference that Swift's acquaintance with Mrs. Brent dated from the time he was Prebendary of Kilroot. Her husband was a printer, and in the days of his power Swift dismissed a suggestion that he was a suitable candidate for the Charter House with much contempt ("Prose Works," ii, 15, 385). According to Nichols ("Works," xv, 87) Swift's mother lodged with them when she came to Ireland after Swift's appointment to Laracor, but at no time does Mrs. Brent seem to have acted as landlady to him, and there is no certainty that she resided with him in the Deanery (*supra*, vol. ii, pp. 256, 288; vol. iii, p. 443). In her will, which is dated 27 July, 1732, the mention of furniture, plate, and household goods tends to show that she had a house of her own.

[2] *I.e.*, Naboth's Vineyard (*supra*, vol. iii, p. 201) and the garden round the Deanery.

confess freely that I have no discontent at living here, beside
what arises from a silly spirit of liberty, which as it neither
sours my drink, nor hurts my meat, nor spoils my stomach
farther than in imagination, so I resolve to throw it off.

You talk of this Dunciad, but I am impatient to have it
volitare per ora.[1] There is now a vacancy for fame; the
Beggar's Opera has done its task, *discedat uti conviva satur.*[2]
Adieu.

DCXCIX. [*Original.*[3]]

SWIFT TO THE EARL OF OXFORD

Dublin, *May* 11, 1728.

MY LORD,

I MUST desire your Lordship's pardon if out of ignorance
I send you medals that are perfect trash, but you have an
easy remedy to throw them out of the windows. There is
a very fair one of Cromwell, which for aught I know may
be as common as a milled shilling.

There is one of a Roman Emperor which is fair, but I
know not of whom; it was given me by a Portuguese
cousin,[4] who brought it with her from Portugal. The small
one seems to be a Saxon. The other two are only Edwards,
and I think very common, but perhaps you may want one
to complete a series. That Portuguese cousin hath likewise
a very fair gold medallion of Titus with a reverse of Domi-
tian when he was Caesar. Some fool, if she does not lie,
offered her three times more than the weight for it, so I
shall not meddle with it, the intrinsic value of it is not
above four pounds.

I have not heard of any coin of this kingdom before the
conquest under Henry the Second. Those since are of no
value or curiosity, not above three or four hundred years
old, with the names of the cities, as *civitas* Waterford,
civitas Dublin, *civitas* Drogheda, etc.[5]

---

[1] See the epitaph of Ennius on himself, quoted by Cicero, "Tuscul.,"
i, 15, 34.

[2] Hor., "Sat.," I, i, 118. But Horace has *cedat*. For the sentiment
cf. Lucretius, iii, 938.

[3] In the possession of the Duke of Portland. *Supra*, vol. ii, p. 160, n. 2.

[4] *I.e.*, Mrs. Lightburne (*supra*, vol. iii, p. 235).

[5] *Supra*, vol. iii, p. 286.

I hope my Lady Oxford and Lady Margaret are in good health as well as your Lordship. You and your family have my daily prayers and good wishes. I am, with great respect, my Lord,

Your Lordship's most obedient and most humble servant,

JONATH. SWIFT.

DCC. [*Original.*[1]]

JOHN GAY TO SWIFT

Bath, *May* 16, 1728.

DEAR SIR,

I HAVE been at the Bath about ten days, and I have played at no game but once, and that at backgammon with Mr. Lewis, who is very much your humble servant. He is here upon account of the ill state of health of his wife,[2] who hath as yet found very little benefit from the waters. Lord and Lady Bolingbroke are here; and I think she is better than when I came here: they stay, as I guess, only about a fortnight longer. They both desired me to make their compliments; as does Mr. Congreve, who is in a very ill state of health, but somewhat better since he came here. Mr. Lewis tells me, that he is promised to receive a hundred pounds upon your account at his return to London; he having, upon request, complied to stay for the payment till that time.[3] The two hundred pounds you left with me are in the hands of Lord Bathurst, together with some money of mine, all which he will repay at Midsummer, so that we must think of some other way of employing it; and I cannot resolve what to do.

I do not know how long I shall stay here, because I am now, as I have been all my life, at the disposal of others. I drink the waters, and am in hopes to lay in a stock of health, some of which I wish to communicate to you. Dr. Delany[4] told me you had been upon a journey, and I really fancy taking horse is as good as taking the waters;

---

[1] In the British Museum. See Preface.
[2] *Supra*, vol. iii, p. 284.
[3] The reference is to the profit from "Gulliver's Travels" (*supra*, p. 4).
[4] *Supra*, p. 14.

I hope you have found benefit by it.[1] The Beggar's Opera
is acted here; but our Polly hath got no fame, but the
actors have got money. I have sent by Dr. Delany,[2] the
opera, Polly Peachum, and Captain Macheath. I would
have sent you my own head, which is now graving to
make up the gang, but it is not yet finished. I suppose you
must have heard that I have had the honour to have had a
sermon preached against my works by a Court chaplain,
which I look upon as no small addition to my fame.[3] Direct
to me here when you write; and the sooner that is, the
sooner you will make me happy.

Addressed—To the Revd. Dr. Swift, Dean of St. Patrick's,
in Dublin, Ireland.

DCCI. [*Elwin.*]

SWIFT TO ALEXANDER POPE

June 1, 1728.

I LOOK upon my Lord Bolingbroke and us two, as a peculiar triumvirate, who have nothing to expect or to fear; and
so far fittest to converse with one another, only he and I
are a little subject to schemes, and one of us, I will not say
which, upon very weak appearances, and this you have
nothing to do with. I do profess without affectation, that
your kind opinion of me as a patriot, since you call it so,

---

[1] As appears from the second number of the "Intelligencer" which
was published about that time ("Prose Works," ix, 311), Swift and
Sheridan had shortly before, probably during the Easter holidays,
which fell late that year, made a tour through the south-eastern part
of Ireland. While passing through the town of Gorey in the county of
Wexford, Swift's life had been endangered by the reckless driving of
the coachman of one of the local magnates, and as his master's name
and character gave opportunity for raillery, the occurrence was chosen
by Sheridan as the subject of his first contribution to his and Swift's
joint venture.

[2] Who then returned to Ireland.

[3] The Court chaplain was Dr. Thomas Herring, afterwards successively Archbishop of York and Canterbury. In the third number of
the "Intelligencer" it is remarked that Gay's opera would probably
do more good than "a thousand sermons of so stupid, so injudicious,
and so prostitute a Divine," but according to a less biased critic the
sermon was a fine one ("Memoirs of a Royal Chaplain," edited by
Albert Hartshorne, p. 120).

is what I do not deserve; because what I do is owing to
perfect rage and resentment, and the mortifying sight of
slavery, folly, and baseness about me, among which I am
forced to live. And I will take my oath that you have
more virtue in an hour than I in seven years; for you
despise the follies and hate the vices of mankind without
the least ill effect on your temper, and with regard to particular men, you are inclined always rather to think the
better, whereas with me it is always directly contrary. I
hope, however, this is not in you from a superior principle
of virtue, but from your situation, which has made all
parties and interests indifferent to you; who can be under
no concern about High and Low Church, Whig and Tory,
or who is first Minister.

Your long letter was the last I received till this by Dr.
Delany, although you mention another since.[1] The Doctor
told me your secret about the Dunciad, which does not
please me, because it defers gratifying my vanity in the
most tender point, and perhaps may wholly disappoint it.[2]
As to one of your inquiries, I am easy enough in great
matters, but have a thousand paltry vexations in my little
station, and the more contemptible the more vexatious.
There might be a Lutrin writ upon the tricks used by my
Chapter to tease me. I do not converse with one creature
of station or title, but I have a set of easy people whom I
entertain when I have a mind, I have formerly described
them to you; but when you come you shall have the honours of the country as much as you please, and I shall, on
that account, make a better figure as long as I live. Pray
God preserve Mrs. Pope for your sake and ease; I love and
esteem her too much to wish it for her own. If I were five-
and-twenty, I would wish to be of her age, to be as secure
as she is of a better life. Mrs. Patty Blount has writ to
me,[3] and is one of the best letter-writers I know; very
good sense, civility and friendship, without any stiffness or
constraint. The Dunciad has taken wind here,[4] but if it

---

[1] The last letter from Pope now forthcoming is the one dated
March 23 (*supra*, p. 17).
[2] The first edition of the "Dunciad" was published without the
"inscriptio" (*supra*, p. 11).
[3] *Supra*, p. 28.
[4] As Mr. Courthope tells us in the Introduction to the "Dunciad"
(Pope's "Works," iv, 18), one of Pope's many subterfuges was to re-

had not, you are as much known here as in England, and the University lads will crowd to kiss the hem of your garment. I am grieved to hear that my Lord Bolingbroke's ill health forced him to the Bath. Tell me, is not temperance a necessary virtue for great men, since it is the parent of ease and liberty, so necessary for the use and improvement of the mind, and which philosophy allows to be the greatest felicities of life? I believe, had health been given so liberally to you, it would have been better husbanded without shame to your parts.

DCCII. [*Elwin.*]

ALEXANDER POPE TO SWIFT

Dawley, *June* 28, 1728.

I NOW hold the pen for my Lord Bolingbroke, who is reading your letter [1] between two haycocks, but his attention is somewhat diverted by casting his eyes on the clouds, not in admiration of what you say, but for fear of a shower. He is pleased with your placing him in the triumvirate between yourself and me; though he says that he doubts he shall fare like Lepidus, while one of us runs away with all the power, like Augustus, and another with all the pleasures, like Anthony. It is upon a foresight of this that he has fitted up his farm, and you will agree that his scheme of retreat at least is not founded upon weak appearances. Upon his return from the Bath, all peccant humours, he finds, are purged out of him, and his great temperance and economy are so signal, that the first is fit for my constitution, and the latter would enable you to lay up so much money as to buy a bishopric in England. As to the return of his health and vigour, were you here, you might inquire of his haymakers, but as to his temperance, I can answer that, for one whole day, we have had nothing for dinner but mutton broth, beans and bacon, and a barn-door fowl.

present that poem as originally printed in Dublin. The first edition was issued in London on 28 May with the following title: " The Dunciad, an heroic poem, in three books; Dublin printed, London reprinted for A. Dodd 1728."
[1] The preceding one.

Now his Lordship is run after his cart, I have a moment left to myself to tell you, that I overheard him yesterday agree with a painter for two hundred pounds to paint his country hall with trophies of rakes, spades, prongs, etc., and other ornaments, merely to countenance his calling this place a farm.[1] Now turn over a new leaf.

He bids me assure you, he should be sorry not to have more schemes of kindness for his friends than of ambition for himself. There, though his schemes may be weak, the motives at least are strong; and he says farther, if you could bear as great a fall and decrease of your revenues, as he knows by experience he can, you would not live in Ireland an hour.

The Dunciad is going to be printed in all pomp, with the inscription, which makes me proudest.[2] It will be attended with *Proeme, Prolegomena, Testimonia Scriptorum, Index Authorum,* and Notes *Variorum.* As to the latter, I desire you to read over the text, and make a few in any way you like best; whether dry raillery, upon the style and way of commenting of trivial critics; or humorous, upon the authors in the poem; or historical, of persons, places, times; or explanatory; or collecting the parallel passages of the ancients. Adieu. I am pretty well, my mother not ill. Dr. Arbuthnot vexed with his fever by intervals. I am afraid he declines, and we shall lose a worthy man. I am troubled about him very much. I am, etc.

DCCIII. [*Original.*[3]]

JOHN GAY TO SWIFT

Bath, *July* 6, 1728.

DEAR SIR,

THE last news I heard of you was from Mr. Lancelot, who was at this place with Lord Sussex, who gave me

---

[1] Writing to Bathurst four months later Pope says that "there are all the insignia and instruments of husbandry painted now in the hall, that one could wish to see in the fields of the most industrious farmer in Christendom" (Pope's "Works," viii, 333).

[2] That edition did not appear, however, until the following year.

[3] In the British Museum. See Preface.

hopes of seeing you the latter end of this summer.[1] I wish
you may keep that resolution, and take the Bath in your
way to town. You, in all probability, will find here some
or most of those you like to see. Dr. Arbuthnot wrote to
me to-day from Tunbridge, where he is now for the recovery
of his health, having had several relapses of a fever: he tells
me that he is much better, and that in August he intends
to come hither. Mr. Lewis will be here the beginning of
August, and I have some hope of seeing Mr. Pope too.
Mr. Congreve and I often talk of you, and wish you health
and every good thing; but often, out of self-interest, we
wish you with us. In five or six days I set out upon an
excursion to Herefordshire, to Lady Scudamore's,[2] but shall
return here in the beginning of August. I wish you could
meet me at Goodrich.

The Bath did not agree with Lady Bolingbroke, and she
went from hence much worse than she came. Since she
went to Dawley, by her own inclination, without the advice
of physicians, she hath taken to a milk diet, and she hath
writ me an account of prodigious good effects both of recovery of her appetite and spirits. The weather is extremely
hot, the place is very empty. I have an inclination to study,
but the heat makes it impossible. The Duke of Bolton, I
hear, hath run away with Polly Peachum, having settled
four hundred pounds a year upon her during pleasure, and
upon disagreement two hundred pounds a year.[3] Mr. Pope
is in a state of persecution for the Dunciad; I wish to be
witness of his fortitude, but he writes but seldom. It would
be a consolation to me to hear from you. I have heard but
once from Mrs. Howard these three months, and I think
but once from Mr. Pope. My portrait mezzotinto is published from Mrs. Howard's painting. I wish I could con-

[1] Talbot Yelverton, second Viscount de Longueville and sixteenth
Baron Grey de Ruthyn, who was created Earl of Sussex by George I,
died three years later at the age of forty. There is no indication as to
the calling of Patty Rolt's husband (*supra*, vol. iii, p. 410). His death
is thus announced in the " Gentleman's Magazine " for 1743: " Aug. 7.
William Lancelot, Esq., of New Bond Street."

[2] Lady Scudamore, the widow of the third Viscount Scudamore,
was an aunt of Pope's friend, Robert Digby, and is mentioned more
than once in Pope's correspondence. At her seat, Hom Lacy on the
Wye, Pope is said to have become acquainted with the existence of
the Man of Ross.

[3] *Supra*, p. 16.

trive to send you one, but I fancy I could get a better impression at London.

I have ten thousand things to talk to you, but few to write, but defer writing to you no longer, knowing you interest yourself in everything that concerns me so much, that I make you happy, as you will me, if you can tell me you are in good health, which I wish you to hear every morning as soon as I wake. I am, dear Sir,

Yours most affectionately.

Addressed—To the Reverend Dr. Swift, Dean of St. Patrick's, in Dublin, Ireland.

DCCIV. [*Elwin.*]

SWIFT TO ALEXANDER POPE

July 16, 1728.

I HAVE often run over the Dunciad, in an Irish edition [1]— I suppose full of faults—which a gentleman sent me. [2] The notes I could wish to be very large, in what relates to the persons concerned; for I have long observed that twenty miles from London nobody understands hints, initial letters, or town facts and passages, and in a few

---

[1] *Supra*, p. 34, n. 4.

[2] Swift had then been for more than a month the guest of Sir Arthur Acheson at his seat, now known as Gosford Castle, near Armagh. The visit seems to have been contrived by Sheridan, who possibly was known to Acheson as his sons' schoolmaster, but there was an old tie between Lady Acheson and Swift, as her father, the Right Hon. Philip Savage, who was for more than twenty years Chancellor of the Exchequer in Ireland, is mentioned in the Journal to Stella as one of Swift's friends, and was vindicated by him in the " Short Character of the Earl of Wharton " from insinuations against his character (" Prose Works," ii, 70; v, 19, 28). Acheson shared with his father-in-law Tory opinions, and after the accession of George I the Irish executive had prevented the transfer to him of Savage's office on the ground that he had always been deemed "a professed Jacobite," and was reported " to have gone the most extravagant lengths in declaring his affection that way, even so far as to debauch others from their allegiance " (State Papers Ireland, 24 December, 1715). But milder councils prevailed when this letter was written, and Acheson, who had been elected in the preceding year member for the borough of Mullingar, was then serving as high sheriff of his own county.

years not even those who live in London. I would have
the names of those scribblers printed indexically at the
beginning or end of the poem, with an account of their
works, for the reader to refer to. I would have all the
parodies, as they are called, referred to the author they
imitate. When I began this long paper, I thought I should
have filled it with setting down the several passages I had
marked in the edition I had, but I find it unnecessary, so
many of them falling under the same rule. After twenty
times reading the whole, I never in my opinion saw so
much good satire, or more good sense, in so many lines.
How it passes in Dublin I know not yet, but I am sure it
will be a great disadvantage to the poem, that the persons
and facts will not be understood till an explanation comes
out, and a very full one. I imagine it not to be published
till towards winter, when folks begin to gather in town.
Again I insist, you must have your asterisks filled up with
some real names of real dunces.

I am now reading your preceding letter of June 28th,
and find that all I have advised above is mentioned there.
I would be glad to know whether the quarto edition is to
come out anonymously, as published by the commentator,
with all his pomp of prefaces, etc., and among many complaints of spurious editions? I am thinking whether the
editor should not follow the old style of "this excellent
author," etc., and refine in many places when you meant
no refinement; and into the bargain, take all the load of
naming the dunces, their qualities, histories, and performances.

As to yourself, I doubt you want a spurrer-on to exercise
and to amusements; but to talk of decay at your season of
life is a jest. But you are not so regular as I. You are the
most temperate man God-ward, and the most intemperate
yourself-ward, of most I have known. I suppose Mr. Gay
will return from the Bath with twenty pounds more flesh,[1]
and two hundred less in money. Providence never designed
him to be above two-and-twenty, by his thoughtlessness
and cullibility. He has as little foresight of age, sickness,
poverty, or loss of admirers, as a girl at fifteen. By the
way, I must observe, that my Lord Bolingbroke, from the

---

[1] In a skit entitled "The Female Faction or the Gay Subscribers,"
published in 1729 (Royal Irish Academy Tracts), Gay is described
as: "A bard as bulky in renown as size."

effects of his kindness to me, argues most sophistically. The fall from a million to a hundred thousand pounds is not so great as from eight hundred pounds a year to one: besides he is a controller of fortune, and poverty dares not look a great Minister in the face under his lowest declension. I never knew him live so greatly and expensively as he has done since his return from exile; such mortals have resources that others are not able to comprehend. But God bless you, whose great genius had not so transported you as to leave you to the courtesy of mankind; for wealth is liberty, and liberty is a blessing fittest for a philosopher, and Gay is a slave just by two thousand pounds too little, and Horace was of my mind, and let my Lord contradict him if he dares.

DCCV. [*Manuscripts of the Marquis of Bath.*[1]]

THE EARL OF OXFORD TO SWIFT

July 27, 1728.

IT is now complete two months since I received the favour of your letter,[2] and a very great one I esteem it, and also some medals which were of use to me in my collection; please to accept my thanks for them. Mr. Clayton[3] has been going this six weeks, which was one reason of my not writing, and I think I should not give you the trouble of two letters upon the same subject resolving to write by him whenever he went. I have heard some kind of whisper as if the Dean of St. Patrick's would be in England this winter. I wish he may, but it is too good news to be true, I fear. Mr. Pope stands by himself, *Athanasius contra mundum.* There is never a newspaper comes out but he is favoured with a letter, a poem, an epigram, even to a distich, from the numerous herd of dunces and blockheads that are in and about London and the suburbs thereof. I saw him the other day. He is as to his health much the same as you left him. He has at last taken a resolution of going to the Bath this season. I hope it will be of service to him. My wife and Peggy are much your humble ser-

---

[1] Hist. MSS. Com., vol. i, p. 253.   [2] *Supra*, p. 31.
[3] *Supra*, vol. iii, p. 260, n. 2.

vants. My wife goes this next season to the Bath. I hope
it will do her good for the badness of her stomach. I hope
this will find you very well wherever it be, for I hear you
often make excursions into the country. I shall be glad to
hear that you are free from your deafness you complained
of when you went out of England last.

DCCVI. [*Sheridan.*]

SWIFT TO THE REV. THOMAS SHERIDAN

Market Hill, *August* 2, 1728.

OUR friends here,[1] as well as myself, were sadly disappointed
upon hearing the account of your journey. Nobody in
town or country, as we were informed, knew where you
were, but I persuaded our family, that you were certainly
in a way of making yourself easy, and had got that living
you mentioned, and accordingly we were grieved, and re-
joiced at the loss and settlement of a friend. But it never
entered into our heads, that you were bestowing forty days
in several stages between constable and constable, without
any real benefit to yourself, farther than of exercise,[2] and
we wished that nobody should have had the benefit of your
long absence from your school but yourself, by a good living, or we by your good company, much less than the

---

[1] *I.e.*, the Achesons (*supra*, p. 38, n. 2).

[2] It appears from a letter addressed to him by Archbishop King on
25 July that Sheridan had been in Cork. The letter conveys a rebuke
represented as coming from a third person in the manner characteristic
of King. " I received yours without date. I spake to the Registrar in
your behalf, and he told me you never yet appeared on the proper day
when school-masters were summoned; that it is expected that clergymen who know the rules and canons of the Church should give the
most exact obedience to them, and be an example to other people, and
when they fail deserve most to be made examples; he intimated further
that the pretenders to be the Highest Churchmen are commonly the
most negligent and refractory, by which they encourage such as profess less regard to religion to contemn the ecclesiastical jurisdiction. I
did not know what to answer to this, but the Court being adjourned to
the 8th of next month, I will take care to have an *expectator* put upon
you, and do hope when you come to Dublin you will take care to
make yourself *rectus in curia.*"

pleasure of spiteing T[ighe] had been your great motive.[1]
I heartily wish you were settled at Hamilton's Bawn,[2] and
I would be apt to advise you not to quit your thoughts
that way, if the matter may be brought to bear, for by a
letter I just received from the Bishop of Cork,[3] which was
short and dry, with the stale excuse of pre-engagements, I
doubt you can hope nothing from him. As to what you
call my exercise,[4] I have long quitted it: it gave me too
much constraint, and the world does not deserve it. We
may keep it cold till the middle of winter.

As to my return, there are many speculations. I am well
here, and hate removals; my scheme was, that you should
come hither, as you say, and I return with you in your
chaise. Sir Arthur, on hearing your letter, pressed me to
stay longer.[5] I am a very busy man, such as at Quilca,
which you will know when you come; yet I would contrive to be pressed more to stay till Christmas, and that
you may contrive to be here again, and take me back with
you time enough for my own visitation, and my reason of
staying is, to be here the planting and pruning time, etc.
I hate Dublin, and love the retirement here, and the civility
of my hosts. This is my state and humour upon it, and
accordingly you are to manage my scheme. However, I
would have you keep your vacation of September here;
and let Mrs. Brent send me a dozen guineas, half of them
half guineas, by you, and a periwig, and a new riding-gown
and cassock, and whatever else I may want by a longer

[1] The eighth and tenth numbers of the "Intelligencer" are devoted
to Tighe (*supra*, vol. iii, p. 272, n. 1), and are mainly occupied by two
of Swift's poetical effusions on him.
[2] A suggestion that Sheridan should remove his school to the celebrated Bawn was evidently then under consideration. The word bawn
is an Anglicized form of the Irish *bábhun*, an enclosure for cattle, and
has come to signify an enclosure formed by walls flanked with towers.
Some valuable notes on the origin and construction of these fortified
structures by the Rev. A. T. Lee and the well-known Irish scholar
John O'Donovan will be found in the "Ulster Journal of Archaeology"
(I, vi, 125).
[3] *I.e.*, Peter Browne (*supra*, vol. iii, p. 244).
[4] *I.e.*, the "Intelligencer."
[5] The verses, which open by describing Swift's arrival at Market
Hill in response to a casual invitation three days before he was expected, and Lady Acheson's artifices to terminate a stay that had been
prolonged "a week, a month, a quarter," were probably written at
that time ("Poetical Works," ii, 93).

absence, provided you will resolve and swear that I shall stay.

I had all Mrs. Brent's packets by Mr. Little. My service to Mrs. Dingley. I cannot say that I have more to say than to say that I am, etc.

DCCVII. [*Sheridan.*]

SWIFT TO THE REV. THOMAS SHERIDAN

September 18, 1728.

MY continuance here is owing partly to indolence, and partly to my hatred to Dublin.[1] I am in a middling way, between healthy and sick, hardly ever without a little giddiness or deafness, and sometimes both: so much for that. As to what you call my lesson, I told you I would think no more of it, neither do I conceive the world deserves so much trouble from you or me. I think the sufferings of the country for want of silver deserves a paper,[2] since the remedy is so easy, and those in power so negligent. I had some other subjects in my thoughts, but truly I am taken up so much with long lampoons on a person, who owns you for a back, that I have no time for anything else, and if I do not produce one every now and then of about two hundred lines, I am chid for my idleness, and threatened with you.[3] I desire you will step to the Deanery, speak to Mrs. Brent, bid her open the middle great drawer of Ridgeway's escritoire in my closet,[4] and then do you take out from thence the History in folio, marble cover;[5] and two thin folios fairly writ, I forget the titles, but you have read them, one is an account of the proceedings of Lord Oxford's Ministry, and the other to the same purpose.[6] There

---

[1] Swift is apparently answering a reply to the preceding letter.

[2] The nineteenth number of the "Intelligencer," which was written by Swift, deals with this subject.

[3] The reference is probably to "My Lady's Lamentation and Complaint against the Dean" which is dated July 28, 1728 ("Poetical Works," ii, 95). That poem contains two hundred and thirty-six lines.

[4] Ridgeway was the husband of Mrs. Brent's daughter.

[5] The "History of the Four Last Years of the Queen."

[6] The "Memoirs relating to that Change in the Queen's Ministry" and the "Enquiry into the Behaviour of the Queen's Last Ministry."

are foul copies of both in the same drawer, but do you take out the fair ones, not in my hand. Let them be packed up and brought hither by the bearer. My lady is perpetually quarrelling with Sir Arthur and me, and shows every creature the libels I have writ against her.

Mr. Worrall sent me the particulars of the havoc made in Naboth's vineyard. The dam burst, etc.[1] I think Lady Dun's burning would be an admirable subject to show how hateful an animal a human creature is that is known to have never done any good. The rabble all rejoicing, etc., which they would not have done at any misfortune to a man known to be charitable.[2]

I wish you could get in with the Primate, on the account of some discourse about you here to-day with Whaley and Walmsley.[3] Whaley goes to Dublin on Monday next in order for England. I would have you see him. I fancy you may do some good with the Primate as to the first good vacant school, if you wheedle him, and talk a little Whiggishly.

[1] On account of its situation on a river called the Poddle, St. Patrick's Cathedral was in ancient times styled *in insula*. The inundations from this river were in the past often attended with disastrous results (Bishop Bernard's " St. Patrick's," p. 101).

[2] The residence of Sir Patrick Dun's widow (*supra*, vol. i, p. 137, n. 1) in Dublin had been consumed by fire on the 1st of that month, and Swift had doubtless seen an extraordinary account of the conflagration which appeared in the " Dublin Intelligence." After describing the havoc made by the fire and the depredations of a gang of thieves the reporter says: " So great a loss as was here was not sustained by any fire in this city these many years, the house being full of exceeding valuable goods as well as clothes, plate and linen, little of which were saved for the owner, that part of them which was unconsumed being mostly taken away; several of the mob barbarously expressing there was no pity due for that loss, the sum total being mostly the right of others than the possessor, besides such other taunting language which in their ravaging they used, notwithstanding all the care and pains which are taken to the contrary by many well-minded persons."

[3] *Supra*, vol. iii, pp. 54, 128.

DCCVIII. [*Copy.*[1]]

Swift to the Earl of Oxford

September 21, 1728.

My Lord,

Mr. Clayton sent me your Lordship's letter[2] to the north of this kingdom, where I have been these three months and still continue, in the same degree with Yorkshire and where codlins will sometimes grow ripe, provided it be a favourable season. I shall not accept your Lordship's thanks because I have not even so much merit as the poor man who presented his Prince with a greater turnip than ordinary. If I desire them on any account it is for having given you so many opportunities of showing your generosity and goodness.

I intended to have passed this winter in London, but my health is so uncertain with the frequent returns of those two impertinent disorders, giddiness and deafness, that I am forced to prefer a scurvy home where I can command people to speak as loud as I please, before the vexation of making a silly figure and tearing the lungs of my friends.

I hear that myself and one or two more have a share in the scurrilities that the Dunciad hath occasioned, as a just punishment for the friendship we have with Mr. Pope. These are usual events. For about six months ago, a pamphlet was sent me by post, and to my great cost not franked, but no doubt from some special well-wisher, wherein I was handled with the like decency upon the account of a mere trifle, only for joining with some great confederates to break the present Ministry, and utterly destroy Sir Robert Walpole;[3] whereas God knows, I was at that time quiet with Mr. Pope: I cannot say better employed, but much more to my own satisfaction.[4]

---

[1] In the Forster Collection.
[2] *Supra*, p. 40.
[3] The pamphlet was possibly one entitled "An Essay upon the Taste and Writings of the present Times, but with a more particular View to Political and Dramatick Writings occasion'd by a late Volume of Miscellanies by A. Pope, Esq., and Dr. Swift," which was published in that year (Royal Irish Academy Pamphlets).
[4] At that time it had been rumoured in Dublin that he was apprehended. "A like account we have by report without other foundation,"

I pray God send my Lady Oxford success at the Bath, and that she may soon and long increase the market bills in your Lordship's family, and take corporeal food like us mortals, which I cannot charge my memory to have ever seen her do. I desire to present my most humble service to her Ladyship, and to my Lady Marget. I am ever, with great respect, my Lord,

Your Lordship's most obedient and most humble servant,
JONATH. SWIFT.

This letter will be delivered to your Lordship by Mr. Whaley, who was a fellow of Wadham in your Lordship's time, and invited over hither by the late Primate Lindsay, by whom he was preferred. He has now an appeal before the House of Lords for a Church living of near a thousand pounds a year, of which he has been long and legally possessed, and his adversary, one Dean Daniel, is the greatest puppy and vilest poet alive, with a very bad cause to be supported by a party.[1] Mr. Whaley is so worthy a person that I could not refuse his request of recommending him to your Lordship's favour on this occasion, and your credit with the Lords of your acquaintance to attend at the cause when it will be of most use.

Addressed—To the Right Honourable the Earl of Oxford.

Endorsed—Delivered by Dr. Whaley, Nov. 11, 1728, in Dover Street.

says the " Dublin Intelligence " of 20 June, 1727, "that D . . . Sw . . . was committed to the custody of a messenger, or to the Tower of London, on account of some paper lately published in that city, to the great surprise of many of our inhabitants here, who have an entire love and respect to that worthy gentleman, and whom we assure this should not be inserted, but that we fear some gross abusive person should pretend to confirm this publicly for which there is no certain nor real foundation."

[1] In addition to Donoughmore (*supra*, vol. iii, p. 54), Whaley had been given by Primate Lindsay the rectory of Armagh, but the Government claimed the right of presentation, and nominated one of their own supporters Richard Daniel, who was appointed at the same time Dean of Armagh. His published works include a poem occasioned by the death of William III, another on the return of George I from Hanover in 1717, and paraphrases of a number of the Psalms (Leslie's "Armagh Clergy," pp. 20, 114).

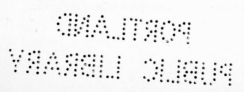

DCCIX. [*Original.*[1]]

SWIFT TO THE REV. JOHN WORRALL

September 28, 1728.

I HAD all the letters given me by my servants, so tell Mrs. Brent and Dr. Sheridan ; and I thank you for the great care you had in the commissions I troubled you with.[2] I imagine Mrs. Brent is gone into the country, but that you know where to send to her. I desire you will pay her four pounds, and sixteen pounds to Mrs. Dingley, and take their receipts. I beg Mrs. Dingley's pardon for not remembering her debt sooner; and my humble service to her. I desire Mrs. Brent to send me the best receipt she has for making mead: she may send me her receipt for making the strong mead, and that for making the next strong, and the third strong. Hers was always too strong, and on that account she was so wilful I would suffer her to make no more.

There is a vexatious thing happened about the usquebaugh for my Lord Bolingbroke. It seems, you only directed it for the Earl of Berkeley, but I thought I had desired you to add " for Lord Bolingbroke "; but there is nothing in that, for I wrote to the Earl of Berkeley, to give him notice. But Mr. Gavan, who married a daughter of Mrs. Kenna, who keeps the inn at Chester,[3] hath just sent me a letter, informing me that the usquebaugh came to Parkgate, within seven miles of Chester, and that Mr. Whittle, the owner of the ship, was to deliver it himself; but he sent it by a man of a noted bad character, who, as Mrs. Kenna supposes, kept it some time, and opened it before he delivered it. For, immediately upon the delivery of it, Mrs. Kenna sent to Parkgate, to have the usquebaugh brought up to Chester, but was told that the fellow had brought it away, that he said, he sent it as directed, but that no doubt he must have some view of paying himself for the trouble, which made him so busy, but whether it was by changing the usquebaugh, or overrating the charges of it, Mr. Gavan cannot tell, but adds that, if I should hear of anything amiss, I should write to Mrs. Kenna, his

---

[1] In the British Museum. See Preface.
[2] *Supra*, p. 43.   [3] *Supra*, vol. iii, p. 363.

mother, who will endeavour to make the fellow do me justice. All this I have transcribed from Mr. Gavan's letter; and I desire you will call upon his father, Mr. Luke Gavan, who is a known man in Dublin,[1] and desire him, when he writes to his son, to give my service to him and Mrs. Kenna, and let them know I will do as they direct. I am very unfortunate in this affair, but have no remedy; however, I will write to Lord Bolingbroke, though I fear I am cheated of it all, for I do not find that the fellow demanded anything from Mrs. Kenna, or came to her at all.

Your new fancies of making my riding-gown and cassock, I mean Mrs. Brent's fancies, do not please me at all, because they differ so much from my old one. You are a bad packer of bad grapes. Mrs. Dingley says she cannot persuade Mrs. Brent to take a vomit. Is she not—do not tell her—an old fool? She has made me take many a one without mercy. Pray give Mrs. Worrall a thousand thanks from me, for her kind present and workmanship of her fairest hands in making me two nightcaps. We have a design upon Sheridan. He sent us in print a ballad upon Ballyspellan, in which he has employed all the rhymes he could find to that word; but we have found fifteen more, and employed them in abusing his ballad, and Ballyspellan too.[2] I here send you a copy, and desire you will get it printed privately, and published. I am ever yours, etc.

Your periwig-maker is a cursed rogue. The wig he gave you is an old one with a new caul, and so long that I cannot wear it, and the curls all fallen. I just tried it on my head, but cannot wear it.

Addressed—To the Revd. Mr. Worrall at his house in Big Sheep Street, Dublin.

[1] He was a merchant and shipowner, and the father of seven sons.
[2] Ballyspellan, which lies eight miles to the north-west of Kilkenny, possesses a chalybeate spring which was then in high repute, and gained for the place the name of the Irish Spa. Dissertations upon its properties with directions for its use were published by local physicians, and recommended to the public by a display of much learning. See an "Essay on the Waters and Air of Ballyspellan," by John Burges, M.D. (Royal Irish Academy Tracts, and Rutty's "Mineral Waters of Ireland," p. 170). The rhymes will be found in the "Poetical Works," ii, 368, 371.

DCCX. [*Elwin.*]

ALEXANDER POPE TO SWIFT

Bath, *Oct.* 12, 1728.

I HAVE passed six weeks in quest of health, and found it not, but I found the folly of solicitude about it in a hundred instances; the contrariety of opinions and practices, the inability of physicians, the blind obedience of some patients, and as blind rebellion of others. I believe at a certain time of life, men are either fools or physicians for themselves; and zealots or divines for themselves.

It was much in my hopes that you intended us a winter's visit, but last week I repented that wish, having been alarmed with a report of your lying ill on the road from Ireland, from which I am just relieved by an assurance that you are still at Sir Arthur Acheson's planting and building—two things that I envy you for, beside a third, which is the society of a valuable lady. I conclude, though I know nothing of it, that you quarrel with her, and abuse her every day, if she is so. I wonder I hear of no lampoons upon her, either made by yourself, or by others, because you esteem her.[1] I think it a vast pleasure that whenever two people of merit regard one another, so many scoundrels envy and are angry at them; it is bearing testimony to a merit they cannot reach, and if you knew the infinite content I have received of late, at the finding yours and my name constantly united in any silly scandal, I think you would go near to sing *Io Triumphe*, and celebrate my happiness in verse, and I believe if you will not, I shall.

The inscription to the Dunciad is now printed, and inserted in the poem. Do you care I should say anything farther how much that poem is yours, since certainly without you, it had never been?[2] Would to God we were together for the rest of our lives! The whole weight of scribblers would just serve to find us amusement, and not more. I hope you are too well employed to mind them. Every stick you plant, and every stone you lay, is to some purpose; but

---

[1] Pope had learned through Sheridan of the verses on Lady Acheson.   [2] *Supra*, p. 4, n. 4.

IV   E

the business of such lives as theirs, is but to die daily, to
labour, and raise nothing. I only wish we could comfort
each other under our bodily infirmities, and let those who
have so great a mind to have more wit than we, win it and
wear it. Give us but ease, health, peace, and fair weather!
I think it is the best wish in the world, and you know
whose it was. If I lived in Ireland, I fear the wet climate
would endanger more than my life, my humour and health,
I am so atmospherical a creature.

I must not omit acquainting you, that what you heard
of the words spoken of you in the drawing-room was not
true.[1] The sayings of Princes are generally as ill related as
the sayings of wits. To such reports little of our regard
should be given, and less of our conduct influenced by
them.

DCCXI. [*Nichols.*]

SWIFT TO THE REV. THOMAS WALLIS

Market Hill, *November* 16, 1728.

SIR,

I AM extremely obliged to you for your kind intention
in the purchase you mention; but it will not answer my
design, because these lands are let in leases renewable for
ever, and consequently can never have the rent raised,
which is mortal to all estates left for ever to a public use,[2]
and is contrary to a fundamental maxim of mine, and
most corporations feel the smart of it.

I have been here several months to amuse me in my
disorders of giddiness and deafness, of which I have frequent
returns, and I shall hardly return to Dublin till Christmas.

I am truly grieved at your great loss.[3] Such misfortunes
seem to break the whole scheme of man's life, and although
time may lessen sorrow, yet it cannot hinder a man from
feeling the want of so near a companion, nor hardly supply
it with another. I wish you health and happiness, and that

---

[1] The reference to which this paragraph is a reply has been lost.
[2] Swift had probably formed the intention of bequeathing his property for such a purpose before Stella's death.
[3] By the death of his wife, to whom he was not long married (*supra*
vol. iii, p. 82).

the pledge[1] left you may prove a comfort. I am, with great sincerity,
　　　Your most obliged and most humble servant,
　　　　　　　　　　　　　　　　　　JON. SWIFT.

DCCXII. [*Original.*[2]]

JOHN GAY TO SWIFT

London, *December* 2, 1728.

　　DEAR SIR,

I THINK this is my fourth letter, I am sure it is the third, without any answer.[3] If I had had any assurance of your health, I should have been more easy. I should have writ to you upon this subject above a month ago, had it not been for a report that you were upon the road in your way to England, which I fear now was without any foundation. Your money, with part of my own, is still in the hands of Lord Bathurst, which I believe he will keep no longer, but repay upon his coming to town, when I will endeavour to dispose of it as I do of my own, unless I receive your orders to the contrary. Lord and Lady Bolingbroke are in town: she hath lately been very ill, but is now somewhat better.

I have had a very severe attack of a fever, which, by the care of our friend Dr. Arbuthnot, hath, I hope, now almost left me. I have been confined about ten days, but never to my bed, so that I hope soon to get abroad about my business, which is, the care of the second part of the Beggar's Opera, which was almost ready for rehearsal, but Rich received the Duke of Grafton's commands, upon an information he was rehearsing a play improper to be represented, not to rehearse any new play whatever, till his Grace hath seen it.[4] What will become of it I know not, but I am sure

---

[1] A son who is said to have become a barrister.
[2] In the British Museum. See Preface.
[3] Only two have been preserved (*supra*, pp. 32, 36).
[4] The scene of the sequel to the "Beggar's Opera" is laid in the Plantations, and many of the old characters are introduced, including Macheath, who is hanged, and Polly, who obtains another husband. The sequel is called "Polly," and its suppression is said to have been due to Walpole's resentment at the identification of Gay's heroine with his friend Miss Maria Skerrett ("D. N. B.," lix, 205).

I have written nothing that can be legally suppressed, unless the setting vices in general in an odious light, and virtue in an amiable one, may give offence. I passed five or six months this year at the Bath with the Duchess of Marlborough, and then, in the view of taking care of myself, writ this piece. If it goes on in case of success, I have taken care to make better bargains for myself. I tell you this, because I know you are so good to interest yourself so warmly in my affairs, that it is what you would want to know.

I saw Mr. Pope on Friday, who, as to his health, is just as you left him. His mother, by his account, is much the same. Mr. Lewis, who is very much your servant, as are all I have mentioned, tells me further time is still desired of him about the hundred pounds. Dr. Arbuthnot particularly desires his compliments, and Mrs. Howard often asks after you. Prince Frederick is expected over this week.[1] I hope to go abroad in two or three days. I wish I could meet with you either abroad or at home.

DCCXIII. [*Deane Swift.*]

—— TO SWIFT

Montrose, *December* 17, 1728.

SIR,[2]

SOME people here having flattered me that I have a genius for poetry, and my circumstances a little favouring it, I have resolved to turn my thoughts that way. I have already tried my talent on some little amusements, and have had the pleasure in secret to see them pretty well re-

---

[1] The news of his arrival in England reached Dublin on the 13th, and was received "with universal joy, the fine character of that Prince charming everybody " ("Dublin Intelligence"). This adulation is finely satirized by Swift in his poem "On how to write a Birthday Ode" ("Poetical Works," i, 335):

> "Now sing his little Highness Freddy
> Who struts like any king already."

[2] "As this letter seems to have been written by some very young adventurer in poetry," says Deane Swift, "we choose to suppress his name."

ceived; but few here being much conversant in that study, can be proper judges, and as I would not venture my character abroad in the world without the advice of those who have succeeded in it, I thought I could not more properly apply than to you, who have been pretty happy that way. What I mean is, that you would be pleased to furnish me with a theme to try my genius, with what rules you may think necessary. I expect your compliance with this, as it is the first, at least of this nature, you ever had from this place; and as soon as it is finished, you may expect a copy of the performance from, Sir,

Your most humble servant.

DCCXIV. [*Hawkesworth.*]

SWIFT TO THE REV. JOHN WORRALL

Market Hill, *January* 4, 1728-9.

I HAD your long letter, and thank you heartily for your concern about my health. I continue very deaf and giddy; but, however, I would certainly come to town, not only for my visitation,[1] but because in these circumstances, and in winter, I would rather be at home. But it is now Saturday night, and that beast Sheridan is not yet come, although it has been thawing since Monday.[2] If I do not come, you know what to do. My humble service to our friends, as usual.

DCCXV. [*Hawkesworth.*]

SWIFT TO THE REV. JOHN WORRALL

Market Hill, *January* 13, 1728-9.

I JUST received your letter, and should never have done, if I returned you thanks so often as I ought for your care

---

[1] The reference is to Swift's visitation of his Cathedral as Dean, which took place early in that month (*supra*, vol. iii, p. 188).

[2] A great quantity of snow had fallen in Dublin before Christmas, and had been followed by severe frost. Although a thaw is said to have set in at the close of the year, the "Dublin Intelligence" announces on 11 January that the roads continued so bad as "to retard the coming in of our posts."

and kindness. Both my disorders still continue; however, I desire that Mrs. Brent may make things ready, for my raggedness will soon force me away. I have been now ill about a month, but the family are so kind as to speak loud enough for me to hear them, and my deafness is not so extreme as you have known when I have fretted at your mannerly voice, and was only relieved by Mrs. Worrall.

I send you enclosed the fruit of my illness, to make an Intelligencer; I desire you will enclose it in a letter to Mrs. Harding,[1] and let your letter be in an unknown hand, and desire her to show it to the author of the Intelligencer, and to print it if he thinks fit. There is a letter, you will find, that is to be prefixed before the verses, which letter is grounded on a report, and if that report be false, the former part of the letter will be unseasonable, but the latter will not, and therefore the Intelligencer must be desired to alter it accordingly. It should be sent soon, to come time enough for the next Intelligencer.[2] Pray, in your letter to Mrs. Harding, desire her to make her people be more correct, and that the Intelligencer himself may look over it, for that everybody who reads those papers, are very much offended with the continual nonsense made by her printers. I am,

Yours,

J. SWIFT.

DCCXVI. [*Hawkesworth.*]

SWIFT TO THE REV. JOHN WORRALL

Market Hill, *January* 18, 1728-9.

I HAVE yours of the 14th instant, but you had not then received my last, in which was enclosed a paper for the

---

[1] The "Intelligencer" was issued from the same press as the Drapier Letters (*supra*, vol. iii, p. 266).

[2] The nineteenth number of the "Intelligencer," with which the Dublin edition in a collected form concludes, is dated 2 December, 1728, and a twentieth number entitled "Dean Smedley gone to seek his fortune," which is included in the London edition, was apparently not issued until the following May. The verses to which Swift here refers are "The Journal of a Modern Lady" ("Poetical Works," i, 172), which were issued about that time as a separate publication under the title of "The Journal of a Dublin Lady."

Intelligencer, which I hope you have disposed of as desired. My disorder still continues the same for this fortnight past, and am neither better nor worse. However, I resolved to return on the first mending of the weather; these three last days there being as violent a storm as I have known, which still continues. We have been told my Lord Mountcashell is dead at Drogheda, but believe it to be a lie. However, he *is so tender, and affects so much vigour and fatigue, that we have been in pain about him.[1]

I had a letter two days ago, which cost me six shillings and fourpence; it consisted of the probate of a will in Leicestershire, and of two enclosed letters, and was beyond the weight of letters franked. When I went a lad to my mother, after the Revolution, she brought me acquainted with a family where there was a daughter with whom I was acquainted.[2] My prudent mother was afraid I should be in love with her; but when I went to London, she married an inn-keeper in Loughborough, in that county, by whom she had several children. The old mother died, and left all that she had to her daughter aforesaid, separate from her husband. This woman, my mistress with a pox, left several children,[3] who are all dead but one daughter, Anne by name. This Anne, for it must be she, about seven years ago writ to me from London, to tell me she was daughter of Betty Jones, for that was my mistress's name, till she was married to one Perkins, inn-keeper, at the George in Loughborough, as I said before. The subject of the girl's letter was, that a young lady of good fortune was courted by an Irishman, who pretended to be barrack-master-general of Ireland, and desired me as an old acquaintance of her mother Betty Jones, *alias* Perkins, to inquire about this Irishman. I answered, that I knew him not, but supposed he was a cheat; I heard no more.

[1] The rumour of the death of Sheridan's show pupil (*supra,* vol. iii, p. 402, n. 1) at that time was without foundation, but only anticipated the event by a few years. He was the last representative of the family of Davys which contributed many distinguished servants to the public service in Ireland, and was the second son of the first holder of the title which was conferred by George I.

[2] *Supra*, vol. i, p. 2.

[3] Notwithstanding the word "left," the subsequent paragraph shows that so far as Swift knew, Betty Perkins was still alive.

But now comes a letter to me from this Betty Jones, *alias* Perkins, to let me know that her daughter, Anne Giles, married an Irishman, one Giles, and was now come over to Ireland to pick up some debts due to her husband, which she could not get; that the young widow, for her husband Giles is dead, has a mind to settle in Ireland, and to desire I would lend her daughter Giles three guineas, which her mother will pay me when I draw upon her in England, and Mrs. Giles writes me a letter to that purpose. She intends to take a shop, and will borrow the money from Mrs. Brent, whose name she has learned, and pay me as others do.[1] I was at first determined to desire you would, from me, make her a present of five pounds, on account of her mother and grandmother, whom my mother used to call cousin. She has sent me an attested copy of her mother's will, which, as I told you, cost me six shillings and fourpence. But I am in much doubt, for by her mother's letters, she is her heiress, and the grandmother left Betty Jones, *alias* Perkins, the mother of this woman in Dublin, all she had, as a separate maintenance from her husband, who proved a rogue, to the value of five hundred pounds. Now, I cannot conceive why she would let her only daughter and heiress come to Ireland, without giving her money to bear her charges here, and put her in some way. The woman's name is Anne Giles, she lodges at one Mrs. Wilmot's, the first house in Molesworth Court, on the right hand, in Fishamble Street. I have told you this long story, to desire you will send for the woman, this Anne Giles, and examine her strictly, to find if she be the real daughter of Elizabeth Jones, *alias* Perkins, or not, and how her mother, who is so well able, came to send her in so miserable a condition to Ireland. The errand is so romantic, that I know not what to say to it. I would be ready to sacrifice five pounds, on old acquaintance, to help the woman. I suspect her mother's letters to be counterfeit, for I remember she spells like a kitchen maid. And so I end this worthy business.

My bookseller, Mr. Motte, by my recommendation, dealt with Mr. Hyde; there are some accounts between them, and Hyde is in his debt. He has desired me to speak to Mr. Hyde's executors to state the account, that Mr.

[1] *Supra*, vol. iii, p. 99.

Motte may be in the way to recover the balance.[1] I wish
you would step to Mr. Hyde's house, and enquire how
that matter stands, and how Mr. Motte is to be paid. I
suppose Mr. Hyde died in good circumstances, and that
there will be no danger of his creditors suffering by his
death. I enclose a letter to Mr. Motte, which you will be
so kind to send to the post-office.

I desire, likewise, that you will make Mrs. Brent buy a
bottle of usquebaugh, and leave it with the woman who
keeps Sir Arthur Acheson's house in Capel Street,[2] and
desire her to deliver it to Captain Creichton,[3] who lodges
at the Pied Horse, in Capel Street, and is to bring down
other things to my Lady Acheson. My most humble service to Mrs. Worrall, Mrs. Dingley, and love to Mrs. Brent.
I wish you all a happy new year.

DCCXVII. [*Elwin.*]

SWIFT TO ALEXANDER POPE

Dublin, *February* 13, 1728-9.

I LIVED very easily in the country.[4] Sir Arthur is a man
of sense, and a scholar,[5] has a good voice, and my Lady a
better. She is perfectly well bred and desirous to improve
her understanding, which is very good, but cultivated too
much like a fine lady. She was my pupil there, and
severely chid when she read wrong.[6] With that, and walk-

---

[1] The will of "John Hide of the city of Dublin stationer" was proved
just a week before (*supra*, vol. iii, pp. 33, 438).

[2] A street in the northern part of Dublin which has been already
mentioned (vol. ii, p. 420, n. 1) and which dates from the latter part of
the seventeenth century when the Earl of Essex was viceroy. It is
now occupied by business houses, but was then a residential quarter.

[3] The hero of the "Memoirs of Captain John Creichton" ("Prose
Works," xi, 165).

[4] This letter is evidently a reply to one from Pope that has been suppressed (*supra*, vol. iii, p. 452).

[5] *Cf.* his verses to Swift, "Poetical Works," ii, 92. He was a graduate
of Dublin University.

[6]
> "Put a word out of joint,
> Or miss but a point,
> He rages and frets,
> His manners forgets,

ing, and making twenty little amusing improvements,[1] and writing family verses of mirth by way of libels on my Lady, my time passed very well and in very great order; infinitely better than here, where I see no creature but my servants and my old Presbyterian housekeeper, denying myself to everybody, till I shall recover my ears.

The account of another Lord Lieutenant was only in a common newspaper, when I was in the country;[2] and if it should have happened to be true, I would have desired to have had access to him as the situation I am in requires. But this renews the grief for the death of our friend Mr. Congreve,[3] whom I loved from my youth, and who surely, beside his other talents, was a very agreeable companion. He had the misfortune to squander away a very good constitution in his younger days, and I think a man of sense and merit like him, is bound in conscience to preserve his health for the sake of his friends, as well as of himself. Upon his own account I could not much desire the continuance of his life, under so much pain, and so many infirmities. Years have not yet hardened me, and I have an addition of weight on my spirits since we lost him, though I saw him so seldom, and possibly if he had lived on, should never had seen him more.

I do not only wish, as you ask me, that I was unacquainted with any deserving person, but almost that I never had a friend. Here is an ingenious good-humoured

> And as I am serious
> Is very imperious."
>
> "Poetical Works," ii, 97.

[1]
> "How proudly he talks
> Of zigzags and walks,
> And all the day raves
> Of cradles and caves,
> And boasts of his feats,
> His grottos and seats."
>
> *Ibid.*, ii, 98.

[2] Pope had probably alluded to a rumour that Carteret was to be superseded. In the following April it was reported that Swift's old friend the Duke of Argyll was to be sent over to Ireland as Lord Lieutenant ("Dublin Intelligence," 5 April, 1729).

[3] It is possible that Pope's letter had informed Swift of Congreve's death, which had occurred in London on 29 January from the effects of a carriage accident while he had been at Bath.

physician,[1] a fine gentleman, an excellent scholar, easy in his fortunes, kind to everybody, has abundance of friends, entertains them often and liberally. They pass the evening with him at cards, with plenty of good meat and wine, eight or a dozen together. He loves them all, and they him. He has twenty of these at command. If one of them dies, it is no more than " poor Tom "! He gets another, or takes up with the rest, and is no more moved than at the loss of his cat. He offends nobody, is easy with everybody. Is not this the true happy man? I was describing him to my Lady Acheson, who knows him too; but she hates him mortally by my character, and will not drink his health. I would give half my fortune for the same temper, and yet I cannot say I love it, for I do not love my Lord ——, who is much of the Doctor's nature.

I hear Mr. Gay's second opera, which you mention, is forbid;[2] and then he will be once more fit to be advised, and reject your advice.   Adieu.

DCCXVIII. [*Elwin*.]

SWIFT TO ALEXANDER POPE

March 6, 1728-9.

SIR,

IF I am not a good correspondent, I have bad health, and that is as good.[3] I passed eight months in the country, with Sir Arthur and my Lady Acheson, and had at least half-a-dozen returns of my giddiness and deafness, which lasted me about three weeks apiece, and, among other inconveniences, hindered me from visiting my Chapter,[4] and punishing enormities, but did not save me the charges of a visitation dinner. This disorder neither hinders my sleeping, nor much my walking, yet is the

---

[1] The reference is to Dr. Helsham. He followed twelve months later the example of his friend Delany in retiring from his fellowship and retaining his professorship, which was the chair of Natural and Experimental Philosophy, endowed by Erasmus Smith (*supra*, p. 1, n. 2).   [2] *Supra*, p. 51.

[3] As appears from the concluding paragraph, this letter is a reply to one from Charles Ford, whose handwriting had been mistaken by Swift for that of Pope.   [4] *Supra*, p. 53.

most mortifying malady I can suffer. I have been just a
month in town, and have just got rid of it in a fortnight,
and, when it is on me, I have neither spirits to write, or
read, or think, or eat. But I drink as much as I like, which
is a resource you cannot fly to when you are ill. And I
like it as little as you; but I can bear a pint better than
you can a spoonful. You were very kind in your care for
Mr. Whaley, but I hope you remembered, that Daniel is a
damnable poet, and consequently a public enemy to mankind.[1] But I despise the Lords' decree, which is a jest
upon common sense, for what did it signify to the merits of
the cause, whether George the old, or the young, were on
the throne? [2]

No, I intended to pass last winter in England, but my
health said no; and I did design to live a gentleman, and,
as Sancho's wife said, to go in my coach to Court.[3] I know
not whether you are in earnest to come hither in spring;
if not, pray God you may never be in jest! Dr. Delany
shall attend you at Chester, and your apartment is ready;
and I have a most excellent chaise, and about sixteen
dozen of the best cider in the world; and you shall command the town and kingdom, and *digito monstrari*, etc.;
and, when I cannot hear, you shall have choice of the best
people we can afford, to hear you, and nurses enough; and
your apartment is on the sunny side.

The next paragraph strikes me dumb. You say I am to
blame, if I refuse the opportunity of going with my Lady
Bolingbroke to Aix-la-Chapelle. I must tell you, that a
foreign language is mortal to a deaf man. I must have
good ears to catch up the words of so nimble a tongued
race as the French, having been a dozen years without
conversing among them. Mr. Gay is a scandal to all lusty
young fellows with healthy countenances;[4] and, I think,
he is not intemperate in a physical sense. I am told he
has an asthma, which is a disease I commiserate more than

---

[1] *Supra*, p. 46.
[2] Owing to the death of George I, after the writ had been served
and before an answer had been made, the Lords had ten days before
decreed that a new writ must be issued (Nichols, "Works," xviii, 12).
[3] "If I am put to it, I'll go to Court, and set up a coach like all the
world; for she who has a governor for a husband may very well have
one and keep one" (Ormsby, *op. cit.*, iv, 127).
[4] As will be seen from subsequent letters, Gay was at that time
seriously ill.

deafness, because it will not leave a man quiet either sleeping or waking. I hope he does not intend to print his opera before it is acted;[1] for I defy all your subscriptions to amount to eight hundred pounds;[2] and yet, I believe, he lost as much more, for want of human prudence.

I told you some time ago that I was dwindled to a writer of libels on the lady of the family where I lived, and upon myself;[3] but they never went farther, and my Lady Acheson made me give her up all the foul copies, and never gave the fair ones out of her hands, or suffered them to be copied. They were sometimes shown to intimate friends to occasion mirth, and that was all. So that I am vexed at your thinking I had any hand in what could come to your eyes. I have some confused notion of seeing a paper called Sir Ralph the Patriot,[4] but am sure it was bad or indifferent; and as to the Lady at Quadrille, I never heard of it. Perhaps it may be the same with a paper of verses, called the Journal of a Dublin Lady, which I writ at Sir Arthur Acheson's, and leaving out what concerned the family, I sent it to be printed in a paper which Doctor Sheridan had engaged in, called the Intelligencer,[5] of which he made but sorry work, and then dropped it. But the verses were printed by themselves, and most horridly mangled in the press, and were very *mediocre* in themselves; but did well enough in the manner I mentioned, of a family jest. I do sincerely assure you, that my frequent old disorder, and the scene where I am, and the humour I am in, and some other reasons which time has shown, and will show more if I live, have lowered my small talents with a vengeance, and cooled my disposition to put them in use. I want only to be rich, for I am hard to be pleased; and for want of riches, people grow every day less solicitous to please me. Therefore I keep humble company, who are happy to come where they can get a bottle of wine without paying for it. I give my vicar[6]

---

[1] *Supra*, p. 51.

[2] The reference is to the profit from "The Beggar's Opera" (*supra*, p. 16).

[3] *Supra*, p. 58.

[4] It is to the twelfth number of the "Intelligencer" that Swift alludes. The verses which it contains are said to have originally been published in an English periodical called "The Country Journal."

[5] *Supra*, p. 33, n. 1. [6] *I.e.*, Worrall.

a supper, and his wife a shilling, to play with me an hour at backgammon once a fortnight. To all people of quality, and especially of titles, I am not within; or, at least, am deaf a week or two after I am well. But on Sunday evenings it costs me six bottles of wine to people whom I cannot keep out.

Pray, come over in April, if it be only to convince you that I tell no lies; and the journey will be certainly for your health. Mrs. Brent, my housekeeper, famous in print for digging out the great bottle,[1] says she will be your nurse; and the best physicians we have shall attend you without fees, although I believe you will have no occasion but to converse with one or two of them, to make them proud. Your letter came but last post, and you see my punctuality. I am unlucky at everything I send to England. Two bottles of usquebaugh were broken. Well, my humble service to my Lord Bolingbroke, Lord Bathurst, Lord Masham, and his lady my dear friend, and Mr. Pulteney, and the Doctor, and Mr. Lewis, and our sickly friend Gay, and my Lady Bolingbroke, and very much to Patty, who, I hope, will learn to love the world less before the world leaves off to love her. I am much concerned to hear of my Lord Peterborough being ill. I am exceedingly his servant; and pray God recover his health! As for your courtier, Mrs. Howard, and her mistress, I have nothing to say, but that they have neither memory nor manners, else I should have some mark of the former from the latter, which I was promised about two years ago; but, since I made them a present, it would be mean to remind them.[2] I am told poor Mrs. Pope is ill. Pray God preserve her to you, or raise you up as useful a friend!

This letter is an answer to Mr. Ford, whose hand I mistook for yours, having not heard from him this twelve-month. Therefore you are not to stare; and it must not be lost, for it talks to you only. Again, forgive my blunders; for, reading the letter by candle-light, and not dreaming of a letter from Mr. Ford, I thought it must be yours, because it talks of our friends. The letter talks of Gay, and Mr. Whaley, and Lord Bolingbroke, which made me conclude

---

[1] See the verses addressed to Stella on her birthday in 1723 ("Poetical Works," ii, 38).

[2] The reference is to a medal which was promised to him by Queen Caroline before he sent her the poplin (*supra*, vol. iii, p. 374).

it must be yours; so all the answering part must go for nothing.

DCCXIX. [*Deane Swift.*]

FRANCIS GEOGHEGAN TO SWIFT

March 10, 1728-9.

SIR,[1]

YOUR time is precious, your curiosity not very small, my esteem of you very great: therefore come not within the walls of the Four Courts in hopes a hearing a matrimonial decree in this reign; for on Monday, viz. that is to say, the 10th of this instant March 1728, his Excellency Thomas Wyndham, Esq., Lord High Chancellor of Ireland,[2] pronounced, after your back was turned, and not with the assistance of the two Chiefs, his decree in the case of Stewart *v.* Stewart, on a Powell, to this effect.[3] He said there was a full consent till such time as the draft of the settlement was sent down to Mrs. Stewart, to be considered by her and her friends, and after she had considered it, she shall not be at liberty to make any objections, for all

---

[1] The writer was a member of the Irish bar. He was a native of the county of Westmeath.

[2] Wyndham, who was a member of the distinguished Wiltshire family of that name, and is buried in Salisbury Cathedral where his virtues are commemorated on a monument by Rysbrack, had come to Ireland about the same time as Primate Boulter in the capacity of Chief Justice of the Common Pleas, and had subsequently been promoted to the Woolsack. When this letter was written he was regarded as a mere creature of the Primate, but during his tenure of the great seal he developed Irish sympathies, and enjoyed the privilege of numbering Swift amongst the guests at his table (Journal of the Roy. Soc. of Ant., Ireland, xxxiv, 3). The Primate's friend, Ambrose Philips, acted as Wyndham's purse bearer.

[3] This suit concerned the will of a gentleman who had died seven years before, leaving a widow and two daughters, and originated in the widow's seeking to enforce a provision that his daughters' enjoyment of his estate should be conditional on their marrying with their mother's consent (Chancery Bill, 18 June, 1728). Swift's interest in the cause was probably due to the fact that the widow was by a previous marriage the mother of his friend Le Hunte (*supra*, vol. iii, p. 126). Powell, whose Christian name was Charles, and who was a Chancery official, now extinct, known as a Six Clerk, was the prospective bridegroom.

restrictions of marriage are odious in the civil law, and not favoured by the common law, especially after the age of one-and-twenty;[1] therefore marry they may, and let Mr. Nutley[2] be a lawyer for Mrs. Rebecca Stewart, the plaintiff, to take care of the settlement for her advantage, and let Powell choose another lawyer for himself, though, by the by, Mr. Nutley would serve for both; and it is not necessary to inquire what Powell makes by his practice, although he assured the mother it amounted to one thousand four hundred pounds per annum.[3]

> Ovid, 'tis true, successfully imparts
> The rules to steal deluded virgins' hearts;
> But oh! ye fair ones, pious Nutley's skill
> Instructs you to elude, by magic bill,
> The laws of God, and gratify your will.

You will, I hope, excuse this liberty in one, who, to resent the indignity offered to you by Ram's coachman,[4] made him drunk soon after at Gorey, which so incensed the aforesaid Ram, that he discharged him his service, and he is now so reduced, that he has no other way of getting his bread but by crying in this city, "Ha' you any dirt to carry out?" I am, Sir,

Your sincere friend and humble servant,

FRANCIS GEOGHEGAN.

[1] The mother admitted that the daughter in question, who was the eldest, came of age shortly after her husband's death. It was the only admission favourable to her daughter made by the mother, who was evidently of a litigious disposition, and was involved in another lawsuit, in which her daughters were the defendants, as to the maintenance of the family seat.

[2] Richard Nutley, who died in the following November (*supra*, vol. ii, p. 60).

[3] According to the mother's statements Powell had assured her that he had, by his business and practice, acquired an undoubted and unquestionable fortune of £10,000, and for some years had made yearly by his practice as a Six Clerk £1,400 or £1,500.

[4] The reference is to the occurrence related in the second number of the "Intelligencer" (*supra*, p. 33, n. 1).

DCCXX. [*Copy.*[1]]

SWIFT TO KNIGHTLEY CHETWODE

Dublin, *March* 15, 1728-9.

SIR,

I HAD the favour of yours of the 5th instant when I
had not been above a fortnight recovered from a disorder
of giddiness and deafness, which hardly leaves me a month
together. Since my last return from England I never had
but one letter from you while I was in the country,[2] and
that was during a time of the same vexatious ailment,
when I could neither give myself the trouble to write or to
read. I shall think very unwise in such a world as this, to
leave planting of trees and making walks, to come into it.
I wish my fortune had thrown me anywhere rather than
into this town and no town, where I have not three acquaintances, nor know any person whom I care to visit. But I
must now take up with a solitary life from necessity as
well as inclination, for yesterday I relapsed again, and am
now so deaf that I shall not be able to dine with my
Chapter on our only festival in the year, I mean St.
Patrick's Day.[3]

As to any scurrilities published against me, I have no
other remedy than to desire never to hear of them, and
then the authors will be disappointed, at least it will be the
same thing to me as if they had never been writ; for I
will not imagine that any friend I esteem can value me the
less upon the malice of fools and knaves, against whose
republic I have always been at open war.[4] Every man is

---

[1] In the Forster Collection. *Supra*, vol. ii, p. 241, n. 1.

[2] Swift had probably forgotten the letters which he received from
Chetwode in the autumn of 1727, and is referring to one sent him
during the previous year.

[3] The menu on one of these occasions will be found in Appendix III.

[4] A pamphlet entitled "Some Memoirs of the Amours and Intrigues
of a Certain Irish Dean who Liv'd and Flourish'd in the Kingdom of
Ireland not many Hundred Years since, interspers'd with the Gal-
lantries of Two Berkshire Ladies," was then extensively advertised in
the Irish newspapers. It was issued in two parts and was dedicated to
the Countess of Pembroke by the writer, who is said to have been a
lady well acquainted "in those days" with the Dean. Vanessa is the
principal figure in it, but Polidore, as Swift is called, is represented as

IV   F

safe from evil tongues, who can be content to be obscure, and men must take distinction as they do land, *cum onere.* I wish you happy in your retreat, and hope you will enjoy it long and am your etc.

Addressed—To Knightley Chetwode, Esq., at his house at Woodbrooke, near Mountmellick.

DCCXXI. [*Deane Swift.*]

WILLIAM FLOWER TO SWIFT

Ashbrook, *March* 18, 1728-9.

SIR,[1]
As I have been honoured with some of your letters, and as you are my old acquaintance, though to my sorrow not intimately so, I trust you will pardon this presumption. Perhaps you may be at a loss to guess what title I have to an old acquaintance with you; but as several little accidents make indelible impressions upon the minds of schoolboys, near thirty years ago, when I was one, I remember I was committed to your care from Sheen to London.[2] We took water at Mortlake, the commander of the little skiff was very drunk and insolent, put us ashore at Hammersmith, yet insisted, with very abusive language, on his fare, which you courageously refused; the mob gathered; I expected to see your gown stripped off, and for want of a blanket, to take a flight with you in it, but

> Tum pietate gravem ac meritis si forte virum quem
> Conspexere, silent, arrectisque auribus astant:
> Iste regit dictis animos, et pectora mulcet.
> VIRG., Æn., i, 155.

---

carrying on intrigues with many other ladies including Abigail, under which name Stella is evidently denoted (Royal Irish Academy Pamphlets).

[1] William Flower, on whom the barony of Castle Durrow, now merged in the viscounty of Ashbrook, was conferred, was known to Swift through his mother, who was a niece of Sir William Temple and a sister of the first Viscount Palmerston. The family mansion in the county of Kilkenny, which is said to have been built by him, is now known as Castledurrow, but would appear to have been then called Ashbrook.

[2] Flower's maternal grandfather, Sir John Temple (*supra*, vol. i, p. 54, n. 2), resided at Sheen for some years before his death.

By your powerful eloquence you saved your bacon and money, and we happily proceeded on our journey.

But it is not an inclination purely to tell you this old story, which persuades me to write. A friend from Dublin lately obliged me with a very entertaining paper, entitled, The Intelligencer; it is numbered twenty, a posthumous work of Nestor Ironside; a correspondent mentioning these papers in a letter, raising my curiosity, with the specimen I had of them, to read the rest.[1] For my part, I have buried myself in the country, and know little of the world, but what I learn from newspapers; you, who live so much in it, and from other more convincing proofs, I am satisfied are acquainted with the Intelligencer. I wish his zeal could promote the welfare of his poor country, but I fear his labour is in vain.

The miseries of the North, as represented, demand the utmost compassion, and must soften the malice of the most bitter enemy.[2] I hope they, whose interest it is, if they rightly considered it, to relieve those miserable wretches, will redress so public a calamity; to which if, as I have heard, some of the clergy, by exacting of tithes, have contributed, they deserve as great censure, as a certain dean, who lends several sums without interest to his poor parishioners, has gained credit and honour by his charitable beneficence.[3] Bad men, to be sure, have crept in, and are of that sacred and learned order. The blackest of crimes, forgery, treason, and blasphemy, recently prove this. Such should be spewed out of it with utmost contempt, and punished according to their demerit with severe justice. If this allegation be true, I hope to see them censured by the Intelligencer, and recommend to him the words of Jeremiah to expatiate upon, chap. x, ver. 21, chap. xii, ver. 10, 11.[4] I imagine the poor widow, his

---

[1] The paper which Flower had first seen was probably one published "under the title of the Intelligencer No. XX." It is mentioned in the "Dublin Intelligence" of 14 January, 1728-9, as a flagitious production for which the editor, one Golden, was about to be prosecuted.

[2] Writing at that time Primate Boulter says: "the scarcity and dearness of provision still increases in the North; many have eaten the oats they should have sowed their land with" ("Letters," i, 229).

[3] *Supra*, vol. iii, p. 99, n. 1.

[4] "For the pastors are become brutish and have not sought the Lord: therefore they shall not prosper, and all their flocks shall be scattered. . . . Many pastors have destroyed my vineyard, they have

printer,[1] is in danger of punishment. She suffered very cruelly for the Drapier's works. I hope several contributed to ease her misfortunes on that occasion. I confess I am sorry I did not, but if you will give her a piece of gold, not in my name I beg, being unwilling to vaunt of charity, but as from a friend of yours, I shall by the first safe hand send one; in return I expect the Drapier's works entire.

I am sorry that, for the benefit of the ladies, the author[2] has not given us the English of

> Motus doceri gaudet Ionicos
> Matura virgo.[3]

Not having Creech's Horace,[4] a gentleman prevailed on me to attempt translating it in a couple of distichs. The science, which the compound English and Greek word signifies, little concerns a widower, but I should be glad to see it improved by good proficients in the Ionic jig. I own, in my little reading, I never met with this word, which puts me in mind of a passage on the Thames. My younger uncle, the grave Mr. Flower, his wife and mine, and Parson Dingle, one day made the tour of the city: we saw Bedlam, the lions, and what not, and finished with a view of that noble engine under London Bridge.[5] Then we took water for Whitehall, rowed very silently to opposite the glasshouse, where a dyer, his boat at anchor, was angling. Poor Jack unfortunately asked, addressing himself to our waterman, what that man was fishing for. The wag answered very brisk, "For ——, Master, will you buy any?" You are a man of too much humour not to be pleased with the reply. I never can think of it without a laugh, and am sure need not describe the scene to you. He is since called in our family by the name of Jack Fisher.

trodden my portion under foot, they have made my pleasant portion a desolate wilderness. They have made it desolate, and being desolate it mourneth unto me; the whole land is made desolate, because no man layeth it to heart."

[1] *I.e.*, Mrs. Harding (*supra*, p. 54).

[2] The reference is apparently to the author of Golden's paper.

[3] Hor. "Od.," iii, 6, 21.

[4]   "Plain truth, dear Murray, needs no flower of speech,
        So take it in the very words of Creech."

[5] By which water was pumped up to the city.

DCCXXII. [*Original.*[1]]

JOHN GAY TO SWIFT

From the Duke of Queensberry's in Burlington
Gardens, *March* 18, 1728-9.

DEAR SIR,

I HAVE writ to you several times, and having heard
nothing from you, makes me fear my letters have miscarried.
Mr. Pope's letter hath taken off my concern in some
degree, but I hope good weather will entirely re-establish
you in your health.[2] I am but just recovered from the
severest fit of sickness that ever anybody had who escaped
death. I was several times given up by the physicians and
everybody that attended me, and upon my recovery, was
judged to be in so ill a condition that I should be miserable for the remainder of my life; but contrary to all
expectation, I am perfectly recovered, and have no re-
mainders of the distempers that attacked me, which were,
at the same time, fever, asthma, and pleurisy. I am now
in the Duke of Queensberry's house, and have been so ever
since I left Hampstead, where I was carried at a time
that it was thought I could not live a day. Since my
coming to town, I have been very little abroad, the weather
hath been so severe. I must acquaint you, because I know
it will please you, that during my sickness I had many of
the kindest proofs of friendship, particularly from the Duke
and Duchess of Queensberry, who, if I had been their
nearest relation and nearest friend, could not have treated
me with more constant attendance then, and they continue the same to me now.

You must undoubtedly have heard that the Duchess
took up my defence with the King and Queen in the cause
of my play, and that she hath been forbid the Court for
interesting herself to increase my fortune, for the publication of it without being acted.[3] The Duke too has given up

---

[1] In the British Museum. See Preface.   [2] *Supra*, p. 59.

[3] "The Duchess of Queensberry, to the great amazement of the
admiring world," writes Mrs. Delany on the 4th of that month, "is
forbid the Court, only for being solicitous in getting a subscription for
Mr. Gay's sequel of the Beggar's Opera. The Duchess is a great
friend of Gay's, and has thought him much injured, upon which, to

his employment, which he would have done, if the Duchess had not met with this treatment, upon account of ill usage from the Ministers, but this hastened him in what he had determined.[1] The play is now almost printed, with the music, words, and basses, engraved on thirty-one copper-plates, which, by my friends' assistance, hath a probability to turn greatly to my advantage. The Duchess of Marlborough hath given me a hundred pounds for one copy,[2] and others have contributed very handsomely; but, as my account is not yet settled, I cannot tell you particulars.

For writing in the cause of virtue, and against the fashionable vices, I am looked upon at present as the most obnoxious person almost in England. Mr. Pulteney tells me I have got the start of him. Mr. Pope tells me that I am dead, and that this obnoxiousness is the reward for my inoffensiveness in my former life. I wish I had a book ready to send you, but, I believe, I shall not be able to complete the work till the latter end of the next week.

make him some amends, for he is poor, she promised to get a subscription for his play, if he would print it. She indiscreetly has urged the King and Queen in his behalf, and asked subscriptions in the drawing-room, upon which she is forbid the Court—a thing never heard of before to one of her rank; one might have imagined her beauty would have secured her from such treatment" (Mrs. Delany's Correspondence, i, 193).

[1]   " The gay Amanda let us now behold,
In thy defence, a lovely, banish'd scold;
What tributary numbers can thy Muse,
To this bright championess of wit refuse?
To her, who greatly Empire's frowns defies,
And bids her late disgrace new point her eyes;
Who makes her tender Lord her quarrel join,
And the fair honours of his post resign,
To let thy foes her soul's high temper see
That holds no sacrifice too rich for thee.
Paint her each beauty o'er and o'er again,
Strong as when first she charmed in Prior's strain,
When kind Mamma indulged her heart's desire,
And then, as now, she set the world on fire."
                    " The Female Faction " (*supra*, p. 39, n. 1).

[2] In the verses just cited the second Duchess of Marlborough is represented as looking upon Gay as a second Congreve:

" First in thy list does great Almeria stand,
And deal her favours with a lavish hand,
Her bury'd bard's resemblance does she see,
And think Alphonso still survives in thee."

Your money is still in Lord Bathurst's hands, but, I believe, I shall receive it soon. I wish to receive your orders how to dispose of it. I am impatient to finish my work, for I want the country air, not that I am ill, but to recover my strength, and I cannot leave my work till it is finished. While I am writing this, I am in the room next to our dining-room, with sheets all around it, and two people from the binder folding sheets. I print the book at my own expense, in quarto, which is to be sold for six shillings, with the music.[1] You see I do not want industry, and I hope you will allow, that I have not the worst economy. Mrs. Howard hath declared herself strongly, both to the King and Queen, as my advocate.[2] The Duchess of Queensberry is allowed to have shown more spirit, more honour, and more goodness, than was thought possible in our times; I should have added too, more understanding and good sense. You see my fortune, as I hope my virtue will, increases by oppression. I go to no Courts, I drink no wine, and am calumniated even by Ministers of State, and yet am in good spirits. Most of the courtiers, though otherways my friends, refused to contribute to my undertaking, but the city and the people of England take my part very warmly, and, I am told, the best of the citizens will give me proofs of it by their contributions.

I could talk to you a great deal more, but I am afraid I should write too much for you, and for myself. I have not writ so much together since my sickness. I cannot omit telling you that Dr. Arbuthnot's attendance and care of me showed him the best of friends. Dr. Hollings, though entirely a stranger to me, was joined with him, and used me the kindest and most handsome manner.[3] Mr. and Mrs. Pulteney were greatly concerned for me, visited me, and showed me the strongest proofs of friendship. When I see you I will tell you of others, as of Mr. Pope, Mrs.

---

[1] The volume is as described; the text occupies seventy-two pages, the music thirty-one.

[2] In the "Female Faction" she is represented as imitating the Duchesses:

> "On chaste Calista let us cast our eye,
> By their example thine and Wit's ally."

[3] John Hollings, who was one of George II's physicians, had a reputation for scholarship and culture as well as for knowledge of his profession.

Blount, Mr. and Mrs. Rollinson,[1] Lord and Lady Bolingbroke, etc. I think they are all your friends and well-
wishers. I hope you will love them the better upon my
account; but do not forget Mr. Lewis, nor Lord Bathurst,
Sir William Wyndham, and Lord Gower,[2] and Lord Oxford
among the number. My service to Dr. Delany and Mr.
Stopford.

DCCXXIII. [*Original.*[3]]

JOHN ARBUTHNOT TO SWIFT

London, *March* 19, 1728-9.

THIS is the second or third time, dear Sir, that I have
wrote to you without hearing a word of you, or from you;
only, in general, that you were very much out of order
sometimes of your two old complaints, the vertigo and
deafness, which I am very sorry for. The gentleman who
carries this has come better off than I did imagine.[4] I used
my little interest as far as it would go, in his affair. He
will be able to give you some account of your friends,
many of whom have been in great distress this winter.
John Gay, I may say with vanity, owes his life, under God,
to the unwearied endeavours and care of your humble
servant; for a physician who had not been passionately his
friend could not have saved him. I had, beside my personal concern for him, other motives of my care. He is
now become a public person, [a little Sacheverell; and
I took the same pleasure in saving him as Radcliffe did
in preserving my Lord Chief Justice Holt's wife, whom
he attended out of spite to the husband, who wished her
dead.[5]
The inoffensive John Gay is now become one of the

---

[1] *Supra,* vol. iii, p. 325.
[2] He was a kinsman of the Duchess of Queensberry, and is mentioned in Pope's " Works " as a friend of Fenton and devotee to the
ladies.
[3] In the British Museum. See Preface.
[4] *I.e.,* Whaley (*supra,* p. 46).
[5] This story has been adopted by Lord Campbell as well founded
(" Lives of the Chief Justices," ii, 177). He says that some persons
maliciously accounted for Holt's unwearied devotion to business by
his dislike of the society of his wife.

obstructions to the peace of Europe, the terror of the Ministers, the chief author of the Craftsman, and all the seditious pamphlets which have been published against the government.[1] He has got several turned out of their places; the greatest ornament of the Court banished from it for his sake;[2] another great lady in danger of being *chasée* likewise;[3] about seven or eight Duchesses pushing forward, like the ancient Circumcelliones[4] in the Church, who shall suffer martyrdom upon his account first. He is the darling of the city. If he should travel about the country, he would have hecatombs of roasted oxen sacrificed to him. Since he became so conspicuous, Will Pulteney hangs his head to see himself so much outdone in the career of glory. I hope he will get a good deal of money by printing his play, but, I really believe, he would get more by showing his person; and I can assure you, this is the very identical John Gay, whom you formerly knew, and lodged with in Whitehall two years ago. I have been diverting myself with making an extract out of a history, which will be printed in the year 1948. I wish I had your assistance to go through with it; for I can assure you, it riseth to a very solemn piece of burlesque.

As to the condition of your little club, it is not quite so desperate as you might imagine, for Mr. Pope is as high in favour, as I am afraid the rest are out of it. The King, upon the perusal of the last edition of his Dunciad, declared he was a very honest man. I did not know till this moment that I had so good an opportunity to send you a letter; and now I know it, I am called away, and obliged to end with my best wishes and respects, being

Most sincerely yours.

Addressed—To the Reverend the Dean of St. Patrick's, Dublin.

---

[1] In the Preface to " Polly," Gay says that he has been accused of having written disaffected libels and seditious pamphlets, although it had ever been his utmost ambition, if that word may be used on that occasion, to lead a quiet and inoffensive life.

[2] *I.e.*, the Duchess of Queensberry.

[3] *I.e.*, Mrs. Howard.

[4] *I.e.*, African fanatics of the fourth century.

DCCXXIV. [*Original.*[1]]

—— TO SWIFT

Philad[elphia], March 29, 1729.

FRIEND JONATHAN SWIFT,

HAVING been often agreeably amused by thy Tale, etc., etc., and being now loading a small ship for Dublin, I have sent thee a gammon, the product of the wilds of America, which perhaps may not be unacceptable at thy table, since it is only designed to let thee know that thy wit and good parts are here in esteem at this distance from place of thy residence. Thee need ask no questions who this comes from, since I am a perfect stranger to thee.

Addressed—To Jon. Swift in Dublin.

Endorsed—Received May 22, 1729; Quaker's letter from Philadelphia with a ham.

DCCXXV. [*Deane Swift.*]

LADY JOHNSON TO SWIFT

[*March* 30, 1729.]

HON^D S^R,[2]

I AM a Huckster and Lives in Strand Street and has Dealings with Several familys; a saturday Night a Case of Instruments was sent me in pawn by a Certain person in Marys Street, for two Rowls, a print of Butter, four Herrings and three Nagins of strong Watters; My foster brother who ply's about that End of the town tells Me, he wanst saw it in your hand, fearing Hawkins's[3] whip I send it to

---

[1] In the Forster Collection.

[2] Lady Johnson was an aunt of Sir Arthur Acheson. Her husband, who resided at Gilford in the county of Down, had been knighted soon after the accession of George I, and had died some years before this letter was written. Their grandson was created a baronet.

[3] The Keeper of Newgate prison in Dublin, whose iniquities soon afterwards attracted the attention of Parliament and led to the institution of criminal proceedings.

you, and will take an Other Course to gett My Money, so I
Remain your Hon^rs

Humble Sarv^t to Command

ye 30   MARTHA SHARP.

Addressed—To the Rev. the Dean of St. PaTricks.

Endorsed by Swift—The best letter I ever read.

DCCXXVI. [*Elwin.*]

SWIFT TO VISCOUNT BOLINGBROKE AND ALEXANDER
POPE

Dublin, *April* 5, 1729.

TO BOLINGBROKE

I DO not think it could be possible for me to hear better
news than that of your getting over your scurvy suit, which
always hung as a dead weight on my heart.[1] I hated it in
all its circumstances, as it affected your fortune and quiet,
and in a situation of life that must make it every way
vexatious. And as I am infinitely obliged to you for the
justice you do me in supposing your affairs do at least
concern me as much as my own, so I would never have
pardoned your omitting it. But before I go on, I cannot
forbear mentioning what I read last summer in a newspaper, that you were writing the history of your own times.
I suppose such a report might arise from what was not
secret among your friends, of your intention to write
another kind of history, which you often promised Mr. Pope
and me to do.[2] I know he desires it very much, and I am
sure I desire nothing more, for the honour and love I
bear you, and the perfect knowledge I have of your public
virtue.

My Lord, I have no other notion of economy than that [it]
is the parent of liberty and ease, and I am not the only friend
you have who has chid you in his heart for the neglect of
it, though not with his mouth, as I have done. For there
is a silly error in the world, even among friends otherwise

---

[1] The suit concerned the first Lady Bolingbroke's property.
[2] A history of the Tory administrations in Queen Anne's reign.

very good, not to intermeddle with men's affairs in such nice matters. And, my Lord, I have made a maxim, that should be writ in letters of diamonds, that a wise man ought to have money in his head, but not in his heart.[1] Pray, my Lord, inquire whether your prototype, my Lord Digby, after the Restoration, when he was at Bristol, did not take some care of his fortune,[2] notwithstanding that quotation I once sent you out of his speech to the House of Commons?[3] In my conscience, I believe fortune, like other drabs, values a man gradually less for every year he lives. I have demonstration for it; because if I play at piquet for sixpence with a man or woman two years younger than myself, I always lose; and there is a young girl of twenty who never fails of winning my money at backgammon, though she is a bungler, and the game be ecclesiastic.

As to the public, I confess nothing could cure my itch of meddling with it, but these frequent returns of deafness, which have hindered me from passing last winter in London; yet I cannot but consider the perfidiousness of some people, who I thought when I was last there, upon a change that happened, were the most impudent in forgetting their professions that I have ever known. Pray will you please to take your pen, and blot me out that political maxim from whatever book it is in, that *res nolunt diu male administrari*. The commonness makes me not know who is the author, but sure he must be some modern.

I am sorry for Lady Bolingbroke's ill health, but I protest I never knew a very deserving person of that sex, who had not too much reason to complain of ill health. I never wake without finding life a more insignificant thing than it was the day before, which is one great advantage I get by living in this country, where there is nothing I shall be sorry to lose. But my greatest misery is recollecting the scene of twenty years past, and then all on a sudden dropping into the present. I remember, when I was a little boy, I felt a great fish at the end of my line which I drew up almost on the ground, but it dropped in, and the

---

[1] In this remark, observes a writer in the "Church Quarterly Review," xxxiii, 442, Swift shows his Yorkshire origin.

[2] Two months after the Restoration his valet-de-chambre was a suitor for the place of Collector of Customs at Bristol (S. P. Domestic).

[3] *Supra*, vol. iii, p. 111.

disappointment vexes me to this very day, and I believe it was the type of all my future disappointments. I should be ashamed to say this to you, if you had not a spirit fitter to bear your own misfortunes than I have to think of them. Is there patience left to reflect, by what qualities wealth and greatness are got, and by what qualities they are lost? I have read my friend Congreve's verses to Lord Cobham, which end with a vile and false moral, and I remember is not in Horace to Tibullus which he imitates, that all times are equally virtuous and vicious,[1] wherein he differs from all poets, philosophers, and Christians that ever writ. It is more probable that there may be an equal quantity of virtues always in the world, but sometimes there may be a peck of it in Asia, and hardly a thimbleful in Europe. But if there be no virtue, there is abundance of sincerity; for I will venture all I am worth, that there is not one human creature in power, who will not be modest enough to confess that he proceeds wholly upon a principle of corruption. I say this, because I have a scheme, in spite of your notions, to govern England upon the principles of virtue, and when the nation is ripe for it, I desire you will send for me. I have learned this by living like a hermit, by which I am got backward about nineteen hundred years in the era of the world, and begin to wonder at the wickedness of men. I dine alone upon half a dish of meat, mix water with my wine, walk ten miles a day, and read Baronius.[2] *Hic explicit epistola ad Dominum* Bolingbroke, *et incipit ad amicum* Pope.

TO POPE

Having finished my letter to Aristippus, I now begin to you. I was in great pain about Mrs. Pope, having heard from others that she was in a very dangerous way, which

---

[1]   " Not wondering at the world's new wicked ways,
Compar'd with those of our forefathers' days,
For virtue now is neither more or less,
And vice is only varied in the dress.
Believe it, men have ever been the same,
And all the golden age is but a dream."

[2] His works are comprised in twelve folio volumes, and cost Swift £6. See Dean Swift's Library by Mr. T. P. Le Fann (Journal of the Roy. Soc. of Ant., Ireland, xxvi, 115).

made me think it unseasonable to trouble you. I am ashamed to tell you, that when I was very young I had more desire to be famous than ever since; and fame, like all things else in this life, grows with me every day more a trifle. But you who are so much younger, although you want that health you deserve, yet your spirits are as vigorous as if your body were sounder. I hate a crowd, where I have not an easy place to see and be seen. A great library always makes me melancholy, where the best author is as much squeezed, and as obscure, as a porter at a coronation. In my own little library, I value the compilements of Grævius and Gronovius, which make thirty-one volumes in folio, and were given me by my Lord Bolingbroke, more than all my books besides, because whoever comes into my closet, casts his eyes immediately upon them, and will not vouchsafe to look upon Plato or Xenophon.[1] I tell you it is almost incredible how opinions change by the decline or decay of spirits, and I will further tell you, that all my endeavours, from a boy, to distinguish myself, were only for want of a great title and fortune, that I might be used like a Lord by those who have an opinion of my parts—whether right or wrong, it is no great matter, and so the reputation of wit or great learning does the office of a blue ribbon, or of a coach and six horses. To be remembered for ever on the account of our friendship, is what would exceedingly please me; but yet I never loved to make a visit, or be seen walking with my betters, because they get all the eyes and civilities from me. I no sooner writ this than I corrected myself, and remembered Sir Fulke Greville's epitaph, Here lies, etc., who was friend to Sir Philip Sidney.[2] And therefore I most heartily thank you for your desire that I would record our friendship in verse, which, if I can succeed in, I will never desire to write one more line in poetry while I live. You must present my humble service to

---

[1] It is noted in Swift's catalogue that the works of Grævius and Gronovius cost £40. Swift's purchase of his Plato has been mentioned. He was evidently proud of his bargain as he boasted of it to Fountaine (*supra*, vol. i, p. 182).

[2] The inscription, which was his own composition, is still to be read in St. Mary's Church at Warwick: "Fulke Greville, servant to Queen Elizabeth, councillor to King James, and friend to Sir Philip Sidney. Tropaeum Peccati."

Mrs. Pope, and let her know I pray for her continuance in the world, for her own reason, that she may live to take care of you.

DCCXXVII. [*Original.*[1]]

ANDREW RAMSAY TO SWIFT

London, *April* 10, 1729.

SIR,[2]

ONE of the greatest pleasures I proposed to myself in a journey to England, was that of seeing you at London, and it is a very sensible mortification to me to find myself disappointed in so agreeable an expectation. It is now many years since I had the highest esteem of your genius and writings, and when I was very young, I found in some of them certain ideas, that prepared me for relishing those principles of universal religion, which I have since endeavoured to unfold in Cyrus. I could not let our common friend Mr. Leslie[3] go back to Ireland, without seizing the opportunity of acknowledging the obliging zeal you have shown to make my work esteemed. Such marks of friendship do me a great deal of honour as well as pleasure, and I hope I have a thorough sense of them. As I have much enlarged my book, I am going to publish a new edition by subscription. I have given a hundred copies of the proposals to our friend, and flatter myself that I may count upon the continuation of your friendship. I am, with great respect, Sir,

Your most obliged and most obedient humble servant,

A. RAMSAY.

[1] In the British Museum. See Preface.
[2] See Ramsay's former letter (*supra*, vol. iii, p. 405).
[3] The son of the non-juror.

DCCXXVIII. [*Original.*¹]

JOHN ARBUTHNOT TO SWIFT

London, *May* 8, 1729.

DEAR SIR,

I HAVE wrote three times to Mr. Dean of St. Patrick's, without receiving so much as an acknowledgement of the receipt of my letters. At the same time, I hear of other letters, which his acquaintances receive from him. I believe I should hardly have brought myself to have wrote this, were it not to serve you and a friend at the same time. I recommended one Mr. Mason, son of Mason, gentleman of the Queen's Chapel, a baritone voice, for the vacancy of a singer in your Cathedral. This letter was wrote from Bath last September. The same Mason informs me that there is another vacancy: therefore I renew my request.² I believe you will hardly get a better. He has a pleasant mellow voice, and has sung several times in the King's chapel this winter, to the satisfaction of the audience. I beg at least your answer to this.

Your friends in town, such as I know, are well. Mr. Pope is happy again, in having his mother recovered. Mr. Gay is gone to Scotland with the Duke of Queensberry. He has about twenty lawsuits with booksellers for pirating his book. The King goes soon to Hanover. These are all the news I know. I hope you do not imagine I am so little concerned about your health, as not to desire to be informed of the state of it from yourself. I have been tolerably well this winter, I thank God. My brother Robin is here, and longs, as well as I, to know how you do. This with my best wishes and respects, from, dear Sir,

Your most faithful humble servant,

JO. ARBUTHNOT.

Addressed—To the Reverend Dr. Swift, Dean of St. Patrick's, Dublin, Ireland.

---

¹ In the British Museum. See Preface.

² John Mason became subsequently a vicar-choral in both the Dublin Cathedrals, and held his place in them for over fifty years. He was also for part of that time a vicar-choral of Armagh Cathedral.

WOODBROOKE

From a photograph by Mr. Wynne.

DCCXXIX. [*Copy*.[1]]

SWIFT TO KNIGHTLEY CHETWODE

Dublin, *May* 17, 1729.

SIR,

THAT I did not answer your former letter [2] was because I did not know it required any, and being seldom in a tolerable humour by the frequent returns or dreads of deafness, I am grown a very bad correspondent. As to the passage you mentioned in that former letter, and desired my opinion, I did not understand the meaning, and that letter being mislaid I cannot recollect it, though you refer to it in the last. I shall not make the usual excuses on the subject of lending money, but as I have not been master of thirty pounds for thirty days this thirty years, so I have actually borrowed several small sums for these two or three years past for board-wages to my servants and common expenses. I have within these ten days borrowed the very poor-money lodged in my hands to buy clothes for my servants, and left my note in the bag in case of my death. These pinches are not peculiar to me, but to all men in this kingdom, who live upon tithes or high rents, for as we have been on the high road to ruin these dozen years, so we have now got almost to our journey's end. And truly I do expect and am determined in a short time to pawn my little plate, or sell it, for subsistence.

I have had the same request you make me from several others, and have desired the same favour from others, without success; and I believe there are hardly three men of any figure in Ireland, whose affairs are so bad as mine, who now pay interest for a thousand pounds of other people's money which I undertook to manage, without receiving one farthing myself, but engaged seven years in a lawsuit to recover it.[3] This is the fairest side of my circumstances, for they are worse than I care to think of, much less to tell, and if the universal complaints and despair of all people

---

[1] In the Forster Collection. *Supra*, vol. ii, p. 241, n. 1.

[2] Swift had received two letters from Chetwode since writing to him in March (*supra*, p. 65).

[3] The reference is to the money invested in South Sea Stock (*supra*, vol. ii, p. 148).

have not reached you, you have yet a vexation to come.[1] I
am in ten times a worse state than you, having a lawsuit
on which my whole fortune depends, and put to shifts for
money which I thought would never fall to my lot. I have
been lately amazed as well grieved at some intimate friends,
who have desired to borrow money of me, and whom I could
not oblige, but rather expected the same kindness from
them. Such is the condition of the kingdom, and such is
mine. I am,

Yours etc.

Addressed—To Knightley Chetwode, Esq., at Woodbrooke,
near Mountmellick.

DCCXXX. [*Copy.*[2]]

SWIFT TO THE EARL OF BURLINGTON

Deanery House, Dublin,
May 22, 1729.

MY LORD,
    THE two last times I was in England I often mentioned
to your Lordship the repairing the monument of the first
Earl of Cork, your ancestor, which you readily complied
with, and promised to send an order to some of your managers here that it might be done.[3]

---

[1] At that time the poverty of Ireland, which was never greater,
occupied Swift's mind almost to the exclusion of every other subject,
and his prose writings are entirely occupied with the miseries of that
country, their causes, and schemes for their abatement. About the
time of Stella's death his "Short View of the State of Ireland" had
been issued from the press, and two months later his answer to
Browne's paper (*supra*, p. 24, n. 3) had appeared. Then the "Intelligencer," which was inspired when not actually written by Swift, had
given opportunity for further passionate pictures of the impoverish-
ment of the country, and since his return from the north in February
the cause of the weavers had once more received support from his
pen ("Prose Works," vii, *passim*).

[2] In the Chapter Book of St. Patrick's Cathedral, from which it has
been extracted by the kind permission of the Dean and Chapter.

[3] This monument, which now stands at the western end of the
Cathedral, was erected early in the reign of Charles I by the first Earl
of Cork in memory of his second wife. It is made of black marble and
alabaster, and is very lofty and elaborate, with numerous effigies

I did then likewise humbly propose to your Lordship to settle some small rent on the Dean and Chapter of St. Patrick's and their successors, not exceeding five pounds a year, in trust for keeping the said monument in repair for ever, and if your Lordship should please to comply with this last request, we are of opinion that the said five pounds a year should not be a rent charge, but a small quantity of land now worth at a full rent five pounds a year, because it would always be of the same intrinsic value, whether money or land should rise or fall, and the Dean and Chapter will enter into the Chapter book the said gift as a standing record, and oblige themselves to apply the whole rent of the said land to no other use than to the preservation of the said monument entire and in good order. I believe your Lordship will agree that the Dean and Chapter can have no other design in making this request than the desire of preserving a monument which does some honour to your Lordship's family, and is an ornament to the Cathedral.

I send your Lordship a copy of the order of the Dean and Chapter, by which I am desired to write to you upon this occasion.[1] I am, with great respect, my Lord,

Your Lordship's most obedient and most humble servant,

J. S.

To the Right Honble. the Earl of Burlington.

arranged in four tiers. The design was made by the Irish pursuivant of the time, who received a fee of £40, and the work was executed at a cost of £400 by a stonecutter who resided at Chapelizod, near Dublin. The monument is of historic interest, as a dispute with regard to its original situation, which was behind the communion table, helped to bring the Earl of Strafford to his doom (see Bishop Bernard's " St. Patrick's Cathedral," p. 47, and Litton Falkiner's " Illustrations of Irish History," p. 378).

[1] " Ordered by the aforesaid Dean and Chapter that the Dean do write to the several persons hereafter named to request their compliance for repairing and erecting monuments in the aforesaid Cathedral Church in remembrance of their ancestors, which will more fully appear by a copy of each letter herein entered."

DCCXXXI. [*Copy.*[1]]

SWIFT TO LADY CATHERINE JONES

Deanery House, Dublin,
May 22, 1729.

MADAM,[2]

THE monument to your Ladyship's grandfather, the Earl of Ranelagh, in the Cathedral Church of St. Patrick's, Dublin, whereof I have the honour to be Dean, being much out of repair, I was desired by an order of the Dean and Chapter, of which I send you a copy, to apply to your Ladyship that you would please to direct one of your receivers here to repair the said monument, which will do an honour to the memory of your Ladyship's family, and be some ornament to our Cathedral without any considerable expense.[3]

Although I am a stranger to your Ladyship's person, yet I have heard much of your piety and good works, and your Ladyship will easily believe that neither the Chapter nor I can have any other view in this request than the honour of your family, whereof one was Archbishop of Dublin,[4] and the care we have of keeping our Cathedral as decently as we can. I am, with great respect, Madam,

Your Ladyship's etc.

J. S.

To the Right Honble. the Lady Catherine Jones.

[1] In the Chapter Book of St. Patrick's Cathedral. *Supra*, p. 82, n. 2.

[2] The recipient was a daughter of the Earl of Ranelagh (*supra*, vol. i, p. 314).

[3] The monument is similar to that of the Earl of Cork, although of smaller dimensions, and was erected about the same time. It contains effigies of the first Viscount Ranelagh, who was Lady Catherine's great-grandfather, and of his father, who was Archbishop of Dublin. Her father was the only earl of his line.

[4] Archbishop Jones had been one of Swift's predecessors, and in that capacity was stigmatized by Swift with the appellation " rascal." See Appendix IV.

DCCXXXII. [*Copy.*[1]]

SWIFT TO THE COUNTESS OF HOLDERNESS

Deanery House, Dublin,
May 22, 1729.

MADAM,[2]

I TOOK the liberty of writing to your Ladyship some years ago upon the note of an old acquaintance, but you were not so good as to return me an answer, although my letters were altogether intended to the honour of your Ladyship's family, and particularly of that great person the Duke of Schomberg, your grandfather, whose body lies in a vault of St. Patrick's Cathedral, where I have the honour to be Dean.

The Chapter and I having reflected with much concern that the remains of a general so renowned all over Europe, and so highly deserving both of England and this kingdom, should lie so obscurely without any monument over him, have made a formal order in full assembly, whereof I send you a copy annexed, that I should be desired to represent this matter to your Ladyship, and to request that you would please to assign what moderate sum you think fit to erect a plain marble monument over his Grace. It shall be submitted to your Ladyship whether you will choose to get an epitaph drawn by some friend of your own or leave it to us. Your Ladyship may be firmly assured that the money shall be laid out with the utmost good management, because it is a matter which the Chapter and I have much at heart.

I send this letter under a cover to Sir Conyers Darcy,[3] being wholly ignorant where to address your Ladyship. I am, with great respect, Madam, etc.

J. S.

To the Right Honble. the Countess of Holderness now
Countess Fitzwalter.[4]

---

[1] In the Chapter Book of St. Patrick's Cathedral. *Supra,* p. 82, n. 2.

[2] The recipient has been already mentioned as one of the Vanhomrighs' friends (*supra,* vol. iii, p. 459). She married first, in 1715, Robert Darcy, fifth Earl of Holderness, and secondly, in 1724, Benjamin Mildmay, the nineteenth Lord Fitzwalter.

[3] Her first husband's brother.

[4] Her second husband was created an Earl, but not until the following year.

DCCXXXIII. [*Original.*[1]]

JOHN ARBUTHNOT TO SWIFT

London, *June* 9, 1729.

DEAR SIR,

THIS is given you by Mr. Mason, whom I believe you will find answer the character I gave of him; which really was not partial, for I am not so much as acquainted with his father or himself.[2] I explained everything to him according to the tenor of the letter which I received from you some time ago, and for which I most heartily thank you. Let him now speak for himself. I have been inquiring about a counter-tenor, but have, as yet, no intelligence of any.

I am really sensibly touched with the account you give of Ireland.[3] It is not quite so bad here, but really bad enough. At the same time, we are told, that we are in great plenty and happiness. Your friends, whom you mention in yours, are well. Mr. Gay is returned from Scotland, and has recovered his strength by his journey. Mr. Pope is well. He had got an injunction in Chancery against the printers, who had pirated his Dunciad. It was dissolved again, because the printer could not prove any property, nor did the author appear. That is not Mr. Gay's case, for he has owned his book. Mr. Pulteney gives you his service. They are all better than myself, for I am now so bad of a constant convulsion in my heart, that I am like to expire sometimes. We have no news that I know of. I am apt to believe that, in a little time, this matter of the provisional treaty will be on or off.[4] The young man waits for my letter. I shall trouble you no more at present, but remain with my best wishes, and most sincere affection, dear Sir,

Your most faithful humble servant,

J. ARBUTHNOT.

My family all send you their love and service.

[1] In the British Museum. See Preface.
[2] *Supra*, p. 80.   [3] *Supra*, p. 82, n. 1.
[4] The negotiations which resulted in the Treaty of Seville were then in progress.

DCCXXXIV. [*Original.*[1]]

LADY CATHERINE JONES TO SWIFT

Chelsea, *June* 11, 1729.

SIR,

I RECEIVED the favour of your letter the 22nd of May, and own my obligation to Mr. Dean for the information of the decay of my grandfather's monument in the Cathedral Church of St. Patrick. Mr. French, the present receiver of my father's estate,[2] will be, some time next month, in that kingdom, whom I order to wait upon you for your direction in that affair; in which, when he has informed me of the expense, I shall immediately give direction to have it done, agreeably to the desire of the Dean and Chapter, as well as the duty due to the memory of my grandfather, without adding farther trouble to Mr. Dean, from his

Most humble and obedient servant,
CATHERINE JONES.

Addressed—To the Reverend Dean Swift, at the Deanery House in Dublin, Ireland, *and readdressed to him* at Sir Arthur Acheson's, Bart., at Market Hill, in the county of Armagh, by Newry.[3]

DCCXXXV. [*Copy.*[4]]

SWIFT TO KNIGHTLEY CHETWODE

August 9, 1729.

SIR,

YOUR letter of July 30th I did not receive till this day. I am near sixty miles from Dublin,[5] and have been so these ten weeks. I am heartily sorry for the two occasions of the difficulties you are under. I knew Mrs. Chetwode from her

---

[1] In the British Museum. See Preface.
[2] He is said to have been Humphrey French who became Lord Mayor of Dublin and was much extolled by Swift.
[3] As appears from the next letter Swift had gone at the beginning of June for the second time on a visit to the Achesons.
[4] In the Forster Collection. *Supra*, vol. ii, p. 241, n. 1.
[5] Market Hill is sixty Irish miles from Dublin.

childhood, and knew her mother and sisters, and although I saw her but few times in my life, being in a different kingdom, I had an old friendship for her, without entering into differences between you, and cannot but regret her death.[1] As to Mr. Jackman I have known him many years; he was a good-natured, generous and gentlemanly person, and a long time ago, having a little money of my own, and being likewise concerned for a friend, I was inclined to trust him with the management of both, but received some hints that his affairs were even then not in a condition so as to make it safe to have any dealings of that kind with him.[2] For these fourteen years past, he was always looked on as a gone man, for which I was sorry, because I had a personal inclination towards himself, but seldom saw him of late years, because I was only a general acquaintance, and not of intimacy enough to advise him, or meddle with his affairs, nor able to assist him. I therefore withdrew, rather than put my shoulders to a falling wall, which I had no call to do.

This day upon reading your letter I asked a gentleman just come from Dublin, who told me the report was true, of Jackman's being gone off. Now, Sir, I desire to know, how it is possible I can give you advice being no lawyer, not knowing how much you stand engaged for, nor the situation of your own affairs. I presume the other security is a responsible person, and I hope Mr. Jackman's arrears cannot be so much as to endanger your sinking under them. It is to be supposed that Mr. Shirley will give time, considering the case. I think there is a fatality in some people to embroil themselves by their good nature. I know what I would do in the like condition. It would be, upon being pressed, to be as open as possible, and to offer all in my power to give satisfaction, provided I could have the allowance of time. I know all fair creditors love free and open

---

[1] Chetwode's separation from his wife (*supra*, vol. iii, p. 227) had no doubt continued up to the time of her death. She was an only child, and it is to her half sisters, Stopford's whole sisters, that Swift refers (*supra*, vol. ii, p. 243). She had probably not been known to him until after her mother married Stopford's father.

[2] As subsequently appears, Jackman had induced Chetwode to become surety for him. He was agent for a great estate in the north of Ireland near Carrickmacross, which was granted by Queen Elizabeth to the Earl of Essex, and descended from him to the first Earl Ferrers, who bequeathed it to his younger sons. As the site of Lough Fea, the

dealings, and that staving off by the arts of lawyers makes all things worse at the end. I will write to Mr. Stopford by the next post, in as pressing a manner as I can.[1] He is as honest and benevolent a person as ever I knew. If it be necessary for you to retrench in your way of living, I should advise, upon supposing that you can put your affairs in some settlement here under the conduct of your son assisted by some other friends, that you should retire to some town in England in a good country and far from London, where you may live as cheap as you please, and not uncomfortably, till this present storm shall blow over. This is all I can think of after three times reading your letter. I pray God direct you. I am,

Ever, etc.

Addressed—To Knightley Chetwode, Esq., at Woodbrooke, near Mountmellick.

DCCXXXVI. [*Elwin.*]

SWIFT TO ALEXANDER POPE

August 11, 1729.

I AM very sensible that in a former letter I talked very weakly of my own affairs, and of my imperfect wishes and desires,[2] which however I find with some comfort do now daily decline, very suitably to my state of health for some months past, for my head is never perfectly free from giddiness, and especially towards night. Yet my disorder is very moderate, and I have been without a fit of deafness this half-year; so I am like a horse, which, though off his mettle, can trot on tolerably, and this comparison puts me in mind to add that I am returned to be a rider, wherein I wish you would imitate me.

As to this country, there have been three terrible years'

Irish home of Mr. Evelyn Philip Shirley, the distinguished antiquary, the estate became widely known in the last century.

[1] Chetwode would seem to have desired his brother-in-law's acquiescence in any step he might take.

[2] The reference is presumably to the letter written in April to Bolingbroke and Pope (*supra*, p. 75). Pope had probably sent a reply to it which has been suppressed.

dearth of corn, and every place strewed with beggars; but dearths are common in better climates, and our evils here lie much deeper. Imagine a nation the two thirds of whose revenues are spent out of it, and who are not permitted to trade with the other third, and where the pride of women will not suffer them to wear their own manufactures, even where they excel what come from abroad.[1] This is the true state of Ireland in a very few words. These evils operate more every day, and the kingdom is absolutely undone, as I have been telling often in print these ten years past. What I have said requires forgiveness, but I had a mind for once to let you know the state of our affairs, and my reason for being more moved than perhaps becomes a clergyman, and a piece of a philosopher, and perhaps the increase of years and disorders may hope for some allowance to complaints, especially when I may call myself a stranger in a strange land.

As to poor Mrs. Pope, if she be still alive, I heartily pity you and pity her. Her great piety and virtue will infallibly make her happy in a better life, and her great age has made her fully ripe for Heaven and the grave, and her best friends will most wish her eased of her labours, when she has so many good works to follow them. The loss you will feel by the want of her care and kindness, I know very well; but she has amply done her part, as you have yours. One reason why I would have you in Ireland when you shall be at your own disposal, is that you may be master of two or three years' revenues, *provisae frugis in annos copia*, so as not to be pinched in the least when years increase, and perhaps your health impairs. And when this kingdom is utterly at an end, you may support me for the few years I shall happen to live; and who knows but you may pay me exorbitant interest for the spoonful of wine, and scraps of a chicken, it will cost me to feed you? I am confident you have too much reason to complain of ingratitude; for I never yet knew any person, one tenth part so heartily disposed as you are to do good offices to others, without the least private view.

[1] As has been already mentioned Swift had renewed his crusade in favour of Irish manufactures (*supra*, p. 82, n. 1). His "Proposal that all the Ladies and Women of Ireland should appear constantly in Irish Manufactures" was written about that time ("Prose Works," vii, 191).

Was it a gasconade to please me, that you said your fortune was increased one hundred pounds a year since I left you?[1] You should have told me how. Those *subsidia senectuti* are extremely desirable if they could be got with justice, and without avarice; of which vice, though I cannot charge myself yet, nor feel any approaches towards it, yet no usurer more wishes to be richer, or rather to be surer of his rents. But I am not half so moderate as you, for I declare I cannot live easily under double to what you are satisfied with.

I hope Mr. Gay will keep his three thousand pounds and live on the interest without decreasing the principal one penny; but I do not like your seldom seeing him. I hope he is grown more disengaged from his intentness on his own affairs, which I ever disliked, and is quite the reverse to you, unless you are a very dextrous disguiser. I desire my humble service to Lord Oxford, Lord Bathurst, and particularly to Mrs. Blount, but to no lady at Court.[2] God bless you for being a greater dupe than I. I love that character too myself, but I want your charity. Adieu.

DCCXXXVII. [*Copy*.[3]]

SWIFT TO KNIGHTLEY CHETWODE

August 30, 1729.

SIR,

I RECEIVED your letter by a man that came from Dublin with some things for me.[4] This is the first post since. I come now to answer your questions. First whether you shall marry. I answer that if it may be done with advantage to your fortune, to a person where the friendship and good usage will be reciprocal, and without loss to your present children, I suppose all your friends, as I, would approve it. As to the affair of letter of licence, etc., I profess I am not master of it. I understand it is to be given by all the creditors before the debtor can be secure; why it is desired of you, I know not, unless as a creditor, and how you are a creditor, unless as being bound for him, I am as ignorant,

---

[1] *Supra*, p. 6.   [2] *I.e.*, Mrs. Howard.
[3] In the Forster Collection. *Supra*, vol. ii, p. 241, n. 1.
[4] An answer to Swift's letter of the 9th of that month (*supra*, p. 87).

and how Jackman in his condition can be able to indemnify you is as hard to conceive; I doubt his rich friends will hardly do it. This is all I can see after half blinding myself with reading your clerk's copies.

As to your leaving Ireland, doubtless your first step should be to London for a final answer from the lady. If that fails, I think you can live more conveniently in some distant southern county of England, though perhaps cheaper in France. To make a conveyance of your estate, etc., there must, I suppose, be advice of good lawyers. Mr. Stopford will be a very proper person,[1] but you judge ill in thinking on me who am so old and crazy that for several years I have refused so much as to be executor to three or four of my best and nearest friends both here and in England. I know not whether Mr. Stopford received my letter, but I will write to him again. You cannot well blame him for some tenderness to so near a relation, but I think you are a little too nice and punctilious for a man of this world, and expect more from human race than their corruptions can afford. I apprehend that whatever the debt you are engaged for shall amount to, any unsettled part of your estate will be liable to it, and it will be wise to reckon upon no assistance from Jackman, and if you shall be forced to raise money and pay interest, you must look only towards how much is left, and either retrieve by marriage or live retired in a thrifty way.

No man can advise otherwise than as he follows himself. Every farthing of any temporal fortune I have is upon the balance to be lost. The turn I take is to look on what is left, and my wisdom can reach no higher. But as you ill bear public mortifications, it will be best to retire to some other country where none will insult you on account of your living in an humbler manner. In the country of England one may live with repute, and keep the best company, for a hundred pounds a year. I can think of no more at present. I shall soon leave this place,[2] the weather being cold, and an Irish winter country is what I cannot support. I am, Sir,

Your most, etc.

Addressed—To Knightley Chetwode, Esq., at Woodbrooke, near Mountmellick.

[1] To act as a trustee.   [2] *I.e.*, Market Hill.

DCCXXXVIII. [*Copy.*[1]]

SWIFT TO THE REV. JAMES STOPFORD

Market Hill, *August* 30, 1729.

I HAVE received two letters from Mr. Chetwode upon a great distress he is under by being bound for Mr. Jackman, who is withdrawn. Jackman was receiver for Mr. Shirley, a son of Lord Ferrers. Upon Mr. Shirley's coming over, Jackman being in arrear went off. What the arrear is, Mr. Chetwode knows not. He writ twice for my advice on that and other parallel matters, and desired I would persuade you to write to him, which I would not have done if his children did not demand some of your care, as your nephews. You know his temper, and how far you will think fit to offer in concerning yourself with his affairs. I writ to you before, but believe my letter miscarried. I hope your health is fixed, without any dread of your late ailment returning. I know not where you are, but I direct at a venture. I intend to be soon in town. My humble services to your lady,[2] and all others about you of my acquaintance. If you should have occasion to write, enclose to me under a cover to Sir Arthur Acheson at Market Hill, by Newry.

Addressed—To the Reverend Mr. James Stopford at Colonel Butler's [3] house in Dawson Street, Dublin.

---

[1] In the Forster Collection.

[2] Although he had failed to obtain the best or any college living, Stopford had entered the married state (*supra*, vol. iii, pp. 322, 347), and had twelve months before resigned his fellowship. He had been subsequently appointed by Archbishop King vicar of Finglas, the parish near Dublin formerly held by Dilly Ashe and Parnell (*supra*, vol. iii, p. 18, n. 2).

[3] A son of the first Viscount Lanesborough (*supra*, vol. ii, p. 242). The Viscount's brother, Lord Newtown-Butler, had married an aunt of Stopford's wife.

DCCXXXIX. [*Copy.*[1]]

KNIGHTLEY CHETWODE TO SWIFT

[*September* 10, 1729.]

SIR,

A PERSON of some figure and distinction, whom probably you saw every day you lived when in London,[2] came hither the morning I proposed to acknowledge your favour of the 30th; so that I was compelled to lose post to hear him talk of fine pictures, distant prospects, and Elysian fields. He pressed me hard to hasten to England at least; but at last it came almost to Paul and Agrippa, for when I walked him through Versailles' labyrinth,[3] and through some of my other improvements, [and] that he had gorged himself with what he called better fruit than he eat in England or abroad, [and] flew the hawks at my partridge which in almost every field I sprang for him, he swore I was happier than if crowned, and that he would willingly quit the world, and come into my retreat. But for God's sake is it true, as he says, that your friend Lewis is married to my friend Bateman,[4] whom you so merrily described to me with a shining face as if a calf had licked it? He tells me of a lady I valued, who has ran through thirty thousand pounds in a single state, quitted our Church, gone into France, and shut herself in religion, as they term it, there. In short he gave me a full natural day to hear him relate unnatural things, and then left me at gaze like a boy who had lost his bird. He tells me Shirley, with whom I am likely to have more dealings than I like, is a worthy honest man, and married to your Lord Bathurst's sister,[5] and that your friend Ford, who he says is in Dublin, knows him, and

---

[1] In the Forster Collection. *Supra*, vol. ii, p. 241, n. 1.

[2] *I.e.*, Charles Jervas (*supra*, vol. iii, p. 124).

[3] From a note appended to this letter by Mr. Edward Wilmot-Chetwode it appears that the labyrinth in imitation of the one at Versailles was in a very fine beech grove that still exists at Woodbrooke. All trace of the labyrinth has, however, now disappeared. Mr. Wilmot-Chetwode mentions that Swift planted at Woodbrooke many of the trees that dated from Knightley Chetwode's time.

[4] Erasmus Lewis's wife (*supra*, vol. iii, p. 285) was the widow of one Thomas Bateman.

[5] Shirley's relationship to Lord Bathurst was through the marriage of his sister to Lord Bathurst's brother.

has he believes some interest in him. I have none in Mr.
Ford; you have.

But to leave his chimerical world, at least a world I have
so long lived out of, as to have forgot as much of it as old
Serjeant Maynard said he had of his law,[1] I return to what
I can say I know and feel. I am to acquaint you that along
with your letter I got one from a lady who mentions you.
I am sorry for it, for she says that even Lady Acheson has
not preserved you from being broke and shattered terribly,
which agrees too well with what you write me in excuse
for your non-compliance with what I desired from you, but
I am inexpressibly troubled at what you write that every
farthing of any temporal fortune you have is upon the
balance to be lost. I suppose you mean at Drapier's Hill;[2]
take care it comes up to Cooper's. I remember a certain
person talked twice or thrice to me of some money in the
South Sea, and Ben Tooke said somewhat of it to me in
England, but as I had no commission from you, I little
noticed it more than decorum and good breeding obliged
me to in regard to the Sec[retary].[3]

I received the other day a letter from brother Stopford
which pleased me. He says in it he will be plain with me;
and I have been so with him, upon your assuring me he
was as honest, benevolent a person as you ever knew, and I
have told him so. I meant to please him, for your recommendation will ever direct me in my choice of friends, and
I wish you had sooner interested yourself in it. I have
often reflected whether as you say I am not too punctilious
for a man of this world, and expect more from human race
than their corruptions can afford, for pretty near the same
thing has been urged to me, by at least half a dozen of the

---

[1] Chetwode refers presumably to Maynard's remark to Jeffreys that
he had forgotten more law than Jeffreys ever knew.
[2] His proposed investment near Market Hill:

"A purchase which will bring him clear
Above his rent four pounds a year;
Provided to improve the ground,
He will but add two hundred pound,
And from his endless hoarded store,
To build a house, five hundred more."

("Poetical Works," ii, 107.)

[3] The reference is evidently to Bolingbroke with whom Chetwode
had no doubt intercourse when he was living abroad.

most considerable men I ever corresponded or conversed
with, of which old Duke of Buckingham and your patron
Oxford were two.[1] I aver that from them I had almost the
same thing in almost the same words. But few men I
really believe know as well as I do what comfort there is
in lying down in a content arising from the following
motives: that I cannot accuse myself of one wilful breach of
honour in the whole course of my life; that the secrets,
lives, and fortunes of some have been safely in my keeping;
and that even the quickness of my passions by nature or
acquired pride could never provoke me, even when I was
assured I was laughed to scorn, to break in upon my integrity in any of these points. This is a matter of solid
comfort to me amidst the vexations of sundry crosses and
disappointments, how ill soever I am qualified to bear public mortifications. But as you have formerly charged me
with being a great refiner, and in that article compared me
to a person whose principles I hate, though I admire his
fine parts and other accomplishments, and whom I cannot
help esteeming a Judas, though you own you love him, I
must desist since I know this will not please you, and what
I could say will not come within the compass of a letter.

When I had got so far I was obliged to see Lord and
Lady Mountrath, who have taken a house for a year within
a mile of me.[2] Before we parted I saw a nose enter, which
upon inquiry I found belonged to Dan Jackson, for whom
his patron[3] had sent his coach. I must now acquaint you
that I have received another letter from Fletcher, the
schoolmaster, pressing me upon Jackman's affair. I hope
you will not only excuse my troubling you on that head,
but that you will in generosity and kindness to me, as your
friend and servant, try to think of some expedient to extricate me out of this damned affair, since a part of your
trade, if I may so say, is to save sinners, and in this I have,
I allow, sinned against prudence, God and the Dean. Forgive me upon repentance, whereby I forsake this sin, stead-
fastly purposing to lead a new life in this article _à l'avenir_.

---

[1] Oxford and John of Bucks (_supra_, vol. iii, p. 74) were not the only
great persons with whom Chetwode was acquainted. See Appendix V.
[2] The reference is to the sixth Earl of Mountrath. He occupied a
seat in the British House of Commons as well as in the Irish House
of Lords.
[3] George Rochfort (_supra_, vol. iii, p. 103, n. 4).

For God's sake think of me, write to me, advise me, assist me; the rather since I freely own I am so nice that I cannot bring myself to go whither my other interests and a call requires, lest it looks like a dishonourable flight, till I have ended this affair of Jackman's now depending. I hope this will find you safe and sound in Dublin. I am ever, dear Mr. Dean,

Your faithful etc.

DCCXL. [*Original.*[1]]

VISCOUNT BOLINGBROKE TO SWIFT

[Dawley, *October* 5, 1729.[2]]

Aix-la-Chapelle, *Aug.* 30 [O.S. 19], 1729.

I TOOK a letter of yours from Pope,[3] and brought it to this place, that I might answer at least a part of it. I begin to-day; when I shall finish I know not, perhaps when I get back to my farm. The waters I have been persuaded to drink, and those which my friends drink, keep me fuddled or employed all the morning. The afternoons are spent in airings or visits, and we go to bed with the chicken.

Brussels, *September* 27 [O.S. 16].

I have brought your French acquaintance[4] thus far on her way into her own country, and considerably better in health than she was when she went to Aix. I begin to entertain hopes that she will recover such a degree of health as may render old age supportable. Both of us have closed the tenth lustre, and it is high time to determine how we shall play the last act of the farce. Might not my life be entitled much more properly a What-d'ye-call-it than a farce?[5] Some comedy, a great deal of tragedy, and the

---

[1] In the British Museum. See Preface.
[2] As appears from the concluding paragraph this letter was eventually despatched to Swift from Dawley on the date named.
[3] The letter of 5 April (*supra*, p. 75).
[4] *I.e.*, his wife.
[5] The reference is to Gay's play, described by Dr. Johnson (*op. cit.*, x, 243) as a mock tragedy in which the images are comic and the actors grave.

IV   H

whole interspersed with scenes of Harlequin, Scaramouche, and Dr. Baloardo, the prototype of your hero Oxford.[1] I used to think sometimes formerly of old age and of death; enough to prepare my mind, not enough to anticipate sorrow, to dash the joys of youth, and to be all my life a-dying. I find the benefit of this practice now, and shall find it more as I proceed on my journey; little regret when I look backwards, little apprehension when I look forwards. You complain grievously of your situation in Ireland. I could complain of mine too in England, but I will not, nay, I ought not, for I find, by long experience, that I can be unfortunate, without being unhappy.

I do not approve your joining together the figure of living, and the pleasure of giving, though your old prating friend Montaigne does something like it in one of his rhapsodies:[2] to tell you my reasons would be to write an essay, and I shall hardly have time to write a letter; but, if you will come over and live with Pope and me, I will show you in an instant why those two things should not *aller de pair*, and that forced retrenchments on both may be made, without making us even uneasy. You know that I am too expensive, and all mankind knows that I have been cruelly plundered; and yet I feel in my mind the power of descending, without anxiety, two or three stages more. In short, Mr. Dean, if you will come to a certain farm in Middlesex, you shall find that I can live frugally without growling at the world, or being peevish with those whom fortune has appointed to eat my bread, instead of appointing me to eat theirs; and yet I have naturally as little disposition to frugality as any man alive. You say you are no philosopher, and I think you are in the right to dislike a word which is so often abused; but I am sure you like to follow reason, not custom, which is sometimes the reason, and oftener the caprice of others, of the mob of the world. Now, to be sure of doing this, you must wear your philosophical spectacles as constantly as the Spaniards used to wear theirs. You must make them part of your dress, and sooner part with your broad-brimmed beaver, your gown, scarf, or even that emblematical vestment your

---

[1] These characters were, as Elwin observes (*op. cit.*, vii, 154), the standing ones in Italian comedies; the doctor being always "the personification of pedantic vanity." The scaramouche was a clown.

[2] Cf. "Essays," Book I, chap. xxvii: Of Friendship.

surplice. Through this medium you will see few things to
be vexed at, few persons to be angry at.

Ostend, October 5 [O.S. September 24].

And yet there will frequently be things which we ought
to wish altered, and persons whom we ought to wish
hanged. Since I am likely to wait here for a wind, I
shall have leisure to talk with you more than you will like
perhaps. If that should be so, you will never tell it me
grossly; and my vanity will secure me against taking a hint.

In your letter to Pope, you agree that a regard for fame
becomes a man more towards his exit, than at his entrance
into life; and yet you confess that the longer you live, the
more you grow indifferent about it. Your sentiment is true
and natural; your reasoning, I am afraid, is not so upon
this occasion. Prudence will make us desire fame, because
it gives us many real and great advantages in all the affairs
of life. Fame is the wise man's means; his ends are his
own good, and the good of society. You poets and orators
have inverted this order: you propose fame as the end, and
good, or at least great actions, as the means. You go
farther: you teach our self-love to anticipate the applause
which we suppose will be paid by posterity to our names,
and with idle notions of immortality you turn other heads
beside your own; I am afraid this may have done some
harm in the world.

Calais, October 9 [O.S. September 28].

I go on from this place, whither I am come in hopes of
getting to sea, which I could not do from the port of
Ostend. Fame is an object which men pursue successfully
by various and even contrary courses. Your doctrine leads
them to look on this end as essential, and on the means as
indifferent; so that Fabricius and Crassus, Cato and Cæsar,
pressed forward to the same goal. After all, perhaps it may
appear, from a consideration of the depravity of mankind,
that you could do no better, nor keep up virtue in the world
without calling this passion, or this direction of self-love,
in to your aid. Tacitus has crowded this excuse for you,
according to his manner, into a maxim, *Contemptu famae
contemni virtutes.*[1] But now, whether we consider fame as a

---

[1] "Ann.," iv, 38.

useful instrument in all the occurrences of private and public life, or whether we consider it as the cause of that pleasure which our self-loves is so fond of, methinks our entrance into life, or, to speak more properly, our youth, not our old age, is the season when we ought to desire it most, and therefore when it is most becoming to desire it with ardour. If it is useful, it is to be desired most when we have, or may hope to have, a long scene of action open before us; toward our exit, this scene of action is, or should be closed, and then methinks it is unbecoming to grow fonder of a thing which we have no longer occasion for. If it is pleasant, the sooner we are in possession of fame, the longer we shall enjoy this pleasure; when it is acquired early in life, it may tickle us on till old age, but when it is acquired late, the sensation of pleasure will be more faint, and mingled with the regret of our not having tasted it sooner.

From my Farm, October 5.

I am here: I have seen Pope, and one of my first inquiries was after you. He tells me a thing I am sorry to hear: you are building, it seems, on a piece of land you have acquired for that purpose, in some county of Ireland.[1] Though I have built in a part of the world, which I prefer very little to that where you have been thrown and confined by our ill fortune and yours, yet I am sorry you do the same thing. I have repented a thousand times of my resolution, and I hope you will repent of yours before it is executed. Pope tells me he has a letter of yours, which I have not seen yet.[2] I shall have that satisfaction shortly, and shall be tempted to scribble to you again, which is another good reason for making this epistle no longer than it is already. Adieu, therefore, my old and worthy friend. May the physical evils of life fall as easily upon you as ever they did on any man who lived to be old, and may the moral evils which surround us make as little impression on you, as they ought to make on one who has such superior sense to estimate things by, and so much virtue to wrap himself up in

My wife desires not to be forgot by you; she is faithfully

---

[1] I.e., on Drapier's Hill (supra, p. 95). This information appears to have been sent in Swift's letter of 11 August, but to have been omitted from the printed version.

[2] No doubt the one of 11 August.

your servant, and zealously your admirer. She will be concerned, and disappointed, not to find you in this island at her return; which hope both she and I had been made to entertain before I went abroad.

DCCXLI. [*Elwin.*]

ALEXANDER POPE TO SWIFT

October 9, 1729.

IT pleases me that you received my books at last; but you have never once told me if you approve the whole, or disapprove not of some parts, of the commentary, etc.[1] It was my principal aim in the entire work to perpetuate the friendship between us, and to show that the friends or the enemies of one were the friends or enemies of the other. If in any particular, anything be stated or mentioned in a different manner from what you like, pray tell me freely, that the new editions now coming out here may have it rectified. You will find the octavo rather more correct than the quarto, with some additions to the notes and epigrams cast in, which I wish had been increased by your acquaintance in Ireland.

I rejoice in hearing that Drapier's Hill is to emulate Parnassus. I fear the country about it is as much impoverished. I truly share in all that troubles you, and wish you removed from a scene of distress, which I know works your compassionate temper too strongly. But if we are not to see you here, I believe I shall once in my life see you there. You think more for me and about me than any friend I have, and you think better for me. Perhaps you will not be contented, though I am, that the additional hundred pounds a year is only for my life.

My mother is yet living, and I thank God for it. She will never be troublesome to me, if it but please God she be not

---

[1] This letter is evidently a reply to Swift's letter of 11 August, from which several passages have been no doubt omitted. The books were copies of the second edition of the "Dunciad," which was issued ni March.

so to herself; but a melancholy object it is to observe the gradual decays both of body and mind, in a person to whom one is tied by the links of both. I cannot tell whether her death itself would be so afflicting. You are too careful of my worldly affairs; I am rich enough, and I can afford to give away a hundred pounds a year. Do not be angry; I will not live to be very old; I have revelations to the contrary. I would not crawl upon the earth without doing a little good when I have a mind to do it. I will enjoy the pleasure of what I give, by giving it alive, and seeing another enjoy it. When I die, I should be ashamed to leave enough to build me a monument, if there were a wanting friend above ground.

Mr. Gay assures me his three thousand pounds is kept entire and sacred. He seems to languish after a line from you, and complains tenderly. Lord Bolingbroke has told me ten times over he was going to write to you. Has he, or not? The Doctor is unalterable, both in friendship and quadrille. His wife has been very near death last week; his two brothers buried their wives within these six weeks.[1] Gay is sixty miles off, and has been so all this summer, with the Duke and Duchess of Queensberry. He is the same man. So is every one here that you know: mankind is unamendable. *Optimus ille qui minimis urgetur.* Poor Mrs. Blount is like the rest, she cries at the thorn in her foot, but will suffer nobody to pull it out.[2] The Court lady I have a good opinion of, yet I have treated her more negligently than you would do, because you like to see the inside of a Court, which I do not. I have seen her but twice. You have a desperate hand at dashing out a character by great strokes, and at the same time a delicate one at fine touches. God forbid you should draw mine, if I were conscious of any guilt; but if I were conscious only of folly, God send it, for as nobody can detect a great fault so well as you, nobody would so well hide a small one. But after all, that lady means to do good, and does no harm, which is a vast deal for a courtier. I can assure you that Lord Peterborough always speaks kindly of you, and certainly has as

[1] Their marriages have been mentioned; one three years before (*supra*, vol. iii, p. 320), the other only one year before (*supra*, p. 11).

[2] As Elwin observes (*op. cit.*, vii, 160), Pope had urged Martha Blount to separate from her mother and sister.

great a mind to be your friend as any one. I must throw
away my pen: it cannot, it will never tell you, what I
inwardly am to you. *Quod nequeo monstrare, et sentio
tantum.*

DCCXLII. [*Copy.*[1]]

KNIGHTLEY CHETWODE TO SWIFT

October 25, 1729.

SIR,

THE last letter I had the honour to receive from you
bore date the 30th August; the post after it came to my
hands I answered it, viz., on the 10th of September.[2] As you
then designed soon for Dublin, I deferred my congratulatory
compliments till I should know certainly you were arrived.
I hear you are there and well, which affords me great satisfaction.[3] I consulted you on two affairs I conceive of great
consequence to my well-being ; you advised me, and I
retain a grateful sense of the favour. Will you now consent
I send you two letters to read, and afford me your opinion
upon them? I would not send to you upon it, without your
permission. I shall ever treat you with the greatest defer-
ence and respect. I would have everybody else do the like,
and if I could, I would have the nation's public thanks to
you recorded for the evil you have delivered us all from.
But it is easier for a man to mend his own than the faults
of the public, and I conceive the public is exceedingly

---

[1] In the Forster Collection. *Supra*, vol. ii, p. 241, n. 1.

[2] *Supra*, pp. 91, 94.

[3] Swift had returned to Dublin on the 8th of that month, and had
been greeted with much rejoicing. " On Wednesday last the Reverend
Dr. Swift arrived in town from Sir A. Acheson's country seat where
he resided for some time, and was received with great joy by many of
our principal citizens, who also on the same occasion caused the bells
to ring in our cathedrals, and had bonfires and other illuminations." A
contested election was then proceeding in Dublin, and both candidates
claimed to have the support of the Drapier. The successful candidate,
an ancestor of Lord Athlumney, was alleged to have been in favour of
the indictment of that " inimitable writer," but won the day by issuing
a letter purporting to be addressed to him by Swift, which served
" its turn for a day," and induced the weavers to rally to his support
(" Dublin Intelligence," Oct. 11 and 14).

faulty in neglecting you. If you will favour me with the answer to my last and this letter, it will be very satisfactory and obliging to me, who am truly,

Your, etc.

DCCXLIII. [*Elwin.*]

SWIFT TO VISCOUNT BOLINGBROKE

Dublin, October 31, 1729.

I RECEIVED your lordship's travelling letter of several dates, at several stages, and from different nations, languages, and religions.[1] Neither could anything be more obliging than your kind remembrance of me in so many places. As to your ten lustres, I remember, when I complained in a letter to Prior, that I was fifty years old, he was half angry in jest, and answered me out of Terence, *ista commemoratio est quasi exprobratio.*[2] How then ought I to rattle you, when I have a dozen years more to answer for, all monastically passed in this country of liberty and delight, and money, and good company! I go on answering your letter. It is you were my hero, but the other[3] never was. Yet if he were, it was your own fault, who taught me to love him, and often vindicated him, in the beginning of your Ministry, from my accusations. But I granted he had the greatest inequalities of any man alive, and his whole scene was fifty times more a What-d'ye-call-it, than yours: for I declare yours was *unie*, and I wish you would so order it, that the world may be as wise as I upon that article. And Mr. Pope wishes it too, and I believe there is not a more honest man in England, even without wit. But you regard us not.

I was forty-seven years old when I began to think of death,[4] and the reflections upon it now begin when I wake in the morning, and end when I am going to sleep. My Lord, I writ to Mr. Pope, and not to you. My birth, although from a family not undistinguished in its time, is many degrees inferior to yours; all my pretensions from person and parts infinitely so; I a younger son of younger

---

[1] *Supra*, p. 97.   [2] "Andria," i, 1, 17.
[3] *I.e.,* Oxford.   [4] *I.e.,* when Queen Anne's death occurred.

sons,[1] you born to a great fortune. Yet I see you, with all
your advantages, sunk to a degree that you could never
have been without them, but yet I see you as much
esteemed, as much beloved, as much dreaded, and perhaps
more, though it be almost impossible, than ever you were
in your highest exaltation, but I grieve like an alderman
that you are not so rich. And yet, my Lord, I pretend to
value money as little as you, and I will call five hundred
witnesses, if you will take Irish witnesses, to prove it. I
renounce your whole philosophy, because it is not your
practice. By the figure of living, if I used that expression
to Mr. Pope, I do not mean the parade, but a suitableness
to your mind; and as for the pleasure of giving, I know
your soul suffers when you are debarred of it. Could you,
when your own generosity and contempt of outward things
—be not offended, it is no ecclesiastical but an Epictetian
phrase—can you, could you, when these have brought you
to it, come over and live with Mr. Pope and me at the
Deanery? I could almost wish the experiment were tried.
No, God forbid, that ever such a scoundrel as Want should
dare to approach you. But, in the mean time, do not brag;
retrenchments are not your talent. But as old Weymouth[2]
said to me in your Ministry, and in his lordly Latin,
Philosophia verba, ignava opera; I wish you could learn
arithmetic, that three and two make five, and will never
make more. My philosophical spectacles which you advise
me to, will tell me that I can live on fifty pounds a year,
wine excepted, which my bad health forces me to; but I
cannot endure that *otium* should be *sine dignitate*.

My Lord, what I would have said of fame is meant of
fame which a man enjoys in his life; because I cannot be
a great lord, I would acquire what is a kind of *subsidium*. I
would endeavour that my betters should seek me by the
merit of something distinguishable, instead of my seeking
them. But the desire of enjoying it in after times is owing
to the spirit and folly of youth; but with age we learn to
know the house is so full, that there is no room for above
one or two at most in an age, through the whole world. My

---

[1] This expression is, in my opinion, to be read figuratively, and not
literally. At the same time it deserves notice that a resident in the
east of England claimed to stand to Swift in the relationship of
brother. See Appendix VI.

[2] *Supra*, vol. ii, p. 41.

Lord, I hate and love to write to you; it gives me pleasure, and kills me with melancholy. The d—— take stupidity that it will not come to supply the want of philosophy.

DCCXLIV. [*Elwin.*]

SWIFT TO ALEXANDER POPE

October 31, 1729.

YOU were so careful of sending me the Dunciad, that I have received five of them, and have pleased four friends.[1] I am one of everybody who approve every part of it, text and comment; but am one abstracted from everybody, in the happiness of being recorded your friend, while wit and humour, and politeness, shall have any memorial among us. As for your octavo edition we know nothing of it, for we have an octavo of our own, which has sold wonderfully, considering our poverty, and dulness the consequence of it.

I writ this post to Lord Bolingbroke, and tell him in my letter, that, with a great deal of loss for a frolic, I will fly as soon as build.[2] I have neither years, nor spirits, nor money, nor patience for such amusements.[3] The frolic is gone off, and I am only a hundred pounds the poorer. But this kingdom is grown so excessively poor, that we wise men must think of nothing but getting a little ready money. It is thought there are not two hundred thousand pounds of specie in the whole island; for we return thrice as much to our absentees as we get by trade, and so are all inevitably undone, which I have been telling them in print these ten years, to as little purpose as if it came from the pulpit. And this is enough for Irish politics, which I only mention, because it so nearly touches myself.

I must repeat, what I believe I have said before, that I pity you much more than Mrs. Pope. Such a parent and friend hourly declining before your eyes, is an object very

---

[1] This letter is an answer to Pope's letter of the 9th (*supra*, p. 101).
[2] This passage has been omitted from the letter to Bolingbroke in the printed version.
[3] In his verses (" Poetical Works," ii, 107) Swift attributes his change of intention to Sir Arthur Acheson's incompatibility of temperament.

unfit for your health, and duty, and tender disposition; and I pray God it may not affect you too much. I am as much satisfied that your additional hundred pounds per annum is for your life as if it were for ever. You have enough to leave your friends; I would not have them glad to be rid of you, and I shall take care that none but my enemies will be glad to get rid of me. You have embroiled me with Lord Bolingbroke about the figure of living, and the pleasure of giving. I am under the necessity of some little paltry figure in the station I am, but I make it as little as possible. As to the other part, you are base, because I thought myself as great a giver as ever was of my ability; and yet in proportion you exceed, and have kept it till now a secret even from me, when I wondered how you were able to live with your whole little revenue. Adieu.

Lord Carteret, who does his duty of a good governor in enslaving this kingdom as much as he can, talks to me of you as he ought.[1]

DCCXLV. [*Original.*[2]]

JOHN GAY TO SWIFT ·

Middleton Stoney,[3] *November* 9, 1729.

I HAVE long known you to be my friend upon several occasions, and particularly by your reproofs and admonitions. There is one thing, which you have often put me in mind of, the overrunning you with an answer before you had spoken. You find I am not a bit the better for it, for I still write and write on, without having a word of an answer. I have heard of you once by Mr. Pope: let Mr. Pope hear of you the next time by me. By this way of treating me, I mean by your not letting me know that you remember me, you are very partial to me; I should have said very just to me. You seem to think, that I do not

---

[1] Carteret had returned for the third time to Ireland in September.
[2] In the British Museum. See Preface.
[3] One of the Duke of Queensberry's residences (*supra*, vol. iii, p. 340).

want to be put in mind of you, which is very true, for I think of you very often, and as often wish to be with you.

I have been in Oxfordshire with the Duke of Queensberry for these three months, and have had very little correspondence with any of our friends. I have employed my time in new writing a damned play, which I wrote several years ago, called the Wife of Bath.[1] As it is approved or disapproved of by my friends, when I come to town, I shall either have it acted, or let it alone, if weak brethren do not take offence at it. The ridicule turns upon superstition, and I have avoided the very words bribery and corruption. Folly indeed is a word, that I have ventured to make use of; but that is a term that never gave fools offence. It is a common saying, that he is wise that knows himself. What hath happened of late, I think, is a proof that it is not limited to the wise.

My Lord Bathurst is still our cashier: when I see him, I intend to settle our accounts, and repay myself the five pounds out of the two hundred that I owe you. Next week I believe I shall be in town; not at Whitehall, for those lodgings were judged not convenient for me, and disposed of.[2] Direct to me at the Duke of Queensberry's, in Burlington Gardens, near Piccadilly. You have often twitted me in the teeth with hankering after the Court. In that you mistook me, for I know by experience that there is no dependence that can be sure, but a dependence upon one's self. I will take care of the little fortune I have got. I know you will take this resolution kindly, and you see my inclinations will make me write to you, whether you will write to me or not. I am, dear Sir,

Yours most sincerely, and most affectionately,

J. G.

To the lady I live with, I owe my life and fortune; think of her with respect, value and esteem her as I do, and never more despise a fork with three prongs; I wish too you would not eat from the point of your knife.[3] She has so much goodness, virtue, and generosity, that if you

---

[1] This play, which was brought upon the stage in 1713 and in 1730, failed to attract the public taste.

[2] By the government, on account of the publication of " Polly."

[3] *Supra*, p. 10, n. 2.

knew her, you would have a pleasure in obeying her as I do. She often wishes she had known you.

Addressed—To the Revd. Dr. Swift, Dean of St. Patrick's, Dublin, Ireland.

DCCXLVI. [*Faulkner.*]

Viscount Bolingbroke to Swift

November 19, 1729.

I FIND that you have laid aside your project of building in Ireland,[1] and that we shall see you in this island *cum zephyris, et hirundine prima.* I know not whether the love of fame increases as we advance in age; sure I am that the force of friendship does. I loved you almost twenty years ago: I thought of you as well as I do now, better was beyond the power of conception, or to avoid an equivoque, beyond the extent of my ideas. Whether you are more obliged to me for loving you as well when I knew you less, or for loving you as well after loving you so many years, I shall not determine. What I would say is this: while my mind grows daily more independent of the world, and feels less need of learning on external objects, the ideas of friendship return oftener, they busy me, they warm me more. Is it that we grow more tender as the moment of our great separation approaches? Or is it that they who are to live together in another state, for *vera amicitia non nisi inter bonos*, begin to feel more strongly that divine sympathy which is to be the great band of their future society? There is no one thought which soothes my mind like this. I encourage my imagination to pursue it, and am heartily afflicted when another faculty of the intellect comes boisterously in, and wakes me from so pleasing a dream, if it be a dream. I will dwell no more on economics than I have done in my former letter. Thus much only I will say, that *otium cum dignitate* is to be had with five hundred pounds a year as well as with five thousand pounds: the difference will be found in the value of the man, and not in that of the estate.

[1] *Supra*, p. 106.

I do assure you, that I have never quitted the design of collecting, revising, improving, and extending several materials which are still in my power; and I hope that the time of setting myself about this last work of my life is not far off. Many papers of much curiosity and importance are lost, and some of them in a manner which would surprise and anger you. However, I shall be able to convey several great truths to posterity, so clearly and so authentically, that the Burnets and the Oldmixons of another age might rail, but not be able to deceive.[1] Adieu, my friend. I have taken up more of this paper than belongs to me, since Pope is to write to you; no matter, for upon recollection the rules of proportion are not broken; he will say as much to you in one page as I have said in three. Bid him talk to you of the work he is about.[2] I hope in good earnest, it is a fine one; and will be in his hands an original. His sole complaint is, that he finds it too easy in the execution. This flatters his laziness, it flatters my judgement, who always thought that, universal as his talents are, this eminently and peculiarly his, above all the writers I know, living or dead; I do not except Horace.

Adieu.

DCCXLVII. [*Elwin.*[3]]

SWIFT TO JOHN GAY

Dublin, *November* 20, 1729.

IN answer to your kind reproaches of the 9th instant, I declare myself to have not received above two letters from you at most since I left England. I have every letter by me that you writ since I first knew you, although neither those, nor of some other friends, are in such order as I have long intended them. But one thing you are to con-

[1]   " From these the world will judge of men and books,
    Not from the Burnets, Oldmixons, and Cookes."

[2] The poem on which Pope was then engaged was, in the opinion of Mr. Courthope (*op. cit.*, v, 238), the one now known as the Fourth Moral Essay, which was originally published as an Epistle on Taste, and gained great notoriety from the supposition that the Duke of Chandos was pictured in the character of Timon.

[3] By permission of Mr. John Murray. *Supra*, vol. iii, p. 148, n. 1.

sider, because it is an old compact, that when I write to
you or Mr. Pope, I write to both, and if you are such
a vagabond and truant as not to see your friends above
once a quarter, who is to blame? Who could write to you
in Scotland?[1] Yet I am glad you were in a country nine
times worse than this, wherein I speak very favourably of
the soil, the climate, and the language. But you were
among a brave people and defenders of their liberty, which
outbalances all our advantages of nature. Here I will
define Ireland a region of good eating and drinking, of
tolerable company, where a man from England may
sojourn some years with pleasure, make a fortune, and
then return home with the spoils he has got by doing us
all the mischief he can, and by that make a merit at
Court. Pray tell Mr. Pope what a wise thing he has done.
He gave my Lord Allen's lady a commission to buy him
here a bed of Irish stuff.[2] Like a right Englishman, he
did not imagine any nation of human creatures were deprived of sending their own goods abroad. But we cannot
send an inch of wrought woollen to any foreign place without the penalty of five hundred pounds and forfeiture of
the stuff, and the English sea-publicans grumble if we

---

[1] *Supra*, p. 80.
[2] This nobleman and his wife set at that time the fashion in Dublin.
Their house at Stillorgan, on the southern side of Dublin, overlooking
Dublin Bay, was the finest mansion in the metropolitan county, and
the demesne, by which it was surrounded, was unsurpassed for its
extent and beauty. All that remains, however, of the buildings are the
walls of vast grottos and a lofty obelisk, designed by the architect of
the Irish Houses of Parliament, and the demesne, which was inherited
from the Allens by the Proby family, and is now known as the Carys-
fort estate, has become a populous suburb. In the attack which he
made subsequently upon Swift, Lord Allen merely acted as might be
expected from his antecedents. The peerage, to which he had succeeded three years before, had been conferred upon his father for his
devotion to the House of Hanover, and the experiences of his earlier
progenitors in Ireland were calculated to make him dread the return
of Stuart rule. His great grandfather, who had introduced into Ireland
the architectural tastes of Holland, had been ruined by the great
rebellion, and his grandfather, who was one of the chief merchants in
Dublin, had suffered much loss under James II. In regard to them
Swift's pen has run riot (" Poetical Works," ii, 243). There is ample
evidence that the first was a man of good parts and handsome person,
and that the second was in his time one of the leading merchants
and bankers in Dublin, whose only acquaintance with the trade of a
butcher was the export of salt meat.

carry our own night-gowns, unless they be old. Lady Allen used all endeavours but found it impossible, and I told her she was a fool to attempt it. But if he will come over, he shall lie in one of mine.

I have heard of the Wife of Bath; I think in Shakespeare.[1] If you wrote one it is out of my head. I had not the cant word damned in my head; but if it were acted and damned and printed, I should not be your counsellor to new lick it. I wonder you will doubt of your genius. The world is wider to a poet than to any other man, and new follies and vices will never be wanting, any more than new fashions. *Je donne au diable* the wrong notion that matter is exhausted; for as poets in their Greek names are called creators, so in one circumstance they resemble the great Creator by having an infinity of space to work in.

Mr. Pope has been teased ten times to pay your five guineas, and in his last letter he says it is done. But you say otherwise. However, I do not understand Lord Bathurst to be my cashier, but my cully and creditor upon interest, else you are a bad manager, and our money had better have been in the funds. I assure you I will give Lord Carteret a note on him for nine guineas, which his Excellency has squeezed from many of us for a job to Buckley, the Gazetteer, who in conjunction with a Jacobite parson, is publishing a most monstrous, unreasonable edition of Thuanus. I understand the parson is only to be paid as a corrector of the press, but Buckley is to have all the profit. The parson's name is Carte. I wish you would occasionally inquire into this matter, for the subscribers on your side are many and glorious.[2]

I cannot be angry enough with my Lord Burlington. I sent him an order of the Chapter of St. Patrick's, desiring the Dean would write to his Lordship about his ancestor's monument in my Cathedral.[3] The gentlemen are all persons of dignity and consequence, of birth and fortune, not like those of your hedge-chapters in England; and it be-

---

[1] Although Elwin (*op. cit.*, vii, 167) implies that in the insertion of Shakespeare for Chaucer Swift showed his ignorance of the former author, it is quite possible that it was done intentionally as a joke.

[2] The reference is to the "History of Thuanus," published by Dr. Mead in seven folio volumes. It contains a letter addressed to Mead signed by Thomas Carte.

[3] *Supra*, p. 83.

came him to send an answer to such a body on an occasion
where only the honour of his family is concerned. I desired
in England that he would order the monument to be repaired, which may be done for fifty pounds, and that he
would bestow a bit of land not exceeding five pounds a
year, to repair it for ever, which I would have ordered to
be entered in our records in the most solemn manner. This
he promised me. I believe the Dean and Chapter are worth
in preferments and real estates above ten thousand pounds
a year, they being twenty-five and the Dean, and he cannot imagine they would cheat his posterity to get about
three shillings and sixpence a man. Pray tell him this in
the severest manner, and charge it all upon me, and so let
the monument perish.

So they have taken away your lodgings. This is a
sample of Walpole's magnanimity. When princes have a
private quarrel with their subjects, they have always the
worst of the fray. You have sent us over such a cargo of
violent colds, that the well are not sufficient to tend the
sick, nor have we servants left to deliver our orders. I
apprehend myself to be this moment seized, for I have
coughed more these three minutes past, than I have done
in as many years.

I wish for her own sake that I had known the Duchess
of Queensberry, because I should be a more impartial judge
than you; but it was her own fault, because she never made
me any advances. However, as to you, I think the obligation lies on her side by giving her an opportunity of acting
so generous and honourable a part and so well becoming
her dignity and spirit. Pray tell her Grace that the fault
was in Mr. Pope's poetical forks, and not in my want of
manners; and that I will rob Neptune of his trident rather
than commit such solecism in good breeding again; and
that when I return to England I will see her at the tenth
message which is one fewer than what I had from another
of her sex.[1] With my humble respects to her Grace, I beg
she will be your guardian, take care to have your money
well put out, and not suffer you to run in debt or encroach
on the principal. And so God continue to you the felicity
of thriving by the displeasure of Courts and Ministries;
and to your goddess, many disgraces that may equally re-

[1] *I.e.*, the Queen (*supra*, vol. iii, p. 303).

dound to her through her honour with the last. My most humble service to my Lord Peterborough, Lord Oxford, Lord Bolingbroke, Lord Masham, Lord Bathurst, Mr. Pulteney, the Doctor, Mr. Pope, and Mr. Lewis. Alas! poor Alderman Barber; I doubt he has left me nothing.[1]

DCCXLVIII. [*Elwin.*]

ALEXANDER POPE TO SWIFT

November 28, 1729.

THIS letter, like all mine, will be a rhapsody; it is many years ago since I wrote as a wit. How many occurrences or informations must one omit, if one determined to say nothing that one could not say prettily! I lately received from the widow of one dead correspondent, and the father of another,[2] several of my own letters of about fifteen and twenty years old; and it was not unentertaining to myself to observe, how and by what degrees I ceased to be a witty writer, as either my experience grew on the one hand, or my affection to my correspondents on the other. Now as I love you better than most I have ever met with in the world, and esteem you too the more the longer I have compared you with the rest of the world, so inevitably I write to you more negligently, that is more openly, and what all but such as love one another, will call writing worse. I smile to think how Curll would be bit, were our epistles to fall into his hands, and how gloriously they would fall short of every ingenious reader's expectations.

You cannot imagine what a vanity it is to me, to have something to rebuke you for in the way of economy. I love the man that builds a house *subito ingenio*, and makes a wall for a horse; then cries, "We wise men must think of nothing but getting ready money." I am glad you ap-

[1] Since he was last noticed (*supra*, vol. iii, p. 67) Barber had given up his trade as a printer and spent some years in Italy. The announcement of his death, which was without foundation, had appeared in the "Dublin Intelligence" of 22 November: "Alderman Barber died the 11th instant; he was one of the sheriffs for the present year, and very rich which he acquired by printing." He did ultimately leave Swift a legacy.

[2] Edward Blount and the Hon. Robert Digby.

prove my annuity; all we have in this world is no more than an annuity, as to our own enjoyment; but I will increase your regard for my wisdom, and tell you that this annuity includes also the life of another, whose concern ought to be as near to me as my own, and with whom my whole prospects ought to finish. I throw my javelin of hope no farther. *Cur brevi fortes jaculamur aevo*, etc.

The second, as it is called, but indeed the eighth edition of the Dunciad, with some additional notes and epigrams, shall be sent you if I know any opportunity. If they reprint it with you, let them by all means follow that octavo edition. The Drapier's Letters are again printed here, very laudably, as to paper, print, etc., for you know I disapprove Irish politics, as my commentator tells you, being a strong and jealous subject of England. The lady you mention,[1] you ought not to complain of for not acknowledging your present; she having lately received a much richer present from Mr. Knight of the South Sea,[2] and you are sensible she cannot ever return it to one in the condition of an outlaw. It is certain, as he never can expect any favour, his motive must be wholly disinterested.[3] Will not this reflection make you blush? Your continual deplorings of Ireland make me wish you were here long enough to forget those scenes that so afflict you: I am only in fear if you were, you would grow such a patriot here too as not to be quite at ease, for your love of old England. It is very possible your journey, in the time I compute, might exactly tally with my intended one to you, and if you must soon again go back, you would not be unattended. For the poor woman decays perceptibly every week, and the winter may too probably put an end to a very long, and a very irreproachable life. My constant attendance on her does indeed affect my mind very much, and lessen extremely my desires of long life; since I see the best that

---

[1] *I.e.*, the Queen. The reference to her has been omitted from Swift's letter (*supra*, p. 106).

[2] The former treasurer of the South Sea Company, who was living on his ill-gotten gains in France with other refugees of the same character:

> "Gone ev'ry blush, and silent all reproach,
> Contending Princes mount them in their coach."

[3] Knight's efforts were eventually successful, and permission was given to him twelve years later to return to England.

can come of it is a miserable benediction at most so that
I look upon myself to be many years older in two years
since you saw me. The natural imbecility of my body, joined
now to this acquired old age of the mind, makes me at
least as old as you, and we are the fitter to crawl down the
hill together. I only desire I may be able to keep pace
with you. My first friendship, at sixteen, was contracted
with a man of seventy, and I found him not grave enough
or consistent enough for me, though we lived well to his
death. I speak of old Mr. Wycherley, some letters of
whom, by the by, and of mine, the booksellers have got
and printed, not without the concurrence of a noble friend
of mine and yours.[1] I do not much approve of it; though
there is nothing for me to be ashamed of, because I will
not be ashamed of anything I do not do myself, or of anything that is not immoral, but merely dull, as for instance,
if they printed this letter I am now writing, which they
easily may, if the underlings at the post-office please to
take a copy of it. I admire on this consideration, your
sending your last to me quite open, without a seal, wafer,
or any closure whatever, manifesting the utter openness of
the writer. I would do the same by this, but fear it would
look like affectation to send two letters so together. I will
fully represent to our friend, and, I doubt not, it will touch
his heart, what you so feelingly set forth as to the badness
of your Burgundy, etc.[2] He is an extreme honest man, and
indeed ought to be so, considering how very indiscreet and
unreserved he is; but I do not approve this part of his
character, and will never join with him in any of his idlenesses in the way of wit.

You know my maxim to keep as clear of all offence as
I am clear of all interest in either party. I was once displeased before at you, for complaining to Mr. Doddington of my not having a pension,[3] and am so again at

---

[1] There has been already reference to Pope's friendship with
Wycherley, which was not so uninterrupted as Pope wished Swift to
believe (*supra*, vol. iii, p. 295). According to Elwin (*op. cit.*, vi,
xxxviii) Pope's noble friend, Lord Oxford, could not have acted the
part attributed to him, as a copy of Pope's correspondence was not in
his possession at the time Wycherley's correspondence was published.

[2] As appears from subsequent letters, the friend was John Arbuthnot, and the wine, which was Hermitage, had been sent to Swift by
George Arbuthnot (*supra*, p. 11, n. 2).

[3] Swift appears to have made the acquaintance of George Bubb

your naming it to a certain Lord.[1] I have given some proofs in the course of my whole life, from the time when I was in the friendship of Lord Bolingbroke and Mr. Craggs,[2] even to this when I am civilly treated by Sir Robert Walpole, that I never thought myself so warm in any party's cause as to deserve their money, and therefore would never have accepted it, but give me leave to tell you, that of all mankind the two persons I would least have accepted any favour from are those very two, to whom you have unluckily spoken of it. I desire you to take off any impressions which that dialogue may have left on his Lordship's mind, as if I ever had any thought of being beholden to him, or any other, in that way. And yet you know I am no enemy to the present constitution; I believe as sincere a well-wisher to it, nay even to the Church established, as any minister in or out of employment whatever; or any bishop of England or Ireland. Yet I am of the religion of Erasmus, a Catholic. So I live, so I shall die; and hope one day to meet you, Bishop Atterbury, the younger Craggs, Dr. Garth,[3] Dean Berkeley, and Mr. Hutchinson,[4] in that place, to which God, of his infinite mercy, bring us and everybody.

Lord Bolingbroke's answer to your letter I have just received, and join it to this packet. The work he speaks of with such abundant partiality is a system of ethics in the Horatian way.[5]

Doddington, who has been mentioned in connection with his uncle (*supra*, vol. i, p. 102), while staying with Pope, and was on sufficiently intimate terms with him to take from his table the note-book in which he wrote the "Holyhead Journal" ("Prose Works," xi, 392).

[1] *I.e.*, Carteret (*supra*, p. 107).

[2]   "Statesman, yet friend to truth! of soul sincere,
         In action faithful, and in honour clear."

[3]   "Accept, O Garth! the muse's early lays,
         That adds this wreath of ivy to thy bays;
         Hear what from love unpractised hearts endure,
         From love, the sole disease thou canst not cure."

[4] The author of "Moses's Principia."
[5] *Supra*, p. 110.

DCCXLIX. [*Sheridan.*]

SWIFT TO ROBERT PERCIVAL

January 3, 1729-30.

SIR,[1]

SEEING your frank on the outside, and your address in the same hand, it was obvious who was the writer, and before I opened it, a worthy friend being with me, I told him the contents of the difference between us: that your tithes being generally worth five or six pounds per annum, and by the terror of squireship, frightening my agent to take what you graciously thought fit to give, you wronged me of half my due every year; that having held from your father an island worth threepence a year, which I planted and paid two shillings annually for, and being out of possession of the said island seven or eight years, there could not possibly be above four shillings due to you, for which you have thought proper to stop three or four years tithe, at your own rate of two pounds five shillings a year, as I remember, and still continue to stop it, on pretence that the said island was not surrendered to you in form, although you have cut down more plantations of willows and abeles, than would purchase a dozen such islands.[2] I told my friend, that this talent of esquires prevailed very much formerly in the country; that as to yourself, from the badness of your education,[3] against all my advices and endeavours, and from the cast of your nature, as well as another circumstance which I shall not mention, I expected nothing from you that became a gentleman; that I had expostulated this scurvy matter very gently with you; that I conceived this letter was an answer; that from the prerogative of a good estate, however gotten, and the practice of lording over a few Irish wretches, and from the natural want of better thinking, I was sure your answer

---

[1] The recipient was the eldest son of Swift's old friend and neighbour at Laracor who had died in 1718. He had been elected member for Trim in his father's room.

[2] In this action he appears to have imitated his father (*supra*, vol. ii, p. 240).

[3] Percival does not appear to have been a graduate of any University.

would be extremely rude and stupid, full of very bad language in all senses; that a bear in a wilderness will as soon fix on a philosopher as on a cottager, and a man wholly void of education, judgement, or distinction of persons, has no regard, in his insolence, but to the passion of fear; and how heartily I wished that, to make you show your humility, your quarrel had rather been with a captain of dragoons than the Dean of St. Patrick's. All this happened before my opening your letter; which being read, my friend told me, I was an ill guesser; that you affirmed you despised me only as a clergyman, by your own confession; and that you had reason, because clergymen pretend to learning, wherein you value yourself as what you are an utter stranger to.

I took some pains in providing and advising about your education, but, since you have made so ill use of my rules, I cannot deny, that according to your own principles, your usage of me is just. You are wholly out of my danger: the weapons I use will do you no hurt, and to that which would keep nicer men in awe, you are insensible. A needle against a stone wall can make no impression. Your faculty lies in making bargains: stick to that. Leave your children a better estate than your father left you, as he left you much more than your grandfather left him. Your father and you are much wiser than I, who gave among you fifty years purchase for land, for which I am not to see one farthing. This was intended as an encouragement to a clergyman to reside among you, whenever any of your posterity shall be able to distinguish a man from a beast. One thing I desire you will be set right in: I do not despise all squires. It is true, I despise the bulk of them.[1] But pray take notice, that a squire must have some merit before I shall honour him with my contempt; for I do not despise a fly, a maggot, or a mite. If you send me an answer to this, I shall not read it, but open it before company, and in their presence burn it; for no other reason but the detestation of bad spelling, no grammar, and that pertness which proceeds from ignorance and an invincible want of taste.

---

[1] The "Character of an Irish Squire," which has been included in the "Prose Works," xi, 193, was probably written at the same time as this letter.

I have ordered a copy of this letter to be taken, with an intention to print it as a mark of my esteem for you, which, however, perhaps I shall not pursue, for I could willingly excuse our two names from standing in the same paper, since I am confident you have as little desire of fame as I have to give it you. I wish many happy New Years to you and your family, and am, with truth,

Your friend and humble servant.

Let me add something serious; that, as it is held an imprudent thing to provoke valour, so, I confess, it was imprudent in me to provoke rudeness, which, as it was my own standing rule never to do, except in cases where I had power to punish it, so my error proceeded from a better opinion of you than you have thought fit to make good, for, with every fault in your nature, your education, and your understanding, I never imagined you so utterly devoid of knowing some little distinction between persons.

DCCL. [*Elwin.*[1]]

SWIFT TO ALEXANDER POPE

Dublin, February 6, 1729-30.

THERE are three citizens' wives in this town; one of them whose name is Grierson, a Scotch bookseller's wife. She is a very good Latin and Greek scholar, and has lately published a fine edition of Tacitus, with a Latin dedication to the Lord Lieutenant; and she writes *carmina Anglicana non contemnenda.*[2] The second is one Mrs. Barber, wife to

---

[1] By permission of Mr. John Murray. *Supra*, vol. iii, p. 148, n. 1.

[2] The origin of this remarkable woman is enveloped in mystery, and has excited much curiosity in Ireland. Her edition of Tacitus has received a high encomium, and was not her only work of the kind ("D. N. B.," xxiii, 220). Hebrew is said to have been one of her accomplishments, but the accuracy of the statement is doubted by Mrs. Delany ("Correspondence," ii, 576). She studied obstetrics under the father of Swift's friend Mrs. Pilkington, and appears to have been introduced to him by her future husband (Mrs. Pilkington's "Memoirs," i, 23). The fact that her son, who was known to Dr. Johnson, bore the name of Abraham suggests that she may have been of Jewish extraction (*cf.* "The Irish Book-Lover," ii, 136).

a woollen draper, who is our chief poetess and, upon the whole, has no ill genius. I fancy I have mentioned her to you formerly.[1] The last is the bearer hereof, and the wife of a surly, rich husband, who cheeks her vein; whereas Mrs. Grierson is only well to pass, and Mrs. Barber, as it becomes the chief poetess, is but poor. The bearer's name is Sican. She has a very good taste of poetry, has read much, and, as I hear, has writ one or two things with applause which I never saw, except about six lines she sent me unknown, with a piece of sturgeon, some years ago, on my birthday.[2] Can you show such a triumfeminate in London? They are all three great friends and favourites of Dr. Delany, and at his desire, as well as from my own inclination, I give her this passport to have the honour and happiness of seeing you, because she has already seen the ostrich, which is the only rarity at present in this town,[3] and her ambition is to boast of having been well received by you upon her return; and I do not see how you can well refuse to gratify her, for if a Christian will be an ostrich, and the only ostrich in a kingdom, he must suffer himself to be seen, and what is worse, without money.

I writ this day to Mr. Lewis, to settle that scrub affair with Motte. It is now at an end, and I have all the money or receipts for it, except twenty pounds, which is in Mr. Lewis's hands, so that I have come off better than you.[4] I

---

[1] *Supra*, p. 22.

[2] The modern inquirer has been as unsuccessful as Swift in finding proof of Mrs. Sican's talents as a poetess. She was evidently, however, a clever woman and a true friend. In his lines on Pysche (" Poetical Works," i, 282) Swift celebrates her as a domestic economist, and in verses written during her illness Mrs. Barber testifies (" Poems," p. 134) to her goodness of heart. Sheridan gives (" Life," p. 323) her as his authority for his account of the marriage ceremony between Swift and Stella, and says that she was a great favourite of Stella as well as of Swift, but the present reference indicates that she could have been known to her, if at all, only in the slightest way. Her husband was one of the grand jury that defied Chief Justice Whitshed and sent up a presentment against Wood's halfpence (" Prose Works," vi, 234).

[3] The following paragraph, which appeared in the " Dublin Intelligence" for 28 October, 1729, explains this allusion: "We are informed that there is an ostrich lately brought into this city, as is supposed for a show, that though but young, picks fourteen or fifteen foot high, and when it spreads its wings fills a large room."

[4] The reference is in the one case to the proceeds from " Gulliver's Travels" and in the other to those from the " Miscellanies."

am inquiring an opportunity to send your four bottles of usquebaugh. Pray God bless Mrs. Pope. I despair of seeing her in this world, and I believe the most pious person alive would be glad to share with her in the next. You will see eighteen lines relating to yourself, in the most whimsical paper that ever was writ, and which was never intended for the public.[1] I do not call this a letter, for I know I long owe you one. I protest you must allow for the climate, and for my disposition from the sad prospect of affairs here, and the prostitute slavery of the representers of this wretched country. I have not been deaf these ten months, but my head is an ill second to my feet in the night.

DCCLI. [*Copy.*[2]]

SWIFT TO KNIGHTLEY CHETWODE

Dublin, *February* 12, 1729-30.

SIR,

I DID not come to town till October, and I solemnly protest that I writ to you since I came, with the opinion I was able to give on the affairs you consulted me about;[3] indeed I grow every day an ill retainer of memory even in my own affairs, and consequently much more of other peoples, especially where I can be of little or no service. I find you are a great intelligencer, and charge me at a venture with twenty things which never came into my head. It is true I have amused myself sometimes both formerly and of late, and have suffered from it by indiscretion of people. But I believe that matter is at an end, for I would see all the little rascals of Ireland hanged rather than give them any pleasure at the expense of disgusting one judicious friend.

[1] The paper was the "Libel on the Reverend Dr. Delany and his Excellency Lord Carteret" ("Poetical Works," i, 320) and the lines those beginning:

> " Hail happy Pope ! whose generous mind,
> Detesting all the statesmen kind,
> Contemning courts, at courts unseen,
> Refused the visits of a Queen."

[2] In the Forster Collection. *Supra*, vol. ii, p. 241, n. 1.

[3] Swift had probably in his mind the letter which he wrote from Market Hill in the previous August (*supra*, p. 91).

I have seen Mr. Jackman twice in the Green,[1] and therefore suppose there hath been some expedient found for an interval of liberty, but I cannot learn the state of his affairs. As to changing your single life, it is impossible to advise without knowing all circumstances both of you and the person. Archbishop Sheldon advised a young Lord to be sure to get money with a wife, because he would then be at least possessed of one good thing. For the rest, you are the only judge of person, temper and understanding. And those who have been married may form juster ideas of that estate than I can pretend to do. I am, Sir,

Your most obedient, etc.

Addressed—To Knightley Chetwode, Esq., at Woodbrooke, near Mountmellick.

DCCLII. [*Original.*[2]]

LORD BATHURST TO SWIFT

February 12, 1729-30.

DEAR DEAN,

I HAVE this moment received a letter from you: but it is the first I can call a letter: the other scraps were only to direct me to convey your correspondence to others, and I thought I answered them best by obeying your demands.[3] But now you have deigned to send me one in form, with a proper beginning and ending, I will not wait even for a post-day, but I have taken pen and ink immediately to tell you, how much I think myself obliged to you, and how sincerely I am ——

[1] St. Stephen's Green, the largest open space in Dublin.
[2] In the British Museum. See Preface.
[3] During Oxford's ministry Swift bestowed no more than a passing notice on Bathurst as one of the new peers and a member of the Brothers' Club (" Prose Works," ii, *passim*), and little appreciated then, like others, that remarkable man who, in the words of Lord Campbell (*op. cit.*, vii, 119), " acted a distinguished part in public life during four reigns, and is celebrated in prosaic verses by Pope, and in poetical prose by Burke." But Bathurst's political consistency and admiration for genius had no doubt impressed Swift during his last visits to England, and induced Swift to do him the rare honour of opening a correspondence with him.

Well, I might end here if I would; but I cannot part with you so soon, and I must let you know, that as to your money affairs, though I have paid off John Gay, I still keep your two hundred pounds, for which I have given him a note. I have paid him interest to this time for it, which he must account to you for.[1] Now you must imagine, that a man who has nine children to feed, cannot long afford *alienos pascere nummos*; but I have four or five, that are very fit for the table. I only wait for the Lord Mayor's day to dispose of the largest; and I shall be sure of getting off the youngest, whenever a certain great man makes another entertainment at Chelsea.[2] Now you see, though I am your debtor, I am not without my proper ways and means to raise a supply answerable to your demand.

I must own to you, that I should not have thought of this method of raising money, but that you seemed to point it out to me. For, just at the time that scheme came out, which pretended to be calculated only for Ireland,[3] you gave me a hint in one of your envelopes (*Anglice* covers) that you wished I might provide for my numerous family; and in this last you harp upon the same string. I did immediately propose it to Lady Bathurst, as your advice, particularly for her last boy, which was born the plumpest, finest thing, that could be seen; but she fell in a passion, and bid me send you word, that she would not follow your direction, but that she would breed him up to be a parson, and he should live upon the fat of the land, or a lawyer, and then, instead of being eat himself, he should devour

---

[1] *Supra*, p. 108.

[2] The allusion is to a banquet given by Walpole at his Chelsea house in the previous summer to the Queen and royal family. It is said to have been the most sumptuous ever seen in England.

[3] Swift's "Modest Proposal for preventing the Children of Poor People from being a Burthen to their Parents or Country, and for making them Beneficial to the Publick" ("Prose Works," vii, 201) had been issued from the press in the preceding October. Its appearance was thus announced in the "Dublin Intelligence" of 8 November: "The late apparent spirit of patriotism, or love to our country, so abounding of late, has produced a new scheme, said in public to be written by D—— S——, wherein the author . . . ingenuously advises that one fourth part of the infants under two years old, be forthwith fattened, brought to market, and sold for food, reasoning that they will be dainty bits for landlords, who as they have already devoured most of the parents, seem to have best right to eat up the children. N.B. This excellent treatise may be had at the printer's hereof."

others. You know women in passion never mind what they say; but, as she is a very reasonable woman, I have almost brought her over to your opinion now, and having convinced her, that as matters stood, we could not possibly maintain all the nine, she does begin to think it reasonable the youngest should raise fortunes for the eldest.[1]

And upon that foot a man may perform family duty with more courage and zeal; for, if he should happen to get twins, the selling of one might provide for the other, or if, by any accident, while his wife lies in with one child, he should get a second upon the body of another woman, he might dispose of the fattest of the two, and that would help to breed up the other. The more I think upon this scheme, the more reasonable it appears to me; and it ought by no means to be confined to Ireland; for, in all probability, we shall, in a very little time, be altogether as poor here as you are there. I believe, indeed, we shall carry it farther, and not confine our luxury only to the eating of children; for I happened to peep the other day into a large assembly[2] not far from Westminster Hall, and I found them roasting a great fat fellow.[3] For my own part, I had not the least inclination to a slice of him; but, if I guessed right, four in five of the company had a devilish mind to be at him. Well, adieu. You begin now to wish I had ended, when I might have done it so conveniently.

DCCLIII. [*Elwin.*[4]]

SWIFT TO ALEXANDER POPE

Dublin, *February* 26, 1729-30.

MY memory is so bad that I cannot tell whether I answered a letter from you, and another from Lord Bolingbroke that

---

[1] Bathurst is said by Elwin (Pope's "Works," *passim*) to have been a pleasure seeker and gallant, but a man devoid of domestic virtues could hardly have penned this passage, and proof that he was not such as he has been represented is to be found in the fact that his son, who was Lord Chancellor in Lord North's administration, desired that his parents' names might be inscribed upon his tomb with the words "his ambition was to render himself not unworthy of such parents."

[2] *I.e.*, the House of Commons.   [3] *I.e.*, Walpole.

[4] By permission of Mr. John Murray. *Supra*, vol. iii, p. 148, n. 1.

I received in January last.[1] I have read them so often that
I should think I answered them, and yet I cannot recall
one particular of what I said to either of you. I find you
have been a writer of letters almost from your infancy; and,
by your own confession, had schemes even then of epistolary
fame. Montaigne says, that if he could have excelled in
any kind of writing, it would have been in letters;[2] but I
doubt they would not have been natural, for it is plain that
all Pliny's letters were written with a view of publishing,
and I accuse Voiture himself of the same crime, although
he be an author I am fond of. They cease to be letters
when they become a *jeu d'esprit*.

I am innocent of half your reproaches on the subject of
economy. It is true I did some years ago, at a great expense, build a wall to enclose a field for horses,[3] being tired
with the knavery of grooms, who foundered all my horses
and hindered me from the only remedy against increasing
ill health. But the house is no more than a plan, and shall
never be more, for *sublata causa tollitur effectus*. I wish
these were the worst parts of my management; for I am
in danger of losing every groat I have in the world by
having put my whole fortune, no less than sixteen hundred
pounds, into ill hands, upon the advice of a lawyer and a
friend. I have absolutely got clear of Motte, and have all
the money in my hands or paid to Mr. Lewis.[4] I believe
he is poor, or too great an undertaker, and rich only in the
worst kind of stock. I have not seen the new octavo
Dunciad, nor do I believe they will reprint it here. The
kingdom cannot afford it. I think you have had some
correspondence with my Lady Allen.[5] Her Lord has shown
an odd instance of his madness. He has for some years
professed a particular friendship for me; but a penny paper
having been lately printed, called a Libel on D—— D——
and a certain great Lord, meaning, as is supposed, Dr. Delany
and the Lord Lieutenant,[6] this same Allen, about a fortnight
ago, at the Privy Council, the Lord Mayor being sent for,
accused me for the author, and reproached the city for their
resolution of giving me my freedom in a gold box, calling

---

[1] *Supra*, pp. 109, 114.   [2] *Cf.* "Essays," i, xxxix.
[3] From this passage it would appear that there was a utilitarian
object in the construction of Naboth's Vineyard (*supra*, vol. iii, p. 201).
[4] *Supra*, p. 121.   [5] *Supra*, p. 111.   [6] *Supra*, p. 122, n. 1.

me a Jacobite, libeller, etc.,[1] and has now brought the same affair into the House of Lords, that the printer, etc., may be prosecuted; and there is a circumstance in this affair, that when it is over, may be worth your hearing. There is not much in the paper, and they say it was printed in London before we had it.

I have done with Court ladies and their mistress. Yet I think to write a moral letter to our half-discarded friend.[2] I suppose it was purposely intended as a slur, what was in some of the prints, that she was to be preferred to the place of maid of honour. I allow the great disinterestedness of the other, which is fully acknowledged by the most loyal Whigs among us. I have some usquebaugh ready to be sent to you on the first opportunity. These happen so seldom that I am out of patience. There are but four quart bottles, for the lightness of carriage from Chester; but since they were packed up, I am advised to send them by long sea, and directed to Lord Bathurst, because a Lord's name will give them a sanction. But this I have mentioned to his Lordship, and so may you, that he may not be at a loss. My coming to England depends on two things: the settlement of my health, and of my little affairs. The times are so miserable, I can get in no money, and among us clergy here, all go to wreck in absence; for although tithes be of divine institution, they are of diabolical execution; and God knows how long my lawsuit may last for my sixteen hundred pounds. As much as I love you, to establish your health I would load you, not from myself, with half-a-score years, yet on condition not to abate one grain of your genius. For, a mischief on it, I find neither prose nor rhyme will come to me as it used; but that is not the worst, for I am daily harder to please, and less care taken whether I am pleased or not. I dine alone, or only with my house-keeper. I go to my closet immediately after dinner, there

---

[1] It had been resolved on 16 January by the civic assembly that the freedom voted to Swift some years before (*supra*, vol. iii, p. 234, n. 1), should be presented to him in a gold box, for which a sum of twenty-five pounds was allowed. From the "Advertisement by Dr. Swift in his defence against Joshua, Lord Allen" ("Prose Works," vii, 174), it appears that the words used by Lord Allen in addressing the Lord Mayor were "My Lord, you and your city can squander away the public money in giving a gold box to a fellow, who hath libelled the government."

[2] *I.e.*, Mrs. Howard.

sit till eleven, and then to bed. The best company here grows hardly tolerable, and those who were formerly tolerable are now insupportable. This is my life five nights in seven. Yet my eyes are hurt with reading by candle-light, so that I am forced to write and burn whatever comes into my head. If I sent my last letter without a seal, it was an honest, pure blunder, of which I make fifty every day, and what increases them is my fear of increasing them. I will hold a crown that in revising this letter I shall be forced to make thirty verbal corrections. Yet I hope to mend a little, being cured of Irish politics by despair, and I have ordered in my will that my body shall be buried at Holyhead, with an epitaph whereof this is a part.

As to my Hermitage misfortune,[1] it is a very afflicting trifle, whereof your abstemiousship is no judge; but I am very serious in telling you, that I expect the Doctor will this very summer make his brother give me ample satisfaction. I suppose he is rich, else it would not be contemptible if he got the custom of several persons here, who liked my first Hermitage so well, which was sent by Robin Arbuthnot, that they resolved to send for cargoes if I succeeded in my second; and I tell you that good wine is ninety per cent in living, in Ireland. But in you I sing to the deaf. I will refer it to your friend Gay, who has writ to me lately, and you must promise my answer. I have not writ to Lord Burlington, but will soon with a vengeance, unless you prevent it. Sure, I answered your last before, about what you say of Doddington, etc. I would not be so nice about poking in a sore eye as in doing anything wrong in so tender a point, neither am I guilty in the least; but the Lieutenant knows himself, and has often known from me your spirit in this matter. I hope your ethic system is towards the umbilicum. I will write to Lord Bolingbroke. My most humble service to him and Lord Masham, Lord Oxford, Mr. Pulteney, the Doctor, Mr. Lewis. I will write to Lord Bathurst, from whom I received a very kind letter.

[1] *Supra*, p. 116, n. 2.

DCCLIV. [*Original.*[1]]

JOHN GAY TO SWIFT

London, *March* 3, 1729-30.

DEAR SIR,

I FIND you are determined not to write to me according to our old stipulation. Had I not been every post for some time in expectation to have heard from you, I should have writ to you before to have let you know the present state of your affairs, for I would not have you think me capable of neglecting yours, whatever you think of me as to my own. I have received twenty-one pounds, thirteen shillings, and four pence interest from Lord Bathurst for your two hundred pounds from October 1727 to Christmas 1729, being two years and two months, at five pounds per cent. Lord Bathurst gave me a note for your two hundred pounds again, and to allow interest for the same, dated January 15, 1729-30.[2] If you would have me dispose of your money any other way, I shall obey your orders. Let me know what I shall do with the interest-money I have received. What I have done for you, I did for myself, which will be always the way of my transacting anything for you.

My old vamped play got me no money; for it had no success.[3] I am going very soon into Wiltshire with the Duke of Queensberry, with an intention to stay there till the winter. Since I had that severe fit of sickness, I find my health requires it; for I cannot bear the town as I could formerly. I hope another summer's air, and exercise, will reinstate me. I continue to drink nothing but water, so that you cannot require any poetry from me. I have been very seldom abroad since I came to town, and not once at Court. This is no restraint upon me, for I am grown old enough to wish for retirement. I saw Mr. Pope, a day or two ago, in good spirits, and with good wishes for you; for we always talk of you. The Doctor does the same. I have left off all great folks but our own family; perhaps you will think all great folks little enough to leave off us in our present situation. I do not hate the world, but I

---

[1] In the British Museum. See Preface.
[2] *Supra*, p. 124.   [3] *Supra*, p. 108.

laugh at it; for none but fools can be in earnest about a
trifle. I am, dear Sir,

Yours most affectionately.

Direct for me at the Duchess of Queensberry's, in Burlington Gardens.

Addressed—To the Revd. Dr. Swift, Dean of St. Patrick's,
in Dublin, Ireland.

DCCLV. [*Elwin.*]

ALEXANDER POPE TO SWIFT

March 4, 1729-30.

THIS is a letter extraordinary, to do and say nothing but
recommend to you as a clergyman, and a charitable one,
a pious and a good work, and for a good and an honest
man. Moreover, he is above seventy, and poor, which you
might think included in the word honest. I shall think it a
kindness done myself if you can propagate Mr. Wesley's
subscription for his Commentary on Job among your
divines—Bishops excepted, of whom there is no hope—and
among such as are believers, or readers of Scripture.[1] Even
the curious may find something to please them, if they
scorn to be edified. It has been the labour of eight years
of this learned man's life. I call him what he is, a learned
man, and I engage you will approve his prose more than
you formerly could his poetry.[2] Lord Bolingbroke is a
favourer of it, and allows you to do your best to serve an
old Tory, and a sufferer for the Church of England, though
you are a Whig as I am.

We have here some verses in your name, which I am

---

[1] The Rev. Samuel Wesley, to whom Pope refers, did not obtain
more credit from this work, which was not published until after his
death, than from his contributions to the "Athenian Gazette" (*supra*,
vol. i, p. 7, n. 1). His only title to fame is in being the father of the
founder of Methodism.

[2] Wesley had the temerity to attempt a life of our Saviour in heroic
verses.

angry at. Sure you would not use me so ill as to flatter
me? I therefore think it is some other weak Irishman.[1]

DCCLVI. [*Deane Swift.*]

THE EARL OF OXFORD TO SWIFT

Dover Street, *March* 4, 1729-30.

GOOD MR. DEAN,

IT is now above a whole year and six months since I
have had the favour and pleasure of a line from your own
self,[2] and I have not troubled you with one from myself.
The answer that you would naturally make is very obvious,
why do you then trouble me now? I reply, it is to join with
my friend Mr. Pope in recommending the person concerned
in the enclosed proposal to your favour and protection,[3]
and to entreat that you would be so good as to promote
his interest. I have not sent you any of his receipts; but
will when you please to let me know what number you can
dispose of. I believe that your Bishops have more learning,
at least would be thought to have more, than our bench
here can pretend to; so I hope they will all subscribe. The
person concerned is a worthy honest man; and, by this
work of his, he is in hopes to get free of the load which has
hung upon him some years. This debt of his is not owing
to any folly or extravagance of his, but to the calamity of
his house being twice burnt, which he was obliged to re-
build, and having but small preferment in the Church, and
a large family of children, he has not been able to extricate
himself out of the difficulties these accidents have brought
upon him. Three sons he has bred up well at Westminster,
and they are excellent scholars. The eldest has been one
of the ushers in Westminster school since the year 1714.[4]
He is a man in years, yet hearty, and able to study many
hours in a day. This, in short, is the case of an honest,
poor, worthy clergyman; and I hope you will take him

---

[1] The reference is to the Libel on D—— D——. Pope had not received Swift's last two letters (*supra*, pp. 120, 125).
    [2] *Supra*, p. 45.   [3] *I.e.*, Samuel Wesley.
    [4] John Wesley's eldest brother, who was an attached friend of
Atterbury and became a few years later Master of Blundell's School,
disapproved of his brother's views which he foresaw must lead to
schism.

under your protection. I cannot pretend that my recommendation should have any weight with you, but as it is joined to and under the wing of Mr. Pope.

I took hold of this opportunity to write to you, to let you know you had such an humble servant in being that often remembers you, and wishes to see you in this island. My family, I thank God, is well. My daughter had last summer the small-pox really, and in the natural way, and she is not marked at all. My wife and daughter desire that you will accept of their humble services, and say that they want much to see you. I obeyed your commands, and did Mr. Whaley all the little service I was capable of. It was little enough that was in my power, God knows. He comes again before us soon after Easter. He seems to be in great hopes; I wish they may be well founded. I think it is now time to release you, which I will not do until I have told you, I may say repeat to you, that I have a house for you, or house-room, come when you please, provided you come soon. I am, with true respect and esteem,

Your most obliged and most humble servant,

OXFORD.

Your Lord Lieutenant would do well to encourage this poor man. He deserves it better than Buckley.[1]

DCCLVII. [*Elwin.*[2]]

SWIFT TO JOHN GAY

Dublin, *March* 19, 1729-30.

I DENY it.[3] I do write to you according to the old stipulation; for, when you kept your old company, when I writ to one I writ to all. But I am ready to enter into a new bargain since you are got into a new world, and will answer all your letters. You are first to present my most humble respects to the Duchess of Queensberry, and let her know that I never dine without thinking of her, although it be with some difficulty that I can obey her when I happen to

---

[1] *Supra*, p. 112.
[2] By permission of Mr. John Murray. *Supra*, vol. iii, p. 148, n. 1.
[3] *Supra*, p. 129.

dine with forks that have but two prongs, and when the sauce is not very consistent;[1] and I desire she will order Lady Charlotte Hyde[2] to read before me, when I go next to my Lord Clarendon's, for when I saw her last she behaved herself like a young sempstress, or a country-parson's daughter. You must likewise tell her Grace that she is a general toast among all honest folks here, and particularly at the Deanery, even in the face of my Whig subjects. I will leave my money in Lord Bathurst's hands, and the management of it, for want of better, in yours; but I hope you have paid yourself the five guineas, and pray keep the interest-money in a bag wrapped up and sealed by itself, for fear of your own fingers under your carelessness and necessities. I pay an annuity of fifteen pounds per annum in Surrey,[3] and shall soon send you a direction for part of it; and besides, my Lord Lieutenant has forced me against my will to pay nine guineas for the new edition of Thuanus, which I know to be a job for Buckley,[4] and I shall put the payment on you or Mr. Lewis, who likewise has some money of mine in his hands. And now I have learnt a way of making my friends write. It is but letting them keep my money, for till then I never had a line from Mr. Lewis nor hardly from you.

Mr. Pope talks of you as a perfect stranger; but the different pursuits and manners and interests of life, as fortune has pleased to dispose them, will never suffer those to live together, who by their inclinations ought never to part. I hope, when you are rich enough, you will have some little economy of your own either in town or country, and be able to give your friend a pint of port and a bit of mutton; for the domestic season of life will come on. We are taught to hope here that events may happen in no long time which may give the Court another face with regard to you, as well as all well-wishers to their country; but I hope you will be wise enough after you have got your bit to go decently off. I had never much hopes of your vamped play, although Mr. Pope seemed to have, and although it were

[1] *Supra*, p. 108.
[2] A younger sister of the Duchess of Queensberry. As will be seen from a subsequent sentence in this letter Swift was not quite certain of her relationship to the Duchess of Queensberry.
[3] Probably to his sister.
[4] *Supra*, p. 112.

ever so good; but you should have done like the parsons, and changed your text—I mean the title, and the names of the persons. After all, it was an effect of idleness, for you are in the prime of life, when invention and judgement go together. I wish you had a hundred pounds a year more for horses. I ride and walk whenever good weather invites me, and am reputed the best walker in this town, and five miles round. I writ lately to Mr. Pope. I wish you had a little villakin in his neighbourhood; but you are yet too volatile, and any lady with a coach and six horses would carry you to Japan.

I complain to you as I did to Mr. Pope of the Doctor's Rouen brother,[1] who sent me one hundred and fifty bottles of Hermitage, that by the time they got into my cellar cost me twenty-seven pounds, and in less than a year all turned sour, though what I had formerly from his brother Robin was not fit to drink till two years, and grew better at seven, as a few left yet show. For this I expect satisfaction. The disappointment is five times more than the loss. But what care you for this, who have left off drinking wine, and would not now think it hard if Mr. Pope should tell us towards the bottom of a pint, "Gentlemen, I will leave you to your wine." And by the way, this is an ill encouragement for me to come among you, if my health and business would permit. Mr. Pope's usquebaugh is, I hope, at sea, and directed to my Lord Bathurst. Tell his Lordship I will write to him soon, with one enclosed to my Lord Boling-broke, whose address I do not well know, and wish you would tell me. My humble service to the Doctor. What other acquaintances of mine you see I know not, except Mr. Pulteney, whose humble servant I shall ever be in all fortunes, and he is another of our stock healths. I know not your Duke,[2] but love him for his spirit. In my con-science, I forget whether your Duchess be daughter of my mistress Rochester or no.[3] Pray venture on horseback

---

[1] *Supra*, p. 128.

[2] His father has been already mentioned as a member of Oxford's administration, and was doubtless known to Swift (*supra*, vol. i, p. 266). Gay's friend was only a boy of thirteen at the time of his father's death.

[3] As the ladies of the Hyde family greatly outnumbered the males, Swift might be pardoned for some doubt about their genealogy. Edward Hyde, third Earl of Clarendon, sometime Governor of New

when you are in Wiltshire. There is very cold riding if you
are near Salisbury. Adieu, and God preserve you.

DCCLVIII. [*Elwin.*]

SWIFT TO VISCOUNT BOLINGBROKE

Dublin, *March* 21, 1729-30.

YOU tell me you have not quitted the design of collecting,
writing, etc.[1] This is the answer of every sinner who defers
his repentance. I wish Mr. Pope were as great an urger as
I, who long for nothing more than to see truth, under your
hands, laying all detraction in the dust. I find myself disposed every year, or rather every month, to be more angry
and revengeful; and my rage is so ignoble, that it descends
even to resent the folly and baseness of the enslaved people
among whom I live. I knew an old Lord in Leicestershire,
who amused himself with mending pitchforks and spades
for his tenants gratis.[2] Yet I have higher ideas left, if I
were nearer to objects on which I might employ them;
and contemning my private fortune, would gladly cross the
channel and stand by while my betters were driving the
boars out of the garden, if there be any probable expectation of such an endeavour. When I was of your age I often
thought of death, but now, after a dozen years more, it is
never out of my mind, and terrifies me less. I conclude
that Providence has ordered our fears to decrease with our
spirits; and yet I love *la bagatelle* better than ever, for,

---

York, who died in 1723, his uncle Laurence Hyde, first Earl of
Rochester, who died in 1711 (*supra*, vol. i, p. 262), and his uncle's son,
Henry Hyde, second Earl of Rochester, who succeeded to the title of
Clarendon on his cousin's death, had all daughters. The wife of the
last, one of the daughters of Sir William Leveson-Gower, was the
mother of the Duchess of Queensberry (*supra*, p. 10, n. 2), and the lady
to whom Swift refers here and in the Journal to Stella as his mistress.
She was famous for her beauty and for scandal about her conjugal
fidelity (*cf.* "D. N. B.," xxviii, 394, and "Complete Peerage," vi, 311).
Her death had taken place five years before.

[1] *Supra*, p. 110.

[2] The reference is probably to the second Viscount Carrington of
Burford, whose seat, Ashby Folville, was near the parish in Leicester-
shire of which Swift's uncle was vicar (*supra*, vol. i, p. 3, n. 4). Lord
Carrington died in 1701 at the age of eighty.

finding it troublesome to read at night, and the company here growing tasteless, I am always writing bad prose, or worse verses, either of rage or raillery, whereof some few escape to give offence, or mirth, and the rest are burnt. They print some Irish trash in London, and charge it on me, which you will clear me of to my friends, for all are spurious except one paper, for which Mr. Pope very lately chid me.[1]

I remember your Lordship used to say, that a few good speakers would in time carry any point that was right; and that the common method of a majority, by calling to the question, would never hold long when reason was on the other side. Whether politics do not change like gaming, by the invention of new tricks, I am ignorant; but I believe in your time you would never, as a Minister, have suffered an Act to pass through the House of Commons, only because you were sure of a majority in the House of Lords to throw it out, because it would be unpopular, and consequently a loss of reputation. Yet this, we are told, has been the case in the Qualification Bill relating to Pensioners.[2] It should seem to me that corruption, like avarice, has no bounds. I had opportunities to know the proceedings of your Ministry better than any other man of my rank; and having not much to do, I have often compared it with these last sixteen years of a profound peace all over Europe, and we running seven millions in debt. I am forced to play at small game, to set the beasts here a-madding, merely for want of better game. *Tentanda via est qua me quoque possim*, etc.[3] The d—— take those politics, where a dunce might govern for a dozen years together. I will come in person to England if I am provoked, and send for the dictator from the plough. I disdain to say, *O mihi praeteritos*, but *cruda deo viridisque senectus*.[4]

Pray, my Lord, how are the gardens? Have you taken down the mount, and removed the yew hedges? Have you not bad weather for the spring corn? Has Mr. Pope gone

---

[1] *Supra*, p. 131.
[2] The object of this Bill was to make previous legislation effective in preventing the election to the House of Commons of persons in receipt of pensions from the Crown. The procedure to which Swift alludes was Walpole's policy, and increased the dissension between him and Townshend (Leadam, *op. cit.*, p. 341).
[3] Virg., "Georg.," iii, 9.   [4] "Aen.," vi, 304; viii, 560.

farther in his ethic poems? And is the headland sown with wheat? And what says Polybius? And how does my Lord St. John, which last question is very material to me, because I love Burgundy, and riding between Twickenham and Dawley?[1] I built a wall five years ago, and when the masons played the knaves, nothing delighted me so much as to stand by while my servants threw down what was amiss.[2] I have likewise seen a monkey overthrow all the dishes and plates in a kitchen, merely for the pleasure of seeing them tumble, and hearing the clatter they made in their fall. I wish you would invite me to such another entertainment; but you think, as I ought to think, that it is time for me to have done with the world, and so I would if I could get into a better before I was called into the best, and not die here in a rage, like a poisoned rat in a hole. I wonder you are not ashamed to let me pine away in this kingdom, while you are out of power.

I come from looking over the *mélange* above-written, and declare it to be a true copy of my present disposition, which must needs please you, since nothing was ever more displeasing to myself. I desire you to present my most humble respects to my Lady.

DCCLIX. [*Original.*[3]]

JOHN GAY TO SWIFT

March 31, 1730.

DEAR SIR,

I EXPECT in about a fortnight to set out for Wiltshire, and am as impatient, as you seem to be to have me, to get on horseback.[4] I thought proper to give you this intelligence, because Mr. Lewis told me last Sunday that he was in a day or two to set out for the Bath; so that very soon you are likely to have neither of your cashiers in town. Continue to direct to me at this house: the letters will be sent to me, wherever I am. My ambition, at present, is levelled to the same point that you direct me to; for I am every day building villakins, and have given over that of castles.

---

[1] *Supra*, p. 12, n. 1.   [2] *Supra*, vol. iii, p. 201.
[3] In the British Museum. See Preface.   [4] *Supra*, p. 134.

If I were to undertake it in my present circumstance, I should, in the most thrifty scheme, soon be straitened, and I hate to be in debt, for I cannot bear to pawn five pounds worth of my liberty to a tailor or a butcher. I grant you, this is not having the true spirit of modern nobility, but it is hard to cure the prejudice of education.

I have made your compliments to Mr. Pulteney, who is very much your humble servant. I have not seen the Doctor, and am not likely to see his Rouen brother very soon; for he is gone to China. Mr. Pope told me, he had acquainted the Doctor with the misfortune of the sour Hermitage. My Lord Oxford told me, he at present could match yours, and from the same person. The Doctor was touched with your disappointment, and hath promised to represent this affair to his brother at his return from China. I assure you too, for all your gibes, that I wish you heartily good wine, though I can drink none myself. When Lord Bolingbroke is in town, he lodges at Mr. Chetwynd's,[1] in Dover Street. I do not know how to direct to him in the country. I have been extremely taken up of late in settling a steward's account. I am endeavouring to do all the justice and service I can for a friend; so I am sure you will think I am well employed. Upon this occasion, I now and then have seen Joe Taylor,[2] who says he hath a demand upon you for rent, you having taken his house in the country, and he being determined not to let it to anybody else, and he thinks it but reasonable, that you should either come and live in it, or pay your rent. I neither ride nor walk; but I design to do both this month, and to become a laudable practitioner.

The Duchess wishes she had seen you, and thinks you were in the wrong to hide yourself, and peep through the window that day she came to Mr. Pope's. The Duke, too, is obliged to you for your good opinion, and is your humble servant. If I were to write, I am afraid I should again incur the displeasure of my superiors, for I cannot for my life think so well of them as they themselves think they deserve. If you have a very great mind to please the Duchess, and at the same time to please me, I wish you would write

---

[1] Probably the eldest brother of Lord Chetwynd (*supra*, vol. iii p. 338) who succeeded him in the title.
[2] *Supra*, p. 22, n. 3.

a letter to her, to send to her brother, Lord Cornbury,[1] to advise him in his travels; for, she says, she would take your advice rather than mine, and she remembers, that you told her in the Park, that you loved and honoured her family.[2] You always insisted upon a lady's making advances to you; I do not know whether you will think this declaration sufficient. Then too, when you were in England, she writ a letter to you, and I have been often blamed since for not delivering it.

The day the Pension Bill was thrown out of the House of Lords,[3] Lord Bathurst spoke with great applause. I have not time to go to Mr. Pope's: in a day or two very probably I shall see him, and acquaint him about the usquebaugh. I will not embezzle your interest money; though, by looking upon accounts, I see how money may be embezzled. As to my being engaged in an affair of this kind, I say nothing for myself, but that I will do all I can: for the rest I leave Joe Taylor to speak for me. To-day I dine with Alderman Barber, the present sheriff, who holds his feast in the city.[4] Does not Charteris's misfortunes grieve you? For that great man is like to save his life, and lose some of his money.[5] A very hard case!

I am just now come from the alderman's feast, who had a very fine dinner, and a very fine appearance of company. The post is just going away.

Addressed—To the Reverend Dr. Swift, Dean of St. Patrick's, in Dublin, Ireland.

---

[1] He died before their father, and is well known as a friend of Pope and Bolingbroke:

" Disdain whatever Cornbury disdains;
Be virtuous, and be happy for your pains."

[2] This remark was no doubt made to her by Swift when he met her as a child (*supra*, p. 21).

[3] *Supra*, p. 136, n. 2.   [4] *Supra*, p. 114, n. 1.

[5] Colonel Charteris was then lying under sentence of death, but as Gay predicted, escaped with a short imprisonment and some confiscations by which Barber, as sheriff, benefited (" Life of John Barber," p. 51).

DCCLX. [*Elwin.*[1]]

ALEXANDER POPE AND VISCOUNT BOLINGBROKE
TO SWIFT

April 9, 1730.

POPE

DEAR SIR,

I HAVE received two or three letters of one kind or other from you, and answered them either jointly or separately as I could.[2] I also saw a letter of one Mrs. Sican,[3] but missed the sight of the lady by an accident. She came from London one night, sent yours to my house about seven, it raining very hard. I sent word I would be at home all the next day at her service. The next morning it raining still, I sent my servant by nine, to ask at what hour I should send a chariot for her, and she was gone two hours before, back to London. So she has seen no greater monster yet than the ostrich. I do not wonder if people from all parts should flock to see me, after the picture lately drawn of me by a very peculiar painter in Ireland, who has made the finest show-board of me in the world.[4] I forgive that painter, though there may be others who do not, and though he flatters my virtue, which is a greater sin sure than to flatter one's vanity. I am pleased to see however your partiality, and it is for that reason I have kept some of your letters, and some of those of my other friends. These, if I put together in a volume, for my own secret satisfaction, in reviewing a life passed in innocent amusements and studies, not without the good will of worthy and ingenious men, do not therefore say I aim at epistolary fame. I never had any fame less in my head; but the fame I most covet indeed is that which must be derived to me from my friendships.

I am truly and heartily concerned at the prospect of so great a loss as you mention, in your fortune, which I wish you had not told me, since I cannot contribute to help it

---

[1] By permission of Mr. John Murray. *Supra,* vol. iii, p. 148, n. 1.

[2] The present letter appears to be in the main an answer to Swift's letter of 26 February (*supra,* p. 125).

[3] *Supra,* p. 120.   [4] By the Libel on D. D.

by any remedy. For God's sake acquaint me if you come off well. I shall be thoroughly uneasy till I know the event. If there be any virtue in England, I would try to stir it up in your behalf, but it dwells not with power. It is got into so narrow a circle that it is hard, very hard, to know where to look for it. Among your friends I have been seeking it, and have hopes some occasion may arise, which will not be neglected, to invite you to us once again. I do not dislike your writing a moral letter to a courtier, provided you enclose it to me; but the slur you mention in the news was not levelled at her but at a poor maid of honour. As to your writing to Lord Burlington, I would by no means have you. It will tend to no good, and only anger, not amend. You are both of you positive men.[1] I showed Arbuthnot the passage in two of your letters about the bad wines. His answer I doubt not will be fully satis-factory to you. He owned the wines were execrable; for, said he, so were all the wines my brother had at that time. And to make you amends he thinks highly reasonable, which, said he, "my brother will surely do as soon as he returns from China, whither he set out some three weeks since. In the mean time, if the Dean will step and see my brother at his house in China, I am sure he will make him welcome to the best wine the country affords." What can a man desire more? You make me smile at appealing to Gay rather than to me, for pitying any distress in a friend; but particularly this of your bad wine. Do not you know that he has wholly abstained from wine almost these two years, and I drink nothing else? I am really heartily vexed at this piece of ill luck, and wish you would come and revenge it upon our good wines here rather than follow the Doctor's direction to China. If your law suit—*quod deus bene vertat* —can be finished, why not? You will see here more of what you like, or less of what you hate at least. I am in hope your health is tolerable, and cannot be worse in a better clime, for so I believe ours is in respect to deafness, as the air is rather clearer.

Dr. Whaley has given me his cases again upon a rehearing, and you may be confident, I will do him whatever service

---

[1] According to Mrs. Pilkington (" Memoirs," i, 62) the last time he was in London Swift had given proof of this trait by persisting in asking Lady Burlington to sing for him, until she burst into tears and left the room.

I can.[1] I lately saw your cousin, Lancelot, who is a man extremely affectionated to you and to me.[2] Every man here asks of you. Lord Oxford lately wrote to you in behalf of a very valuable clergyman's father's book.[3] I wish you could promote it, but expect little from poor Ireland by your accounts of it. The best thing it affords is what you have sent me,—its usquebaugh, but we hear nothing yet of it, nor by what ship it comes.

BOLINGBROKE

I did not take the pen out of Pope's hands, I protest to you. But since he will not fill the remainder of the page, I think I may without offence. I seek no epistolary fame, but am a good deal pleased to think that it will be known hereafter that you and I lived in the most friendly intimacy together. Pliny writ his letters for the public, so did Seneca, so did Balsac, Voiture, etc. Tully did not, and therefore these give us more pleasure than any which have come down to us from antiquity. When we read them, we pry into a secret which was intended to be kept from us. That is a pleasure. We see Cato, and Brutus, and Pompey, and others, such as they really were, and not such as the gaping multitude of their own age took them to be, or as historians and poets have represented them to ours. That is another pleasure. I remember to have seen a procession at Aix-la-Chapelle, wherein an image of Charlemagne is carried on the shoulders of a man, who is hid by the long robe of the imperial saint. Follow him into the vestry, you see the bearer slip from under the robe, and the gigantic figure dwindles into an image of the ordinary size and is set by among other lumber.

I agree much with Pope, that our climate is rather better than that you are in, and perhaps your public spirit would be less grieved, or oftener comforted, here than there. Come to us, therefore, on a visit at least. It will not be the fault of several persons here if you do not come to live with us. But great goodwill, and little power, produce such slow and feeble effects, as can be acceptable to Heaven alone and heavenly men. I know you will be angry with me if I say nothing to you of a poor woman, who is still on the

[1] *Supra*, p. 132.   [2] *Supra*, p. 37, n. 1.   [3] *Supra*, p. 131.

other side of the water in a most languishing state of health. If she regains strength enough to come over, and she is better within these few weeks, I shall nurse her in this farm with all the care and tenderness possible. If she does not, I must pay her the last duties of friendship where-ever she is, though I break through the whole plan of life which I have formed in my mind. Adieu. I am,

Most faithfully and affectionately yours.

DCCLXI. [*Hawkesworth.*]

SWIFT TO LORD CARTERET

[*April*, 1730.][1]

MY LORD,

I TOLD your Excellency that you were to run on my errands. My Lord Burlington has a very fine monument of his ancestor, the Earl of Cork, in my Cathedral, which your Excellency has seen. I and the Chapter have written to him in a body to have it repaired, and I in person have desired he would do it ;[2] and I desired likewise, that he would settle a parcel of land, worth five pounds a year, not an annuity, to keep it always in repair. He said he would do anything to oblige me, but was afraid that, in future times, the five pounds a year would be misapplied, and secured by the Dean and Chapter to their own use. I answered that a Dean and twenty-four members of so great a Chapter, who, in livings, estates, etc., had about four thousand pounds a year amongst them, would hardly divide four shillings among them to cheat his posterity; and that we could have no view but to consult the honour of his family.[3] I therefore command your Excellency to lay this before him, and the affront he has put upon us, in not answering a letter written to him by the Dean and Chapter in a body.

[1] This letter is said not to have been dated but to have been en-dorsed "To Lord Lieutenant Carteret before his going off." Carteret left Ireland finally on 20 April. Although he set out early, the "Dublin Intelligence" says that he was attended "by most of our nobility and gentry to the water-side."

[2] *Supra*, p. 82.

[3] Swift, in writing to Gay (*supra*, p. 113), had estimated the endow-ment as £10,000 a year, and, Elwin considers (*op. cit.*, vii, 169), is less positive here as to Burlington's promise.

The great Duke of Schomberg is buried under the altar in my Cathedral. My Lady Holderness is my old acquaintance, and I writ to her about a small sum to make a monument for her grandfather.[1] I writ to her myself; and also there was a letter from the Dean and Chapter to desire she would order a monument to be raised for him in my Cathedral. It seems Mildmay, now Lord Fitzwalter, her husband, is a covetous fellow; or whatever is the matter, we have had no answer. I desire you will tell Lord Fitzwalter that if he will not send fifty pounds to make a monument for the old Duke, I and the Chapter will erect a small one of ourselves for ten pounds, wherein it shall be expressed, that the posterity of the Duke, naming particularly Lady Holderness and Mr. Mildmay, not having the generosity to erect a monument, we have done it of ourselves. And if, for an excuse, they pretend they will send for his body, let them know it is mine; and rather than send it, I will take up the bones, and make of it a skeleton, and put it in my register office, to be a memorial of their baseness to all posterity. This I expect your Excellency will tell Mr. Mildmay, or, as you now call him, Lord Fitzwalter; and I expect likewise, that he will let Sir Conyers Darcy know how ill I take his neglect in this matter, although, to do him justice, he averred that Mildmay was so avaricious a wretch, that he would let his own father be buried without a coffin, to save charges.

I expect likewise, that if you are acquainted with your successor,[2] you will let him know how impartial I was in giving you characters of clergymen, without regard to party, and what weight you laid on them, and that having but one clergyman who had any relation to me, I let him pass unpreferred;[3] and lastly, that you will let your said successor know, that you lament the having done nothing for Mr. Robert Grattan, and give him such a recommendation, that he may have something to mend his fortune.[4]

---

[1] *Supra*, p. 85.

[2] It is evident that it had then been arranged that Carteret was not to return. His resignation has been connected with that of Lord Townshend, but the latter did not retire until 15 May.

[3] Presumably his cousin the Rev. Stafford Lightburne (*supra*, vol. iii, p. 235).

[4] Robert Grattan was appointed that year to a more valuable prebend in St. Patrick's Cathedral than he had hitherto held (*supra*, vol. ii,

These are the matters I leave in charge to your Excellency; and I desire that I, who have done with Courts, may not be used like a courtier, for, as I was a courtier when you were a schoolboy, I know all your arts. And so God bless you, and all your family, my old friends; and remember, I expect you shall not dare to be a courtier to me. I am, etc.

DCCLXII. [*Hawkesworth.*]

SWIFT TO LADY WORSLEY

April 19, 1730.

MADAM,[1]

MY Lady Carteret, if you know such a lady, commands me to pursue my own inclination; which is, to honour myself with writing you a letter, and thereby endeavouring to preserve myself in your memory, in spite of an acquaintance of more years than, in regard to my own reputation as a young gentleman, I care to recollect. I forgot whether I had not some reasons to be angry with your Ladyship, when I was last in England. I hope to see you very soon the youngest great-grandmother in Europe; and fifteen years hence, which I shall have nothing to do with, you will be at the amusement of " Rise up, daughter, etc." You are to answer this letter, and to inform me of your health and humour, and whether you like your daughter better or worse, after having so long conversed with the Irish world, and so little with me. Tell me what are your amusements at present; cards, Court, books, visiting, or fondling—I humbly beg your ladyship's pardon, but it is between ourselves—your grandchildren? My Lady Carteret has been the best Queen we have known in Ireland these many years; yet is she mortally hated by all the young girls, because, and it is your fault, she is handsomer than all of them together. Pray, do not insult poor Ireland on this occasion;

p. 262) and resigned St. Bride's (*supra*, vol. iii, p. 157). He appears to have been in no want of money, as he retired a few years later from clerical life and adopted the *rôle* of a country gentleman at Belcamp.

[1] Contrary to expectation Lady Worsley did not come to Ireland to grace her daughter's court (*supra*, vol. iii, p. 233), but Swift had renewed his acquaintance with her during his last visits to England.

for it would have been exactly the same thing in London. And therefore I shall advise the King, when I go next to England, to send no more of her sort, if such another can be found, for fear of turning all his loyal female subjects here against him.

How is our old friend Mrs. Barton? I forget her new name. I saw her three years ago, at Court, almost dwindled to an echo, and hardly knew her;[1] while your eyes dazzled me as much as when I first met them, which, considering myself, is a greater compliment than you are aware of. I wish you may have grace to find it. My Lady Carteret has made me a present, which I take to be malicious, with a design to stand in your place.[2] Therefore I would have you to provide against it by another, and something of your own work, as hers is. For you know, I always expect advances and presents from ladies. Neither was I ever deceived in this last article by any of your sex but the Queen, whom I taxed three years ago with a present of ten pounds value. Upon taking my leave, she said, she intended a medal for me, but it was not finished. I afterwards sent her, on her own commands, about five and thirty pounds worth of silk, for herself and the Princesses; but never received the medal to this day. Therefore, I will trust your sex no more.

You are to present my most humble service to my old friend Sir Robert Worsley. I hope my friend Harry is well, and fattening in the sun, and continuing a bachelor, to enrich the poor Worsley family.[3] I command you to believe me to be, with the greatest truth and respect, etc.

[1] Catherine Barton (*supra*, vol. i, p. 143) had married some twelve years previously John Conduitt, who succeeded her uncle Sir Isaac Newton as Master of the Mint. Some letters addressed to Lady Sundon (Mrs. Thomson, "Memoirs," ii, 295) show that she retained her vigour of mind if not of body. In one of them, referring to an election in Nottinghamshire, she expresses the opinion that "an accusation which is founded upon good works is of the same nature as the sin against the Holy Ghost," from which she prays they may be delivered.

[2] As appears from a subsequent letter to Lady Worsley, the present was a tea-caddy.

[3] Her brother-in-law (*supra*, vol. ii, p. 71), who was governor of Barbadoes from 1722 to 1728.

DCCLXIII. [*Original.*[1]]

SWIFT TO THE EARL OF OXFORD

Dublin, *April* 28, 1730.

MY LORD,

I HAD the honour of your Lordship's letter dated the 4th of March last, and I deferred my acknowledging it thus long to see what success I could have in recommending Mr. Wesley's book. I have the fewest acquaintance in this kingdom of any man who is condemned to live in it. I am hated mortally by every creature in power, and by all their followers. The author's name is utterly unknown here, except by some who read verses and have chanced to read some where he is distinguished as an unfortunate meddler in poetry. I gave the proposals to a clergyman who knows more of his tribe than I do; but such is the poverty, the indifference, the ignorance and the pride of people among us, that he hath not got me one subscriber. Therefore I fear it will all terminate in my desiring Mr. Pope to subscribe for me. That I do not trouble your Lordship with my letters, is the greatest mark I can give you of my respect. It is not possible for any person in this kingdom to be either of use or entertainment, and particularly to your Lordship, who are wholly a stranger as well to the people as to the concerns of so wretched a scene. And I am almost in the same case; I do not visit one Lord either temporal or spiritual, nor am acquainted with above three squires and half-a-dozen parsons. If my own little affairs, I mean the whole small fortune I have, had not been embroiled by law, and yet in peril of being entirely lost, I believe I should have ventured this summer to have waited on your Lordship, and quartered once more on my good friend Mr. Pope; for although my health is uncertain, I am still an excellent walker and a tolerable rider. But I have other difficulties besides my private affairs to detain me. No offence to your Lordship, I am not very fond of the public situation. I see

---

[1] In the possession of the Duke of Portland. *Supra,* vol. ii, p. 160, n. 2.

nails that I thought might be pulled out, now more strongly
rivetted than ever. I heartily congratulate with your Lordship and my Lady Oxford for Lady Margaret's good success
in coming out so happily from a disease so ruinous to ladies
as the small-pox, and without being obliged to the Turkish
manner of inoculating. I hope my Lady Oxford eats more
than she did when I was a witness to her starving. If she
does not promise to mend in that article, I beg your Lordship will burn her barge.

I have a very fair medal, worth sixpence, of Edward the
Third; I know not whether it be worth putting into your
series of English Kings. Pray my Lord, look upon me as
the Greek Emperor did upon the countryman who offered
him a very large turnip; you commanded me to enquire
into coins here, and as an ignorant man I may do ignorant
things. Your Lordship acted your own part, a Harley part,
in your generosity and favour to Mr. Whaley, and I had
the honour to act on the same principle when I entreated
your Lordship to befriend an honest Oxford gentleman
against the rigour and cruelty of the common law. The
loser sends complaints hither that he was overcome by
party. I wish it were true, for then there would be some
hopes of a better world; but I believe the event will show
that the loser will be a gainer, and that they will take care
to see a most abominable poet and a strong party man re-
imbursed by a bishopric. Our friend Carteret is gone, and
we are in the clouds, apprehending he will not be rewarded
according to his merit, which, as I have often told him, is
excessively great, according to the best merits of a chief
governor here, which are to put on more chains and to get
more money, wherein none of his predecessors ever equalled
him, nor met with more stupid, slavish, complying beasts
to manage.[1] Mr. Wesley will not be encouraged by the
person you mention from the same principle that Buckley
was. I most humbly thank your Lordship for the favourable invitation you are pleased to give me, but time and
the miseries I see about me have made me almost as stupid
as the people I am among, and altogether disqualified me
from living with better. I desire to present my most humble

---

[1] This passage tends to show that Carteret's retirement was voluntary (*supra*, p. 144, n. 2). He was afterwards offered the post of Lord
Steward, which he declined.

respect to my Lady Oxford and Lady Marget. I am with the truest respect, my Lord,
  Your Lordship's most obedient and most humble servant,
                                        JON. SWIFT.

DCCLXIV. [*Elwin.*[1]]

SWIFT TO ALEXANDER POPE

Dublin, *May* 2, 1730.

I HAVE yours, mentioning one Mrs. Sican,[2] whom, at her earnest request, I ventured to recommend, that she might come back full of vanity with the honour of seeing you. It is to be understood that the only women of taste here are three shop-keepers' wives. Of the other two, one is both a scholar and a poet, the other a poet only, and Mrs. Sican but a good reader and a judge. Mrs. Barber, who is a poet only, but not a scholar, is going to England; but I shall give her no letter of recommendation, and you will pardon me for what I did to Mrs. Sican. I must tell you that the mortal sin of your painter was praising a Papist; for we have no other zeal or merit than what arises from the utter detestation of your religion. Ludlow, in his Memoirs, mentions one Lord Fitzwilliam with this character, that he was a civil person, though a Papist.[3]

  The lawyers say I have absolutely recovered my fortune, for my creditor has done what you understand not, he has

---

[1] By permission of Mr. John Murray. *Supra*, vol. iii, p. 148, n. 1.

[2] *Supra*, p. 140.

[3] The peer, to whom Ludlow refers, belonged to a family whose name enters largely into the nomenclature of the present residential quarter in Dublin, and which is represented in a female line by the Earl of Pembroke. He was the second holder of an Irish viscountcy, and was promoted by Charles II to an earldom with the title of Tyrconnell, an honour that became extinct on his death and was afterwards conferred on James II's favourite, Dick Talbot. Through his marriage to a daughter of the house of Holles, Lord Fitzwilliam had gained access to the Commonwealth rulers, and by an offer to mediate between Ludlow and Cromwell caused the former to reflect on the strange revolution of affairs that had made "the interest of a gentleman who had been lieutenant-general in the army of the Irish rebels" greater than his own with "the general of the army of the Commonwealth" ("Memoirs of Edmund Ludlow," edited by Professor Firth, i, 421).

levied a fine [1] and suffered a recovery to sell his estate; and my money, with costs and interest, will be paid me at Michaelmas, and I hope I shall never complain again upon my own affairs, like friend Gay, except I am compelled by sickness. But the noise will not be loud enough for you to hear it. As to virtue, you have more charity than I, who never attempt to seek it, and if I had lost all my money I would disdain to seek relief from power. The loss would have been more to some wanting friends and to the public than myself. Besides, I find that the longer I live I shall be less expensive. It is growing with me as with Sir John Mennes, who, when he grew old, boasted of his happiness to a friend that a groat would make him as drunk as half-a-crown did formerly,[2] and so with me, half-a-pint of wine will go as far as a pint did some years ago, and probably I shall soon make up an abstemious triumvirate with you and Mr. Gay. Your usquebaugh is set out by long sea a fort-night ago. I wish I may be once lucky in my commissions from hence. Some rascal in London has packeted me as far as two shillings with a paper writ in favour of Wood the copperman, on a project of his to make iron with pit-coal.[3]

I shall not, upon third thoughts, trouble your female courtier with a letter any more than Lord Burlington. As to the wine, I give it up; for, positively, I will not go to China till I receive my law money. Nothing could keep me from seeing you but the dread of my deafness return-ing; although I must tell you that almost three years in my share of life to come make a difference as much as an inch in a man's nose. Yet I hitherto walk as much and ride oftener than formerly. I intend to make no distant journey this summer even here, nor be above two nights out of the power of returning to my home.[4] I certainly expect that neither tithes or lands, let to the full value, will in a year or

---

[1] *I.e.*, compromised a fictitious suit for the possession of his lands, a mode of conveyance, says the Oxford Dictionary, formerly in use when other modes were not available or equally efficacious.

[2] Mennes was an admiral and verse maker of the seventeenth century, to whom Pepys often alludes as a "very good, harmless, honest gentleman," but hopeless administrator ("D. N. B.," xxxvii, 253).

[3] "An account of Mr. Wood's iron made with pulverized ore and pit-coal" is possibly the paper mentioned. There are also letters from a "merchant at Whitehaven" on the same subject.

[4] But Swift changed his mind and went two months later once more to Market Hill, and remained with the Achesons for three months.

two yield any money at all. All my comfort is, that I have two hundred and fifty pounds a year, which I receive from lands of above three times the value, and that will support me in some sort while there is any remnant of trade or money left among us. And so much for my scurvy domestic.

It is current here that the Duke of Dorset will be Lieutenant. I have known him from his youth.[1] But see the misfortune. There is one Lady Allen whom you employed in a commission.[2] Her Lord and she have been some years caressing me in the most friendly manner, when the Lord on a sudden, without the least provocation, railed at me in the Privy Council and House of Lords as a Jacobite and libeller of the government, etc. He has been worried by some well-wisher of mine in a paper called a Vindication of Lord Carteret, etc.,[3] and all this is laid on me. The libel is that paper of verses where you are mentioned; the other thing is prose. Now this lady has been an old favourite of the Duke of Dorset,[4] and consequently will use all means to put me on a worse foot than my station requires me to be with a chief governor; and who can help it, for I shall not so much as desire Lady Betty Germain[5] to mend the matter, but rather when the Parliament sits here a year and a half hence, I will, if my health permits, pass that winter between you and London.

I writ to my Lord Oxford the other day,[6] and told him

---

[1] The report was soon officially confirmed. As a reward for conveying the intelligence of Queen Anne's death (*supra*, vol. ii, p. 211) Dorset had been appointed by George I first Lord of the Bedchamber, and subsequently was created Duke of Dorset, and became Lord Steward of the Household.

[2] *Supra*, p. 111.

[3] The "Vindication of his Excellency the Lord C——t from the charge of favouring none but Tories, High-Churchmen, and Jacobites." In it Traulus was first gibbeted and his dissection in the verses that bear his name, "all for threepence," was predicted ("Prose Works," vii, 236).

[4] It is said that her marriage to Lord Allen was accomplished by a stratagem of the Duke of Dorset, and that Lord Allen refused at first to acknowledge her as his wife. By another trick, the circulation of a rumour that she had succeeded to a large fortune, she overcame his scruples, and through her masterful character soon obtained complete ascendency over him ("Prose Works," vii, 175).

[5] There has been already reference to her connection with Dorset (*supra*, vol. i, p. 110, n. 1).

[6] *Supra*, p. 147.

sincerely that I had not credit to get one subscriber for Mr. Wesley except myself. I am not acquainted with one Lord, either temporal or spiritual, nor with three squires. Half-a-dozen middling clergymen are all the cronies I have, who never will be worth a guinea beforehand. I will say nothing to my Lord Bolingbroke here, but write to him enclosed, as this is, to my debtor.[1] It is the safest way to his Lordship and you, though it may reach you later.

There is a knot of little fellows here, either in the University or among the younger clergy, who deal in verse, and sometimes shrewdly enough. These have been pestering Dr. Delany for several months past, but how they have been provoked I know not, unless by envy of seeing him so very domestic with the Lord Lieutenant. The Doctor, as a man of much strictness in his life, was terribly mortified with two or three of the first squibs, but now his gall is broke.[2] He has a country house, very agreeable, within a mile of this town, fit to lodge you, in a fine country, much more retired than Twickenham.[3] But the Deanery is your habitation. He is a man of the easiest and best conversation I ever met with in this island—a very good listener, a right reasoner, neither too silent nor talkative, and never positive, but has too many acquaintance. I am now told I may drag on five years more without my money. My most humble service to Lord Burlington, Lord Bathurst, Lord Masham, Mr. Pulteney, the Doctor, Mr. Lewis, and friend Gay. None to Lord Bolingbroke, for I will write to him; and my particular service to Mrs. Pope, and love to Patty Blount, and to Mrs. Howard, if you please, when you see her; and Mrs. Howard, if she has a mind, may present my duty to the Queen. And by the way, is her Majesty angry at the line where your painter has named her with relation to you, or has she by chance heard of it? Pray God bless you and restore and preserve your health.

---

[1] *I.e.*, Bathurst.
[2] Swift's lines to "Dr. Delany on the libels written against him" contributed no doubt to that end.
[3] *I.e.*, Delville (*supra*, vol. iii, p. 239).

DCCLXV. [*Copy.*[1]]

SWIFT TO KNIGHTLEY CHETWODE

Dublin, *June* 24, 1730.

SIR,

I HAD yours,[2] but it came a little later than usual. You are misinformed; I have neither amused myself with opposing or defending anybody. I live wholly within myself; most people have dropped me, and I have nothing to do, but fence against the evils of age and sickness as much as I can, by riding and walking. Neither have I been above six miles out of this town this nine months; except once at the Bishop's visitation in Trim. Neither have I any thought of a villa either near or far off, having neither money, youth, nor inclination for such an achievement. I do not think the country of Ireland a habitable scene without long preparation and great expense. I am glad your trees thrive so well. It is usual when good care is taken, that they will at last settle to the ground.

I cannot imagine how you procure enemies, since one great use of retirement is to lose them, or else a man is no thorough retirer. If I mistake you not, by your sixty friends, you mean enemies. I knew not Webb. As to your information of passages in private life, it is a thing I never did nor shall pursue; nor can envy you or any man for knowledge in it, because it must be liable to great mistakes, and consequently wrong judgements. This I say, though I love the world as little, and think as ill of it as most people; and I would as lief peep three hours a morning into a jail. Mr. Cusack died a week after I left Trim, and is much lamented by all parties.[3] What embroilments you had with him I know not, but I always saw him act the

---

[1] In the Forster Collection. *Supra*, vol. ii, p. 241, n. 1.
[2] An answer to Swift's letter in February (*supra*, p. 122).
[3] The reference is to one of Swift's neighbours in the county of Meath, Christopher Cusack of Rathaldron, in respect of whose property a grant of administration had been issued on the 13th of that month. The Cusacks were amongst the earliest Anglo-Norman settlers in Ireland, and have displayed in many generations distinguished abilities.

part of a generous, honest, good-natured, reasonable, obliging man. I find you intended to treat of a marriage by proxy in England and the lady is dead. I think you have as ill luck with burying your friends, as good with burying your enemies. I did expect that would be the event when I heard of it first from you. I know not what advertisements you read of any libels or stories against me, for I read no news, nor any man tells me of such things, which is the only way of disappointing such obscure slanderers. About three years ago I was shown an advertisement to some such purpose,[1] but I thought the person who told me had better let it alone. I do not know but they will write Memoirs of my actions in war. These are natural consequences that fall upon people who have writings laid to their charge, whether true or not.

I am just going out of town, to stay nowhere long, but go from house to house, whether inns or friends, for five or six weeks merely for exercise.[2] I am, Sir,

Your most obedient, etc.

I direct to Maryborough by guess, never remembering whether that or Mountmellick be right.

Addressed—To Knightley Chetwode, Esq., at Woodbrooke, near Mountmellick.

Endorsed—A serious letter when he was ill and leaving town.

DCCLXVI. [*Elwin.*]

ALEXANDER POPE TO SWIFT

June, 1730.

MY Lord has spoken justly of his lady; why not I of my mother?[3] Yesterday was her birthday, now entering on the

---

[1] The advertisement of the " Memoirs of a Certain Irish Dean" was still issued (*supra*, p. 65, n. 4). An Irish edition, in which it was proposed to print the name of the subscribers, had been published and evidently had met with an extensive sale (" Dublin Intelligence," 1 February, 1728-9, 10 April, 1730, *et passim*).

[2] Swift appears, however, to have spent the next three months entirely with the Achesons.

[3] A letter from Bolingbroke has probably been lost.

ninety-first year of her age; her memory much diminished, but her senses very little hurt, her sight and hearing good. She sleeps not ill, eats moderately, drinks water, says her prayers. This is all she does. I have reason to thank God for continuing so long to me a very good and tender parent, and for allowing me to exercise for some years those cares which are now as necessary to her, as hers have been to me. An object of this sort daily before one's eyes very much softens the mind, but perhaps may hinder it from the willingness of contracting other ties of the like domestic nature, when one finds how painful it is even to enjoy the tender pleasures. I have formerly made some strong efforts to get and to deserve a friend; perhaps it were wiser never to attempt it, but live extempore, and look upon the world only as a place to pass through, just pay your hosts their due, disperse a little charity, and hurry on. Yet am I just now writing, or rather planning, a book to make mankind look upon this life with comfort and pleasure, and put morality in good humour.[1] And just now too I am going to see one I love very tenderly; and to-morrow to entertain several civil people, whom if we call friends, it is by the courtesy of England. *Sic, sic juvat ire sub umbras.* While we do live we must make the best of life. *Cantantes licet usque, minus via laedat, eamus,* as the shepherd said in Virgil[2] when the road was long and heavy. I am,

Yours.

DCCLXVII. [*Original.*[3]]

LORD BATHURST TO SWIFT

June 30, 1730.

DEAR DEAN,
   I RECEIVED a letter from you some time ago which gave me infinite pleasure,[4] and I was going to return you an answer immediately, but when I sat down to write, I found my thoughts rolled upon the trifles, which fill the scene of life in that busy, senseless place,[5] where I then was, and

---

[1] The allusion is to the "Essay on Man" (*supra*, vol. iii, p. 269). By some writers the scheme has been ascribed entirely to Bolingbroke.
[2] "Ecl.," ix, 64.   [3] In the British Museum. See Preface.
[4] An answer to Bathurst's letter in February (*supra*, p. 123).
[5] *I.e.*, Parliament. Bathurst was writing from Cirencester.

though I had nothing to do there, at least nothing worth doing, and time lay upon my hands, I was resolved to defer writing to you, till I could clear my head from that rubbish which every one must contract in that place. I cannot but fancy, if one of our heads were dissected after passing a winter's campaign there, it would appear just like a pamphlet shop: you would see a collection of treaties, a bundle of farces, a parcel of encomiums, another of satires, speeches, novels, sermons, bawdy songs, addresses, epigrams, proclamations, poems, divinity-lectures, quack-bills, historical accounts, fables, and God knows what.

The moment I got down here, I found myself quite clear from all those affairs; but really, the hurry of business which came upon me after a state of idleness for six months, must excuse me to you. Here I am absolute monarch of a circle of above a mile round, at least one hundred acres of ground, which, to speak in the style of one of your countrymen, is very populous in cattle, fish, and fowl. To enjoy this power, which I relish extremely, and regulate this dominion, which I prefer to any other, has taken up my time from morning to night. There are Yahoos in the neighbourhood; but having read in history, that the southern part of Britain was long defended against the Picts by a wall, I have fortified my territories all round. That wise people the Chinese, you know, did the same thing to defend themselves against the Tartars. Now I think of it, as this letter is to be sent to you, it will certainly be opened; and I shall have some observations made upon it, because I am within three miles of a certain castle.[1] Therefore I do hereby declare, that nothing herein contained shall extend, or be construed to extend, so far; and furthermore, I think myself in honour bound to acknowledge, that under our present just and prudent Ministry, I do not fear the least molestation from that quarter. Neither are the fortifications aforementioned in anywise designed to keep them out; for I am well satisfied they can break through much stronger fences than these, if they should have a mind to it.

Observe how naturally power and dominion are attended with fear and precaution. When I am in the herd, I have

[1] The reference is probably to the borough of Cirencester. It was represented by Tories, but was often assailed by the Whigs. On one occasion the author of the "Night Thoughts" was put forward as their champion.

as little of it about me as anybody; but now that I am in
the midst of my own dominions, I think of nothing but
preserving them, and grow fearful lest a certain great man
should take a fancy to them, and transport them into
Norfolk, to place them as an island in one of his new-made
fish-ponds.[1] Or, if you take this for too proud a thought, I
will only suppose it to be hung out under a great bow-
window.[2] In either case I must confess to you, that I do
not like it. In the first place, I am not sure his new-made
ground may hold good; in the latter case, I have some
reason to doubt the foundations of his house are not so
solid as he may imagine. Now, therefore, I am not so
much in the wrong as you may conceive, to desire that my
territory may remain where it is; for, though I know you
could urge many arguments to show the advantages I
might reap by being so near him, yet I hold it as a maxim,
that he who is contented with what he has, ought not to
risk that, even though he should have a chance to augment
it in any proportion. I learned this from our friend Erasmus;
and the corrupt notions, that money is power, and therefore every man ought to get as much as he can, in order to
create more power to himself, have no weight with me.

But now, to begin my letter to you, I have received four
bottles of usquebaugh, and sent three of them to Mr. Pope;
so that I have detained only one for myself. I do not believe such an instance of honesty, punctuality, disinterestedness, and self-denial, can be given in this age. The whole
being in my power, I have withheld but the quarter part.
I expect, if ever I come to be a great man, you will write
a vindication of me, whether I am aspersed or not. Till
then, I remain,

Your most faithful and most obedient servant.

[1] Walpole was then building the mansion-house, and laying out
the demesne, at Houghton. In a very interesting description of his
improvements it is observed that there was "not a drop of water for
ornament" (Carlisle Manuscripts, Hist. MSS. Com., p. 85).

[2] About that time Walpole built also his lodge in Richmond Park,
and appears to have adopted a design in which bow-windows were a
feature (Chancellor's "History of Richmond," p. 217). In the description just cited, the house at Houghton is said to have been without any
relief of that kind.

DCCLXVIII. [*Original.*[1]]

John Gay to Swift

Amesbury, near Salisbury, *July* 4, 1730.

DEAR SIR,

You tell me that I have put myself out of the way of all my old acquaintance, so that unless I hear from you, I can know nothing of you.[2] Is it not barbarous then to leave me so long without writing one word to me? If you would not write to me for my sake, methinks you might write for your own. How do you know what is become of your money? If you had drawn upon me when I expected it, you might have had your money, for I was then in town; but I am now at Amesbury, near Salisbury in Wiltshire, at the Duke of Queensberry's. The Duchess sends you her services. I wish you were here. I fancy you would like her and the place. You might fancy yourself at home; for we have a Cathedral near us, where you might find a Bishop of the same name.[3] You might ride upon the Downs, and write conjectures upon Stonehenge. We are but five and twenty miles from the Bath; and I was told this very evening by General Dormer,[4] who is here, that he heard somewhere or other, that you had some intentions of coming there the latter season. I wish anything would bring us together, but your want of health.

I have left off wine and writing; for I really think that man must be a bold writer, who trusts to wit without it. I

---

[1] In the British Museum. See Preface.

[2] *Supra*, p. 132.

[3] Swift's old correspondent, Archbishop King, had died in the previous year, and had been succeeded in the see of Dublin by a brother of the famous Hoadly, then Bishop of Salisbury. The "ceremony of his induction" had taken place at St. Patrick's six months before, and had been attended "by a great company of divines and abundance of gentlemen and ladies" ("Dublin Intelligence," 24 Jan.).

[4] General James Dormer, who saw much service under Marlborough and in Spain, raised, soon after the accession of George II, the regiment known now as the King's Hussars. It was at first called Dormer's Horse, and was stationed in Ireland during a great part of the eighteenth century. A portrait of Dormer, who was a bibliophile and a member of the Kit-Cat Club, has been reproduced by Colonel H. B. Hamilton in his "Historical Record of the 14th Hussars."

took your advice, and some time ago took to love, and made some advances to the lady you sent me to in Soho,[1] but I met no return, so I have given up all thoughts of it, and have now no pursuit or amusement. A state of indolence is what I do not like: it is what I would not choose. I am not thinking of a Court or preferment; for I think the lady I live with is my friend, so that I am at the height of my ambition. You have often told me there is a time of life that every one wishes for some settlement of his own. I have frequently that feeling about me, but I fancy it will hardly ever be my lot, so that I will endeavour to pass away life as agreeably as I can, in the way I am. I often wish to be with you, or you with me; and I believe you think I say true.

I am determined to write to you, though those dirty fellows of the post-office do read my letters; for, since I saw you, I am grown of that consequence to be obnoxious to the men I despise, so that it is very probable in their hearts they think me an honest man. I have heard from Mr. Pope but once since I left London. I was sorry I saw him so seldom, but I had business that kept me from him. I often wish we were together again. If you will not write, come. I am, dear Sir,

Yours most sincerely and affectionately.

DCCLXIX. [*Deane Swift.*]

The Earl of Oxford to Swift

Dover Street, *July* 15, 1730.

REVEREND SIR,

MR. CLAYTON[2] telling me he was going for Ireland, I could not forbear sending you a few lines by him; although I may punish you, yet it is so great a pleasure to me to think of you, and to converse with you even in this manner, that I must expect you will be so good as to forgive the trouble this gives you.

I do not know what notions you entertain of us here; I fear and believe you are in a very bad way. This is my

---

[1] Mrs. Barber, who had arrived in England and lodged in that part of London.

[2] *Supra*, vol. iii, p. 260.

thought, that devoured we certainly shall be,[1] but only this will be the difference, we shall have that great favour and instance of mercy that we shall have the honour to follow you, and be the last devoured; and though this is so plain, and that demonstrable, yet we have so many unthinking, unaccountable puppies among us, that to them everything seems to go well as it should do, and [they] are so pleased with this thought, or rather do not think at all, that it is in vain to say anything to them. This is a very disagreeable subject, and I will therefore leave it.

My wife is, I thank God, pretty well. Her stomach is rather better than it was. Peggy is very well. Both desire you will accept of their humble service. You mention your law affairs: I know so much of that sort of people called lawyers, that I pity most heartily anyone that is obliged to be concerned with them; if you are not already, I hope you will be soon safe out of their hands. I suppose Master Whaley is, by this time, got safe to his living, and enjoying the fruit of his victory, peace and quietness.[2] I believe he has enough of law, of lawyers, and of Lords both spiritual and temporal. I hope he is well; if you see him, my service to him. I wish you would come over here, that we might have the pleasure of seeing you. Why should you not pass the winter here? I should think it would be more agreeable to you than where you are. Lord Bathurst has had a fever, but he is now well again. Pope I saw yesterday; he is pretty well. I am, with true respect and esteem, Sir,

Your most affectionate humble servant,

OXFORD.

DCCLXX. [*Original.*[3]]

SWIFT TO THE EARL OF OXFORD

From the north part of Ireland [4]
August 28, 1730.

MY LORD,

I AM the only man since the first Villiers Duke of Buckingham that ever succeeded in favour from a father to a

---

[1] The "Modest Proposal" (*supra*, p. 124) evidently caught the fancy of Swift's English friends.

[2] *Supra*, p. 148.

[3] In the possession of the Duke of Portland. *Supra*, vol. ii, p. 160, n. 2.

[4] *I.e.*, Market Hill (*supra*, p. 154, n. 2).

THE DEAN'S WELL AT GOSFORD CASTLE
From a photograph by Mr. H. Allison

THE GROVE AT WOODBROOKE
From a photograph by Mr. Wynne

son, for I can boast myself to have been in the good graces
of two Earls of Oxford. But I have one advantage over
the Duke that I am in no danger to be stabbed on account
of the kindness and distinction you are pleased to show me.
Your letter was sent me by Mr. Clayton to a friend's house
here in the North, where I have been passing a cool summer
these two months, and shall finish the third before I return
to Dublin. Neither my present condition of health or private
fortune will suffer me to make larger journeys. I have had
your Lordship's letter near a month, and by the return of
an old disorder, a giddiness in my head, I have wanted
spirits to make my acknowledgments for the honour you
have done me. God forgive my revengeful temper if I am
not sorry for any mortifications on your side. Your Ministers
have ruined this country, which your Lordship's father from
principles of justice, prudence and humanity, took care to
preserve. You will forgive me, my Lord, for the zeal of
liberty hath eaten me up, and I have nothing left but ill
thoughts, ill words, and ill wishes, of all which I am not
sparing, and like roaring in the gout, they give me some
imaginary ease.

I hope to recover my little fortune in two or three months,
and have no other value for it than that upon any public
distress or any strains of power that may affect my conscience, I may have somewhat independent to keep my
nag, myself, and a glass of ale in Wales. What should I
do in England, when I find myself entirely ruined at Court,
and in utter disgrace with the Ministers? If they would pay
what they honestly owe me,[1] I would be just their humble
servant as much as I am already. If a scribble comes out
complaining of our hardships here, it is infallibly laid at
my door. It is well I have the rabble on my side: that
hath been very lately told them, and they affect not to
believe it. There is a fellow here from England, one Saw-
bridge, he was last term indicted for a rape.[2] The plea he
intended was his being drunk when he forced the woman;
but he bought her off. He is a dean and I name him to
your Lordship, because I am confident you will hear of his

---

[1] The *douceur* of Queen Anne's time (*supra*, vol. iii, p. 315).
[2]   " A holier priest ne'er was rapt up in crape,
        The worst you can say, he committed a rape."
                        " Poetical Works," i, 190.

IV   M

being a bishop; for, in short, he is just the counterpart of
Charteris, that continual favourite of Ministers.[1] I congratulate with my Lord Bathurst for his recovery from a fever.
It is the disease of a young man, and foretells a long life,
if that be any satisfaction in such a world.

The good account you are pleased to give me of my
Lady Oxford's health hath removed a great load from my
shoulders, for I was ever in pain about her Ladyship's want
of appetite, and could often hardly forbear acting the
physician, by prescribing my only remedy which I take
twice a day in fair weather and once in foul; I mean exercise, which although it be the cheapest of all drugs, yet you
great people are seldom rich enough to purchase. Pray
God preserve my Lady Margaret and your Lordship in the
health you possess. I must expect that your Lordship will
please to present my most humble respects and services to
both their Ladyships. Your whole family have my constant
prayers. I am with great respect and gratitude for a
thousand favours, my Lord,

Your Lordship's most obedient and most humble
servant,

JONATH. SWIFT.

Addressed—To the Right Honourable the Earl of Oxford,
Dover Street, London.

DCCLXXI. [*Original.*[2]]

LORD BATHURST TO SWIFT

Cirencester, *September* 9, 1730.

DEAR SIR,

YOU have taken all the precaution, which a reasonable
man could possibly take, to break off an impertinent correspondence, and yet it will not do. One must be more stupid
than a Dutch burgomaster, not to see through the design
of the last letter:[3] " I show all your letters to our Irish wits;
one of them is going to write a treatise of English bulls

---

[1] *Supra*, p. 139, n. 5.
[2] In the British Museum. See Preface.
[3] An answer to Bathurst's letter in June (*supra*, p. 155).

and blunders ";[1] and for farther security, you add at last:
"I am going to take a progress, God knows where, and
shall not be back again, God knows when." I have given
you a reasonable breathing-time, and now, I must at you
again. I receive so much pleasure in reading your letters,
that, according to the usual good-nature and justice of mankind, I can dispense with the trouble I give you in reading
mine. But if you grow obstinate, and will not answer me, I
will plague and pester you, and do all I can to vex you. I
will take your works to pieces, and show you that they are
all borrowed or stolen. Have you not stolen the sweetness
of your numbers from Dryden and Waller? Have not you
borrowed thoughts from Virgil and Horace? At least, I am
sure I have seen something like them in those books. And
in your prose writings, which they make such a noise about,
they are only some little improvements upon the humour
you have stolen from Miguel de Cervantes and Rabelais.
Well, but the style—a great matter indeed, for an Englishman to value himself upon, that he can write English; why,
I write English too, but it is in another style.

But I will not forget your political tracts. You may
say, that you have ventured your ears at one time, and
your neck at another, for the good of your country. Why,
that other people have done in another manner, upon less
occasion, and are not at all proud of it. You have over-
turned and supported Ministers; you have set kingdoms in
a flame by your pen. Pray, what is there in that, but having
the knack of hitting the passions of mankind? With that
alone, and a little knowledge of ancient and modern history,
and seeing a little farther into the inside of things than the
generality of men, you have made this bustle. There is no
wit in any of them: I have read them all over, and do not
remember any of those pretty flowers, those just antitheses,
which one meets with so frequently in the French writers;
none of those clever turns upon words, nor those apt quotations out of Latin authors, which the writers of the last age
among us abounded in; none of those pretty similes, which
some of our modern authors adorn their works with, that
are not only a little like the thing they would illustrate, but
are also like twenty other things. In short as often as I
have read any of your tracts, I have been so tired with

[1] *I.e.*, Sheridan.

them, that I have never been easy till I got to the end of them. I have found my brain heated, my imagination fired, just as if I was drunk. A pretty thing, indeed, for one of your gown to value himself upon, that with sitting still an hour in his study, he has often made three kingdoms drunk at once.

I have twenty other points to maul you upon, if you provoke me; but if you are civil and good-natured, and will send me a long, a very long letter, in answer to this, I will let you alone a good while. Well, adieu now; if I had had a better pen, I can tell you, that I should not have concluded so soon.

DCCLXXII. [*Original.*[1]]

Lady Elizabeth Germain to Swift

London, *September* 19, 1730.

Had I not been retired into the country, yours should have been answered long before.[2] As to your poetess, I am her obliged servant, and must confess the fact just as you state it. It is very true I was gaming, and upon the dapper youth's[3] delivering me a paper, which I just opened, found they were verses, so slunk them into my pocket, and there truly they were kept exceeding private, for I cannot accuse myself of showing them to a mortal. But let me assure you, it was not out of modesty, but in great hopes that the author would have divulged them, which, you know, would have looked decenter and prettier than trumpeting my own fame. But it seems unhappily we were both bit, and judged wrong of each other. However, since you desire it, you may be very sure she shall not fail of my entreaties to his Grace of Dorset for her, though you have not yet let me

---

[1] In the British Museum. See Preface.

[2] Lady Betty Germain, who had then been a widow for thirteen years, had no doubt been staying at her stately seat in Northamptonshire. Swift had evidently overcome his unwillingness to use her as a means of communication with the Duke of Dorset (*supra*, p. 151), and had written to ask her to intercede with his Grace for Mrs. Barber (*supra*, p. 159, n. 1).

[3] Probably Mrs. Barber's son.

into the secret of what her request is; so till my Lord
Carteret does his part, or that I hear from you again, it
will be but a blind sort of a petition. I have not seen his
Grace this great while, and he is now at Windsor, and I
choose rather to speak to him on all accounts, having not
so fine a talent of writing, as that same Lord's lady; and
whether just or no, I will not attempt disputing with her
Ladyship.[1] But as you are commonly esteemed by those
who pretend to know you, to have a tolerable share of
honesty and brains, I do not question your doing what is
right by him; nor his paying you all the civility and kindness you can desire. Nor will I hope their influence ever
can make him do otherwise, though he has the unfashionable quality of esteeming his old friends, but however
partial to them, yet not to be biased against his own sense
and judgement and the consequence of this I hope, will be
your coming to England, and meeting often with him, in
Lady Betty's chamber,[2] where the happy composition[3]
shall exert her skill in ordering dinner; and I will not mistake oil of amber for the spirit of it, but continue as I ever
was,

Your sincere friend, as well as faithful humble servant,

E. GERMAIN.

Addressed—To the Revd. Mr. Dean Swift at the Deanery
  of St. Patrick's, Dublin.

---

[1] In the Journal to Stella ("Prose Works," ii, 128) Swift speaks of
Lady Betty as a fine woman, possessed of much "good breeding and
nature," but little wit.

[2] Lady Betty recalls "Mrs. Frances Harris's Petition" ("Poetical
Works," i, 37):

"'Lord help me!' says Mary, 'I never stirr'd out of this place!'
'Nay,' said I, 'I had it in Lady Betty's chamber, that's a plain case.'"

[3]   "Jove mix'd up all, and the best clay employ'd;
        Then call'd the happy composition Floyd."
                          "Poetical Works," i, 50.

DCCLXXIII. [*Copy.*[1]]

SWIFT TO LORD BATHURST

[*October*, 1730.]

MY LORD,

I HAD the honour of your letter[2] three days before I returned from the northern parts of this kingdom, where I passed three months in search of cold weather and exercise; but deferred my acknowledgments till I returned to town, and am now, from riding three times a week to settle an ill head, resumed my old Cathedral formalities, constantly at morning prayers by nine, and superintending my vicars.[3]

Your Lordship hath done me an unspeakable injury. I happened to let fall in one of my letters that I showed yours to all comers as a boast of my corresponding with you, and your Lordship in the highest degree of malice hath written to me in such a manner that I cannot communicate the particulars to my nearest friends. When Sir William Temple writ an Essay preferring the Ancient Learning to the Modern,[4] it was said that what he writ showed he was mistaken, because he discovered more learning in that Essay than the ancients could pretend to. This I think was too great a compliment. But it is none to tell you that I would give the best thing I ever was supposed to publish, in exchange to be author of your letters. I pretend to have been an improver of irony on the subject of satire and praise, but I will surrender up my title to your Lordship. Your injustice extends further. You accuse me of endeavouring to break off all correspondence with you, and at the same time demonstrate that the accusation is against yourself. You threaten to pester me with letters if I will not write. If I were sure that my silence would force you to one letter in a quarter of a year, I would be wise enough never to write to you as long as I live.

---

[1] In the Forster Collection.

[2] *Supra*, p. 162.

[3] As evidence that Swift's discharge of his duties was appreciated by the public, it may be mentioned that a few years before Archbishop King wrote to a friend that a thousand persons attended St. Patrick's Cathedral "every Lord's day" (8 October, 1725).

[4] "Prose Works," i, 156.

I swear your Lordship is the first person alive that ever
made me lean upon my elbow when I was writing to him,
and by consequence this will be the worst letter I ever
writ. I have never been so severely attacked, nor in so
tender a point, nor by weapons against which I am so ill
able to defend myself, nor by a person from whom I so
little deserved so cruel a treatment, and who in his own
conscience is so well convinced of my innocence upon
every article. I have endorsed your letter with your name
and date, and shall leave it to my executors to be published
at the head of all the libels that have been writ against me,
to be printed in five volumes in folio after my death. And
among the rest a very scrub one in verses lately written by
myself; for having some months ago much and often
offended the ruling party, and often worried by libellers, I
was at the pains of writing one in their style and manner,
and sent it by an unknown hand to a Whig printer who
very faithfully published it.[1] I took special care to accuse
myself but of one fault of which I am really guilty, and so
shall continue as I have done these sixteen years till I see
cause to reform;[2] but in the rest of the satire I chose to
abuse myself with the direct reverse of my character, or at
least in direct opposition to one part of what you are pleased
to give me.[3]

---

[1] The libel to which Swift alludes was no doubt " A Panegyric on
the Reverend D—n S—t in Answer to the Libel on Dr. D—y and a
certain great Lord." In order to throw the reader off the scent, Swift
has in this poem made use of triplets, for which he expresses such great
contempt, but a reference to his old enemy, Archbishop Sharp, betrays
the author:

> " 'Twas therefore cruel hard, by Jove,
> Your industry no better throve,
> Nor could achieve the promised lawn,
> Though Robin's honour was in pawn ;
> Because it chanced an old grave Don
> Believed in God, and you in none."

[2] " Where'er the wind of Favour sits,
> It still your constitution hits ;
> If fair it brings you safe to port,
> And when 'tis foul affords you sport."

[3] *I.e.*, that he possessed wit in which the poem labours to prove he
was deficient :

> " Rightly you show that wit alone
> Advances few, enriches none,

I am afraid your Lordship is spending the latter end of a summer *par manière d'acquit* among your neighbouring squires at Cirencester, without my lady or your olive branches.

What I mentioned in a former letter is true: that a certain wag, one of my followers, is collecting materials for a tolerable volume of English bulls, in revenge of the reproaches you throw on us upon the article. The author is a great reader of jest books, and in those of poor Robin he hath met several passages of Mr. Abdy, the famous bull-maker of his time:[1] all these are to be gathered, others invented, and many transplanted from hence to England. All the bulls fathered upon names at length with their places of abode. Your Lordship as an old offender against me shall have half a dozen blunders charged upon your groom and coachman, no matter which, and there must be a long introduction proving the native Irish rabble to have a better tact for wit than the English, for which philosophical causes shall be assigned, and many instances produced.

I will tell you further that I have another operator, a smart ingenious young fellow, who is employed to collect all the clever things written in verse and prose for four or five years past, such as libels on the public, complaints of oppression, and the like, under the title of the Dublin Miscellany; and I will put down you Lordship among a dozen or two more of my friends on your side for subscribers, merely to shame you, though we get not one of your crowns, I mean Mr. Pope, Gay, the Doctor, Lords Oxford, Burlington, Masham, Bolingbroke, Dartmouth, Orrery, Mr. Pulteney, etc., etc. And how will you help yourselves? And if you advertise, we will readvertise, and

> And 'tis as true, or story lies,
> Men seldom by their good deeds rise;
> From whence the consequence is plain
> You never had commenced a Dean,
> Unless you other ways had trod
> Than those of wit or trust in God."

[1] The reference is probably to a book entitled "Poor Robin's Jests or the Compleat Jester," of which only one copy is known. It is said to have been compiled by William Winstanley, and to have been incorporated in "England's Witty and Ingenious Jester by W. W., gent." ("D. N. B.," lxii, 210), but the name Abdy does not occur in the latter work.

reply and rejoin to the world's end. And a little young poetical parson, who has a littler young poetical wife, shall have the whole profit. And take notice that the word littler is no blunder. And the young parson aforesaid hath very lately printed his own works, all in verse and some not unpleasant; in one or two of which I have the honour to be celebrated, which cost me a guinea and two bottles of wine.[1]

Thus we contrive to keep up our spirits in the most miserable country upon earth, where a man of fifteen hundred pounds a year cannot command as many shillings, except he be a Bishop, a soldier, a commissioner of the revenue or a vicar-choral in my Cathedral, who touches more ready money than his Dean; so that if any kingdom was ever in a right situation of breeding poets, it is this, whither you and your crew unpardonably sent me sixteen years ago, and where I have been ever since, studying as well as preaching revenge, malice, envy, and hatred, and all uncharitableness. And I desire, by grace, Lady Bathurst may not be angry, for I do assure her upon the word of a Dean that it is all the pure uncorrupt fruit of a true public spirit.

I reckon this season is driving you up to St. James's Square, where this letter will find you, where Mr. Pope

---

[1] Swift mentions here for the first time the Rev. Matthew Pilkington and his wife Letitia, who on account of their diminutive size were styled by him "the mighty Thomas Thumb and her Serene Highness of Lilliput." They had not been long known to him. In the previous November, relying on a slight acquaintance on her husband's part, she had sent him some verses on his birthday, and had subsequently been brought to Delville by Mrs. Barber and introduced to him. Swift showed small judgement in making confidants of persons of their character, but he was not so mistaken as has been supposed in his first estimate of Pilkington's abilities. Writers have vied in trying to prove that Pilkington was devoid of brains, and in asking their readers carefully to distinguish him from the author of a much applauded work, the "Complete Dictionary of Painters," but in spite of their efforts the fact remains that his capacity was sufficient to enable him to become a scholar of Dublin University, and to be the author of the book for which they have endeavoured to deprive him of credit ("Notes and Queries," II, vi, 65). His volume of poems, which was issued in August of that year, is also by no means contemptible. It opens with a poem addressed to Pilkington by William Dunkin, who became afterwards one of Swift's favourites, and it is possible that he is the "ingenious young fellow" to whom Swift refers at the beginning of the paragraph.

will tell you that there is an Irish poetess now in London soliciting the Duke of Dorset for an employment, though she be but a woollen-draper's wife;[1] and that we have another, the wife of a bookseller, who has lately published a fine edition of Tacitus with a Latin dedication to Lord Carteret.[2] These two will much enrich our Miscellany. *I nunc et verbis virtutem illude superbis.* I will not this time employ your Lordship as a postman, but as a *salutigerulus* —read Plautus[3]—to present my humble services to Lord Bolingbroke, Mr. Pulteney, Lord Masham, the Doctor, etc. I will answer Mr. Pope's last letter very soon. My most humble service to my Lady Bathurst, and all my best prayers and wishes for you and your whole family. I am ever, with the truest respect,

Your most obedient, etc.

DCCLXXIV. [*Original.*[4]]

JOHN ARBUTHNOT TO SWIFT

[November, 1730.]

DEAR SIR,

THE passage in Mr. Pope's letter[5] about your health does not alarm me: both of us have had the distemper these thirty years. I have found that steel, the warm gums, and the bark, all do good in it. Therefore, first take the vomit *a*; then every day the quantity of a nutmeg, in the morning, of the electuary marked *b*, with five spoonfuls of the tincture marked *d*. Take the tincture, but not the electuary, in the afternoon. You may take one of the pills marked *c*, at any time when you are troubled with it, or thirty of the drops marked *e*, in any vehicle, even water. I had a servant of my own, that was cured merely with vomiting. There is another medicine not mentioned, which you may try: the *pulvis radicis valerianae sylvestris*, about a scruple of it twice a day.

---

[1] Mrs. Barber (*supra*, p. 164).
[2] *I.e.*, Mrs. Grierson (*supra*, p. 120, n. 2).
[3] "Aul.," 3, 5, 28.
[4] In the British Museum. See Preface.
[5] Arbuthnot refers to a letter that has been suppressed.

How came you to take it in your head that I was
Queen's physician? When I am so, you shall be a bishop,
or anything you have a mind to. Pope is now the great
reigning poetical favourite. Your Lord Lieutenant[1] has a
mind to be well with you. Lady Betty Germain complains
you have not writ to her since she wrote to you.[2] I have
showed as much civility to Mrs. Barber as I could, and she
likewise to me.[3] My family, especially Nanny, gives you
[their] service. I have no more paper, but what serves to
tell you, that I am, with great sincerity,

Your most faithful humble servant,

J. ARBUTHNOT.

I recommended Dr. Helsham to be physician to the
Lord Lieutenant.[4] I know not what effect it will have. My
respects to him and Dr. Delany.

Addressed—To the Reverend the Dean of St. Patrick's,
Dublin.

Endorsed—Received November 13 1730.

Enclosure:

(*a*) ℞ pulv. rad. ipecacuanhæ ℈s.

(*b*) ℞ conserv. flavedin. aurant., absynth. Rom. ana ℥vj.
rubigin. Martis in pulverem redact. ℥iij. syrup. succi
kermes, q. s.

(*c*) ℞ as. fœtid. ℥ij. tinctur. castor q. s. m. fiant pilulæ
xxiv.

(*d*) ℞ cortic. Peruviani, elect. rubigin. Martis ana ℥j.
digere tepide in vini alb. Gallic. ℔ij per 24 horas: postea
fiat colatura.

(*e*) ℞ sp. cor. cerv., sp. lavandul., tinctur. castor. ana ℥ij.
misce.

---

[1] *I.e.*, Dorset (*supra*, p. 151).
[2] By an endorsement on her letter (*supra*, p. 164), it appears that
Swift sent a reply on 10 November.
[3] *Supra*, p. 159, n. 1.
[4] Helsham had then resigned his fellowship and was relying on his
practice as a physician (*supra*, p. 59, n. 1).

DCCLXXV. [*Original.*[1]]

JOHN GAY AND THE DUCHESS OF QUEENSBERRY
TO SWIFT

Amesbury, near Salisbury in Wiltshire,
November 8, 1730.

GAY

DEAR SIR,

SO you are determined never to write to me again; but, for all that, you shall not make me hold my tongue.[2] You shall hear from me, the post-office willing, whether you will or not. I see none of the folks you correspond with, so that I am forced to pick up intelligence concerning you as I can, which hath been so very little that I am resolved to make my complaints to you as a friend, who I know loves to relieve the distressed, and in the circumstances I am in, where should I apply but to my best friend? Mr. Pope, indeed, upon my frequent inquiries, has told me that the letters that are directed to him concern me as much as himself; but what you say of yourself, or of me, or to me, I know nothing at all.

Lord Carteret was here yesterday, in his return from the Isle of Wight, where he had been a shooting,[3] and left seven pheasants with us. He went this morning to the Bath, to Lady Carteret, who is perfectly recovered. He talked of you for three hours last night, and told me that you talk of me. I mean that you are prodigiously in his favour, as he says, and I believe that I am in yours, for I know you to be a just and equitable person, and it is but my due. He seemed to take to me, which I take to proceed from your recommendation; though, indeed, there is another reason for it, for he is now out of employment, and my friends have been generally of that sort, for I take to them, as being naturally inclined to those who can do no mischief. Pray, do you come to England this year? He thinks you do. I wish you would; and so does the Duchess of Queensberry. What would you have more to induce

---

[1] In the British Museum. See Preface.
[2] Swift had apparently not written since March (*supra*, p. 132).
[3] On the property of his father-in-law, Sir Robert Worsley, by whom the erection of Appuldurcombe House was begun.

you? Your money cries, come spend me, and your friends cry, come see me. I have been treated barbarously by you. If you knew how often I talk of you, how often I think of you, you would now and then direct a letter to me, and I would allow Mr. Pope to have his share in it. In short, I do not care to keep any man's money that serves me so. Love or money I must have; and if you will not let me have the comfort of the one, I think I must endeavour to get a little comfort by spending some of the other. I must beg that you would call at Amesbury, in your way to London, for I have many things to say to you; and I can assure you, you will be welcome to a three-pronged fork.[1]

I remember your prescription, and I do ride upon the Downs, and at present I have no asthma. I have killed five brace of partridges, and four brace and a half of quails; and I do not envy either Sir Robert or Stephen Duck, who is the favourite poet of the Court.[2] I hear sometimes from Pope, and from scarce anybody else. Were I to live here never so long, I believe I should never think of London; but I cannot help thinking of you. Were you here, I could talk to you, but I would not; for you shall have all your share of talk, which was never allowed you at Twickenham. You know this was a grievance you often complained of; and so, in revenge, you make me write all, and answer nothing. I beg my compliments to Dr. Delany. I am, dear Sir,

Yours most affectionately,
J. GAY.

I ended the letter as above, to go to the Duchess, and she told me, I might go down, and come a quarter of an hour hence. I had a design to have asked her to sign the invitation that I have made you. As I do not know how much she may have to say to you, I think it will be prudent to leave off, that she may not be stinted for want of room. So much I will say, that whether she signs it or not, both the Duke and Duchess would be very glad you would come to Amesbury; and you must be persuaded, that I say this without the least private view. For what is

---

[1] *Supra*, p. 133.

[2] "Thrice happy Duck, employed in threshing stubble, Thy toil is lessened, and thy profits double."

"Poetical Works," i, 192.

it to me whether you come or not? For I can write to you, you know.

THE DUCHESS

I would fain have you come. I cannot say you will be welcome, for I do not know you, and perhaps I shall not like you, but if I do not, unless you are a very vain person, you shall know my thoughts as soon as I do myself.

C. Q.

DCCLXXVI. [*Elwin.*[1]]

SWIFT TO JOHN GAY

Dublin, *November* 10, 1730.

WHEN my Lord Peterborough, in the Queen's time, went abroad upon his embassies, the Ministry told me that he was such a vagrant they were forced to write at him by guess, because they knew not where to write to him.[2] This is my case with you; sometimes in Scotland, sometimes at Ham walks, sometimes God knows where. You are a man of business, and not at leisure for insignificant correspondence. It was I got you the employment of being my Lord Duke's *premier ministre*; for his Grace, having heard how good a manager you were of my Bathurst revenue, thought you fit to be intrusted with ten talents.[3] I have had twenty times a strong inclination to spend a summer near Salisbury Downs, having rode over them more than once, and with a young parson of Salisbury reckoned twice the stones of Stonehenge, which are either ninety-two or ninety-three.[4]

[1] By permission of Mr. John Murray. *Supra*, vol. iii, p. 148, n. 1.
[2]   "A messenger comes all a-reek,
          Mordanto at Madrid to seek,
          He left the town above a week."
                    "Poetical Works," i, 49.
[3] *Supra*, p. 138.
[4] If tradition may be believed, Swift paid a secret visit to Salisbury during Oxford's ministry, and wrote in chalk on a tombstone in the close an epitaph on Burnet (Hist. MSS. Com. Rept., vi, App., p. 468). The concluding lines were:
          " If such a soul to Heaven stole,
          And passed the Devil's clutches,
          I do presume there may be room
          For Marlboro' and his Duchess."

I thank you for offering me the neighbourhood of another Hoadly. I have enough of one. He lives within twenty yards of me. Our gardens join, but I never see him except on business.[1]

I desire to present my most humble acknowledgements to my Lady Duchess in return of her civility. I hear an ill thing, that she is *matre pulchra filia pulchrior*: I never saw her since she was a girl, and would be angry she should excel her mother, who was long my principal goddess.[2] I desire you will tell her Grace that the ill-management of forks is not to be helped when they are only bidental, which happens in all poor houses, especially those of poets; upon which account a knife was absolutely necessary at Mr. Pope's, where it was morally impossible, with a bidental fork, to convey a morsel of beef, with the incumbrance of mustard and turnips, into your mouth at once. And her Grace hath cost me thirty pounds to provide tridents for fear of offending her, which sum I desire she will please to return me.[3]

I am sick enough to go to the Bath, but have not heard it will be good for my disorder. You remember me giddy sometimes, and very violently. I am now constantly so, not to so high a degree. I ride often every week, and walk much, but am not better. I thank God the pain is not great, nor does it spoil my sleep. But I grow listless, and good for nothing. I have a strong mind to spend my two hundred pounds next summer in France. I am glad I have it, for there is hardly twice that sum left in this kingdom. I have left off writing, but not wine, though I have lost six hogsheads that grew muddy in the bottles, and I have not one family upon whom I can sponge.

You want no settlement—I call the family where you live, and the foot you are upon, a settlement—till you increase your fortune to what will support you with ease and plenty, a good house and a garden. The want of this

---

[1] A road now divides the site of St. Sepulchre's Palace (*supra*, vol. i, p. 60, n. 2) from the garden of the Deanery. Its construction was one of the improvements which the Cathedral owed to the generosity of the late Sir Benjamin Lee Guinness.

[2] *Supra*, p. 134, n. 3.

[3] According to Faulkner ("Works," xi, 255), Swift had a service of plate that might have cost £1,000. In a manuscript note (Forster Collection, No. 579), Lyon adds that his dishes, plates, covers and wine-coolers were all silver.

I much dread in you; for I have often known a she-cousin of a good family and small fortune passing months among all her relations, living in plenty and taking her circles till she grew an old maid, and everybody weary of her. Mr. Pope complains of seldom seeing you, but the evil is unavoidable, for different circumstances of life have always separated those whom friendship would join. God hath taken care of this to prevent any progress towards real happiness here, which would make life more desirable, and death too dreadful. I hope you have now one advantage that you always wanted before, and the want of which made your friends as uneasy as it did yourself: I mean the removal of that solicitude about your own affairs which perpetually filled your thoughts and disturbed your conversation. For if it be true what Mr. Pope seriously tells me that you are principal manager of the Duke's affairs, you will have opportunity of saving every groat of the interest you receive; and so by the time he and you grow weary of each other you will be able to pass the rest of your wineless life in ease and plenty, with as good a house and garden as Mr. Pope, and with the additional triumphal comfort of never having received a penny from a tasteless ungrateful Court from which you deserved so much, and which deserve no better geniuses than those by whom they are celebrated. So let the post rascals open this letter, and let Walpole read it.

Mr. Ford is with us upon the death of his mother, who has left him money enough to supply the not receiving of rent for two years in London.[1] He tells me that he heard I was out of favour with the Queen. The loss is not great. I made a present, or rather it was begged from me, of about thirty-five pounds. The trifle promised me, worth about fifteen pounds, was never remembered, and after I had made my present, shame would not suffer me to remind

---

[1] Her will was proved by Ford on 21 October. As already mentioned (*supra*, p. 94), he had also been in Ireland in the preceding autumn, and called at the Deanery when Mrs. Pilkington was paying her first visit to Swift ("Memoirs," i, 65). She says that he was "the oddest little mortal" that she had ever met, didactic in manner, and prone to the habit of exaggeration for which Irishmen are proverbial. In proof of these characteristics she describes him as laying down the law about Rome, which he could do without fear of contradiction, as he was the only one of the company that had been there, and asserting that the bases of the pillars in St. Peter's covered half an acre.

them of theirs.[1] If you see Mr. Cæsar present my humble service to him,[2] and let him know that the scrub libel printed against me here, and reprinted in London, for which he showed a kind concern to a friend of us both, was written by myself, and sent to a Whig printer;[3] it was in the style and genius of such scoundrels, when the humour of libelling ran in this town against a friend of mine whom you know. But my paper is ended. My most humble service to Lord Peterborough, Bolingbroke, Masham, Bathurst, Lord Oxford, Mr. Pulteney, the Doctor, Mr. Lewis, Mr. Pope, etc.

Ever yours.

Lord Burlington never remembers the request made him in a solemn manner about his ancestor's tomb. However, he owed, in civility, an answer to a letter from so considerable a body. He that would not sacrifice twenty acres out of two hundred thousand to the honour of his family, may live to see them not return him two hundred thousand pence, towards which I believe he feels enough already.

DCCLXXVII. [*Sheridan.*]

SWIFT TO THE EARL OF CHESTERFIELD

November 10, 1730.

MY LORD,[4]

I WAS positively advised by a friend,[5] whose opinion has much weight with me, and who has a great veneration for your Lordship, to venture a letter of solicitation, and it is the first request of this kind that I ever made, since the public changes in times, persons, measures, and opinions, drove me into distance and obscurity. There is an honest man, whose name is Lancelot; he has been long a servant to my Lord Sussex;[6] he married a relation of mine, a

---

[1] *Supra*, p. 146.

[2] Charles Cæsar, who was Treasurer of the Navy in Oxford's administration, and whose pardon Swift begged for mentioning Brutus in his presence (" Prose Works," ii, 415).

[3] *Supra*, p. 167, n. 1.

[4] After the accession of George II, who insisted upon employment being found for him, Chesterfield (*supra*, vol. iii, p. 348) had been given the English embassy at the Hague, and had been appointed that summer Lord Steward in room of the Duke of Dorset.

[5] *I.e.*, Pope.   [6] *Supra*, p. 37, n. 1.

widow, with a tolerable jointure, which, depending on a lease which the Duke of Grafton suffered to expire about three years ago, sunk half her little fortune. Mr. Lancelot had many promises from the Duke of Dorset, while his Grace held that office, which is now in your Lordship, but they all failed, after the usual fate that the bulk of Court suitors must expect.

I am very sensible that I have no manner of claim to the least favour from your Lordship, whom I have hardly the honour to be known to, although you were always pleased to treat me with much humanity, and with more distinction than I could pretend to deserve. I am likewise conscious of that demerit which I have largely shared with all those who concerned themselves in a Court and Ministry, whose maxims and proceedings have been ever since so much exploded. But your Lordship will grant me leave to say that in those times, when any persons of the ejected party came to Court, and were of tolerable consequence, they never failed to succeed in any reasonable request they made for a friend. And when I sometimes added my poor solicitations, I used to quote the then Ministers a passage in the Gospel:—The poor—meaning their own dependents—you have always with you, etc.

This is the strongest argument I have to entreat your Lordship's favour for Lancelot, who is a perfectly honest man, and as loyal as you could wish. His wife, my near relation, has been my favourite from her youth, and as deserving as it is possible for one of her level. It is understood that some little employments about the Court may be often in your Lordship's disposal, and that my Lord Sussex will give Mr. Lancelot the character he deserves: and then let my petition be, to speak in my own trade, a drop in the bucket. Remember, my Lord, that although this letter be long, yet what particularly concerns my request is but of a few lines.

I shall not congratulate with your Lordship upon any of your present great employments, or upon the greatest that can possibly be given to you; because you are one of those very few who do more honour to a Court, than you can possibly receive from it, which I take to be a greater compliment to any Court than it is to your Lordship. I am, my Lord, etc.

DCCLXXVIII. [*Elwin.*]

SWIFT TO JOHN GAY AND THE DUCHESS OF QUEENSBERRY

Dublin, *November* 19, 1730.

TO GAY

I WRIT to you a long letter about a fortnight past[1] concluding you were in London, from whence I understood one of your former was dated; nor did I imagine you were gone back to Amesbury so late in the year, at which season I take the country to be only a scene for those who have been ill used by a Court on account of their virtues, which is a state of happiness the more valuable, because it is not accompanied by envy, although nothing deserves it more. I would gladly sell a dukedom to lose favour in the manner their Graces have done. I believe my Lord Carteret, since he is no longer Lieutenant, may not wish me ill, and I have told him often that I only hated him as Lieutenant. I confess he had a genteeler manner of binding the chains of this kingdom, than most of his predecessors, and I confess, at the same time, that he had, six times, a regard to my recommendation, by preferring so many of my friends in the Church, and the two last acts of his power were to add to the dignities of Dr. Delany and Mr. Stopford, the last of whom was by you and Mr. Pope put into Mr. Pulteney's hands.[2] I told you in my last, that a continuance of giddiness, though not in a violent degree, prevented my thoughts of England at present. For in my case a domestic life is necessary, where I can with the centurion say to my servant, go, and he goeth, and do this, and he doth it. I now hate all people whom I cannot command, and consequently a Duchess is at this time the hatefulest lady in the world to me, one only excepted, and I beg her Grace's pardon for that exception, for, in the way I mean, her Grace is ten thousand times more hateful.[3]

[1] *Supra*, p. 174.

[2] On 8 June Delany had received an additional preferment, that of Chancellor in Swift's Cathedral, and about the same time Stopford was appointed Provost of Tuam, a dignity peculiar in Ireland to that diocese.

[3] The exception was the Queen, for whom he had no respect.

I confess I begin to apprehend you will squander my money, because I hope you never less wanted it; and if you go on with success for two years longer, I fear I shall not have a farthing of it left. The Doctor hath ill informed me, who says that Mr. Pope is at present the chief poetical favourite,[1] yet Mr. Pope himself talks like a philosopher, and one wholly retired. But the vogue of our few honest folks here is, that Duck is absolutely to succeed Eusden in the laurel,[2] the contention being between Concanen or Theobald, or some other hero of the Dunciad.[3] I never charged you for not talking, but the dubious state of your affairs in those days was too much the subject, and I wish the Duchess had been the voucher of your amendment. Nothing so much contributed to my ease as the turn of affairs after the Queen's death, by which all my hopes being cut off, I could have no ambition left, unless I would have been a greater rascal than happened to suit with my temper. I therefore sat down quietly at my morsel, adding only thereto a principle of hatred to all succeeding measures and ministries by way of sauce to relish my meat; and I confess one point of conduct in my Lady Duchess's life has added much poignancy to it. There is a good Irish practical bull toward the end of your letter, where you spend a dozen lines in telling me you must leave off, that you may give my Lady Duchess room to write, and so you proceed to within two or three lines of the bottom; though I would have remitted you my two hundred pounds to have left place for as many more.

To the Duchess

Madam,

My beginning thus low is meant as a mark of respect, like receiving your Grace at the bottom of the stairs. I am glad you know your duty; for it has been a known and established rule above twenty years in England, that the first advances have been constantly made me by all ladies who

---

[1] *Supra*, p. 171.

[2] Eusden (*supra*, vol. iii, p. 22) had died on 27 September.

[3]   " That hapless Shakespear, yet of Tibbald sore,
            Wish'd he had blotted for himself before
            .   .   .   .
            True to the bottom see Concanen creep,
            A cold long-winded native of the deep."

aspired to my acquaintance, and the greater their quality, the greater were their advances. Yet, I know not by what weakness, I have condescended graciously to dispense with you upon this important article, though Mr. Gay will tell you that a nameless person sent me eleven messages[1] before I would yield to a visit: I mean a person to whom he is infinitely obliged, for being the occasion of the happiness he now enjoys under the protection and favour of my Lord Duke and your Grace. At the same time I cannot forbear telling you, Madam, that you are a little imperious in your manner of making your advances. You say, perhaps you shall not like me. I affirm you are mistaken, which I can plainly demonstrate; for I have certain intelligence, that another person dislikes me of late, with whose likings yours have not for some time past gone together. However, if I shall once have the honour to attend your Grace, I will out of fear and prudence appear as vain as I can, that I may not know your thoughts of me. This is your own direction, but it was needless; for Diogenes himself would be vain, to have received the honour of being one moment of his life in the thoughts of your Grace. I am, with the greatest respect, your Grace's etc.

DCCLXXIX. [*Original.*[2]]

SWIFT TO MRS. HOWARD

Dublin, *November* 21, 1730.

MADAM,

I DO not now pity the leisure you have to read a letter from me;[3] and this letter shall be a history. First, therefore, I call you to witness, that I did not attend on the Queen till I had received her own repeated messages, which, of course, occasioned my being introduced to you.

---

[1] *I.e.*, the Queen (*supra*, vol. iii, p. 303).

[2] British Museum, Addit. MSS., 22625, f. 20.

[3] Although Pope had told Swift that it did not relate to Mrs. Howard, the newspaper paragraph which had appeared many months before seems to have been Swift's authority for an assumption that she was no longer in favour at Court (*supra*, pp. 127, 141). The subject was a most delicate one, and could hardly have been mentioned except with the intention of causing her annoyance. So far as her ostensible position at Court was concerned, no change had taken place.

I never asked anything till, upon leaving England the first time, I desired from you a present worth a guinea,[1] and from her Majesty one worth ten pounds, by way of a memorial. Yours I received, and the Queen, upon my taking my leave of her, made an excuse that she had intended a medal for me, which not being ready, she would send it me the Christmas following; yet this was never done, nor at all remembered when I went back to England the next year, and by her commands, attended her as I had done before. I must now tell you, Madam, that I will receive no medal from her Majesty, nor anything less than her picture at half length, drawn by Jervas, and if he takes it from another original, the Queen shall sit at least twice for him to touch it up. I desire you will let her Majesty know this in plain words, although I have heard that I am under her displeasure. But this is a usual thing with Princes, as well as Ministers, upon every false representation; and so I took occasion to tell the Queen, upon the quarrel Mr. Walpole had with our friend Gay, the first time I ever had the honour to attend her.

Against you I have but one reproach, that when I was last in England, and just after the present King's accession, I resolved to pass that summer in France, for which I had then a most lucky opportunity, from which those who seemed to love me well dissuaded me, by your advice;[2] and when I sent you a note, conjuring you to lay aside the character of a courtier and a favourite upon that occasion, your answer positively directed me not to go in that juncture; and you said the same thing to my friends, who seemed to have power of giving me hints that I might reasonably hope for a settlement in England; which, God knows, was no very great ambition, considering the station I should leave here of greater dignity, and which might have easily been managed to be disposed of as the Crown pleased. If these hints came from you, I affirm, you then acted too much like a courtier. But I forgive you, and esteem you as much as ever. You had your reasons, which I shall not inquire into, because I always believed you had some virtues, besides all the accomplishments of mind and person that can adorn a lady.

I am angry with the Queen for sacrificing my friend Gay

---

[1] *I.e.*, a ring (*supra*, vol. iii, p. 353).   [2] *Supra*, vol. iii, p. 396.

to the mistaken piques of Sir Robert Walpole, about a libel writ against him, although he were convinced at the same time of Mr. Gay's innocence; and although, as I said before, I told her Majesty the whole story. Mr. Gay deserved better treatment among you, upon all accounts, and particularly for his excellent unregarded Fables, dedicated to Prince William,[1] which I hope his Royal Highness will often read for his instruction. I wish her Majesty would a little remember what I largely said to her about Ireland, when, before a witness, she gave me leave and commanded to tell here what she spoke to me upon that subject; and ordered me, if I lived to see her in her present station, to send her our grievances; promising to read my letter, and do all good offices in her power for this miserable and most loyal kingdom, now at the brink of ruin, and never so near as now. As to myself, I repeat again, that I never asked anything more than a trifle, as a memorial of some distinction which her Majesty graciously seemed to make between me and every common clergyman; but that trifle was forgotten, according to the usual method of Princes, although I was taught to think myself upon a foot of pretending to some little exception.

As to yourself, Madam, I most heartily congratulate with you for being delivered from the toil, the envy, the slavery, and vexation, of a favourite; where you could not always answer the good intentions that I hope you had. You will now be less teased with solicitations, one of the greatest evils in life. You possess an easy employment, with quiet of mind, although it be by no means equal to your merit, and if it shall please God to establish your health, I believe and hope you are too wise to hope for more. Mr. Pope has always been an advocate for your sincerity; and even I, in the character I gave you of yourself, allowed you as much of that virtue as could be expected in a lady, a courtier, and a favourite. Yet, I confess, I never heartily pledged your health as a toast, upon any other regards than beauty, wit, good sense, and an unblemished character. For, as to friendship, truth, sincerity, and other trifles of that kind, I never concerned myself about them; because I knew them to be only parts of the lower morals, which are altogether useless at Courts. I am content that

---

[1] *Supra*, vol. iii, p. 295, n. 3.

you should tell the Queen all I have said of her, and in my own words, if you please.

I could have been a better prophet in the Character I gave you of yourself, if it had been good manners, in the height of your credit, to put you in mind of its mortality, for you are not the first, by at least three ladies, whom I have known to undergo the same turn of fortune.[1] It is allowed, that ladies are often very good scaffoldings; and I need not tell you the use that scaffoldings are put to by all builders, as well political as mechanic. I should have begun this letter by telling you, that I was encouraged to write it by my best friend, and one of your great admirers,[2] who told me, that, from something which had passed between you, he thought you would not receive it ill. After all, I know no person of your sex, for whom I have so great an esteem, as I do and believe I shall always continue to bear for you; I mean a private person, for I must except the Queen, and it is not an exception of form, because I have really a very great veneration for her great qualities, although I have reason to complain of her conduct to me, which I could not excuse although she had fifty kingdoms to govern. I have but room to conclude with my sincere professions of being, with true respect, Madam,

Your most obedient humble servant,

J. S.

If you were a Lord or Commoner I would have sent you this in an envelope.[3]

DCCLXXX. [*Original.*[4]]

THE EARL OF CHESTERFIELD TO SWIFT

Hague, *December* 15 [O. S. 4], 1730.

SIR,

YOU need not have made any excuses to me for your solicitation, on the contrary, I am proud of being the first

---

[1] The editor of the "Countess of Suffolk's Letters" suggests (i, 402) that Swift refers to Lady Orkney, the Duchess of Marlborough, and Lady Masham.

[2] *I.e.*, Pope (*supra*, p. 141).

[3] It was, however, ultimately enclosed in one.

[4] In the British Museum. See Preface.

person to whom you have thought it worth your while to apply, since those changes, which, you say, drove you into distance and obscurity.[1] I very well know the person you recommend to me, having lodged at his house a whole summer at Richmond. I have always heard a very good character of him, which alone would incline me to serve him, but your recommendation, I can assure you, will make me impatient to do it. However, that he may not again meet with the common fate of Court suitors, nor I lie under the imputation of making Court promises, I will exactly explain to you how far it is likely that I may be able to serve him.

When first I had this office, I took the resolution of turning out nobody, so that I shall only have the disposal of those places that the death of the present possessors will procure me. Some old servants that have served me long and faithfully, have obtained the promises of the first four or five vacancies; and the early solicitations of some of my particular friends have tied me down for about as many more. But, after having satisfied those engagements, I do assure you Mr. Lancelot shall be my first care. I confess his prospect is more remote than I could have wished it, but as it is so remote he will not have the uneasiness of a disappointment, if he gets nothing, and if he gets something, we shall both be pleased.

As for his political principles, I am in no manner of pain about them. Were he a Tory, I would venture to serve him in the just expectation, that should I ever be charged with having preferred a Tory, the person who was the author of my crime would likewise be the author of my vindication. I am, with real esteem,

Your most obedient humble servant,
CHESTERFIELD.

[1] *Supra*, p. 177.

DCCLXXXI. [*Original.*[1]]

JOHN GAY AND THE DUCHESS OF QUEENSBERRY TO SWIFT

Amesbury, *December* 6, 1730.

GAY

DEAR SIR,

BOTH your letters, to my great satisfaction, I have received.[2] You were mistaken as to my being in town, for I have been here ever since the beginning of May. But the best way is to direct my letters always to the Duke's house in London, and they are sent hither by his porter. We shall stay here till after the holidays. You say we deserve envy: I think we do, for I envy no man, either in town or out of it. We have had some few visitors, and every one of them such that one would desire to visit. The Duchess is a more severe check upon my finances than ever you were; and I submit, as I did to you, to comply to my own good. I was a long time before I could prevail with her to let me allow myself a pair of shoes with two heels; for I had lost one, and the shoes were so decayed that they were not worth mending. You see by this, that those, who are the most generous of their own, can be the most covetous for others. I hope you will be so good to me, as to use your interest with her, for, whatever she says, you seem to have some, to indulge me with the extravagance suitable to my fortune.

The lady you mention, that dislikes you, hath no discernment.[3] I really think, you may safely venture to Amesbury, though indeed the lady here likes to have her own way as well as you, which may sometimes occasion disputes; and I tell you beforehand that I cannot take your part. I think her so often in the right, that you will have great difficulty to persuade me she is in the wrong. Then there is another thing that I ought to tell you, to deter you from this place, which is, that the lady of the house is not given to show civility to those she does not

[1] In the British Museum. See Preface.
[2] *Supra*, pp. 174, 179.
[3] *I.e.*, the Queen (*supra*, p. 176).

like. She speaks her mind, and loves truth. For the un-
commonness of the thing, I fancy your curiosity will prevail over your fear, and you will like to see such a woman.
But I say no more till I know whether her Grace will fill
up the rest of the paper.

THE DUCHESS

Write I must, particularly now, as I have an opportunity
to indulge my predominant passion, contradiction. I do, in
the first place, contradict most things Mr. Gay says of me,
to deter you from coming here, which if you ever do, I
hereby assure you that, unless I like my own way better,
you shall have yours; and in all disputes you shall convince me, if you can. But, by what I see of you, this is not
a misfortune that will always happen; for I find you are a
great mistaker. For example, you take prudence for im-
periousness: it is from this first, that I determined not to
like one who is too giddy-headed for me to be certain
whether or no I shall ever be acquainted with [him]. I have
often known people take great delight in building castles
in the air; but I should choose to build friends upon a
more solid foundation. I would fain know you; for I often
hear more good likeable things [of you] than it is possible
anyone can deserve. Pray come, that I may find out something wrong; for I, and I believe most women, have an incon-
ceivable pleasure to find out any faults except their own.
Mr. Cibber is made Poet Laureate.[1] I am, Sir, as much your
humble servant as I can be to any person I do not know.

C. Q.

Mr. Gay is very peevish that I spell and write ill; but I
do not care, for the pen nor I can do no better. Besides,
I think you have flattered me, and such people ought to be
put to trouble.

GAY

Now I hope you are pleased, and that you will allow, for
so small a sum as two hundred pounds, you have a lump-
ing pennyworth.

Addressed—For the Reverend Dr. Swift, Dean of St.
Patrick's in Dublin, Ireland. By way of London.

---

[1] In room of Eusden (*supra*, p. 180, n. 2).

DCCLXXXII. [*Original.*[1]]

LADY ELIZABETH GERMAIN TO SWIFT

December 24, 1730.

SINCE you, with a modest assurance, affirm you understand and practise good manners better than any other person in either kingdom, I wish you would therefore put into very handsome terms my excuse to Dean Swift, that I have not answered his letter I received before the last;[2] for even Prebendary Head assured my brother Harry,[3] that he, in all form and justice, took place of a colonel, as being a major-general in the Church, and therefore you need not have called a council to know whether you or I were to write last; because, as being but a poor courtesy lady,[4] [I] can pretend to no place but what other people's goodness gives me. This being settled, I certainly ought not to have writ again; but however, I fear I should have been wrong enough to have desired the correspondence to be kept up, but that I have been ill this fortnight, and of course lazy, and not in a writing mood.

First, as to Mrs. Barber; as I told you before, so I tell you the same again, that upon your recommendation, I shall be very glad to serve her, though I never did see her, and as I had not your letter till I went from Tunbridge, she passed unmarked by me in the crowd, nor have I met with her since.[5] She writ to me to present [Pilkington]'s

---

[1] In the British Museum. See Preface.

[2] Swift had apparently written twice to Lady Betty Germain since receiving her letter in September (*supra*, p. 164).

[3] Henry Head, who was then a canon of Bristol, had been for many years Lord Berkeley's vicar in Gloucestershire, and had been probably known in that capacity to Swift. Lady Betty's brother, the Honble. Henry Berkeley, was then one of the colonels of the Horse Guards and a representative of Gloucestershire in Parliament. He had seen service at Blenheim and elsewhere under Marlborough.

[4] The reference is to her title as an Earl's daughter.

[5] As appears from her volume of poems, Mrs. Barber (*supra*, p. 159) had spent some time at Tunbridge Wells. In the hope of attracting Lady Betty's attention she had inscribed upon the rocks there some

poems¹ to the Duke and Duchess of Dorset. I answered
her letter, and obeyed her commands. And as to her own,
I shall most willingly subscribe; though I am of the opinion
we ladies are not apt to be good poets, especially if we
cannot spell, but that is by way of inviolable secret between
you and me. So much for this letter.² Now to your last
epistle, for which it seems I am to give you thanks, for
honouring me with your commands. Well I do so, because
this gets a proof, that after so many years' acquaintance,
there is one that will take my word, which is a certain
sign that I have not often broke it. Therefore, behold the
consequence is this; I have given my word to the Duke of
Dorset that you would not so positively affirm this fact
concerning Mr. Fox,³ without knowing the certain truth,
that there is no deceit in this declaration of trust. And
though it has been recommended to him, as you say, he
never did give any answer to it, nor design it, till he was
fully satisfied of the truth; and even then, I believe, would
not have determined to have done it, because it is an easy
way of securing a place for ever to a family, and were this
to be an example, be it so many pence or so many pounds,
for the future they would be inheritances. So now, not to
show my power with his Grace, in spite of his dependents
who may cast their eyes on it, for that I dare affirm there
never will be need of where justice or good-nature is
necessary, but to show you his dependence on your honour
and integrity, he gives me leave to tell you, it shall certainly
be done; nor does this at all oblige you to give the thanks
you seem to be so desirous to save, for at any time, when-
soever you have any business, service, or request to make

lines in which she laments her country's wretched state until the God of
Wit appears:

> " Suspend, he cries, thy care awhile;
> My Sackville soon shall bless your isle;
> No longer talk of barren bays;
> Remember, 'tis a Dorset sways."

¹ The name, which was written in full, has been obliterated. There
can be little doubt, however, that the poems were those which Pilkington had recently published (*supra*, p. 169).
² It was evidently to Swift's influence, and not to the notable effort
just cited, that Mrs. Barber was able to include Lady Betty amongst
the subscribers to her volume for no less than five copies.
³ Probably the choir-man (*supra*, p. 16, n. 5), who sought some post
in the viceregal household.

to his Grace of Dorset, whether my proper business or no, till you two are better acquainted with one another's merits, I shall be very glad to show how sincerely I am,

Your friend and faithful humble servant,

E. GERMAIN.

Addressed—To the Revd. Dean Swift, at Dublin, Ireland.

DCCLXXXIII. [*Deane Swift.*]

SWIFT TO MRS. WHITEWAY

December 28, 1730.

YOU might give a better reason for restoring my book, that it was not worth keeping.[1] I thought by the superscription that your letter was written by a man; for you have neither the scrawl nor the spelling of your sex. You live so far off, and I believe are so seldom at home, and I am so ill a visitor, that it is no wonder we meet so seldom; but if you knew what I say of you to others, you would believe it was not want of inclination; I mean what I say of you as I knew you formerly, for as to what you are now, I know but little. I give you the good wishes of the season; and am, with true esteem and affection,

Yours, etc.

J. SWIFT.

---

[1] As appears from this letter Swift's cousin, although living in Dublin, had seen little of him for many years. It has been already mentioned that she was the daughter of his uncle Adam (*supra*, vol. i, p. 24, n. 2) who had been returned to the Irish Parliament the year before his death as member for Newry. She was twice married. Her first husband was the Rev. Theophilus Harrison who died seven years after their marriage in 1714, while rector of Killallon in the diocese of Meath. He has been often confounded with his father, who bore the same name and who was remarkable for the number of his preferments even in the days of pluralism. Probably he became known to his future wife through his stepmother, who was the widow of her uncle Godwin (*supra*, vol. i, p. 371, n. 3). Two years after Harrison's death Swift's cousin married Edward Whiteway, who was still alive when this letter was written.

DCCLXXXIV. [*Sheridan.*]

SWIFT TO THE EARL OF CHESTERFIELD

January 5, 1730-1.

MY LORD,

I RETURN your Lordship my most humble thanks for the honour and favour of your letter;[1] and desire your justice to believe, that, in writing to you a second time, I have no design of giving you a second trouble. My only end at present is to beg your pardon for a fault of ignorance. I ought to have remembered that the arts of Courts are like those of play, where, if the most expert be absent for a few months, the whole system is so changed that he has no more skill than a new beginner. Yet I cannot but wish that your Lordship had pleased to forgive one, who has been an utter stranger to public life above sixteen years. Bussy Rabutin himself, the politest person of his age, when he was recalled to Court after a long banishment, appeared ridiculous there,[2] and what could I expect, from my antiquated manner of addressing your Lordship, in the prime of your life, in the height of fortune, favour, and merit, so distinguished by your active spirit, and greatness of your genius? I do here repeat to your Lordship, that I lay the fault of my misconduct entirely on a friend, whom I exceedingly love and esteem, whom I dare not name, and who is as bad a courtier by nature, as I am grown by want of practice. God forbid that your Lordship should continue in an employment however great and honourable, where you only can be an ornament to the Court so long, until you have an opportunity to provide offices for a dozen low people like the poor man whom I took the liberty to mention, and God forbid that in one particular branch of the King's family, there should ever be such a mortality, as to take away a dozen of his meaner servants in less than a dozen years.

Give me leave, in farther excuse of my weakness, to confess that beside some hints from my friends, your Lordship is in great measure to blame for your obliging

---

[1] *Supra*, p. 184.
[2] *Supra*, vol. iii, p. 178.

manner of treating me in every place where I had the honour to see you, which I acknowledge to have been a distinction that I had not the least pretence to, and consequently as little to ground upon it the request of a favour. As I am an utter stranger to the present forms of the world, I have imagined more than once that your Lordship's proceeding with me may be a refinement introduced by yourself; and that, as in my time the most solemn and frequent promises of great men usually failed, against all probable appearances, so that single slight one of your Lordship may, by your generous nature, early succeed against all visible impossibilities. I am, etc.

DCCLXXXV. [*Scott.*[1]]

SWIFT TO SAMUEL GERRARD

Dublin, *January* 6, 1730-1.

SIR,[2]

IT was with great concern that I first heard a dubious, and then a certain account of the death of our common friend Mr. Cusack,[3] whom, in an acquaintance of many years, I never found otherwise than a gentleman of honour, sincerity, candour, and every other good quality that can recommend a man to the friendship and esteem of all worthy persons. He is a great example of the uncertainty of life, for except an aptness he complained of to take cold in his head, I have known few persons likelier to live long. I am but too sensible of his unhappy family's loss in him, and particularly of the condition of his lady, who I hope will not live under the tyranny of that odious old woman.[4] To her poor Mr. Cusack owed that he never passed one happy day at home, while she was under his roof. I must needs condole with you particularly for your loss in so worthy a friend; a thing so scarce in the country of Ire-

---

[1] The original was then in the possession of a Miss Cusack, a granddaughter of the gentleman to whom this letter relates.

[2] The recipient belonged to a well-known Meath family. Their seat, Gibbstown, near Navan, was then owned by his eldest brother.

[3] *Supra*, p. 153.

[4] The reference is possibly to Cusack's mother, to whom administration was granted for the benefit of his widow and six children.

land, where the neighbouring squires are usually the most disagreeable of all human creatures.[1]

You know, Sir, that last year he let me have a little mare, which I have rode ever since. I have often desired him to let me know the value he put on her. He answered, it was a present to him, and should be so to me; I protested I would suffer no such thing. He likewise sent me another young mare, which he was breeding up for me. I hope she will be good when she is cured of her starting, and in the mean time is very proper for a servant. I desire you will give your judgement what they both are worth, and I will pay the money immediately to the unfortunate widow's order, who may perhaps have occasion for it under her present circumstances. I shall continue for some weeks in town, and then, if my health permits, wander for a month or two in the country to preserve it. I am much obliged to our poor friend for bringing me acquainted with you, and he was a good judge of men, as I find by the character he often gave me of you; and I hope you will never come to this town while I am in it, without doing me the favour of calling on me. I am Sir, with true esteem,

Your most faithful humble servant,

J. SWIFT.

DCCLXXXVI. [*Elwin.*[2]]

SWIFT TO ALEXANDER POPE

Dublin, January 15, 1730-1.

I HAVE just finished a letter to my Lord Bolingbroke. It is one of my many evenings when I have nothing to do, and can do nothing. Read at night I dare not for my eyes, and to write anything but letters, and those to any but a

---

[1] To show the consequence which the Irish have always attached to the minutest particulars of Swift's life, Sir Walter Scott tells (" Works," xix, 292) that it is traditionally related that when going to dine on a fast-day with Mr. Cusack, who according to Sir Walter was a Roman Catholic, Swift provided himself with a leg of mutton, and that on the way the joint was intercepted by a near relation of an Irish judge, and plunged into his own pot, from which Swift, in an outrageous passion, rescued it and carried it off in a half boiled condition to Cusack's house.

[2] By permission of Mr. John Murray. *Supra*, vol. iii, p. 148, n. 1.

few friends, I find all inclination is gone. I awake so indifferent to anything which may pass either in the world,
or my own little domestic, that I hardly think it worth my
time to rise, and would certainly lie all day a-bed if decency
and dread of sickness did not drive me thence. This I owe
not so much to years, at least I would hope so, as to the
scene I am in. I dine *tête-à-tête* five days a week with my
old Presbyterian housekeeper,[1] whom I call Sir Robert and
so do all my friends and neighbours. I am in my chamber
at five, there sit alone till eleven, and then to bed. I write
pamphlets and follies merely for amusement, and when
they are finished, or I grow weary in the middle, I cast
them into the fire, partly out of dislike, and chiefly because
I know they will signify nothing. I walk much every day,
and ride once or twice a week, and so you have the whole
state of my life.[2]

What you dislike in the letter you saw to a lady,[3] I
ought also to dislike, and shall do so, although my conscience be clear. For I meant only a reproach in a matter
long since at an end; for I did ill explain myself, if it was
not understood that I talked of schemes long since at an
end; for sure if I had any the least hopes left, I would not
have writ in a manner to render them desperate, as I think
I did, and as I am sure I intended, both in what related to
her, and her mistress; and therefore I intreat when you see

[1] *Supra*, p. 30, n. 1.
[2] Swift's life at that time was not so solitary and cheerless as he
would have had Pope believe. He had spent the Christmas vacation
with the Grattans, and is represented by Mrs. Pilkington (" Memoirs,"
iii, 87) as indulging while with them in the most extraordinary buf-
foonery. On going to dinner at Belcamp one day with her husband
and Dr. Delany, she became the victim. According to her account
she was introduced to the company, which comprised twelve clergymen, as a wench whom her companions had picked up on the road,
was ordered to take off her shoes in order to be measured, had to
submit to her face being smeared with resin, and was forced to hold a
pipe in her mouth while others were smoking. As compensation the
guests were informed that the essay on " Polite Conversation " would
owe something to her advice. On his return to Dublin Swift's
intimates were impanelled as a jury to try his servants for killing the
Grattans' favourite hen, and kept alive by twenty other "agreeable
whims " of the same kind. In this relation there must be some vein
of truth, and of the date of its occurrence there can be no question
(*infra*, p. 261, n. 1).
[3] *I.e.*, Swift's letter to Mrs. Howard (*supra*, p. 181). Pope had evidently accused Swift of still seeking Court favours.

her next, to let her know that from the moment I saw her last to the moment I writ to her last, and from that moment to this moment, I never had one single imagination that the least regard would ever be shown for me.

You reproach me very unjustly for my apology in giving you an account of myself and my little affairs;[1] and yet in your letter there is not a syllable that concerns your health, which I know is always so precarious, and so seldom as it should be. I can walk eight or ten miles a day and ride thirty Irish ones. You cannot ride a mile nor walk two. Will you dare to think that this does not hang on my spirits? I am unhappy in sickly friends. There are my Lord and Lady Bolingbroke, the Doctor, you, and Mr. Gay, are not able to contribute amongst you to make up one sturdy healthy person. If I were to begin the world, I would never make an acquaintance with a poor, or sickly man, with whom there might be any danger of contracting a friendship; for I do not yet find that years have begun to harden me. Therefore I argue that avarice and hardness of heart are the two happiest qualities a man can acquire who is late in his life, because by living long we must lessen our friends, and may increase our fortunes.

I have inquired for Mr. Brandreth, but cannot hear he is yet landed.[2] I shall be very glad of such an acquaintance, if he be but one half of what he is described to you; but I shall probably have more need of his countenance than he of mine. Yet, with all his merits, the Duke of Dorset, if I had been his counsellor, would have waited till himself came over,—at least, it would have been more popular to have bestowed those middling preferments at first to persons of this kingdom, as well as the first great one;[3] and yet he has already acted otherwise in both, though he has time enough before him.

[1] Swift's letter has disappeared as well as Pope's reply.
[2] The Rev. John Brandreth, who had been tutor to the Duke of Dorset's eldest son, was preferred by his patron to a succession of valuable dignities in Ireland. On a monument to his memory in the church of Kilmore in the diocese of Armagh, it is recorded that "he loved our nation and hath built us a synagogue" (Leslie's "Armagh Clergy," p. 21).
[3] The allusion is to the bishopric of Ossory, which had fallen vacant since Dorset's nomination as viceroy and had been filled by the appointment of one of the King's chaplains, a nephew of Archbishop Tennison.

Lord T[ownshend], in what you write of him, acts directly suitable to his character. He has treated twenty persons in the like manner.[1] Pray tell me whether your Colonel Cleland be a tall Scots gentleman, walking perpetually in the Mall, and fastening upon everybody he meets, as he has often done upon me? As to his letter before the Dunciad I know not the secret, but should not suspect him for it.[2] I must tell you how affairs pass between Lord Chesterfield and me. By your encouragement I writ to him, but named you not.[3] He sent me a long and gracious answer. As to the point it was that he had five dependents, and as many prior engagements, after which he would provide for Mr. Lancelot. This I took as a jest, but my answer was thankful, and serious,—that I hoped his Lordship would not continue in any post where he could be only an ornament to the Court so long till a dozen vacancies should fall, and God forbid there should be ever such a mortality in any one branch of the King's family that a dozen people in low offices should die in less than a dozen years. So I suppose he finds that we understand each other, and there is an end of the matter. I have writ to Mr. Pulteney to congratulate with him on his son.[4] I wait but an opportunity to supply Sir C. Cotterell's refusal, and when you receive them it will be left entirely to you, provided you will be as severe a judge as becomes so good and dear a friend.[5] My humble service—I must still name them—to my Lord Bathurst, Oxford, Peterborough (how is his health?), Mr. Pulteney, the Doctor, Mr. Lewis, and Mr. Gay; and particularly Mrs. Pope. And pray tell Patty Blount, that I am her constant lover and admirer.

[1] There seems little doubt that Townshend, who had retired from office in the previous year, is the person to whom Swift alludes.

[2] William Cleland, who had seen service in Spain and was afterwards a revenue official, is mentioned in the Journal to Stella as "laying long traps" to secure Swift's interest (see Mr. Aitken's edition of the Journal, p. 532). The public, as well as Swift, recognized that the signature was Cleland's only part in the letter.

[3] *Supra*, p. 177.

[4] He was Pulteney's only son and predeceased him.

[5] As Elwin suggests (*op. cit.*, vii, 215) the reference seems to be to a contribution from Swift towards a further volume of Miscellanies. It is possible that Pope had endeavoured to obtain some of Elijah Fenton's papers. Fenton had died a few months before, and Sir Clement Cotterell, who was master of the ceremonies, an office held by his family for five generations, was a mutual friend.

I had a letter lately from Mr. Budgell, the direction a feigned hand and enclosed to Mr. Tickell.[1] He desires I would write to some of my great friends in England to get him into the House of Commons there, where he will do wonders. What shall I do? I dare not answer him, and fear he will be angry. Can nobody tell him that I have no great friends in England, and dare not write to him?

DCCLXXXVII. [*Elwin.*]

VISCOUNT BOLINGBROKE TO SWIFT

January 17, 1730-1.

I BEGIN my letter by telling you that my wife has been returned from abroad about a month, and that her health, though feeble and precarious, is better than it has been these two years. She is much your servant, and as she has been her own physician with some success, imagines she could be yours with the same. Would to God you was within her reach! She would, I believe, prescribe a great deal of the *medicina animi*, without having recourse to the books of Trismegistus.[2] Pope and I should be her principal apothecaries in the course of the cure; and though our best botanists complain, that few of the herbs and simples which go to the composition of these remedies are to be found at present in our soil, yet there are more of them here than in Ireland. Besides, by the help of a little chemistry, the most noxious juices may become salubrious, and rank poison a specific. Pope is now in my library with me, and writes to the world, to the present and to future ages, while I begin this letter which he is to finish to you.[3] What good he will do to mankind I know not; this comfort he may be sure of, he cannot do less than you have done before him. I have sometimes thought, that if preachers, hang-men, and moral writers, keep vice at a stand, or so much

---

[1] Budgell (*supra*, vol. iii, p. 150) had joined the Opposition, and was then writing for the "Craftsman."

[2] *I.e.*, the syncretistic writings issued under the pseudonym of the thrice great Hermes.

[3] Whatever part Bolingbroke may have had in the conception of the "Essay on Man" (*supra*, p. 155, n. 1), it cannot be questioned that he gave essential help in the execution.

as retard the progress of it, they do as much as human nature admits. A real reformation is not to be brought about by ordinary means; it requires these extraordinary means which become punishments as well as lessons. National corruption must be purged by national calamities. Let us hear from you. We deserve this attention, because we desire it, and because we believe that you desire to hear from us.

DCCLXXXVIII. [*Original.*[1]]

WILLIAM PULTENEY TO SWIFT

London, *February* 9, 1730-1.

DEAR SIR,

AMONG the many compliments I have received from my friends on the birth of my son, I assure you none gave me greater pleasure than the kind letter you honoured me with on the occasion.[2] When you was last in England, your stay was so short that I scarce had time, and very few opportunities, to convince you how great a desire I had to bear some share of your esteem; but, should you return this summer, I hope you will continue longer among us. Lord Bolingbroke, Lord Bathurst, Pope, myself, and others of your friends, are got together in a country neighbourhood, which would be much enlivened, if you would come and live among us. Mrs. Pulteney joins with me in the invitation, and is much obliged to you for remembering her. She bid me tell you, that she is determined to have no more children unless you will promise to come over and christen the next. You see how much my happiness, in many respects, depends upon your promise. I have always desired Pope, when he wrote to you, to remember my compliments; and I can assure you, with the greatest truth, though you have much older acquaintances, that you have not in England a friend that loves and honours you more than I do, or can be with greater sincerity than I am,

Your most humble and obedient servant,

WM. PULTENEY.

If any of our pamphlets, with which we abound, are ever

[1] In the British Museum. See Preface.
[2] *Supra,* p. 196, n. 4.

sent over to Ireland, and you think them worth reading, you will perceive how low they are reduced in point of argument on one side of the question. This has driven certain people to that last resort of calling names. Villain, traitor, seditious rascal, and such ingenious appellations, have frequently been bestowed on a couple of friends of yours. Such usage has made it necessary to return the same polite language; and there has been more Billingsgate stuff uttered from the press within these two months, than ever was known before. Upon this Dr. Arbuthnot has written a very humorous treatise,[1] which he showed me this morning, wherein he proves, from many learned instances, that this sort of altercation is ancient, elegant and classical, and that what the world falsely imagines to be polite, is truly gothic and barbarous. He shows how the gods and goddesses used one another—dog, bitch, and whore, were pretty common expressions among them; kings, heroes, ambassadors, and orators, abused one another much in the same way; and concludes, that it is [a] pity this method of objurgation should be lost. His quotations from Homer, Demosthenes, Æschines, and Tully are admirable, and the whole is very humorously conducted.[2] I take it for granted, he will send it you himself, as soon as it is printed.

DCCLXXXIX. [*Original.*[3]]

Lady Elizabeth Germain to Swift

February 23, 1730-1.

NOW was you in vast hopes you should hear no more of me, I being slow in my motions? But do not flatter yourself; you began the correspondence, set my pen a-going, and God knows when it will end; for I had it by inheritance from my father ever to please myself when I could, and though I do not just take the turn my mother did of

---

[1] "A Brief Account of Mr. John Ginglicut's Treatise concerning the Altercation or Scolding of the Ancients."

[2] In the opinion of Mr. Aitken ("Life of Arbuthnot," p. 132) Pulteney was partial to Arbuthnot, and bestowed exaggerated praise upon the tract.

[3] In the British Museum. See Preface.

fasting and praying, yet to be sure that was her pleasure too, or else she would not have been so greedy of it.[1] I do not care to deliver your messages this great while to Lieutenant Head, he having been dead these two years, and though he had, as you say, a head, I loved him very well, but, however, from my Dame Wadgar's[2] first impression, have ever had a natural antipathy to spirits.

I have not acquaintance enough with Mr. Pope, which I am sorry for, and expect you should come to England, in order to improve it. If it was the Queen, and not the Duke of Grafton, that picked out such a Laureate,[3] she deserves his poetry in her praises.

Your friend Mrs. Barber has been here. I find she has some request, but neither you nor she has yet let it out to me what it is. For certainly you cannot mean that by subscribing to her book; if so, I shall be mighty happy to have you call that a favour, for surely there is nothing so easy as what one can do one's self, nor nothing so heavy as what one must ask other people for; though I do not mean by this, that I shall ever be unwilling, when you require it, yet shall be much happier, when it is in my own power to show how sincerely I am my old friend's

Most faithful, humble servant,

E. GERMAIN.

Mrs. Floyd is much yours; but dumber than ever, having a violent cold.

Addressed—To the Revd. Dean Swift, at Dublin, Ireland.

DCCXC. [*Copy.*[4]]

KNIGHTLEY CHETWODE TO SWIFT

[*February* 1730-1.]

SIR,

I CAME to town the 12th of December and leave it the 12th of March, and could never see you but in the street.

---

[1] *Supra*, vol. i, p. 238.

[2] *I.e.*, the deaf housekeeper mentioned in " Mrs. Frances Harris's Petition " (" Poetical Works," i, 37).

[3] *I.e.*, Cibber (*supra*, p. 187). Grafton was Lord Chamberlain.

[4] In the Forster Collection. *Supra*, vol. ii, p. 241, n. 1.

The last time I met you I merrily thought of Horace's ninth satire, and upon it pursued you to your next house though not *prope Caesaris hortos.*[1] I had a desire to catch you by your best ear for half an hour, and something to tell you, which I imagined would surprise and please you, but with the cunning of experienced courtiers, grown old in politics, you put me off with a " I will send to you," which probably you never intended.

I am now returning to Woodbrooke from an amour which has proved little profitable to myself. Business here I have none but with women; those pleasures have not with me as yet [lost] their charms. And though when I am at home I do not like my neighbourhood, and shall therefore probably seldom stir beyond the limits of my gardens and plantations, which are full big enough for my purse, or what is even more insatiable my ambition, yet if my amusements there are scanty, my thoughts are unmolested, I see not the asperity of rascals, I hear not the complaints of the worthy, I enjoy the sun and fresh air without paying a fruitless attendance upon his Eminence of St. Patrick, my fruit will bloom, my herbs be fragrant, my flowers smile though the Dean frowns, and looks gloomy. Take this as some sort of return for the greatest neglect of me I have met since my last coming to this town, [together with] many ill offices, and what is far more extraordinary with half a dozen females, who have cleared up the truth of it to a mathematical demonstration.[2] This causes me to reflect upon the Jewish method formerly to make proselytes, which, I think, St. Ambrose well expresses in the following words: *Hi arte immiscent se hominibus, domos penetrant, ingrediuntur praetoria, aures judicum et publica inquietant, et ideo magis praevalent quo magis impudenter.*

I saw you pass last Friday by my window like a lady to

---

[1]   " Nil opus est te
Circumagi; quendam volo visere non tibi notum;
Trans Tiberim longe cubat is, prope Caesaris hortos."

[2] The reference is apparently to Mrs. Pilkington and the other female wits, "the seraglio of very virtuous women," who then frequented the Deanery. By his mention of the " Memoirs" (*supra*, p. 65, n. 4) Chetwode had increased Swift's estrangement from him, and by the present letter started a final breach in their friendship. From his experience in the case of "Cadenus and Vanessa" (*supra*, vol. iii, p. 306) he ought to have foreseen that such was likely to be the result.

take horse, with your handkerchief and whip in your hand
together; your petticoats were of the shortest and you
wanted a black cap, or I might have thought of Lady
Harriott Harley, now Lady Oxford.

DCCXCI. [*Elwin.*[1]]

SWIFT TO GAY AND THE DUCHESS OF QUEENSBERRY

Dublin, *March* 13, 1730-1.

TO GAY

BEFORE I go to answer your letter[2] I must tell you that
I am perpetually battling against my disorders by riding
and walking, whether the weather favours or no. I have
not for almost two years been rid of a kind of giddiness,
which, though not violent as formerly, keeps me low in
spirits and humour, and makes me a bad walker whenever
it grows towards night. This and some small returns of
deafness have hindered me from acknowledging yours of
above two months old; but that I matter not. What is
more, I have wanted courage to return my humblest thanks
to her Grace the Duchess of Queensberry, which I shall leave
till I come to her Grace's part.

Mr. Pope in all his letters complains he has no acquaintance with you and is utterly ignorant of your affairs. Your
situation is an odd one. The Duchess is your treasurer, and
Mr. Pope tells me you are the Duke's; and I had gone a
good way in some verses on that occasion, prescribing
lessons to direct your conduct in a negative way, not to do
so and so, etc., like other treasurers; how to deal with servants, tenants, or neighbouring squires, which I take to be
courtiers, parliaments, and princes in alliance, and so the
parallel goes on, but grew too long to please me.[3] I will
copy some lines:

> Let some reward[4] to merit be allowed,
> Nor with your kindred half the palace crowd;

---

[1] By permission of Mr. John Murray. *Supra*, vol. iii, p. 148, n. 1.

[2] Of 6 December (*supra*, p. 186).

[3] The verses were however completed and published under the title
of "An Epistle to Mr. Gay" ("Poetical Works," i, 214).

[4] In the published version "due reward" is substituted.

Nor think yourself secure in doing wrong,
By telling noses with a party strong.
Be rich, but of your wealth make no parade,
At least before your master's debts are paid;
Nor in a palace, built with charge immense,
Presume to treat him at his own expense.

Then I prove that poets are the fittest persons to be
treasurers and managers to great persons, from their virtue
and contempt of money, etc.[1] Pray why did you not get a
new heel to your shoe, unless you would make your court
at St. James's by affecting to imitate the Prince of Lilliput?
But the rest of your letter being wholly taken up in a very
bad character of the Duchess, I shall say no more to you,
but apply myself to her Grace.

To the Duchess

Madam,

Since Mr. Gay affirms that you love to have your
own way, and since I have the same perfection, I will
settle that matter immediately, to prevent those ill consequences he apprehends. Your Grace shall have your
own way in all places except your own house, and the
domains about it. There, and there only, I expect to have
mine, so that you have all the world to reign in, bating
only two or three hundred acres, and two or three houses
in town or country. I will likewise, out of my special grace,
certain knowledge, and mere motion, allow you to be in
the right against all human kind except myself, and to be
never in the wrong, but when you differ from me. You
shall have a greater privilege in the third article of speaking your mind, which I shall graciously allow you now
and then to do even to myself, and only rebuke you when
it does not please me.

Madam, I am now got as far as your Grace's letter,
which having not read this fortnight, having been out of
town, and not daring to trust myself with the carriage of
it, the presumptuous manner in which you begin had
slipped out of my memory. But I forgive you to the
seventeenth line, where you begin to banish me for ever
by demanding me to answer all the good character some

---

[1] The order was eventually reversed, and this argument was placed
before the lines just given.

partial friends have given me. Madam, I have lived sixteen years in Ireland, with only an intermission of two
summers in England, and consequently am fifty years
older than I was at the Queen's death, and fifty thousand
times duller, and fifty million times more peevish, perverse,
and morose; so that under these disadvantages I can only
pretend to excel all your other acquaintance about some
twenty bars' length. Pray, Madam, have you a clear voice;
and will you let me sit at your left hand, at least within
three of you, for of two bad ears my right is the best? My
groom tells me that he likes your park, but your house is
too little.[1] Can the parson of the parish play at backgammon, and hold his tongue? Is any one of your women a
good nurse, if I should fancy myself sick for four-and-twenty
hours? How many days will you maintain me and my
equipage? When these preliminaries are settled, I must
be very poor, very sick, or dead, or to the last degree unfortunate, if I do not attend you at Amesbury. For I profess you are the first lady that ever I desired to see since
the 1st of August, 1714,[2] and I have forgot the date when
that desire grew strong upon me, but I know I was not
then in England, else I would have gone on foot for that
happiness as far as to your house in Scotland. But I can
soon recollect the time, by asking some ladies here the
month, the day, and the hour, when I began to endure
their company, which, however, I think was a sign of my
ill judgement, for I do not perceive they mend in anything
but envying or admiring your Grace.

I dislike nothing in your letter but an affected apology
for bad writing, bad spelling, and a bad pen, which you
pretend Mr. Gay found fault with, wherein you affront Mr.
Gay, you affront me, and you affront yourself. False
spelling is only excusable in a chambermaid, for I would
not pardon it in any of your waiting-women. Pray God
preserve your Grace and family, and give me leave to expect that you will be so just to number me among those
who have the greatest regard for virtue, goodness, prudence,
courage, and generosity; after which you must conclude
that I am, with the greatest respect and gratitude, Madam,
Your Grace's most obedient and most humble servant, etc.

---

[1] Swift's groom had apparently acquaintance with Amesbury.
[2] *I.e.*, since Queen Anne died.

To Gay

I have just got yours of February 25th, with a postscript by Mr. Pope.[1] I am in great concern for him, for I did not know that the rheumatism was in the number of his disorders. I owe him for a letter some time ago that I had from Mr. Brandreth,[2] who is gone to his preferments that are about three hundred pounds per annum, if any money is to be got by lands or tithes in this most miserable country. God knows I have inducements enough to be with you, besides the uneasiness of beggary and desolation in every scene and person round me. But that lawsuit of mine, wherein almost my whole fortune depends, is still on foot; for land is to be sold to pay me, and that is still delayed, but I am told will be done in May. I hope from drinking wine by advice you will arrive to drink it by inclination, else I shall be a bad companion: for I do it indeed only by advice, for I love ale better. I find Mr. Pope dictated to you the first part of what he would say, and with great difficulty some days after added the rest. I see his weakness by his hand-writing. How much does his philosophy exceed mine! I could not bear to see him; I will write to him soon. I received lately a very friendly letter from Mr. Pulteney.[3] Adieu. Pray God preserve you both. Dr. Delany keeps much at his villa about two miles from this town.[4] He will be very happy with Mr. Pope's kind remembrance of him. I am not perfectly master how to direct to the Duke's house. Pray tell me.

DCCXCII. [*Original.*[5]]

John Gay to Swift

March 20, 1730-1.

I think it is above three months that I wrote to you, in partnership with the Duchess. About a fortnight since I wrote to you from Twickenham, for Mr. Pope and myself.[6]

---

[1] Evidently owing to the postscript this letter has been suppressed.
[2] *Supra*, p. 195.   [3] *Supra*, p. 198.
[4] *I.e.*, Delville (*supra*, p. 152).
[5] In the British Museum. See Preface.
[6] The letters to which Swift had replied in the preceding one.

He was then disabled from writing by a severe rheumatic pain in his arm; but is now pretty well again, and at present in town. Lord Oxford, Lord Bathurst, he, and I, dined together yesterday at Barnes, with old Jacob Tonson,[1] where we drank your health. I am again, by the advice of physicians, grown a moderate wine-drinker after an abstinence of above two years; and now I look upon myself as qualified for society as before.

I formerly sent you a state of the accounts between us.[2] Lord Bathurst this day has paid me your principal and interest. The interest amounted to twelve pounds, and I want your directions how to dispose of the principal, which must lie dead, till I receive your orders. I had a scheme of buying two lottery tickets for you,[3] and keeping your principal entire; and as all my good fortune is to come, to show you that I consult your advantage, I will buy two more for myself, and you and I will go halves in the ten thousand pounds. That there will be a lottery is certain: the scheme is not yet declared, but I hear it will not be the most advantageous one, for we are to have but three pounds per cent. I solicit for no Court favours, so that I propose to buy the tickets at the market-price, when they come out, which will not be these two or three months. If you do not like to have your money thus disposed of, or if you like to trust to your own fortune rather than to share in mine, let me have your orders, and at the same time, tell me what I shall do with the principal sum.

I came to town the 7th of January last with the Duke and Duchess, about business, for a fortnight. As it depended upon others, we could not get it done till now. Next week we return to Amesbury in Wiltshire for the rest of the year; but the best way is always to direct to me at the Duke's in Burlington Gardens, near Piccadilly. I am ordered by the Duchess to grow rich in the manner of Sir John Cutler.[4] I have nothing, at this present writing,

---

1   " Thou, Jacob Tonson, were to my conceiving,
        The cheerfullest, best, honest fellow living."

[2] *Supra*, p. 129.
[3] Gay is said to have remained until that year a commissioner of the lottery.
[4] The meanness of this great merchant of Restoration times has become proverbial through Pope's reference to it in the third of his *Moral Essays*. It has been shown by modern authorities that he com-

but my frock that was made at Salisbury, and a bob periwig. I persuade myself that it is shilling weather[1] as seldom as possible; and have found out, that there are few Court visits that are worth a shilling. In short, I am very happy in my present independency. I envy no man, but have the due contempt for the voluntary slaves of birth and fortune. I have such a spite against you that I wish you may long for my company, as I do for yours. Though you never write to me, you cannot make me forget you; so that if it is out of friendship you write so seldom to me, it doth not answer the purpose. Those who you would like should remember you, do so whenever I see them. I believe they do it upon their own account, for I know few people who are solicitous to please or flatter me. The Duchess sends you her compliments, and so would many more, if they knew of my writing to you.

Addressed—To the Rev. Dr. Swift, Dean of St. Patrick's, in Dublin, Ireland.

DCCXCIII. [*Elwin.*]

VISCOUNT BOLINGBROKE AND ALEXANDER POPE TO SWIFT

March 20, 1731.

BOLINGBROKE

I HAVE delayed several posts answering your letter of January last,[2] in hopes of being able to speak to you about a project which concerns us both, but me the most, since the success of it would bring us together.[3] It has been a good while in my head, and at my heart; if it can be set a-going, you shall hear more of it. I was ill in the beginning of the winter for near a week, but in no danger

---

bined with his penuriousness "large benevolence and public spirit" (cf. "D. N. B.," xiii, 364; Pope's "Works," iii, 154). Wimpole had belonged to Cutler.

[1] *I.e.*, such as rendered the hire of a hackney coach necessary.

[2] The letter to which Swift refers in his last letter to Pope (*supra*, p. 193).

[3] *I.e.*, securing for Swift English preferment.

either from the nature of my distemper, or from the attendance of three physicians. Since that bilious intermitting fever, I have had, as I had before, better health than the regard I have paid to health deserves. We are both in the decline of life, my dear Dean, and have been some years going down the hill. Let us make the passage as smooth as we can. Let us fence against physical evil by care, and the use of those means which experience must have pointed out to us. Let us fence against moral evil by philosophy. I renounce the alternative you propose. But we may, nay, if we will follow nature, and do not work up imagination against her plainest dictates, we shall of course grow every year more indifferent to life, and to the affairs and interests of a system out of which we are soon to go. This is much better than stupidity. The decay of passion strengthens philosophy, for passion may decay, and stupidity not succeed. Passions, says our divine Pope, as you will see one time or other, are the gales of life.[1] Let us not complain that they do not blow a storm. What hurt does age do us in subduing what we toil to subdue all our lives? It is now six in the morning. I recall the time, and am glad it is over, when about this hour I used to be going to bed, surfeited with pleasure, or jaded with business: my head often full of schemes, and my heart as often full of anxiety. Is it a misfortune, think you, that I rise at this hour, refreshed, serene, and calm; that the past, and even the present, affairs of life stand like objects at a distance from me, where I can keep off the disagreeable so as not to be strongly affected by them, and from whence I can draw the others nearer to me? Passions in their force would bring all these, nay, even future contingencies, about my ears at once, and reason would but ill defend me in the scuffle.

I leave Pope to speak for himself, but I must tell you how much my wife is obliged to you. She says she would find strength enough to nurse you, if you were here, and yet God knows, she is extremely weak. The slow fever works under, and mines the constitution. We keep it off sometimes, but still it returns, and makes new breaches

---

[1] In the second epistle of the " Essay on Man ":

> " On life's vast ocean diversely we sail,
> Reason the card, but passion is the gale."

before nature can repair the old ones. I am not ashamed
to say to you, that I admire her more every hour of my
life. Death is not to her the king of terrors; she beholds
him without the least. When she suffers much, she wishes
for him as a deliverer from pain; when life is tolerable,
she looks on him with dislike, because he is to separate her
from those friends to whom she is more attached than to
life itself. You shall not stay for my next as long as you
have for this letter; and in every one Pope shall write
something much better than the scraps of old philosophers,
which were the presents, *munuscula*, that stoical fop
Seneca used to send in every epistle to his friend Lucilius.

POPE

My Lord has promised too much for me. I can write
nothing, not even so much as good scraps; for I am become but a scrap of myself, and quite exhausted by a
long pain and confinement. The Doctor puts me into
asses' milk, and I must neither use study nor exercise; I
am too weak. I am to do nothing but sleep and eat, if I
can. Were my life my own, even without health, I would
come and show you the last of me in Ireland. My spirits
continue good, and fear is a stranger to me.

Mrs. Barber desires I would correct her verses. Truly I
should do it very ill; for I can give no attention to anything. Whatever service I can render her, by speaking
well, etc., I will. Whatever friends I can get to subscribe
to her, I will. But you know my circle is vastly contracted,
as I seldom have been out of the country these two years.
All your friends she will have without me, and all their
friends. But I will do all I can. I must in return press
you to speak well, as you justly may, of an abridgement of
the Roman History, a subscription for which is going on in
Ireland, and the profit of which the gentleman, who is a
very valuable man and my particular friend, gives to the
repairing of St. Mary's Hall in Oxford.[1] Pray also desire
Mr. Brandreth [2] from me to promote it what he can.

---

[1] In the opinion of Elwin (*op. cit.*, vii, 223) this work was projected
by Walter Harte, a writer who enjoyed the friendship of Dr. Johnson
as well as Pope (" D. N. B.," xxv, 65), but it was never issued by him.

[2] *Supra*, p. 209.

My hearty services to Dr. Delany. I writ to you the first time I was able, with Mr. Gay, about two weeks since.[1] My mother is yours, and at this present better than I. I hope your lawsuit is well ended. How is your health? Adieu.

DCCXCIV. [*Original.*[2]]

John Gay and the Duchess of Queensberry to Swift

April 11, 1731.

GAY

DEAR SIR,

THE fortune of the person you interest yourself in [3] amounts to at present, all debts paid, above three thousand four hundred pounds; so that, whatever other people think, I look upon him, as to fortune, to be a happy, that is to say, an independent creature. I have been in expectation, post after post, to have received your directions about the disposal of your money, which Lord Bathurst paid into my hands some time ago. I left that sum, with two hundred of my own, in Mr. Hoare's [4] hands at my coming out of town. I shall go to town for a few days very soon. If I hear nothing from you, I will do with it as I do with my own. I made you a proposal about purchasing lottery-tickets in partnership with myself, that is to say, four tickets between us.[5] This can be done with overplus, with the interest-money I have received; but in this I will do nothing till I hear from you.

I am now got to my residence at Amesbury; getting health and saving money. Since I have got over the impediment to a writer of water-drinking, if I can persuade myself that I have any wit, and find I have inclination, I intend to write, though as yet I have another impediment, for I have not provided myself with a scheme. Ten to one but I shall have a propensity to write against vice, and who

[1] The suppressed letter of 25 February (*supra*, p. 205).
[2] In the British Museum. See Preface.
[3] *I.e.*, Gay himself.
[4] Afterwards Sir Richard Hoare, the grandfather of the historian of Wiltshire.
[5] *Supra*, p. 206.

can tell how far that may offend? But an author should consult his genius rather than his interest, if he cannot reconcile them. Just before I left London I made a visit to Mrs. Barber.[1] I wish I could anywise have contributed to her subscription. I have always found myself of no consequence, and am now of less than ever; but I have found out a way, in one respect, of making myself of more consequence, which is by considering other people of less. Those who have given me up, I have given up; and in short, I seek after no friendships, but am content with what I have in the house; and they have subscribed. I proposed it before Joe Taylor,[2] who, upon hearing she was a friend of yours, offered his subscription, and desired his compliments to you. I believe she hath given you an account that she hath some prospect of success from others' recommendations to those I know, and I have not been wanting upon all occasions to put in my good word, which I fear avails but little.

Two days ago I received a letter from Dr. Arbuthnot, which gave me but a bad account of Mr. Pope's health. I have writ to him, but have not heard from him since I came into the country. If you knew the pleasure you gave me, you would keep your contract of writing more punctually, and especially you would have answered my last letter, as it was about a money affair, and you have to do with a man of business. Your letter was more to the Duchess than to me, so I now leave off to offer her the paper.

THE DUCHESS

It was Mr. Gay's fault that I did not write sooner, which, if I had, I should hope you would have been here by this time; for I have to tell you that all your articles are agreed to, and that I only love my own way when I meet not with others whose ways I like better. I am in great hopes that I shall approve of yours, for to tell you the truth, I am at present a little tired of my own. I have not a clear or distinct voice except when I am angry; but I am a very good nurse when people do not fancy themselves sick. Mr. Gay knows this, and he knows too how to play at backgammon.

[1] *Supra*, p. 159.   [2] *Supra*, p. 22, n. 3.

Whether the parson of the parish can, I know not; but if
he cannot hold his tongue, I can. Pray set out the first
fair wind, and stay with us as long as ever you please. I
cannot name any fixed time that I shall like to maintain
you and your equipage; but if I do not happen to like you,
I know I can so far govern my temper as to endure you
for about five days. So come away directly; for at all
hazards you will be allowed a good breathing-time. I shall
make no sort of respectful conclusion; for till I know you
I cannot tell what I am to you.

GAY

The direction is to the Duke of Queensberry's, in Burlington Gardens in Piccadilly. Now I have told you this
you have no excuse from writing but one, which is coming.
Get over your lawsuit and receive your money.

THE DUCHESS

He shall not write a word more.

From Amesbury in Wiltshire.

Your groom was mistaken, for the house is big enough,
but the park is too little.

Addressed—To the Revd. Dr. Swift, Dean of St. Patrick's
in Dublin, Ireland. By London.

DCCXCV. [*Scott.*]

SWIFT TO THE REV. JOHN BLACHFORD

Dublin, *April* 16, 1731.

SIR,[1]

I BEGGED some mutton of you, and you put me off with
a barrel of ale; these disappointments we must endure.

---

[1] Blachford, who was a scholar and graduate of Dublin University,
had been for more than twelve years a member of Swift's chapter, and
held at that time the prebend of Wicklow. He was evidently a man of
good abilities, which he transmitted to Mrs. Tighe, the poetess, who
was his granddaughter. There is a mezzotint of him by MacArdell,
and verses of a very laudatory kind were written upon him after his
death (Hughes's " St. Werburgh's," p. 63).

But the main business is, whether it be of your own brewing, and here is another *silentium*. I knew we must not look a gift horse in the mouth, but ale must look into ours. There is another point; I would fain know what title you have to send me ale or anything else, when you hardly ever see the inside of the Deanery, or taste my bad wine.

I have had intentions to drink some of your Wicklow ale upon the place, because I fancy it is better where it grows; and in such a case, it will not be improper that the minister should be actually residing. I shall observe your directions of keeping it, and Mr. John Grattan [1] will be delighted

> With ale
> Strong and stale,
> Or beer
> Stout and clear.

You are a stranger to these proverbs. I am truly obliged to you for remembering me; although it be the duty of you country-folks, as it is of us town-folks, to forget you, and therefore we have a legal title to your presents. However, for once I will break this rule, by assuring you, that I have been, am, and shall be always

> Your obedient and obliged servant.

Addressed—To the Rev. Mr. Blachford at Wicklow.

DCCXCVI. [*Original.*[2]]

LORD BATHURST TO SWIFT

April 19, 1731.

I NEVER designed to have written to you any more, because you bantered and abused me so grossly in your last.[3] To flatter a man from whom you can get nothing, nor expect anything, is doing mischief for mischief sake, and consequently highly immoral. However I will not carry my resentments so far, as to stand by and see you undone, without giving you both notice and advice. Could any man

---

[1] John Grattan (*supra*, vol. ii, p. 262, n. 3) had become one of Swift's prebendaries.
[2] In the British Museum. See Preface.
[3] *Supra*, p. 166.

but you think of trusting John Gay with his money? None of his friends would ever trust him with his own whenever they could avoid it. He has called in the two hundred pounds I had of yours: I paid him both principal and interest. I suppose by this time he has lost it. I give you notice, you must look upon it as annihilated.

Now, as I have considered that your deanery brings you in little or nothing, and that you keep servants and horses, and frequently give little neat dinners, which are more expensive than a few splendid entertainments, beside which, you may be said to water your flock with French wine, which altogether must consume your substance in a little while, I have thought of putting you in a method that you may retrieve your affairs. In the first place, you must turn off all your servants, and sell your horses; I will find exercise for you. Your whole family must consist of only one sound wholesome wench. She will make your bed, and warm it; beside washing your linen, and mending it, darning your stockings, etc. But to save all expense in housekeeping, you must contrive some way or other, that she should have milk; and I can assure you, it is the opinion of some of the best physicians that woman's milk is the wholesomest food in the world.

Besides this regimen, take it altogether, will certainly temper and cool your blood. You will not be such a *boute-feu*, as you have been, and be ready, upon every trifling occasion, to set a whole kingdom in a flame. Had the Drapier been a milksop, poor Wood had not suffered so much in his reputation and fortune. It will allay that fervour of blood, and quiet that hurry of spirits, which breaks out every now and then into poetry, and seems to communicate itself to others of the Chapter. You would not then encourage Delany and Stopford in their idleness, but let them be as grave as most of their order are with us. I am convinced they will sooner get preferment than in the way they now are. And I shall not be out of hopes of seeing you a bishop in time, when you live in the regular way, which I propose. In short, in a few years, you may lay up money enough to buy even the bishopric of Durham. For, if you keep cows instead of horses, in that high-walled orchard, and cultivate by your own industry a few potatoes in your garden, the maid will live well, and be able to sell more butter and cheese, than will answer her wages. You may

preach then upon temperance with a better grace, than
now, that you are known to consume seven or eight hogsheads of wine every year of your life. You will be mild
and meek in your conversation, and not frighten Parliament-
men, and keep even Lord Lieutenants in awe. You will
then be qualified for that slavery, which the country you
live in, and the order you profess, seem to be designed for.
It will take off that giddiness in your head, which has disturbed yourself and others. The disputes between Sir
Arthur and my Lady,[1] will for the future be confined
to prose, and an old thorn may be cut down in peace, and
warm the parlour chimney,[2] without heating the heads of
poor innocent people, and turning their brains. You ought
to remember what St. Austin says, *Poesis est vinum
daemonum.*[3] Consider the life you now lead: you warm all
that come near you with your wine and conversation; and
the rest of the world, with your pen dipped deep in St.
Austin's *vinum daemonum.*

So far for your soul's health. Now, as to the health of
your body, I must inform you, that part of what I prescribe to you, is the same which our great Friar Bacon
prescribed to the Pope who lived in his days. Read his
" Cure of Old Age, and Preservation of Youth," chapter
twelve.[4] You used to say, that you found benefit from
riding. The French, an ingenious people, use the word
chevaucher, instead of *monter à cheval,* and they look upon
it as the same thing in effect. Now, if you will go on after
this, in your old ways, and ruin your health, your fortune,
and your reputation, it is no fault of mine. I have pointed
out the road which will lead you to riches and preferment,
and that you may have no excuse from entering into this
new course of life, upon pretence of doubting whether you

---

[1] *I.e.,* Sir Arthur and Lady Acheson.
[2] The allusions are to " The Grand Question Debated: Whether
Hamilton's Bawn should be turned into a Barrack or Malt House "
and the verses on " Cutting down the Thorn at Market Hill " (" Poetical
Works," ii, 89, 101).
[3] *Cf.* " De Civitate Dei," II, xiv.
[4] This work, of which the English version was published in 1683 by
Richard Brown, is believed to have been addressed to Pope Nicolas the
Fourth, and to have been written "to atone the enraged and angry
mind " of that Pontiff, who had kept Roger Bacon in prison for many
years. The twelfth chapter treats of the incident in David's life
recorded in 1 Kings, i, 1-4.

can get a person properly qualified to feed you, and compose your new family, I will recommend you to John Gay, who is much better qualified to bring increase from a woman, than from a sum of money. But if he should be lazy, and he is so fat, that there is some reason to doubt him, I will without fail supply you myself, that you may be under no disappointment. Bracton[1] says, *Conjunctio maris et foeminae est jure naturae.* *Vide* Coke upon Littleton; Calvin's case, first volume Reports.[2]

This I send you from my closet at Ritchings,[3] where I am at leisure to attend serious affairs; but when one is in town, there are so many things to laugh at, that it is very difficult to compose one's thoughts, even long enough to write a letter of advice to a friend. If I see any man serious in that crowd, I look upon him for a very dull or designing fellow. By the by, I am of opinion, that folly and cunning are nearer allied than people are aware of. If a fool runs out his fortune, and is undone, we say the poor man has been outwitted. Is it not as reasonable to say of a cunning rascal, who has lived miserably, and died hated and despised, to leave a great fortune behind him, that he has outwitted himself? In short, to be serious about those trifles, which the majority of mankind think of consequence, seems to me to denote folly, and to trifle with those things which they generally treat ludicrously, may denote knavery. I have observed that in comedy, the best actor plays the part of the droll, while some scrub rogue is made the hero, or fine gentleman. So, in this farce of life, wise men pass their time in mirth, while fools only are serious. Adieu. Continue to be merry and wise; but never turn serious, or cunning.

Addressed—To the Revd. Dr. Swift, Dean of St. Patrick's, Dublin.

Endorsed by Swift—It is too late for me to turn serious now.

---

[1] Henry de Bracton, who flourished in the thirteenth century and was the earliest writer on English law.

[2]   " Calvin, Scotch *ante nati* aliens were,
       But *post nati* in England subjects are."
                    " Coke's Reports in Verse," vii, 1.

[3] Bathurst's seat in Buckinghamshire to which there has been previous reference (*supra*, vol. iii, p. 312, n. 5).

DCCXCVII. [*Elwin.*[1]]

SWIFT TO ALEXANDER POPE

Dublin, *April* 20, 1731.

FROM your own letters,[2] as well as one I just had from Mr. Gay, I have by no means a good account of your health. The common saying of life being a farce is true in every sense but the most important one, for it is a ridiculous tragedy, which is the worst kind of composition. I know but one temporal felicity that has fallen to your share, which is, that you never were a struggler for bread. As to the rest, I mean the esteem of friends, and enemies of your own and other countries, your patience and fortitude, and a long *et cetera*, they are all spiritual blessings. The misfortune I most lament is your not being able, by exercise, to battle with your disorders, as I do by riding and walking, at which, however, I repine, and would not do it merely to lengthen life, because it would be ill husbandry, for I should save time by sitting still, though I should die seven years sooner; but the dread of pain and torture makes me toil to preserve health from hand to mouth as much as a labourer to support life. I am glad you are got into asses' milk. It is a remedy I have a great opinion of, and wish you had taken it sooner. And I wish, too, you were rich enough to keep a coach, and use it every day you are able; and this you might do if your private charities were less extensive, or at least suspended, till you were able *nare sine cortice*. I believe you have as good reason as any Christian man to be a stranger to fear. But I cannot endure the thought that you should live in pain, and I believe when Horace said, *quisquis erit vitae, scribam, color*,[3] he understood that pain was to be excepted.

Mrs. Barber acted weakly in desiring you to correct her verses. I desired her friends here to warn her against everything of that kind. I believe there was a great combat between her modesty and her ambition. I can learn nothing of this Roman history. You did not tell me the gentleman's name, and I know not where to inquire.

---

[1] By permission of Mr. John Murray. *Supra*, vol. iii, p. 148, n. 1.
[2] *Supra*, p. 209.   [3] "Sat.," 2, i, 60.

Mr. Brandreth is gone to his livings, and will stay there till the Duke of Dorset's arrival hither, or at least till towards the end of the summer. Perhaps you may hear that I and my Chapter are erecting a stone over the body of the old Duke of Schomberg, killed at the Boyne. We had applied often to the Countess of Holderness, now Lady Fitzwalter, for a monument over her grandfather, and could receive no answer. The Latin inscription has been printed by the news-writers here, and has, I suppose, reached England, and I hear the relations are angry.[1] Let them take it for their pains. I have ordered the stone to be fixed up.

I long to know the success of your asses' milk. If it hinders you from study, the world will be the chief sufferer. Descend, in the name of God, to some other amusements, as common mortals do. Learn to play at cards, or tables, or bowls; get talking females, who will go on or stop at your commands; contrive new trangrams in your garden, or in Mrs. Howard's, or my Lord Bolingbroke's; or, when you are able, go down to Amesbury, and forget yourself for a fortnight with our friend Gay and the Duchess. Sweeten your milk with mirth and motion. For my own part, I think when a man is sick or sickly, great Lords and Ladies, let them be ever so civil, so familiar, and so friendly, are not half so commodious as middling folks, whom one may govern as one pleases, and who will think

---

[1] On the 14th of that month the following paragraph had appeared in the "Dublin Intelligence": "We hear that his Reverence Doctor Jonathan Swift, Dean of St. Patrick's, having a long time sued in vain to the daughters of the great Duke of Schomberg for a monument to be placed over his body in that church, at length with the Chapter agreed that the following inscription, in elegant Latin, should be there deposited, which for the public satisfaction we give thus rendered, as a matter to be fully reflected on: 'Here underneath lieth the body of Frederick, Duke of Schomberg, who was slain at the Boyne in the year 1690. The Dean and Chapter [of St. Patrick's] did most earnestly, over and over again, request that the heirs of the Duke would be pleased to erect a monument, however plain and small, to his memory, but when after long and frequent solicitations, both by letters and by friends, they found that nothing could be obtained, grieved for the indignity offered to the memory of so great a man, they fixed up this stone, that thou, O stranger! mightest know in how poor a cell the ashes of so great a General lie neglected, to the reproach of his heirs. So much could the admiration of his virtues avail with strangers more than the nearest ties of blood with his own relations.'"

it an honour and happiness to attend us, to talk or be silent, to laugh or look grave, just as they are directed. The old Lord Sunderland was never without one or more of these; Lord Somers had a humdrum parson, with whom he was used to forget himself for threepence at backgammon; and our friend Addison had a young fellow, now of figure in your Court, whom he made to dangle after him, to go where, and to do whatever, he was bid.[1] I often thought you wanted two or three of either sex in such an employment, when you were weary, or sick, or solitary; and you have my *probatum est*, if that be of any value. My old Presbyterian housekeeper tells me, that if you could bring your stomach to woman's milk, it would be far better than asses'. I would have you contrive to get as much of summer air as it is possible, of which we have yet had nothing here, but a long run of north-east winds, that have almost ruined my fruit; for I suffer peach, and nectarine, and pearweeds to grow in my famous garden of Naboth's Vineyard, that you have heard me boast of.

I protest to you that nothing so much discourages me from an English journey as the prospect of domestic ailments when I am from home, and at a distance of such a kind that I cannot come back but by the pleasure of waves and winds. However, if my health and law will permit me, I shall venture once more to see you. For, as to my law, the land of my creditor is not sold, but after a dozen hopes, I have the thirteenth, that it will be done in a month. Yet then I know not what to do with the money; for Mr. Gay tells me I can hardly expect even four per cent, besides the trouble of returning it, and safely putting it out, and here I hope to have six per cent on good security of land, if land continues to yield anything at all, for, without a miracle, we are just at our last gasp, beyond the imagination of anyone who does not live in this kingdom. And most of my sorry revenues being of the tithe kind, I am forced to watch my agents and farmers constantly, to get anything. This, and years, and uncertain health, have sunk my spirits, and I often wish myself a vicar in Wales. I ride constantly here, but cannot afford to support a couple

---

[1] The reference is to Walter Carey, who figures in several of Pope's poems under the sobriquet of *Umbra*. He was then member for Dartmouth, and came to Ireland a few months later in the capacity of Chief Secretary to Dorset.

of horses in England. Pardon this particular impertinence of relating my difficulties so contrary to my desires. I was just reading one of your letters, three months old, wherein you are hard on me for saying you were a poet in favour at Court. I profess it was writ to me either by Lord Bolingbroke or the Doctor.[1] You know favour is got by two very contrary qualities,—one is by fear, the other by ill taste. As to Cibber, if I had any inclination to excuse the Court, I would allege that the Laureate's place is entirely in the Lord Chamberlain's gift; but who makes Lord Chamberlains is another question. I believe, if the Court had interceded with the Duke of Grafton[2] for a fitter man, it might have prevailed. I am at the end of my paper. You are in my constant prayers for your health. I hope you will present my humble service to my list,—Lord Peterborough, Lord Oxford, Lord Bolingbroke and lady, Lord Bathurst, Lord Masham, Mr. Pulteney, the Doctor, Mr. Lewis, Mrs. Pope, and Patty, very heartily. Nothing to Mrs. Howard; you drew me in to write to her, and see how she has served me, for which she is a ——.

DCCXCVIII. [*Original.*[3]]

JOHN GAY TO SWIFT

Amesbury, *April* 27, 1731.

DEAR SIR,

YOURS without a date[4] I received two days after my return to this place from London, where I stayed only four days. I saw Mr. Pope, who was much better. I dined with him at Lord Oxford's, who never fails drinking your health, and is always very inquisitive after everything that concerns you. Mr. Pulteney had received your letter,[5] and seemed very much pleased with it; and I thought you very much too in the good graces of the lady. Sir William

---

[1] The allusion is in Arbuthnot's letter of the preceding November (*supra*, p. 171). Neither Swift's letter nor Pope's rejoinder is forthcoming.

[2] Who then held the office of Lord Chamberlain.

[3] In the British Museum. See Preface.

[4] This letter has disappeared.

[5] Probably a reply to Pulteney's letter of 9 February (*supra*, p. 198).

Wyndham, who you will by this time have heard hath buried Lady Catherine,[1] was at Dawley in great affliction. Dr. Arbuthnot I found in good health and spirits. His neighbour, Mr. Lewis, was gone to the Bath. Mrs. Patty Blount I saw two or three times, who will be very much pleased when she knows you so kindly remember her. I am afraid Mrs. Howard will not be so well satisfied with the compliments you send her. I breakfasted twice with her at Mrs. Blount's, and she told me that her indisposition had prevented her answering your letter. This she desired me to tell you, and that she would write to you soon; and she desires you will accept of her compliments in the mean time by me. You should consider circumstances before you censure. It will be too long for a letter to make her apology; but when I see you, I believe I shall convince you that you mistake her.

This day, before I left London, I gave orders for buying two South-Sea or India bonds for you, which carry four pounds per cent and are as easily turned into ready money as bank bills which, by this time, I suppose is done. I shall go to London again for a few days in about a fortnight or three weeks, and then I will take care of the twelve pound affair with Mrs. Lancelot,[2] as you direct; or, if I hear of Mr. Pope's being in town, I will do it sooner, by a letter to him. When I was in town, after a bashful fit, for having writ something like a love-letter, and in two years not making one visit, I writ to Mrs. Drelincourt,[3] to apologise for my behaviour, and received a civil answer, but had not time to see her. They are naturally very civil, so that I am not so sanguine to interpret this as any encouragement. I find by Mrs. Barber, that she very much interests herself in her affair; and indeed from everybody who knows her, she answers the character you first gave me.

Whenever you come to England, if you will put that confidence in me to give me notice, I will meet you at your landing-place, and conduct you hither. You have experience of me as a traveller; and I promise you I will not drop

---

[1] Lady Catherine Wyndham, who was a daughter of " the proud " Duke of Somerset, died on the 9th of that month. There is a reference in the Journal to Stella to her escaping barefoot from the fire that destroyed her husband's richly furnished house in the Haymarket (" Prose Works," ii, 347).

[2] *Supra*, p. 37, n. 1.   [3] *Supra*, vol. iii, p. 408.

you upon the road for any visit whatever. You tell me of thanks that I have not given. I do not know what to say to people who will be perpetually laying one under obligations. My behaviour to you shall convince you that I am very sensible of them, though I never once mention them. I look upon you as my best friend and counsellor. I long for the time when we shall meet and converse together. I will draw you into no great company, beside those I live with. In short, if you insist upon it, I will give up all great company for yours. These are conditions that I can hardly think you will insist upon, after your declarations to the Duchess, who is more and more impatient to see you, and all my fear is that you will give up me for her, which after my ungallant declaration, would be very ungenerous. But we will settle this matter together when you come to Amesbury. After all, I find I have been saying nothing; for, speaking of her, I am talking as if I were in my own power. You used to blame me for over-solicitude about myself. I am now grown so rich, that I do not think myself worth thinking on, so that I will promise you never to mention myself, or my own affairs; but you owed it all to the inquisitiveness of your friendship, and ten to one but every now and then you will draw me in to talk of myself again. I sent you a gross state of my fortune already. I have not room to draw it out in particulars. When you come over, the Duchess will state it you. I have left no room for her to write, so that I will say nothing till my letter is gone; but she would not forgive me, if I did not send her compliments.

Addressed—To the Revd. Dr. Swift, Dean of St. Patrick's, in Dublin, Ireland. By way of London.

DCCXCIX. [*Notes and Queries.*[1]]

SWIFT TO LADY WORSLEY

Dublin, *May* 1, 1731.

MADAM,

IT is now three years and a half since I had the honour to see your Ladyship, and I take it very ill that you have

---

[1] I, iv, 218.

not finished my box above a month.[1] But this is always
the way that you ladies treat your adorers in their absence.
However upon Mrs. Barber's account, I will pardon you,
because she tells me it is the handsomest piece of work she
ever saw, and because you have accepted the honour to be
one of her protectors, and are determined to be one of her
principal recommenders and encouragers. I am in some
doubt whether envy had not a great share in your work, for
you were I suppose informed that my Lady Carteret had
made for me with her own hands the finest box in Ireland,
upon which you grew jealous, and resolved to outdo her
by making for me the finest box in England, for so Mrs.
Barber assures me. In short, I am quite overloaden with
favours from your Ladyship and your daughter, and what
is worse, those loads will lie upon my shoulders as long as
I live. But I confess myself a little ungrateful, because I
cannot deny your Ladyship to have been the most constant
of all my Goddesses, as I am the most constant of all your
worshippers.

I hope the Carterets and the Worsleys are all happy and
in health, and you are obliged to let Sir Robert Worsley
know that I am his most humble servant, but you need
say nothing of my being so long his rival. I hear my friend
Harry is returning from the fiery Zone;[2] I hope with more
money than he knows what to do with, but whether his
vagabond spirit will ever fix is a question. I beg your
Ladyship will prevail on Sir Robert Worsley to give me a
vicarage in the Isle of Wight,[3] for I am weary of living at
such a distance from you. It need not be above forty
pounds a year.

As to Mrs. Barber, I can assure you she is but one of
four poetesses in this town, and all citizens' wives,[4] but she
has the vogue of being the best, yet one of them is a
scholar, and hath published a new edition of Tacitus, with
a Latin dedication to my Lord Carteret. I require that your

---

[1] Swift had been informed by Mrs. Barber that Lady Worsley had
obeyed the injunction in his letter to her twelve months before (*supra*,
p. 146). As will be seen from a subsequent letter the box proved to
be an escritoire. It is preserved in St. Patrick's Deanery.

[2] *I.e.*, Barbadoes (*supra*, p. 146, n. 4).

[3] The connection of the Worsleys with the Isle of Wight has been
already mentioned (*supra*, p. 172, n. 3).

[4] It was probably by the addition of Mrs. Pilkington's name that the
Dublin poetesses (*supra*, p. 120) had been increased to four.

Ladyship shall still preserve me some little corner in your memory, and do not think to put me off only with a box, which I can assure you will not contribute in the least to [increase] my esteem and regard for your Ladyship, [since] I have been always, and shall ever remain, Madam,

Your Ladyship's [most] obedient and [very] humble servant,

JONATH. SWIFT.

DCCC. [*Copy*.[1]]

SWIFT TO KNIGHTLEY CHETWODE

Dublin, *May* 8, 1731.

SIR,

YOUR letter[2] hath lain by me without acknowledging it much longer than I intended, or rather this is my third time of writing to you, but the two former I burned in an hour after I had finished them,[3] because they contained some passages which I apprehended one of your pique might possibly dislike, for I have heard you approve of one principle in your nature, that no man had ever offended you against whom you did not find some opportunity to make him regret it, although perhaps no offence were ever designed. This perhaps, and the other art you are pleased with, of knowing the secrets of families, which as you have told me was so wonderful that some people thought you dealt with old Nick, hath made many families so cautious of you.

And to say the truth, your whole scheme of thinking, conversing, and living, differs in every point from mine. I have utterly done with all great names and titles of Princes and Lords and Ladies and Ministers of State, because I conceive they do me not the least honour; wherein I look upon myself to be a prouder man than you, who expect that the people here should think more honourably of you

---

[1] In the Forster Collection. *Supra*, vol. ii, p. 241, n. 1.
[2] *Supra*, p. 200.
[3] One of these letters escaped, however, the flames, and will be found in Appendix VII.

THE DEAN'S CHAIR AT GOSFORD CASTLE

THE DEAN'S WALK AT GOSFORD CASTLE
From photographs by Mr. H. Allison

by putting them in mind of your high acquaintance, whereas the spirits of our Irish folks are so low and little and malicious that they seldom believe a syllable of what we say on these occasions, but score it all up to vanity, as I have known by experience, whenever by great chance I blabbed out some great name beyond one or two intimate friends; for which reason I thank God that I am not acquainted with one person of title in this whole kingdom, nor could I tell how to behave myself before persons of such sublime quality. Half a dozen middling clergymen, and one or two middling laymen make up the whole circle of my acquaintance.

That you returned from an amour without profit, I do not wonder, nor that it was more pleasurable, if the lady as I am told be sixty, unless her literal and metaphorical talents are very great; yet I think it impossible for any woman of her age, who is both wise and rich, to think of matrimony in earnest. However I easily believe what you say that women have not yet lost all their charms with you, who could find them in a Sibyl. I am sorry for what you say, that your ambition is unsatiate, because I think there are few men alive so little circumstanced to gratify it. You made one little essay in a desperate cause much to the disadvantage of your fortune, and which would have done you little good if it had succeeded; and I think you have no merit with the present folks, though some affect to believe it to your disadvantage. I cannot allow you my disciple; for you never followed any one rule I gave you. I confess the Queen's death cured all ambition in me, for which I am heartily glad, because I think it little consists either with ease or with conscience.

I cannot imagine what any people can propose by attempts against you, who are a private country gentleman, who can never expect any employment or power. I am wondering how you came acquainted with Horace or St. Ambrose, since neither Latin nor Divinity have been your studies; it seems a miracle to me. I agree with that gentleman, whoever he is, that said to answer letters was a part of good breeding, but he would agree with me, that nothing requires more caution, from the ill uses that have been often made of them, especially of letters without common business. They are a standing witness against a man, which is confirmed by a Latin saying, for words pass but letters

IV   Q

remain. You hint, I think, that you intend for England;[1] I shall not enquire into your motives. My correspondence there is but with a few old friends, and of these but one who is in employment, and he hath lately dropped me too, and he is in right; for it is said I am out of favour, at least, what I like as well, I am forgotten, for I know not anyone who thinks it worth the pains to be my enemy; and it is mere charity in those who still continue my friends, of which however not one is in power, nor will ever be during my life. I am ashamed of this long letter, and desire your pardon. I am, Sir,

Your, etc.

Addressed—To Knightley Chetwode, Esq., at Woodbrooke, near Mountmellick.

Endorsed—A very extraordinary letter designed, I suppose, to mortify me.

DCCCI. [*Copy.*[2]]

KNIGHTLEY CHETWODE TO SWIFT

[*May*, 1731.]

SIR,

UPON my return from a visit I found yours of the 8th. The principle you say I approve in my nature, that no person ever offended me against whom I did not find some opportunity to make him repent it, would be of very little signification, did not the offending parties aid and assist me. Had not Whitshed by corruption taken a servant out [of] my service into his, I had probably never suspected that servant capable of being corrupted. But as I found he designed him for a Judas to betray his master, and would give but, basely, forty pieces of silver, I thought it justifiable to give one piece more, by which I fixed Whitshed in a lodging at Pall Mall, to be cured of a dirty distemper, and had accounts every packet of his progress in the cure, and when he got abroad of his applications to preside in our Chancery, upon his brazen merit in favour

---

[1] The passage in Chetwode's letter to which Swift refers has apparently been lost.

[2] In the Forster Collection. *Supra*, vol. ii, p. 241, n. 1.

of his friend Wood's halfpence.[1] This Brodrick, the Chancellor, told me pinched Whitshed more than Scrogg's censure thrown into his coach, or even the two letters to the Right Honourable ——, and swore by God, it was the best stratagem imaginable, and that he should love me for it, as long as he lived.[2] Raymond, that uninformed lump of clay, did cruelly disoblige and offend me, which compelled me to bring upon the *tapis* Nanny Neary *cum sociis*, to come at the cause of his mad disorders, and when discovered he, to keep me silent and in humour, betrayed everybody, and all he knew, saw, heard or believed.[3] I know no family so cautious as you say, but some weak people [who are] subject to first impressions, and who, though clad in glass doublets, will be throwing of stones.

The objection of great names and titles is a threadbare pretext for abusing me. I am extremely sensible how low, little and malicious a spirit reigns amongst some folks, and am as sensible how difficult it is to live and converse with that difficult and mutable creature man; and yet I have done enough in the two great scenes of my life to convince such, who are not proof against conviction, that it is my way to act according to my reason without being driven to anything contrary to my inclination. I can easily bear to be laughed at, for what I am sure is right; besides I have reason to value myself that a person of honour would condescend to make me a subject of jest, and then I have company for my comfort, for I could tell you another

---

[1] Whitshed's ambition to preside in that court has been already noticed (*supra*, vol. iii, p. 65).

[2] The Irish chancellorship was resigned in 1725 very unwillingly by Brodrick, otherwise Lord Midleton, and sought unsuccessfully by Whitshed. The latter is compared by Swift in the sixth Drapier's Letter ("Prose Works," vi, 173) to Chief Justice Scroggs, and a censure passed by the English House of Commons upon Scroggs for conduct similar to that of Whitshed in dismissing the Grand Jury before the conclusion of their business had been printed and circulated. The letters to the Right Honourable —— are those signed with the initials N. N., to which Swift alluded in writing to Chetwode at the time of their publication (*supra*, vol. iii, p. 229).

[3] Whatever Chetwode may have discovered to Raymond's disadvantage does not appear to have interrupted the friendship between Swift and the rector of Trim (*supra*, vol. i, p. 120). In his will, which is dated 21 October, 1725, and was proved 28 May, 1726, Raymond, who was then resident in London, refers to his "very good friend Dr. Swift, Dean of St. Patrick's," and in bequeathing to him a gold ring says that he owes him "the greatest obligations."

besides, whom honour has rendered ridiculous as well as
me. Here is a riddle for you, but you have a key for
it, but as matters are circumstanced between you and
me you must take care to turn it dexterously, in a distinction of honour in the concrete, and honour in the abstract—
a distinction I could not for my blood pass over: I mean
my vanity to show you I understand a little logic, as well
as Latin and Divinity. You are merry upon my late amour,
and allow that women have not lost all their charms with
me, who could find any in a Sibyl. But if you could do
for me as Maro did by Æneas, and bring Sibylla Cumæa
to conduct me to the golden branch,[1] *non solus Cadenus, sed
eris mihi magnus Apollo.*

What essays I have made, and what to the disadvantage
of my fortune, I know better than any other man living
can. Whether I have any merit with the present folks is
not of one farthing signification to the world; though I
have heard frequently of a set of puppies, who, as you say,
affect to believe the first to my dishonour. As to my being
employed, I may answer as Lady Anne did to Gloucester
in Shakespeare's Richard the Third, it is permitted to all
men to hope.[2] I cannot help what you say that you cannot
imagine what people can propose by attempts against me,
but the present attempt is to represent me as poor that I
may the more easily be rendered ridiculous, as well knowing that the loss of an ounce of credit is the loss of a pound
of power. [As to] what you observe of great names, etc., it
has always been my opinion that *principibus placuisse viris
non ultima laus est,* and Horace, with whom my becoming
acquainted seems so great a miracle to you, says

tamen me
Cum magnis vixisse invita fatebitur usque
Invidia.[3]

---

[1]   " thick woods, and gloomy night,
Conceal the happy plant from human sight;
One bough it bears, but wondrous to behold,
The ductile rind, and leaves of radiant gold."
Dryden, " Æneid," vi, 208.

[2]   " *Glouc.* But shall I live in hope?
Anne. All men, I hope, live so."
" Richard III," ii, 199.

[3] " Sat.," 2, i, 76.

Your accounts in some of your latest letters to me, that everybody has dropped you, that you are out of favour, that you are forgotten and the like, minds me of the favourite of Augustus, who was so great a master in the art of declining envy. It is, I think, verily in Dr. Swift the merriest affectation I ever met, that you who were bred under Sir William Temple, and have been much about Court, especially [the] four last years of Queen Anne, should not know, how to behave in presence of Traulus,[1] and other sublime Irish quality. What think you of the Countess of Kerry since her trip to France?[2] As to many things which regard me, I think reason furnishes means sufficient to confound some, who refuse to believe unless they can comprehend, and that they are unwilling to do to my advantage. I meet some who love themselves too much to love a friend, and I have often thought, whether this, and some other conduct, has not been designed to take me off the expectation of friendship.

I did say, as you write, that I intend for England. I cannot guess who the Devil succeeds superannuated Manley in his intelligencer's place of writing everything into England,[3] but it has been writ that I was to be at Chester such a day, and a person came [up for me] in his coach, and writes me a letter filled with kind severity for having disappointed him in what I never promised. I received a letter along with yours from Dulman, the parson,[4] intended I suppose more to disturb than please me, wherein he says he received a letter about me wherein his correspondent tells him that I see, and feel, and hear, imagine, suspect, penetrate, and foresee everything so well that a man would be tempted to believe that every one of my passions was guided by a sort of magic, peculiar to me. I think I have read these very words, or something very like them, somewhere, which this coxcomb would apply to me, but cannot for my blood, recollect where. He adds that he heard me terribly fallen

---

[1] *I.e.*, Lord Allen (*supra*, p. 111, n. 2).

[2] From a letter written two years later to Swift by his old friend Lady Kerry (*supra*, vol. ii, p. 299, n. 5), it would appear that she was in ill health and apprehensive of losing her sight.

[3] Stella's friend Isaac Manley, the postmaster, was still living in Dublin. He died there in 1735.

[4] Possibly the allusion is to his brother-in-law Stopford.

upon, and attacked about so many folks, who had offended
me, dying in so short a time. I am,

Your humble servant,

K. C.

DCCCII. [*Original.*[1]]

SWIFT TO THE REV. PHILIP CHAMBERLAIN

Deanery House, *May* 20, 1731.

SIR,[2]

ONE of the Grattans told me to-day, that you were so
kind to object against some passages in the monument
intended over Duke Schomberg.[3] The first was *ut haeredes
Ducis.* I varied that expression often, but made it equivocal
whether the heirs or the Chapter desired such a monument
might be made. I have changed the word *erigi* for *erigendum,* as Mr. Grattan said you desired. *Hunc ipsi lapidem,* that is to avoid being equivocal, *ipsi* meaning the
Chapter.[4] *Quantilla in cellula,*[5] these diminutives I was
wrong advised in, because it was rightly observed by

---

[1] In the possession of Mr. Thomas P. Le Fanu, of Abingdon, Bray,
co. Wicklow. The letter was contributed in the early part of the last
century by his uncle, J. Sheridan Le Fanu, the well-known novelist,
to the pages of the " Dublin University Magazine" (vol. xii, p. 269).

[2] The recipient of this letter, who was a member of Swift's Chapter,
has been frequently mentioned in the correspondence between Swift
and Archdeacon Walls (*supra,* vol. ii, p. 279, *et seq.*). His only
daughter married Thomas Sheridan the younger, and was the mother
of Richard Brinsley Sheridan. She has left some reputation as a
dramatist and novelist.

[3] The following is the inscription which was eventually engraved
upon the stone: " Hic infra situm est corpus Frederici, Ducis de
Schomberg, ad Bubindam occisi, A.D. 1690. Decanus et Capitulum
maximopere etiam atque etiam petierunt, ut hæredes Ducis monu-
mentum in memoriam Parentis erigendum curarent: sed postquam
per epistolas, per amicos, diu ac sæpe orando nil profecere, hunc
demum lapidem statuerunt, saltem ut scias, hospes, ubinam terrarum
Schombergenses cineres delitescunt. Plus potuit fama virtutis apud
alienos quam sanguinis proximitas apud suos. A.D. 1731."

[4] As will be seen " hunc demum lapidem " was substituted.

[5] The words in the concluding lines originally stood: " Saltem ut
sciat viator indignabundus, quantilla in cellula tanti ductoris cineres
delitescunt." According to his own account Delany had " the felicity"
to prevail upon Swift to alter this sentence (" Observations," p. 186).

another friend, that the cell was good enough,—it was in Lord Cork's tomb,—but the fault was that the ashes lay unhonoured and forgotten, and therefore I have changed that passage in the copy on the other side.

I forgot to mention that some of the Chapter, going with me into the church to-day, disliked the place intended for the monument, which was a space of white wall between the bottom of the east window and the top of the altar-piece, and, therefore, another place was resolved on, which is over the arched door which carries you the shortest way from the Chapter House to the altar, and is three yards distant westward from Lord Cork's tomb, therefore, instead of *Hic infra situm est*, I begin, *Sub altari situm est*.[1]

This trouble given you is a just punishment for your skill in criticism. It is dangerous writing on marble, where one cannot make errata, or mend in a second edition. I showed to many persons what I first writ, and was printed; but except one friend, no other would find any fault. I am therefore much obliged to you, and desire by your skill to save me from the reproach of blunders.[2] I send you the first copy as it was printed, and the second as I altered some parts, and the third at the back of this, where I altered more. I intreat your judgement and correction, for I shall have all the scandal upon any slip. If you please to send me your opinion to-morrow, I shall be much obliged to you. I am, with true esteem, Sir,

Your most obedient, humble servant,

JONATH. [SWIFT].

Addressed—To the Reverend Mr. Chamberlain, at Grange-gorman.[3]

---

[1] Lord Cork's vault was under the communion table, and his monument was at first only transferred from the east to the south wall of the sacrarium (*supra*, p. 82, n. 3). As the distance from the vault was so inconsiderable, it was evidently not considered necessary to alter the original wording of the inscription for the Schomberg monument. In the last century it was placed in the north choir aisle.

[2] Swift's opinion of Chamberlain, who was a scholar and graduate of Dublin University, had undergone a great change since his correspondence about him with Walls (*supra*, vol. ii, p. 322).

[3] Grangegorman is situated in the northern part of Dublin near the terminus of the Midland Great Western Railway.

DCCCIII. [*Original.*[1]]

LADY ELIZABETH GERMAIN TO SWIFT

June 5, 1731.

I FANCY you have comforted yourself this long time with the hopes of hearing no more from me; but you may return your thanks to a downright fit of the gout in my foot, and as painful a rheumatism that followed immediately after in my arm, that bound me to my good behaviour. So you may perceive I should make but a sad nurse to Mr. Pope, who find the effects of age and a crazy carcass already. However, if it is true what I am informed, that you are coming here soon, I expect you should bring us together; and if he will bear me with patience, I shall hear him with pleasure.

I do not know what number of chaplains the Duke of Dorset intends to carry over; but, as yet, I have heard of but one that he has sent, and he as worthy, honest, sensible [a] man, as any I know, Mr. Brandreth, who, I believe, was recommended to your acquaintance.[2] I have not been in a way of seeing Mrs. Barber this great while; but I hear, and I hope it is so, that she goes on in her subscription very well; nor has the lady she so much feared done her any harm, if she endeavoured it, which is more than I know that she did.[3] I believe you will find by my writing, that it is not quite easy to me, so I will neither tease you, nor trouble myself longer, who am most sincerely,

Your faithful humble servant,

E. GERMAIN.

Addressed—To the Revd. Dr. Swift, Dean of St. Patrick's, Dublin.

---

[1] In the British Museum. See Preface.

[2] *Supra,* p. 195.

[3] The allusion is possibly to Mrs. Clayton, who appears about that time to have been accused of obstructing Mrs. Barber in her canvass for subscribers (*infra,* p. 243, n. 1).

DCCCIV. [*Elwin*.[1]]

SWIFT TO JOHN GAY AND THE DUCHESS OF QUEENSBERRY

Dublin, *June* 29, 1731.

To Gay

DEAR FRIEND,

EVER since I received your letter,[2] I have been upon a balance about going to England, and landing at Bristol, to pass a month at Amesbury, as the Duchess has given me leave. But many difficulties have interfered. First, I thought I had done with my lawsuit, and so did all my lawyers, but my adversary, after being in appearance a Protestant these twenty years, has declared he was always a Papist, and consequently by the law here cannot buy, nor, I think, sell; so that I am at sea again, for almost all I am worth. But I have still a worse evil; for the giddiness I was subject to, instead of coming seldom and violently, now constantly attends me more or less, though in a more peaceable manner, yet such as will not qualify me to live among the young and healthy; and the Duchess, in all her youth, spirit, and grandeur, will make a very ill nurse, and her women not much better. Valetudinarians must live where they can command and scold. I must have horses to ride, I must go to bed and rise when I please, and live where all mortals are subservient to me. I must talk nonsense when I please, and all who are present must commend it. I must ride thrice a week, and walk three or four miles besides every day.

I always told you Mrs. Howard was good for nothing but to be a rank courtier. I care not whether she ever writes me or no. She has cheated us all; and may go hang herself, and so may her mistress, and you may tell this to the Duchess, and I hate to see you so charitable, and such a cully, and yet I love you for it, because I am one myself. A p— on her for hindering me from going to France, where I might have recovered my health, and she did it in a most treacherous manner, when I laid it on her honour. You are the silliest lover in Christendom. If you like Mrs.

---

[1] By permission of Mr. John Murray. *Supra*, vol. iii, p. 148, n. 1.
[2] *Supra*, p. 220.

Drelincourt, why do you not command her to take you? If she does not, she is not worth pursuing. You do her too much honour; she has neither sense nor taste if she dares to refuse you, though she had ten thousand pounds. I do not remember to have told you of thanks that you have not given, nor do I understand your meaning, and I am sure I had never the least thoughts of any myself. If I am your friend, it is for my own reputation, and from a principle of self-love; and I do sometimes reproach you for not honouring me in letting the world know we are friends.

I see very well how matters go with the Duchess in regard to me. I heard her say, " Prithee Mr. Gay, fill your letter to the Dean, that there may be no room for me; the frolic is gone far enough, I have writ thrice, I will do no more. If the man has a mind to come let him come. What a clutter is here! Positively I will not write a syllable more. The jest is grown stale." She is an ungrateful Duchess, considering how many adorers I have procured her here, over and above the thousands she had before. I cannot allow you rich enough till you are worth seven thousand pounds, which will bring you three hundred pounds per annum, and this will maintain you, with the perquisite of sponging while you are young, and when you are old will afford you a pint of port at night, two servants and an old maid, a little garden, and pen and ink—provided you live in the country. You never mentioned whether you were seriously a manager for my Lord Duke in his estate, which the Doctor and Mr. Pope absolutely affirm. And pray what will you do with my two hundred pounds? Will it yield nothing in the funds? And what are you doing towards increasing your fame and your fortune? Have you no scheme either in verse or prose? The Duchess should keep you at hard meat, and by that means force you to write, and so I have done with you.

To the Duchess

MADAM,

SINCE I began to grow old, I have found all ladies become inconstant, without any reproach from their consciences. If I wait on you, I declare that one of your women, whichever it is that has designs upon a chaplain, must be my nurse, if I happen to be sick or peevish at your house, and in that case you must suspend your domineering claim till I recover. Your omitting the usual appendix to Mr. Gay's letters has done me infinite mischief here; for while you continued them, you would wonder how civil the ladies here were to me, and how much they have altered since. I dare not confess that I have descended so low as to write to your Grace, after the abominable neglect you have been guilty of; for, if they but suspected it, I should lose them all. One of them, who had an inkling of the matter—your Grace will hardly believe it—refused to beg my pardon upon her knees, for once neglecting to make my rice-milk. Pray, consider this, and do your duty, or dread the consequence. I promise you shall have your will six minutes in every hour at Amesbury, and seven in London, while I am in health, but if I happen to be sick I must govern to a second. Yet, properly speaking, there is no man alive with so much truth and respect,

Your Grace's most obedient and devoted servant,
THE DEAN.

To Gay

PRAY tell her Grace that Mr. Ford, whose affairs keep him here against his heart,[1] toasts her every day, which is a great matter, for he has thrown off all except her Grace and Harietta Pitt.[2]

DCCCV. [*Copy.*[3]]

SWIFT TO LORD BATHURST

[Dublin, *July* 17, 1731.]

I MAKE your Lordship my humblest acknowledgement for your letter,[4] and the most excellent advice it contains, which last I wish had been given to me when I had first the honour to see you, and had life enough before me.

As to my two hundred pounds I know not by what authority your Lordship paid it to Mr. Gay. I have been

---

[1] *Supra*, p. 176.
[2] Lord Chatham's sister, who married an ancestor of the Earl of Kilmorey.
[3] In the Forster Collection. [4] *Supra*, p. 213.

at law these ten years and still continue so, and have learnt enough to know that I expect my money from you, and the constant interest too, besides loss and damage at *valorem centum liberum* sterling. The aggravation is that you know Mr. Gay very well, for his first offer to me, after he received the money, was to throw off the interest at hazard with the government, till I entreated he would employ it in paying a debt.

As to the regimen you prescribe, I must complain to your Lordship of the hard circumstances I lie under. I have an old Presbyterian Tory housekeeper, whom the neighbourhood call Sir Robert Walpole.[1] She will not suffer a female in the house who is younger than herself, under the pretence that if it were otherwise my men and the maids together would multiply my family too much. Then this same Sir Robert hath half a dozen parsons, and two or three squires who corrupt her to let them in. She hath made one of the squires my head butler, and one of the parsons my under butler; and these are all preaching how absolutely necessary wine and company are to my health. Sir Robert delivers them the keys, and in recompense they send her a glass out of every bottle.[2] I have sent my men one after another twenty times to buy me a wife in the market; but she privately orders them to come back with flams and lying stories that there is not one to be sold; and when I complain of these hardships to these very knaves that drink up my wine, they are all unanimously against me.

One thing I take ill of your Lordship, that you did not begin your prescription with me but with Dr. Delany. I say this because I am confident that the two or three sermons he lately preached against black pudding were owing to some directions from ——. He will not eat a chicken except its throat hath been cut: he says the blood of other animals inflames our own and disposeth us to

---

[1] *I.e.*, Mrs. Brent (*supra*, p. 30, n. 1).

[2] Mrs. Pilkington relates that one Sunday soon after the Belcamp visit (*supra*, p. 194, n. 2) she was installed as mistress of the cellar, and sent to draw some precious ale with a particular order to allow the candle to drop into the tankard and to leave the spigot loose; but that frail lady was discovered entertaining Delany and Sheridan on the sly, and notwithstanding that "with all the moving eloquence of a female orator" she pleaded, "the parsons seduced me and I did drink," she was deposed and Nim Rochfort appointed in her room.

cruelty. This is in your own doctrine to me whom you call an inflamer.[1]

I beg, my Lord, you will leave me a little wine, because time hath already reformed me in poetry; and I can bring lawful witnesses that I was lately searching three days for a rhyme in vain, that I have not written a libel these six months, and that I kept this summer at home rather than [to] go to Sir A. Acheson's, and write lampoons on him and his lady, as to my shame I confess I did for two seasons together,[2] of which some false brother hath maliciously informed you.

I have gotten into your direction about milk, only with the addition of a little rice, sugar, and nutmeg, in which I hope you will be so good as to indulge me. I approve your way of getting preferment; but for some reasons I am a little in haste, and humbly propose that I may be allowed to pay the expense annually out of the premises, giving my bond and judgement and a mortgage if it be required. There is another advantage in this expedient, that of being impatient to go out of debt. I shall grow covetous and busy, have neither time to write verses or pamphlets, nor heart to allow myself any better drink than small beer.

If you had read the notes upon that passage, perhaps, in St. Austin's, you would have found that *vinum daemonum* is only to be understood damn wine such as is drunk in hedge taverns at London. If your *double entente* quibble in French be the same that Friar Bacon prescribed to the Pope, I believe I and the Pope would make the same use of it that David did: "but the King knew her not"; and so much for your *friponnerie*.... Besides I consult my own reputation, being resolved [to avoid the] censure of the world; for what would people say if a [person of my] age and gravity would put on seriousness. But I am not [yet entirely] determined in the article of cunning, because every tradesman [throughout this] kingdom is a rogue to a man, but of the squires not above [one or two

---

[1] Delany maintained "that we are forbidden to eat blood, and that Θῦσον in St. Peter's vision was a command to sacrifice, *i.e.*, to drain off the blood." See an interesting examination of Delany's published works by the Rev. W. G. Carroll in his " Succession of Clergy in the Parish of St. Bride, Dublin," p. 47.

[2] Swift has either purposely or by a slip inserted two instead of three.

in a] hundred, allowing a quantum of ignorance and folly, [that are not knaves,] beggars or fools, and sometimes all three, so that I am well [surrounded].

I saw Lord Orrery to-day;[1] he is come over on the knavery of a [steward or agent]. May all Irish absentees have the same fate! He dines with me [here, I hope, on] Tuesday next. He gives a very indifferent account of [affairs also on] your side. You stick together like sand and cannot agree [in any single] *point de vue*. God be praised, for the condition you are in [is justly brought] upon you by your tyranny and oppression to this kingdom, [which some have the joy to] leave and I the misery, thank my quondam friends, of [lingering till] death in, and God bless some others that shall be [nameless, which I] say with the meaning of a beggar when you call [him friend and] refuse him a penny.

I desire to present my [respectful compliments] to my Lady Bathurst, and God bless you with [your olive branches which would] better become a parson than a peer. I always employ you, my correspondent, to distribute my services occasionally, for instance to Lord Peterborough, Lord Bolingbroke, Lord Oxford, Lord Masham, Mr. Pulteney, Mr. Pope, the Doctor, etc., etc. Are you acquainted with our old brother Lord Lansdown? He hath two daughters here,[2] and I take it ill he did not order them to be acquainted with me. Tell your neighbour Lord Burlington that if he does not repair his ancestor's monument, I will use him worse than I have done Duke Schomberg's granddaughter. I am, with the truest respect,

Your Lordship's most, etc.

[1] The reference is to the father of Swift's biographer, whose arrest in connection with Layer's plot has been noticed (*supra*, vol. iii, p. 140). Although in failing health he had insisted upon coming to Ireland. He stayed there only a week or two, and died within a month of his return to England ("Orrery Papers," i, 88-95).

[2] The marriage of Lord Lansdown's daughter to young Graham, Stopford's pupil (*supra*, vol. iii, p. 238), had taken place before then.

DCCCVI. [*Original.*[1]]

THE DUCHESS OF QUEENSBERRY AND JOHN GAY
TO SWIFT

July 18, 1731.

THE DUCHESS

YOU are my dear friend, I am sure, for you are hard to be found. That you are so, is certainly owing to some evil genius; for, if you say true, this is the very properest place you can repair to.[2] There is not a head upon any of our shoulders that is not at some times worse than yours can possibly be at the worst; and not one to compare with yours when at best, except your friends are your sworn liars; so in one respect, at least, you will find things just as they could be wished. It is farther necessary to assure you, that the Duchess is neither young or healthy. She lives in all the spirits that she can; and with as little grandeur as she can possibly. She too, as well as you, can scold, and command; but she can be silent, and obey, if she pleases; and then for a good nurse, it is out of dispute, that she must prove an excellent one, who has been so experienced in the infirmities of others, and of her own. As for talking nonsense, provided you do it on purpose, she has no objection. There is some sense in nonsense, when it does not come by chance. In short, I am very sure that she has set her heart upon seeing you at this place. Here are women enough to attend you, if you should happen not to approve of her. She has not one fine lady belonging to her, or her house. She is impatient to be governed, and is cheerfully determined that you shall quietly enjoy your own will and pleasure as long as ever you please.

GAY

You shall ride, you shall walk, and she will be glad to follow your example, and this will be doing good at the same time to her and yourself. I had not heard from you so long that I was in fears about you, and in the utmost

---

[1] In the British Museum. See Preface.
[2] *Supra*, p. 233.

impatience for a letter. I had flattered myself your law-suit was at an end, and that your own money was in your own pocket; and about a month ago I was every day ex-pecting a summons to Bristol. Your money is either getting or losing something, for I have placed it in the funds; for I am grown so much a man of business, that is to say, so covetous, that I cannot bear to let a sum of money lie idle. Your friend Mrs. Howard is now Countess of Suffolk.[1] I am still so much a dupe, that I think you mistake her. Come to Amesbury, and you and I will dispute this mat-ter; and the Duchess shall be judge. But I fancy you will object against her; for I will be so fair to you as to own, that I think she is of my side; but, in short, you shall choose any impartial referee you please. I have heard from her; Mr. Pope hath seen her; I beg you would suspend your judgement till we talk over this affair together; for, I fancy, by your letter, you have neither heard from her, or seen her; so that you cannot at present be as good a judge as we are. I will be a dupe for you at any time: there-fore I beg it of you, that you would let me be a dupe in quiet.

As you have had several attacks of the giddiness you at present complain of, and that it hath formerly left you, I will hope that at this instant you are perfectly well; though my fears were so very great, before I received your letter, that I may probably flatter myself, and think you better than you are. As to my being a manager for the Duke, you have been misinformed. Upon the discharge of an unjust steward, he took the administration into his own hands. I own I was called in to his assistance, when the state of affairs was in the greatest confusion. Like an ancient Roman, I came, put my helping hand to set affairs right, and as soon as it was done, I am retired again as a private man.

THE DUCHESS

What you imagined you heard her say, was a good deal in her style. It was a thousand to one she had said so; but

---

[1] Her husband had succeeded his brother on 22 June as ninth Earl of Suffolk. Writing soon afterwards Peter Wentworth says (" Went-worth Papers," p. 465), " I hear she is so well pleased that she hears better already."

I must do her the justice to say, that she did not, either in thought or word. I am sure she wants to be better acquainted with you; for which she has found out ten thousand reasons, that we will tell you, if you will come.

GAY

By your letter, I cannot guess whether we are like to see you or no. Why might not the Amesbury Downs make you better?

THE DUCHESS

DEAR SIR,

Mr. Gay tells me, I must write upon his line for fear of taking up too much room. It was his fault that I omitted my duty in his last letter, for he never told me one word of writing to you, till he had sent away his letter. However, as a mark of my great humility, I shall be ready and glad to ask your pardon upon my knees, as soon as ever you come, though not in fault. I own this is a little mean-spirited, which I hope will not make a bad impression, considering you are the occasion. I submit to all your conditions; so pray, come, for, I have not only promised myself, but Mr. Gay also, the satisfaction to hear you talk as much nonsense as you can possibly utter.

GAY

You will read in the Gazette of a friend of yours, who hath lately had the dignity of being disgraced; for he, and everybody except five or six, look upon it in the same light.[1] I know, were you here, you would congratulate him upon it. I paid the twelve pounds to Mrs. Lancelot, for the uses you directed. I have no scheme at present, either to raise my fame or fortune. I daily reproach myself for my idleness. You know one cannot write when one will. I think and I reject. One day or other, perhaps, I may think on something that may engage me to write. You

---

[1] "Sir Robert wearied by Will Pulteney's teasings,
Who interrupted him in all his leasings,
Resolved that Will and he should meet no more,
Full in his face Bob shuts the Council door."

" Poetical Works," ii, 250.

and I are alike in one particular—I wish to be so in many—
I mean, that we hate to write upon other folks' hints. I love
to have my own scheme, and to treat it in my own way.
This, perhaps, may be taking too much upon myself, and
I may make a bad choice; but I can always enter into a
scheme of my own with more ease and pleasure, than into
that of other bodies. I long to see you; I long to hear
from you; I wish you health; I wish you happiness; and
I should be very happy myself to be witness that you [en-
joyed my wishes].

Addressed—To the Reverend Dr. Swift, Dean of St.
Patrick's, in Dublin, Ireland. By way of London.

DCCCVII. [*Copy.*[1]]

SWIFT TO ALEXANDER POPE

July 20, 1731.

DEAR SIR,
I WRIT you a long letter not many days ago, which,
therefore, did not arrive until after your last that I received
yesterday, with the enclosed from me to the Queen.[2] You
hinted something of this in a former letter. I will tell you
sincerely how the affair stands. I never was at Mrs. Barber's house in my life, except once that I chanced to pass
by her shop, was desired to walk in, and went no farther,
nor stayed three minutes. Dr. Delany has been long her
protector; and he, being many years my acquaintance, desired my good offices for her, and brought her several
times to the Deanery. I knew she was poetically given,

---

[1] In the Forster Collection, No. 549.

[2] In this letter, the genesis of which has given rise to much controversy, the writer opens with the proposition that the misfortunes of
provinces are attributable in a great measure to their being "far removed from the Prince's eye," says that his assertion is illustrated in
the case of Ireland, whose inhabitants find great difficulty in approaching her Majesty even so far as "to enjoy the relief of complaint," and
cites as an instance the failure of many attempts to introduce to her
Majesty's notice Mrs. Barber, "the best female poet of this or perhaps
of any age." The signature purports to be that of Swift, but the letter,
which is printed in Appendix VIII, from the original in the Forster
Collection, is written in a large female hand.

and, for a woman, had a sort of genius that way. She appeared very modest and pious, and I believe was sincere, and wholly turned to poetry. I did conceive her journey to England was on the score of her trade, being a woollen-draper, until Dr. Delany said, she had a design of printing her poems by subscription, and desired I would befriend her, which I did, chiefly by your means, the Doctor still urging me on, upon whose request I writ to her two or three times, because she thought that my countenancing her might be of use. Lord Carteret very much befriended her, and she seems to have made her way not ill.

As for those three letters you mention, supposed all to be written by me to the Queen, on Mrs. Barber's account, especially the letter which bears my name,[1] I can only say, that the apprehensions one may be apt to have of a friend's doing a foolish thing, is an effect of kindness; and God knows who is free from playing the fool some time or other, but in such a degree as to write to the Queen, who has used me ill without any cause, and to write in such a manner as the letter you sent me, and in such a style, and to have so much zeal for one almost a stranger, and to make such a description of a woman as to prefer her before all mankind, and to instance it as one of the greatest grievances of Ireland, that her Majesty has not encouraged Mrs. Barber, a woollen-draper's wife, declined in the world because she has a knack at versifying, was to suppose, or fear, a folly so transcendent, that no man could be guilty of, who was not fit for Bedlam.

You know the letter you sent enclosed is not my hand; and why I should disguise, and yet sign my name, should seem unaccountable, especially when I am taught, and have reason to believe, that I am under the Queen's displeasure on many accounts, and one very late, for having fixed up a stone over the burying-place of the Duke of Schomberg, in my Cathedral, where, however, I was assured by a worthy person, who solicited that affair last summer with some relations of the Duke, that her Majesty, on hearing the matter, said they ought to erect a monument. Yet I am told assuredly, that the King not long ago, on

---

[1] The second letter was "in abuse" of Queen Caroline's friend, Mrs. Clayton, probably for concealing Mrs. Barber's merits from her Majesty, and was unsigned (Mrs. Thomson's "Memoirs of Viscountess Sundon," ii, 71). Of the third letter nothing is known.

the representation and complaint of the Prussian envoy with a hard name, who has married a grand-daughter of the Duke,[1] said publicly in the drawing-room, that I had put up that stone out of malice, to raise a quarrel between his Majesty and the King of Prussia. This perhaps may be false, because it is absurd: for I thought it was a Whiggish action to honour Duke Schomberg, who was so instrumental in the Revolution, and was stadtholder of Prussia, and otherwise in the service of that electorate, which is now a kingdom.

You will observe the letter sent me concluded, "Your Majesty's loyal subject," which is absolutely absurd, for we are only subjects to the King, and so is her Majesty herself. I have had the happiness to be known to you above twenty years; and I appeal, whether you have known me to exceed the common indiscretions of mankind; or that, when I conceived myself to have been so very ill used by her Majesty, whom I never attended but on her own commands, I should turn solicitor to her for Mrs. Barber? If the Queen had not an inclination to think ill of me, she knows me too well to believe in her own heart that I should be such a coxcomb. I am pushed on by that unjust suspicion to give up so much of my discretion, as to write next post to my Lady Suffolk on this occasion, and to desire she will show what I write to the Queen, although I have as much reason to complain of her, as of her Majesty, upon the score of her pride and negligence, which make her fitter to be an Irish lady than an English one. You told me, she complained that I did not write to her; when I did, upon your advice, and a letter that required an answer,[2] she wanted the civility to acquit herself.

I shall not be less in the favour of God, or the esteem of my friends, for either of their Majesties' hard thoughts, which they only take up from misrepresentations. The first time I saw the Queen, I took occasion, upon the subject of Mr. Gay, to complain of that very treatment which innocent persons often receive from Princes and great Ministers, that they too easily receive bad impressions, and although they are demonstrably convinced that those impressions had no grounds, yet they will never shake them

[1] Lady Holderness's sister married Christoph Martin von Degenfeld.
[2] *Supra*, p. 181.

off. This I said upon Sir Robert Walpole's treatment of
Mr. Gay about a libel; and the Queen fell entirely in with
me, yet now falls into the same error. . . .[1]

Endorsed by Swift—Letter to Mr. Pope about my pretended letter to the Queen.[2]

DCCCVIII. [*Scott.*[3]]

SWIFT TO THOMAS TICKELL

I have marked the figures 1, 2, 3, in your original:

1. For "when," I would advise "where."
2. I do not well understand this line.
3. I see what "this" and "that" refer to. But in the line
   just before, there are two words, "present" and "past,"
   and in the next line above "viscus," and "leach," which
   will make some difficulty to a common reader.

Deanery House, *July* 20, 1731.

SIR,
AFTER frequent reading with as much care as I could, I
found but the three remarks above mentioned that I could
possibly make. Only I would sink nine of the "ten thousand
fathom," and call it a thousand. I desire you will please to
finish it.[4] I have been riding out to-day, as well as yesterday, for my health, but find myself much disordered. If I
grow better, I will wait on you to-morrow; if not, I will send
the paper by a safe hand. I am, Sir,

Your, etc.

[1] The end of the paper is torn, leaving only the following words:
" As the letter . . . of accidents and out of perfect commiseration."
[2] The endorsement disposes of the comment of Dr. Johnson, who
believed that Swift himself wrote the letter to the Queen (*op. cit.*, xi,
28): " When he was charged with this letter, he laid hold of the inaccuracies, and urged the improbability of the accusation, but never
denied it; he shuffles between cowardice and veracity, and talks big
when he says nothing."
[3] *Supra*, vol. iii, p. 198, n. 1.
[4] The piece does not appear among Tickell's published poems.

DCCCIX. [*Original.*[1]]

SWIFT TO THE COUNTESS OF SUFFOLK

Dublin, *July* 27, 1731.

MADAM,

I GIVE you joy of your new title,[2] and of the consequences it may have, or hath had, on your rising at Court, whereof I know nothing but by common fame; for, you remember how I prophesied of your behaviour, when you should come to be a great lady, at the time I drew your Character, and hope you have kept it. I writ to you some time ago, by the advice of Mr. Pope: I writ to you civilly, but you did not answer my letter, although you were not then a Countess, and if you were, your neglect was so much the worse; for your title hath not increased your value with me, and your conduct must be very good, if it will not lessen you. Neither should you have heard from me now, if it were not on a particular occasion. I find, from several instances, that I am under the Queen's displeasure, and as it is usual among Princes, without any manner of reason. I am told, there were three letters sent to her Majesty in relation to one Mrs. Barber, who is now in London, and soliciting for a subscription to her poems. It seems, the Queen thinks that these letters were written by me, and I scorn to defend myself even to her Majesty, grounding my scorn upon the opinion I had of her justice, her taste, and good sense, especially when the last of those letters, whereof I have just received the original from Mr. Pope, was signed with my name, and why I should disguise my hand, which you know very well, and yet write my name, is both ridiculous and unaccountable.[3]

---

[1] British Museum, Addit. MSS., 22625, f. 22. There is also a copy in the Forster Collection (No. 550) endorsed by Swift: "Copy of a letter to the Countess of Suffolk about the counterfeit letters from me to the Queen."

[2] *Supra*, p. 240, n. 1.

[3] Various suggestions have been made as to the source of these letters. Some writers, while not prepared to go so far as Dr. Johnson (*supra*, p. 245, n. 2), have expressed the opinion that Swift prompted their composition, others have held that Mrs. Barber was herself the author, but the weight of authority has attributed them to a third person. In regard to the letter purporting to be signed by Swift,

Last post, I wrote my whole sentiments on the matter to
Mr. Pope, who tells me, that you and he vindicated me on
all the three letters, which, indeed, was but bare justice in
you both, for he is my old friend, and you are in my debt
on account of the esteem I had for you. I desire you would
ask the Queen, whether, since the time I had the honour
to be known to her, I ever did one single action, or said
one single word, to disoblige her. I never asked her for
anything, and you well know, that when I had an intention
to go to France, about the time that the late King died, I
desired your opinion, not as you were a courtier, whether I
should go or no, and that you absolutely forbid me, as a
thing that would look disaffected, and for other reasons,
wherein I confess I was your dupe as well as somebody's
else, and, for want of that journey, I fell sick, and was
forced to return hither to my unenvied home. I hear the
Queen has blamed me for putting a stone, with a Latin
inscription, over the Duke of Schomberg's burying-place in
my Cathedral, and that the King said publicly, I had done
it in malice, to create a quarrel between him and the
King of Prussia. But the public prints, as well as the thing
itself, will vindicate me, and the hand the Duke had in the
Revolution made him deserve the best monument, neither
could the King of Prussia justly take it ill, who must have
heard that the Duke was in the service of Prussia, and
stadtholder of it, as I have seen in his titles. The first time
I saw the Queen, I talked to her largely upon the conduct
of Princes and great Ministers—it was on a particular occasion—that when they receive an ill account of any person,
although they afterward have the greatest demonstration
of the falsehood, yet, will they never be reconciled, and

Delany, in writing to Mrs. Clayton, absolves Mrs. Barber from all
responsibility, but in regard to the one reflecting on Mrs. Clayton, he
is ambiguous, and relies on her magnanimity in still seeking her good
offices for his *protégée*. He says: "She (Mrs. Barber) hath wrote, it
is said, two letters to the Queen, one in abuse of you without a name,
and another in praise of herself with the name of Dr. Swift; by the
last she hath to my knowledge entirely lost his friendship, and by the
former all hope of yours. As to Dr. Swift I shall content myself to tell
you I know her innocent, but as to you I shall not attempt to acquit
her, let the imputation rest upon her with all its weight." By Deane
Swift the remarkable theory is enunciated that Delany wrote "the
forged letter" (see Mrs. Thomson's "Memoirs of Viscountess Sundon,"
pp. 71, 75).

although the Queen fell in with me upon the hardship of such a proceeding, yet now she treats me directly in the same manner. I have faults enough, but never was guilty of any either to her Majesty or to you, and as little to the King, whom I never saw, but when I had the honour to kiss his hand. I am sensible that I owe a great deal of this usage to Sir Robert Walpole; whom yet I never offended, although he was pleased to quarrel with me very unjustly, for which I showed not the least resentment, whatever I might have in my heart, nor was ever a partaker with those who have been battling with him for some years past.[1]

I am contented that the Queen should see this letter, and would please to consider how severe a censure it is to believe I should write thrice to her, only to find fault with her Ministry, and recommend Mrs. Barber, whom I never knew until she was recommended to me by a worthy friend to help her to subscribers, which, by her writings, I thought she deserved. Her Majesty gave me leave, and even commanded me, above five years ago, if I lived until she was Queen, to write to her on behalf of Ireland, for the miseries of which kingdom she appeared then to be much concerned. I desired the friend[2] who introduced me to be a witness of her Majesty's promise. Yet that liberty of writing to her I never took, although I had too many occasions; and is it not wonderful, that I should be suspected of writing to her in such a style, in a counterfeit hand, and my name subscribed, upon a perfect trifle, at the same time that I well

---

[1] If it be the case, as Mr. Temple Scott believes (" Prose Works," vii, 392), that Swift was the author of the " Answer of the Right Hon. William Pulteney, Esq., to the Right Hon. Sir Robert Walpole" this statement cannot be considered a candid one. The authority for including the Answer amongst Swift's works, that of Deane Swift, is however far from an infallible one, and the composition, although resembling Swift's in its power, lacks the lighter touches which he introduced into controversy of the kind. Besides, as the Correspondence has shown, at the time the Answer was written, 15 October, 1730, Swift was either in the north of Ireland or had only just returned to Dublin, and *vive la bagatelle* was his ruling passion at the moment. The fragments entitled a " Proposal for Virtue " and an " Account of the Court and Empire of Japan " (*ibid.*, pp. 376, 382) indicate certainly an intention on Swift's part to give the Opposition literary assistance after the death of George I, but the former is evidently the heads for a pamphlet which Swift contemplated but never wrote, and the latter breaks off before its point becomes even apparent.

[2] *I.e.*, Arbuthnot (*supra*, vol. iii, p. 303).

knew myself to be very much out of her Majesty's good graces? I am, perhaps, not so very much awed with majesty as others; having known Courts more or less from my early youth, and I have more than once told the Queen that I did not regard her station half so much, as the good under-standing I heard and found to be in her. I am a good Whig, by thinking it sufficient to be a good subject, with little personal esteem for Princes, further than as their virtues deserve; and upon that score, had a most particular respect for the Queen, your mistress. One who asks nothing may talk with freedom, and that is my case. I have not said half that was in my heart, but I will have done; and remembering that you are a Countess, will borrow so much ceremony as to remain, with great respect, Madam,

Your Ladyship's most obedient and most humble servant,
JONATH. SWIFT.

Addressed—To the Right Honourable the Countess of Suffolk at Hampton Court, Middlesex, *via* London.

DCCCX. [*Original.*[1]]

VISCOUNT BOLINGBROKE TO SWIFT

August 2, 1731.

I AM indebted to you, my reverend Dean, for a letter of a very old date;[2] the expectation of seeing you from week to week, which our friend Gay made me entertain, hindered me from writing to you a good while, and I have since deferred it by waiting an opportunity of sending my letter by a safe hand. That opportunity presents itself at last, and Mr. Echlin[3] will put this letter into your hands. You will hear from him, and from others, of the general state of things in this country, into which I returned, and where I am confined for my sins. If I entertained the notion, which by the way I believe to be much older than Popery, or even than Christianity, of making up an account with Heaven, and demanding the balance in bliss, or paying it by good

[1] In the British Museum. See Preface.
[2] A reply probably to Bolingbroke's letter in March (*supra*, p. 207).
[3] Possibly the Rev. John Echlin, who has been already mentioned (*supra*, vol. iii, p. 248).

works and sufferings of my own, and by the merits and sufferings of others, I should imagine that I had expiated all the faults of my life, one way or other, since my return into England. One of the circumstances of my situation, which has afflicted me most and which afflicts me still so, is the absolute inutility I am of to those whom I should be the best pleased to serve. Success in serving my friends would make me amends for the want of it in disserving my enemies. It is intolerable to want it in both, and yet both go together generally.

I have had two or three projects on foot for making such an establishment here as might tempt you to quit Ireland. One of them would have succeeded, and would have been agreeable in every respect, if engagements to my lady's¹ kinsman, who did not, I suppose, deserve to be your clerk, had not prevented it. Another of them cannot take place, without the consent of those, who would rather have you a dean in Ireland, than a parish priest in England, and who are glad to keep you, where your sincere friend, my late Lord Oxford, sent you. A third was wholly in my power; but when I inquired exactly into the value, I found it less than I had believed, the distance from these parts was great, and beside all this, an unexpected and groundless dispute about the right of presentation, but still such a dispute as the law must determine, had arisen. You will please to believe, that I mention these things for no other reason than to show you, how much those friends deserve you should make them a visit at least, who are so desirous to settle you among them. I hope their endeavours will not be always unsuccessful.

I received, some time ago, a letter from Dr. Delany; and very lately Mr. Pope sent me some sheets, which seem to contain the substance of two sermons of that gentleman's.² The *philosophia prima* is above my reach, and especially when it attempts to prove, that God has done, or does so and so, by attempting to prove, that doing so and so is

¹ *I.e.*, his first wife.
² The sheets were no doubt portion of a work entitled " Revelation examined with Candour," of which Delany published the first volume in the next year. " It was his largest work," says the Rev. W. G. Carroll (*op. cit.*, p. 46), " and he seems to have been inordinately proud of it. . . . The book is very florid, declamatory and discursive, and has far more learning than solid reasoning scattered through it."

essential to his attributes, or necessary to his design; and
that the not doing so and so, would be inconsistent with
the former, or repugnant to the latter. I content myself to
contemplate what I am sure he has done, and to adore him
for it in humble silence. I can demonstrate, that every
cavil, which has been brought against the great system of
the world, physical and moral, from the days of Democritus
and Epicurus to this day, is absurd; but I dare not pronounce why things are made as they are, state the ends of
infinite wisdom, and show the proportion of the means.

Dr. Delany, in his letter to me, mentioned some errors in
the critical parts of learning, which he hoped he had corrected, by showing the mistakes, particularly of Sir John
Marsham, on whose authority these errors were built.[1]
Whether I can be of use to him even in this part, I know
not; for, having fixed my opinions long ago concerning all
ancient history and chronology, by a careful examination
into the first principles of them, I have ever since laid that
study totally aside. I confess, in the letter I writ lately to
the Doctor, notwithstanding my great respect for Sir John
Marsham, his authority is often precarious, because he leans
often on other authorities, which are so. But to you I will
confess a little more: I think, nay, I know, that there is no
possibility of making any system of that kind, without
doing the same thing, and that the defect is in the subject,
not in the writer. I have read the writings of some who
differ from him, and of others who undertook particularly
to refute him. It seemed plain to me, that this was the
case. All the materials of this sort of learning are dis-
jointed and broken. Time has contributed to render them
so, and the unfaithfulness of those who have transmitted
them down to us, particularly of that vile fellow Eusebius,[2]

---

[1] In his attempts to rival that eminent chronologist, Sir John
Marsham, Delany propounded some remarkable theories, such as "that
after the flood man was multiplied by twins at the least, and that in
a hundred years the race numbered a million and a half and were
numerous enough to build the Tower of Babel," and "that the pillar
of salt lasted until about the time of Christ, that the cows used to
lick it, and that it replenished itself," in support of which opinion "he
quotes an Austrian historian, physician, and chancellor, who in the
year 1348 saw fifty cow-keepers and the cattle turned into statues of
salt" (*ibid.*).

[2] In spite of his carelessness and inaccuracy in matters of chronology Eusebius accomplished in his "History of the Christian Church"
a monumental work, and thereby gained justly the title of "the Father

has done even more than time itself by throwing these fragments into a different order, by arbitrary interpretations, and it is often impossible to make any others; in short, by a few plausible guesses for the connection and application of them, a man may, with tolerable ingenuity, prove almost anything by them. I tried formerly to prove, in a learned dissertation, by the same set of authorities, that there had been four Assyrian monarchies; that there had been but three; that there had been but two; that there had been but one; and that there never had been any. I puzzled myself, and a much abler man than myself, the friend to whom I lent the manuscript, and who has, I believe, kept it. In short, I am afraid, that I shall not be very useful to Dr. Delany, in making remarks on the work he is about. His communication of this work may be useful, and I am sure it will be agreeable to me. If you and he are still in Ireland, pray give my best services to him; but say no more than may be proper of all I have writ to you.

I know very well the project you mean, and about which you say, that Pope and you have often teased me. I could convince you, as he is convinced, that a publication of anything of that kind would have been wrong on many accounts, and would be so even now. Besides, call it pride if you will, I shall never make, either to the present age, or to posterity, any apology for the part I acted in the late Queen's reign.[1] But I will apply myself very seriously to the composition of just and true relations of the events of those times, in which both I, and my friends and my enemies, must take the merit, or the blame, which an authentic and impartial deduction of facts will assign to us. I will endeavour to write so as no man could write who had not been a party in those transactions, and as few men would write who had been concerned in them. I believe I shall go back, in considering the political interests of the principal powers in Europe, as far as the Pyrenean treaty;[2]

---

of Church History" (see Dr. McGiffert's notice in the "Encyclopaedia Britannica").

[1] From the reference to this subject in Swift's letter two years before (*supra*, p. 75) it is evident that Bolingbroke had intended at one time a history of the Tory administration such as he here disavows.

[2] The treaty made in 1659 between France and Spain respecting the succession to the throne of the latter country.

but I shall not begin a thread of history till the death of
Charles the Second of Spain, and the accession of Queen
Anne to the throne of England. Nay, even from that time
downward, I shall render my relations more full or *piu
magra*, the word is Father Paul's, just as I have, or have
not, a stock of authentic materials. These shall regulate
my work, and I will neither indulge my own vanity, nor
other men's curiosity, in going one step farther than they
carry me. You see, my dear Swift, that I open a large
field to myself. With what success I shall expatiate in it, I
know as little, as I know whether I shall live to go through
so great a work, but I will begin immediately, and will
make it one principal business of the rest of my life. This
advantage, at least, I shall reap from it, and a great advantage it will be, my attention will be diverted from the
present scene. I shall grieve less at those things which I
cannot mend, I shall dignify my retreat, and shall wind up
the labours of my life in serving the cause of truth.[1]

You say that you could easily show, by comparing my
letters for twenty years past, how the whole system of
philosophy changes by the several gradations of life. I
doubt it. As far as I am able to recollect, my way of
thinking has been uniform enough for more than twenty
years. True it is, to my shame, that my way of acting has
not been always conformable to my way of thinking. My
own passions, and the passions and interests of other men
still more, have led me aside. I launched into the deep
before I had loaded ballast enough. If the ship did not
sink, the cargo was thrown overboard. The storm itself
threw me into port. My own opinion, my own desires
would have kept me there. The opinion, the desires of
others, sent me to sea again. I did, and blamed myself for
doing, what others, and you among the rest, would have
blamed me, if I had not done. I have paid more than I
owed to party, and as much at least as was due to friendship. If I go off the stage of public life without paying all
I owe to my enemies, and to the enemies of my country, I
do assure you the bankruptcy is not fraudulent. I conceal
none of my effects.

Does Pope talk to you of the noble work, which, at my
instigation, he has begun in such a manner, that he must

---

[1] Of this history not a trace now survives.

be convinced, by this time, I judged better of his talents than he did?[1] The first epistle, which considers man, and the habitation of man, relatively to the whole system of universal being; the second, which considers him in his own habitation, in himself, and relatively to his particular system; and the third, which shows how,

> a universal cause
> Works to one end, but works by various laws;

how man, and beast, and vegetable are linked in a mutual dependency, parts necessary to each other and necessary to the whole, how human societies were formed, from what spring true religion and true policy are derived, how God has made our greatest interest and our plainest duty indivisibly the same—these three epistles, I say, are finished. The fourth he is now intent upon. It is a noble subject; he pleads the cause of God, I use Seneca's expression,[2] against that famous charge which atheists in all ages have brought, the supposed unequal dispensations of Providence—a charge which I cannot heartily forgive your divines for admitting. You admit it indeed for an extreme good purpose, and you build on this admission the necessity of a future state of rewards and punishments. But what if you should find, that this future state will not account, in opposition to the atheist, for God's justice in the present state, which you give up? Would it not have been better to defend God's justice in this world, against these daring men, by irrefragable reasons, and to have rested the proof of the other point on revelation? I do not like concessions made against demonstration, repair or supply them how you will. The epistles I have mentioned will compose a first book; the plan of the second is settled. You will not understand by what I have said, that Pope will go so deep into the argument, or carry it so far as I have hinted.

You inquire so kindly after my wife, that I must tell you something of her. She has fallen upon a remedy, invented by a surgeon abroad, and which has had great success in

---

[1] "The Essay on Man" (*supra*, p. 197).

[2] Bolingbroke is again quoting from L'Estrange's version (*op. cit.*, p. 486): "It is a Common Argument against the Justice of Providence, in the matter of Reward and Punishment; *the Misfortune of Good Men in this World and the Prosperity of the Wicked*; But it is an easie matter to vindicate the cause of the Gods."

cases similar to hers. This remedy has visibly attacked the
original cause of all her complaints, and has abated, in
some degree, by one gentle and uniform effect, all the
grievous and various symptoms. I hope, and surely with
reason, that she will receive still greater benefit from this
method of cure, which she will resume as soon as the great
heat is over. If she recovers, I shall not, for her sake, abstract
myself from the world more than I do at present in this
place. But if she should be taken from me, I should most
certainly yield to that strong desire, which I have long had,
of secluding myself totally from the company and affairs of
mankind; of leaving the management, even of my private
affairs, to others; and of securing, by these means, for the
rest of my life, an uninterrupted tenor of philosophical
quiet.

I suppose you have seen some of those volumes of scur-
rility, which have been thrown into the world against Mr.
Pulteney and myself, and the Craftsman, which gave occasion to them. I think, and it is the sense of all my friends,
that the person who published the Final Answer,[1] took a
right turn, in a very nice and very provoking circumstance.
To answer all the falsities, misrepresentations, and blunders,
which a club of such scoundrels, as Arnall, Concanen, and
other pensioners of the Minister,[2] crowd together, would
have been equally tedious and ridiculous, and must have
forced several things to be said, neither prudent, nor
decent, nor perhaps strictly honourable to be said. To have
explained some points, and to have stopped at others,
would have given strength to that impertinent suggestion:
guilt alone is silent in the day of inquiry. It was therefore
right to open no part of the scene of the late Queen's reign,
nor submit the passages of her administration, and the conduct of any of her Ministers, to the examination of so vile
a tribunal. This was still the more right, because, upon
such points as relate to subsequent transactions, and as
affect me singly, what the Craftsman had said, was justified
unanswerably, and what the remarker had advanced, was
proved to be infamously false. The effect of this paper has
answered the design of it; and, which is not common, all

[1] His own " Final Answer to the Remarks on the Craftsman's
Vindication of his two honourable Patrons."

[2] As has been mentioned both Concanen and Arnall figure in the
" Dunciad " (*supra*, p. 9, n. 2 ; p. 180, n. 2).

sides agree, that the things said ought to have been said, and that more ought not to have been said. The public writers seem to be getting back, from these personal alter- cations, to national affairs, much against the grain of the Minister's faction. What the effect of all this writing will be, I know not; but this I know, that when all the informa- tion which can be given is given, when all the spirit which can be raised, is raised and all to no purpose, it is to no purpose to write any more. Even you men of this world have nothing else to do, but to let the ship drive till she is cast away, or till the storm is over. For my own part, I am neither an owner, an officer, nor a foremastman. I am but a passenger, said my Lord Carbery.[1]

It is well for you I am got to the end of my paper; for you might else have a letter as long again from me. If you answer me by the post, remember, while you are writing, that you write by the post. Adieu, my reverend friend.

DCCCXI. [*Scott.*[2]]

SWIFT TO THOMAS TICKELL

Deanery House, Tuesday morning [*August* 1731].

SIR,

As you have been very obliging to me on all occasions, gratitude would not suffer me to be careless to anything relating to your credit. The last time you were here, you mentioned a foolish scribble printed in Mr. Pilkington's Poems.[3] When you were gone I immediately looked into the book, and as I had told you could not find it. I then sent to Mr. Pilkington, who brought me an edition printed

---

[1] The reference is to the first holder of that peerage, which is an Irish one. He became possessed of property in England through his wife, and occupied a seat in the British House of Commons.

[2] *Supra*, vol. iii, p. 198, n. I.

[3] An edition of Pilkington's poems (*supra*, p. 169, n. I) published in London in that year contains a prose composition entitled "The Plague of Wealth, or the Poet's Diary, in a letter to Dr. Delany." The Diary originated in a gratuity of fifty pounds given to Pilkington by Lord Carteret for an ode on the King's birthday, and pictures the recipient as overwhelmed by his accession to such unaccustomed riches.

in London, where I found it at the end of the book. The story of the thing is this. When that money was ordered by my Lord Carteret, Pilkington, not used to such sums, told his patron, Dr. Delany, all the particulars of his fear, joy, etc., on the matter, which so diverted the Doctor, that he made the young man to write it down, that Lord Carteret might see it; and when his Lordship went to England, he writ to the Doctor to send him a copy, which his Lordship having shown to several persons, was transcribed, and by the impertinence of the bookseller, printed at the end of the poems, against Pilkington's knowledge and much to his vexation, for the character he gives himself in it is a very mean one, and must be remembered, and much to his disadvantage, if ever he rises in the world.

As for your part in it, I must declare my thoughts that it does not affect you in the least. You are said to be sick, and could not be seen, and the complaint is of the usual kind made by all who attend at Courts.[1] The young man was sorry, as he had reason, to see it in print, lest it might possibly offend a person of your reputation and consequence. He appears to me to be a modest, good-natured man. I know but little of him. Dr. Delany brought him to me first, and recommended him as one whom I might safely countenance. He is in the utmost pain at hearing that you imagine there was the least design to affront you; since, as it would be the basest thing in itself, so such a treatment would be the surest method to ruin his interests. I could not forbear telling you this out of perfect pity to the young man.

I desire to present my humble service to Mrs. Tickell, and am with great esteem, Sir,

Your most obedient humble servant,

JONATH. SWIFT.

I am just going out of town for a few weeks,[2] but I have

---

[1] The gratuity was to be paid to Pilkington by Tickell, who was "confined to his chamber" at the time, and unable to see him for a week. During that time the Diary represents Pilkington as consumed with melancholy, and regarding Tickell as a proud man,

"Who, grown a Minister of State,
Sees Poets at his levee wait."

[2] As appears from the following letter Swift was then going to stay with one of the members of his Chapter at Powerscourt (*supra*, vol. ii,

ordered that Mrs. Tickell shall have her annual tribute of peaches and nectarines, which will be ripe in a few days, if the sun is favourable, and thieves will spare them.

DCCCXII. [*Elwin.*[1]]

SWIFT TO JOHN GAY AND THE DUCHESS OF QUEENS-
BERRY

The Country,[2] *August* 28, 1731.

TO GAY

YOU and the Duchess use me very ill, for I profess I cannot distinguish the style or the hand-writing of either.[3] I think her Grace writes more like you than herself, and that you write more like her Grace than yourself. I would swear the beginning of your letter was writ by the Duchess, though it is to pass for yours, because there is a cursed lie in it, that she is neither young nor healthy, and besides, it perfectly resembles the part she owns. I will likewise swear that what I must suppose is written by the Duchess is your hand; and thus I am puzzled and perplexed between you, but I will go on in the innocency of my own heart. I am got eight miles from our famous metropolis to a country parson's, to whom I lately gave a city living such as an English chaplain would leap at.[4] I retired hither for the public good, having two great works in hand: one to reduce the whole politeness, wit, humour, and style of England into a short system for the use of all persons of quality, and particularly the maids of honour;[5] the other is of almost equal importance, I may call it the Whole Duty of Servants, in about twenty several stations, from

p. 272), which lies on the border of the counties of Wicklow and Dublin.

[1] By permission of Mr. John Murray. *Supra*, vol. iii, p. 148, n. 1.

[2] *I.e.*, at Powerscourt.

[3] *Supra*, p. 239.

[4] The living of Powerscourt, known ecclesiastically as Stagonil, formed a prebend in Swift's Cathedral. It was then held by John Towers, to whom Swift had given the living of St. Luke (*supra*, vol. ii, p. 51, n. 1).

[5] "A Complete Collection of Genteel and Ingenious Conversation by Simon Wagstaff" ("Prose Works" xi, 195).

the steward and waiting-woman down to the scullion and pantry-boy.[1]

I believe no mortal had ever such fair invitations as I to be happy in the best company of England; I wish I had liberty to print your letter with my own comments upon it. There was a fellow in Ireland, called Conolly, who, from a shoe-boy, grew to be several times one of the chief governors, wholly illiterate, and with hardly common sense.[2] A Lord Lieutenant told the first King George that Conolly was the greatest subject he had in both kingdoms; and truly his character was gotten and preserved by Conolly's never appearing in England, which was the only wise thing he ever did, except purchasing sixteen thousand pounds a year. Why, you need not stare; it is easily applied. I must be absent in order to preserve my credit with her Grace. One thing I like well enough—that you and the Duchess absolutely govern the family, for I have not heard one syllable of my Lord Duke, who I take for granted submits to all your decrees. I writ some time ago to your new Lady Suffolk, and old friend,[3] but have received no answer. She will probably be more civil when she comes to be a Duchess. But I do not think her sincerity worth disputing, nor will disturb you in your dupery, because it is of no consequence. Besides, my quarrel with her is partly good manners, and she is a good servant, who does the office of a shrew. Lo, here comes in the Duchess again—I know her by her *dds*, but I am a fool for discovering my art—to defend herself against my conjecture of what she said.

To the Duchess

Madam,

I WILL imitate your Grace, and write to you upon the same line. I own it is a base, unromantic spirit in me to suspend the honour of waiting at your Grace's feet till I can finish a paltry lawsuit. It concerns, indeed, almost all

[1] " Directions to Servants in General, and in Particular to the Butler," etc. (" Prose Works," xi, 303).

[2] Conolly (*supra*, vol. ii, p. 370, n. 2) had died in 1729 a few months after Archbishop King. It is hardly necessary to observe that Swift's character of him is not to be accepted literally. The positions to which he attained show that neither his origin nor abilities were such as Swift represents them.

[3] *Supra*, p. 246.

my whole fortune. It is equal to half Mr. Pope's, and two-thirds of Mr. Gay's, and about six weeks' rent of your Grace's. This cursed accident has drilled away the whole summer. But, Madam, understand one thing, that I take all your ironical civilities in a literal sense, and whenever I have the honour to attend you, shall expect them to be literally performed, though perhaps I shall find it hard to prove your hand-writing in a court of justice; but that will not be much for your credit. How miserably has your Grace been mistaken in thinking to avoid envy by running into exile, where it haunts you more than ever it did even at Court. *Non te civitas, non regia domus in exilium miserunt, sed tu utrasque.* So says Cicero, as your Grace knows, or so he might have said.

To Gay

SIR,

I PROFESS it was in my thoughts to have writ that congratulatory letter you mention. I never saw the paper which occasioned the disgrace. It was not suffered to be visible here; but I am told there was something wrong in it that looked like betraying private conversation. Two Ministers may talk with freedom of their master's wrong notions, etc., and it would hardly agree with honour to communicate what was spoken to any third person, much less to the public. This I say at a venture, for all things are here misrepresented, and I wish myself better informed.[1]

I am told that the Craftsman, in one of his papers, is offended with the publishers of, I suppose, the last edition of the Dunciad; and I was asked whether you and Mr. Pope were as good friends to the new disgraced person as formerly? This I know nothing of, but suppose it the consequence of some Irish mistake. As to writing, I look on you just in the prime of life for it, the very season when judgement and invention draw together. But schemes are perfectly accidental. Some will appear barren of hints and matter, but prove to be fruitful, and others the contrary; and what you say is past doubt, that every one can best find hints for himself, though it is possible that sometimes a friend may give you a lucky one, just suited to your own

---

[1] In Lord Stanhope's opinion (*op. cit.*, ii, 238), the disclosure was not without justification, and ought not to have led to Pulteney's removal from the Privy Council.

imagination. But all this is almost past with me. My invention and judgement are perpetually at fisticuffs, till they have quite disabled each other; and the merest trifles I ever wrote are serious philosophical lucubrations in comparison to what I now busy myself about, as, to speak in the author's phrase, the world may one day see.

I must desire you, raillery apart, to let my Lady Duchess know that no man is or can be more sensible than myself of her Grace's undeserved civility, favour, and condescension with my thanks for all which I could fill this paper, and twenty more to the bottom, but an opportunity just happening to end this letter—for I am out of post-roads—I must here conclude.

DCCCXIII. [*Mrs. Pilkington's Memoirs.*]

SWIFT TO MRS. PILKINGTON

[*September* 6, 1731.]

MADAM,[1]

I SEND you a piece of plum-cake, which I did intend should be spent at your christening; if you have any objection to the plums, or do not like to eat them, you may return them to, Madam,

Your sincere friend and servant,

J. SWIFT.

DCCCXIV. [*Mrs. Pilkington's Memoirs.*]

MRS. PILKINGTON TO SWIFT

SIR,

I HAVE heard that ostriches could digest iron, but you gave me a harder task, when you bid me eat gold, but sup-

[1] In a passage that does not err on the side of refinement, Mrs. Pilkington tells us that during her visit to Belcamp (*supra*, p. 194, n. 2) she obtained a promise from Swift that he would be godfather to her next child if it was a boy. She goes on to relate that at a time when Swift was in the country the child appeared and proved to be of the right sex, but only lived five days, to the truth of all which the register of St. Andrew's Church, Dublin, testifies: "1731 August 28 Buried Jonathan, the son of the Rev. Matthew and Letitia Pilkington." A fortnight after the child's birth Swift appeared at the Pilkingtons' house, and on hearing of its death expressed much joy that he was saved expense, but no sooner had he returned to the Deanery than he despatched this letter and a piece of cake with four guineas stuck in it.

pose I should, like the pure streams of Tagus, flow potable
gold, the interpretation of which is, that I mean to drink
your health this minute in a glass of sack, and am, with
the utmost respect, Sir,

Your ever devoted servant,

L. PILKINGTON.

DCCCXV. [*Original.*]

LADY ELIZABETH GERMAIN TO SWIFT

Drayton, *September* 7, 1731.

TO show how strictly I obey your orders, I came from the
Duchess of Dorset's country-house [2] to my own, where I
have rid and walked as often as the weather permitted me;
nor am I very nice in that, for, if you remember, I was not
bred up very tenderly, nor a fine lady, for which I acknowledge myself exceedingly obliged to my parents, for had
I had that sort of education, I should not have been so
easy and happy, as I thank God, I now am. As to the
gout, indeed, I believe I do derive it from my ancestors;
but I may forgive even that, since it waited upon me no
sooner; and especially since I see my elder and two younger
brothers so terribly plagued with it; so that I am now the
only wine-drinker in my family, and upon my word, I am
not increased in that since you first knew me.

I am sorry you are involved in lawsuits; it is the thing
on earth I most fear, and I wish you had met with as complaisant an adversary as I did; for my Lord Peterborough
plagued Sir John all his lifetime, but declared, if ever he
gave the estate to me, he would have done with it, and
accordingly has kept his word, like an honourable man. [3] I
saw Mrs. Barber the day before I came out of town, and
should be mighty glad to serve her; but I cannot say so
much by her husband, whom, for her sake, I recommended
to the Duke of Dorset to buy his liveries on. The first

---

[1] In the British Museum. See Preface.

[2] *I.e.*, Knole.

[3] As brother of Sir John Germain's first wife the Earl of Peterborough had embarked in two unsuccessful lawsuits for the recovery
of the property which she had brought to her husband.

thing he did was to ask a greater price than anybody else, and when we were at Whitchurch, where I attended their Graces,[1] he was informed he had not cloth near enough in his shop, and they feared they would not be ready against he came over.

I hope in God I shall soon hear of their safe landing; and I do not question the people of Ireland's liking them as well as they deserve. I desire no better for them; for, if you do not spoil him there, which I think he has too good sense to let happen, he is the most worthy, honest, good-natured, great-souled man that ever was born. As to my Duchess, she is so reserved, that perhaps she may not be at first so much admired; but, upon knowledge, I will defy anybody upon earth, with sense, judgement, and good nature, not only [not] to admire her, but must love and esteem her as much as I do, and every one else, that is really acquainted with her. You know him a little, so, for his own sake, you must like him; and till you are better acquainted with them both, I hope you will like them for mine.[2] Your friend Biddy is just the same as she was: laughs sedately, and makes a joke slily, and I am, as I ever was, and hope I ever shall be,

Your most sincere friend, and faithful humble servant,

E. GERMAIN.

DCCCXVI. [Original.[3]]

THE COUNTESS OF SUFFOLK TO SWIFT

Hampton Court, *September* 25, 1731.

SIR,

You seem to think that you have a natural right to abuse me, because I am a woman, and a courtier.[4] I have

---

[1] Travellers to Ireland took frequently then a route through Whitchurch in Shropshire.

[2] The Duke and Duchess of Dorset landed in Ireland for the first time on 11 September. Writing on the 28th Bishop Clayton says: "He lives very magnificently, and seems hitherto to be very acceptable to the people. His tongue is not so lavish of promises, nor his hand so full of squeezes as the late Lord Lieutenant; but I think in the end it will answer better. . . . Her behaviour is with less hauteur; it is more polite and less proud" (Mrs. Thomson's "Memoirs of Viscountess Sundon," ii, 83).

[3] In the British Museum. See Preface.   [4] *Supra*, p. 246.

taken it as a woman and as a courtier ought, with great resentment, and a determined resolution of revenge. The number of letters that have been sent, and thought by many to be yours, and thank God they were all silly ones, has been a fair field to execute it. Think of my joy to hear you suspected of folly; think of my pleasure when I entered the list for your justification. Indeed I was a little disconcerted to find Mr. Pope took the same side; for I would have had the man of wit, the dignified divine, the Irish Drapier, have found no friend but the silly woman and the courtier. Could I have preserved myself alone in the list, I should not have despaired, that this monitor of Princes, this Irish patriot, this excellent man at speech and pen, should have closed the scene under suspicions of having a violent passion for Mrs. Barber, and Lady M——[1] or Mrs. Haywood[2] have writ the progress of it. Now, to my mortification I find everybody inclined to think you had no hand in writing those letters; but I every day thank Providence that there is an epitaph in St. Patrick's Cathedral, that will be a lasting monument of your imprudence. I cherish this extremely; for, say what you can to justify it, I am convinced I shall as easily argue the world into the belief of a courtier's sincerity, as you, with all your wit and eloquence, will be able to convince mankind of the prudence of that action.

I expect to hear if peace shall ensue, or war continue between us. If I know but little of the art of war, yet you see I do not want courage; and that has made many an ignorant soldier fight successfully. Besides, I have a numerous body of light-armed troops to bring into the field, who, when single, may be as inconsiderable as a Lilliputian, yet ten thousand of them embarrassed Captain Gulliver. If you send honourable articles, they shall be signed. I insist that you own that you have been unjust to me, for I have never forgot you, but made others send my compliments, because I was not able to write myself. If I cannot justify the advice I gave you from the success of it, yet you know I gave you my reasons for it: and it was your business to have judged of my capacity by the solidity of my arguments. If the principle was false, you ought not to have acted upon it. So you have only

---

[1] *I.e.*, Swift's old flame, Lady Mary Wortley Montagu.
[2] A lady damned to everlasting celebrity in the "Dunciad."

been the dupe of your own ill judgement, and not to my falsehood. Am I to send back the crown and the plaid,[1] well packed up, in my own Characters, or am I to follow my own inclination, and continue

Very truly and very much your humble servant,

H. SUFFOLK.

DCCCXVII. [*Original.*[2]]

SWIFT TO THE COUNTESS OF SUFFOLK

October 26, 1731.

MADAM,

YOUR Ladyship's letter made me a little grave, and in going to answer it, I was in great danger of leaning on my elbow, I mean my left elbow, to consider what I should write, which posture I never used except when I was under a necessity of writing to fools, or lawyers, or Ministers of State, where I am to consider what is to be said, but as I write to a person whom I esteem, I am in no pain at all.

It would be an injury to you and Mr. Pope, to give thanks to either of you for justifying me about those letters sent to the Queen, because to think me guilty would disgrace your understandings, and as he is my best friend, so your Ladyship owes me no malice, except that of raillery, and good raillery is always sincere. And if her Majesty were deceived, it would lessen my opinion of her judgement; which would no otherwise affect me, than by making me sorry upon her own account. But what your Ladyship would have me discover, through all your refined civilities, is my great imprudence in ordering that monument to be fixed in my Cathedral. I shall not trouble you with a long story; but if ever a numerous venerable body of dignified clergymen had reason to complain of the highest repeated indignity, in return of the greatest honour offered by them, to persons they were wholly strangers to, then my Chapter is not to be blamed, nor I, who proposed the matter to them; which, however, I could have done by my own authority, but rather chose it should be the work of us all.

---

[1] The trinket and poplin sent to her by Swift in the autumn of 1726 (*supra*, vol. iii, pp. 354, 369).

[2] British Museum Addit. MSS., 22625, f. 24.

And I will confess it was upon their advice that I omitted the only two passages which had much bitterness in them; and which a Bishop here, one after your own heart, blamed me very much for leaving out, declaring that the treatment given us by the Schomberg family deserved a great deal worse. Indeed, Madam, I shall not attempt to convince England of anything that relates to this kingdom. The Drapier, whom you mention, could not do it in relation to the halfpence, neither can the Parliament here convince you that we ought not to be put in so miserable condition in every article of distress. Why should the Schomberg family be so uneasy at a thing they were so long warned of, and were told they might prevent for fifty pounds?

But here I wish your Ladyship would put the Queen in mind of what passed between her Majesty and me, upon the subject of Ireland, when she appeared so much to pity this distressed kingdom, and gave me leave to write to her if ever I lived to see her Queen, [said] that she would answer my letters, and promised that in such a case she would use all her credit to relieve us; whereupon I desired Dr. Arbuthnot, who was present, to be witness of what she said, and her Majesty confirmed it. I will not ask what the event has been. If any state scribble writ here should happen to reach London, I entreat your Ladyship would continue to do me the justice of believing my innocence, because I lately assured the Duke of Dorset that I would never have a hand in any such thing, and I gave him my reason before his Secretary, that looking upon this kingdom's condition as absolutely desperate, I would not prescribe a dose to the dead.[1]

Some parts of your letter I do not understand. Mrs. Barber was recommended to me by Dr. Delany, who is now in London, and whom I once presented to you at Marble Hill. She seems to be a woman of piety and a poetical genius; and though I never visited her in my life, yet was I disposed to do her good offices on the Doctor's account, and her own good character. By Lady M—— I cannot guess whom you mean. Mrs. Haywood I have heard

---

[1] The Duke of Dorset's secretary, Walter Carey (*supra*, p. 219, n. 1) considered himself the most important member of the Irish government, and used to speak of "his administration" (Mrs. Thomson's "Memoirs of Viscountess Sundon," ii, 23).

of as a stupid, infamous, scribbling woman, but have not seen any of her productions. And now, Madam, I utterly acquit your Ladyship of all things that may regard me, except your good opinion, and that very little share I can pretend to in your memory. I never knew a lady who had so many qualities to beget esteem, but how you act as a friend, is out of my way to judge. As to the Queen, whom I never offended, since it would be presumption to imagine I ever voluntarily came into her thoughts, so it must be a mortification to think, when I happen to be named in her presence, it is usually to my disadvantage. I remember to have once told her Majesty, how hard a thing it was, that when a Prince, or great Minister, had once received an ill impression of any person, although from the most false information, although the Prince were demonstrably convinced of the person's innocence, yet the impression still continued; and her Majesty readily condemned the severity of such a proceeding. I had said the same thing before to Sir Robert Walpole, who, upon reporting it to others, was pleased to give it a turn that I did not deserve.[1]

I remember the plaid, but I forget the crown, and the meaning of it. If you had thought fit to have sent me as much of the plaid, as would have made me a morning-cap, before it fell to the share of the lowest of your women, I should have been proud that my head should have worn your livery. But if you are weary of your Character, it must lie upon my head, for I know no other whom it will fit. And if your Ladyship will not allow it to be a character, I am sure it may pass for a prediction. If you should put the same fancy into the Queen's head, I must send her a much larger character, and in royal paper, otherwise she will not be able to wrap the bundle in it. I fear so long a letter is beyond your mercy to forgive; but your Ladyship is sure to be easy till Mr. Pope shall tell me that you are content to receive another. I should be heartily sorry, if your increase in honour and employment hath not been accompanied with increase of health. Let Mr. Pope, in all his letters, give me a particular account on this head, and pray God I may never have the least motive to pity you. For as a courtier, I forgive your *âme endurcie*, which I once charged on my Lord Chesterfield, and he did not dislike it.

---

[1] *I.e.*, that Swift was referring to himself, instead of to Gay.

And you have not a favourite or flatterer, who makes more outward offers of wishes for your ease and happiness than I do prayers from the bottom of my heart, which proceed entirely from that real respect, and esteem, wherewith I am, Madam,

Your Ladyship's most obedient humble servant,

JONATH. SWIFT.

Addressed—To the Right Honourable the Countess of Suffolk, Groom of the Stole to her Majesty,[1] at St. James's, London.

DCCCXVIII. [*Original.*[2]]

LADY ELIZABETH GERMAIN TO SWIFT

November 4, 1731.

I BELIEVE in my conscience, that though you had answered mine before, the second was never the less welcome. So much for your *topscript*, not postscript; and in very sincere earnest I heartily thank you for remembering me so often.[3] Since I came out of the country, my riding days are over; for I never was for your high park courses, although my courage serves me very well at a hand-gallop in the country, six or seven miles, with one horseman, and a ragged lad, a labourer's boy, that is to be clothed when he can run fast enough to keep up with my horse, who has yet only proved his dexterity by escaping from school. But my courage fails me for riding in town, where I should have the happiness to meet with plenty of your very pretty fellows, that manage their own horses to show their art, or that think a postilion's cap, with a white frock, the most becoming dress. These and their grooms I am most bitterly afraid of, because, you must know, if my complaisant friend,

---

[1] Lady Suffolk, a few days after her accession to that title, was appointed Mistress of the Robes, an office previously held by the Duchess of Dorset.

[2] In the British Museum. See Preface.

[3] Apparently Lady Betty had sent him a letter, which arrived while he was answering the one of 7 September (*supra*, p. 262).

your Presbyterian housekeeper, can remember anything like such days with me, that is a very good reason for me to remember that time is past;[1] and your fops would rejoice to see a horse throw an ancient gentlewoman.

I am sorry to hear you are no wiser in Ireland than we English; for our birthday was as fine as hands could make us, but I question much whether we all paid ready money.[2] I mightily approve of my Duchess's being dressed in your manufacture; if your ladies will follow her example in all things, they cannot do amiss. And I dare say you will soon find that the more you know of them both, the better you will like them, or else Ireland has strangely depraved your taste, and that my own vanity will not let me believe, since you still flatter me.

Why do you tantalize me? Let me see you in England again, if you dare, and choose your residence, summer or winter, St. James's Square or Drayton. I defy you in all shapes; be it Dean of St. Patrick's governing England or Ireland, or politician Drapier, but my choice should be the parson in Lady Betty's chamber. Make haste then, if you have a mind to oblige,

　　　　Your ever sincere and hearty old friend,
　　　　　　　　　　　　　LADY BETTY.

[1] Mrs. Brent (*supra*, p. 30, n. 1) had evidently reminded Swift of Lady Betty's appearance on horseback when she was in Ireland.

[2] George II's birthday, which fell in October, had been celebrated in Dublin with much splendour. All Ireland was invited to a ball at the Castle. The architect who had just completed the Irish Houses of Parliament was employed to restore the great hall, which had been long disused, and under his direction a scheme of decoration and lighting was carried out. The great monuments of Egypt, which had contributed so largely to the success of his achievements, were seen in perspective on the walls, and the hall, through his skill, proved "as light as a summer's day." Scoffers said the room would be better than the company, but found themselves in the wrong. " I believe more rich clothes were never seen together except at St. James's," says the Duke of Dorset to Lady Suffolk, "and some of them so well chosen that one would have sworn a certain Countess of my acquaintance had given her assistance upon this occasion." Mrs. Delany, who was then in Dublin, and foremost at every amusement, was greatly impressed by the whole entertainment, and in one of her lively letters tells us that a vast profusion of meat and drink gained the hearts of the guzzlers, and crowding and confusion added to the enjoyment of all the guests (cf. "Countess of Suffolk's Letters," ii, 34; Mrs. Delany's "Correspondence," i, 309).

DCCCXIX. [*Original.*[1]]

JOHN GAY AND THE DUKE OF QUEENSBERRY TO SWIFT

[*November* 1731.[2]]

GAY

FOR about this month or six weeks past, I have been rambling from home, or have been at what I may not improperly call other homes, at Dawley, and at Twickenham; and I really think at every one of my homes you have as good a pretension as myself; for I find them all exceedingly disappointed by the lawsuit that has kept you this summer from us. Mr. Pope told me that affair was now over, that you have the estate which was your security. I wish you had your own money; for I wish you free from every engagement that keeps us from one another. I think you deciphered the last letter we sent you very judiciously.[3] You may make your own conditions at Amesbury, where I am at present. You may do the same at Dawley, and Twickenham, you know, is your own. But, if you rather choose to live with me, that is to say, if you will give up your right and title, I will purchase the house you and I used to dispute about over against Ham Walks, on purpose to entertain you.[4] Name your day, and it shall be done. I have lived with you, and I wish to do so again in any place, and upon any terms. The Duchess does not know of my writing, but I promised to acquaint the Duke the next time I wrote to you, and for aught I know he may tell the Duchess, and she may tell Sir William Wyndham, who is now here, and for fear they should all have something to say to you, I leave the rest of the paper till I see the Duke.

THE DUKE

MR. GAY tells me you seem to doubt what authority my wife and he have to invite a person hither, who, by agreement, is to have the government of the place during his stay, when at the same time it does not appear, that the

---

[1] In the British Museum. See Preface.
[2] It is endorsed as received on the 8th.   [3] *Supra*, p. 258.
[4] From the reply it would appear that this house was owned by the Countess of Suffolk. Possibly the reference is to Marble Hill.

present master of these demesnes hath been consulted in it. The truth of the matter is this, I did not know whether you might not have suspected me for a sort of a pert coxcomb, had I put in my word in the late correspondence between you and my wife. Ladies, by the courtesy of the world, enjoy privileges not allowed to men; and in many cases the same thing is called a favour from a lady, which might perhaps be looked upon as impertinence from a man. Upon this reflection I have hitherto refrained from writing to you, having never had the pleasure of conversing with you otherways; and as that is a thing I most sincerely wish, I would not venture to meddle in a negotiation that seemed to be in so fair a way of producing that desirable end. But our friend John has not done me justice, if he has never mentioned to you how much I wish for the pleasure of seeing you here; and though I have not till now avowedly taken any steps toward bringing it about, what has passed conducive to it has been all along with my privity and consent, and I do now formally ratify all the preliminary articles and conditions agreed to on the part of my wife, and will undertake for the due observance of them. I depend upon my friend John to answer for my sincerity. I was not long at Court. I have been a country gentleman for some time.

THE DUCHESS

Poll manu sub linus darque dds.
Sive nig tig gnipite gnaros.

Addressed—To the Revd. Doctor Swift, Dean of St. Patrick's, in Dublin, Ireland.

DCCCXX. [*Elwin.*[1]]

SWIFT TO JOHN GAY AND THE DUKE AND DUCHESS
OF QUEENSBERRY

December 1, 1731.

TO GAY

IF your ramble was on horseback, I am glad of it on account of your health; but I know your arts of patching

---

[1] By permission of Mr. John Murray. *Supra*, vol. iii, p. 148, n. 1.

up a journey between stage-coaches and friends' coaches; for you are as arrant a cockney as any hosier in Cheapside, and one clean shirt with two cravats, and as many handkerchiefs, make up your equipage; and as for nightgown, it is clear from Homer that Agamemnon rose without one. I have often had it in my head to put it into yours, that you ought to have some great work in scheme, which may take up seven years to finish, beside two or three under-ones that may add another thousand pounds to your stock; and then I shall be in less pain about you. I know you can find dinners, but you love twelvepenny coaches too well without considering that the interest of a whole thousand pounds brings you but half-a-crown a day. I find a greater longing than ever to come among you; and reason good when I am teased with Dukes and Duchesses for a visit, all my demands complied with, and all excuses cut off. You remember: O happy Don Quixote! Queens held his horse, and Duchesses pulled off his armour, or something to that purpose.[1] He was a mean-spirited fellow. I can say ten times more: O happy, etc.! Such a Duchess was designed to attend him, and such a Duke invited him to command his palace.

Nam istos reges ceteros
Memorare nolo, hominum mendicabula.

Go read your Plautus,[2] and observe Strobilus vapouring after he had found the pot of gold.

I will have nothing to do with the house over against Ham Walks, or with the owner of it. I have long hated her on your account, and the more because you are so forgiving as not to hate her. I writ her a long letter lately in answer to her last,[3] and let her know I would write to her no more, although she has good qualities enough to make her esteemed, but not one piece of truth or honour. I only wish she were a fool as she is a knave.

---

[1]

"Oh, never, surely was there knight
So served by hand of dame,
As served was he, Don Quixote hight,
When from his town he came;
With maidens waiting on himself,
Princesses on his hack."

Ormsby, *op. cit.*, i, 120.

[2] Aul., 4, 8, 2.   [3] *Supra*, p. 265.

I have been several months writing near five hundred lines on a pleasant subject, only to tell what my friends and enemies will say on me after I am dead.[1] I shall finish it soon, for I add two lines every week, and blot out four and alter eight. I have brought in you and my other friends, as well as enemies and detractors.

It is a great comfort to see how corruption and ill conduct are instrumental in uniting virtuous persons and lovers of their country of all denominations. Lord Bolingbroke with William Pulteney, Sir William Wyndham with the Amesbury, Whig and Tory, High and Low Church, as soon as they are left to think freely, all joining in opinion. If this be disaffection, pray God send me always among the disaffected; and I heartily wish you joy of your scurvy treatment at Court, which has given you leisure to cultivate both public and private virtue, neither of them likely to be soon met within the walls of St. James's or Westminster. But I must here dismiss you, that I may pay my acknowledgements to the Duke for the great honour he has done me.

To the Duke

My Lord,

I could have sworn that my pride would be always able to preserve me from vanity, of which I have been in great danger to be guilty for some months past, first by the conduct of my Lady Duchess, and now by that of your Grace, which had like to finish the work; and I should have certainly gone about showing my letter under the charge of secrecy to every blab of my acquaintance, if I could have the least hope of prevailing on any of them to believe that a man in so obscure a corner, quite thrown out of the present world and within a few steps of the next, should receive such condescending invitations from two such persons to whom he is an utter stranger, and who know no more of him than what they have heard by the partial representations of a friend. But in the mean time I must desire your Grace not to flatter yourself that I waited for your consent to accept the invitation. I must be ignorant indeed not to know that the Duchess, ever since you met, has been most politically employed in increasing those

[1] The poem, entitled "On the Death of Dr. Swift" ("Poetica Works," i, 247), contains now five hundred and fifty lines.

forces and sharpening those arms with which she subdued you at first, and to which, the braver and wiser you grow, you will more and more submit. Thus I know myself on the secure side, and it was a mere piece of my good manners to insert that clause, of which you have taken the advantage. But as I cannot forbear of informing your Grace that the Duchess's great secret in her art of government has been to reduce both your wills into one, so I am content, in due observance to the forms of the world, to return my most humble thanks to your Grace for so great a favour as you are pleased to offer me, and which nothing but impossibilities shall prevent me from receiving, since I am with the greatest reason, truth, and respect, my Lord,
                Your Grace's most obedient, etc.

To the Duchess

    Madam,

I have consulted all the learned in occult sciences of my acquaintance, and have sat up eleven nights to discover the meaning of those two hieroglyphical lines in your Grace's hand at the bottom of the last Amesbury letter, but all in vain. Only it is agreed that the language is Coptic, and a very profound Behmist assures me the style is poetic, containing an invitation from a very great person of the female sex to a strange kind of man whom she never saw, and this is all I can find, which, after so many former invitations, will ever confirm me in that respect, wherewith I am, Madam,
                Your Grace's most obedient, etc.

DCCCXXI. [*Elwin.*]

John Gay and Alexander Pope to Swift

                                        December 1, 1731.
                GAY

You used to complain that Mr. Pope and I would not let you speak: you may now be even with me, and take it out in writing.[1] If you do not send to me now and then, the

----
[1] As has been noticed, the preceding letter which crossed this one was an answer to a letter which Gay had sent in August.

post-office will think me of no consequence, for I have no correspondent but you. You may keep as far from us as you please, you cannot be forgotten by those who ever knew you, and therefore please me by sometimes showing that I am not forgot by you. I have nothing to take me off from my friendship to you. I seek no new acquaintance, and court no favour; I spend no shillings in coaches or chairs to levees or great visits, and, as I do not want the assistance of some that I formerly conversed with, I will not so much as seem to seek to be a dependent. As to my studies, I have not been entirely idle, though I cannot say that I have yet perfected anything. What I have done is something in the way of those Fables I have already published.[1] All the money I get is by saving, so that by habit there may be some hopes, if I grow richer, of my becoming a miser. All misers have their excuses. The motive to my parsimony is independence. If I were to be represented by the Duchess, she is such a downright niggard for me, this character might not be allowed me; but I really think I am covetous enough for any who lives at the Court end of the town, and who is as poor as myself: for I do not pretend that I am equally saving with Selkirk.[2]

Mr. Lewis desired you might be told that he has five pounds of yours in his hands, which he fancies you may have forgot, for he will hardly allow that a verseman can have a just knowledge of his own affairs. When you got rid of your lawsuit, I was in hopes that you had got your own, and was free from every vexation of the law, but Mr. Pope tells me you are not entirely out of your perplexity, though you have the security now in your own possession; but still your case is not so bad as Captain Gulliver's, who was ruined by having a decree for him with costs.[3] I have an injunction for me against pirating booksellers, which I am sure to get nothing by, and will, I fear, in the end drain me of some money. When I began this

[1] Gay was then writing the second volume of his Fables, which was not published until after his death.

[2] Charles Douglas, second Earl of Selkirk, who is said by Luttrell ("Brief Relation," 10 August, 1703) to have married Gay's old employer the Duchess of Monmouth (*supra*, vol. ii, p. 144). He is satirized as Harfax in Pope's Epistle to Lord Bathurst.

[3] This experience enabled Gulliver to give the King of Brobdingnag a graphic picture of judicial procedure in England ("Prose Works," viii, 133).

prosecution, I fancied there would be some end of it, but the law still goes on, and it is probable I shall some time or other see an attorney's bill as long as the book. Poor Duke Disney is dead, and has left what he had among his friends, among whom are Lord Bolingbroke, five hundred pounds, Mr. Pelham, five hundred pounds, Sir William Wyndham's youngest son, five hundred pounds, General Hill, five hundred pounds, Lord Masham's son, five hundred pounds.[1]

You have the good wishes of those I converse with; they know they gratify me, when they remember you, but I really think they do it purely for your own sake. I am satisfied with the love and friendship of good men, and envy not the demerits of those who are most conspicuously distinguished. Therefore, as I set a just value upon your friendship, you cannot please me more than letting me now and then know that you remember me—the only satisfaction of distant friends!

POPE

Mr. Gay's is a good letter; mine will be a very dull one; and yet what you will think the worst of it is what should be its excuse, that I write in a headache that has lasted three days. I am never ill but I think of your ailments, and repine that they mutually hinder our being together; though in one point I am apt to differ from you, for you shun your friends when you are in those circumstances, and I desire them. Your way is the more generous, mine the more tender. Lady Suffolk took your letter[2] very kindly, for I had prepared her to expect no answer under a twelvemonth; but kindness, perhaps, is a word not applicable to courtiers. However, she is an extraordinary woman there, who will do you common justice. For God's

---

[1] The facetious Disney had been buried on 25 November in the east cloister of Westminster Abbey (Chester's "Registers," p. 334), "Having given to Major General Hill, Samuel Masham, Esq. (afterwards second Lord Masham), and Percy Wyndham, Esq. (afterwards Earl of Thomond) considerable legacies, he made them his residuary legatees. His other bequests were exclusively to members of the nobility, military friends, and servants." Lady Masham's brother (*supra*, vol. i, p. 336) had seen military service with Disney, and had been admitted a member of the Brothers' Club on the same day ("Prose Works," ii, 288).

[2] *Supra*, p. 265.

sake why all this scruple about Lord Bolingbroke's keeping your horses, who has a park; or about my keeping you on a pint of wine a day?[1] We are infinitely richer than you imagine. John Gay shall help me to entertain you, though you come like King Lear with fifty knights.[2] Though such prospects as I wish, cannot now be formed for fixing you with us, time may provide better before you part again. The old Lord may die,[3] the benefice may drop, or, at worst, you may carry me into Ireland.

You will see a work of Lord Bolingbroke's, and one of mine, which, with a just neglect of the present age, consult only posterity, and, with a noble scorn of politics, aspire to philosophy.[4] I am glad you resolve to meddle no more with the low concerns and interests of parties, even of countries, for countries are but larger parties. *Quid verum atque decens, curare, et rogare, nostrum sit.* I am much pleased with your design upon Rochefoucauld's maxim; pray finish it.[5] I am happy whenever you join our names together; so would Dr. Arbuthnot be, but at this time he can be pleased with nothing, for his darling son is dying in all probability, by the melancholy account I received this morning.[6] The

---

[1] The present letter is apparently a reply to one that has been suppressed.

[2]
        " I'll go with thee,
Thy fifty yet doth double five and twenty,
And thou art twice her love."
            " King Lear," II, iv, 255.

[3] *I.e.*, Bolingbroke's father, who was possibly one of the obstacles to securing preferment in England for Swift (*supra*, p. 250).

[4] The allusion is to the " Essays on Philosophy," which Bolingbroke wrote at that time for circulation amongst his friends, and Pope's " Essay on Man " (*supra*, p. 208).

[5] The reference is to the poem on his own death (*supra*, p. 273), in which Rochefoucauld's maxim is thus rendered:

    " In all distresses of our friends,
    We first consult our private ends;
    While nature kindly bent to ease us,
    Points out some circumstance to please us."

[6] Arbuthnot's second son, Charles, died the day after this letter was written. He had been a student of Christ Church, Oxford, and was one of those Swift met when dining there with Stratford (*supra*, vol. iii, p. 386, n. 2). Verses by him addressed to the King are prefixed to his father's " Tables of Ancient Coins." His untimely death is thought to have been at least in part due to a wound which he had received in a duel (see Aitken's " Life of Arbuthnot," p. 136).

paper you ask me about is of little value.[1] It might have been a seasonable satire upon the scandalous language and passion with which men of condition have stooped to treat one another. Surely they sacrifice too much to the people, when they sacrifice their own characters, families, etc., to the diversion of that rabble of readers.

I agree with you in my contempt of most popularity, fame, etc. Even as a writer I am cool in it, and whenever you see what I am now writing, you will be convinced I would please but a few, and, if I could, make mankind less admirers, and greater reasoners. I study much more to render my own portion of being easy, and to keep this peevish frame of the human body in good humour. Infirmities have now quite unmanned me, and it will delight you to hear they are not increased, though not diminished. I thank God, I do not very much want people to attend me, though my mother now cannot. When I am sick, I lie down; when I am better, I rise up: I am used to the headache, etc. If greater pains arrive, such as my late rheumatism, the servants bathe and plaster me, or the surgeon scarifies me, and I bear it, because I must. This is the evil of nature, not of fortune. I am just now as well as when you were here: I pray God you were no worse. I sincerely wish my life were passed near you, and such as it is, I would not repine at it. All you mention remember you, and wish you here.

DCCCXXII. [*Original.*[2]]

LADY ELIZABETH GERMAIN TO SWIFT

January 11, 1731-2.

IT is well for Mr. Pope your letter came as it did,[3] for else I had called for my coach, and was going to make a thorough search at his house; for I was most positively assured, that you was there in private, the Duke of Dorset can tell you. *Non credo* is all the Latin I know, and the most useful word upon all occasions to me. However, like

---

[1] Arbuthnot's "Brief Account of Mr. John Ginglicut's Treatise" (*supra*, p. 199).

[2] In the British Museum. See Preface.

[3] A reply no doubt to her letter in November (*supra*, p. 268).

most other people, I can give it up for what I wish; so for
once I believed, or at least went half way in what I hoped
was true, and then, for the only time, your letter was un-
welcome. You tell me you have a request, which is purely
personal to me; *non credo* for that, for I am sure you would
not have been so disagreeable as not to have made it, when
you know it is a pleasure and satisfaction to me to do anything you desire, by which you may find you are not *sans
consequence* to me.

I met with your friend Pope the other day. He complains of not being well, and indeed looked ill. I fear his
wit nor sense does not arm him enough against being hurt
by malice, and that he is too sensible of what fools say:
the run is much against him on the Duke of Chandos's
account, but I believe their rage is not kindness to the
Duke, but glad to give it vent with some tolerable pretence.[1] I wish your presence would have such a miraculous
effect as your design on Biddy's[2] speech; you know formerly her tongue was not apt to run much by inclination,
but now every winter it is kept still perforce, for she commonly gets a violent cold that lasts her all winter. But as
to that quarrelsome friend of the Duke of Dorset's, I will
let her loose at you, and see which can get the better.[3]
Miss Kelly was a very pretty girl when she went from
hence, and the beaux show their good taste by liking her.
I hear her father is now kind to her, but if she is not
mightily altered, she would give up some of her airs and
equipage to live in England.[4]

[1] The "Epistle on Taste" (*supra*, p. 110) had appeared in the preceding December, and brought upon Pope a storm of criticism:

> " Let Pope no more what Chandos builds deride,
> Because he takes not Nature for his guide;
> Since wondrous critic! in thy form we see,
> That Nature may mistake as well as he."

[2] *I.e.*, Biddy Floyd.

[3] Possibly the reference is to Lady Allen (*supra*, p. 151).

[4] The lady to whom Lady Betty alludes was the only child of Dennis
Kelly, who was sent to the Tower for alleged complicity in Layer's plot
(*supra*, vol. iii, p. 140, n. 6). She is said by Mrs. Delany (" Correspondence," i, 396) to have been distinguished for beauty and wit. As will
be seen from subsequent letters her health gave way before long, and
her death took place at the end of the following year. Although he
refers in terms of affection to her in his will, her father, who was
separated from his wife, does not appear to have treated her with all
the consideration that her condition deserved.

Since you are so good as to inquire after my health, I ought to inform you I never was better in my life than this winter, and I have escaped both headaches and gout; and that yours may not be in danger by reading such a long letter, I will add no more, but bid adieu to my dear Dean,

E. Germain.

Addressed—To the Revd. Doctor Swift, Dean of St. Patrick's, at Dublin, Ireland.

DCCCXXIII. [*Original.*¹]

John Gay to Swift

London, *January* 18, 1731-2.

Dear Sir,²

It is now past nine o'clock. I deferred sitting down to write to you, in expectation to have seen Mr. Pope, who left me two or three hours ago to try to find Lord Burlington, within whose walls I have not been admitted this year and a half, but for what reason I know not.³ Mr. Pope is just this minute come in, but had not the good luck to find him, so that I cannot give you any satisfaction in the affair you writ last about. He designs to see him to-morrow, and if anything can be done, he says you shall hear from him. By the beginning of my letter you see how I decline in favour, but I look upon it as my particular distinction, that as soon as the Court gains a man I lose him. It is a mortification I have been used to, so I bear it as a philosopher should.

The letter which you writ to me and the Duke, I received;⁴ and Mr. Pope showed me that directed to him,⁵

---

¹ In the British Museum. See Preface.

² As appears from this letter Swift had written to ask Gay to speak to Lord Burlington about Lord Cork's monument. He despaired evidently of assistance from Lord Bathurst (*supra*, p. 238).

³ Lord Burlington, with whom Gay was living when he opened the correspondence with Swift (*supra*, vol. iii, p. 145), appears to have answered Dr. Johnson's description of a patron. "I went to visit him," remarked Arbuthnot while Gay was at Burlington House, "and ordered him a poultice for his swelled face. He said Lord and Lady Burlington were very good to him, but the poor creature eat his poultice for hunger."

⁴ *Supra*, p. 271.

⁵ This letter has been suppressed.

which gave me more pleasure than all the letters you have writ since I saw you, as it gives me hopes of seeing you soon. Were I to acquaint the Duke and Duchess of my writing, I know that they would have something to say to you, and perhaps would prevent my sending the letter this post, so I choose to say nothing about it. You are in great favour and esteem with all that love me, which is one great reason that I love and esteem them.

Whenever you will order me to turn your fortune into ready money, I will obey you, but I choose to leave it where it is till you want it, as it carries some interest, though it might be now sold to some advantage, and is liable to rises and falls with the other stocks. It may be higher as well as lower, so I will not dispose of it till I hear from you. I am impatient to see you, so are all your friends. You have taken your resolution, and I shall henceforth every week expect an agreeable surprise. The bellman rings for the letter, so I can say no more.

Addressed—To the Reverend Dr. Swift, Dean of St. Patrick's, in Dublin, Ireland.

DCCCXXIV. [*Original.*[1]]

SWIFT TO THE REV. JOHN WINDER

Dublin, *February* 19, 1731-2.

SIR,[2]

I HAD the favour of yours of the 6th instant. I have been above a fortnight confined by an accidental strain,[3] and neither ride nor walk, nor easily write, else you should have heard from me sooner. I am heartily sorry for your disorders, and am the more sensible by those I have myself, though not of the same kind, but a constant dispo-

---

[1] It is preserved by Mr. John Murray amongst Swift's letters to Archdeacon Walls. See Preface.

[2] Winder may have seen Swift since the Kilroot days. The sermon to which there has been allusion (*supra*, vol. i, p. 23, n. 1), and which shows him to have been a supporter of Oxford's administration, was preached by him in Dublin in the summer of 1714 (Royal Irish Academy Tracts).

[3] It appears from a subsequent letter that the strain was to one of his legs, and was occasioned by a slip on the stairs. Swift suffered from the effects of it throughout that year.

sition to giddiness, which I fear my present confinement, with the want of exercise, will increase.

I am afraid you could not light upon a more unqualified man to serve you, or my nearest friends, in any manner, with people in power; for I have the misfortune to be not only under the particular displeasure both of the King and Queen, as everybody knows, but likewise of every person both in England and Ireland who are well with the Court, or can do me good or hurt. And although this and the two last Lieutenants here [1] were of my old acquaintance, yet I never could prevail with any of them to give a living to a sober grave clergyman, who married my near relation, and has been long in the Church, so that he is still my curate,[2] and I reckon this present governor will do like the rest. I believe there is not any person you see from this town, who does not know that my situation is as I describe. If you or your son [3] were in favour with any bishop or patron, perhaps it might be contrived to have them put in mind, or solicited; but I am no way proper to be the first mover, because there is not one spiritual or temporal Lord in Ireland whom I visit, or by whom I am visited, but am as mere a monk as any in Spain; and there is not a clergyman on the top of a mountain who so little converses with mankind, or is so little regarded by them, on any other account except showing malice. All this I bear as well as I can; eat my morsel alone like a King, and am constantly at home when I am not riding or walking, which I do often, and always alone.

I give you this picture of myself out of old friendship; from whence you may judge what share of spirits and mirth are now left me. Yet I cannot read at nights, and am therefore forced to scribble something, whereof nine things in ten are burned next morning. Forgive this tediousness in the pen, which I acquire by the want of spending it in talk; and believe me to be, with true esteem and friendship,

Your most obedient humble servant, etc.

Addressed—To the Reverend Mr. Winder at Belfast.

[1] *I.e.*, Dorset, Carteret, and Grafton.
[2] *I.e.*, Stafford Lightburne (*supra*, vol. iii, p. 152).
[3] Winder had two sons, Edward and Peter, who took holy orders, and two daughters, Jane, who married the Rev. Edward Benson, and Elizabeth, who married George Macartney, and was mother of the illustrious Earl Macartney.

DCCCXXV. [*Original.*[1]]

LADY ELIZABETH GERMAIN TO SWIFT

February 23, 1731-2.

I LIKE to know my power, if it is so, that I can make you uneasy at my not writing, though I shall not often care to exert it, lest you should grow weary of me and my correspondence; but the slowness of my answer does not come from the emptiness of my heart, but the emptiness of my head, and that you know is nature's fault, not mine.[2] I was not learned enough to know *non credo* has been so long in fashion, but every day convinces me more of the necessity of it, not but that I often wish against myself; as *par exemple*, I would fain believe you are coming to England, because most of your acquaintance tells me so; and yet I turn, and wind, and sift your letters to find anything like it being true, but instead of that, there I find a lawsuit, which is a worse tie by the leg than your lameness. And pray what is " this hurt above my heel "?[3] Have you had a fellow-feeling with my Lord Lieutenant of the gout, and call it a sprain, as he does, who has lied so long and often to disguise it, that I verily think he has not a new story left? Does he do the same in Ireland, for there I hoped he would have given a better example?

I find you are grown a horrid flatterer, or else you could never have thought of anything so much to my taste as this piece of marble you speak of for my sister Penelope, which I desire may be at my expense.[4] I cannot be exact, neither as to the time nor year, but she died soon after we came there, and we did not stay quite two year, and were in England some months before King William died.[5] I

---

[1] In the British Museum. See Preface.

[2] At that time no letters gave Swift more pleasure than those from his old friend Lady Betty. Only a month had elapsed since he received her last letter (*supra*, p. 278).

[3] *Supra*, p. 281, n. 3.

[4] As appears from subsequent letters Swift, who had then monuments on the brain, had proposed to erect one to the memory of a sister of Lady Betty, who had died while their father was a Lord Justice of Ireland, and had been buried in St. Andrew's Church in Dublin.

[5] According to the inscription placed eventually on the slab Lady

wish I had my Dame Wadgar, or Mr. Ferris's memorandum head, that I might know whether it was at "the time of gooseberries."[1]

Surely your Irish air is very bad for darts, if Mrs. Kelly's are blunted already; make her cross father let her come over, and we would not use her so in England. If my Duchess[2] sees company in a morning, you need not grumble at the hour, for it must be purely from great complaisance, for that never was her taste here, though she is as early a riser as the generality of ladies are, and I believe there is not many dressing-rooms in London, but mine, where the early idle come. Adieu abruptly; for I will have no more formal humble servants, with your whole name at the bottom, as if I was asking you your catechism.

Addressed—To the Revd. Doctor Swift, Dean of St. Patrick's, at Dublin, Ireland.

DCCCXXVI. [*Original.*[3]]

JOHN GAY TO SWIFT

March 13, 1731-2.

DEAR SIR,

I HOPE this unlucky accident of hurting your leg will not prevent your coming to us this spring, though you say nothing about it.[4] All your friends expect it, and particularly my landlord and landlady, who are my friends as much as ever, and I should not think them so, if they were not as much yours. The Downs of Amesbury are so smooth that neither horse nor man can hardly make a wrong step, so that you may take your exercise with us with greater security. If you can prevail with the Duchess to ride and walk with you, you will do her good, but that is a motive I could never prevail with her to comply with. I wish you would try whether your oratory could get over

Betty's sister died within a few weeks of their father's arrival in Ireland (*supra*, vol. i, p. 31, n. 1). Lord Berkeley returned to England nearly a year before King William died.

[1] See "Mrs. Frances Harris's Petition" ("Poetical Works," i, 37).
[2] *I.e.*, of Dorset.
[3] In the British Museum. See Preface.
[4] The letter to which the present one is a reply is not forthcoming.

this difficulty. General Dormer, Sir Clement Cotterell, and I set out to-morrow morning for Rousham, in Oxfordshire, to stay ten days or a fortnight.[1] The Duchess will undertake to recommend the Lords of her acquaintance to attend Mr. Ryves's cause, if it should come on before our return. The Duke will do the same.[2] Her Grace, too, hath undertaken to answer your letter. I have not disposed of your South Sea bonds. There is a year's interest due at Lady-day. But if I were to dispose of them at present, I should lose a great deal of the premium I paid for them; perhaps they may fall lower, but I cannot prevail with myself to sell them. The rogueries that have been discovered in some other companies, I believe, make them all have less credit.

I find myself dispirited, for want of having some pursuit. Indolence and idleness are the most tiresome things in the world, and I begin to find a dislike to society. I think I ought to try to break myself of it, but I cannot resolve to set about it. I have left off almost all my great acquaintance, which saves me something in chair-hire, though in that article the town is still very expensive. Those who were your old acquaintance are almost the only people I visit, and, indeed, upon trying all, I like them best. Lord Cornbury refused the pension that was offered him.[3] He is chosen to

---

[1] General James Dormer (*supra*, p. 158, n. 4) was a cousin of Sir Clement Cotterell (*supra*, p. 196), and ultimately bequeathed to him Rousham, which is said by Pope to have been the prettiest place for waterfalls, jets, ponds and beautiful scenes of green and hanging wood that ever he saw. It was then in the possession of the General's elder brother, Colonel James Dormer, to whom Swift's "Imitation of the second epistle of the second book of Horace" was addressed:

"Dear Colonel, Cobham's and your country's friend,
    You love a verse, take such as I can send."

[2] The reference is to a suit between William Ryves and David Bindon, which had led to an appeal to the British House of Lords (Nichols, "Works," xviii, 218). Ryves was a son of Sir Richard Ryves, who had occupied a seat on the bench of the Exchequer in Ireland under William III, and was a nephew of Swift's old friend, Dean Ryves (*supra*, vol. i, p. 45). Swift's interest in him was, however, attributable to the fact that he was through his mother, who was a sister of Philip Savage, a cousin of Lady Acheson.

[3] It is to his conduct on this occasion that Pope alludes in his lines on him (*supra*, p. 139, n. 1): "How could you tell, my Lord," Cornbury said to his brother-in-law, Lord Essex, who conveyed the offer, "that I was to be sold, or at least how could you know my price so exactly?"

represent the University of Oxford, in the room of Mr. Bromley,[1] without opposition. I know him, and I think he deserves it. He is a young nobleman of learning and morals, which is so particular, that I know you will respect and value him; and, to my great comfort, he lives with us in our family. Mr. Pope is in town, and in good health. I lately passed a week with him at Twickenham. I must leave the rest to the Duchess;[2] for I must pack up my shirts, to set out to-morrow, being the 14th of March, the day after I received your letter. If you would advise the Duchess to confine me four hours a day to my own room, while I am in the country, I will write; for I cannot confine myself as I ought.

Addressed—To the Rev. Dr. Swift, Dean of St. Patrick's, in Dublin.

DCCCXXVII. [*Faulkner.*]

SWIFT TO GEORGE FAULKNER

Deanery House, *March* 29, 1732.

MR. FAULKNER,[3]

WITHOUT the least regard to your wager, I do assure you, upon my word and reputation, that I am not the author of one single line or syllable of that pamphlet, called an Infallible Scheme to pay the Debts of the Nation;[4] and, as it is very unjust, so it is equally an im-

[1] William Bromley, who had been so well known to Swift first as Speaker, and afterwards as Secretary of State in Oxford's administration, died that year.

[2] As is subsequently mentioned she was prevented finishing the letter by being summoned to Winchester to attend on her son, Lord Drumlanrig, who had contracted the smallpox.

[3] The Hibernian Atticus, as Lord Chesterfield used to call this celebrated printer, had probably made Swift's acquaintance when he delivered the letter from Pope (*supra*, vol. iii, p. 343). Faulkner, who was by birth and education an Irishman, was then returning to Dublin after serving for a time in William Bowyer's office, and opened soon afterwards a bookselling and printing establishment of his own in that city. On the death of Hyde Swift appears to have transferred the business to him.

[4] The "Infallible Scheme to pay the Public Debt of this Nation in Six Months humbly offered to the Consideration of the present Parlia-

prudent and fallible proceeding, to pronounce determin-
ately on our taste and knowledge of style or manner of
writing, where very good judges are often deceived, and in
this case, few men have suffered so much as myself, who
have borne the reproach of many hundred printed papers,
which I never saw. I do likewise protest in the same manner, that I did not write the epigram upon Taylor, nor
heard of it until Mr. Pilkington showed it me in manuscript.[1] Therefore pray desire your wagerer from me to be
more cautious in determining on such matters, and not to
venture the loss of his money and credit with so much
odds against him. I am,

Your affectionate[2] servant,

J. SWIFT.

If this fancy should hold, of taxing me with all the
papers that come out, and at the same time I should take a
fancy to be a writer, I shall be discovered when I have no
mind, for it will be only to catechise me whenever I am
suspected.

DCCCXXVIII. [*Deane Swift.*]

SWIFT TO LADY ACHESON

Saturday Morning [*April* 1], 1732.

A GENTLEMAN called here last night upon some business, who took Mr. ——'s house yesterday at dinner in his
return from Wicklow.[3] He tells me that Mrs. —— was

ment" (Royal Irish Academy Tracts) came from the pen of Pilkington.
It proposes the imposition of a tax on such vices as perjury, fornica-
tion, drunkenness, swearing, slander, infidelity, fraud and blasphemy,
which was suggested to the author by a scheme of one of the pro-
jectors in the Academy of Lagado ("Prose Works," viii, 197).

[1] A celebrated charlatan, the Chevalier Taylor, visited Ireland at
that time, and was the victim of some very unsavoury horseplay. It
is described in a tract called "The English Imposter Detected, or the
History of the Life and Fumigation of the Renowned Mr. J—— T——,
Occulist" (Dublin, 1732), and in "An Elegy on the much Lamented
Death of Mr. T——r, the famous occulist, who was suffocated by a
new Method of Fumigation at the College, the first of this instant
April 1732."

[2] It seems improbable that Faulkner was thus honoured. Possibly
the adjective is due to editing on his part.

[3] As appears from the reply Lady Acheson was then residing in

brought to bed yesterday morning at five o'clock of half a child, just as if it were divided in two equal parts. It had one eye, half a nose and a mouth, one leg, and so from top to bottom. They could see it was a boy, or rather half a boy. It was dead born, but she is very well. It was thought that this was the cause of all her colics. Mrs. Brent tells me she has known the like more than once. I am glad the poor woman had her mother and sister with her.

Are you not undone for want of Monky?[1] How are you? Does your milk agree with you? We shall see you no more at church until Monky returns. Adieu, etc. I mend a little.

Endorsed—An April-fool letter.

DCCCXXIX. [*Deane Swift.*]

LADY ACHESON TO SWIFT

Saturday Morning [*April* 1], 1732.

I AM greatly surprised at the account you gave me of poor Mrs. ——; but since it was so, I am heartily glad she has got rid of it. Mrs. Morris's gout seized her all over on Thursday, so that she keeps her bed. None of them know anything of this matter. They sent a boy yesterday to Delgany[2]—I will not mention this thing to them till he returns—to let them know she was not able to go to the country. I am sorry that you mend but a little. This bad weather has increased my cough; the milk agrees very well with me. I will be at your church to-morrow. I am,

Yours, etc.

Dublin, and a lady who was living with her had intended to go on a visit to the house which is here denoted, and which belonged to her brother-in-law.

[1] The reference is evidently to Lady Acheson's companion, whose name, as will be seen by the reply, was Morris. She is mentioned in the " Epistle to Two Friends " (" Poetical Works," ii, 373) as a member of St. Patrick's congregation.

[2] Delgany lies about half-way between Dublin and Wicklow. It was the home of Chief Justice Whitshed, by whose representatives his lands are still owned.

DCCCXXX. [*Elwin.*]

VISCOUNT BOLINGBROKE AND ALEXANDER POPE TO SWIFT

[*April*, 1732.]

BOLINGBROKE

YOU may assure yourself, that if you come over this spring, you will find me not only got back into the habits of study, but devoted to that historical task, which you have set me these many years.[1] I am in hopes of some materials which will enable me to work in the whole extent of the plan I propose to myself. If they are not to be had, I must accommodate my plan to this deficiency. In the mean time Pope has given me more trouble than he or I thought of, and you will be surprised to find that I have been partly drawn by him, and partly by myself, to write a pretty large volume upon a very grave and very important subject;[2] that I have ventured to pay no regard whatever to any authority, except sacred authority, and that I have ventured to start a thought which must, if it is pushed as successfully as I think it is, render all your metaphysical theology both ridiculous and abominable. There is an expression in one of your letters to me, which makes me believe you will come into my way of thinking on this subject, and yet I am persuaded that divines and freethinkers would both be clamorous against it, if it was to be submitted to their censure, as I do not intend that it shall. The passage I mean is that where you say you told Dr. Delany the grand points of Christianity ought to be taken as infallible revelations, etc.[3]

It has happened that whilst I was writing this to you the Doctor came to make me a visit from London, where I

---

[1] As appears from his former letter the task was, however, not exactly the one which Swift was anxious that he should undertake (*supra*, p. 252).

[2] His "Essays on Philosophy" (*supra*, p. 277, n. 4). "Their object," says Churton Collins, "was to demolish theological and philosophical dogma, to purify philosophy from mysticism, and to reconstruct on an entirely new basis the science of metaphysics" ("Bolingbroke," p. 217).

[3] "Whatever Swift may have said Bolingbroke wanted him to acknowledge that revelation was not to be reconciled to reason, or to our moral ideas" (Elwin, *op. cit.*, vii, 262).

heard he was arrived some time ago. He was in haste to return, and is, I perceive, in great haste to print. He left with me eight dissertations, a small part, as I understand, of his work,[1] and desired me to peruse, consider, and observe upon them against Monday next, when he will come down again. By what I have read of the two first, I find myself unable to serve him. The principles he reasons upon are begged in a disputation of this sort, and the manner of reasoning is by no means close and conclusive. The sole advice I could give him in conscience would be that which he would take ill and not follow. I will get rid of this task as well as I can, for I esteem the man, and should be sorry to disoblige him where I cannot serve him.

As to retirement, and exercise, your notions are true. The first should not be indulged so much as to render us savage, nor the last neglected so as to impair health. But I know men, who, for fear of being savage, live with all who will live with them; and who, to preserve their health, saunter away half their time. Adieu. Pope calls for the paper.

POPE

I hope what goes before will be a strong motive to your coming. God knows if ever I shall see Ireland. I shall never desire it, if you can be got hither, or kept here. Yet I think I shall be too soon a free man. Your recommendations I constantly give to those you mention; though some of them I see but seldom, and am every day more retired. I am less fond of the world, and less curious about it; yet no way out of humour, disappointed, or angry, though in my way I receive as many injuries as my betters; but I do not feel them, therefore I ought not to vex other people, nor even to return injuries. I pass almost all my time at Dawley and at home. My Lord—of which I partly take the merit to myself—is as much estranged from politics as I am. Let philosophy be ever so vain, it is less vain now than politics, and not quite so vain at present as divinity. I know nothing that moves strongly but satire, and those who are ashamed of nothing else are so of being ridiculous. I fancy, if we three were together but for three years, some good might be done even upon this age.

[1] *I.e.*, "Revelation Examined with Candour" (*supra*, p. 250, n. 2).

I know you will desire some account of my health. It is as usual, but my spirits rather worse. I write little or nothing. You know I never had either a taste or talent for politics, and the world minds nothing else. I have personal obligations, which I will ever preserve, to men of different sides, and I wish nothing so much as public quiet, except it be my own quiet. I think it a merit, if I can take off any man from grating or satirical subjects, merely on the score of party; and it is the greatest vanity of my life that I have contributed to turn my Lord Bolingbroke to subjects moral, useful, and more worthy his pen. Dr. Delany's book is what I cannot commend so much as Dean Berkeley's,[1] though it has many things ingenious in it, and is not deficient in the writing part; but the whole book, though he meant it *ad populum*, is, I think, purely *ad clerum*. Adieu.

DCCCXXXI. [*Manuscripts of Mrs. Stopford Sackville.*[2]]

SWIFT TO THE DUKE OF DORSET

Deanery House, *April* 20, 1732.

MY LORD,

I RETURN my most humble acknowledgements to your Grace and my Lady Duchess for your great condescension in inquiring after me at a time when you are so much taken up in crowds and ceremony.[3] I can make no wishes for either of you but a good voyage without sickness or accidents; for as to honour, fortune, favour, and the like, I can only pray for the continuance of them. That I so seldom troubled your Grace I am sure you will approve as a matter of conscience in me, not to disturb your hours, which in the business of some months left so few for your own leisure and diversions.

---

[1] Berkeley had returned at the close of the preceding year from his expedition to found a college in the West Indies, on which he had set out three years before ("Memoirs of Viscountess Sundon," ii, 165). Within a few months of his arrival he published his "Alciphron or the Minute Philosopher."

[2] Hist. MSS. Com., vol. i, p. 149.

[3] Two days later the Duke and Duchess set sail for England.

DCCCXXXII. [*Copy.*[1]]

KNIGHTLEY CHETWODE TO SWIFT

[*April*, 1732.]

SIR,[2]

I AM truly concerned at your having been so long lame, whence you say I cannot see you, though I imputed it to your having taken something amiss in my last letter, wherein when I thought I was only plain perhaps I have been blunt, and that is a fault, for I am of opinion with my old friend Wycherley, that some degree of ceremony should be preserved in the strictest friendship.[3] However I write again to you, upon my old maxim that he who forbears to write because his last letter is unanswered shows more regard to forms and punctilios than to friendship. I have met you handed about in print, and as the coffeehouses will have it of your own doing.[4] I am afraid your using your leg too soon will not let it be too soon well, the very shaking of a chair, though you had a stool under it, I believe harmed you, for you see by your accident at the Archbishop's, and exertion,[5] how small a thing throws you back. Beware I pray you of this hurt in time for if a

---

[1] In the Forster Collection. *Supra*, vol. ii, p. 241, n. 1.

[2] This letter is printed by Birkbeck Hill (" Unpublished Letters," p. 147), but in his arrangement it precedes the last one from Swift to Chetwode (*supra*, p. 224). In a review of Hill's book in the "Athenæum" (1899, pt. i, p. 460) the opinion was expressed that the order of these letters ought to have been reversed, and this conclusion is confirmed by the discovery of Chetwode's bitter retort. To that effort of Swift's exasperated correspondent there is evident allusion in the present letter, of which the date can be determined with approximate certainty by mention in it of the hurt to Swift's leg. As will be seen Chetwode had come to Dublin, and had endeavoured through friends to obtain access once more to the Deanery, but without success.

[3] "Society, which should beget love and friendship, grows to familiarity, which breeds contempt; till friendship becomes enmity, and men grow the worse friends the better they know one another" (" Posthumous Works," Lond., 1728, p. 64).

[4] The reference is no doubt to " The Grand Question debated: whether Hamilton's Bawn should be turned into a Barrack or a Malt House," which was published at that time. In a subsequent letter Swift attributes its appearance to the carelessness of Lord Carteret in handing about a copy which had been given to him.

[5] According to the copy used by Birkbeck Hill these words should read "Archbishop's visitation."

swelling should fix in your legs, an access of a dropsy may be apprehended. I should be glad to see you if it were convenient and agreeable to you and not else,[1] though I am,

Your well wisher and humble servant,

K. C.

DCCCXXXIII. [*Elwin.*[2]]

SWIFT TO JOHN GAY

Dublin, *May* 4, 1732.

DEAR SIR,

I AM now as lame as when you writ your letter, and almost as lame as your letter itself, for want of that limb from my Lady Duchess, which you promised, and without which I wonder how it could limp hither.[3] I am not in a condition to make a true step even on Amesbury Downs, and I declare that a corporeal false step is worse than a political one; nay, worse than a thousand political ones, for which I appeal to Courts and Ministers, who hobble on and prosper without the sense of feeling. To talk of riding and walking is insulting me, for I can as soon fly as do either. I desire you will manage my South Sea estate as you would do if it were your own—I mean in every circumstance except gaming with the public; that is, buying or selling lottery tickets, as you once proposed to me from your own practice.[4] I love Mr. Lewis's device, *piano, piano.*

It is your pride or laziness, more than chair-hire, that makes the town expensive. No honour is lost by walking in the dark; and in the day, you may beckon a blackguard boy under a gate, near your visiting place,[5] *experto crede,* save elevenpence, and get half-a-crown's worth of health. The worst of my present misfortune is, that I eat and drink, and can digest neither for want of exercise; and, to increase my misery, the knaves are sure to find me at home, and make huge void spaces in my cellars. I congratulate with you for losing your great acquaintance. In

---

[1] So far as is known there was never any further communication between Chetwode and Swift.

[2] By permission of Mr. John Murray. *Supra*, vol. iii, p. 148, n. 1.

[3] *Supra*, p. 286.   [4] *Supra*, p. 206.

[5] As Elwin observes (*op. cit.*, vii, 265) "to black his shoes."

such a case, philosophy teaches that we must submit and be content with good ones. I like Lord Cornbury's refusing his pension, but I demur at his being elected for Oxford, which, I conceive, is wholly changed, and entirely devoted to new principles, directly contrary to those for which Lord Cornbury refused a pension, and it appeared to me a most corrupt seminary the two last times I was there.

I find by the whole cast of your letter that you are as giddy and as volatile as ever, just the reverse of Mr. Pope, who has always loved a domestic life from his youth. I was going to wish you had some little place that you could call your own, but I profess I do not know you well enough to contrive any one system of life that would please you. You pretend to preach up riding and walking to the Duchess, yet, from my knowledge of you after twenty years, you always joined a violent desire of perpetually shifting places and company, with a rooted laziness, and an utter impatience of fatigue. A coach and six horses is the utmost exercise you can bear, and this only when you can fill it with such company as is best suited to your taste; and how glad would you be if it could waft you in the air to avoid jolting, while I, who am so much later in life, can, or at least could, ride five hundred miles on a trotting horse. You mortally hate writing, only because it is the thing you chiefly ought to do; as well to keep up the vogue you have in the world, as to make you easy in your fortune. You are merciful to everything but money, your best friend, whom you treat with inhumanity. Be assured I will hire people to watch all your motions and to return me a faithful account. Tell me, have you cured your absence of mind? Can you attend to trifles? Can you at Amesbury write domestic libels to divert the family and neighbouring squires for five miles round, or venture so far on horseback without apprehending a stumble at every step? Can you set the footmen a laughing as they wait at dinner, and do the Duchess's women admire your wit? In what esteem are you with the vicar of the parish? Can you play with him at backgammon? Have the farmers found out that you cannot distinguish rye from barley, or an oak from a crab tree? You are sensible that I know the full extent of your country skill is in fishing for roaches or gudgeons at the highest. I love to do you good offices with your friends, and therefore desire you will show this letter to the Duchess, to improve her Grace's good opinion of your qualifications, and convince her how useful you are like to be in the family.

I suppose you have seen Dr. Delany, who has been long amongst you, and we hear is printing many sermons against freethinkers, besides one or more against eating blood. I advised him against preaching on those subjects to plain believing Christians, but that he might print if he pleased. This I suppose hindered him from taking me as his adviser, and he rather chooses Lord Bolingbroke. We hear he has published a poem inscribed to one of the Princesses.[1] Pray how does Dr. Berkeley's book pass amongst you? It is too speculative for me.[2] I hope you still see Lady Suffolk in her grandeur, and think her as much your friend as ever, in which you do her justice. I desire to present my most humble respect to the Duke and Duchess. Her Grace shall have the honour of my correspondence again when she goes to Amesbury. Hear a piece of Irish news. I buried the famous General Meredyth's father last night in my Cathedral. He was ninety-six years old; so that Mrs. Pope may live seven years longer.[3] You saw Mr. Pope in health; pray is he generally more healthy than when I was among you? I would know how your own health is, and how much wine you drink in a day? My stint in company is a pint at noon, and half as much at night, but I often dine at home like a hermit, and then I drink little or none at all. Yet I differ from you, for I would have society, if I could get what I like, people of middle understanding and middle rank, very complying, and consequently such as I can govern.

Lord knows where this letter will find you; but I think

[1] Literary labours were not Delany's only occupation at that time (*supra*, p. 290). In the hope of securing Court favour he was busy ingratiating himself with Mrs. Clayton, to whom he had no doubt been introduced by her kinsman the Bishop of Killala, and did not venture to deliver a sermon until it had received her imprimatur (Mrs. Thomson's "Memoirs of the Viscountess Sundon," i, 402).

[2] *Supra*, p. 291, n. 1.

[3] Although the General is said to have drunk destruction to the Tory administration, and to have fired a pistol at a representation of the great Oxford, Swift had a kindly feeling for him (*cf.* "Prose Works," ii, 346). The fact that the Meredyths were a Meath family accounts no doubt for this weakness, and also for Swift's officiating at the interment of the General's father, who displays in his will a strong leaning towards Dissent.

your will is that I should direct always to the Duke's in Burlington Gardens. There is a Lord[1] for you wholly out of my favour, whom I will use as I did Schomberg's heiresses. So adieu.

Ever yours.

DCCCXXXIV. [Original.[2]]

LADY ELIZABETH GERMAIN TO SWIFT

London, May 13, 1732.

I AM sorry my writing should inconvenience your eyes, but I fear, it is rather my style, than my ink, that is so hard to be read; however, if I do not forget myself, I will enlarge my hand to give you the less trouble.[3] Their Graces are at last arrived in perfect health, in spite of all their perils and dangers;[4] though I must own they were so long in their voyage that they gave me an exceeding heart-ache, and if that would be any hindrance, they shall never have my consent to go back to Ireland, and remain here, be only king of Knole and Drayton,[5] and I do not think it would be the worse for him, either in person or pockets. I dare say, he would not need a remembrance office for anything you have spoke to him about, but however, I will not fail the part that you have set me.

I find you want a strict account of me how I pass my time. But first, I thank you for the nine hours out of the

---

[1] I.e., Burlington (supra, p. 280).

[2] In the British Museum. See Preface.

[3] Swift's strictures on Lady Betty's writing shows that there was reason for his complaints as to loss of sight. Her hand is easily read, and the writing is even to-day quite clear.

[4] The "imminent danger" which the Duke and Duchess of Dorset encountered in crossing to England on that occasion was twenty years later still vividly recollected ("Orrery Papers," ii, 260), and was commemorated at the time in verses which represent Heaven as allowing the tempest to delay but not to harm Dorset, the "darling viceroy" of Ireland, and the "favourite son" of England ("London Magazine," 1732, p. 89). They set sail from Dublin on Saturday evening, 22 April, for Parkgate, but having met with very bad weather, during which the seas ran so high that they broke "into the state room where their Graces were in bed," they were driven back to the Irish coast, and on Monday evening put into Carrickfergus. There they remained for some days, and did not reach Parkgate until the following Saturday.

[5] Lady Betty's own seat (supra, p. 164, n. 2).

twenty-four you bestowed on me for sleeping; one or two of them I will willingly present you back again. As to quadrille, though I am, generally speaking, a constant attendant to it every day in the week, not one excepted, yet I will most thankfully submit to your allowance of time; for, when complaisance draws me on farther, it is with great yawnings, and a vast expense of my breath, in asking, who plays, who's called, and what's trumps, and if you can recollect anything of my former way of life, such as it was, so it is. I never loved to have my hands idle; they were either full of work or had a book, but as neither sort was the best or most useful, so you will find forty years and a way bit[1] have done no more good to my head, than it has to my face.

Your old friend Biddy is much your humble servant, and could she get rid of her cough, her spleen would do her nor her friend no harm; for she loves a sly sedate joke, as well as ever you knew her do. The Duke and Duchess are just come in, who both present their services to you, and will take it as a favour, if you will bestow any of your time that you can spare upon Lord George.[2] Adieu, for the Duchess the Countess of Suffolk, Mr. Chardin,[3] and I, are going to quadrille.

DCCCXXXV. [Hawkesworth.]

SWIFT TO THE REV. THOMAS SHERIDAN

[May 13, 1732.]

DOMINE,

AUDIVI quod abra foeminae nobilis et mihi amicae offendendo pedem ad paxillum vel ridicam, vel, ut alii dicunt,

---

[1] *Hibernice* a wee bit.

[2] Lady Betty Germain's heir, whose conduct at Minden left a stigma that great abilities as an administrator and debater could not remove, had been entered as a student in Dublin University, and evidently remained in Dublin when his parents returned to England. His matriculation entry is dated 3 August, 1731, and states that he was then sixteen years of age, had been born in London, and was educated at Westminster School. His college tutor was Dr. Whitcombe, who was raised by Dorset to the episcopal bench, and became Archbishop of Cashel. Lord George is described about that time by Mrs. Delany ("Correspondence," i, 393) as "a comical spark."

[3] Probably the second son of the well-known Eastern traveller. His eldest son had been created before then a baronet.

rutabulum; valdè laesit uropygium, et est miserè catax.[1]
Novi ejus patrem, capitularem, et sublestum, et carnarium,
qui suratus erat hornotinum per ostium clathratum, et, ut
meruit, a vulgo occillatus.[2] Pauper enim erat, gaunaco et
decotibus vestitus; pernionibus claudicans laboravit.[3] Fre-
quentavit sui similes, propolas nempe, arilatores, cociones,
imò salisubsulos et labdas, omnes, ut meruerant, tribonibus
vestitos.[4]

Pridiè tabellio ad me attulit epistolam de stlata et catta
in portu obrutis, unde miser perdidi cadiscum strobilorum
plerum, duo haustra, calpar, decem scutellas, calignam, et,
quod maximè dolet, crocotulam nuper uxori emptam, sed
spero me redhostiturum fore.[5]

Amicus noster catulaster lepidissimus hominum miserè
vivit in domuncula vescarum plena, proficiebus pascitur,
operando strigans et conquiniscens, et turundis pullos pascit
in tuguriolo serphorum pleno.[6]

---

[1] "As the words, in this and the following letter," says Hawkesworth, "which cause any difficulty, are extremely uncommon; we presume, it will not be amiss to print a glossary, in order to save our
readers the plague and trouble of turning over a dictionary."
Abra, a waiting-woman : *quod sit* delicata, *non vulgaris Ancilla.*
Paxillus, a stake, pale, or post. *Ridica*, the prop of a vine, etc. *Rutabulum*, a maukin, a cole-rake to make clean an oven, an oven-swoop,
a skealing-stick. *Uropygium*, the narrowest and lowest part of the
chine, the rump. *Catax*, lame, hip-halt.

[2] *Capitularis*, a tax-gatherer, an exciseman. *Sublestus*, weak, feeble ;
of no esteem or account. *Carnarius*, a butcher. *Hornotinus*, a fawn
or hind-calf. *Clathratus*, latticed, barred, grated. *Occillo*, to buffet, or
beat and maul.

[3] *Gaunacum*, a thick shag rug to cover one with, an Irish mantle.
Decotes, togae detritae, garments worn bare. *Pernio*, a kibe on the heel.

[4] *Propola*, a huckster, or retailer, a forestaller, a regrater, etc.
Arilator, a pedlar. *Cocio*, a higler. *Salisubsulus*, a morris-dancer, any
one who dances and capers to music. *Labda*, any sort of vile, filthy
rascal. *Tribon*, a threadbare cloak.

[5] *Tabellio*, a carrier of letters. *Stlata*, a float, a hoy, a flat boat.
Catta, nomen navis. Cadiscus, a rundlet, a kilderkin, or little barrel.
Strobilus, a pine-apple. *Plerus*, idem quod *plenus. Haustrum*, a bucket;
also a kind of pot, or jug, to draw drink with. *Calpar*, an earthen
vessel, or tun. *Scutella*, any kind of dish or platter. *Caligna*, as this
word seems to be derived from καλὸν, *lignum*, perhaps it signifies a
large wooden bowl. *Crocotula*, a little saffron-coloured, or yellow garment. *Redhostio*, to requite a courtesy, to return like for like : but
here it may signify, to make a present of just such another garment.

[6] *Catulaster*, a little whelp. *Vesca*, a cobweb. *Proficies*, perhaps it
may signify a supply, or subsidy, given as a present. *Strigo*, to breathe,
or rest in work, to stop or stand still, as oxen sometimes do at plough

Hesterna nocte cecidit terribilissima labes mantissa, quae inlices omnes implevit.[1]

Sum humilissimus, etc.

DCCCXXXVI. [*Hawkesworth.*]

The Rev. Thomas Sheridan to Swift

[*May* 15, 1732.]

DOCTISSIME DECANE,

FORBUM tabellarum methodium vestrarum lagonopono me fermè affecit, quocirca hostire vestrae reverentiae gerras aggredior.[2] Quid mea refert si uropygium abrae ignobilis sit laesum? Ejusmodi etenim mulieres plerumque sunt exbuae, atque rimarum non minùs plenae quàm excernicula; profectò non mihi injucundum foret si tu esses illi iatraliptes.[3] Si vero curam suscipias, non abs re fuerit illius crotaphitas ambabus calidè manibus fricare ne spiritus deficiant, atque inde porrò ad podicem descendens, postquam complutum aquâ vitae feceris, applicueris emplastrum calligoni, mattiacarum tritarum, daucorum, sussitieteridis, gethyonum.[4] Caveo interim ne tibi manus im-

in the middle of a furrow. *Conquinisco,* to duck the head, to bow or bend the body, to stoop. *Turunda,* a pellet of bread, dough, or paste, wherewith capons are crammed. *Serphus,* a kind of vermin like an ant.

[1] *Labes,* a great fall, or pash of rain or hail, etc. *Mantissa,* qu. *manutensa,* eo quod manu porrigitur; over-measure, advantage, the vantage or over-weight; the Welsh call it *Ispine. Inlex, inlices canales,* gutters in streets.

[2] *Forbus,* calidus, *serv.*; formus a θερμος: Æol. φερμος, aliter a *forbo,* vel *forvo,* i.e., *ferveo,* hot, warm. *Tabella,* a letter, or epistle. *Methodium,* a trick, a cheat, a cunning fetch. *Lagonoponos,* fretting to the gutts. *Hostio,* to recompense, to return like for like. *Gerrae,* hurdles, or twigs filled up with earth, for fortifying a place; gabions, etc.

[3] *Exbuae,* tippling-gossips. *Excerniculum,* a sieve. *Iatraliptes,* a physician or surgeon that cures by ointments and frictions.

[4] *Crotaphitae,* the two muscles that are in the temples. *Complutus,* wetted all over. *Calligonum,* way-grass, knot-grass. *Mattiacae,* [pilae dict. quòd praestantissimae apud Mattiacum Germaniae oppidum conficerentur,] soap-balls, wash-balls. *Tritus,* common, much used. *Daucus,* a kind of wild carrot. *Sussitieteridis.* As there is no such word as this to be found in the common dictionaries, it is imagined to have been coined by Doctor *Sheridan,* when he was writing this letter, in order to amuse and puzzle his correspondent: or, if it be not too wild a conjecture, let us suppose the word to be thus divided, *sussiti et eridis*; and then it may refer to the rest of the ingredients of the

bulbitaverit, aut imbubinaverit, partiliter quandò praedicti spiritus urticam senserit; sed ne forsan obliviscaris, te moneo, ut pars crepidinis dorsi interior sit fissiculanda.[1] Memini illius patrem ex infimâ plebis ruderatione gingrinatorem; lucuntes olim vendidit, admodum fuit procellulus, eximius autem pilicrepus; sed salaconem atque dosonem nimiùm se ostendendo, minuit hanc gloriam quam exercitiis meruit.[2] Si vis ut nostra denuo amicitia inolescat, te mecum cràs prandere prorito; habebis sympinium vel applam vini non vulgaris absque flocibus, cum cervisia aequè pellucidum ac glaesum.[3] Saepissimè futabas in aedibus meis neque unquam inanias, de quibus mentionem in epistolâ vestrâ fecisti, in ullâ nostrarum conspexisti camerarum. Hesterno die nimiùm ambulando flegmine laboro, quod ex stomachi ventositate evenisse comperio, ideoque magnam git quantitatem, ut postico emurmuret, deglutire statuo.

Sum tibi humillimus, etc.

Manaco Maii 15°, 1732.[4]

plaster, and especially to the severe poignancy of the onions, in the next and last article. And then, perhaps, the latter part of the sentence may be thus paraphrastically interpreted : "You might apply to the part affected a plaster of knot-grass, common wash-ball, wild carrot and among the rest of the ingredients," [for Συσσιτος signifies a Companion] "by way of giving the whole a poignancy," [for Ἔρις signifies a contention for victory] "you should take care that a mixture of onion predominate in the composition." The word *Urtica*, in the following period, seems to favour his conjecture. *Gethyon*, a kind of onions, hollow leeks.

[1] *Imbulbito*, to defile one's self with any thing detestable; vide Dictionary. *Imbubino*, to defile with any thing abominable; vide Dict. *Partiliter*, particularly, with exactness or subtility. *Urtica*, a nettle, or any tickling pain like the sting of a nettle. *Crepido, dorsi crepido*, the rump. *Fissiculandus*, to be cleft, or cut open.

[2] *Ruderatio*, rubbish. *Gingrinator*, a piper or minstrel. *Lucuns*, a kind of meat, or rather some baked thing; a spice-cake. *Pilicrepus*, a ball-player. *Salacon*, a great boaster, who, being extremely poor, would be thought very rich. *Doso*, a great promiser, but who does nothing.

[3] *Inolesco*, ut *coalesco*, to grow together, to stick one to another. *Prorito*, to provoke, stir up, egg on. *Sympinium*, a kind of wooden vessel for wine, used of old in their holy rites and divine services; a stone-jug, or pitcher, a drinking-cup. *Appla*, ab *ad* et *pleo*, ut sit vas quod subinde impletur et depletur, a kind of vessel used at table. *Floces*, pl. the dregs or lees of wine. *Cervisia*, vel *cerevisia, cerealis*, liquor, ale, beer, etc. *Glaesum*, a kind of amber.

[4] *Futo*, to blame or reprove. *Inaniae*, emptinesses, cobwebs. *Flegmen*, an inflammation or swelling in the legs, tired by overmuch walking. *Git*, vel *gith*, indecl. a kind of cockle, a small seed. *Posticum*, a backdoor. *Manacus*, a month.

DCCCXXXVII. [*Original.*[1]]

JOHN GAY TO SWIFT

London, *May* 16, 1732.

DEAR SIR,

TO-MORROW we set out for Amesbury, where I propose to follow your advice, of employing myself about some work against next winter. You seemed not to approve of my writing more fables. Those I am now writing, have a prefatory discourse before each of them, by way of epistle, and the morals of most of them are of the political kind, which makes them run into a greater length than those I have already published. I have already finished fifteen or sixteen; four or five more would make a volume of the same size as the first. Though this is a kind of writing that appears very easy, I find it is the most difficult of any that I ever undertook. After I have invented one fable, and finished it, I despair of finding out another; but I have a moral or two more, which I wish to write upon. I have also a sort of scheme to raise my finances by doing something for the stage.[2] With this, and some reading, and a great deal of exercise, I propose to pass my summer. I am sorry it must be without you. Why cannot you come and saunter about the Downs a horseback, in the autumn, to mark the partridges for me to shoot for your dinner?

Yesterday I received your letter,[3] and notwithstanding your reproaches of laziness, I was four or five hours about business, and did not spend a shilling in a coach or chair. I received a year's interest on your two bonds, which is eight pounds. I have four of my own. I have deposited all of them in the hands of Mr. Hoare, to receive the half year's interest at Michaelmas. The premium of the bonds is fallen a great deal since I bought yours. I gave very near six pounds on each bond, and they are now sold for about fifty shillings. Everything is very precarious, and I have no opinion of any of their public securities, but I do not

---

[1] In the British Museum. See Preface.
[2] In the opinion of Mr. Austin Dobson ("D. N. B.," xxi, 89), the allusion is to the opera of "Achilles," which was acted at Covent Garden shortly after Gay's death.
[3] *Supra*, p. 293.

know what to do with our money. I believe, the Parliament next year intend to examine the South Sea scheme. I do not know, whether it will be prudent to trust our money there till that time. I did what I could to assist Mr. Ryves, and I am very glad that he hath found justice.[1] Lord Bathurst spoke for him, and was very zealous on bringing on his cause. The Duchess intended to write in my last letter, but she set out all on a sudden, to take care of Lord Drumlanrig, who was taken ill of the smallpox at Winchester school. He is now perfectly well recovered, for he had a favourable kind, to the great joy of our family. I think she ought, as she intends, to renew her correspondence with you at Amesbury. I was at Dawley on Sunday. Lady Bolingbroke continues in a very bad state of health, but still retains her spirits. You are always remembered there with great respect and friendship. Mrs. Pope is so worn out with old age, but without any distemper, that I look upon her life as very uncertain. Mr. Pope's state of health is much in the same way as when you left him. As for myself, I am often troubled with the colic. I have as much inattention, and have, I think, lower spirits than usual, which I impute to my having no one pursuit in life.

I have many compliments to make you from the Duke and Duchess, and Lords Bolingbroke, Bathurst, Sir William Wyndham, Mr. Pulteney, Dr. Arbuthnot, Mr. Lewis, etc. Every one of them is disappointed in your not coming among us. I have not seen Dean Berkeley, but have read his book, and like many parts of it, but in general think, with you, that it is too speculative, at least for me. Dr. Delany I have very seldom seen; he did not do me the honour to advise with me about anything he hath published. I like your thoughts upon these sorts of writing; and I should have advised him, as you did, though I had lost his good opinion. I write in very great haste; for I have many things to do before I go out of town. Pray make me as happy as you can, and let me hear from you often. But I am still in hopes to see you, and will expect a summons one day or other to come to Bristol, in order to be your guide to Amesbury.

---

[1] It appears from Swift's reply that this letter was conveyed to him by Ryves (*supra*, p. 285, n. 2).

DCCCXXXVIII. [*Barrett's Essay.*[1]]

Swift to the Rev. Henry Jenney

Dublin, *June* 8, 1732.

Sir,[2]

It is true that some weeks ago a manuscript paper of verses was handed about this town, and afterwards printed. The subject was my great ingratitude and breach of hospitality in publishing a copy of verses called Hamilton's Bawn. The writer hath likewise taken severe notice of some other verses published many years ago by the indiscretion of a friend, to whom they were sent in a letter. It was called a Journal, and writ at Mr. Rochfort's; and the consequences drawn from both by this late writer is, that the better I am used in any family the more I abuse them, with other reflections that must follow from such a principle. I was originally as unwilling to be libelled as the nicest man can be, but having been used to such treatment ever since I unhappily began to be known, I am now grown hardened; and while the friends I have left will continue to use me with any kindness, I shall need but a small degree of philosophy to bear me up against those who are pleased to be my enemies on the score of party zeal, and the hopes of turning that zeal to account.

One thing, I confess, would still touch me to the quick; I mean, if any person of true genius would employ his pen against me; but if I am not very partial to myself, I cannot remember that among at least two thousand papers full of

---

[1] The original is said to have been then in the possession of Viscount Cremorne, an ancestor of the Earl of Dartrey.

[2] Jenney, who had been known to Swift for many years (*supra*, vol. iii, p. 163), had evidently written to him to say that he was not the author of a poem entitled "An Answer to Hamilton's Bawn: or a Short Character of Dr. S—t" (Haliday Tracts) which was published at that time. The opening lines are as follows:

> "Gallstown is long in wish'd oblivion lost,
> The only vict'ry death o'er him can boast,
> In dust deserv'd that odious journal lies,
> O! had it ne'er appear'd to mortal eyes,
> Unsullied then had stood the Drapier's name,
> And unborn tongues proclaim'd the patriot's fame,
> Now fresh alas! the black remembrance lives,
> Gallstown again in Market Hill revives."

groundless reflections against me, hundreds of which I have seen, and heard of more, I never saw any one production that the meanest writer could have cause to be proud of; for which I can assign a very natural reason, that during the whole busy time of my life, the men of wit, in England, were all my particular friends, although many of them differed from me in opinions of public persons and proceedings. As to Ireland, where I lived very little before the Queen's death, and ever since in perfect retirement, I remember to have published nothing but what is called the Drapier's Letters, and some few other trifles relating to the affairs of this miserable and ruined kingdom. What other things fell from me, chiefly in verse, were only amusements in hours of sickness or leisure, or in private families, to divert ourselves and some neighbours, but were never intended for public view, which is plain from the subjects and the careless way of handling them: neither, indeed, can it answer the true ends of vanity or desire of praise, to let the world see such little sallies of fancy or humour, because if they be ill or indifferently performed, which must often be the case, the loss of reputation is certain; and however well executed, after a week's vogue, they are utterly forgot.

I know not how I come to be led so far from the subject of your letter. I confess there were some few persons who made random conjectures that you might possibly be concerned in the paper you hint at, but they were such who knew very little of you or me; for others who were better acquainted with us both have always cleared you, because they did not look upon that paper any way equal to your known good sense and candour, or talent of writing. And as to myself, I had further conviction, because I knew how well you were acquainted with the whole history and occasion of writing those verses on the Barrack; how well pleased the master and lady of the family were with it; that you had read it more than once; that it was no secret to any neighbour, nor any reserve but that against giving a copy. You know well by what incidents that reserve was broken, by granting a copy to a great person, and from thence how it fell into other hands, and so came, as it is the constant case, to be published, and is now forgot.

I confess my own conjectures about this late libel against me lay towards another gentleman, who, I am informed, hath since cleared himself, I mean Dr. Tisdall, but that

suspicion was first taught me by others: and yet I know
very well that for at least fifteen years past, he hath been
often engaged in a kind of flirting war of satiric burlesque
verse with certain wags both in town and country, who, it
seems, were provoked with his faculty of jibing, and used to
answer him in his own way.[1] Yet I have been assured that
in these combats, he was generally mistaken in his adversaries, falling foul upon many persons who never dipped a
pen either for or against him, and I think you, among
others, had some marks of his favour. But, as to me, who,
I solemnly profess, was always entirely innocent, during
the whole time that his pen and tongue took this unhappy
turn, as well as before and since, I could never be one
month at peace for his wit.[2] Whatever was writ to ridicule
him, was laid at my door, and only by himself, with a
further declaration, much to my honour, that he knew my
style, would trouble himself to inquire no further, and, using
my surname, said, I was his man. Some of his performances
I have seen, and have heard of more, besides the great
number he kept *in petto*; so that five or six gentlemen have
often and very lately assured me, that in one evening-sitting,
he has produced a dozen of his libels wholly against me,
desiring I might be told of it, and assuring those gentlemen
that the whole dozen should be published, if I would not
let him alone. This was a little hard upon me who had
never one single moment in my life the least inclination to
enter the lists with him, at those or any other weapons
whatsoever, any more than I would venture to sit four
hours disputing with him any point of controversy. I confess this keenness of the Doctor in determining, whenever
he was attacked, to fix on me for his adversary, incline me

---

[1] Eight years before Tisdall had published "Tom Pun-sibi Meta-
morphosed, or the Gibber Gibb'd" in which Sheridan is represented as a
mere creature of Swift:

> "What he shou'd do, he couldn't guess,
>   Sw—t us'd him like a pawn at chess;"

and this poem was answered by "The Rivals" in which Tisdall is
represented as actuated by jealousy and as having formerly been
proud to occupy a similar position (Trinity College Library).

[2] "Tom Pun-sibi" is included in "Gulliveriana" and is said to have
been written "by a very ingenious clergyman of Ireland in contempt
of Gulliver's insolence to his friends and acquaintances, and to expose
the servile behaviour of the Captain's underlings." It is probable that
Swift had treated Tisdall with contempt when he met him in Cope's
company. See Appendix IX.

IV   X

to conceive that he might have probably writ this last
paper, and other people had the same thought; but I hear
he hath utterly denied it, and I believe him, for I am confident he is an honest man, but unhappily misled through
the whole course of his life, by mistaking his talent, which
he hath against nature applied to wit and raillery, and
rhyming.[1] Besides which, his incurable absence of mind on
all occasions, and in all companies, hath led him into ten
thousand errors, especially of that kind, which are mortal
to all agreeable or improving conversation, and which hath
put him upon such a foot with every friend, that I heartily
lament the situation he is in.

I entreat your pardon for the length and insignificancy
of this letter, but my solitary way of life is apt to make me
talkative upon paper. I desire you would believe, first, that
I have so frequently been libelled, that my curiosity to
know the authors is quite extinct, though that of some
friends is not; secondly, that I am not hasty in judging of
men's style, or matter, or malice. I can venture to say, that
a thing is not written by such a person, because it is much
below his good sense, and to look among the herd of
dunces is endless. As to yourself, I hope you will be my
witness that I have always treated you with particular distinction, and if we differ in opinions relating to public proceedings, it is for very good reasons. You are an expectant
from the world and from power. I have long done with
both, having been an original offender against all principles
set up since the death of the Queen, I could not think it
worth my while to quit my old ones, and must have done
it with an ill grace, though honour and conscience had been
out of the question. Whoever really believes that things are
well, is many ways happy. He is pleased with the world,
as I was formerly, and the world with him; his merit is
allowed, and favour will certainly follow, which I heartily
wish you, only desiring, that in what appears to my eyes a
very dirty road, you would pick out the cleanest stages you
can, and believe me to be, with much esteem, Sir,

Your most obedient humble servant,

J. S.

Addressed—To the Rev. Dr. Henry Jenney at his house in
Armagh.

---

[1] " Preach, preach, that is certainly your talent" (*supra*, vol. i, p. 44).

DCCCXXXIX. [*Elwin.*]

SWIFT TO ALEXANDER POPE

Dublin, *June* 12, 1732.

I DOUBT habit has little power to reconcile us with sickness attended by pain. With me the lowness of spirits has
a most unhappy effect: I am grown less patient with soli-
tude, and harder to be pleased with company, which I
could formerly better digest, when I could be easier without it than at present. As to sending you anything that I
have written since I left you, either verse or prose, I can
only say, that I have ordered by my will, that all my papers
of any kind shall be delivered you to dispose of as you
please.[1] I have several things that I have had schemes to
finish, or to attempt, but I very foolishly put off the trouble,
as sinners do their repentance; for I grow every day more
averse from writing, which is very natural, and when I take
a pen say to myself a thousand times, *non est tanti.*

As to those papers of four or five years past, that you are
pleased to require soon, they consist of little accidental
things writ in the country, family amusements, never intended farther than to divert ourselves and some neighbours, or some effects of anger on public grievances here,
which would be insignificant out of this kingdom. Two or
three of us had a fancy, three years ago, to write a weekly
paper, and call it an Intelligencer. But it continued not
long; for the whole volume—it was reprinted in London,
and I find you have seen it—was the work only of two,
myself and Dr. Sheridan. If we could have got some ingenious young man to have been the manager, who should
have published all that might be sent to him, it might have
continued longer, for there were hints enough. But the
printer here could not afford such a young man one farthing
for his trouble, the sale being so small, and the price one
halfpenny; and so it dropped. In the volume you saw, to
answer your questions, the first, third, fifth [and] seventh were

---

[1] It was originally intended that the Miscellanies should extend to
four volumes, and Pope had evidently written in a letter that has been
destroyed to remind Swift of its completion. The first three volumes
had been distinguished as one, two, and "the last." The volume
which was subsequently published was described as the third.

mine.[1] Of the eighth I writ only the verses, very incorrect, but against a fellow we all hated, the ninth mine, the tenth only the verses, and of those not the four last slovenly lines; the fifteenth is a pamphlet of mine printed before, with Dr. Sheridan's preface, merely for laziness, not to disappoint the town, and so was the nineteenth, which contains only a parcel of facts relating purely to the miseries of Ireland, and wholly useless and unentertaining.[2]

As to other things of mine, since I left you, there are, in prose, a View of the State of Ireland, a Project for Eating Children, and a Defence of Lord Carteret;[3] in verse, a Libel on Dr. Delany and Lord Carteret, a Letter to Dr. Delany on the Libels writ against him,[4] the Barrack (a stolen copy),[5] the Lady's Journal, the Lady's Dressing-room (a stolen copy), [and] the [Place] of the Damned (a stolen copy).[6] All these have been printed in London. I forgot to tell you that the Tale of Sir Ralph was sent from England.[7] Besides these there are five or six, perhaps more, papers of verses writ in the North, but perfect family things, two or three of which may be tolerable, the rest but indifferent, and the humour only local, and some that would

---

[1] The first number was introductory in its character, the third was on the subject of the "Beggar's Opera," and the fifth and seventh comprised the "Essay on the Fates of Clergymen" ("Prose Works," iii, 290; ix, 313).

[2] The verses were on Tighe and are those entitled "The Dialogue between Mad Mullinix and Timothy" and "Tim and the Fables" ("Poetical Works," ii, 226, 234). The ninth number was the "Essay on Modern Education," and the fifteenth the "Short View of the State of Ireland" ("Prose Works," vii, 80; xi, 48). The nineteenth was principally concerned with the question of the coinage (*ibid.*, ix, 323). Mr. Temple Scott assumes from Swift's words here that it had been printed before, but the date appended to it seems to show that it was written specially for the "Intelligencer," and in my opinion Swift intends in its case to apply only the concluding words of the previous sentence.

[3] "Prose Works," vii, 79, 201, 225.

[4] "Poetical Works," i, 320, 326.

[5] *I.e.*, the "Grand Question Debated" (*ibid.*, ii, 101).

[6] *Ibid.*, i, 172, 193, 212. Of the various pieces mentioned here Pope included in the new volume of the Miscellanies only the Essays on Clergymen and Education, the "Dialogue between Mad Mullinix and Timothy," the "Defence of Lord Carteret," the "Letter to Dr. Delany," the "Barrack," and the "Lady's Journal." The word "Place" has been hitherto printed "Plea."

[7] He had already disclaimed responsibility for this poem (*supra*, p. 61).

give offence to the times. Such as they are, I will bring them, tolerable or bad, if I recover this lameness, and live long enough to see you either here or there. I forget again to tell you that the Scheme of paying Debts by a Tax on Vices, is not one syllable mine, but of a young clergyman whom I countenance:[1] he told me it was built upon a passage in Gulliver, where a projector hath something upon the same thought. This young man is the most hopeful we have. A book of his poems was printed in London. Dr. Delany is one of his patrons; he is married and has children, and makes up about a hundred pounds a year, on which he lives decently. The utmost stretch of his ambition is, to gather up as much superfluous money as will give him a sight of you, and half an hour of your presence; after which he will return home in full satisfaction, and, in proper time, die in peace.

My poetical fountain is drained, and I profess I grow gradually so dry that a rhyme with me is almost as hard to find as a guinea, and even prose speculations tire me almost as much. Yet I have a thing in prose, begun above twenty-eight years ago, and almost finished. It will make a four shilling volume, and is such a perfection of folly that you shall never hear of it till it is printed, and then you shall be left to guess. Nay, I have another of the same age, which will require a long time to perfect, and is worse than the former, in which I will serve you the same way.[2] I heard lately from Mr. Gay, who promises to be less lazy in order to mend his fortune. But women who live by their beauty, and men by their wit, are seldom provident enough to consider that both wit and beauty will go off with years, and there is no living upon the credit of what is past.

I am in great concern to hear of my Lady Bolingbroke's ill health returned upon her, and I doubt my Lord will find Dawley too solitary without her. In that neither he nor you are companions young enough for me, and I believe the best part of the reason why men are said to grow children when they are old, is because they cannot entertain themselves with thinking; which is the very case of

---

[1] *I.e.*, Pilkington (*supra*, p. 256, n. 3). The Scheme was inserted in the new volume of the Miscellanies.

[2] The reference is to the " Collection of Genteel and Ingenious Conversation" and the "Directions to Servants" (" Prose Works," xi, 195, 303).

little boys and girls, who love to be noisy among their
playfellows. I am told Mrs. Pope is without pain, and I
have not heard of a more gentle decay, without uneasiness
to herself or friends. Yet I cannot but pity you, who are
ten times the greater sufferer, by having the person you
most love so long before you, and dying daily; and I pray
God it may not affect your mind or your health.

DCCCXL. [*Original.*[1]]

LADY CATHERINE JONES TO SWIFT

June 15, 1732.

THE return of my humble thanks to Mr. Dean by the date
it bears looks more like a slumber of gratitude than the
quick sense of that rare virtue which I owe to you, Sir, for
the trouble you have so willingly undertaken in executing
what I so much desired; since the manner you have
done it, answers my wishes in every respect.[2] The proposal you made, I acquainted my sister Kildare, and niece
Fanny Coningsby with, for I being but one part of the
family, cannot act farther than they will consent, which is,
that they will settle twenty shillings per year during your
life, that you may never be liable to any more trouble upon
the same occasion.[3]

I need not inform Mr. Dean that the world teaches us
that relations and friends look like two different species,
and though I have the honour to be allied to my Lord
Burlington, yet since the death of my good father and his,
the notice he takes of me is as if I was a separated blood,
or else I am vain enough to say, we are sprung from one

---

[1] In the British Museum. See Preface.
[2] Swift had evidently written to tell Lady Catherine that the monument to her ancestors had been repaired, and to request that an
annual allowance might be made for its care in the future (*supra*,
p. 87). At the same time he appears to have expressed the hope that
she would induce Lord Burlington to follow her example.
[3] Lady Catherine had two sisters. The eldest, who was then a
widow, had married the nineteenth Earl of Kildare, and the younger,
who was then dead, had married Earl Coningsby and had left two
daughters, of whom Lady Frances was the younger.

ancestor, whose ashes keep up a greater lustre than those
that are not reduced to it.[1]

I cannot conclude without saying, that was I worthy in
any way to have the pleasure of seeing Dean Swift, I do
not know any passion, even envy, would not make innocent, in my ambition of seeing the author of so much wit
and judicious writing, as I have had the advantage to reap
from.

Your most humble and obliged servant,
CATHERINE JONES.

Your opinion of Mr. French is just, and his due.

Addressed—To the Revd. the Dean of St. Patrick's, at
Dublin.

DCCCXLI. [*Barrett's Essay.*[2]]

SWIFT TO DEAN BRANDRETH

June 30, 1732.

SIR,[3]

IF you are not an excellent philosopher, I allow you
personate one perfectly well, and if you believe yourself, I
heartily envy you, for I never yet saw in Ireland a spot of
earth two feet wide, that had not in it something to dis-
please. I think I once was in your county, Tipperary,[4]

---

[1] Lady Catherine's grandmother was a daughter of the great Earl
of Cork. Her relationship to the Earl of Burlington was only that
of a second cousin once removed.

[2] Although Sir Walter Scott claimed to give a more correct version
of this letter, the original of which was then in the possession of the
Rev. Edward Mangin, the copy made by Barrett bears evidence of
greater accuracy.

[3] Brandreth had been appointed a few months before by his patron
Dorset (*supra*, p. 195, n. 2) to the deanery of Armagh, which had been
vacated by the promotion of Richard Daniel to the deanery of Down.
He continued to hold, however, his original preferments a prebend in
the diocese of Ossory and the rectory of Knocktopher in the county
of Kilkenny, and appears to have written to Swift from the latter
place a glowing account of the surrounding country.

[4] Swift was probably under the impression that Knocktopher was
in the county of Tipperary, to which it is adjacent. His knowledge of
that county had been possibly acquired during the visit which he is
said to have made to Thomastown (*supra*, vol. iii, p. 34, n. 3).

which is like the rest of the whole kingdom, a bare face of nature, without houses or plantations; filthy cabins, miserable, tattered, half-starved creatures, scarce in human shape; one insolent ignorant oppressive squire to be found in twenty miles riding; a parish church to be found only in a summer day's journey, in comparison of which, an English farmer's barn is a cathedral; a bog of fifteen miles round; every meadow a slough, and every hill a mixture of rock, heath, and marsh; and every male and female, from the farmer, inclusive to the day-labourer, infallibly a thief, and consequently a beggar, which in this island are terms convertible. The Shannon is rather a lake than a river, and has not the sixth part of the stream that runs under London bridge. There is not an acre of land in Ireland turned to half its advantage, yet it is better improved than the people; and all these evils are effects of English tyranny, so your sons and grandchildren will find it to their sorrow. Cork indeed was a place of trade, but for some years past is gone to decay, and the wretched merchants instead of being dealers, are dwindled to pedlars and cheats.

I desire you will not write such accounts to your friends in England. Did you ever see one cheerful countenance among our country vulgar, unless once a year at a fair, or on a holiday, where some poor rogue happened to get drunk, and starved the whole week after? You will give a very different account of your winter campaign, when you cannot walk five yards from your door without being mired to your knees, nor ride half a mile without being in slough to your saddle skirts; when your landlord must send twenty miles for yeast, before he can brew or bake; and the neighbours five miles round must club to kill a mutton. Pray take care of damps, and when you leave your bed-chamber, let a fire be made to last till night, and, after all, if a stocking happens at night to fall off a chair, you may wring it next morning. *I nunc et versus tecum meditare canoros.*[1] I have not said all this out of any malicious intention, to put you out of conceit with the scene where you are, but merely for your credit, because it is better to know you are miserable, than to betray an ill taste. I consult your honour, which is dearer than life; therefore I demand that you shall not relish one bit of victuals, or drop of

[1] Hor., " Ep.," ii, 2, 76.

drink, or the company of any human creature within thirty miles round Knocktopher, during your residence in those parts, and then I shall begin to have a tolerable opinion of your understanding.

My lameness is very slowly recovering, and if it be well when that the year is out, I shall gladly compound, yet I made a shift to ride about ten miles a-day, by virtue of certain implements called gambadoes,[1] where my feet stand firm as on a floor, and I generally dine alone, like a king or a hermit, and continue alone until I go to bed; for even my wine will not purchase company, and I begin to think the lame are forsaken as much as the poor and blind. Mr. Jebb never calls at the Deanery of late; perhaps he hath found out that I like him, as a modest man, and of very good understanding.[2] This town is neither large nor full enough to furnish events for entertaining a country correspondent. A murder now and then is all we have to trust to. Our fruit is all destroyed with the spring north-east winds, and I shall not have the tenth part of my last year's fruit. Miss Hoadly hath been nine days in the small-pox, which I never heard of till this minute, but they say she is past danger. She would have been a terrible loss to the Archbishop.[3] Dr. Felton of Oxford hath writ a very large octavo about Revelations, etc. I know not his character. He sent over four copies to me, one of which was for Mr. Tickell, two for the Bishops of Cork and Waterford, and one to myself, by way of payment for sending the rest, I suppose, for he sent me no letter. I know him not.[4] Whenever you are in this town, I hope you will mend your

---

[1] *I.e.*, large boots fastened to the saddle to protect the rider's legs and feet from the wet and cold.

[2] The reference is to the Rev. John Jebb, who then held, like Brandreth, a prebend in the diocese of Ossory, and became afterwards Dean of Cashel. He was father of John Jebb, who took an active part in promoting the movement for the abolition of clerical subscription and was in later life known as a parliamentary reformer and prison philanthropist (" D. N. B.," xxix, 258).

[3] She was the Archbishop's only child, and married a nephew of the first Earl of Shannon.

[4] Henry Felton, who published at that time "The Christian Faith asserted against Deists, Arians, and Socinians" was then Principal of Edmund Hall. He had graduated, like Tickell, from Queen's College, and had been a pupil of Thomas Mills, who still held the see of Waterford. Of the Bishop of Cork, Peter Browne, he knew probably only by reputation.

usage of me, by coming often to a philosophic dinner at the Deanery. This I pretend to expect, for the sake of our common Princess, Lady Elizabeth Germain, to whom I have the happiness of your acquaintance, and, on her account, I expect your justice to believe me to be, with truest esteem,

Your most obedient humble servant,

J. S.

Addressed—To the Rev. the Dean of Armagh at Knocktopher, in the county of Kilkenny.

DCCCXLII. [*Elwin.*[1]]

SWIFT TO JOHN GAY AND THE DUCHESS OF QUEENSBERRY

Dublin, *July* 10, 1732.

DEAR SIR,

I HAD your letter by Mr. Ryves a long time after the date, for I suppose he stayed long in the way.[2] I am glad you determine upon something that will bring you money. But you have quite misunderstood me; for there is no writing I esteem more than fables, nor anything so difficult to succeed in, which, however, you have done excellently well, and I have often admired your happiness in such a kind of performance, which I have frequently endeavoured at in vain. I remember I acted as you seem to hint; I found a moral first, and then studied for a fable, but could do nothing that pleased me, and so left off that scheme for ever. I remember one, which was to represent what scoundrels rise in armies by a long war, wherein I supposed the lion was engaged; and having lost all his animals of worth, at last Sergeant Hog came to be brigadier, and Corporal Ass a colonel, etc. I agree with you likewise about getting something by the stage, which, when it succeeds, is the best crop for poetry in England. But, pray take some new scheme, quite different from anything you have already touched. The present humour of the players, who hardly, as I was told in London, regard any new play, and your

---

[1] By permission of Mr. John Murray. *Supra*, vol. iii, p. 148, n. 1.
[2] *Supra*, p. 302.

present situation at the Court, are the difficulties to be overcome; but those circumstances may have altered, at least the former, since I left you.

My scheme was to pass a month at Amesbury, and then go to Twickenham, and live a winter between that and Dawley, and sometimes at Ritchings, without going to London, where I now can have no occasional lodgings,[1] but I am not yet in any condition for such removals. I believe I told you that I had been about a month able to ride in gambadoes, which give my feet a support like a floor, but I can no more stand tiptoe on my left leg than I can dance the rope, nor know when I shall; for I mend slowly, and limp when I walk. For these reasons I would fain have you get enough against you grow old, to have two or three servants about you and a convenient house. It is hard to want those *subsidia senectuti*, when a man grows hard to please, and few people care whether he be pleased or not. I have a large house, yet I should hardly prevail to find one visitor if I were not able to hire him with a bottle of wine; so that, when I am not abroad on horseback, I generally dine alone, and am thankful if a friend will pass the evening with me over a bottle. I am now with the remainder of my pint before me, that I drank with water at dinner, with no creature but two servants attending while I eat about half a chicken, and so here is your health, and the second and chief is to my Tunbridge acquaintance, my Lady Duchess.[2] And I tell you that I fear my Lord Bolingbroke and Mr. Pope, a couple of philosophers, would starve me; for even of port wine I should require half a pint a day, and as much at night; and you were growing as bad, unless your Duke and Duchess have mended you. You have not forgot " Gentlemen, I will leave you to your wine," which was but the remainder of a pint when four glasses were drunk. I told that story to everybody in commendation of Mr. Pope's abstemiousness.

If you please to manage my two hundred pounds as your own, though I believe you are just such a manager as myself, I shall be obliged to you. Yet if it ever comes to

---

[1] As the government had deprived Gay of his rooms in Whitehall (*supra*, p. 113).

[2] He means that she would only recognize his existence when she was in the country. Except the undecipherable passage (*supra*, p. 271) the Duchess had not written to him since July 1731.

be at par I will, against my former maxims return it hither, where I can get ten per cent by the exchange, and six per cent interest, or five and a half with great safety. But probably I shall have occasion to spend it, for our tithes hardly yield us anything, and my land rents are not half sufficient to maintain me.

I congratulate with my Lady Duchess on her son's passing so easily through the smallpox. I am heartily concerned for the lady at Dawley; I fear she is in a bad way. I owe her much gratitude for many civilities I received from her, and have a great esteem for her good sense. Your colic is owing to intemperance of the philosophical kind; you eat without care, and if you drink less than I, you drink too little. But your inattention I cannot pardon, because I imagined the cause was removed, for I thought it lay in your forty millions of schemes by Court-hopes and Court-fears. Yet Mr. Pope has the same defect, and it is of all others the most mortal to conversation. Neither is my Lord Bolingbroke untinged with it: all for want of my rule, *Vive la bagatelle*! But the Doctor is the king of inattention! What a vexatious life should I lead among you! If the Duchess be a *reveuse*, I will never go to Amesbury; or, if I do, I will run away from you both to one of her women and the steward and chaplain. Pray God bless you, and your land-lord and landlady, with the whole family. I am,

Ever sincerely yours.

To the Duchess

Madam,

I mentioned something to Mr. Gay of a Tunbridge acquaintance, whom we forget of course when we return to town, and yet I am assured that, if they meet again next summer, they have a better title to resume their commerce. Thus I look on my right of corresponding with your Grace to be better established upon your return to Amesbury; and I shall at this time descend to forget, or at least suspend, my resentments of your neglect all the time you were in London, though I still keep in my heart that Mr. Gay had no sooner turned his back, than you left the place in his letter void which he had commanded you to fill; though your guilt confounded you so far, that you wanted presence of mind to blot out the last line, where that command stared you in the face. But I own it is my misfortune to quarrel with all my acquaintance, and always come by the worst; and fortune is ever against me, but never so much as by pursuing me out of mere partiality to your Grace, for which you are to answer. By your connivance, she has pleased, by one stumble on the stairs, to give me a lameness that six months have not been able perfectly to cure; and thus I am prevented from revenging myself by continuing a month at Amesbury, and breeding confusion in your Grace's family. No disappointment through my whole life has been so vexatious by many thousand degrees; and God knows whether I shall ever live to see the invisible lady to whom I was obliged for so many favours, and whom I never beheld since she was a brat in hanging sleeves. I am and shall be ever, with the greatest respect and gratitude, Madam,

Your Grace's most obedient and most humble, etc.

I entreat your Grace to present my most humble respects to my Lord Duke, and pray God of his mercy preserve you to see a Court worthy of your appearing in it.

DCCCXLIII. [*Gentleman's Magazine.*[1]]

SWIFT TO BENJAMIN MOTTE

Dublin, *July* 15, 1732.

SIR,[2]

I RECEIVED your letter but two days ago, and will first answer the material part of it. Upon my word, I never intended that any but yourself should be concerned as printer or bookseller in anything that shall be published with my consent while I am alive, or after my death by my executors. As to my posthumous things I shall intrust them to Mr. Pope, but with a strong recommendation that you alone may be employed, supposing and being assured of your honest and fair dealing, which I

---

[1] N. S., xliii, 258.

[2] Since receiving Swift's last letter (*supra*, p. 307) Pope had been in communication with Motte as to the additional volume of the Miscellanies, and had proposed only to give him the right of publishing in it Swift's lighter writings.

have always found. I am likewise desirous that some time
or other all that I acknowledge to be mine in prose and
verse, which I shall approve of, with any little things that
shall be thought deserving, should be published by themselves by you during my life, if it contains any reasonable
time, provided you are sure it will turn to your advantage;
and this you may say to Mr. Pope, as my resolution, unless he hath any material objections to it, which I would
desire to know. For I ever intended the property as a
bookseller should be only in you, as long as you shall act
with justice and reason, which I never doubted in the
least, and I conceive that Mr. Pope's opinion of you is the
same with mine.

I am so well recovered of my lameness that I can ride
in gambadoes[1] and hope in some time to come to my stirrups. I ride twice or thrice a week about ten miles at a
time, and I begin to walk the town, but with halting a little.
I tried your remedy a good while, only not with red-lead;
but I use at present only a soap plaster. If I should be able
before summer is spent to ride with stirrups, and get more
strength in the sinew above my left heel, so as to be able
to get in and out of a ship and a boat without danger of a
new wrench, by several of which my cure hath been much put
back, I did propose to go over and pass a month at Amesbury, and then the winter with Mr. Pope; but God knows
whether I shall find it possible. Pray thank Mrs. Motte in
my name, for her kind remembrance, with my humble
service. I had lately a letter from my cousin Lancelot, in
answer to one I sent by Mr. Jackson,[2] who I believe forgot
to give her a small present I troubled him to carry over:
it was only a piece of gold that goes here for forty shillings,
but with you is worth something less.

I received the box with the Bibles and Dr. Felton's
books.[3] The Bibles I think are very good; I hope you
have included the charge of carriage to Chester, for I shall
send you a bank-bill in two or three days of eight pounds,
twelve shillings, and six pence. If there be any more for
the carriage, Mr. Jackson shall pay you. I desire my
humble service and thanks to Dr. Felton; I have delivered

[1] *Supra*, p. 313, n. 1.
[2] Probably the vicar of Santry was then again in London (*supra*,
p. 6, n. 5).
[3] *Supra*, p. 313.

the three books as he has directed. I will write to cousin
Lancelot soon. I am,

> Your assured friend and very humble servant,
>
>   J. SWIFT.

	£	s.	d.
I will add to bank-bill the sixteen shillings	8	12	6
for the telescopes,[1] which I might have forgot	0	16	0
if I had not kept your letters.			
	£9	8	6

Addressed—To Mr. Benjamin Motte, bookseller, at the
Middle Temple Gate in Fleet Street, London.

DCCCXLIV. [*Original.*[2]]

VISCOUNT BOLINGBROKE TO SWIFT

July 18, 1732.

I WRITE this letter in hopes that Pope, a man scattered
in the world, according to the French phrase, will soon
procure me an opportunity of conveying it safely to you,
my reverend Dean. For my own part half this wicked
nation might go to you, or half your beggarly nation might
come to us, and the whole migration be over before I knew
anything of the matter. My letter will concern neither
affairs of State, nor of party; and yet I would not have it fall
into the hands of our Ministers; it might pass in their excellent noddles for a piece of a plot against themselves, if
not against the State, or, at least, it might furnish them
with an opportunity of doing an ill-natured, and disappointing a good-natured thing, which being a pleasure to the
malicious and the base, I should be sorry to give it on any
occasion, and especially on this, to the *par nobile fratrum*.[3]

---

[1] Writing to his London publisher in February Pilkington says:
"I desire you to present my services to Dr. Delany, and tell him that
the Dean designs to trouble him to buy a convenient microscope that
he may find out both myself and my house with greater ease than he
can at present, because we are both so excessively small that he can
scarce discover either." See Appendix X.

[2] In the British Museum. See Preface.

[3] Sir Robert Walpole's brother Horatio had resigned his embassy
to France two years before, and was then in England.

After this preamble, I proceed to tell you that there is in my neighbourhood in Berkshire,[1] a clergyman, one Mr. Talbot, related to the Solicitor General, and protected by him.[2] This man has now the living of Burghfield, which the late Bishop of Durham held before, and, for aught I know, after he was Bishop of Oxford. The living is worth four hundred pounds per annum, over and above a curate paid, as Mr. Correy, a gentleman who does my business in that country, and who is a very grave authority, assures me. The parsonage house is extremely good, the place pleasant, and the air excellent, the distance from London a little day's journey, and from hence—give me leave to think this circumstance of some importance to you—not much above half a day's, even for you who are no great jockey.[3] Mr. Talbot has many reasons, which make him desirous to settle in Ireland for the rest of his life, and has been looking out for a change of preferments some time. As soon as I heard this, I employed one to know whether he continued in the same mind, and to tell him that an advantageous exchange might be offered him, if he could engage his kinsman to make it practicable at Court. He answered for his own acceptance, and his kinsman's endeavours.

I employed next some friends to secure my Lord Dorset, who very frankly declared himself ready to serve you in anything, and in this if you desired it. But he mentioned a thing, at the same time, wholly unknown to me, which is, that your deanery is not in the nomination of the Crown, but in the election of the Chapter. This may render our affair perhaps more easy—more hard, I think, it cannot be; —but in all cases, it requires other measures to be taken. One of these, I believe, must be to prepare Hoadly, Bishop of Salisbury, if that be possible, to prepare his brother, Archbishop of Dublin. The light, in which the proposition must be represented to him and our Ministers, if it be made to them, is this, that though they gratify you, they

[1] *I.e.*, near his first wife's property.

[2] The office of Solicitor General was at that time filled by Charles Talbot, who was promoted in the following year over his colleague, the great Hardwick, to the Woolsack, and earned, before his death a few years later, the reputation of being one of its most successful occupants. His father, who had recently died, had been successively Bishop of Oxford, Salisbury, and Durham.

[3] Burghfield lies a few miles to the south-west of Reading. Bolingbroke was no doubt writing from Dawley.

THE OLD GATEWAY AT GOSFORD CASTLE

From a photograph by Mr. H. Allison

gratify you in a thing advantageous to themselves and silly in you to ask. I suppose it will not be hard to persuade them that it is better for them you should be a private parish priest in an English county, than a dean in the metropolis of Ireland, where they know, because they have felt, your authority and influence. At least this topic is a plausible one for those who speak to them to insist upon, and coming out of a Whig mouth may have weight. Sure I am, they will be easily persuaded that quitting power for ease, and a greater for a less revenue, is a foolish bargain, which they should by consequence help you to make.

You see now the state of this whole affair, and you will judge better than I am able to do of the means to be employed on your side of the water; as to those on this, nothing shall be neglected. Find some secure way of conveying your thoughts and your commands to me; for my friend has a right to command me arbitrarily, which no man else upon earth has. Or rather dispose affairs so as to come hither immediately. You intended to come some time ago. You speak, in a letter Pope has just now received from you, as if you still had in view to make this journey before winter. Make it in the summer, and the sooner the better. To talk of being able to ride with stirrups is trifling: get on Pegasus, bestride the hippogriff, or mount the white nag in the Revelation. To be serious; come any how, and put neither delay nor humour in a matter which requires dispatch and management. Though I have room, I will not say one word to you about Berkeley's or Delany's book. Some part of the former is hard to be understood; none of the latter is to be read.[1] I propose, however, to reconcile you to metaphysics, by showing how they may be employed against metaphysicians, and that whenever you do not understand them, nobody else does, no not those who write them.

I know you are inquisitive about the health of the poor woman who inhabits this place; it is tolerable, better than it has been in some years. Come and see her; you shall be nursed, fondled, and humoured. She desires you to accept this assurance, with her humble service. Your horses shall be grazed in summer, and foddered in winter; and you and your man shall have meat, drink, and lodging.

[1] *Supra*, p. 291.

IV   Y

Washing I cannot afford, Mr. Dean; for I am grown saving, thanks to your sermon about frugality.

DCCCXLV. [*Original.*[1]]

LADY ELIZABETH GERMAIN TO SWIFT

Drayton, *July* 19, 1732.

I BELIEVE you will not wonder at my long silence, when I tell you that Mrs. Floyd came ill here, but that she kept pretty much to herself; and ever since she has been here, till within these two or three days, I have had no hopes of her life. You may easily guess what I must have suffered for a so long tried, prudent, useful, agreeable companion and friend. And God knows now she is excessively weak, and mends but slowly; however, I have now great hopes, and I am very good at believing what I heartily wish. As I dare say you will be concerned for her, you may want to know her illness, but that is more than I can tell you. She herself has fancied herself in a consumption a great while; but though she has had the most dreadful cough I ever heard in my life, all the doctors said it was not that; but none of them did say what it was. The doctor here, who is an extraordinary good one, but lives fourteen long long miles off, has lately been left ten thousand pounds, and now hates his business; he says, it is a sharp humour that falls upon her nerves, sometimes on her stomach and bowels; and indeed what he has given her has, to appearance, had much better effect than the millions of things she has been forced to take. After this, you will not expect I should have followed your orders, and rid, for I have scarcely walked; although I durst not be very much in her room, because she constrained herself to hide her illness from me.

The Duke and Duchess of Dorset have not been here yet, but I am in hopes they will soon. I do not know whether you remember Mrs. Crowther[2] and Mrs. A'Court;[3]

[1] In the British Museum. See Preface.

[2] Possibly the widow of Swift's noisy friend (*supra*, vol. i, p. 134). Her husband had died in 1730.

[3] Possibly the widow of Pierce A'Court, an ancestor of Lord Heytesbury.

they and Mr. Pursade [1] are my company; but as I love my
house full, I expect more still, and my Lady Suffolk talks
of making me a short visit. I have been so full of Mrs.
Floyd that I had like to have forgot to tell you, that I am
such a dunderhead, that I really do not know what my
sister Pen's age was; but I think she could not be above
twelve years old.[2] She was the next to me, but whether
two or three year younger I have forgot; and what is more
ridiculous, I do not exactly know my own, for my mother
and nurse used to differ upon that notable point. And I
am willing to be a young lady still, so will not allow myself
to be more than forty-eight next birth-day; but if I make
my letter any longer, perhaps you will wish I had never
been born. So adieu, dear Dean.

DCCCXLVI. [*Nichols.*]

SWIFT TO JOHN BARBER

Dublin, *July* 22, 1732.

MR. ALDERMAN,[3]

THERE is a young gentleman of the clergy here, for
whom I have great regard, and I cannot but wish this
young gentleman, for whose learning and oratory in the
pulpit I will engage, might have the honour to be your
chaplain in your mayoralty. His name is Matthew Pilkington; he is some years under thirty, but has more wit,
sense, and discretion, than any of your London parsons ten
years above his age.[4] He has a great longing to see England, and appear in the presence of Mr. Pope, Mr. Gay, and
others, in which I will venture to befriend him. You are

---

[1] The death of a Dr. Pursade, sub-preceptor to the Duke of
Gloucester, is mentioned in 1729.

[2] Swift had evidently asked the question with the object of inserting
Lady Penelope's age in the inscription for the tablet (*supra*, p. 283).
It was eventually not mentioned.

[3] Barber, who had gained much popularity by his lavish hospitality
(*supra*, p. 139), had before then been chosen to serve as Lord Mayor
of London for the ensuing year.

[4] According to his matriculation entry Pilkington (*supra*, p. 169, n. 1)
was born in 1700. If Swift was correct, Pilkington must have been
ordained before the canonical age.

not to tell me of prior engagements, because I have some
title, as an old acquaintance, to expect a favour from you.
Therefore pray let me know immediately that you have
complied with my request before you had read half my letter.
I expect your answer to my satisfaction and the happiness
of the young gentleman, and am, with great sincerity,

Your most obedient servant,
JON. SWIFT.

You need not be afraid of Mr. Pilkington's hanging upon
you, for he has some fortune of his own, and somewhat
in the Church, but he would be glad to see England, and
be more known to those who will esteem him, and may
raise him.

DCCCXLVII. [*Original.*[1]]

JOHN GAY AND THE DUCHESS OF QUEENSBERRY TO SWIFT

Amesbury, July 24, 1732.

GAY

DEAR SIR,

As the circumstances of our money affairs are altered, I
think myself obliged to acquaint you with them as soon as
I can, which, if I had not received your letter last post,[2] I
should have done now. I left your two South Sea bonds,
and four of my own, in Mr. Hoare's hands,[3] when I came
out of town, that he might receive the interest for us, when
due; or, if you should want your money, that you might
receive it upon your order. Since I came out of town, the
South Sea Company have come to a resolution to pay off
fifty per cent of their bonds, with the interest of the fifty
per cent to Michaelmas next. So that there is now half of
our fortunes in Mr. Hoare's hands at present, without any
interest going on. As you seem to be inclined to have
your money remitted to Ireland, I will not lay out the sum
that is paid into his hands in any other thing, till I have

---

[1] In the British Museum. See Preface.

[2] *Supra*, p. 314.

[3] As already mentioned, the reference is to the future Sir Richard
Hoare, grandfather of the historian of Wiltshire.

your orders. I cannot tell what to do with my own. I believe I shall see Mr. Hoare in this country very soon, for he hath a house not above six miles from us,[1] and intend to advise with him; though in the present situation of affairs, I expect to be left to take my own way. The remaining fifty per cent were it to be sold at present, bears a premium; but the premium on the fifty that was paid in is sunk. I do not know whether I write intelligibly upon this subject. I cannot send you the particulars of your account, though I know I am in debt to you for interest, beside your principal; and you will understand so much of what I intend to inform you, that half of your money is now in Mr. Hoare's hands without any interest. So since I cannot send you the particulars of your account, I will now say no more about it.

I shall finish the work I intended, this summer, but I look upon the success in every respect to be precarious. You judge very right, by my present situation, that I cannot propose to succeed by favour; and I do not think, if I could flatter myself that I had any degree of merit, much could be expected from that unfashionable pretension. I have almost done everything I proposed in the way of fables, but not set the last hand to them. Though they will not amount to half the number, I believe they will make much such another volume as the last. I find it the most difficult task I ever undertook; but I have determined to go through with it; and, after this, I believe I shall never have courage enough to think any more in this way.

Last post I had a letter from Mr. Pope, who informs me he hath heard from you, and that he is preparing some scattered things of yours and his for the press. I believe I shall not see him till the winter; for, by riding and walking, I am endeavouring to lay in a stock of health, to squander in the town. You see, in this respect, my scheme is very like the country gentlemen in regard to their revenues. As to my eating and drinking, I live as when you knew me, so that in that point we shall agree very well in living together; and the Duchess will answer for me that I am cured of inattention, for I never forget anything she says to me.

---

[1] *I.e.*, at Stourhead.

THE DUCHESS

For he never hears what I say, so cannot forget. If I served him the same way, I should not care a farthing ever to be better acquainted with my Tunbridge acquaintance, which, by my attention to him, I have learned to set my heart upon. I began to give over all hopes, and from thence began my neglect. I think this a very good philosophical reason, though there might be another given. When fine ladies are in London, it is very genteel and allowable to forget their best friends, which, if I thought modestly of myself, must needs be you, because you know little of me. Till you do more, pray do not persuade Mr. Gay that he is discreet enough to live alone, for I do assure you he is not, nor I either. We are of great use to one another, for we never flatter nor contradict, but when it is absolutely necessary, and then we do it to some purpose; particularly the first agrees mightily with our constitutions. If ever we quarrel, it will be about a piece of bread and butter, for somebody is never sick, except he eats too much of it. He will not quarrel with you for a glass or so, for by that means he hopes to gulp down some of that forty millions of schemes that hindered him from being good company. I would fain see you here, there is so fair a chance that one of us must be pleased; perhaps both, you with an old acquaintance, and I with a new one. It is so well worth taking a journey for, that if the mountain will not come to Mahomet, Mahomet must come to the mountain. But before either of our journeys are settled, I desire you would resolve me one question, whether a man, who thinks himself well where he is, should look out for his house and servants before it is convenient, before he grows old, or before a person with whom he lives, pulls him by the sleeve in private, according to oath, and tells him that they have enough of his company? He will not let me write one word more, but that I have a very great regard for you, etc.

The Duke is very much yours, and will never leave you to your wine. Many thanks for Drum.[1] I wish to receive your congratulations for the other boy, you may believe.

Addressed—For the Revd. Dr. Swift, Dean of St. Patrick's, in Dublin, Ireland. By way of London.

[1] *I.e.*, her son Lord Drumlanrig.

DCCCXLVIII. [*Sheridan.*]

SWIFT TO CHARLES WOGAN

[*August* 2, 1732.]

SIR,[1]

I RECEIVED your packet at least two months ago, and took all this time not only to consider it maturely myself, but to show it to the few judicious friends I have in this kingdom. We all agreed that the writer was a scholar, a man of genius and of honour. We guessed him to have been born in this country from some passages, but not from the style, which we were surprised to find so correct in an exile, a soldier, and a native of Ireland. The history of yourself, although part of it be employed in your praise and importance, we did not dislike, because your intention was to be wholly unknown, which circumstance exempts you from any charge of vanity. However, although I am utterly ignorant of present persons and things, I have made a shift, by talking in general with some persons, to find out your name, your employments, and some of your actions, with the addition of such a character as would give full credit to more than you have said, I mean of yourself, in the dedicatory epistle.

You will pardon a natural curiosity on this occasion, especially when I began with so little that I did not so

---

[1] The recipient of this letter, who was then one of the Jacobite refugees in the service of Spain, belonged to a well-known Irish family, that traced descent from a viceroy in the reign of Henry III. His principal claim to fame is as a knight errant in connection with the marriage of the Pretender, who conferred upon him the title of a baronet ("D. N. B.," lxii, 284). Of the communication which led to this letter Mrs. Pilkington gives the following account ("Memoirs," iii, 100): "Just when he had fixed Mr. Pilkington to be chaplain to Alderman Barber, the Dean received from one Mr. Wogan, a green velvet bag, in which was contained the adventures of Eugenius, as also an account of the courtship and marriage of the Chevalier to the Princess Sobiesky, wherein he represents himself to have been a principal negotiator; it was written in the novel style, but a little heavily. There was also some of the Psalms of David, paraphrased in Miltonic verse, and a letter to the Dean with remarks on the Beggar's Opera, in which he says he believes the people of England and Ireland had quite lost all remains of elegance and taste, since their top entertainment was composed of scenes of highwaymen and prostitutes, who all remain unpunished and triumphant in their crimes. He concluded with paying the Dean the compliment of entreating him to correct the work."

much as untie the strings of the bag for five days after I received it, concluding it must come from some Irish friar in Spain filled with monastic speculations, of which I have seen some in my life; little expecting a history, a dedication, a poetical translation of the penitential Psalms, Latin poems, and the like, and all from a soldier. In these kingdoms you would be a most unfashionable military man, among troops where the least pretension to learning, or piety, or common morals, would endanger the owner to be cashiered. Although I have no great regard for your trade, from the judgement I make of those who profess it in these kingdoms, yet I cannot but highly esteem those gentlemen of Ireland, who with all the disadvantages of being exiles and strangers, have been able to distinguish themselves by their valour and conduct in so many parts of Europe, I think above all other nations, which ought to make the English ashamed of the reproaches they cast on the ignorance, the dulness, and the want of courage, in the Irish natives; those defects, wherever they happen, arising only from the poverty and slavery they suffer from their inhuman neighbours, and the base corrupt spirits of too many of the chief gentry, etc. By such events as these, the very Grecians are grown slavish, ignorant, and superstitious. I do assert that from several experiments I have made in travelling over both kingdoms, I have found the poor cottagers here, who could speak our language, to have a much better natural taste for good sense, humour, and raillery, than ever I observed among people of the like sort in England. But the millions of oppressions they lie under, the tyranny of their landlords, the ridiculous zeal of their priests, and the general misery of the whole nation, have been enough to damp the best spirits under the sun.

I return to your packet. Two or three poetical friends of mine have read your poems with very good approbation, yet we all agree some corrections may be wanting, and at the same time we are at a loss how to venture on such a work. One gentleman of your own country, name, and family, who could do it best, is a little too lazy,[1] but, however, something shall be done, and submitted to you. I have been only a man of rhymes, and that upon trifles,

---

[1] Except Swift's correspondent, no member of the Wogan family in that century attained to literary fame. Possibly the reference is to a scion of the house who was then a student in Trinity College.

never having written serious couplets in my life, yet never any without a moral view. However, as an admirer of Milton,[1] I will read yours as a critic, and make objections where I find anything that should be changed. Your directions about publishing the epistle and the poetry will be a point of some difficulty. They cannot be printed here with the least profit to the author's friends in distress. Dublin booksellers have not the least notion of paying for a copy. Sometimes things are printed here by subscription, but they go on so heavily, that few or none make it turn to account. In London, it is otherwise, but even there the authors must be in vogue, or, if not known, be discovered by the style; or the work must be something that hits the taste of the public, or what is recommended by the presiding men of genius. When Milton first published his famous poem, the first edition was very long going off; few either read, liked, or understood it, and it gained ground merely by its merit. Nothing but an uncertain state of my health, caused by a disposition to giddiness, which, although less violent, is more constant, could have prevented my passing this summer into England to see my friends, who hourly have expected me; in that case I could have managed this affair myself, and would have readily consented that my name should have stood at length before your epistle, and by the caprice of the world, that circumstance might have been of use to make the thing known, and consequently better answer the charitable part of your design by inciting people's curiosity. And in such a case, I would have writ a short acknowledgement of your letter, and published it in the next page after your epistle, but giving you no name, nor confessing my conjecture of it. This scheme I am still upon, as soon as my health permits me to return to England.

As I am conjectured to have generally dealt in raillery and satire, both in prose and verse, if that conjecture be right, although such an opinion has been an absolute bar

---

[1] As in the case of Shakespeare, some commentators have assumed that Swift had only a superficial knowledge of Milton, and on account of an ironical passage in one of his contributions to the "Tatler," have even included him amongst Milton's detractors. But apart from his annotation of Milton's works for Stella (*supra*, vol. ii, p. 328, n. 2), there is ample evidence in his "Letter to a Young Poet" and in his "Remarks on Burnet's History of his Own Times" that Swift held Milton in high esteem, and was a student of his works ("Prose Works," *passim*).

to my rising in the world, yet that very world must suppose that I followed what I thought to be my talent, and charitable people will suppose I had a design to laugh the follies of mankind out of countenance, and as often to lash the vices out of practice. And then it will be natural to conclude, that I have some partiality for such kind of writing, and favour it in others. I think you acknowledge, that in some time of your life, you turned to the rallying part, but I find at present your genius runs wholly into the grave and sublime, and therefore I find you less indulgent to my way by your dislike of the Beggar's Opera, in the persons particularly of Polly Peachum and Macheath, whereas we think it a very severe satire upon the most pernicious villainies of mankind. And so you are in danger of quarrelling with the sentiments of Mr. Pope, Mr. Gay the author, Dr. Arbuthnot, myself, Dr. Young, and all the brethren whom we own. Dr. Young is the gravest among us, and yet his satires have many mixtures of sharp raillery.[1] At the same time you judge very truly, that the taste of England is infamously corrupted by shoals of wretches who write for their bread; and therefore I had reason to put Mr. Pope on writing the poem, called the Dunciad, and to hale those scoundrels out of their obscurity by telling their names at length, their works, their adventures, sometimes their lodgings, and their lineage; not with *A*s and *B*s according to the old way, which would be unknown in a few years.

As to your blank verse, it has too often fallen into the same vile hands of late. One Thomson, a Scotchman, has succeeded the best in that way, in four poems he has writ on the four seasons, yet I am not over fond of them, because they are all description, and nothing is doing,[2] whereas Milton engages me in actions of the highest importance, *modo me Romae, modo ponit Athenis,* and yours on the seven Psalms, etc. have some advantages that way.

You see Pope, Gay, and I, use all our endeavours to make folks merry and wise, and profess to have no enemies,

---

[1] In the light of to-day it is rather amusing to find Swift insisting on a preponderance of gravity in Young's case, and it may be well to recall that the "Night Thoughts" were not published until many years later, and that his principal work then was the "Universal Passion," in which ridicule was his object, and "the gaiety of Horace" has been not unsuccessfully imitated.

[2] "The Seasons" had been published in a collected form two years before that time.

except knaves and fools. I confess myself to be exempted from them in one article, which was engaging with a Ministry to prevent, if possible, the evils that have overrun the nation, and my foolish zeal in endeavouring to save this wretched island. Wherein though I succeeded absolutely in one important article, yet even there I lost all hope of favour from those in power here, and disobliged the Court of England, and have in twenty years drawn above one thousand scurrilous libels on myself, without any other recompense than the love of the Irish vulgar, and two or three dozen signposts of the Drapier in this city, beside those that are scattered in country towns, and even these are half worn out. So that, whatever little genius God has given me, I may justly pretend to have been the worst manager of it to my own advantage of any man upon earth.

August 2.

What I have above written has long lain by me, that I might consider farther, but I have been partly out of order, and partly plagued with a lawsuit of ten years standing, and I doubt very ill closed up, although it concerns two thirds of my little fortune. Think whether such periods of life are proper to encourage poetical or philosophical speculations.

I shall not therefore tire you any longer, but, with great acknowledgement for the distinction you please to show me, desire to be always thought, with great truth and a most particular esteem, Sir,

Your most obedient and obliged servant,

JON. SWIFT.

We have sometimes editions printed here of books from England, which I know not whether you are in a way of getting. I will name some below, and if you approve of any, I shall willingly increase your library; they are small, consequently more portable in your marches, and which is more important, the present will be cheaper for me.

Dr. Young's Satires.
Mr. Gay's Works.
Mr. Pope's Works.
Pope's Dunciad.

Gay's Fables.
Art of Politics,[1] and some other trifles in verse, etc.

[1] The Rev. James Bramston's imitation of the "Ars Poetica."

DCCCXLIX. [*Original.*[1]]

Mrs. Cæsar to Swift

August 6, 1732.

Permit me to congratulate you upon the return of Mrs. Barber, with thanks for pleasures enjoyed in her company; for had she not come recommended by the Dean of St. Patrick's, likely I had passed her by unheeded, being apt to follow a good author, in shunning those of my own coat. But hold, I must look if it runs not from corner to corner, which I more fear than length. For Pope says, though sometimes he finds too many letters in my words, never too many words in my letters. So with Mr. Cæsar's, and my best wishes, thou worthy, witty, honest Dean, adieu.

M. Adelmare Cæsar.[2]

DCCCL. [*Original.*[3]]

Lady Worsley to Swift

August 6, 1732.

Sir,

I flatter myself that if you had received my last letter, you would have favoured me with an answer; therefore I take it for granted it is lost.[4]

I was so proud of your commands, and so fearful of being supplanted by my daughter that I went to work immediately, that her box might not keep her in your remembrance, while there was nothing to put you in mind of an old acquaintance, and humble servant. But Mrs. Barber's long stay here, who promised me to convey it to

[1] In the British Museum. See Preface.
[2] The writer was the wife of the Treasurer of the Navy (*supra*, p. 177, n. 2). He was descended from a physician of Venetian origin, Cesare Adelmare, and seems to have revived the use of his patronymic which had been discarded by Adelmare's children. There is a letter from her in Pope's "Works."
[3] In the British Museum. See Preface.
[4] Her former letter was no doubt an answer to Swift's letter in the previous year (*supra*, p. 222).

you, has made me appear very negligent. I doubt not but you think me unworthy of the share, you once told me, I had in your heart, but I am yet vain enough to think I deserve it better than all those flirting girls you coquette with. I will not yield, even, to dirty Patty, whom I was the most jealous of when you was last here. What if I am a great-grandmother, I can still distinguish your merit from all the rest of the world, but it is not consistent with your good breeding to put me in mind of it, therefore I am determined not to use my interest with Sir Robert for a living in the Isle of Wight, though nothing else could reconcile me to the place.[1] But if I could make you Archbishop of Canterbury, I should forget my resentment, for the sake of the flock, who very much want a careful shepherd.

Are we to have the honour of seeing you, or not? I have fresh hopes given me, but I dare not please myself too much with them, lest I should be again disappointed. If I had it as much in my power, as my inclination, to serve Mrs. Barber, she should not have been kept thus long attending, but I hope her next voyage may prove more successful. She is just come in, and tells me you have sprained your foot, which will prevent your journey till the next summer, but assure yourself the Bath is the only infallible cure for such an accident. If you have any regard remaining for me, you will show it by taking my advice; if not, I will endeavour to forget you, if I can. But, till that doubt is cleared, I am as much as ever, the Dean's obedient humble servant,

F. WORSLEY.

Endorsed by Swift—With a present of a writing-box, japanned by herself.

DCCCLI. [*Nichols.*]

SWIFT TO JOHN BARBER

Dublin, *August* 10, 1732.

MR. ALDERMAN,
I AM very angry with my friend Doctor Delany, for not applying to you sooner, as I desired him, in favour of Mr.

[1] *Supra*, p. 172, n. 3.

Matthew Pilkington, a young clergyman here, who has a great ambition to have the honour of being your chaplain in your mayoralty.[1] I waited for the Doctor's answer before I could write to you, and it came but last night. He tells me you have been so very kind as to give him a promise upon my request; I will therefore tell my story. This gentleman was brought to me by the Doctor about four years ago, and I found him so modest a young man, so good a scholar and preacher, and of so hopeful a genius, and grew still better upon my hands the more I knew him, that I have been seeking all opportunities to do him some real service, from no other motive in the world, but the esteem I had of his worth. And I hope you know me long enough to believe me capable of acting as I ought to do in such a case, however contrary it may be to the present practice of the world. He has a great longing to see England, and appear in the presence of Mr. Pope, Mr. Gay, Dr. Arbuthnot, and some other of my friends, wherein I will assist him with my recommendations. He is no relation or dependent of mine. I am not putting you upon a job, but to encourage a young man of merit upon his own account as well as mine. He will be no burden upon you, for he has some fortune of his own, and will have a much better from his father, and has also a convenient establishment in a church in this city.

Mr. Pilkington will be ready to attend you upon your command, and I wish he may go as soon as possible, that he may have a few weeks to prepare him for his business, by seeing the Tower, the Monument, and Westminster Abbey, and have done staring in the streets. I am so entirely out of the world, that I cannot promise a hope ever to requite your favour, otherwise than with hearty thanks for conferring this obligation upon me. And I shall ever remain, with true esteem,

Your most obedient, and obliged humble servant,

JONATH. SWIFT.

[1] It would appear that the letter sent by Swift three weeks before had been enclosed to Delany.

DCCCLII. [*Elwin.*[1]]

SWIFT TO JOHN GAY AND THE DUCHESS OF
QUEENSBERRY

Dublin, *August* 12, 1732.

TO GAY

I KNOW not what to say to the account of your steward-
ship, and it is monstrous to me that the South Sea should
pay half their debts at one clap.[2]   But I will send for the
money when you put me into the way, for I shall want it
here, my affairs being in a bad condition by the miseries of
the kingdom, and my own private fortune being wholly
embroiled and worse than ever; so that I shall soon petition the Duchess, as an object of charity, to lend me three
or four thousand pounds to keep up my dignity.   That one
hundred pounds will buy me six hogsheads of wine, which
will support me a year; *provisae frugis in annum copia.*
Horace desired no more: for I will construe *frugis* to be
wine.   You are young enough to get some lucky hint which
must come by chance, and it shall be a thing of importance,
quod et hunc in annum vivat et in plures, and you shall not
finish it in haste, and it shall be diverting and usefully
satirical, and the Duchess shall be your critic; and betwixt
you and me, I do not find she will grow weary of you till
this time seven years.   I had lately an offer to change for
an English living,[3] which is just too short by three hundred
pounds a year, and that must be made up out of the Duchess's pin-money before I can consent.   I want to be minister
of Amesbury, Dawley, Twickenham, Ritchings, and Prebendary of Westminster, else I will not stir a step, but
content myself with making the Duchess miserable three
months next summer.   But I keep ill company: I mean the
Duchess and you, who are both out of favour; and so I
find am I, by a few verses[4] wherein Pope and you have your

---

[1] In the possession of Mr. John Murray.   *Supra*, vol: iii, p. 148, n. 1.
[2] *Supra*, p. 324.
[3] The exchange suggested by Bolingbroke (*supra*, p. 320).
[4] The "Libel on Delany and Carteret" (*supra*, p. 122), in which
Gay is introduced:

"Thus Gay, the hare with many friends,
Twice seven long years the Court attends,

parts. And though the [Court] told me five years ago they would make me easy amongst you, I find they take a pretence to be angry to such a degree that they will not give me the medals they promised me, yet wheedled me out of a present that cost me forty pounds.

If my leg had been so well two months ago, I should have been able to see Amesbury this summer, for with a little pain I can walk, and ride without gambadoes. You hear Dr. Delany has got a wife with sixteen hundred pounds a year.[1] I, who am his governor,[2] cannot take one under two thousand. I wish you would inquire of such a one in your neighbourhood. See what it is to write godly books! I profess I envy you above all men in England; you want nothing but three thousand pounds more, to keep you in plenty when your friends grow weary of you. To prevent which last evil at Amesbury, you must learn to domineer and be peevish, to find fault with their victuals and drink, to chide and direct the servants, with some other lessons which I shall teach you, and always practised myself with success. I believe I formerly desired to know whether the Vicar of Amesbury can play at backgammon? Pray ask him the question and give him my service.

To the Duchess

MADAM,

I WAS the most unwary creature in the world when, against my old maxims, I writ first to you upon your return to Tunbridge; for Mr. Gay will depose that all ladies of great quality ever made me the first advances. I beg that this condescension of mine may go no farther, and that you will not pretend to make a precedent of it. I never knew any man cured of any inattention, although the pretended causes were removed. When I was with Mr. Gay last in

> Who, under tales conveying truth,
> To virtue form'd a princely youth,
> Who paid his courtship with the crowd,
> As far as modest pride allow'd,
> Rejects a servile usher's place,
> And leaves St. James's in disgrace."

[1] "We hear that the Revd. Dr. Delany, minister of St. Werburgh's," says "Pue's Occurrences" (July 25-29), "was lately married in London to the widow Tennison of this kingdom, a lady of great fortune."

[2] As the Dean of the Cathedral in which Delany was the Chancellor.

London, talking with him on some poetical subjects, he
would answer, "Well, I am determined not to accept the
employment of gentleman-usher to the Princess;"[1] and of
the same disposition were all my poetical friends, and if
you cannot cure him I utterly despair. As to yourself, I
will say to you, though comparisons be odious, what I said
to the Queen, that your quality should be never any
motive of esteem to me. My compliment was then lost, but
it will not be so to you, for you reason wrong. I know you
more by any one of your letters, than I could by six
months conversing; for your pen is always more natural
and sincere and unaffected than your tongue. In writing
you are too lazy to give yourself the trouble of acting a
part, and have indeed acted so indiscreetly that I have you
at mercy; and although you should arrive at such a height
of immorality as to deny your hand, yet, whenever I
produce it, the world will unite in swearing this must come
from the —— of ——.

I will answer your question. Mr. Gay is not discreet
enough to live alone, but he is too discreet to live alone;
and yet, unless you mend him, he will live alone even in
your Grace's company. Your quarrelling with each other
upon the subject of bread and butter is the most usual
thing in the world. Parliaments, Courts, cities, and kingdoms quarrel for no other cause. From hence, and from
hence only, arise all the quarrels between Whig and
Tory; between those who are in the Ministry and those
who are out; between all pretenders to employment in
the Church, the law, and the army. Even the common
proverb teaches you this, when we say, it is none of my
bread and butter, meaning it is no business of mine.
Therefore I despair of any reconcilement between you
till the affair of bread and butter be adjusted, wherein I
would gladly be a mediator. If Mahomet should come to
the mountain, how happy would an excellent lady be who
lives a few miles from this town! As I was telling of Mr.
Gay's way of living at Amesbury, she offered fifty guineas
to have you both at her house for one hour over a bottle
of Burgundy, which we were then drinking. To your ques-

---

[1] The official notification did not reach Gay until after Swift's
departure from London (*supra*, vol. iii, p. 426), but some intimation
that the place was likely to be offered to him may have come to him
before that time.

tion, I answer that your Grace should pull me by the sleeve till you tore it off, and when you said you were weary of me, I would pretend to be deaf, and think, according to another proverb, that you tore my clothes to keep me from going. I never will believe one word you say of my Lord Duke unless I see three or four lines in his own hand at the bottom of yours. I have a concern in the whole family, and Mr. Gay must give me a particular account of every branch, for I am not ashamed of you though you be Duke and Duchess, though I have been of others who are, etc., and I do not doubt but even your own servants love you, even down to your postilions; and when I come to Amesbury, before I see your Graces I will have an hour's conversation with the Vicar, who will tell me how familiarly you talk to Goody Dobson and all the neighbours as if you were their equal, and that you were godmother to her son Jacky. I am, and shall be ever, with the greatest respect and gratitude,

Your Grace's most obedient, etc.

DCCCLIII. [*Nichols.*]

JOHN BARBER TO SWIFT

London, *August* 24, 1732.

SIR,

I WISH Dr. Delany had complied with your request sooner in acquainting me with your intentions in favour of Mr. Pilkington.[1] I could have been glad also that he had acquainted you, as I desired him, with the particulars how I stood circumstantiated in relation to the chaplain, for I flatter myself that your usual good nature would have induced you to comply with my request, in writing a letter to me, in an authoritative way, in your recommendation of Mr. Pilkington, which would have given me a good excuse for my refusing a gentleman, whom my deputy and common councilmen had recommended to me above six months ago.

Another accident happened in this affair, by the Doctor's

---

[1] *Supra*, p. 323.

not receiving a letter I sent him, which, by mistake, came not to his hands, though at home, until many hours after my man had left it at his lodgings, which letter, had he seen in time, would have prevented some little difficulties I lie under in this affair, and which I must get over as well as I can. For, Sir, when I reflect on the many obligations I have to you, which I shall ever acknowledge, I am glad of any occasion to show my gratitude; and do hereby, at your request, make Mr. Pilkington my chaplain, when Mayor. I wish it may answer his expectations, for the profits are not above one hundred and twenty pounds, if so much, as I am told. He constantly dines with the Mayor, but I am afraid cannot lie in the hall, the rooms being all of state. For your sake I will show him all the civilities I can. You will recommend him to Joe, Doctor I mean, Trapp.[2] The Mayor's Day is the 30th of October; so that he may take his own time.

It would add very much to my felicity, if your health would permit you to come over in the spring, and see a pageant of your own making. Had you been here now, I am persuaded you would have put me to an additional expense, by having a raree show, or pageant, as of old, on the Lord Mayor's Day. Mr. Pope and I were thinking of having a large machine carried through the city, with a printing press, author, publishers, hawkers, devils, etc., and a satirical poem printed and thrown from the press to the mob, in public view, but not to give offence; but your absence spoils that design.

Pray God preserve you long, very long, for the good of your country, and the joy and satisfaction of your friends, among whom I take the liberty to subscribe myself, with great sincerity, Sir,

Your most obedient and most humble servant,

J. BARBER.

[1] The Rev. Joseph Trapp, who is mentioned frequently in the Journal to Stella, was a very small person when Swift first knew him, but was now possessed of livings of much profit and dignity in London. Both as a poet and pamphleteer he was held in great contempt by Swift, but he seems to have attained some measure of success as a preacher.

DCCCLIV. [*Original.*[1]]

JOHN GAY AND THE DUCHESS OF QUEENSBERRY
TO SWIFT

Amesbury, *August* 28, 1732.

DEAR SIR,

MR. HOARE hath a hundred and odd pounds of yours in his hands, which you may have whenever you will please to draw upon me for it.[2] I know I am more indebted to you, I mean beside the South Sea bond of a hundred that still subsists; but I cannot tell you exactly how your account stands till I come to town. I have money of my own too in Mr. Hoare's hands, which I know not at present how to dispose of. I believe I shall leave it without interest till I come to town, and shall then be at the same loss how to dispose of it as now. I have an intention to get more money next winter, but am prepared for disappointments, which I think it very likely I shall meet with, yet as you think it convenient and necessary that I should have more than I have, you see I resolve to do what I can to oblige you. If my designs should not take effect, I desire you will be as easy under it as I shall be; for I find you so solicitous about me, that you cannot bear my disappointments as well as I can. If I do not write intelligibly to you, it is because I would not have the clerks of the post-office know everything I am doing. If you would have come here this summer, you might, with me, have helped to have drunk up the Duke's wine, and saved your money. I am growing so saving of late, that I very often reproach myself with being covetous; and I am very often afraid that I shall have the trouble of having money, and never have the pleasure of making use of it.

I wish you could live among us; but not unless it could be to your ease and satisfaction. You insist upon your being minister of Amesbury, Dawley, Twickenham, Richings, and Prebendary of Westminster. For your being minister in those places, I cannot promise you; but I know you might have a good living in every one of them. Gambadoes I have rid in, and I think them a very fine and useful invention;

---

[1] In the British Museum. See Preface.
[2] This letter is an answer to Swift's letter of the 12th.

but I have not made use of them since I left Devonshire.
I ride and walk every day to such excess, that I am afraid
I shall take a surfeit of it. I am sure, if I am not better in
health after it, it is not worth the pains. I say this, though
I have this season shot nineteen brace of partridges. I have
very little acquaintance with our Vicar; he does not live
among us, but resides at another parish. And I have not
played at backgammon with anybody since I came to
Amesbury, but Lady Harold and Lady Bateman.[1] As Dr.
Delany has taken away a fortune from us, I expect to be
recommended in Ireland. If authors of godly books are
entitled to such fortunes, I desire you would recommend
me as a moral one; I mean, in Ireland, for that recommendation would not do in England.

THE DUCHESS

THE Duchess will not lend you two or three thousand
pounds to keep up your dignity, for reasons [known] to
Strada del Po;[2] but she had much rather give you that, or
ten thousand times more, than lay it out in a fine petticoat
to make herself respected. I believe, for all you give Mr.
Gay much good advice, that you are a very indiscreet
person yourself, or else you would come here to take care
of your own affairs, and not be so indiscreet as to send for
your moneys over to a place where there is none. Mr. Gay
is a very rich man; for I really think he does not wish to
be richer, but he will, for he is doing what you bid him,
though, if it may not be allowed, he will acquire greater
honour, and less trouble. His covetousness, at present, is
for health, which he takes so much pains for, that he does
not allow himself time [to enjoy it]. Neither does he allow
himself time to be either absent or present. When he began
to be a sportsman, he had like to have killed a dog; and
now every day I expect he will kill himself, and then the
bread and butter affair can never be brought before you.
It is really an affair of too great consequence to be trusted

---

[1] Lady Harold was the Duke of Kent's daughter-in-law. She was
then a widow, and married subsequently the Duchess of Queensberry's
kinsman, Lord Gower. Lady Bateman, whose husband was a viscount
in the Irish peerage, was a granddaughter of the first Duke of Marlborough, a daughter of the third Earl of Sunderland.

[2] According to Elwin (*op. cit.*, vii, 285) a synonym for Lombard
Street. There is a street of the name in Turin.

in a letter; therefore pray come on purpose to decide it. If you do, you will not hear how familiar I am with Goody Dobson; for I have seen Goody Dobson play at that with so ill a grace, that I was determined never to risk anything so unbecoming. I am not beloved, neither do I love any creature, except a very few, and those, not for having any sort of merit, but only because it is my humour; in this rank, Mr. Gay stands first, and yourself next, if you like to be respected upon these conditions. Now do you know me? He stands over me, and scolds me for spelling ill; and is very peevish, and sleepy, that I do not give him up the pen, for he has yawned for it a thousand times. We both once heard a lady, who at that time we both thought well of, wish that she had the best living in England to give you. It was not I; but I do wish it with all my heart, if Mr. Gay does not hang out false lights for his friend.[1]

GAY

I HAD forgot to tell you, that I very lately received a letter from Twickenham, in which was this paragraph: "Motte and another idle fellow, I find, have been writing to the Dean to get him to give them some copyright, which surely he will be not so indiscreet as to do, when he knows my design, and has done these two months and more. Surely I should be a properer person to trust the distribution of his works with, than to a common bookseller. Here will be nothing but the ludicrous and l[ittle thing]s; none of the political, or any things of consequence, which are wholly at his own disposal. But, at any rate, it would be silly in him to give a copyright to any, which can only put the manner of publishing them hereafter out of his own and his friend's power, into that of mercenaries."[2] I really think this a very

---

[1] In his reply Swift assumes the reference to be to Queen Caroline. The last sentence is taken by Elwin (*op. cit.*, vii, 286) to mean "if Mr. Gay does not misrepresent your own desire," but seems as likely to have meant "does not misrepresent your merit."

[2] The correspondence between Swift and Pope regarding the publication of the last volume of the Miscellanies has been destroyed. From other sources it is, however, evident that in the negotiations Pope made profit the first consideration, and forgot Swift's reputation in his desire for gain. He wished also to give as little as possible of his own work to the joint venture, and from a letter which he addressed on the 16th of that month to Motte, may be suspected of having played off one publisher against another to obtain an excessive fee for the small

useful precaution, considering how you have been treated by these sort of fellows. The Duke is fast asleep, or he would add a line.

Addressed—To the Revd. Dr. Swift, Dean of St. Patrick's, in Dublin, Ireland. By way of London.

DCCCLV. [*Original.*[1]]

SIR WILLIAM FOWNES TO SWIFT

Island-bridge, *September* 9, 1732.

DEAR SIR,[2]

IT has been the observation of travellers, as I have been frequently told, that in all the countries they have seen,

contribution which he eventually made. As regards Swift, the position is not so clear, but it seems probable that Motte's letter (*supra*, p. 317) had raised a doubt in his mind of Pope's disinterestedness, and that he took a tortuous, and as it proved unsuccessful, course to prevent further progress with Pope's design. From two letters addressed that month by Pilkington to his London publisher, Bowyer, it appears that Pilkington had become possessed of the pieces which Swift had mentioned in his letter of 12 June to Pope, with the exception of the "Short View of the State of Ireland" and the "Place of the Damned," and had offered them with Swift's knowledge and approval to Bowyer, together with an assignment of copyright under Swift's own hand. This offer had been accepted by Bowyer without loss of time. So far as Swift was concerned there was no question of remuneration, but Pilkington received a handsome present. Thus the transaction became apparently on Swift's part an attempt to obtain for his poor friend some benefit from the disposal of his writings, and under the cloak of charity it would have enabled him, if his scheme had succeeded, to regain control of their publication and to surround them with the affectation of anonymity which he so often adopted. (See for the letters cited Appendix X.)

[1] In the British Museum. See Preface.

[2] Sir William Fownes, who was then one of the civic patriarchs of Dublin, had long been prominent amongst the moneyed men of Ireland. From his candidature for the representation of Dublin (*supra*, vol. ii, p. 75, n. 1) he appears to have been an ardent Tory, but he owed to the Whigs a knighthood and a baronetcy, the former conferred upon him while he was Lord Mayor by the Earl of Wharton, and the latter granted to him during the opening months of Lord Carteret's viceroyalty. His town residence was near the Parliament House, where the recollection of his connection is preserved in streets called after him and his son-in-law Cope (*supra*, vol. iii, p. 54, n. 2), and he had also a villa, from which this letter is dated, near the Phœnix

they never met with fewer public charitable foundations than in this kingdom.[1] Private charities, no doubt, will have their reward; but public are great incitements, and good examples often draw others on, though grudgingly, and so a good work be done, no matter who are the workmen. When I was Lord Mayor, I saw some miserable lunatics exposed to the hazard of others, as well as themselves. I had six strong cells made at the Workhouse for the most outrageous, which were soon filled, and by degrees, in a short time, those few drew upon us the solicitations of many, till by the time the old corporation ceased, we had, in that house, forty and upward.[2] The door being opened, interest soon made way to let in the foolish, and such like, as mad folks. These grew a needless charge upon us, and had that course gone on, by this time, the house had been filled with such. The new corporation got rid of most of these by death, or care of friends, and came to a resolution not to admit any such for the future, and the first denial was to a request of the Earl of Kildare,[3] which put a full stop to further applications, as I take it. There are at this time a number of objects which require assistance, and probably many may be restored, if proper care could be taken of them. There is no public place for their reception, nor private undertakers, as about London. Friends and relations here would pay the charge of their support and attendance, if there were a place for securing such lunatics.

Park. Besides he was the owner of an estate amidst the picturesque scenery in the neighbourhood of the town of Wicklow, for which he sat in Queen Anne's reign for some years. His hereditary honour became extinct on the death of his grandson who succeeded him, and his property was united with that of the Tighes of Woodstock, who are the representatives of Swift's political opponent, the Right Hon. Richard Tighe, as well as of his political friend.

[1] A reproach that can be no longer brought against that country.

[2] A Workhouse and Foundling Hospital were established in Dublin in the early years of Queen Anne's reign, with a governing body of nearly two hundred persons, "to relieve, regulate, set to work, and inflict reasonable punishment on all vagabonds and beggars," and "to detain and keep in their service any poor children found or taken up, and to apprentice them out afterwards to honest persons being Protestants." The board or corporation, of which Swift was a member, underwent in 1729 reconstitution. Wodsworth's "Foundling Hospital of Dublin," pp. 2, 3.

[3] Robert, nineteenth Earl of Kildare, whose good deeds are commemorated on "a sumptuous monument" in Christ Church Cathedral, Dublin. His son was created Duke of Leinster.

I own to you, I was for some time averse to our having a public Bedlam, apprehending we should be overloaded with numbers under the name of mad. Nay, I was apprehensive our case would soon be like that in England; wives and husbands trying who could first get the other to Bedlam. Many, who were next heirs to estates, would try their skills to render the possessor disordered, and get them confined, and soon run them into real madness. Such like consequences I dreaded, and therefore have been silent on the subject till of late. Now I am convinced that regard should be had to those under such dismal circumstances; and I have heard the Primate[1] and others express their concern for them; and no doubt but very sufficient subscriptions may be had to set this needful work on foot. I should think it would be a pleasure to any one, that has intentions this way, to see something done in their lifetime, rather than leave it to the conduct of posterity. I would not consent to the proceeding on such a work in the manner I have seen our Poorhouse, and Dr. Steeven's Hospital,[2] viz., to have so an expensive foundation laid, that the expense of the building should require such a sum, and so long a time to finish, as will take up half an age.

My scheme for such an undertaking should be much to this effect. First, I would have a spot of ground fixed on, that should be in a good open air, free from neighbourhood of houses; for the cries and exclamations of the outrageous would reach a great way, and ought not to disturb neighbours, which was what you did not think of, when you mentioned a spot in a close place, almost in the heart of the city. There are many places, in the outskirts of the city, I can name, very proper.

Next to the fixing of a proper spot, I would, when that is secured, which should be a good space, have it well enclosed with a high wall, the cost of all which must be known. Then I would have the cells at the Royal Hospital Infirmary,[3] lately made for mad people, be examined how convenient, and in all points they are adapted to the purpose, with the cost of these cells, which I take to be six or eight. Then I would proceed to the very needful house

[1] *I.e.*, Archbishop Boulter.
[2] *Supra*, vol. iii, pp. 200, 204.
[3] The Chelsea Hospital of Ireland, which is situated at Kilmainham close to the site of Fownes's villa.

for the master and the proper servants. Then another building, to which there should be a piazza for a stone gallery, for walking dry; and out of that several lodging cells for such as are not so outrageous, but melancholy, etc. This may be of such a size that it may be enlarged in length, or by a return; and overhead the same sort of a gallery, with little rooms or cells, opening the doors into the gallery; for, by intervals, the objects affected may be permitted to walk at times in the galleries. This is according to the custom of London. Annexed to the master's house must be the kitchen and offices. This proceeding may be so contrived, as to be enlarged from time to time, as there shall be a fund and occasion requireth additions. There is no necessity for any plans or architects; but an ordinary capacity may contrive those enlargements. Perhaps there may appear some well-disposed persons who will say, they will make this enlargement, and so others, and, by such helps, there may be sufficiently done to answer all purposes.

It comes just now into my head, that there is a very proper spot, which I think the Chapter of St. Patrick lets to one Leigh, a bricklayer or builder. It lies back of Aungier Street east, comes out of York Street, down a place called the Dunghill, runs down to the end of King Street, facing William Street;[1] at the north end of which some alms-houses are built by Dowling and others. Also there stands, to the front of the street, a large stone building, called an alms-house, made by Mrs. Mercer; though by the by, I hear she is weary of her project, and does little in supplying that house, or endowing it. Perhaps this ground may be easily come at from Leigh's heirs; and, by your application, I know not but Mrs. Mercer may give her house up to promote so good a work.[2] This will go a good way, and being followed by subscriptions, a great and speedy progress may be made, in which I will readily join my

---

[1] This land belonged to the Vicars Choral, and has been already mentioned in connection with the Earl of Abercorn (*supra*, vol. ii, p. 113).

[2] Two years later Miss Mercer gave her house for the reception of lunatics and persons whose distempers were of "tedious and doubtful cure," such as those afflicted with "cancer, King's evil, leprosy and falling sickness," and appointed Swift as one of the governors, but the hospital became soon general in its scope, and is now one of the best known medical charities in Dublin.

interest and labour. If that spot fail, we will pitch upon another.

Whatsoever may be your future intentions, do not deny me the consideration of the good your appearance and help may now do. I would not make a step in this affair, if it shall not be agreed, that all matters, which require the consent by votes, shall be determined by the method of a balloting-box, that no great folks, or their speeches, should carry what they please, by their method of scoring upon paper, and seeing who marks, etc., too much practised. If there be nothing in this paper worth your attention, you know how to dispose of it. You have the thoughts of

Your assured humble servant,

W. FOWNES.

THE PROPOSAL

(i) That an hospital, called Bedlam, be built in the city of Dublin, or liberties, for the reception of lunatics from any parts of the kingdom.

(ii) In order to promote so good a work, subscriptions to be taken in Dublin, and in every city and town in the kingdom; and that the chief magistrate of each place be desired to recommend the subscription-paper sent to him for that purpose.

(iii) That when public notice is given in print, that ground is secured for building the hospital of Bedlam, the subscription money be collected, and sent to Dublin, and paid into the hands of (query) Mr. Thorne, steward to the Blue Coat Hospital, a very proper person.

(iv) That upon notice given by Mr. Thorne, that he has received two hundred pounds, a meeting shall be held of all subscribers who happen to be in Dublin, at a proper time and place.

(v) Such persons as subscribe five pounds or upwards, to have a vote at such a meeting.

(vi) That Mr. Thorne, giving security, be continued to receive and pay out the money subscribed for one year, and be allowed only sixpence per pound, for receiving and paying.

(vii) That the money first laid out shall be for the building of six or eight strong cells, for outrageous lunatics to be confined in, and after the form of those made at the Infirmary of the Royal Hospital.

(viii) That the College of Physicians be desired to contribute to this good work, by appointing two or three of their body to be present at their first meeting, and to give their opinion as to the conveniency of the cells, what boilers are proper to be set up in a kitchen, and what food is proper to be provided for such lunatics.

(ix) That near the cells be made a kitchen, small at first, and in such manner as capable to be enlarged. That over this kitchen be a middle room, and over it a garret, to lodge the cook-maid, and one other maid.

(x) That adjoining the kitchen may be made one room, of eighteen feet by eighteen, which may serve for Mr. Thorne to attend in, and where the doctors, or any subscribers, may meet on occasion. And over this room another, to serve for a store-room; and the garret to lodge a porter or two, that must attend the lunatics.

(xi) That these buildings be made plain and strong, with as little cost as can be.

(xii) That the charge of these be computed separately, and the inside necessaries; so that the work may go on as fast as the subscription-fund can be got in.

(xiii) That the subscribers, at the first meeting, do elect seven of their number, such as are knowing in the carrying on of the work, and willing to attend at needful times. That any three or more, at any meeting at the hospital, may give directions for proceeding on the buildings agreed upon to be made at the first meeting of the subscribers; at which first meeting a second meeting may be agreed upon, and so from time to time.

The walling-in of the piece of ground intended for this use may go on as the funds will bear, without obstructing the first useful buildings. And whereas there are lunatics of several kinds, as the melancholy, etc., and some that are unruly by fits, a building must be designed for these sorts; the floors not lofty, but made sufficiently airy, twenty feet wide, whereof ten for a gallery, and ten for lodges; each lodge eight or ten feet broad; as there is a fund [collected] so many go on.

DEAR SIR,

HEREWITH you have my thoughts of the affair you mentioned to me. I wish I could prevail on you to patronize

it, and lay down your own scheme. I am most confident
it cannot fail going on briskly. You have friends and
interest enough to set it agoing, although there may be
some grandees had rather other hands had the conduct of
it; yet the work speaks so much for itself, they must be
ashamed not to contribute, much more to obstruct it. In
the paper called the Proposal, I have considered the pri-
vatest and least expensive way of going to work, avoided
public forms, and grandees interposing. Tom Thorne by
chance I thought upon for that reason, and for preventing
jobs, etc.[1] Do what you please with my papers. I am just
ditto.

Addressed—For the Revd. the Dean of St. Patrick's, this.

DCCCLVI. [*Nichols.*]

SWIFT TO JOHN BARBER

Dublin, *September* 11, 1732.

MY LORD ELECT,
I ANTICIPATE your title, because perhaps it may be your
due before your chaplain, Mr. Pilkington, can attend you,
and besides I have a mind to be the first person who gives
it to you. And, first, I heartily acknowledge your goodness in favouring a young gentleman who has well answered
all the recommendations that have been given me of him,[2]
and I have some years watched all opportunities to do
him a good office, but none of the few things in my own
gift that would be proper for him have fallen in my way
since I knew him; and power with others you know,
or may believe, I have none. I value Mr. Pilkington as
much for his modesty, as his learning and sense, or any
good quality he has. And it would be hard, after your
sending us over so many worthless bishops, all bedangled
with their pert illiterate relations and flatterers, if you

[1] Amusing instances of Thorne's fidelity are given by Sir Frederick
Falkiner ("Hospital of King Charles II," pp. 171, 178). In the previous
year he had detected the contractor for the boys' cassocks in most
shameless swindling, and proved that the governors had been for many
years charged for four and a half yards of stuff more than each
cassock contained.
[2] *Supra*, p. 338.

would not suffer us to lend you, at least for one year, one sample of modesty, virtue, and good sense; and I am glad it falls to your Lordship to give the first precedent. I will write to Dr. Trapp in Mr. Pilkington's favour, but whether I have any credit with him I cannot tell, although, perhaps, you will think I may pretend to some. It is by my advice that Mr. Pilkington goes over somewhat sooner, for I would have him know a little of your end of the town, and what he is to do; but he will not give you any trouble or care till you please to command him, which I suppose will not be till you are settled in your office.

Nothing but this cruel accident of a lameness could have hindered me from attending your ceremonial as a spectator, and I should have forwarded to the utmost Mr. Pope's scheme, for I never approved the omission of those shows. And I think I saw, in my youth, a Lord Mayor's show with all that pomp, when Sir Thomas Pilkington,[1] of your chaplain's name and family, made his procession. I have advised your chaplain to send you this letter, and not present it, that you may be in no pain about him, for he shall wait on you the next morning, when he has taken a lodging for himself, till you come into your mayoralty. I cannot conclude without repeating my acknowledgements for your kind remembrance of me. We were both followers of the same Court and the same cause, and exiles, after a sort, you a voluntary one, and I a necessary; but you have out-thrown me many a hundred bars' lengths. I heartily wish the continuance of your good success, and am, with great truth,

Your most constant friend, and most obedient humble servant,

JONATH. SWIFT.

[1] Pilkington, who had been prominent in opposition to the Court in the civic disputes under Charles II, and suffered four years' imprisonment under James II, was, after the Revolution, elected Lord Mayor three times. The procession which Swift saw was no doubt on the occasion of his second installation, when King William and Queen Mary were entertained by him at the Guildhall. The pageant has been said to have been drawn up by Elkanah Settle, but would appear to have been the work of Matthew Taubman (" D. N. B.," xlv, 300).

DCCCLVII. [*Elwin.*[1]]

SWIFT TO JOHN GAY AND THE DUCHESS OF QUEENSBERRY

Dublin, *October* 3, 1732.

TO GAY

DEAR SIR,

I USUALLY write to friends after a pause of a few weeks, that I may not interrupt them in better company, better thoughts, and better diversions.[2] I believe, I have told you of a great man who said to me, that he never once in his life received a good letter from Ireland, for which there are reasons enough without affronting our understandings. For there is not one person out of this country, who regards any events that pass here, unless he has an estate or employment, except the Court and the chief governors, who delight and endeavour to enslave and ruin us.

I am wondering at the proceeding in the South Sea people to pay off the company's debt at one clap. I will send for the money when you are in town, for all my revenues which depend on tithes are sunk almost to nothing, and my whole personal fortune is in the utmost confusion, so that I believe in a short time I must be driven to live in Wales. God do so and more also to your special friends, who have brought this upon us.

I find some other friends, as well as you, are afraid of the post rascals, and would have me only write by private hands, of which I cannot get a conveniency twice a year. I cannot tell that you or I ever gave the least provocation to the present Ministry, and much less to the Court; and yet I am ten times more out of favour than you. For my own part, I do not see the politics of opening common letters, directed to persons generally known; for a man's understanding would be very weak to convey secrets by the post, if he knew any, which, I declare I do not. And besides, I think the world is already so well informed by plain events, that I question whether the Ministers have any secrets at all. Neither would I be under any apprehension if a letter should be sent me full of treason; because I

---

[1] By permission of Mr. John Murray. *Supra*, vol. iii, p. 148, n. 1.
[2] This letter is an answer to Gay's of 28 August.

cannot hinder people from writing what they please, nor
sending it to me, and although it should be discovered to
have been opened before it came to my hand, I would only
burn it and think no further. I approve of the scheme you
have to grow somewhat richer, though I agree you will
meet with discouragements; and it is reasonable you
should, considering what kind of pens are at this time
only employed and encouraged. For you must allow that
the bad painter was in the right, who, having painted a
cock, drove away all the cocks and hens, and even the
chickens, for fear those who passed by his shop might
make a comparison with his work. And I will say one
thing in spite of the post-officers, that since wit and learning began to be made use of in our kingdoms, they were
never professedly thrown aside, contemned, and punished,
till within your own memory; nor dulness and ignorance
ever so openly encouraged and promoted.

In answer to what you say of my living among you, if I
could do it to my ease, perhaps you have heard of a scheme
for an exchange in Berkshire proposed by two of our
friends.[1] But, beside the difficulty of adjusting certain
circumstances, it would not answer. I am at a time of life
that seeks ease and independence. You will hear my
reasons when you see those friends, and I concluded them
with one saying, that I would rather be a freeman among
slaves, than a slave among freemen. The dignity of my
present station damps the pertness of inferior puppies and
squires, which, without plenty and ease on your side the
channel, would break my heart in a month.

To the Duchess

Madam,

See what it is to live where I do. I am utterly ignorant
of that same *Strada del Po*, and yet, if that author be
against lending or giving money, I cannot but think him a
good courtier, which, I am sure, your Grace is not, no, not
so much as to be a maid of honour. For I am certainly
informed, that you are neither a freethinker, nor can sell
bargains;[2] that you can neither spell, nor talk, nor write,

[1] *Supra*, p. 320.

[2] This phrase is said by the Oxford Dictionary to mean making a
fool of another person, but from Stella's Bon Mots "the sell" would
appear to have consisted in a coarse joke ("Prose Works," xi, 142).

nor think like a courtier; that you pretend to be respected for qualities which have been out of fashion ever since you were almost in your cradle; that your contempt for a fine petticoat is an infallible mark of disaffection;[1] which is further confirmed by your ill taste for wit, in preferring two old-fashioned poets before Duck or Cibber. Besides, you spell in such a manner as no Court lady can read, and write in such an old-fashioned style as none of them can understand.

You need not be in pain about Mr. Gay's stock of health. I promise you he will spend it all upon laziness, and run deep in debt by a winter's repose in town. Therefore I entreat your Grace will order him to move his chops less and his legs more for the six cold months, else he will spend all his money in physic and coach hire. I am in much perplexity about your Grace's declaration of the manner in which you dispose what you call your love and respect, which you say are not paid to merit, but to your own humour. Now, Madam, my misfortune is, that I have nothing to plead but abundance of merit; and there goes an ugly observation, that the humour of ladies is apt to change. Now, Madam, if I should go to Amesbury with a great load of merit, and your Grace happen to be out of humour, and will not purchase my merchandise at the price of your respect, the goods may be damaged, and nobody else will take them off my hands. Besides, you have declared Mr. Gay to hold the first part, and I but the second, which is hard treatment, since I shall be the newest acquaintance by some years; and I will appeal to all the rest of your sex, whether such an innovation ought to be allowed.

I should be ready to say in the common form, that I was much obliged to the lady who wished she could give me the best living, etc., if I did not vehemently suspect it was the very same lady who spoke many things to me in the same style, and also with regard to the gentleman at your elbow when you writ, whose dupe he was as well as

[1] The Duchess's disregard of the changes of fashion is celebrated by William Whitehead in the verses which he addressed to her. She had told him that the preposterous dress of their day was due to the supineness of the men who could only be caught by such vagaries, and he replies that she contradicted her own assertion; as despite her indifference to such arts she had charmed much and charmed long.

of her waiting-woman. But they were both arrant knaves, as I then told him and a third friend, though they will not believe it to this day. I desire to present my most humble respects to my Lord Duke, and with my heartiest prayer for the prosperity of the whole family, remain your Grace's, etc.

To Gay

SIR,

I MUST say something to your few lines at the bottom of your letter, which cites a paragraph from our friend relating to me, to which I give two or three full answers.[1]

DCCCLVIII. [*Mrs. Pilkington's Memoirs.*]

SWIFT TO MRS. PILKINGTON

[*October*, 1732.]

MADAM,[2]

YOU must shake off the leavings of your sex. If you cannot keep a secret and take a chiding, you will quickly be out of my sphere. Corrigible people are to be chid; those who are otherwise may be very safe from any lectures of mine; I should rather choose to indulge them in their follies, than attempt to set them right. I desire you may not inform your husband of what is past, for a reason I

---

[1] This is presumably only the opening sentence of a paragraph which has been suppressed.

[2] According to Mrs. Pilkington ("Memoirs," i, 85) her husband was asked by Pope to stay with him for a fortnight at Twickenham before Barber's inauguration as Lord Mayor. Thence she received from him a letter "filled with Mr. Pope's praises, and the extraordinary regard he showed him, introducing him to several noblemen, and even oppressing him with civilities," but on taking it to the Deanery, she was shown by Swift a letter which had come by the same packet from Pope, expressing surprise that he should have been recommended by Swift as "a modest, ingenious man," one whom he found to be "a most forward, shallow, conceited fellow," and saying that he was "sick of his impertinence before the end of the third day." A stormy scene ensued, as Mrs. Pilkington defended her husband, and said it was highly ungenerous of Pope "to caress and abuse him" at the same time. Next morning she sent Swift an apology, to which this letter is the reply. It will be noticed in subsequent letters that Swift, when referring to Pilkington, adds that he had always found him a modest person.

shall give you when I see you,[1] which may be this evening
if you will. I am,

Very sincerely your friend,
J. SWIFT.

DCCCLIX. [*Notes and Queries.*[2]]

SWIFT TO LADY WORSLEY

Dublin, *November* 4, 1732.

MADAM,[3]

I WILL never tell, but I will always remember how many
years have run out since I had first the honour and happiness to be known to your Ladyship, which however I have
a thousand times wished to have never happened, since it
was followed by the misfortune of being banished from you
for ever. I believe you are the only lady in England that
for a thousand years past hath so long remembered a useless friend in absence, which is too great a load of favour
for me and all my gratitude to support.

I can faithfully assure your Ladyship that I never received from you more than one letter since I saw you last,
and that I sent you a long answer. I often forget what I
did yesterday, or what passed half an hour ago, and yet I
can well remember a hundred particulars in your Ladyship's
company. This is the memory of those who grow old. I
have no room left for new ideas. I am offended with one
passage in your Ladyship's letter, but I will forgive you,
because I do not believe the fact, and all my acquaintance
here join with me in my unbelief. You make excuses for
not sooner sending me the most agreeable present that ever
was made, whereas it is agreed by all the curious and skilful
of both sexes among us, that such a piece of work could
not be performed by the most dextrous pair of hands and
finest eyes in Christendom, in less than a year and a half,
at twelve hours a day. Yet Mrs. Barber, corrupted by the
obligations she hath to you, would pretend that I over-

---

[1] The reason was lest on hearing of Pope's letter, Pilkington "might
resent it to him, and make him an enemy." Pope was then writing to
him in the most friendly manner. See Appendix X.

[2] I, iv, 219.

[3] This letter is an answer to Lady Worsley's of 6 August.

reckon six months, and six hours a day.[1] Be that as it will, our best virtuosi are unanimous that the invention exceeds, if possible, the work itself. But to all these praises I coldly answer, that although what they say be perfectly true, or indeed below the truth, yet if they had ever seen or conversed with your Ladyship, as I have done, they would have thought this escritoire a very poor performance from such hands, such eyes, and such an imagination. To speak my own thoughts, the work itself does not delight me more than the little cares you were pleased to descend to in contriving ways to have it conveyed so far without damage, whereof it received not the least from without; what there was came from within; for one of the little rings that lifts a drawer for wax, hath touched a part of one of the pictures, and made a mark as large as the head of a small pin, but it touches only an end of a cloud, and yet I have been careful to twist a small thread of silk round that wicked ring, who promiseth to do so no more.

Your Ladyship wrongs me in saying that I twitted you with being a great-grandmother. I was too prudent and careful of my own credit to offer the least hint upon that head, while I was conscious that I might have been great-grandfather to you. I beg you, Madam, that there may be no quarrels of jealousy between your Ladyship and my Lady Carteret; I set her at work by the authority I claimed over her as your daughter. The young woman showed her readiness, and performed very well for a new beginner, and deserves encouragement. Besides, she filled the chest with tea, whereas you did not send me a single pen, a stick of wax, or a drop of ink; for all which I must bear the charge out of my own pocket. And after all if your Ladyship were not by, I would say that my Lady Carteret's box, as you disdainfully call it instead of a tea-chest, is a most beautiful piece of work, and is oftener used than yours, because it is brought down for tea after dinner among ladies, whereas my escritoire never stirs out of my closet, but when it is brought for a sight. Therefore I again desire that there may be no family quarrels upon my account.

As to Patty Blount, you wrong her very much. She was

---

[1] Mrs. Barber, who had reached Dublin two months before (Mrs. Delany's "Correspondence," i, 330), had evidently been completely forgiven by Swift for her part in the letters to the Queen, notwithstanding Delany's assertion to the contrary (*supra*, p. 246, n. 3).

a neighbour's child, a good Catholic, an honest girl, and a tolerable courtier at Richmond. I deny she was dirty, but a little careless, and sometimes wore a ragged gown, when she and I took long walks. She saved her money in summer only to be able to keep a chair at London in winter; this is the worst you can say, and she might have a whole coat to her back, if her good-nature did not make her a fool to her mother and sanctified sister Teresa. And she was the only girl I coquetted in the whole half year that I lived with Mr. Pope in Twickenham, whatever evil tongues might have informed your Ladyship, in hopes to set you against me, and after this usage, if I accept the archbishopric of Canterbury from your Ladyship's hands, I think you ought to acknowledge it as a favour.

Are you not weary, Madam? Have you patience to read all this? I am bringing back past times; I imagine myself talking with you as I used to do, but on a sudden, I recollect where I am sitting, banished to a country of slaves and beggars,—my blood soured, my spirits sunk, fighting with beasts like St. Paul, not at Ephesus, but in Ireland. I am not of your opinion, that the flocks, in either kingdom, want better shepherds: for, as the French say, *à telles brebis tel pasteur*, and God be thanked that I have no flock at all, so that I neither can corrupt nor be corrupted. I never saw any person so full of acknowledgement as Mrs. Barber is for your Ladyship's continued favours to her, nor have I known any person of a more humble and grateful spirit than her, or who knows better how to distinguish the persons by whom she is favoured. But I will not honour myself so far, or dishonour you so much, as to think I can add the least weight to your own natural goodness and generosity.

You must, as occasion serves, present my humble respects to my Lord and Lady Carteret, and my Lady Dysart,[1] and to Sir Robert Worsley. I am, and shall be ever, with the truest respect, esteem, and gratitude, Madam,

Your Ladyship's most obedient and most humble servant,   JONATH. SWIFT.

I know not where my old friend Harry Worsley is,[2] but I am his most humble servant.

[1] Lord Carteret's eldest daughter, who had married in 1729 Lionel, third Earl of Dysart.
[2] *Supra*, p. 146, n. 4.

January 8, 1732-3.

MADAM,

I WRIT this Letter two months ago, and was to send it by Mrs. Barber, but she falling ill of the gout, and I deferring from day to day, expecting her to mend, I was at last out of patience.[1] I have sent it among others by a private hand. I wish your Ladyship and all your family many happy new years.

DCCCLX. [*Faulkner.*]

SWIFT TO MRS. CÆSAR

[*November* 4, 1732.]

MADAM,[2]

AMONG a few little vexations, such as beggary, slavery, corruption, ignorance, want of friends, faction, oppression, and some other trifles of the like nature, that we philosophers ought to despise, two or three ladies of long acquaintance, and at a great distance, are still so kind as to remember me, and I was always proud, and pleased to a great degree, that you happened to be one, since constancy is, I think, at least as seldom found in friendship as in love. Mrs. Barber, when I see her, is always telling me wonders of the continual favours you have conferred on her, and that, without your interposition, the success of her errand would have hardly been worth the journey; and I must bear the load of this obligation, without the least possibility of ever returning it, otherwise than by my best wishes for the prosperity and health of you and your family, for, in spite of all your good words, I am the most insignificant man of this most insignificant country. I have been tied by the leg, without being married, for ten months past, by an unlucky strain, which prevented the honour and happiness I proposed to myself of waiting on you oftener during this last summer, and another year at my period of life is like an

---

[1] Nearly a year before Mrs. Barber had announced her intention of settling in Bath, where she proposed that her husband should carry on his trade as a woollen-draper, and that she should let lodgings, and her return to Ireland was for the purpose of transplanting her family thither (Mrs. Delany's "Correspondence," i, 330, 383).

[2] An answer to Mrs. Cæsar's letter of 6 August.

inch in a man's nose, yet I flatter myself that next spring
I may take one voyage more, when you will see me altered
in every disposition of body and mind, except in my respects for you and all that belong to you.

There is one part of Mr. Pope's compliment which I
cannot make you, for I could not with the strictest search
find one letter too many in any of your words, although I
found a thousand words too few in your letter; therefore I
accepted and understood it only as a billet just writ, while
Mrs. Barber stood by in her hood and scarf, just ready to
take her leave and begin her journey, and what is worse, I
suspect that she was forced to solicit you long, because she
wanted a certificate under your hand to convince me that
she was not an impostor. I will not say one word in
Mrs. Barber's behalf, for she will always continue to deserve your protection, and therefore she may be sure you
will always continue to give it her. I hope, Mr. Cæsar is
in good health, and desire he will accept the offer of my
most humble service, with my hearty wishes for your whole
family. I am, with true respect, Madam,

> Your most obedient, and most humble servant,
> JON. SWIFT.

DCCCLXI. [*Gentleman's Magazine.*[1]]

SWIFT TO BENJAMIN MOTTE

Dublin, *November* 4, 1732.

SIR,

IF I did not answer yours of September 4th,[2] as I thought
I did, I will do it now, and indeed I do not find it endorsed
as answered. The other day I received two copies of the
last Miscellany, but I cannot learn who brought them to
the house. Mr. Pope had been for some months before
writing to me that he thought it would be proper to publish
another Miscellany, for which he then gave me reasons that
I did not well comprehend, nor do I remember that I was
much convinced, because I did not know what fund he had

---

[1] N.S., vol. xliii, p. 259.
[2] The letter had doubtless reference to the question of copyright
(*supra*, p. 342, n. 2).

for it, little imagining that some humorous or satirical trifles
that I had writ here occasionally, and sent some to the
press, while others were from stolen copies, would make
almost six-sevenths of the whole verse part in the book,
and the greatest part of the prose was written by other
persons of this kingdom as well as myself.[1] I believe I have
told you, that no printer or bookseller hath any sort of
property here. I have writ some things that would make
people angry. I always sent them by unknown hands. The
printer might guess, but he could not accuse me. He ran
the whole risk, and well deserved the property, if he could
carry it to London and print it there, but I am sure I could
have no property at all. Some things, as that of the Soldier
and Scholar, the Pastoral,[2] and one or two more, were
written at a man-of-quality's house in the North who had
the originals, while I had no copy, but they were given to
the Lord Lieutenant[3] and some others; so copies ran, and
Faulkner got them, and I had no property, but Faulkner
made them his in London. I have sent a kind of certificate
owning my consent to the publishing this last Miscellany,
against my will; and, however it comes to pass, there are
not a few errata that quite alter the sense in those indifferent verses of mine. The best thing I writ, as I think,
is called a Libel on Dr. Delany and Lord Carteret, which I
find is not printed, because it gave great offence here, and
your Court was offended at one line relating to Mr. Pope.[4]
I care not to say any more of this Miscellany, and wish
you may not be a loser by it. I find my name is put at
length in some notes, which I think was wrong; but I am

[1] Pope had apparently issued the new volume of Miscellanies without consulting Swift further in any way as to its contents. The
verse covers a hundred pages, and is all from Swift's pen except
a few epigrams and four short poems, " On the Countess of B—— cutting Paper," " On a Certain Lady at Court," " To a Lady with the
Temple of Fame," and " Verses under the Picture of England's Arch-
poet." The prose pieces, written in Ireland but disclaimed by Swift,
were " God's Revenge against Punning," the " Wonderful Wonder of
Wonders," the " Wonder of all the Wonders," the " Infallible Scheme
to pay the Debts of Ireland," and the sixteenth and seventeenth numbers of the " Intelligencer."

[2] *I.e.*, " The Grand Question Debated: whether Hamilton's Bawn
should be turned into a Barrack or Malt House," and " The Dialogue
between Dermot and Sheelah " (" Poetical Works," ii, 99, 101). " The
Grand Question " was published in England under the title of " The
Soldier and Scholar."

[3] *I.e.*, Lord Carteret.   [4] *Supra*, p. 122.

at too great distance to help it, and must bear what I cannot remedy.

Two days ago I had yours without date, relating to Mr. Ewin. I would fain know what sort of calling or credit he is of. He gave me the account of Mrs. Davys's death; said he was well known at Cambridge, that she left him all her fortune, only her clothes to her sister, one Roda Staunton, a poor beggar who had sixpence a week out of my Cathedral collections. I desired the clothes might be sold, for which he sent four pounds fifteen shillings to you, with that mourning ring.[1] I wonder on what consideration Mrs. Davys left Mr. Ewin her heir, while her own sister lay starving with a lame child and supported by charity. This Ewin writ me another letter, I suppose when he was drunk, for in it he said several things to Mrs. Davys's disadvantage, and it is written with ill manners, among other things that she pretended to have many years ago writ a book, or part of a book, which the world laid upon me.[2] Pray if ever you see him let him show you the letters I writ to her. It is above thirty years since her husband died; for Sir W. Temple was then alive, who died in 169[9],[3] and I was then at his house, and when I went to Ireland with Lord Berkeley she had been some years a widow, and one or two years after she went for mere want to England where she stayed till she died. I saw her once or twice in London, but never after till about five years ago, when my Lord Oxford and I called at Cambridge to dine,[4] and there I saw her an hour; nor do I believe I ever writ her a dozen letters, and those chiefly to tell her I had sent her some money, which I did I believe nine or ten times or oftener.[5]

---

[1] Mary Davys, whose name appears in the lists of Swift's correspondents (*supra*, vol. i, p. 382), wrote some plays and novels. She was the widow of one of Swift's college contemporaries, the Rev. Peter Davys, who became master of the school attached to St. Patrick's Cathedral. Ewin was a grocer, and was the father of a usurer, nicknamed Dr. Squintum, whose transactions with the undergraduates led to his expulsion from Cambridge ("D. N. B.," xiv, 209; xviii, 94).

[2] Probably the "Tale of a Tub."

[3] Davys died on 4 November, 1698, and Temple on 27 January following.

[4] When he visited Lord Oxford at Wimpole (*supra*, vol. iii, p. 409.

[5] Ewin had probably threatened to publish these letters. It is said that there were thirty-six, some of them addressed to Mrs. Davys's husband, and that they were afterwards in the possession of Ewin's son, but all trace of them has been lost.

So that either Ewin lies, or the printers would be much disappointed, for she was a rambling woman with very little taste of wit or humour, as appears by her writings. I believe I have tired you as well as myself. You may please to send me the ring by any opportunity. I believe I shall sell it and give the money to her poor sister, and if Ewin be rich he ought in conscience to relieve her. I am,

Your most humble servant,

J. S.

January 9, 1732-3.

YOU see this letter is of old date; it was to go by Mrs. Barber, who falling ill of the gout, I deferred it in hopes of her mending. This goes by a private hand, with some others which I desire you will send as directed. I had your last with the abstracts about the Test; and by them I suppose it will be needless to publish the old treatise on that subject.[1] I desire you will see Mr. Pilkington, my Lord Mayor's chaplain, and let him know you have power from me to pay him any sum of money as far as twenty pounds, taking his promissory note.

JONATHAN SWIFT.

You will please to convey the enclosed to Mr. Pope in the safest manner you can, for there is another in it to a neighbour of his at Dawley.

To Mr. Motte.

DCCCLXII. [*Original.*[2]]

LADY ELIZABETH GERMAIN TO SWIFT

London, *November* 7, 1732.

I SHOULD have answered yours sooner, but that I every day expected another from you, with your orders to speak

---

[1] During the months of November and December the Dissenters had under consideration the desirability of promoting an agitation for the repeal of the Test Act, but were dissuaded from taking such a step by friends "upon whose approbation the success of their application very much depended" (Boyer, *op. cit.*, xlv, 138). The treatise appears to have been the "Letter concerning the Sacramental Test" (*supra*, vol. i, p. 111, n. 4).

[2] In the British Museum. See Preface.

to the Duke of Dorset; which I should with great pleasure have obeyed, as it was to serve a friend of yours. Mrs. Floyd is now, thank God, in as good health as I have seen her this many years, though she has still her winter-cough hanging upon her; but that, I fear, I must never expect she should be quite free from at this time of day, and all my trouble with her now is, to make her drink wine enough according to the doctor's order, which is not above three or four glasses, such as are commonly filled at sober houses; and that she makes so great a rout with, and makes so many faces, that there is nobody that did not know her perfectly well, but would extremely suspect she drank drams in private.

I am sorry to find our tastes so different in the same person, and as everybody has a natural partiality to their own opinion, so it is surprising to me to find Lady Suffolk dwindle in yours, who rises infinitely higher in mine, the more and the longer I know her.[1] But you say, "you will say no more of Courts, for fear of growing angry"; and indeed, I think you are so already, since you level all without knowing them, and seem to think, that no one who belongs to a Court can act right. I am sure this cannot be really and truly your sense, because it is unjust; and, if it is, I shall suspect there is something of your old maxim in it, which I ever admired and found true, that you must have offended them, because you do not forgive. I have been about a fortnight from Knole, and shall next Thursday go there again for about three weeks, where I shall be ready and willing to receive your commands, who am

Most faithfully and sincerely yours.

Addressed—To the Revd. Dr. Swift, Dean of St. Patrick's, Dublin, Ireland.

---

[1] Lady Betty's mention of the Countess (*supra*, p. 323) had no doubt been seized by Swift as occasion for a denunciation of that lady's insincerity.

DCCCLXIII. [*Original.*[1]]

JOHN GAY TO SWIFT

November 16, 1732.

DEAR SIR,

I AM at last come to London before the family, to follow my own inventions. In a week or fortnight I expect the family will follow me. You may now draw upon me for your money, as soon as you please. I have some of my own too that lies dead, and I protest I do not know which way at present to dispose of it, everything is so precarious. I paid Mr. Lancelot twelve pounds and pay myself the five guineas you had of me, and have deducted your loss by paying off one of the South Sea bonds, and I find I have remaining of yours two hundred and eleven pounds, fifteen shillings, and sixpence. And I believe over and above that sum, there will be more owing to you upon account of interest on the bonds, about four or five pounds. Mr. Hoare has done this for me, but I have not had time to call upon him yet, so that I cannot be more particular. As the money now lies in Mr. Hoare's hands, you see it is ready on demand. I believe you had best give notice when you draw on me for it, that I may not be out of the way.

I have not as yet seen Mr. Pope, but design in a day or two to go to him, though I am in hopes of seeing him here to-day or to-morrow. If my present project succeeds, you may expect a better account of my own fortune a little while after the holidays; but I promise myself nothing, for I am determined, that neither anybody else, or myself, shall disappoint me. I wish the arguments made use of to draw you here, were every way of more consequence. I would not have you change one comfort of life for another. I wish you to keep every one of those you have already, with as many additional ones as you like. When I sit down to consider on the choice of any subject, to amuse myself by writing, I find I have a natural propensity to write against vice, so that I do not expect much encouragement; though I really think, in justice, I ought to be paid for stifling my inclinations; but the great are ungrateful.

[1] In the British Museum. See Preface.

Mr. Pulteney's young son hath had the smallpox, and is perfectly recovered. He is not in town, but is expected in about a week from the Bath. I must answer the letter you writ to the Duchess and me, when her Grace comes to town; for I know she intended to have a part in it. Why cannot you come among us in the beginning of the new year? The company will be then all in town, and the spring advancing upon us every day. What I mean by the company is, those who call themselves your friends, and I believe are so. It is certain the Parliament will not meet till about the middle of January. I have not been idle while I was in the country; and I know your wishes in general, and in particular, that industry may always find its account. Believe me, as I am, unchangeable in the regard, love, and esteem I have for you.

Addressed—To the Revd. Dr. Swift, Dean of St. Patrick's, in Dublin, Ireland.
Endorsed by Swift—He died soon after: his last letter.

DCCCLXIV. [*Elwin.*]

ALEXANDER POPE AND JOHN ARBUTHNOT TO SWIFT

December 5, 1732.

POPE

IT is not a time to complain that you have not answered me two letters, in the last of which I was impatient under some fears.[1] It is not now indeed a time to think of myself, when one of the nearest and longest ties I have ever had is broken all on a sudden, by the unexpected death of poor Mr. Gay. An inflammatory fever hurried him out of this life in three days. He died last night at nine o'clock, not deprived of his senses entirely at last, and possessing them perfectly till within five hours. He asked of you a few hours before, when in acute torment by the inflammation in his bowels and breast. His effects are in the Duke of Queensberry's custody. His sisters, we sup-

---

[1] These letters had probably relation to a claim of copyright which Bowyer made in respect of such pieces as had been assigned to him by Swift, and were printed by Pope in the new volume of the Miscellanies. See Appendix X.

pose, will be his heirs, who are two widows. As yet it is not known whether or no he left a will.[1] Good God! how often are we to die before we go quite off this stage? In every friend we lose a part of ourselves, and the best part. God keep those we have left! Few are worth praying for, and oneself the least of all.

I shall never see you now, I believe. One of your principal calls to England is at an end. Indeed he was the most amiable by far, his qualities were the gentlest, but I love you as well and as firmly. Would to God the man we have lost had not been so amiable, nor so good! But that is a wish for our own sakes, not for his. Sure if innocence and integrity can deserve happiness, it must be his. Adieu. I can add nothing to what you will feel, and diminish nothing from it. Yet write to me, and soon. Believe no man now living loves you better, I believe no man ever did, than

A. POPE.

Dr. Arbuthnot, whose humanity you know, heartily commends himself to you. All possible diligence and affection has been shown, and continued attendance on this melancholy occasion. Once more adieu, and write to one who is truly disconsolate.

ARBUTHNOT

DEAR SIR,

I AM sorry that the renewal of our correspondence should be upon such a melancholy occasion. Poor Mr. Gay died of an inflammation, and, I believe, at last a mortification of the bowels. It was the most precipitate case I ever knew, having cut him off in three days. He was attended by two physicians besides myself. I believed the distemper mortal from the beginning. I have not had the pleasure of a line from you these two years. I wrote one about your health, to which I had no answer. I wish you all health and happiness, being with great affection and respect, Sir,

Yours, etc.

Endorsed—On my dear friend Mr. Gay's death; received December 15, but not read till the 20th, by an impulse foreboding some misfortune.

---

[1] His property was divided between the sisters, Katherine Baller and Joanna Fortescue.

DCCCLXV. [*Gentleman's Magazine.*[1]]

SWIFT TO BENJAMIN MOTTE

December 9, 1732.

SIR,[2]

I THANK you for your packet, and I suppose shall hear of it as soon as it comes. I am not at all satisfied with the last Miscellany, I believe I told you so in a former letter. My part, which in the verses is seven-eighths, is very incorrect. I can assure you I had no advantage by any one of the four volumes, as I once hinted to you, and desire it may be a secret always. Neither do I in the least understand the reasons for printing this. I believe I told you formerly that booksellers here have no property, and I have cause to believe that some of our printers will collect all they think to be mine, and print them by subscription, which I will neither encourage nor oppose. But as to the writings I have had long by me, I intend to leave them to certain friends, and that you shall be the publisher. I must tell you plainly I have now done with writing: verse grows troublesome, and hard to be got, and not worth my time, since they will neither entertain myself nor be of public use.

If you think the Letter you mention [3] will do any service against that destructive design now on foot, I shall leave the matter to your discretion, and if the same wicked project shall be attempted here, I shall so far suspend my laziness as to oppose it to the utmost. I believe in both kingdoms, those who by their function, their conscience, their honour, their oaths, and the interest of their community are most bound to obstruct such a ruin to the Church, will be the great advocates for it; for which, if I shall pray God to forgive them, His divine justice will not suffer Him.

My health is tolerable, and, although I feel my lameness, they tell me I do not limp. I hope your family is well. I desire my service to Mrs. Lancelot: tell her to refresh

---

[1] N.S., vol. xliv, p. 232.

[2] This letter assumes that Motte had received the one of 6 November which did not reach him, as the postscript to it shows, until January.

[3] *I.e.*, " The Letter concerning the Sacramental Test " (*supra*, p. 362, n. 1).

a certain person's memory whenever I write to a certain lady. I am, with great sincerity,

Your assured friend and most humble servant,

J. S.

If you print that piece, I am content you should say, "written many years ago by," etc., and name the author, and get some short preface to show the reasons for printing it now by itself.

Addressed—To Mr. Benjamin Motte, Bookseller, at the Middle Temple Gate, in Fleet Street, London.

DCCCLXVI. [*Nichols.*]

SWIFT TO LORD MAYOR BARBER

Dublin, *December* 14, 1732.

MY LORD,

AFTER obtaining one favour from your Lordship, I am under the necessity of requesting another; which, however, I hope will not give you much trouble. I know that it depends upon chance what employments you may have in your disposal during your mayoralty, but some I presume you will have. It is therefore my request, and will be so likewise of some others among your friends, that if any employment should fall vacant, during your government, which Mr. Barber would be allowed capable of executing well, your Lordship would please that he may have the refusal, with as much favour as will consist with your own generous disposition, adding the friendship you are pleased to profess to me, which I throw heartily into the balance. He is of English birth, a very upright honest man, and his wife has abundance of merit in all respects. They design to settle among you, having turned what fortune they had here into money.[1]

And now, my Lord, I heartily give you joy of governing the noblest city in the world, where I know you are desirous, and able, to do so much good, and to set a worthy pattern for the imitation of those who shall come after you. If my

---

[1] *Supra*, p. 356, n. 1.

health, and the bad situation of my private affairs, will permit, I shall hope to have the honour of being one among your guests next summer. Mr. Pilkington is, in his letters, perpetually full of your great favours to him, and says you will be his voucher that he still continues his modest behaviour, which I always pressed upon him as the best quality in a young man, although I never observed the least want of it in him.

I hope you will take care of your health, which in our city of Dublin is a difficult task for a Lord Mayor to perform, and if your Lordship be under the necessity of drinking as many healths in proportion on public days as are done here, you will be in great danger of ruining your own. I am, with entire friendship and true respect, my Lord,

Your Lordship's most obedient and most humble servant,
JON. SWIFT.

DCCCLXVII. [*Original.*[1]]

ROBERT ARBUTHNOT TO SWIFT

Rouen, *January* 2, 1732-3 [O.S. *December* 22, 1732].

DEAR SIR,[2]

I HAVE flattered myself these many years, that vapours or company would have brought you over seas to Spa, or to some such place, and that you would have taken Paris in your way, and so I should have had the pleasure of seeing you in some place of my own. I wonder much that a person of so much good humour can let yourself grow old, or die without seeing some other country than your own. I am not quite so wicked as to wish you any real illness to bring you to us, though I should not be sorry that you thought you had need of change of air. I wish you a happy new year, and many more; and, whatever interest I have against it, good health, and prosperity, and everything that I can wish to one that I much honour and esteem.

[1] In the British Museum. See Preface.
[2] With "the philanthropic Robert of Rouen," who is so frequently mentioned in his brother's letters, Swift had become acquainted seven years before (*supra*, vol. iii, p. 320).

IV   B B

I recommend to your friendship and acquaintance the bearer, Mr. Delamar. His brother, now dead, has been with you in Ireland, and this gentleman deserves from me that kindness my friends can show him.[1] Adieu, dear Sir. If I can serve you in anything, command me always, for I am, with great esteem,

Your most humble and most obedient servant,
ROB. ARBUTHNOT.

Addressed—To the Reverend Doctor Swift, Dean of St. Patrick's, Dublin.

DCCCLXVIII. [*Deane Swift.*]

CHARLES FORD TO SWIFT

London, *December* 23, 1732.

YESTERDAY I received your letter of the 9th, and am infinitely obliged to you for the constant concern you show for me. I am ashamed to trouble you so much, and so often, in my own affairs, and your great kindness makes me almost ashamed to ask pardon for it.[2] . . .

I am very glad to hear the character you give of Lord Orrery. He was extremely applauded for a speech he made against the Army Bill.[3] There is no danger of repealing the Test. The Court has taken the usual method of gaining the fanatic leaders much against the grain of the body.[4] It is said, the Bishop of Salisbury[5] is the chief en-

---

[1] Members of the family had been settled in Ireland for a considerable time, and were connected by marriage with the Luttrells (*supra*, vol. iii, p. 461).

[2] From some correspondence which is printed by Sir Walter Scott ("Works," xix, 299) it would appear that Swift had acted as arbitrator in a dispute between Ford and a Dublin banker called Burton. In one of the letters Ford speaks of himself as "old and fat."

[3] Swift's biographer, John Boyle, fifth Earl of Orrery, and afterwards fifth Earl of Cork, had come to Ireland in the previous summer to take possession of the property to which, with his first title, he had succeeded on his father's death (*supra*, p. 238, n. 1). He was accompanied by his wife, and while staying at Cork, where they had landed, suffered an overwhelming sorrow by her death. Soon afterwards he appears to have come to Dublin, and to have made Swift's acquaintance.

[4] *Supra*, p. 362, n. 1.   [5] *I.e.*, Hoadly.

courager of them; that the Queen spoke to him, and that
he answered, he can be besmeared, although they would
not suffer him to go the dirty road to Durham. That was
the excuse they made him upon the last vacancy of that
see. I am extremely proud that Lady Acheson does me
the honour to remember her humble servant. I heartily
wish she could be persuaded to keep good hours, having
observed, by many of my acquaintance, that nothing impairs
health so much as sitting up late. I often hear from my
sister. She writes in quite another strain than she talked,
with cheerfulness and good nature. I fancy Ardsallagh has
cured the lady of her spleen.[1] I heartily wish you many
new years, with health and happiness; and am, most entirely, etc.

I am told poor Gay's play is now in rehearsal, and will
please.[2] It was that brought him to town a little before he
died; though, without his fever, he could not probably have
held out long anywhere.

DCCCLXIX. [*Mrs. Pilkington's Memoirs.*]

SWIFT TO MRS. PILKINGTON

Deanery House, *January* 1, 1732-3.

MADAM,[3]
I SEND you your bit of a newspaper, with the verses,
than which I never saw better in their kind. I have the

---

[1] If an account of a mock trial, which is said to have been held
there about that time, is to be credited, the house of Peter Ludlow
(*supra*, vol. iii, p. 12, n. 1) must have been a lively place. Swift acted the
character of the judge, Sheridan that of the prisoner, and the Grattans,
Jacksons, Stopford, and Mrs. Ludlow, filled other parts. So realistic
were the proceedings that the judges, who were on assize at the time,
are said to have complained in turn to the Lord Lieutenant and the
Bishops, but failed in each case to secure redress (Sir Walter Scott,
"Works," xix, 472).

[2] The opera called "Achilles," which was acted at Covent Garden
in the following February (*supra*, p. 301, n. 2).

[3] As the incident resulted in her receiving this letter, Mrs. Pilkington
feels constrained to tell us ("Memoirs," i, 72) that she was shown one
day by a judge's wife "a pretty poem," which was said to have been
written by a daughter of Sir Charles Talbot (*supra*, p. 320), but which
proved to be her own. Although the appearance of the poem is

same opinion of those you were pleased to write upon me, as have also some particular friends of genius and taste, to whom I ventured to communicate them, who universally agree with me. But as I cannot with decency show them, except to a very few, I hope, for both our sakes, others will do it for me. I can only assure you I value your present, as much as either of the others, only you must permit it to be turned into a pen, which office I will perform with my own hand, and never permit any other to use it. I heartily wish you many happy new years; and am, with true esteem, Madam,

Your most obliged friend and servant,

JON. SWIFT.

DCCCLXX. [*Original.*[1]]

SWIFT TO THE EARL OF OXFORD

Dublin, *January* 3, 1732-3.

MY LORD,

THERE is a usual favour which we who live in this kingdom pretend to claim, if we have English acquaintance, especially with Lords. The bearer of this, Mr. Thomas Shaw, will venture to give you a printed paper, called a case; a thing your Lordship is well acquainted with. He is a gentleman of a good estate, for which he is at law with an Irish Lord, called Lord Dunsany, who was a forfeiting person by the rebellion of his ancestors in 1641.[2] But,

---

attributed to one of her friends, it may possibly have been due to the desire of her husband to turn the products of their lighter hours to profit. To her surprise Mrs. Pilkington, who in the innocence of her heart mentioned the circumstance at the Deanery, received a peremptory order from Swift to show him the poem, and chancing to hear of the standish and table-book which Delany and Orrery had just made the occasion for complimentary verses, she thought that she could not do better than follow their example, and accompany the poem by a present of "a fine eagle quill," which gave opportunity for further lines likening Swift's writings to the works of Raphael.

[1] In the possession of the Duke of Portland. *Supra*, vol. ii, p. 160, n. 2.

[2] This litigation had begun in the year 1722 when Shaw was a minor (Irish Chancery Bills). Lord Dunsany was the eleventh peer of his line, and had benefited by the treaty of Limerick, although as a Roman Catholic not eligible to occupy a seat in Parliament.

before I would venture my credit with your Lordship, I consulted with the Attorney General, and another lawyer here, both very eminent in their calling, of fair reputation, and my long acquaintance,[1] whether Mr. Shaw had a just cause; who both assured me he had, and that it was decreed for him here, but renewed by vexatious appeal, and other litigious practices, that I know nothing of. It is now almost a year since I first writ to your Lordship upon this affair, but the cause being by the arts of his adversary put off to the approaching session, Mr. Shaw returned me my letter, and desired a new one, which I would not refuse him. Your Lordship now knows your duty, which is only to attend the hearing of this cause as often as you conveniently can, and to make my Lords Foley[2] and Masham, and all the Lords with whom you have power to do the like. But, as for the decision, I have nothing to say.

I desire to present my most humble service to my Lady Oxford, and to Lady Marget. I am with very great respect, my Lord,

Your Lordship's most obedient and most humble servant,
JONATH. SWIFT.

Addressed—To the Right Honourable the Earl of Oxford in Dover Street.

DCCCLXXI. [*Hawkesworth.*]

SWIFT TO LADY ELIZABETH GERMAIN

January 8, 1732-3.

MADAM,[3]

ALTHOUGH I have but just received the honour of your Ladyship's letter, yet as things stand I am determined

---

[1] The office of Attorney-General was then held by Robert Jocelyn, afterwards Lord Chancellor of Ireland, from whom the Earls of Roden are descended. He had come to Ireland in early life to practise at the bar, and became greatly attached to his adopted country. In Irish historical research he took a most useful interest, and was president of a society which accomplished in the field of topographical history work that remains unsuperseded.

[2] He was Oxford's uncle, and had been raised to the peerage as one of the famous twelve. He died that month.

[3] In this letter, which is an answer to the one from Lady Germain of 7 November, Swift details his grievances against Lady Suffolk at even

against my usual practice to give you no respite, but to answer it immediately, because you have provoked me with your Lady Suffolk. It is six years last spring since I first went to visit my friends in England, after the Queen's death. Her present Majesty heard of my arrival, and sent at least nine times to command my attendance before I would obey, for several reasons not hard to guess, and, among others, because I had heard her character from those who knew her well. At last I went, and she received me very graciously. I told her the first time, that I was informed she loved to see odd persons; and that, having sent for a wild boy from Germany, she had a curiosity to see a wild Dean from Ireland.[1] I was not much struck with the honour of being sent for because I knew the same distinction had been offered to others, with whom it would not give me much pride to be compared. I never went once but upon command, and Mrs. Howard, now Lady Suffolk, was usually the person who sent for me, both at Leicester House and Richmond.

Mr. Pope, with whom I lived, and Mr. Gay were then great favourites of Mrs. Howard, especially the latter, who was then one of her led-captains. He had wrote a very ingenious book of fables, for the use of her[2] younger son, and she often promised to provide for him. But some time before, there came out a libel against Mr. Walpole, who was informed it was written by Mr. Gay, and although Mr. Walpole owned he was convinced that it was not written by Gay, yet he never would pardon him, but did him a hundred ill offices to the Princess. Walpole was at that time very civil to me, and so were all the people in power. He invited me and some of my friends to dine with him at Chelsea. After dinner, I took an occasion to say, what I had observed of Princes and great Ministers, that if they heard an ill thing of a private person, who expected some favour, although they were afterward convinced that the person was innocent, yet they would never be reconciled. Mr. Walpole knew well enough that I meant Mr. Gay. I afterward said the same thing to the Princess, with

greater length than he had done to herself (*supra*, p. 181). Although not sent until the date given above, the letter was written on receipt of Lady Germain's before the news of Gay's death had reached Swift.

[1] *Supra*, vol. iii, p. 304.
[2] *I.e.*, the Queen's.

the same intention, and she confessed it a great injustice. But Mr. Walpole gave it another turn: for he said to some of his friends, and particularly to a Lord, a near relation of yours,[1] that I had dined with him, and had been making apologies for myself: it seems for my conduct in her late Majesty's reign, in which no man was more innocent, and particularly more officious to do good offices to many of that party which was then out of power, as it is well known. Mrs. Howard was then in great favour, and openly protected Mr. Gay, at least she saw him often and professed herself his friend; but Mr. Walpole could hardly be persuaded to let him hold a poor little office for a second year, of commissioner to a lottery.

When I took my leave of her Highness, on coming hither, she was very gracious; told me the medals she had promised me were not ready, but she would send them to me. However, by her commands, I sent her some plaids for herself and the Princesses, and was too gallant to hear of any offers of payment. Next spring I came again to England, was received the same way, and as I had many hints given me that the court at Leicester Fields would endeavour to settle me in England—which I did not much regard—[when]the late King died, I went, by Mrs. Howard's orders, to kiss their new Majesties' hands, and was particularly distinguished by the Queen. In a few weeks, the Queen said to Mrs. Howard, alluding to one of Mr. Gay's fables, that she would take up the hare, and bade her to put her in mind, in settling the family, to find some employment for Mr. Gay, but, in the event, it proved only an offer to be a gentleman-usher to a girl of two years old, which all his friends, and I among the rest, advised him not to accept,[2] and accordingly he excused himself with the utmost respect. This I, and everybody else, were sure must have been a management of Mr. Walpole. As to myself, in a few weeks after the King's death, I found myself not well, and was resolved to take a step to Paris for my health,[3] having an opportunity of doing it with some advantages and recommendations. But my friends advised me first to

---

[1] Probably her brother, the third Earl of Berkeley, who was then a member of Walpole's administration.

[2] *Supra*, p. 337, n. 1.

[3] The resolution was formed before the King's death (*supra*, vol. iii, p. 394).

consult Mrs. Howard; because, as they knew less of Courts
than I, they were strongly possessed that the promise made
me might succeed, since a change was all I desired. I writ
to her for her opinion; and particularly conjured her, since
I had long done with Courts, not to use me like a courtier,
but give me her sincere advice; which she did, both in a
letter, and to some friends. It was, by all means not to go:
it would look singular, and perhaps disaffected; and, to my
friends, [she] enlarged upon the good intentions of the
Court toward me. I stayed; my health grew worse; I left
Mr. Pope's house, went to a private lodging near Hammersmith,[1] and continuing ill I writ to Mrs. Howard with my
duty to the Queen, took coach for Chester, recovered in
my journey, and came over hither, where, although I have
ever since lived in obscurity, yet I have the misfortune,
without any grounds, except misinformation, to lie under
her Majesty's displeasure, as I have been assured by more
than two honourable persons of both sexes; and Mr. Gay
is in the same condition.

For these reasons, as I did always, so I do still think
Mrs. Howard, now my Lady Suffolk, to be an absolute
courtier. Let her show you the Character I writ of her, and
whereof no one else has a copy; and I take Mr. Pope and
Mr. Gay, who judge more favourably, to be a couple of
simpletons. In my answer to the last letter which my Lady
Suffolk honoured me with, I did, with great civility, discharge her from ever giving herself another trouble of that
kind. I have a great esteem for her good sense and taste.
She would be an ornament to any Court, and I do not in
the least pity her for not being a female minister, which I
never looked on as an advantageous character to a great
and wise lady, of which I could easily produce instances.
Mr. Pope, besides his natural and acquired talents, is a
gentleman of very extraordinary candour; and is, consequently, apt to be too great a believer of assurances,
promises, professions, encouragements, and the like words
of course. He asks nothing, and thinks, like a philosopher,
that he wants nothing. Mr. Gay is, in all regards, as honest
and sincere a man as ever I knew; whereof neither Princes
nor Ministers are either able to judge, or inclined to encourage, which, however, I do not take for so high a breach
of politics as they usually suppose, for, however insignificant

---

[1] *Supra,* vol. iii, p. 421.

wit, learning, and virtue, may be thought in the world, it perhaps would do government no hurt to have a little of them on its side. If you have gone thus far in reading, you are not so wise as I thought you to be. But I will never offend again with so much length. I write only to justify myself. I know you have been always a zealous Whig, and so am I to this day, but nature has not given you leave to be virulent. As to myself, I am of the old Whig principles, without the modern articles and refinements.

Your Ladyship says not one syllable to inform me whether you approve of what I sent you to be written on the monument, nor whether you would have it in Latin or English.[1] I am ever, with true respect and high esteem, Madam,

Your ladyship's, etc.

The friend I named, who I was afraid would die, is recovered; and his preferment is by turns in the Crown and the Primate, but the next vacancy will not be in the Crown's disposal.

DCCCLXXII. [*Original.*[2]]

JOHN ARBUTHNOT TO SWIFT

London, January 13, 1732-3.

MY DEAR FRIEND,[3]

I HAD the pleasure of receiving one from you by Mr. [Pilkington].[4] I thank you for the opportunity it gave me of being acquainted with a very agreeable, ingenious man. I value him amongst other things for his music, which you

---

[1] No trace of the monument to the memory of her sister (*supra*, p. 283) is now to be found. It consisted of "a plate of black marble fixed in the wall over the altar-piece," with this inscription: "Underneath lieth the body of the Lady Penelope Berkeley, daughter of the Right Hon. Charles, Earl of Berkeley. She died September the 3rd, 1699."

[2] In the British Museum. See Preface.

[3] As appears from the concluding paragraphs this letter was sent to Swift by the bearer of the one from Robert Arbuthnot (*supra*, p. 370).

[4] Pilkington's name has been erased, as in other cases evidently by Swift when he became ashamed of his *protégé*.

give yourself an air of contemning, and I think I treated him in that way to a degree of surprise. I have had but a melancholy sorrowful life for some time past, having lost my dear child,[1] whose life, if it had so pleased God, I would have willingly redeemed with my own. I thank God for a new lesson of submission to his will, and likewise for what he has left me.

We have all had another loss of our worthy and dear friend Mr. Gay. It was some alleviation of my grief to see him so universally lamented by almost everybody, even by those who knew him only by reputation. He was interred at Westminster Abbey, as if he had been a peer of the realm; and the good Duke of Queensberry, who lamented him as a brother, will set up a handsome monument upon him. These are little affronts put upon vice and injustice, and is all that remains in our power. I believe the Beggar's Opera, and what he has to come upon the stage,[2] will make the sum of the diversions of the town for some time to come. Curll, who is one of the new terrors of death, has been writing letters to everybody for memoirs of his life. I was for sending him some, particularly an account of his disgrace at Court, which I am sure might have been made entertaining, by which I should have attained two ends at once, published truth, and got a rascal whipped for it. I was overruled in this. I wish you had been here, though I think you are in a better country. I fancy to myself, that you have some virtue and honour left, some small regard for religion. Perhaps Christianity may last with you at least twenty or thirty years longer. You have no companies nor stock-jobbing, are yet free of excises;[3] you are not insulted in your poverty, and told with a sneer, that you are a rich and a thriving nation. Every man that takes neither place nor pension, is not deemed with you a rogue, and an enemy to his country.

Your friends of my acquaintance are in tolerable good

---

[1] His son Charles (*supra*, p. 277).

[2] His "Achilles" (*supra*, p. 371, n. 2).

[3] It was then known that Walpole intended to deal with the question of the excise, which had been unaltered since the Restoration. "The name of excise was still associated," says Mr. Lecky (*op. cit.*, ii, 333), "in the popular mind with the hated memory of the Long Parliament which had borrowed the impost from the Dutch, and had first introduced it into England," and the apprehension of an increase in the duties was sufficient to arouse a storm throughout the country.

health. Mr. Pope has his usual complaints of headache and indigestion, I think more than formerly. He really leads sometimes a very irregular life, that is, lives with people of superior health and strength. You will see some new things of his, equal to any of his former productions. He has affixed to the new edition of his Dunciad, a royal declaration against the haberdashers of points and particles assuming the title of critics and restorers, wherein he declares, that he has revised carefully this his Dunciad, beginning and ending so and so, consisting of so many lines, and declares this edition to be the true reading, and it is signed by John Barber, *major civitatis Londini*.[1]

I remember you with your friends, who are my neighbours. They all long to see you. As for news, there is nothing here talked of but the new scheme of excise. You may remember that a Ministry in the Queen's time, possessed of her Majesty, the Parliament, army, fleet, treasury, confederate, etc., put all to the test by an experiment of a silly project in the trial of a poor parson.[2] The same game, in my mind, is playing over again from a wantonness of power. *Miraberis quam pauca sapientia mundus regitur*. I have considered the grievance of your wine. The friend[3] that designed you good wine was abused by an agent that he entrusted his affairs to. It was not this gentleman's brother,[4] whose name is Delamar, to whom show what friendship you can. My brother is getting money now in China, less, and more honestly, than his predecessor's supercargoes, but enough to make you satisfaction, which if he comes home alive, he shall do.

My neighbour the proseman[5] is wiser, and more cowardly and despairing than ever. He talks me into a fit of vapours twice or thrice a week. I dream at night of a chain, and rowing in the gallies. But, thank God, he has not taken from me the freedom I have been accustomed to in my discourse, even with the greatest persons to whom I have access, in defending the cause of liberty, virtue, and religion: for the last, I have the satisfaction of suffering some share of the ignominy that belonged to the first confessors. This has been my lot from a steady resolution I have taken

---

[1] The declaration, which purports to have been made before Barber, is dated January 3, 1732-3 (Pope's " Works," iv, 306).
[2] *I.e.*, Sacheverell.   [3] *I.e.*, his brother George.
[4] *I.e.*, the bearer of the letter.   [5] *I.e.*, Erasmus Lewis.

of giving these ignorant impudent fellows battle upon all occasions. My family send you their best wishes, and a happy new year; and none can do it more heartily than myself, who am, with the most sincere respect,

Your most faithful humble servant.

DCCCLXXIII. [*Elwin.*]

SWIFT TO ALEXANDER POPE

Dublin, *January*, 1732-3.

I RECEIVED yours with a few lines from the Doctor, and the account of our losing Mr. Gay,[1] upon which event I shall say nothing. I am only concerned that long living has not hardened me; for even in this kingdom, and in a few days past, two persons of great merit, whom I loved very well, have died in the prime of their years, but a little above thirty.[2] I would endeavour to comfort myself upon the loss of friends as I do upon the loss of money, by turning to my account-book, and seeing whether I have enough left for my support; but in the former case I find I have not, any more than in the other, and I know not any man who is in a greater likelihood than myself to die poor and friendless. You are a much greater loser than I by his death, as being a more intimate friend, and often his companion, which latter I could never hope to be, except perhaps once more in my life for a piece of a summer. I hope he has left you the care of any writings he may have left, and I wish that, with those already extant, they could be all published in a fair edition, under your inspection.

Your poem on the Use of Riches has been just printed here,[3] and we have no objection but the obscurity of several passages by our ignorance in facts and persons, which make us lose abundance of the satire. Had the printer given me notice, I would have honestly printed the names at

---

[1] *Supra*, p. 365.

[2] It is suggested by Elwin (*op. cit.*, vii, 293) that one of these friends may have been Mrs. Grierson (*supra*, p. 120, n. 2), who died about that time.

[3] It was registered in London at the Stationers' Hall on the 11th of that month.

length, where I happened to know them, and writ explanatory notes, which however would have been but few, for my long absence has made me ignorant of what passes out of the scene where I am. I never had the least hint from you about this work, any more than of your former, upon Taste.[1] We are told here, that you are preparing other pieces of the same bulk to be inscribed to other friends, one, for instance, to my Lord Bolingbroke, another to Lord Oxford, and so on.

Doctor Delany presents you his most humble service; he behaves himself very commendably, converses only with his former friends, makes no parade, but entertains them constantly at an elegant, plentiful table, walks the streets as usual by daylight, does many acts of charity and generosity, cultivates a country house two miles distant, and is one of those very few within my knowledge, on whom a great access of fortune [2] hath made no manner of change. And particularly he is often without money, as he was before. We have got my Lord Orrery among us, being forced to continue here on the ill condition of his estate by the knavery of an agent.[3] He is a most worthy gentleman, whom I hope you will be acquainted with. I am very much obliged by your favour to Mr. Pilkington, which I desire may continue no longer than he shall deserve by his modesty, a virtue I never knew him to want, but is hard for young men to keep, without abundance of ballast.[4]

If you are acquainted with the Duchess of Queensberry, I desire you will present her my most humble service. I think she is a greater loser by the death of a friend than either of us. She seems a lady of excellent sense and spirits. I had often postscripts from her in our friend's letters to me, and her part was sometimes longer than his, and they made up a great part of the little happiness I could have here. This was the more generous, because I never saw her since she was a girl of five years old, nor did I envy poor Mr. Gay for anything so much as being a domestic friend to such a lady. I desire you will never fail to send me a particular account of your health. I dare hardly inquire about Mrs. Pope, who I am told is but just among the living, and consequently a continual grief to you. She is sensible of your tenderness, which robs her of

---

[1] *Supra*, p. 279.   [2] By his marriage (*supra*, p. 336).
[3] *Supra*, p. 370.   [4] *Supra*, p. 354, n. 2.

the only happiness she is capable of enjoying, and yet I
pity you more than her. You cannot lengthen her days,
and I beg she may not shorten yours.

DCCCLXXIV. [*Deane Swift.*[1]]

SWIFT TO THE EARL OF ORRERY

January 25, 1732-3.

MY LORD,[2]

IT is some time since Mrs. Ball gave me, enclosed and
directed to me, your Lordship's verses in your own hand
with the alterations you were pleased to make, for which
I have long deferred my acknowledgement, and if I were to
follow the course of my own nature, the delay should be
longer; because, although I believe no man hath a more
grateful sense of a real honour done him than myself, yet
no man is in more confusion how to express it. Although
I had not the least hand in publishing those verses, which
would have ill become me, yet I shall not be so affected as
to conceal the pride I have in seeing them abroad, whatever enmity they may procure against your Lordship, for
publicly favouring one so obnoxious to present powers, and
turning their hatred into envy, which last, as it is more

[1] The original was sold amongst the autograph letters of the Earl
of Cork and Orrery on 23 November, 1905, by Messrs. Christie, Man-
son and Woods, and was subsequently in the possession of Mr. Sabin,
172, New Bond Street. A number of other letters from Swift to
Orrery were sold at the same time and passed also into the possession
of Mr. Sabin. Extracts from them were printed by Sir Henry Craik
("Life," ii, 342) and by his and Messrs. Macmillan and Co.'s kind
permission are included in the present edition of the Correspondence.

[2] On coming to Dublin (*supra*, p. 370, n. 3) Orrery appears to have
immediately made the acquaintance of Swift, and under Delany's *aegis*
ventured to send him, on his birthday, a table-book and some complimentary verse (Nichols, "Works," xi, 264). The book, in which the
verse is written in Orrery's own handwriting with his signature, was
lately in the possession of Messrs. Maggs of 109, Strand, and is described as containing nearly two hundred leaves, and as being sumptu-
ously bound in red morocco, covered with floral designs and gilt
panels and fastened with silver clasps. From this letter it is evident
that the verse underwent revision after its presentation to Swift, and
its insertion in the book took place subsequently, probably at his own
request.

tormenting to the owners, will better gratify my revenge. And of this advantage I shall make the proper use, leaving your Lordship to shift for yourself, without the least grain of pity for what you may suffer.

In the mean time, I beg you to accept my most humble thanks for the honour done me by so excellent a perform-ance on so barren a subject, by which words I wisely anticipate the censure of all those who love me not: in spite of whom it will be said in future ages that one of Lord Orrery's first essays in poetry were these verses on Dr. Swift. That your Lordship may go on to be the great example, restorer, and patron, of virtue, learning, and wit, in a most corrupt, stupid, and ignorant age and nation, shall be the constant wish, hope, and prayer of, my Lord,

Your most obedient, obliged, and most humble servant,

J. SWIFT.

DCCCLXXV. [*Gentleman's Magazine.*[1]]

SWIFT TO BENJAMIN MOTTE

Dublin, *February* 1, 1732-3.

SIR,

I RECEIVED your last short letter, with an enclosed from Mr. Ewin. What that Ewin is, I know not, but he appears to be a very odd sort of man. I have a letter of his dated last July, which I believe I told you of in one of mine to you.[2] He there says some very silly things, and reflects on Mr. Davys, who left him all he had. I wonder what calling or character the man is of. You can tell him I acknow-ledged the four pounds, fifteen shillings, since you received it. I have advanced it all to the poor sister who would needs have it. In his letter of July, he says he has several letters of mine to Mr. Davys, and a few to his widow; that he hath been importuned to lend them, and has often re-sisted it. Common sense and honesty would have directed him to burn them, or send them to me to do it. In the letter you sent me from him to you, he desires to know what I would have him do with them. Mr. Davys hath been

---

[1] N.S., vol. xliv, p. 233. The original was sold on 15 December, 1906, by Messrs. Sotheby, Wilkinson and Hodge.

[2] *Supra,* p. 361.

dead above thirty-five years. The letters were common letters of friendship among young people, and I believe I writ to her four or five after she was a widow and at Cambridge, and generally some present was mentioned. This Ewin must be a rascal, and has a mind to print them because he thinks they will bring money. Pray desire him to restore them to you to burn them; and, if he will not, let him do what he pleases, for they can be of no consequence, being only the common amusements of young people. I then lived in England, and he was a man I loved very well, but married very indiscreetly.

We have had the poem upon the Use of Riches, which our people here, for want of knowing London, think a little obscure.[1] I desire my love to Mrs. Lancelot. I will answer her letter soon. I find the business of the Test is quite dropped, and am very glad of it. But Satan was the adviser to a general excise, or at least the greatest enemy that he could stir up against the Crown.[2] I am,

Your most humble servant,

J. S.

My service to Mr. Pilkington, when you see him; I hope he continues to please my Lord Mayor and the city. I had your packet of papers from Mrs. Hyde, and kindly thank you for them. I had a letter lately from one Grace Barmby, who says she lives at the King's Arms and Two Bishops, behind St. Clement's Church. I suppose she is the widow of one Barmby, who made my gown in the late Queen's time, when I lived in London. I am very confident I owe her not a farthing, and so I told her or somebody from her when I was last in London. It is against my constant practice to leave a place without paying my debts. Looking at her letter again, I find her demand is for the year 1726, which was the first time I went to England since the Queen's death, which confirms me that I owe her nothing. Her demands are four pounds, six shillings, and eight pence. Pray call at your leisure, and tell her what I say. Perhaps she may be poor. But it is impossible I should be in her debt, for I wanted not money, and the bill is exorbitant, being near eleven pounds for one gown and cassock, more by a third than ever I used to pay. However,

---

[1] *Supra*, p. 380.   [2] *Supra*, p. 378, n. 3.

out of perfect charity, please to let her have two guineas, with a full acquittance for all accounts. I am sorry to give you so much trouble.

Addressed—To Mr. Benjamin Motte, bookseller, at the Middle Temple Gate, in Fleet Street, London.

DCCCLXXVI. [*Deane Swift.*]

MISS KELLY TO SWIFT

Jervis Street,[1] Six o'clock, Friday Evening,
February 2, 1732-3.

SIR,[2]

I DANCED so long last night that I have not been able till this moment to thank you for the goodness you showed me this morning. Be assured the favours you bestow on me are received with the greatest pleasure, and I only am sorry it is not in my power to convince you that nobody can set a higher value on your friendship than I do. Indeed I have an implicit faith in your medicine ; for if only despising the poets can hinder its proving effectual, I must certainly receive from it all the benefit I desire; for really I am quite of the other side, and am a sincere admirer of all the good poets, but am more particularly attached to the best. What I shall do to convince you of the truth of this I cannot determine; but surely the care I shall always take to mend upon your reproofs, will in time let you know that nobody can desire more sincerely to please you than, Sir,

Your most obliged and most faithful humble servant,
F. A. KELLY.

I am half asleep, so do not be angry at these blots. Being

---

[1] A street in the northern part of Dublin near St. Mary's Church.

[2] Since Lady Germain's mention of her (*supra*, p. 279) Miss Kelly had become one of the Deanery circle and a great favourite of Swift. "Miss Kelly's beauty and good-humour have gained an entire conquest over him," writes the future Mrs. Delany, who was still in Dublin, "and I come in only a little by the by" (" Correspondence," i, 396). From the present letter it would appear that Miss Kelly had essayed a poetical composition, and that Swift on its being submitted to him had pronounced an adverse judgement.

out of cash at present, I send you my note, which I hope will satisfy you.

Enclosure—I acknowledge to be indebted to the Reverend Doctor Swift, Dean of St. Patrick's, the sum of £0 1*s*. 1½*d*.[1] for value received, this 2nd day of February 1732-3.

FRANCES ARABELLA KELLY.

DCCCLXXVII. [*Deane Swift.*]

LORD MAYOR BARBER TO SWIFT

London, *February* 6, 1732-3.
Queen Anne's Birthday : the bells all ringing.

BELIEVE me, Sir, and it is with great truth I speak it, that there is not a person in the world I would sooner oblige than yourself, and I should be glad to have it in my power to serve Mrs. Barber in the way you mention;[2] but it is odds it may not be in my power, for many things may fall that her spouse is not fit for, as all places relating to the law he can have no pretensions to. There are a dozen persons in my house, called Lord Mayor's Officers, who wear black gowns, and give from eight to nine hundred pounds for their places, which at first they make about sixty pounds per annum of, and rise in time to three or four hundred pounds, but they are generally young men. These places I suppose, should any one fall, would not be thought good enough. There are many other places in my gift. We have had mayors gone through the office who have not got one hundred pounds, and others have got ten thousand pounds: it is all chance. I have gone through the fourth part of my year, and have got only about two hundred guineas by the deaths of one of the city music and a porter to Guildhall. But suppose a place should fall worth fifteen hundred or two thousand pounds that he may be fit for, one-third of the purchase goes to the city, and must be paid before his admission; the other two-thirds are mine, but I cannot

---

[1] A British shilling, which as a friend points out would be a hangman's wages.
[2] *Supra*, p. 368.

put a less price than was paid before, because the last price is entered in the city books. I know you love particulars, and thus you have the case as it stands.

You will give me leave to add a word or two, which I do in confidence, that I have been for many years plagued with a set of ungrateful monsters called cousins, that I tremble at the name, and though I give yearly pensions to some and monthly and weekly to others, all would not do, and I am insulted and abused by them, and cannot help myself. Now, as Mrs. Barber and her family design to settle here, and she has done me the honour in most places to call me cousin, I hope it will not be expected I should have the care of them. I have very ill health, and any additional care that way would hurt me very much; but for doing her and her family any good offices, I shall never be wanting.

I must now beg leave to return you my thanks for your affectionate and kind wishes. The honour, I own, is very great, I am in possession of, and I am sensible I am placed aloft, and that all my words and actions are scanned; but I will not be discouraged, and hope I shall get through with honour. One motive for making me think so is the great pleasure and satisfaction I have in the hopes of seeing you here, where your advice and example will be of great use; and therefore I hope you will lose no time, but come away, and I will fit up an apartment for you in Queen's Square, and another at Sheen,[1] which I hope you will accept, places that I shall hardly be able to see this year.

Mr. Pilkington gains daily upon us, and comes out a facetious agreeable fellow. I carried him the other day to see her Grace of Bucks in the Park.[2] Her Grace seeing him, asked, who he was. I answered, he was a present from you from Dublin. She smilingly replied, "He is no fool then, I am sure." I shall conclude a long dull letter, with my

---

[1] *I.e.*, in his town and country house.

[2] It was by her husband, John of Bucks (*supra*, vol. iii, p. 74), that the precursor of Buckingham Palace was built. It is said to have been adorned with mottoes without and frescoes within, and was considered both on account of its design and situation one of the beauties of London. The Duchess was an illegitimate daughter of James II, and being immensely proud of her royal descent, used to receive company on the anniversary of the martyrdom of Charles I seated in a chair of state, in deep mourning, attended by her women in like weeds (Hare's " Walks in London," ii, 114).

sincere wishes for your health and prosperity, and that you
would not delay one hour coming to bless your friends here
with your company, which by none is more desired than,
Sir,

Your most obedient and most humble servant,

J. BARBER.

DCCCLXXVIII. [*Original.*[1]]

LADY ELIZABETH GERMAIN TO SWIFT

February 8, 1732-3.

I RECEIVED yours of the 8th of January[2] but last week, so
find it has lain long on the road after the date. It was
brought me whilst at dinner, that very lady sitting close to
me, whom you seem to think such an absolute courtier. She
knew your hand, and inquired much after you, as she always
does; but I, finding her name frequently mentioned, not
with that kindness I am sure she deserves, put it into my
pocket with silence and surprise. Indeed were it in people's
power that live in a Court with the appearance of favour to
do all they desire with their friends, they might deserve
their anger, and be blamed when it does not happen right
to their minds; but that, I believe, never was the case with
anyone, and in this particular of Mr. Gay, thus far I know,
and so far I will answer for, that she was under very great
concern that nothing better could be got for him, and the
friendship upon all other occasions in her own power that
she showed him did not look like a double-dealer.

As to that part concerning yourself and her, I suppose,
it is my want of comprehension that I cannot find out why
she was to blame to give you advice, when you asked it,
that had all the appearance of sincerity, good-nature, and
right judgement. And if after that, the Court did not do
what you wanted, and she both believed and wished they
would, was it her fault? At least, I cannot find out that you
have hitherto proved it upon her. And though you say,
you lamented the hour you had seen her, yet I cannot tell
how to suppose that your good sense and justice can impute
anything to her, because it did not fall out just as she
endeavoured, and hoped it would.

---

[1] In the British Museum. See Preface.   [2] *Supra*, p. 373.

As to your creed in politics, I will heartily and sincerely subscribe to it,—that I detest avarice in Courts, corruption in Ministers, schisms in religion, illiterate fawning betrayers of the Church in mitres,—but, at the same time, I prodigiously want an infallible judge to determine when it is really so; for as I have lived long in the world, and seen many changes, I know those out of power and place always see the faults of those in with dreadful large spectacles; and, I dare say, you know many instances of it in Lord Oxford's time. But the strongest in my memory is Sir Robert Walpole being first pulled to pieces in the year 1720, because the South Sea did not rise high enough, and since that, he has been to the full as well banged about, because it did rise too high. So experience has taught me, how wrong, unjust, and senseless, party factions are; therefore I am determined never wholly to believe any side or party against each other, and to show that I will not, as my friends are in and out of all sides, so my house receives them altogether, and those people meet here, that have, and would fight in any other place. And those of them that have great and good qualities and virtues I love and admire, in which number is Lady Suffolk, and I do like and love her, because I believe, and as far as I am capable of judging, know her to be a wise, discreet, honest and sincere courtier, who will promise no farther than she can perform, and will always perform what she does promise; so, now, you have my creed as to her.

I thought I had told you in my last, at least I am sure I designed it, that I desire you would do just as you like about the monument, and then it will be most undoubtedly approved by

Your most sincere and faithful servant,

E. GERMAIN.

DCCCLXXIX. [*Faulkner.*]

SWIFT TO THE EARL OF OXFORD

Dublin, *February* 16, 1732-3.

MY LORD,

THE bearer, Mr. Faulkner, the prince of Dublin printers, will have the honour to deliver you this.[1] He tells me your

[1] *Supra*, p. 286, n. 3.

Lordship was so gracious as to admit him into your presence, and receive him with great condescension, which encouraged him to hope for the same favour again by my mediation, which I could not refuse. Although for his own profit he is engaged in a work that very much discontents me,[1] yet I would rather have it fall into his hands, than any other's on this side.

I am just recovered, in some degree, of two cruel indispositions of giddiness and deafness, after seven months. I have got my hearing, but the other evil hangs still about me, and I doubt will never quite leave me, until I leave it. I hope your Lordship and Lady Oxford and Lady Margaret, continue in perfect health. I pray God preserve you all, for the good of your friends, and your country. I am, with entire respect and esteem,

Your Lordship's most obedient, and most obliged servant,
JON. SWIFT.

DCCCLXXX. [*Scott.*]

CHARLES WOGAN TO SWIFT

February 27 [O.S. 16], 1732-3.

I HAVE the honour of a very obliging letter from a person whose penetration I flattered myself I could have escaped;[2] although I might assure him with great sincerity, that I never had a more earnest desire for any man's acquaintance and friendship than for his. Upon the late occasion, it is true, my design was to have travelled and been received incognito. I had taken my measures for it in the best manner I could devise. But all my art and travesty was vain. His Mentor was superior to my Uranius, who could not avoid being discovered, as in the story of Telemachus, and striking sail to a more exalted divinity. I own I am somewhat concerned at my being seen in my undress, through all the magnificence of those disguises I had put on. But Mentor has so much the air of a benign and friendly spirit, that my confusion was soon over, and methinks I could be exposed in the midst of all my defects,

---

[1] His edition of Swift's Works, which he began to publish a year later.
[2] *Supra*, p. 327.

without any concern, provided it were only to those whom he judges worthy of his intimacy. . . .[1]

I own I am a little mad, so Mentor must take nothing ill that I say to him. My patience is exhausted, and I have done all I could to tire his. He must blame his own good nature, that has given me room to vent my spleen. As I have no friend here of genius or freedom of thought enough to comprehend these notions, they had rotted in my breast, and thrown me, perhaps, into some dangerous indisposition, if I had not come out with them. I am now setting out upon an expedition against the Moors, since the modern Christians are too hard for me; and whatever may be my fate, it is an exceeding comfort to me to have thus discharged my conscience in regard of these, before I enter the lists against their brethren the Mahometans.

As for the blank verses which I recommended so earnestly to the care of Mentor, I now abandon them to his discretion. If he thinks them worth his correction, he will give them to the public as he proposes, without the name of an author, and with his own, after the epistle to recommend them. It will do me a great deal of honour, and I will take care it shall do him no manner of mischief. If he neglect publishing them, I shall have the mortification of believing the present I took the liberty to make him not worth his while, or that my present liberty of speech is offensive to him. This must not be. We are all brethren in fact; and no man should be angry at another, for using him with all the intimacy of a friend, and opening his whole heart to him without malice or disguise. I beg pardon of Mentor, and of all those great names he mentions, for my censures upon rhyme and raillery, which he may soften or expunge entirely, according to his better judgement. I should be very sorry to make enemies of those whom, of all mankind, I would choose to make my friends. Mr. Pope and I lived in perfect union and familiarity for two or three summers before he entered upon the stage of the world, where he has since gained so great and so just an applause.[2] The

[1] Here follows a disquisition, which occupies nearly fifty pages of Sir Walter Scott's edition of the Correspondence ("Works," xvii, 448-94), on the treatment and position of the Roman Catholics of Ireland. It is in the nature of an essay, and as it has no bearing on the subjects with which the other letters deal, it has been omitted.

[2] In the course of his disquisition Wogan mentions that he had lived with Pope in the Forest of Windsor, and that he had the honour

other geniuses have a right to all my regard by the merit of sharing the affection and esteem of Mentor, who will do me a great deal of honour, if he allow me any place in so learned and polite a society. Without any compliment, they are fitter for the Augustan age than for this. They are at home, and endeavour to give the world a sense of its follies with great humour and gaiety. The cheerfulness of my temper, is, in a great measure, sunk under a long and hopeless exile, which has given it a serious, or, if you will, a supercilious turn. I lash the world with indignation and grief, in the strain of Jeremy. But the world is grown so inveterate in iniquity, that I fear we shall all lose our labour. It will have just the same effect to flog, as to tickle them.

However, if there be any room for a grave, sullen fellow, that has been one of the merriest fellows in Europe, in Mentor's academy, I offer myself, and, to pay my entrance, as I did in Newgate, I send him a kilderkin of the best wine on this side of the country, to drink their healths, and mine, if he pleases. I accept, with a great deal of acknow-ledgement, the present of books offered me by Mentor, and desire he will send along with them Doctor Jonathan Swift's Miscellanies, which they tell me are worth them all. I can give him nothing in return, but some heads of the Saracens of Oran, which I shall be ordered to cut off, because they will not become Christians. I must be their executioner in my own defence; for, with all my spleen and vexation of spirit, I am the most inoffensive creature in the world in regard of religion. I would not shed one ounce of blood in anger or enmity, or wrong any man living of a cracked sixpence, to make all the world Catholics, yet I am as staunch a one myself as any Pope in the universe. I am all for the primitive church, in which people made proof of their religion only at their own expense. But I laugh, with great contempt, at those who will force others to Heaven their way, in spite of charity.

Though I should be in the deserts of Lybia, I can still hear from Mentor. It is not necessary he should submit his criticism or correction to me, since I constitute him my judge, without appeal. The gentleman of my family men-tioned by him, is the honestest, but the idlest fellow breath-ing. I cannot even get a letter from him. Thus my reliance

of bringing him to London, and introducing him at Will's coffee-house.

for the revising and publishing of those pieces is entirely upon Mentor, whom I embrace with all my heart, this 27th of February 1732.

DCCCLXXXI. [*Elwin.*]

ALEXANDER POPE TO SWIFT

February 16, 1732-3.

IT is indeed impossible to speak on such a subject as the loss of Mr. Gay, to me an irreparable one.[1] But I send you what I intend for the inscription on his tomb, which the Duke of Queensberry will set up at Westminster. As to his writings, he left no will, nor spoke a word of them, or anything else, during his short and precipitate illness, in which I attended him to his last breath. The Duke has acted more than the part of a brother to him, and it will be strange if the sisters do not leave his papers totally to his disposal, who will do the same that I would with them. He has managed the Comedy, which our poor friend gave to the playhouse the week before his death,[2] to the utmost advantage for his relations, and proposes to do the same with some fables he left finished.

There is nothing of late which I think of more than mortality, and what you mention, of collecting the best monuments we can of our friends, their own images in their writings; for those are the best, when their minds are such as Mr. Gay's was, and as yours is. I am preparing also for my own, and have nothing so much at heart, as to show the silly world that men of wit, or even poets, may be the most moral of mankind. A few loose things sometimes fall from them, by which censorious fools judge as ill of them as possibly they can, for their own comfort, and indeed, when such unguarded and trifling *jeux d'esprit* have once got abroad, all that prudence or repentance can do, since they cannot be denied, is to put them fairly upon that foot; and teach the public, as we have done in the preface to the four volumes of Miscellanies, to distinguish betwixt our

---

[1] This letter is a reply to the one from Swift in January (*supra*, p. 380).

[2] *I.e.*, Gay's "Achilles" (*supra*, p. 371, n. 2).

studies and our idlenesses, our works and our weaknesses. That was the whole end of the last volume of Miscellanies, without which our former declaration in that preface, that these volumes contained all that we have ever offended in, that way, would have been discredited.[1] It went indeed to my heart to omit what you called the Libel on Dr. Delany, and the best panegyric on myself, that either my own times or any other could have afforded, or will ever afford to me.[2] The book, as you observe, was printed in great haste, the cause whereof was, that the booksellers were doing the same, in collecting your pieces, the corn with the chaff. I do not mean that anything of yours is chaff, but with other wit of Ireland which was so, and the whole in your name. I meant principally to oblige them to separate what you writ seriously from what you writ carelessly, and thought my own weeds might pass for a sort of wild flowers, when bundled up with them.

It was I that sent you those books into Ireland, and so I did my Epistle to Lord Bathurst, even before it was published,[3] and another thing of mine, which is a parody from Horace, writ in two mornings.[4] I never took more care in my life of anything than of the former of these, nor less than of the latter: yet every friend has forced me to print it, though in truth my own single motive was about twenty lines toward the latter end, which you will find out.[5]

I have declined opening to you by letters the whole scheme of my present work, expecting still to do it in a better manner in person; but you will see pretty soon, that the Letter to Lord Bathurst is a part of it, and you will find a plain connection between them, if you read them in the order just contrary to that they were published in.[6] I imitate

---

[1] This passage is evidently a reply to one omitted from Swift's letter.
[2] *Supra*, p. 360.
[3] *I.e.*, the " Epistle on the Use of Riches."
[4] The imitation of the first satire of the second book of Horace addressed to William Fortescue, which was registered at Stationers' Hall two days before this letter is dated.

[5]   " What! armed for Virtue when I point the pen,
        Brand the bold front of shameless guilty men ;
        Dash the proud gamester in his gilded car ;
        Bare the mean heart that lurks beneath a star ; "
                                        etc., etc.

[6] The publication which was to enlighten Swift was the " Epistle to Lord Cobham." It forms the first of the Moral Essays, and Elwin says

those cunning tradesmen, who show their best silks last, or, to give you a truer idea though it sounds too proudly, my works will in one respect be like the works of nature, much more to be liked and understood when considered in the relation they bear with each other, than when ignorantly looked upon one by one; and often those parts which attract most at first sight will appear to be not the most but the least considerable.

I am pleased and flattered by your expression of *orna me*. The chief pleasure this work can give me is, that I can in it, with propriety, decency, and justice, insert the name and character of every friend I have, and every man that deserves to be loved or adorned. But I smile at your applying that phrase to my visiting you in Ireland, a place where I might have some apprehension, from their extraordinary passion for poetry, and their boundless hospitality, of being *adorned* to death, and buried under the weight of garlands, like one I have read of somewhere or other. My mother lives, which is an answer to that point, and, I thank God, though her memory be in a manner gone, is yet awake and sensible to me, though scarce to anything else, which doubles the reason of my attendance, and at the same time sweetens it. I wish, beyond any other wish, you could pass a summer here; I might, too probably, return with you, unless you preferred to see France first, to which country I think you would have a strong invitation. Lord Peterborough has narrowly escaped death, and yet keeps his chamber. He is perpetually speaking in the most affectionate manner of you. He has written you two letters which you never received, and by that has been discouraged from writing more.[1] I can well believe the post-office may do this, when some letters of his to me have met the same fate, and two of mine to him. Yet let not this discourage you from writing to me, or to him, enclosed in the common way, as I do to you. Innocent men need fear no detection of their thoughts, and for my part, I would give them free

(*op. cit.*, vii, 297) gives "unity to the whole from containing the theory of the ruling passion." The "Epistle to Martha Blount" is the second of the Moral Essays, that to Lord Bathurst the third, and that to Lord Burlington the fourth.

[1] In a letter dated 1732 (Pope's "Works," x, 191), Peterborough expresses the greatest impatience to see Swift, and says that he must signify his mind to him by another hand, as no letter of his can come to Swift's hands.

leave to send all I write to Curll, if most of what I write
was not too silly.

I desire my sincere services to Dr. Delany, who, I agree
with you, is a man every way esteemable. My Lord Orrery
is a most virtuous and good-natured nobleman, whom I
should be happy to know. Lord Bolingbroke received your
letter through my hands. It is not to be told you how much
he wishes for you. The whole list of persons to whom you
sent your services return you theirs, with proper sense of
the distinction. Your lady friend is *semper eadem*, and I
have written an epistle to her on that qualification in a
female character,[1] which is thought by my chief critic in
your absence to be my *chef d'œuvre*, but it cannot be
printed perfectly, in an age so sore of satire, and so willing
to misapply characters.

As to my own health, it is as good as usual. I have lain
ill seven days of a slight fever, the complaint here, but recovered by gentle sweats, and the care of Dr. Arbuthnot.
The play Mr. Gay left succeeds very well; it is another
original in its kind. Adieu. God preserve your life, your
health, your limbs, your spirits, and your friendships!

DCCCLXXXII. [*Copy*.[2]]

SWIFT TO THE EARL OF OXFORD

Dublin, *February* 17, 1732-3.

MY LORD,

I WRIT lately to your Lordship upon the subject of an
appeal by a private person,[3] and had no thoughts of troubling you so soon with another. But this is of greater moment,
and wherein I deeply concern myself as a friend to the
privileges of the city wherein I am likely to end my days.
There is one Mr. Vernon, who hath some lands adjoining
to those of the city, and within its jurisdiction, which jurisdiction he disclaims.[4] This controversy is carried by appeal

---

[1] The Epistle just alluded to as the second of the Moral Essays.
[2] In the Forster Collection.
[3] *Supra*, p. 372.
[4] A branch of the family of Vernon has owned for several centuries
the district of Dublin known as Clontarf, which forms the northern
boundary of the bay, and is celebrated as the scene of the great con-

to your House of Lords, and I must with much earnestness intreat your Lordship to attend it, and under that request I include that you are to make your friends to do the same, and if any of them are my friends too, you must command them in my name.

I hope your Lordship enjoys your health. Pray God preserve you, and my Lady Oxford, and Lady Marget, to whom I desire to present my most humble service. I am with the truest respect, my Lord,

Your Lordship's most obedient and most humble servant,
JONATH. SWIFT.

The agent of this city will present a printed case to your Lordship.

DCCCLXXXIII. [*Manuscripts of the Earl of Dartmouth.*[1]]

SWIFT TO THE EARL OF DARTMOUTH

Dublin, *February* 17, 1732-3.

I HAVE a good title to the honour of your friendship, although I have never corresponded with you since the great event that scattered us, and banished me for ever to this miserable country. The title I claim is the great favour you have formerly done me, from whence I may boldly challenge any other in your favour.[2] I am now an interceder for the city of Dublin, which hath always used me well, and whose rights I have always contended for. There is an appeal in your House between one Mr. Vernon and

flict between the Irish and the Scandinavian invaders. The litigation with the city concerned the right to the foreshore on which there were then valuable oyster beds. The owner of Clontarf at that time had only recently become possessed of the property, and on the first riding of the franchises after his succeeding to it had waited on the Lord Mayor and delivered himself of a long speech, in which he said that the claim to jurisdiction over his manor had first been made in the reign of James II, " when not a Protestant durst say his soul was his own" (Speech of Capt. John Vernon amongst " Irish Pamphlets" in Trinity College Library).

[1] Hist. MSS. Com., vol. iii, p. 153.

[2] Dartmouth was one of the members of Oxford's administration best known to Swift (*supra*, vol. ii, p. 65). He is said by Swift to have stood "neuter" in the disputes between Oxford and Bolingbroke, and took little part in public life after the Hanoverian accession.

the city on occasion of bounds, privileges, limits, and immunities. I shall not trouble you with the case, their agent will have the honour to deliver it you; and you are to grant the small favour of your attending this cause constantly and making your friends do the like. This is the utmost we ask, because we all know that every soul of you is consummate in wisdom and justice. I will order the agent to inquire whether your Lordship be as cheerful and healthy as ever. I know little of your domestic affairs, for I do not find your name in my friend's letters, upon which I might justly reproach you.

DCCCLXXXIV. [*Original.*[1]]

THE DUCHESS OF QUEENSBERRY TO SWIFT

February 21, 1732-3.

SIR,

SOON after the death of our friend Mr. Gay I found myself more inclined to write to you, than to allow myself any other entertainment. But, considering that might draw you into a correspondence that most likely might be disagreeable, I left off all thoughts of this kind, till Mr. Pope showed me your letter to him, which encourages me to hope we may converse together as usual,[2] by which advantage I will not despair to obtain in reality some of those good qualities, you say, I *seem* to have. I am conscious of only one, that is being an apt scholar; and if I have any good in me, I certainly learned it insensibly of our poor friend, as children do any strange language. It is not possible to imagine the loss he is to me; but as long as I have any memory, the happiness of ever having such a friend can never be lost to me.

As to himself, he knew the world too well to regret leaving it; and the world in general knew him too little to value him as they ought. I think it my duty to my friend to do him the justice to assure you, he had a most perfect and sincere regard for you. I have learned a good deal of his way of thinking on your account; so that if at any time you have any commands in this part of the world, you will

---

[1] In the British Museum. See Preface.   [2] *Supra*, p. 381.

do me a pleasure to employ me, as you would him, and I
shall wish it could ever be in my power to serve you in anything essential. The Duke of Queensberry meant to write,
if I had not, concerning your money affair. We both thought
of it, as soon as we could of anything, and if you will only
write word what you would have done with your money,
great care shall be taken according to your order. I differ
with you extremely that you are in any likelihood of dying
poor or friendless. The world can never grow so worthless.
I again differ with you, that it is possible to comfort oneself for the loss of friends, as one does upon the loss of
money. I think I could live on very little, not think myself
poor or be thought so, but a little friendship could never
satisfy one, and I could never expect to find such another
support as my poor friend. In almost everything, but friends,
another of the same name may do as well; but friend is
more than a name, if it be anything.

Your letter touched me extremely. It gave me a melancholy pleasure. I felt much more than you wrote, and more
than, I hope, you will continue to feel. As you can give
Mr. Pope good advice, pray practise it yourself. As you
cannot lengthen your friend's days, I must beg you, in your
own words, not to shorten your own; for I do full well
know by experience, that health and happiness depend on
good spirits. Mr. Pope is better in both this year than I
have seen him a good while. This you will believe, unless
he has told you what he tells me, that I am his greatest
flatterer. I hope that news has not reached you; for nothing
is more pleasant than to believe what one wishes. I wish
to be your friend; I wish you to be mine; I wish you may
not be tired with this; I wish to hear from you soon; and
all this, in order to be my own flatterer.

I will believe—— I never write my name. I hope you
have no aversion to blots.

Since I wrote this, the Duke of Queensberry bids me tell
you, that if you have occasion for the money, you need only
draw upon him, and he will pay the money to your order,
and he will take care to have the account of interest settled,
and made up to you. He will take this upon himself that
you may have no trouble in this affair.

Addressed—To the Revd. Dr. Swift, Dean of St. Patrick's,
in Dublin, Ireland.

DCCCLXXXV. [*Deane Swift.*]

THE COUNTESS OF KERRY TO SWIFT

Lixnaw, *March* 4, 1732-3.

THE kind concern and friendly remembrance of the most
esteemed Dean of St. Patrick's, has raised in me a satisfaction and pleasure that I had almost given up, having been
resolved a good while humbly to content myself in a state
of indolence and indifference, and if I could avoid the
pains of body and mind, not to seek farther after those
points in life, I so long and vainly pursued; but you have
invaded my tranquillity in a manner I must not only forgive, but pay my acknowledgements for, since at the same
time you make a melancholy representation of my misfortunes, you strike a light for me from another quarter from
whence to raise hope.[1]

I most heartily rejoice in what you tell me of Mr. Fitz-
maurice, who has indeed given me an undeniable mark of
taste by the sense he has of the honour you do him in
letting him into your society, from whence it is impossible
to come without some good influence. For my part, I grieve
at the interval that necessity seems to call for, to interrupt
such advantage, and it is my study to find an occasion in-

---

[1] The distress of mind which aggravated Lady Kerry's infirmity
arose from the consequences of an imprudent alliance made by her
eldest son. Swift had evidently, from Chetwode's reference to her
(*supra*, p. 229), seen her frequently of late years, and no doubt visited
her when she was staying in Dublin, where her husband owned one of
the great residences of that period known as Kerry House, and spent
the Parliamentary session. She was the moving spirit in her family,
and had delighted her father even when she was a child by her ability
for business, which he hoped would adorn her better than "a suit of
ribbons" and keep her warmer than "a damnable dear manteau" (Fitz-
maurice's "Life of Petty," p. 297). Through her force of character and
ambition her husband was induced to take an active part in public
affairs in Ireland, and to live in a style far surpassing that maintained
by other Irish peers. At his seat at Lixnaw, near the mouth of the
Shannon, which was one of the finest in the south of Ireland, his
establishment was on the scale of feudal times, and a few weeks after
the date of this letter his second son, to whom Lady Kerry refers, was
provided from his father's household and stables with a gorgeous
cavalcade of no less than thirty-five persons when setting out as High
Sheriff to meet the judges of assize (Gilbert's "Hist. of Dublin," iii,
258).

dispensable that he may return; and as I think to be a member of our senate-house, is the best way to lead a young man into the world, I have been watching a good while for some gap in that body, that he might step into. There seems now to offer one on the death of Sir Ralph Gore that may not be impracticable, since it is a very small borough entirely belonging, as I am informed, to the Bishop of Clogher, who I dare say is above disposing of it for Court favour only or to the highest bidder—practices much in fashion of late.[1] Might I not then presume upon your friendship with the Bishop to recommend this young man as an honest one at present, and whom he might devote to his service by so great and seasonable an obligation, beside paying an acknowledgement that in gratitude is due, although the person were never so well qualified? Thus much sure I may say without censure. If I have taken too great liberty in recommending this matter to you, forgive me, and impute it to my zeal in endeavouring to take all opportunities to turn this lad into the world, that I may see what figure he will be likely to make hereafter.

But if I do not succeed in this, or any other attempt, I thank Providence sincerely I can now boast I have attained philosophy enough to take everything with patience as it comes, by no means thinking myself too good to be the sport of higher powers; and my Christian duty will not permit me to look for reasons. As little wisdom as I have bought, I wish I had it sooner; now it is too late, *la farce est joué*, and my curtain almost drawn; so that if I could, I would no more traffic with the world upon my own account. Friendship only is what I still must always value; yours, surely, is more than comes to my share.

You are very good to inquire after my eyes. They are, indeed, well beyond my expectation; but are to me like the miser's gold, hoarded up as imaginary treasure that

---

[1] Sir Ralph Gore, whose son was created Earl of Ross, had succeeded Conolly as Speaker of the Irish House of Commons. He represented the borough of Clogher, which lay not far from his country house, Bellisle on Lough Erne, and which as the seat of the see of Clogher had formerly been practically in the gift of his father-in-law, Bishop Ashe (*supra*, vol. iii, p. 15, n. 3), as it was now likewise in that of Bishop Stearne. Lord Kerry's loss of favour with the government can have been only recent, as he was advanced to an earldom by George I.

one wants, at the same time that one possesses; for so
much as this letter I have not taxed them a long time. I
shall, with attention, observe all you recommend to me in
the way of passing my time, and do daily see reason to
respect *la bagatelle*; yet are there some places where that
is too insipid to be made any use of. I have an excellent
chaplain that I employ in reading, and my domestic.
Handicrafts and gardening do the rest.[1] As for quadrille,
it is a part of entertainment only for strangers. What shall
I say for taking up so much of your time? Forgive, dear
Dean,

Your most real and faithful humble servant,

A. KERRY.

DCCCLXXXVI. [*Craik.*[2]]

SWIFT TO THE EARL OF ORRERY

Dublin, *March* 22, 1732-3.

I HOPE the majority of your subjects is either innocent or
misled, and in that case you need only pass a general
pardon with exceptions. Those who were seen upon the
scaffold, or signed the warrant, must be banished for
ever without mercy, and the second-rate criminals shall
build you a palace in your metropolis.[3] . . .

I had this minute a letter from England telling me that
excise on tobacco is passed, two hundred and sixty-five
against two hundred and four, which was a greater number
of sitters than I can remember.[4] It is concluded they will

---

[1] Lord Kerry's house at Lixnaw, which was of great extent, contained a chapel remarkable for frescoes after Raphael and representations of ancient and modern poets, including Pope. In the gardens and
plantations the horticultural art of the time was conspicuous in canals
and vistas.

[2] *Supra*, p. 382, n. 1.

[3] Orrery had evidently returned to Cork (*supra*, p. 370, n. 3); the
reference is possibly to some local election.

[4] On the 14th of that month Walpole had expounded his excise
scheme in the House of Commons. He said that his designs did
not extend beyond alterations in the duties on wine and tobacco,
and that for the present his proposals would be confined to those on
the latter commodity.

go on in another session to farther articles, and then you will have the honour to be a slave in two kingdoms. Here is a pamphlet just come out in defence of the excise. It was reprinted by a rascal from England in a great office, and at his own charge, to pave the way for the same proceeding here, but I hope our members will think they are slaves enough already, and perhaps somebody or other may be tempted to open folks' eyes.[1]

I sent the Epitaph on Mr. Gay[2] to Mrs. Barber to be copied for your Lordship, and I think there are some lines that might and should be corrected. I am going to write to the author, and shall tell him my opinion. I agree with your Lordship that his imitation of Horace is one of the best things he hath lately writ, and he tells me himself that he never took more pains than in his poem to Lord Bathurst upon the Use of Riches, nor less than in this, which, however, his friends call his *chef d'œuvre*, although he writ it in two mornings, and this may happen when a poet lights upon a fruitful hint, and becomes fond of it. I have often thought that hints were owing as much to good fortune as to invention, and I have sometimes chid poor Mr. Gay for dwelling too long upon a hint, as he did in the sequel of the Beggar's Opera, and this unlucky posthumous production.[3] He hath likewise left a second part of [his] fables, of which I prophesy no good. I have been told that few painters can copy their own originals to perfection. And I believe the first thoughts on a subject that occurs to a poet's imagination are usually the most natural. . . .

A stupid beast in London, one Alexander Burnet, I suppose the Bishop's son, has parodied Mr. Pope's satirical imitation in a manner that makes me envy Mr. Pope for having such an adversary, than whose performance nothing can be more low and scurrilous.[4]

---

[1] The reference is no doubt to "A Letter from a Member of Parliament to his Friends in the Country concerning the Duties on Wine and Tobacco," which is dated 19 February, 1732-3, and was reprinted in Dublin by George Faulkner.

[2] *I.e.*, Pope's epitaph (*supra*, p. 393).

[3] *I.e.*, his "Achilles" (*supra*, p. 371, n. 2).

[4] The parody was published with a criticism on Gay's posthumous play in a pamphlet entitled "Achilles Dissected: being a complete key of the political characters in that new ballad opera, written by Mr. Gay. To which is added the first satire of the second book of Horace

DCCCLXXXVII. [*Hawkesworth.*]

SWIFT TO THE DUCHESS OF QUEENSBERRY

March 23, 1732-3.

MADAM,

I HAD lately the honour of a letter, from your Grace,[1] which was dated just a month before it came to my hand, and the ten days since, I have been much disordered with a giddiness, that I have been long subject to at uncertain times. This hindered me from an acknowledgement of the great favour you have done me. The greatest unhappiness of my life is grown a comfort under the death of my friend, I mean my banishment in this miserable country; for the distance I am at, and the despair I have of ever seeing my friends farther than by a summer's visit, and this, so late in my life, so uncertain in my health, and so embroiled in my little affairs, may probably never happen; so that my loss is not so great as that of his other friends, who had it always in their power to converse with him. But I chiefly lament your Grace's misfortune, because I greatly fear, with all the virtues and perfections which can possibly acquire the highest veneration to a mortal creature from the worthiest of human kind, you will never be able to procure another so useful, so sincere, so virtuous, so disinterested, so entertaining, so easy, and so humble a friend, as that person whose death all good men lament.

I turn to your letter, and find your Grace has the same thoughts. Loss of friends hath been called a tax upon life, and what is worse, it is then too late to get others, if they were to be had, for the younger ones are all engaged. I shall never differ from you in anything longer than till you declare your opinion; because I never knew you wrong in anything, except your condescending to have any regard

imitated in a dialogue between Mr. Pope and the Ordinary of Newgate." It contained such lines as the following:

> " My Twick'nam cot the worst companions grace,
> Attainted peers, commanders out of place,
> And unhanged Savage with his rueful face,"

and appears to have been written by William Guthrie, whose abilities have been praised by Dr. Johnson, but whose character seems to have been a venal one.

[1] *Supra*, p. 398.

for me, and therefore, all you say upon the subject of friendship, I heartily allow. But I doubt you are a perverter; for sure I was never capable of comparing the loss of friends with the loss of money. I think we never lament the death of a friend upon his own account, but merely on account of his friends, or the public, or both; and his, for a person in private life, was as great as possible.

How finely you preach to us who are going out of the world, to keep our spirits, without informing us where we shall find materials! Yet I have my flatterers too, who tell me, I am allowed to have retained more spirits than hundreds of others who are richer, younger, and healthier than myself; which, considering a thousand mortifications, added to the perfect illwill of every creature in power, I take to be a high point of merit, as well as an implicit obedience to your Grace's commands. Neither are those spirits, such as they be, in the least broken by the honour of lying under the same circumstances, with a certain great person, whom I shall not name, of being in disgrace at Court. I will excuse your blots upon paper, because they are the only blots that you ever did, or ever will make in the whole course of your life. I am content, upon your petition, to receive the Duke and your Grace for my stewards for that immense sum; and in proper time I may come to thank you, as a King does the Commons, for your loyal benevolence. In the mean while, I humbly entreat your Grace, that the money may lie where you please, till I presume to trouble you with a bill, as my Lord Duke allows me.

One thing I find, that you are grown very touchy since I lost the dear friend who was my supporter; so that perhaps you may expect I shall be very careful how I offend you in words, wherein you will be much mistaken; for I shall become ten times worse after correction. It seems Mr. Pope, like a treacherous gentleman, showed you my letter wherein I mentioned good qualities that you *seem* to have. You have understroked that offensive word, to show it should be printed in italic. What could I say more? I never saw your person since you were a girl, except once in the dark, to give you a bull of this country, in a walk next the Mall. Your letters may possibly be false copies of your mind; and the universal, almost idolatrous esteem you have forced from every person in two kingdoms, who

have the least regard for virtue, may have been only procured by a peculiar art of your own, I mean that of bribing
all wise and good men to be your flatterers. My literal
mistakes are worse than your blots. I am subject to them
by a sort of infirmity wherein I have few fellow-sufferers,
I mean that my heart runs before my pen, which it will
ever do in a greater degree, as long as I am a servant to
your Grace, I mean to the last hour of my life and senses.
I am, with the greatest respect and utmost gratitude,
Madam,

Your Grace's most obedient, most obliged, and most
humble servant.

I desire to present my most humble respects and thanks
to my Lord Duke of Queensberry. For a man of my level,
I have as bad a name almost as I desire; and I pray God
that those who give it me, may never have reason to give
me a better.

DCCCLXXXVIII. [*Original.*[1]]

LORD CARTERET TO SWIFT

Jermyn Street, *March* 24, 1732-3.

SIR,

I HAD the favour of your letter of the 19th of February.[2] A gentleman left it at my door. I have not heard
from him since, though he said he would call again, and
who he is, I do not know. I showed it to my wife and
Lady Worsley, who will not fail to obey your commands,
and tease me, if I could be forgetful of your orders, to
attend the cause of the city of Dublin when it comes into
the House. I know by experience how much that city
thinks itself under your protection, and how strictly they
used to obey all orders fulminated from the sovereignty of
St. Patrick's. I never doubted their compliance with you
in so trivial a point as a Recorder.[3] You can give anyone

[1] In the British Museum. See Preface.
[2] It was evidently of similar import to those sent to Oxford and
Dartmouth (*supra*, pp. 396, 397).
[3] Eaton Stannard, who became one of Swift's executors, had been
elected Recorder of Dublin on the day Swift had written to Carteret.

law and capacity in half an hour; and if by chance a rake
should get those faculties any other way, you can make the
worthy citizens believe he has them not, and you can
sustain any machine in a furred gown.

I thank you for a letter by Mr. Pilkington. I have
seen him twice at a great entertainment at my Lord
Mayor's, where you was the first toast. I like the young
man very well, and he has great obligations to you, of
which he seems sensible.

I hope Dr. Delany is well, and that you see one another
often, and then the Doctor will not have leisure to pursue
his Dissertations, or to answer the reverend prelate on your
side, who I hear has answered him.[1] As I have not read
the Dissertations, so I shall not read the answer, which, I
hope, without offence I may suppose to be your case. If so,
I hope you will endeavour to keep me well with the Doctor,
who took it a little unkindly of me that I would shut my
eyes to such revelation, so demonstrated. I have a great
esteem for him, to which nothing that he can write upon

Writing about the election Marmaduke Coghill, the Judge of the Prerogative Court, says: "We have lost our Recorder Mr. Stoyte, and
have had a great bustle for a successor. Mr. Forbes, an alderman's
son, and Mr. Stannard, a member of the House of Commons, a zealous
patriot, had the greatest interest, but Mr. Stannard was elected."
In an address which was issued in his favour, and which was possibly
written in part by Swift, Stannard is recommended to the citizens on
account of the opposition which he had offered in the House of Commons to a Bill for the prevention of smuggling, and is described as a
gentleman "of universal learning, of established and known abilities
in the law and in the trade and constitution of the kingdom, of great
virtue and strict honesty, sanguine in doing good, servant in the cause
of liberty and public spirit, and regardless of his own promotion when
put in competition with the prejudice of his country" ("Irish Pamphlets"
in Trinity College Library). Stannard was one of those suggested at
that time to succeed Sir Ralph Gore in the Speaker's chair (Brit. Mus.
Addit. MSS., 21122, vol. ii, pp. 18, 20).

[1] A tract in the collection of the Royal Irish Academy entitled
"The Question about Eating of Blood stated and examined in answer
to two Dissertations in a book entitled 'Revelation examined with
Candour,'" is ascribed in manuscript to Dr. Robert Clayton, Bishop of
Killala. Writing on the subject, Dr. Delany's future wife, who was
then staying with Bishop Clayton, says: "It is hard to know what
judgement one must make in such an affair, where one very learned
man says we must do one thing, and another as learned tells you it is
unnecessary. I hope it is not a point necessary to salvation, for I protest that I am at a loss what to determine; the salvo I have, is that
eating of blood was against the law of God, that the churchmen would
not have given it up" (Mrs. Delany's "Correspondence," i, 395).

those subjects can make any addition, and therefore I would run no risks as to altering my opinion of him by reading his books.

That health and prosperity may attend you, is my sincere wish; and I entreat you to believe that I am, with great truth, Sir,

Your most humble and most obedient servant,

CARTERET.

The whole family of my ladies send their compliments.

DCCCLXXXIX. [*Sheridan.*]

SWIFT TO THE REV. THOMAS SHERIDAN

Dublin, *March* 27, 1733.

I RECEIVED your letter with some pleasure, and a good deal of concern. The condition you are in requires the greatest haste hither, although your school did not;[1] and when you arrive, I will force Dr. Helsham to see and direct you. Your scheme of riding and country air you find hath not answered, and therefore you have nothing to trust to but the assistance of a friendly, skilful doctor. For whether they can do any good or not, it is all we have for it, and you cannot afford to die at present, because the public, and all your family have occasion for you. Besides, I do not like the place you are in, from your account, since you say people are dying there so fast.[2] You cannot afford to lose daily blood, but I suppose you are no more regular than you have been in your whole life. I like the article very much which you propose in your will, and if that takes place forty years hence, and God for the sins of men should continue that life so long, I would have it be still

[1] According to the younger Sheridan ("Life," p. 374), his father used to leave his school in Swift's charge when he went to the country. He was evidently away from Dublin when this letter was written, and apparently, from the postscript, staying with a member of the Irish Parliament.

[2] There was then much sickness in Ireland; two months before it is mentioned that smallpox was raging in Athy, and that there was great mortality in the county of Louth ("Dublin Evening Post," Jan. 23, 27).

inserted, unless you could make it a little sharper.[1] I own you have too much reason to complain of some friends, who next to yourself have done you most hurt, whom still I esteem and frequent, though I confess I cannot heartily forgive.[2] Yet certainly the case was not merely personal malice to you, although it had the same effect, but a kind of I know not what job, which one of them hath often heartily repented, however it came to be patched up.

I am confident your collection of *bon mots*, and *contes à rire*, will be much the best extant; but you are apt to be terribly sanguine about the profits of publishing; however it shall have all the pushing I can give.[3] I have been much out of order with a spice of my giddiness, which began before you left us. I am better of late days, but not right yet, though I take daily drops and bitters. I must do the best I can, but shall never more be a night-walker. You hear they have in England passed the excise on tobacco, and by their votes it appears they intend it on more articles. And care is taken by some special friends here to have it the same way here. We are slaves already. And from my youth upward, the great wise men, whom I used to be among, taught me that a general excise, which they now by degrees intend, is the most direct and infallible way to slavery. Pray G— send it them in his justice, for they well deserve it.

All your friends and the town are just as you left it. I humdrum it on, either on horseback, or dining and sitting the evening at home, endeavouring to write, but write nothing, merely out of indolence and want of spirits. No soul

---

[1] Sheridan's wife was probably the person on whom the anathema was to be pronounced:

> "Come sit by my side, while this picture I draw:
> In chattering a magpie, in pride a jackdaw!
> A temper the devil himself could not bridle,
> Impertinent mixture of busy and idle."
>
> ("Poetical Works," ii, 352.)

[2] The allusion is to the rival school which was opened in Dublin (*supra*, vol. iii, p. 250, n. 3). Delany appears to have been one of those concerned in its establishment.

[3] The novelty of Sheridan's scheme had worn off (*supra*, pp. 163, 168). Amongst the Swift manuscripts belonging to Mr. Locker Lampson ("The Rowfant Library," p. 216), there is one described as English blunders, which was possibly intended as a contribution to the project.

has broke his neck, or is hanged, or married; only Cancerina is dead, and I let her go to her grave without a coffin and without fees.[1] So I am going to take my evening walk after five, having not been out of doors yet. I wish you well and safe at home; pray call on me on Sunday night. I am,

Yours.

I believe there are a hundred literal blunders, but I cannot stay to mend them. So pick as you are able. I am not so *frank* a writer as you.

DCCCXC. [*Original.*[2]]

LORD BATHURST TO SWIFT

Cirencester, *March* 29, 1733.

MY MOST DEAR DEAN,

I AM indebted to you for several scraps of paper, which you have sent me; but I waited to receive a letter from you, and then I would have returned you an answer as well as I could. I obeyed your commands signified in your *penultième*.[3] I attended your cause. Your client happened to be in the right, and we are not a little in the wrong that we gave no costs. I should have moved for them, but I had distinguished myself in pressing Lords to attend, and told so many that I had your commands so to do, that I did not think it proper to take that part upon me, and nobody else would do it; therefore give me leave to tell you that you are bound in conscience to pay that poor man one hundred pounds. He would certainly have had that sum, if you had not interposed in that peremptory manner.

---

[1] She was one of the "seraglio" of poor women, whom Swift distinguished with the names of Cancerina, Stumpanympha, Pullagowna, Fritterilla, Flora, and Stumpantha, and in connection with whom his kindness of heart is said by Delany to have been so conspicuous ("Observations," p. 90).

[2] In the British Museum. See Preface.

[3] It would appear that Swift had sought Bathurst's assistance as well as Oxford's in regard to the appeal of his Meath friend to the House of Lords (*supra*, p. 372).

As to your last orders, in relation to the Dublin cause,[1] I take it for granted you are in the wrong. All corporations of men are perpetually doing injustice to individuals. I will attend it, but am as much prejudiced against them, as it is possible, though I know nothing of the man, nor the matter in question. I have often reflected, from what cause it arises I know not, that though the majority of a society are honest men, and would act separately with some humanity, and according to the rules of morality, yet conjunctively they are hard-hearted determined villains. I know physicians, who if you take them out of their practice, are very good sort of men; but was there ever in the world a consultation of them that tended to anything else than robbery and murder? Do the body of lawyers think of anything else, but to plunder and destroy the rest of mankind? In short there is no corporation to be excepted out of this general rule, but the two Houses of Parliament and all assemblies of divines, wheresoever dispersed over the Christian world. So much for the Dublin cause.

Now, I must tell you I want exceedingly to see you here, and I would have you come just about midsummer. If you come a moment before that time you will find the Parliament sitting, all in a flame about excises, and go into what company you will, you can hear of nothing else. I reckon by that time we shall separate, and then I come down to this place *en famille*, where I am now only a sojourner for three days, and you shall be better accommodated than you were last time you was here. I can assure you, I have made great alterations; and to speak modestly, I think I may say that it is by much the finest place in England. What Ireland may produce I cannot tell. Pope has promised to come down, and it is time for him to retire, for he has made the town too hot to hold him. Poor John Gay! we shall see him no more; but he will always be remembered by those who knew him, with a tender concern.

I want to know how you do, and what you are doing. I suspect you are grown very idle: for I have not heard of any production from that fertile brain of yours a great while, and besides the greatest mark of idleness that I know, is the minding of other people's business. You that

---

[1] *I.e.*, the one between the Corporation of Dublin and Mr. Vernon (*supra*, p. 396).

used to be employed in supporting or pulling down Ministers, in instructing or diverting mankind, in inflaming
kingdoms, or pacifying contending parties, now seem to
be dwindled into an Irish solicitor. I expect to see you in
a dirty brown coat, with a little green bag under your arm.
However, let me see you. If I cannot laugh with you as I
used to do, I will laugh at you; for I am resolved to laugh
as long as I live. So, my dear little pettifogger, adieu.

DCCCXCI. [*Elwin.*[1]]

SWIFT TO ALEXANDER POPE

[*March* 30, 1733.]

I HAVE been out of order for some weeks past with that
giddiness which you have often heard me talk of, and once
saw me in. It was not very violent, but lasted longer, and
now I am pretty near as I was before, an ill walker when
it is dusky. This hindered me from answering your long,
kind letter, that began with your Epitaph upon our deceased
friend.[2] I have not seen in so few lines more good sense, or
more proper to the subject,[3] yet I will tell you my remarks,
and submit them. The whole is intended for an apostrophe
to the dead person, which, however, doth not appear till
the eighth line. Therefore, as I checked a little at the
article " the " twice used in the second line, I imagined it
might be changed into " thy," and then the apostrophe
will appear at first, and be clearer to common readers.[4] My

---

[1] By permission of Mr. John Murray (*supra*, vol. iii, p. 148, n. 1).
There is also a copy in the Forster Collection.

[2] *Supra*, p. 393. In an account-book Swift records, " giddy from
4th, very ill on 14th " (Forster Collection, No. 511).

[3] Dr. Johnson's opinion of the epitaph affords a great contrast to
that of Swift. Hardly a line escapes the censure of the great critic,
and the conception, harmony, and grammar in turn come under his
lash (" Lives of the Poets," ed. G. Birkbeck Hill, iii, 268).

[4] As a result of this criticism the couplet was altered, but still left
it open to Dr. Johnson to say that in the first eight lines " the adjectives
are without any substantive and the epithets without a subject " :

> " Of manners gentle, of affections mild ;
> In wit, a man ; simplicity a child :
> With native humour temp'ring virtuous rage,
> Form'd to delight at once and lash the age ;

Lord Orrery, your great admirer, saith the word "mixed" suits not so properly the heroes' busts as the dust of kings. Perhaps my Lord may be too exact, yet you may please to consider it.[1] The beginning of this last line, "striking their aching bosoms." Those two participles come so near, and sounding so like, I could wish them altered, if it might be easily done. The Scripture expression upon our Saviour's death is, that the people "smote their breasts." You will pardon me, for since I have left off writing, I am sunk into a critic.[2] Some gentlemen here object against the expression in the second line, a child's simplicity; not against the propriety, but in compliance with the vulgar, who cannot distinguish simplicity and folly, and it is argued that your Epitaph, quite contrary to your other writings, will have a hundred vulgar readers for one who is otherwise. I confess I lay little weight upon this, although some friends of very good understanding, and who have a great honour for you, mentioned it to me.[3]

As to our poor friend, I think the Duke of Queensberry hath acted a very noble and generous part. But before he did it, I wish there had been so much cunning used as to have let the sisters know that he expected they would let him dispose of Mr. Gay's writings as himself and other friends should advise; and I heartily wish his Grace had entirely stifled that Comedy,[4] if it were possible, than do an injury to our friend's reputation only to get a hundred or two pounds to a couple of, perhaps, insignificant women. It hath been printed here, and I am grieved to say it is a very poor performance. I have often chid Mr. Gay for not

> Above temptation, in a low estate;
> And uncorrupted, ev'n among the Great:
> A safe companion, and an easy friend,
> Unblam'd thro' life, lamented in thy end.
> These are thy honours! not that here thy bust
> Is mix'd with heroes, or with kings thy dust;
> But that the Worthy and the Good shall say,
> Striking their pensive bosoms—Here lies Gay!"

[1] This couplet is the only one that Dr. Johnson allows to escape without some stricture.

[2] Swift's suggestion led to the insertion of "pensive." "The thought in the last line," says Dr. Johnson, "is so dark that few understand it, and so harsh when it is explained, that still fewer approve."

[3] In Dr. Johnson's opinion the second line raises "no ideas of excellence, either intellectual or moral."

[4] *I.e.*, Gay's "Achilles" (*supra*, p. 403).

varying his schemes, but still adhering to those that he had exhausted, and I much doubt whether the posthumous fables will prove equal to the first. I think it is incumbent upon you to see that nothing more be published of his that will lessen his reputation for the sake of adding a few pence to his sisters, who have already got so much by his death. If the case were mine, my ashes would rise in judgement against you.

I had very lately the great honour and happiness of a long letter from the Duchess, which I have already answered. She is so very good as to promise the continuance of her favour, and to desire a correspondence with me, which would be so useless to her otherwise than upon the accidental occasion it began, that I cannot have the assurance to think of it.

As to mortality it hath never been out of my head eighteen minutes these eighteen years; neither do I value it a rush further than as it parts a man from his friends for ever, and that share of it I have suffered already, and am likely to suffer as long as I live. I only apprehend some difficulties in settling my affairs, which without my fault, have been long embroiled, and the trouble of prudent settling my little fortune to a public use. For the rest, I rely on God's mercy; and will do as little hurt, and as much good as I can, in the scrap of life that may be left me. I am so much of your mind concerning the morality of poets, that I know not whither virtue can possibly find a corner to retire, except in the hearts of men of genius and learning; and what you call their levities have not the least tincture of impiety, but, directly otherwise, tend to drive vice out of the world.

The Libel on Dr. Delany gave great offence here, or, at least, Lord Allen did all he could that might anger the Parliament, but some people of the House of Commons, thinking the kingdom owed the author some gratitude, and knowing that Lord Carteret liked the thing, made them drop it.[1] However, you will make it live, and on your account it shall not be suffered to be forgotten.

March 31.

This day I received the two poems to myself, and one for Dr. Delany. We are not obliged to you; for all your

[1] *Supra*, p. 151.

things come over quickly, and are immediately printed in tolerable wieldable volumes, not your monstrous twelve-penny folio. By comparing kingdoms, I find England just outweighs twenty-four Irelands, for we get a shilling's worth here for a halfpenny; only yours yields a penny. Your Imitation of Horace, the work of two mornings, is reckoned here by the best judges—and with submission we are not without them—to be worth two years of any poet's life except yours; nor are there any objections against that to Lord Bathurst, but that some parts of it are not so obvious to middling readers. That beast called Alexander Burnet, I have read, and may you ever have such adversaries.[1] But the other, supposed to be writ by my Lady Mary, etc., I have not yet seen. They say here it is certainly hers.[2] Faulkner would not print it, nor do I know whether any-body here will, but there are some copies came from your side.

How can I judge of your schemes at this distance? I heard you intended four or five poems, addressed to as many friends, and can easily believe they would together make a system with connection, and a good moral for the conduct of life. But I want to be deep among all yours and your Dawley neighbour's papers for a few months; and my present thought is to come over towards August, and pass the winter there, and return with you hither in spring, if my health and embroilments will any way per-mit me. But, there must be some stipulations for my riding, with other necessary postulatums and ultimatums. I drink less than usual, but to drink as little as you or my Lord Bolingbroke is not to be expected; and yet I do not love wine, but take it purely as a medicine, and I love malt liquor, but dare not touch a drop. All victuals are equal, to my affections, yet I dare not meddle with strong meats; so that you and I are valetudinarians of a direct contrary kind. I am almost every second day on horseback for about a dozen miles. For the rest easy enough, only a most severe critic, and only to my Lord Bolingbroke and

---

[1] *Supra*, p. 403, n. 4.

[2] The allusion is to the "Verses addressed to an Imitator of Horace by a Lady," which are believed to have been written by Lady Mary Wortley Montagu with the assistance of Lord Hervey. "They in-sult," says Sir Leslie Stephen, "Pope's family and person with a brutality only exceeded by his own" ("D. N. B.," xxxviii, 261).

you. I know not whether my spirits, with the addition of six years' weight, will support me to see France. Lady Suffolk stopped that journey; I thank her for it among the rest of her favours. There hath been a strong controversy betwixt me and Lady Elizabeth Germain on the subject of Lady Suffolk's sincerity with regard to our deceased friend, and myself; for you are out of the case, who ask nothing and despise everything that a Court hath to give. But I lately cut that dispute short, and by that means shall probably lose Lady Elizabeth's favour.

I was always proud and pleased with Lord Peterborough's letters, and should never have let any of them gone unanswered; and I humbly acknowledge his favour in saying he had writ twice, for which I shall soon return him my thanks, as I now do my most humble service. I would enclose this to his Lordship, if I knew where to direct to him; for though everybody knows he *is*, yet is it hard to know where, because I think he had no house in town when I saw you last. Dr. Delany entertains his friends once a week in form; and as often as they please on other days. He sticks to his old set, without parade, but great hospitality, and bears a great addition of fortune as well as any man I have known. I never mention to him the singularities of opinions in his books ; and he is as easy a man in conversation as I have known. If Mr. Pilkington continues to preserve that modesty and humanity in his behaviour, which I have so often recommended to him, he will be happy to deserve your countenance and protection.[1]

I hope your Dawley neighbour continues his health and spirits. He laughs at my precepts of thrift, which I am sure you do not, nor ever will at a virtue that brings ease and liberty. He is befathered worse than poor Wycherley, and in that is a very expensive, unthinking young man.[2] I did not scruple sending Lord Orrery a copy of the Epitaph. He is absolutely the most hopeful young gentleman I ever saw, and seems to excel in every virtue, as if he only intended to cultivate any particular one. He is now in the country battling the most villainous agent, next to

---

[1] *Supra*, p. 354, n. 2.

[2] Bolingbroke's father was then eighty-one and lived to be ninety, and Wycherley's father died when his son was nearly sixty years of age.

Waters,[1] that ever ruined Lord or Commoner. Are the verses to Patty a thing to see light? Lords Peterborough, Masham, Bathurst, Oxford, Bolingbroke, Mr. Pulteney, the Doctor, Mr. Lewis, and Patty, are to be presented, as usual, with my most humble service as occasion offers. I have answered the Duchess of Queensberry's letter.

Addressed—For Alexander Pope, Esq., at Twickenham in Middlesex. By way of London.

DCCCXCII. [*Original.*[2]]

SWIFT TO CHARLES FORD

April 5, 1733.

DCCCXCIII. [*Original.*[3]]

LORD AND LADY MASHAM TO SWIFT

London, *April* 7, 1733.

LORD MASHAM

SIR,

I HOPE you will excuse me that I have not answered your letter sooner, but I shall not be backward in obeying your commands, by attending the cause you mentioned, when it comes into the House, and I shall not fail speaking to those few Lords I can be so free with, to attend also, and shall rejoice if it should be determined to your satisfaction,[4] and I have good reason to believe it will, being fully convinced, that you can interest yourself in nothing but where justice is uppermost. We have long flattered ourselves with the hopes of having your good company here. I am sure there is no family in this kingdom wishes

---

[1] *I.e.*, Peter Waters (*supra*, vol. iii, p. 423, n. 1).

[2] It was in the possession of Mr. Sabin of 172, New Bond Street a few years ago.

[3] In the British Museum. See Preface.

[4] Masham was evidently another of the friends to whom Swift had written about the appeal of the Corporation of Dublin to the House of Lords (*supra*, p. 410, n. 3).

to see you more than that of the Mashams, who will
always have you in remembrance, for your health and welfare. I doubt not but you hear from better hands the state
of our affairs, in relation to the excising tobacco and wine,
therefore shall not trouble you upon that subject; and shall
only desire your farther commands wherein I am capable
to serve you, assuring you, that I am, with great esteem
and truth, Sir,

Your most faithful and humble servant,

MASHAM.

LADY MASHAM

SIR,

THERE are few things in life would give me more joy
than to see you again in this part of the world. Let your
friends have that pleasure; for in doing it you will oblige
a vast number of people, but nobody more, my dear
Mr. Dean, than

Your affectionate humble servant,

A. MASHAM.

DCCCXCIV. [*Scott.*[1]]

SWIFT TO SAMUEL GERRARD

Dublin, *April* 7, 1733.

SIR,

I HEARTILY thank you for your kind remembrance of
me in relation to a purchase. But there is one Mr. Swift, a
relation of mine, whose estate is engaged to me for two
thousand pounds, and with whom I am at last come to a
bargain to purchase one hundred and fifty pounds per
annum, for which I must, I fear, borrow some money;[2] and,

---

[1] The original was then in the possession of the Gerrard family
(*supra*, p. 192, n. 2).

[2] The allusion, as the postscript shows, is to his biographer. Deane
Swift, who was baptized in St. Bride's Church, Dublin, on 27 December, 1706, was then a young man of twenty-six. He had been
educated in Dublin University, where he matriculated in 1723, and at
that time failed to win Swift's regard. It is to him that Swift refers in
his letter to Stafford Lightburne (*supra*, vol. iii, p. 235), the reference
being occasioned by litigation concerning Mrs. Lightburne's fortune
which her father had entrusted to his brother Deane, and which her
father's creditors tried to seize (Brit. Mus. Addit. MS., 36148, f. 1).

indeed, as to your proposal, I should never agree to it, from a maxim that is not much thought of. I intend to leave my whole fortune to a public use, in which case I take perpetuities to be the most pernicious, because you are bound for ever to a certain denomination of money, which is of so uncertain a value in all times, occasioned by the increase of silver and gold, and consequently the decrease of both in value. By not observing this caution, most corporations have extremely suffered by granting perpetuities; and so the value of money must decrease in Ireland, let us grow ever so poor, for we must value money by the standard of Europe, and not by our own scarcity. I have formerly considered this matter, and printed my thoughts of it; yet I am much obliged to you for your good intentions. I am, with great truth, Sir,

Your most obedient servant,
J. SWIFT.

I go down on Monday to Castlerickard, within four miles of Trim,[1] to see the land surveyed, and shall return on Thursday following. The land belongs to one Deane Swift, Esq., a relation of mine. I pay seven shillings and sixpence an acre, which I believe is too dear, but I am content to pay somewhat too much out of pity to the difficulties he is under. I had what advice I could get from Mr. Lightburne of Trim, and my proctor at Laracor, who said it might be worth seven shillings per acre round; in that case I pay but ten pounds per annum too much. But I wish I may not pay too much by a shilling, which, in four hundred acres, will make a difference of four hundred pounds at twenty years purchase. I wish you had been my adviser.

Addressed—To Mr. Samuel Gerrard, at Gibbstown, near Navan, County of Meath.

[1] The parish in which Deane Swift's seat was situated (*supra*, vol. i, p. 10, n. 2). In an account-book Swift records that he was at Castlerickard from the 8th to the 11th (Forster Collection, No. 511).

DCCCXCV. [*Original.*[1]]

THE DUCHESS OF QUEENSBERRY TO SWIFT

April 12, 1733.

DEAR SIR,

I RECEIVED yours of the 23rd of March. Perpetual pains in my head have hindered me from writing till this moment, so you see you are not the only person that way tormented. I dare believe there are as many bad heads in England as in Ireland. I am sure none worse than my own; that seems made for pain, and pain for it, for, of late, they have been inseparable. It is a most dispiriting distemper, and brings on pain of mind, whether real or imaginary, it is all one. Whilst I had that very sincere good friend, I could sometimes lay open all my rambling thoughts, and he and I would often view and dissect them; but now they come and go, and I seldom find out whether they be right or wrong, or if there be anything in them. Poor man! he was most truly everything you could say of him. I have lost, in him, the usefulest limb of my mind. This is an odd expression; but I cannot explain my notion otherwise.

I deny that I am touchy; yet am going to seem so again, by assuring you my letters are never false copies of my mind. They are often, I believe, imperfect ones of an imperfect mind; which, however, to do it justice, often directs me better than I act. Though I will not take upon me to declare my way of thinking to be eternally the same, yet whatever I write is at that instant true. I would rather tell a lie than write it down; for words are wind it is said; but the making a memorandum of one's own false heart, would stare one in the face immediately, and should put one out of countenance. Now, as a proof of my unsettled way of thinking, and of my sincerity, I shall tell you, that I am not so much in the wrong as you observed I was in my last; for, my regard to you is lessened extremely, since I have observed you are just like most other people, viz. disobliged at trifles, and obliged at nothings; for what else are bare words? Therefore pray never believe I wish to serve you, till you have tried me; till then protestations are bribes,

---

[1] In the British Museum. See Preface.

by which I may only mean to gain the friendship of a valuable man, and therefore ought to be suspected. I seldom make any for that reason; so that if I have the peculiar happiness to have any wise and good people my flatterers, God knows how I came by it; but sure nothing can equal such glory, except that of having the silly and bad people my enemies.

Here I think we agree. You declare no such can depress your spirits; and if our constitutions are alike, I will not only preach up good spirits, but prescribe the materials that have ever agreed with me. If anybody has done me an injury, they have hurt themselves more than me. If they give me an ill name, without they have my help, I shall not deserve it. If fools shun my company, it is because I am not like them; if people make me angry, they only raise my spirits; and if they wish me ill, I will be well and happy, and wise and handsome, and everything, except a day younger than I am, and that is a fancy I never yet saw becoming to man or woman, so cannot excite envy. Here I have betrayed to you the devilishness of my temper; but I declare to you, nothing ever enlivened me half so much, as unjust ill usage, either directed to myself or to my friends. The very reverse happens to me, when I am too well spoken of; for I am sorry to find I do not deserve it all. This humbleth me as much too much as the other exalts; so I hope you will not be too civil, since I have declared the consequence.

I am in great hopes you will make us a visit this summer; for though I have a sensible satisfaction by conversing with you in this way, yet I love mightily to look in the person's face I am speaking to. By that one soon learns to stop when it is wished, or to mend what is said amiss. Your stewards will take great care of your money; but you must first direct us to your friend Mr. Launcelott, ill spelt to be sure, and order him to give up Mr. Gay's note, on his sister's paying the money to his Grace, who will give him his note for the money, or send it to you as you order; and as to what interest is due to you, I suppose you have kept some account. By this time you must be too much tired, to bear reading one word more; therefore I will make no excuses. Pray employ me; for I want to be certain whether I know my own mind or no, for something or other often tells me, that I should be very happy to be

of any use to you. Whether this be true or false, neither
you nor I can be positive of, till an opportunity shows; but
I do really think, that I am, dear Sir,

                    Most sincerely yours, etc.

Addressed—To the Rev. Doctor Swift, Dean of St. Patrick's,
   in Dublin, Ireland.

DCCCXCVI. [*Deane Swift.*]

CHARLES FORD TO SWIFT

London, *April* 14, 1733.

I AM extremely concerned to hear the bad state of your
health.[1] I have often wished that you would be more
moderate in your walks; for, though riding has always
been allowed to be good for a giddy head, I never heard
walking prescribed for a strain, or any ailment in the leg,
and the violent sweats you put yourself into, are apt to give
colds, and I doubt occasion much of your other disorder. I
am confident you would find yourself better here, and even
the journey would be of great use to you. I was vastly
pleased to hear my Lord Mayor talk of the delight he
should have in seeing you this year, that he might show
you a creature of his own making. He has behaved himself so well in his public capacity, that whether it be his
humility or his pride, he deserves to be gratified. I could
heartily wish your other complaints were as much without
foundation, as that of having lost half your memory, and
all your invention. I will venture to pronounce you have
more left of the first than most men, and of the last than
any man now alive.

While the excises were depending, you were expected
every day;[2] for it was said, why should he not show as
much regard for the liberty of England, as he did for the

---

[1] The letter from Swift had evidently reached Ford (*supra*, p. 417).
[2] The ferment against Walpole's proposals had risen to such a
height that it was said the army could be trusted against the Pretender
but not against the opponents of the excise, and on the 11th of that
month Walpole was forced to announce the postponement of his
measure.

money of Ireland. I wish you had been here, though the
affair, in my opinion, is happily ended. Many people were
offended that the Bills were dropped, and not rejected, and
the authors of the scheme left unpunished. It was absolutely impossible to have carried it otherwise. You have
heard Sir Robert Walpole, and one or two more coming
out of the house, were insulted.[1] A few of that rabble have
been seized, with the ringleader, who proves to be a Norfolk
man—no enemy to excises, but an entire dependent upon
the outraged person. Though the rejoicings were as great,
and as universal as ever were known, there was no violence,
except the breaking a very few windows, whose owners had
shown an untimely thrift of their candles. I foretold Henley
what his joking would come to, but the Mayor of Southampton immediately printed his real letter, which was short,
and extremely proper.[2] His designed opponent at the next
election, having voted for the excise, will not dare to show
himself in the corporation; and Henley, after the division,
thanked him for having, by that vote, bestowed him fifteen
hundred pounds. . . .

I have great hopes this fine mild weather will set you
right, and long to hear you are preparing for your journey.
I am most entirely,

Your grateful, etc.

[1] After the last debate on the Bill, Walpole was surrounded on
leaving the House by "a clamorous mob" of well dressed persons.
Some of them seized his cloak, and as it was tightly fastened round
his throat, nearly strangled him (Coxe's "Memoirs of Pelham," i, 10).

[2] The elder brother of the first Lord Northington, who was then
one of the representatives of Southampton, was, like his father (*supra*,
vol. i, p. 112), addicted to practical jokes, and terminated his political
career by the present one. It consisted in sending an extremely un-
proper reply, as well as the extremely proper one, to a communication
from his constituents about the excise. Of the former the following
extract will suffice: "Gentlemen, I received yours, and am surprised
at your insolence in troubling me about the excise. You know what I
very well know, that I bought you. And I know what perhaps you
think I don't know, you are now selling yourselves to somebody
else. And I know what you don't know, that I am buying another
borough. May God's curse light on you all . . ." ("N. and Q.," 2,
xii, 107).

DCCCXCVII. [*Original.*[1]]

SWIFT TO THE EARL OF ORRERY

Deanery House, *April* 16, 1733.[2]

DCCCXCVIII. [*Original.*]

SWIFT TO THE EARL OF ORRERY

Deanery House, *April* 17, 1733.

I MUST disobey you, because I can do it without hurting me, being somewhat better than I was, though still with a swimming in my head which hinders me from going abroad as I intended on horseback; for your coach I utterly renounce. . . .

DCCCXCIX. [*Original.*]

SWIFT TO THE EARL OF ORRERY

Deanery House, *April* 20, 1733.

. . . THIS is a great day when the Chapter is entertained at the Deanery, and your health was drunk in a company where almost half abhorred your principles. . . .

I was not bound to return you the snuff, nor would for two such boxes.

CM. [*Elwin.*]

ALEXANDER POPE TO SWIFT

April [20], 1733.

YOU say truly, that death is only terrible to us as it separates us from those we love, but I really think those

---

[1] *Supra*, p. 382, n. 1.

[2] Swift had been sent by Orrery a print of his late wife, and writes to thank him for it. Orrery was again in Dublin (*supra*, p. 402), and had been presented on the 3rd of that month with the freedom of that city (" Pue's Occurrences ").

have the worst of it who are left by us, if we are true friends.[1] I have felt more, I fancy, in the loss of Mr. Gay, than I shall suffer in the thought of going away myself into a state that can feel none of this sort of losses. I wished vehemently to have seen him in a condition of living independent, and to have lived in perfect indolence the rest of our days together, the two most idle, most innocent, undesigning poets of our age. I now as vehemently wish you and I might walk into the grave together, by as slow steps as you please, but contentedly and cheerfully. Whether that ever can be, or in what country, I know no more, than into what country we shall walk out of the grave. But it suffices me to know it will be exactly what region or state our Maker appoints, and that whatever is, is right.

Our poor friend's papers are partly in my hands, and for as much as is so, I will take care to suppress things unworthy of him. As to the Epitaph, I am sorry you gave a copy, for it will certainly by that means come into print, and I would correct it more, unless you will do it for me, and that I shall like as well. Upon the whole, I earnestly wish your coming over hither, for this reason among many others, that your influence may be joined with mine to suppress whatever we may judge proper of his papers. To be plunged in my neighbour's and my papers, will be your inevitable fate as soon as you come. That I am an author whose characters are thought of some weight, appears from the great noise and bustle that the Court and town make about any I give; and I will not render them less important, or less interesting, by sparing vice and folly, or by betraying the cause of truth and virtue. I will take care they shall be such as no man can be angry at, but the persons I would have angry. You are sensible with what decency and justice I paid homage to the royal family, at the same time that I satirized false courtiers and spies, etc., about them. I have not the courage, however, to be such a satirist as you, but I would be as much, or more, a philosopher. You call your satires, libels; I would rather call my satires, epistles. They will consist more of morality than of wit, and grow graver, which you will call duller. I shall leave it to my antagonists to be witty, if they can, and content myself to be useful, and in the right. Tell me your opinion

[1] This letter has been hitherto dated 2 April, but is evidently a reply to Swift's letter of 30 March.

as to Lady Mary's or Lord Hervey's performance.[1] They are certainly the top wits of the Court, and you may judge by that single piece what can be done against me; for it was laboured, corrected, pre-commended, and post-disapproved, so as to be disowned by themselves, after each had highly cried it up for the other's. I have met with some complaints, and heard at a distance of some threats occasioned by my verses. I sent fair messages to acquaint them where I was to be found in town, and to offer to call at their houses to satisfy them, and so it dropped. It is very poor in any one to rail and threaten at a distance, and have nothing to say to you when they see you.

I am glad you persist and abide by so good a thing as that poem, in which I am immortal for my morality. I never took any praise so kindly, and yet I think I deserve that praise better than I do any other. When does your Collection come out, and what will it consist of? I have but last week finished another of my epistles, in the order of the system; and this week, *exercitandi gratia*, I have translated, or rather parodied, another of Horace's, in which I introduce you advising me about my expenses, housekeeping, etc.[2] But these things shall lie by, till you come to carp at them, and alter rhymes, and grammar, and triplets, and cacophonies of all kinds. Our Parliament will sit till midsummer, which I hope may be a motive to bring you rather in summer than so late as autumn. You used to love what I hate, a hurry of politics, etc. Courts I see not, courtiers I know not, Kings I adore not, Queens I compliment not; so I am never likely to be in fashion, nor in dependence. I heartily join with you in pitying our poor lady for her unhappiness, and should only pity her more, if she had more of what they at Court call happiness.[3]

---

[1] *Supra*, p. 415, n. 2.

[2] The imitation of the Second Satire of the Second Book addressed to Mr. Bethel:

> "Pray Heaven it last!" cries Swift, "as you go on;
> I wish to God this house had been your own:
> Pity! to build without a son or wife:
> Why, you'll enjoy it only all your life."

[3] Pope chooses to believe that Swift imputed Lady Suffolk's failure to provide for her friends to her want of influence, and not to any want of desire. He had used, five years before in alluding to her, words almost but not quite the same (*supra*, p. 5). It was possible then that the reference was to her relations with her husband, but now it can only be to her relations with the King.

Come then, and perhaps we may go all together into France at the end of the season, and compare the liberties of both kingdoms. Adieu. Believe me, dear Sir, with a thousand warm wishes, mixed with short sighs,

Ever yours.

CMI. [*Original.*[1]]

LADY ELIZABETH GERMAIN TO SWIFT

May 1, 1733.

I SHOULD have answered yours of the 22nd of March long ago, but that I have had some troubles and frights, and the uneasiness I was under made me neglect what, at another time, would have been agreeable to myself, Mrs. Chambers's younger sister having had the small-pox, but is got off perfectly well, though she has hitherto been a very puny sickly girl.[2] Mrs. Floyd too has been excessively bad with her winter-cough and dispiritedness; but country air, I think, has a little revived her.

His Grace of Dorset bids me present his humble service to you, and says, the rectory of Churchtown is at Mr. Stafford Lightburne's service.[3] As to the Countess of Suffolk's affair in dispute, I cannot possibly, according to your own just rule, be angry, because I am in the right. It is you ought to be angry, and never forgive her, because you have been so much in the wrong, as to condemn her without the show of justice; and I wish with all my heart, as a judgement upon you, that you had seen her, as I did, when the news of your friend's death came; for though you are a proud parson, yet give you, devil, your due, you are a sincere, good-natured, honest one. I am extremely Mrs. Kelly's humble servant; but I will never believe she is more valued for her beauty and good qualities in Ireland, than she was in England.

[1] In the British Museum. See Preface.

[2] The reference is to her nieces, the daughters of her eldest sister, who married Thomas Chambers of Hanworth. The eldest married Lord Vere Beauclerk.

[3] The living of Churchtown, which is in the county of Westmeath, near the town of Mullingar, was, before the disestablishment of the Church of Ireland, alternately in the presentation of the Crown and the Bishop of Meath.

The excise you mention has caused great changes here. Some that I am sorry for, though I will not enter into the merits of the cause, because of my aversion to politics. But if you did dislike it, why did you bestow such a costly funeral upon it, as to burn its bones on a sumptuous pile like a Roman emperor?[1] Adieu, my ever honoured old friend, and do not let me see any more respects or Ladyships from you.

CMII. [*Elwin.*]

SWIFT TO ALEXANDER POPE

Dublin, *May* 1, 1733.

I ANSWER your letter[2] the sooner, because I have a particular reason for doing so. Some weeks ago came over a poem called, the Life and Character of Dr. Swift, written by himself. It was reprinted here, and is dedicated to you.[3]

---

[1] "On Tuesday Night last [April 17] a large Bonfire was made on the Steeple of St. Patrick's Church on the News of the Excise Bill being laid aside in England, and another before the Dean's House, where a Barrel of Ale was given, and several Healths drank, as the Drapier's, the City of London who petitioned against the Bill, Prosperity to Ireland by the Return of Gentlemen who spend their Fortunes abroad, the Restoration and flourishing of Trade and confounding of all Projects of Excise, and several other Healths " (" Pue's Occurrences," April 17-21).

[2] *Supra*, p. 424.

[3] On All Fools' Day a poem entitled " The Life and Genuine Character of the Rev. Dr. S—t, D.S.P.D." had been sent to the press with a dedication to Pope signed L. M. from his "chambers in the Inner Temple, London." It is said in the dedication to be the poem written by Swift on "the discourse of the world concerning his character after his death," but is a ridiculous parody of it, little more than a third of its length. According to a categorical account given by Mrs. Pilkington, Swift himself was the author (" Memoirs," i, 88). She tells us that she was accused by him of being responsible for the parody through repeating his own verses which she had learned by heart, that on reading it she saw immediately that " the Dean had burlesqued himself," that on her challenging him to deny that such was the case, she received an evasive answer, and that she learned subsequently from her husband that she had not been mistaken, and that Swift had sent him the parody to be printed in London. Although Elwin (*op. cit.*, vii, 308), who is generally no lenient critic of Swift, takes the view that the *brochure* is more likely to have been concocted by Pilkington, internal evidence tends to prove the truth of Mrs. Pilkington's statement and

It is grounded upon a maxim in Rochefoucauld, and the dedication, after a formal story, says, that my manner of writing is to be found in every line. I believe I have told you, that I writ a year or two ago near five hundred lines upon the same maxim in Rochefoucauld, and was a long time about it, as that impostor says in his dedication, with many circumstances all pure invention. I desire you to believe, and to tell my friends, that in this spurious piece there is not a single line, or bit of a line, or thought, any way resembling the genuine copy, any more than it does Virgil's Æneis; for I never gave a copy of mine, nor lent it out of my sight; and although I showed it to all common acquaintance indifferently, and some of them, especially one or two females, had got many lines by heart, here and there, and repeated them often, yet it happens that not one single line, or thought, is contained in this imposture, although it appears that they who counterfeited me, had heard of the true one. But even this trick shall not provoke me to print the true one, which indeed is not proper to be seen till I can be seen no more. I therefore desire you will undeceive my friends, and I will order an advertisement to be printed here, and transmit it to England, that everybody may know the delusion, and acquit me, as I am sure you must have done yourself, if you have read any part of it, which is mean and trivial, and full of that cant that I most despise. I would sink to be a vicar in Norfolk[1] rather than be charged with such a performance.

Now I come to your letter. When I was of your age, I

---

to show that both the parody and dedication were written by Swift. The strongest ground for that opinion is that the *brochure* evinces the most extraordinary pains on the part of the author, and that no one except Swift is likely to have taken them, but in addition the parody contains rhymes such as he delighted in making, and the dedication comprises a grave, circumstantial recital in his inimitable style. He wished his friends to believe that the parody was a bad copy of his verses, written by some one with an imperfect knowledge of them, but every line displays a close acquaintance with them, and care in making the parody dissimilar. Besides, the date appended to the dedication is a further corroboration of Swift's being the author. It was a festival, as the Correspondence has shown, observed by him, and it is possible that his primary object was to make a fool of Little Matthew in the Sanctuary, and that his success in deluding not only him, but other friends, was far greater than he had expected.

[1] *I.e.*, to be nominated by Walpole.

thought every day of death, but now every minute; and a continual giddy disorder more or less is a greater addition than that of my years. I cannot affirm that I pity our friend Gay, but I pity his friends, I pity you, and would at least equally pity myself, if I lived amongst you; because I should have seen him oftener than you did, who are a kind of hermit, how great a noise soever you make by your ill nature in not letting the honest villains of the times enjoy themselves in this world, which is their only happiness, and terrifying them with another. I should have added in my Libel, that of all men living, you are the most happy in your enemies and your friends, and I will swear you have fifty times more charity for mankind than I could ever pretend to. Whether the production you mention came from the Lady or the Lord, I did not imagine that they were at least so bad versifiers. Therefore, *facit indignatio versus*,[1] is only to be applied when the indignation is against general villainy, and never operates when some sort of people write to defend themselves. I love to hear them reproach you for dulness, only I would be satisfied, since you are so dull, why are they so angry? Give me a shilling, and I will ensure you, that posterity shall never know you had one single enemy, excepting those whose memory you have preserved.

I am sorry for the situation of Mr. Gay's papers. You do not exert yourself as much as I could wish in this affair. I had rather the two sisters were hanged than to see his works swelled by any loss of credit to his memory. I would be glad to see the most valuable printed by themselves, those which ought not to be seen, burned immediately, and the others that have gone abroad, printed separately like opuscula, or rather be stifled and forgotten. I thought your Epitaph was immediately to be engraved, and therefore I made less scruple to give a copy to Lord Orrery, who earnestly desired it, but to nobody else; and he tells me, he gave only two, which he will recall. I have a short epigram of his upon it, wherein I would correct a line or two at most, and then I will send it you, with his permission. I have nothing against yours, but the last line, " striking their aching;" the two participles, as they are so near, seem to sound too like.

I shall write to the Duchess, who has lately honoured me

---

[1] The motto appended to " the production."

with a very friendly letter,[1] and I will tell her my opinion freely about our friend's papers. I want health, and my affairs are enlarged, but I will break through the latter, if the other mends. I can use a course of medicines, lame and giddy. My chief design, next to seeing you, is to be a severe critic on you and your neighbour,[2] but first kill his father that he may be able to maintain me in my own way of living, and particularly my horses. It cost me near six hundred pounds for a wall to keep mine,[3] and I never ride without two servants for fear of accidents; *hic vivimus ambitiosa paupertate*. You are both too poor for my acquaintance, but he much the poorer. With you I will find grass, and wine, and servants, but with him not.

The Collection you speak of is this. A printer[4] came to me to desire he might print my works, as he called them, in four volumes by subscription. I said I would give no leave, and should be sorry to see them printed here. He said they could not be printed in London. I answered they could, if the partners agreed. He said, he would be glad of my permission, but as he could print them without it, and was advised that it could do me no harm, and having been assured of numerous subscriptions, he hoped I would not be angry at his pursuing his own interest, etc. Much of this discourse passed, and he goes on with the matter, wherein I determined not to intermeddle, though it be much to my discontent, and I wish it could be done in England, rather than here, although I am grown pretty indifferent in everything of that kind. This is the truth of the story.

My vanity turns at present on being personated in your *Quae virtus*, etc. You will observe in this letter many marks of an ill head and a low spirit; but a heart wholly turned to love you with the greatest earnestness and truth.

[1] *Supra*, p. 420.
[2] *I.e.*, Bolingbroke.
[3] *I.e.*, the one round Naboth's Vineyard (*supra*, p. 126, n. 2).
[4] *I.e.*, George Faulkner (*supra*, p. 389).

CMIII. [*Deane Swift.*]

MISS KELLY TO SWIFT

Jervis Street, *May* 4, 1733.

SIR,[1]

I AM sure if you knew what I have suffered for having offended you, your anger would be changed into pity; for indeed, Sir, my uneasiness cannot be expressed. Of all the misfortunes I ever met with, this has given me the greatest concern; for your friendship is an honour that the whole world are ambitious of, but I received from it more than ordinary satisfaction. Judge then, Sir, how unhappy I now am, and for God's sake, forgive what is passed, and be assured my future conduct shall be such, that you never again shall have cause of complaint against me. I own you have reason to condemn my impertinence, but as I had not the least intention to offend, I hope it will, in some measure, lessen the fault. Indeed, Sir, if you will be so good to pardon me, I will make any atonement in my power, and it will much add to the other obligations you have already conferred upon me.

My health is so much impaired, that it is but too probable that I shall not live very long, and methinks it would be very hard to have the short time that is allotted for me made more miserable than continual sickness can make it. This must be the case, if you do not once more receive me into your favour; nothing I desire half so much, and do assure you, I spent so bad a night, from the thoughts of my misfortune, that could you have had an idea of it, you would have been sorry for me. You might have seen how depressed I was at supper, but not my indisposition, but your cold behaviour was the real occasion of it. What shall

---

[1] Miss Kelly had before then developed the disease from which she died that year (*supra*, p. 279). Writing two months before, the future Mrs. Delany says ("Correspondence," i, 402): "I have given up the trial with Kelly; her beauty and assiduity have distanced me, and I will not attempt a second heat. At present she is disabled, poor thing, for she is confined to her bed with a pleuritic disorder, but the Dean attends her bedside: his heart must be old and cold indeed if that did not conquer." As appears from this letter she had offended Swift, and was anxious to be reconciled to him before setting out for Bristol, whither she was going for her health.

I say, or do, to influence you to pardon me? If true repentance for my crime, and a firm resolution to be upon my guard for the future against any inadvertent expressions that can give offence, will plead anything in my favour, you will be so good to pardon me; for I can affirm, that I will never offend you again. Try me then, good Sir, and if it is possible, both forget and forgive the errors I have been guilty of.

If you are not determined to continue my unhappiness, I must beg the favour of you to send me a line to assure me of my being pardoned; for my uneasiness cannot be removed without it. I hope too, Sir, that I shall have the honour of seeing you before I go, that I may in person acknowledge how much I owe you, and with what satisfaction I receive your forgiveness, and for God's sake, Sir, look upon me as you were wont to do, for I cannot bear your coldness. I propose, when I go to Bristol, to follow your advice, and should be much obliged to you, if you would recommend me to those books that you think most proper for me, and if it please God that I recover, you shall find that by the honour you have done me in advising me to improve my mind, the deficiencies of my education will be made up, and I shall be more worthy of your esteem. I should beg pardon for the length of this, but that I still could write on to ask your forgiveness; who am, Sir, with true respect and regard,

Your most obliged and most humble servant,

F. A. KELLY.

CMIV. [*Original.*[1]]

SWIFT TO THE EARL OF ORRERY

Deanery House, *May* 28, 1733.

THE appointment made last week at Grange, over a pot of ale, to go to Leslie to-day hath not been cancelled since that I know of, by any subsequent negotiations.[2] I hear

[1] *Supra*, p. 382, n. 1.
[2] The Grange, which is situated near a village called Baldoyle, between Dublin and Howth, was then the residence of Lady Acheson's mother. It had derived its name from having been originally a possession of the Priory of All Saints, the site of whose

my Lady Acheson and her mother came to town last night, and that Lady Betty Brownlow cannot go.[1] What the rest will do I know not, but I was determined to set out with my equipage at all hazards to the place of treaty.

CMV. [*Elwin.*]

ALEXANDER POPE TO SWIFT

May 28, 1733.

I HAVE begun two or three letters to you by snatches,[2] and been prevented from finishing them by a thousand avocations and dissipations. I must first acknowledge the honour done me by Lord Orrery, whose praises are that precious ointment Solomon speaks of, which can be given only by men of virtue. All other praise, whether from poets or peers, is contemptible alike, and I am old enough and experienced enough to know, that the only praises worth having, are those bestowed by virtue for virtue. My poetry I abandon to the critics, my morals I commit to the testimony of those who know me; and therefore I was more pleased with your Libel, than with any verses I ever received. I wish such a collection of your writings could be printed here, as you mention going on in Ireland. I was surprised to receive from the printer that spurious piece called the Life and Character of Dr. Swift, with a letter telling me the person who published it had assured him the dedication to me was what I would not take ill, or else he would not have printed it. I cannot tell who the man is, who took so far upon him as to answer for my way of thinking; though, had the thing been genuine, I should have been greatly displeased at the publisher's part in doing it without your knowledge.

house in Dublin Trinity College occupies, and had become the country residence of a member of Sir Arthur Acheson's family, George Acheson, who had married Lady Acheson's mother as her second husband, and had died a few years before the date of this letter. The friend whom it was proposed to visit was no doubt the son of the Non-juror. He would have been well known to Swift as he was married to a niece of Peter Ludlow, and had probably a house in the vicinity of Dublin.

[1] As already mentioned (*supra*, vol. ii, p. 45, n. 4) she was a daughter of the sixth Earl of Abercorn and was married to an ancestor of Lord Lurgan.

[2] In answer to Swift's letter of the 1st.

I am as earnest as you can be in doing my best to prevent the publishing of anything unworthy of Mr. Gay; but
I fear his friend's partiality. I wish you would come over.
All the mysteries of my philosophical work shall then be
cleared to you, and you will not think that I am not merry
enough, nor angry enough. It will not want for satire, but
as for anger I know it not, or at least only that sort of
which the Apostle speaks, be ye angry, and sin not.

My neighbour's writings have been metaphysical, and
will next be historical. It is certainly from him only that a
valuable history of Europe in these latter times can be expected. Come, and quicken him; for age, indolence, and
contempt of the world, grow upon men apace, and may
often make the wisest indifferent whether posterity be any
wiser than we. To a man in years, health and quiet become
such rarities, and consequently so valuable, that he is apt
to think of nothing more than of enjoying them whenever
he can, for the remainder of life; and this I doubt not has
caused so many great men to die without leaving a scrap
to posterity.

I am sincerely troubled for the bad account you give of
your own health. I wish every day to hear a better, as much
as I do to enjoy my own, I faithfully assure you.

CMVI. [*Deane Swift.*]

Mrs. Pendarves to Swift

London, *May* 29, 1733.

Sir,[1]

You will find, to your cost, that a woman's pen, when
encouraged, is as bad as a woman's tongue. Blame yourself,

---

[1] Mrs. Pendarves, the future Mrs. Delany, who had married at an
early age a Cornish gentleman much older than herself, was then a
young widow of thirty-three years of age. As the daughter of a
younger brother of Lord Lansdown and a cousin of Lord Carteret,
she must have long known Swift by reputation, but she had only
become acquainted with him a few months before. She had been in
Ireland since the autumn of 1731 on a visit to Bishop Clayton and his
wife, but the first reference in her correspondence to meeting Swift
occurs four months before the date of the present letter. In writing

not me; had I never known the pleasure of receiving a letter from you, I should not have persecuted you now. I think, a little to justify this bold attack, that I am obliged by all the rules of civility to give you an account of the letter you charged me with. I delivered it into my Lord Bathurst's hands; he read it before me. I looked silly upon his asking me, what you meant by the Faussett affair, and was obliged to explain it to him in my own defence, which gave him the diversion I believe you designed it should.[1] We then talked of your vineyards. He seemed pleased with every subject that related to you, and I was very ready to indulge him that way. I did not forget to brag of your favours to me; if you intended I should keep them a secret, I have spoiled all, for I have not an acquaintance of any worth that I have not told how happy I have been in your company. Everybody loves to be envied, and this is the only way I have of raising people's envy. I hope, Sir, you will forgive me, and let me know if I have *behaved* myself right.[2]

then to her sister, she says: "On Thursday Phil and I dined at Dr. Delany's; there we met Miss Kelly, Lord Orrery, the Dean of St. Patrick's, Mr. Kit Donnellan, [and] Dr. Helsham, a very ingenious entertaining man. In such company you may believe time passed away very pleasantly. Swift is a very odd companion, if that expression is not too familiar for so extraordinary a genius; he talks a great deal and does not require many answers; he has infinite spirits, and says abundance of good things in his common way of discourse." Two months later she mentions dining again at Dr. Delany's, and says: "The Dean of St. Patrick's was there, in very good humour; he calls himself my 'master,' and corrects me when I speak bad English, or do not pronounce my words distinctly. I wish he lived in England; I should not only have a great deal of entertainment from him, but improvement." Soon afterwards she returned to London (Mrs. Delany's "Correspondence," i, 396, 407).

[1] One of Bishop Clayton's clergy, Robert Faussett, Precentor of Achonry, appears to have made a proposal of marriage to Mrs. Pendarves while she was staying in the summer of 1732 at Killala with the Bishop. In her letters to her sister she refers to an extraordinary affair that had flustered and enraged her not a little, and adds "the whole county knows it, and the wretch is ridiculed to that degree that he has not made his appearance since he wrote the letter" (Mrs. Delany's "Correspondence," i, 373, 381).

[2] Deane Swift appends the following note: "Dr. Swift never could endure to hear anyone say, such a one behaved well, etc. 'Behaved? Behaved what?' he used to ask with some kind of emotion. I remember his giving me an account how he rebuked Lord Carteret for this, and that my Lord promised him not to be guilty of the like for the future."

I think I can hardly do wrong as long as I am, Sir,
    Your most obliged and most obedient servant,
                                M. PENDARVES.

Mrs. Donnellan is much your humble servant,[1] and as vain of your favours as I am.

CMVII. [*Original.*[2]]

SWIFT TO THE EARL OF OXFORD

Dublin, *May* 31, 1733.

MY LORD,
    I WRIT to your Lordship some time ago, upon an occasion wherein we who live in Ireland, and happen to have friends in England, are often employed, I mean the case of an appeal wherein this city is a party,[3] and I being one of its protectors for a long time as a neighbour and confederate Prince,[4] could not forbear my intercession, when at the same time I get an opportunity to pay you my respects and acknowledgements for all the obligations I have received from you and my Lady Oxford.
    This letter will be delivered to you by Mr. Jebb, who I find hath been long known to you, and of whom I have a good opinion.[5] He intends to fix here, and hath lately got a Church preferment of some value from a beast of a Bishop you sent us,[6] but I think it was without the interest of the Archbishop of Dublin,[7] who hath taken Mr. Jebb under his protection. Mr. Jebb hath a very good reputation among us, which I believe he well deserves, and hath naturally good principles, but his friends being on the side

----

[1] Phil Donnellan, who has been mentioned as dining with Mrs. Pendarves at Dr. Delany's, and was her dearest friend, was a sister of Bishop Clayton's wife. They were daughters of a Chief Baron of the Exchequer in Ireland.
    [2] In the possession of the Duke of Portland. *Supra*, vol. ii, p. 160, n. 2.
    [3] *Supra*, p. 396.
    [4] In "the Liberties" of St. Patrick's Cathedral.
    [5] *Supra*, p. 313.
    [6] *I.e.*, Tennison, the Bishop of Ossory.
    [7] *I.e.*, John Hoadly. Swift had written first "by the interest of."

of power, he is forced to tack the prudence of the serpent
to the innocence of the dove. I do not know a more modest,
decent, well-behaved person; I see him often, like him
very well, and can give allowance for the party he is attached to, because I hope and believe he will never go any
lengths unbecoming a man of honour and conscience, and
my hope is much founded upon the favour your Lordship
hath shown him. If he ever deceives me, your Lordship
will be one of my deceivers.

I have often panted for a letter from you, and I excuse
you of any want of good will, but impute your silence
wholly to your laziness. I have felt of late the effects of
time by the return of an old disorder of giddiness which
more or less daily pursues me, but I oppose it by constant
riding and walking, wherein I wish you would follow my
example. This ailment hath hindered me from seeing my
friends in England, for fear of being sick too far from
home, where I can be easy, and do what I please without
troubling others. I heartily wish your Lordship health and
happiness, and the same to my Lady Oxford and Lady
Marget, to whom I desire to present my most humble service. I am with great truth and respect, my Lord,

Your Lordship's most obedient and most obliged humble
servant,

JONATH. SWIFT.

Your Lordship may have seen or heard of a foolish
poem, impudently printed in London as mine, upon what
people will say of me after I am dead.[1] I confess I writ a
poem upon that subject, which I have often shown, and is
above twice as large as this spurious one, but I never gave
it out of my power, and in that which is printed there is
not one single line or thought which resembles the original,
nor is the sham copy so long by three hundred lines.
Therefore I beg your Lordship will please to justify me.

[1] *Supra*, p. 428, n. 3.

CMVIII. [*Original.*[1]]

THE DUCHESS OF QUEENSBERRY TO SWIFT

Amesbury, *May* 31, 1733.

DEAR SIR,

I AM now again your Tunbridge correspondent.[2] His Grace and I have been here this fortnight, with no other company than bricklayers and labourers. We are throwing down a parcel of walls, that blocked us up every way, and making a sunk fence round the house. This will make the place as cheerful again, and we find great entertainment by inspecting the work. Since I came here, even I have often got up by six in the morning—designed it always—and the whole house are fast asleep before twelve. This I call good hours. I walk as much as I am able, sometimes rather more. We sometimes ride, though not often, for the evenings and mornings are very cold, and the middle of the day violently hot. North-east winds continually, and such want of rain that the ground is as hard as iron. I am the most temperate creature in my diet you ever knew; yet, with all my care, I cannot be well, but I believe, if I am never guilty of a greater fault, I shall meet with very little resentment, either public or private. They are the faults in the world the soonest forgot, and the seldomest truly resented.

Let that be as it will, since health is undoubtedly the most valuable thing in life, I shall do all I can to obtain it. This makes me consent to the thing in the world I am most averse to; it is, going to the Spa about a month or six weeks hence. I wish it was good for your complaints, that we might be there together. Really, if you think it will be of any use to you, and that you can order your affairs so as to make it possible, depend upon it we shall make it our study, and a very agreeable one too, to make you as easy and happy as it is in the power of people, not of a very troublesome disposition, to contrive. Your complaint and mine are not very different, as I imagine. Mine is a sort of dizziness, which generally goes off by the headache. Some learned people give it a name I do not know

---

[1] In the British Museum. See Preface.
[2] *Supra*, p. 315, n. 2.

how to spell, a vertico, or virtigo. Pray understand that I, really and truly, do not only say, but mean, that I wish you could either meet us at the Spa, or at London to go on with us; and in this I am sure I shall never change my mind. If it can do you any good, I feel myself enough your friend to resent it extremely if you miss this opportunity. This you would believe, if you knew what obligations I have to you. I am generally poor in spirit, or quarrelling with myself for being good for nothing. When a letter comes from you, it does not only entertain and revive me, but instantly I fancy I ought to have a good opinion of myself, which is of very great use to have, provided it is kept within just bounds.

I shall punctually obey your commands concerning that poem;[1] but I think you may be perfectly easy on that account, for I saw it before I left London, and heard several people talk of it, and the general opinion was, that you had no hand in it, but that the thing happened just as you say. I think you need not have been much disturbed at it. The other troubles you mention I can allow of. Philosophy cannot make such things not be; the most it can pretend to is, to help people to patience. I am heartily sorry you have any particular occasion for any. Is your lawsuit still in being? Perhaps I may be impertinent; but I remember you once mentioned something of that kind.

I am pretty well satisfied anything is bad for the head that fills it too full; therefore I advise you to unbend your thoughts, and ask my advice; if it should prove good, take it; if not, leave it. I should be mighty glad to be of any service to you; in making me so, you would show kindness to the memory of your very sincere friend, and be kind to me. You may depend upon me, both for his sake and your own. I will endeavour to convey your messages to Lady Catherine and Charlotte as soon as possible.[2] The first I have not conversed with this year and a half; I believe she is nobody's friend, but I more than believe that nobody is hers. I have a brother that I dare answer you would like, if you knew him perfectly, not else. I love and honour him, and he deserves it. When his Grace goes to London, which

---

[1] *I.e.*, "The Life and Genuine Character of Dr. S—t" (*supra*, p. 428, n. 3).

[2] Probably the allusion is to a sister of her father, who is mentioned in the Journal to Stella, and her own sister (*supra*, p. 133).

will be very soon, your money shall be as you ordered. He is mightily shocked at so many speeches. He is not by just now, or undoubtedly he would think you deserve to have them returned. It is lucky for me, for I am come to the end of my paper. Note, without an excuse.

Addressed—To the Reverend Dr. Swift, Dean of St. Patrick's, Dublin, Ireland.

CMIX. [*Deane Swift.*]

MISS KELLY TO SWIFT

Bristol Hot Wells, *June* 2, 1733.

SIR,

I HEAR my agreeable fellow traveller has been before-hand with me in paying her compliments to you;[1] but I cannot be surprised at that, for she was formed to get the better of me in everything, but respecting and esteeming you. That, indeed, nobody can do; for both gratitude and taste conspire to make me truly your friend and servant.

I have been, since I came here, very low spirited; the companions I had some part of my journey lessened my illness, or at least I felt not with them the same weight that I did upon their leaving me, and I have often wished myself again in Ireland to enjoy conversation, for I really believe it is one excellent cure for most disorders. This is the dullest place that ever was known; there is not above half a dozen families, and those are cits with great fortunes, or Irish impertinents; the former despise one because their clothes are finer than yours, and the latter have no view in keeping your company, but to report your faults. This makes me avoid all communication with them, and only in the morning I go to the wells, and, I thank God, I can spend my time far better; for either writing to my friends, reading, walking, and riding, find me full employment, and leave me not a wish for such company as the place affords.

---

[1] It is probable that Miss Kelly had crossed to England with Mrs. Pendarves and Miss Donnellan. The latter was a great friend of Miss Kelly, who had "so entirely gained" her as to make Mrs. Pendarves apprehensive of losing her as a companion (Mrs. Delany's "Correspondence," i, 403).

Doctor Lane, who, by character, is a second Æsculapius, and can raise people from the dead, is my physician, and gives me great hopes of a speedy amendment, and as I take his medicines regularly, and am up at six in the morning, breakfast at eight, dine at one, and sup at seven, I hope I may in time find some benefit; nor do either the ass's milk or waters disagree with me, and I think my appetite is rather better.

I wish to Heaven it was agreeable to your affairs to come here; for I am sure you would like the situation of the house that I lodge in. It has the command of such a prospect that I should do it injustice to attempt to describe it; but the variety of the scene is such, that one discovers new beauties in it every day. I hope you will continue your former goodness to me, and let me have the honour of hearing from you sometimes; for, in reality, nobody is more sincerely your well-wisher than, Sir,

Your most obliged and most faithful humble servant,
F. A. KELLY.

Your expedition to Tallaght makes a very fine figure in print;[1] but, since you have made this discovery, I think you ought to fly to us, for, if Dublin be in danger, the Deanery House cannot be a safe retreat for you. I wish anything would send Barber here; for I was at the Bath to see some of my friends, and was forced to swear that only the want of health kept her book from being published. I

---

[1] The following paragraph appeared in many Irish and English newspapers at that time: "On last Saturday, May 12, the Right Honourable the Earl of Orrery, the Reverend Dr. Swift, Dean of St. Patrick's, and the Reverend Dr. Sheridan, rode from Dublin to Tallaght Hill to take a prospect of the adjacent country. As they were mounting a rock, they observed a stream running through the middle of it, which fell into a natural basin, and was thence conveyed through some subterraneous cavities; but they could not anywhere discover by what secret passage it was conveyed out again; so that they concluded the waters were still in some reservoir within the bounds of the hill, which must infallibly come to burst forth in time, and fall directly upon the city. The Doctor sent for a milking-pail to compute what quantity ran out, which held two gallons, and it was filled in the space of a minute, so that it runs in twenty-four hours 2,880 gallons. This multiplied by 365 produces 1,051,200, and shows the quantity that runs from the rock in a year; so that in three years, about the 15th of November, he computed that it must burst the body of the mountain, and emit an inundation which will run to all points of the Boyne, and greatly endanger the city of Dublin."

am sure you would be glad to hear, that a lady of very good understanding, that is a particular friend of mine, comes to me next week to stay while I do: her name is Rooke, Admiral Rooke's son's lady.

CMX. [*Original.*[1]]

LADY ELIZABETH GERMAIN TO SWIFT

June 5, 1733.

HAS Mr. Stafford Lightburne's friend got the gout in his fingers,[2] or is he so busy in measuring the water, and casting a figure to know the exact time when to set his friends a swimming,[3] that he cannot find one moment to let me know that he received my letter, writ a month ago, to inform you that his Grace would cheerfully and readily obey your commands? However, I am again ordered by him to tell you, that the warrant will be sent to Dublin by next post; so pray let Mr. Lightburne be ready to make his personal appearance, lest they should not else know how to find him. It was well you needed no intercessor to his Grace; and that the no promise from him, and the one word from you, is of much more weight than my rhetoric: for I have been so horridly used by a nasty griping brother black coat, in a small three and sixpence affair of my own, that I do not know whether I should not have done like you of the faction, revenge myself of the innocent, for the sake of one bishop and minister, that I say, have cheated, fleeced, and flayed me, just as if they had been South Sea or East India directors.

You are angry if I do not mention Mrs. Floyd to you, so, I must tell you, she is gone for a little time into the country, to try if that will ever cure her cough. I am heartily sorry for your new friend Mrs. Kelly, who writes in a desponding way to Mrs. Chambers about her health, and talks of going to Spa. This is a melancholy subject, and I hate to be vexed. So I will say no more of it, but adieu, my dear Dean, and let me hear from you soon.

Addressed—To the Reverend Dr. Swift, Dean of St. Patrick's, at Dublin, Ireland.

[1] In the British Museum. See Preface.
[2] *Supra*, p. 427.
[3] *Supra*, p. 442, n. 1.

CMXI. [*Faulkner.*]

SWIFT TO GEORGE FAULKNER

June 29, 1733.

I DESIRE Mrs. Pilkington will deliver you the paper relating to Gulliver, which I left with her husband; for, since you intend to print a new edition of that book, I must tell you, that the English printer made several alterations which I much disapprove of, and cannot set them right without those papers.[1] If I am not mistaken, Mr. Pilkington hath an edition of Gulliver, where the true original copy is interleaved in manuscript. I desire I may also see that book. I am,

Your humble servant,
JON. SWIFT.

CMXII. [*Birkbeck Hill.*]

SWIFT TO CHARLES FORD

June 29, 1733.

. . . Now you may please to remember how much I complained of Motte's suffering some friend of his—I suppose it was Mr. Tooke, a clergyman now dead[2]—not only to blot out some things that he thought might give offence, but to insert a good deal contrary to the author's manner and style and intention. I think you had a Gulliver interleaved and set right in those mangled and murdered pages. I enquired of several persons where that copy was. Some said Mr. Pilkington had it, but his wife sent me word that she could not find it.[3] . . . To say the truth, I cannot with patience endure that mingled and mangled manner as it came from Motte's hands, and it will be extremely difficult for me to correct it by any other means, with so ill a memory and so bad a state of health.

---

[1] The Travels formed the third volume of Faulkner's edition of Swift's works (*supra*, p. 390). As appears from subsequent letters, Motte had not made use of the corrections, which Swift had sent him through Ford (*supra*, vol. iii, p. 373).

[2] The Rev. Andrew Tooke, master of the Charterhouse, and translator and editor of various classical works. He was a son of Motte's predecessor, Benjamin Tooke, and had died in the previous year (" D. N. B.," lvii, 39).

[3] See the preceding letter.

SUPPLEMENTAL LETTERS

CMXIIA. [*Original.*[1]]

VISCOUNTESS BOLINGBROKE TO SWIFT

[1728.][2]

MR. POPE m'a fait grand plaisir, Monsieur, de m'assurer que votre santé est bonne; et de me montrer dans une de vos lettres des marques de l'honneur de votre souvenir. Je trouve que vous prenez fort mal votre tems d'habiter votre Dublin pendant que nous habitons notre Dawley. Nous aurions eu grand soin de vous cet hiver, et nous aurions haï ensemble le genre humain, autant qu'il vous auroit plû, car je trouve qu'il n'embellit point au croître. On a fait deux pieces de theatre en France, tirées soi-disant des idées de Gulliver. Je ne vous les envoye point, car elles sont detestable: mais cela prouve au moins, que ce bon voyageur a si bien réussi chez nous, qu'on a crû, qu'en mettant seulement son nom aux plus mauvaises pieces, on les rendroit recommendables au publique. Notre fermier vous embrasse: il a plaint et boude de ce que vous este parti sans qu'il ait pu vous dire adieu; et de ce qu'il a vu une de vos lettres, ou vous ne dites pas un mot pour lui: mais je vous croye comme les coquettes, qui se fiant a leurs charmes ne s'embarassent pas de leurs torts. En effet ils vous seront pardonnés a la premiere lettre, et encore plus aisement a la premiere esperance de vous revoir. Adieu, Monsieur, portez vous bien, et nous serons content. Je ne m'aviseray pas de vous mander des nouvelles de ce pays ci. Je suis étrangère de plus en plus, et je ne serois tentée de me faire naturaliser, que dans ceux où je pourrois vivre avec vous.

---

[1] In the British Museum. See Preface.
[2] This letter must have been written subsequently to Lady Bolingbroke's letter of 1ˢᵗ February, 1726-7, and was probably sent to Swift in the early months of 1728.

445

CMXIIB. [*Original.*[1]]

VOLTAIRE TO SWIFT

SIR,[2]

[1728.]

I SENT the other day a cargo of French dulness to my Lord Lieutenant.[3] My Lady Bolingbroke has taken upon herself to send you one copy of the Henriade. She is desirous to do that honour to my book, and I hope the merit of being presented to you by her hands will be a commendation to it. However, if she has not done it already, I desire you to take one out of the cargo, which is now at my Lord Lieutenant. I wish you a good hearing; if you have got it, you want nothing. I have not seen Mr. Pope this winter, but I have seen the third volume of the Miscellanea,[4] and the more I read your works, the more I am ashamed of mine.[5] I am, with respect, esteem, and gratitude, Sir,

Your most humble obedient servant,

VOLTAIRE.

Addressed—To the Reverend Mr. Swift, Dean of Dublin.

CMXIIC. [*Scott.*]

SWIFT TO THE EARL OF PETERBOROUGH

MY LORD,[6]

[1733.]

I NEVER knew or heard of any person so volatile and so fixed as your Lordship: you, while your imagination is

[1] In the British Museum. See Preface.

[2] It would appear that Swift had not answered Voltaire's last letter (*supra*, vol. iii, p. 438), but he is believed to have written a brief introduction for a Dublin edition of the English essay, which Voltaire had enclosed in it (Ballantyne's "Voltaire's Visit to England," p. 115).

[3] *I.e.*, Carteret.   [4] *Supra*, p. 359.

[5] Voltaire admired Swift greatly, and said that he had the *ridiculum acre*. He is reported to have stated in later life that he lived with him for three months at Lord Peterborough's, but can hardly have forgotten his English visit so far as to make an assertion so inconsistent with fact (Ballantyne's "Voltaire's Visit to England," pp. 105, 306).

[6] This letter is possibly the one which Swift announced his intention of sending when writing to Pope (*supra*, p. 416).

carrying you through every corner of the world, where you have or have not been, can at the same time remember to do offices of favour and kindness to the meanest of your friends, and, in all the scenes you have passed, have not been able to attain that one quality peculiar to a great man, of forgetting everything but injuries. Of this I am a living witness against you; for, being the most insignificant of all your old humble servants, you were so cruel as never to give me time to ask a favour, but prevented me in doing whatever you thought I desired, or could be for my credit or advantage.

I have often admired at the capriciousness of Fortune in regard to your Lordship. She hath forced Courts to act against their oldest and most constant maxims; to make you a general because you had courage and conduct; an ambassador because you had wisdom and knowledge in the interests of Europe; and an admiral on account of your skill in maritime affairs;[1] whereas, according to the usual method of Court proceedings, I should have been at the head of the army, and you of the Church, or rather a curate under the Dean of St. Patrick's.

The Archbishop of Dublin laments that he did not see your Lordship till he was just upon the point of leaving the Bath:[2] I pray God you may have found success in that journey, else I shall continue to think there is a fatality in all your Lordship's undertakings, which only terminate in your own honour, and the good of the public, without the least advantage to your health or fortune.

I remember Lord Oxford's Ministry used to tell me that, not knowing where to write to you, they were forced to write at you. It is so with me; for you are in one thing an evangelical man, that you know not where to lay your head; and I think you have no house.[3] Pray, my Lord, write to me, that I may have the pleasure, in this scoundrel country, of going about, and showing my depending parsons a letter from the Earl of Peterborough. I am, etc.

---

[1] He was appointed an admiral in 1705 (*supra*, vol. iii, p. 371).

[2] "On Wednesday last," says "Pue's Occurrences" (Nov. 21-23, 1732), "his Grace the Archbishop of Dublin with his lady and family embarked on board the Dublin yacht for Chester, from whence they will proceed to Bath."

[3] *Supra*, p. 416.

APPENDIX I

STELLA AND HER HISTORY

THE mystery that surrounds the birth and life of Stella has for nearly two centuries baffled the inquirer. It is not my intention to attempt to solve the insoluble, or to ask others to believe the incredible, but to relate the incidents which cannot be questioned in her history, and to indicate their relation to the traditions which linger round her name.

The first event in Stella's life that does not admit of controversy is her baptism on 20 March, 1680-1, in the parish church of Richmond in the county of Surrey. According to the record in the register she received then the name of Hester, and although she appears to have herself used that of Esther,[1] the inscription on the tablet to her memory in St. Patrick's Cathedral shows that Hester was known to be her rightful designation.[2] Her father was stated to be Edward Johnson, and that he was an actual person, resident in or near Richmond, may be presumed from the record of the baptism of two further children whose paternity is attributed to him. The first on 12 August, 1683, is Stella's sister Anne, and the second on 8 July, 1688, a boy called Edward.[3] " Her father was a younger brother of a good family in Nottinghamshire," says Swift, "her mother of a lower degree, and indeed she had little to boast of her birth."[4] This information Swift's earlier biographers supplement with the statement that Johnson was steward to Sir William Temple, who was then resident at Richmond,[5] and although later writers have assumed that this statement was a mistake arising from the fact that Stella's mother married as her second husband one who had held that position, there seems no reason to suppose that her first husband may not also have done so.

---

[1] She so signs her will. See Wilde's " Closing Years of Swift," p. 97.
[2] *Infra*, p. 462.
[3] The Publications of the Surrey Parish Register Society, i, 78, 85, 117.
[4] " Prose Works," xi, 127. The last words of the sentence are usually understood to apply to Stella, but as Mr. Howard Williams points out (" English Letters and Letter Writers," p. 9) they evidently refer to her mother.
[5] Orrery's " Remarks," p. 22.

But there is a widely prevalent opinion that the introduction of Johnson's name was a subterfuge, and that Stella's father was in reality Sir William Temple. It is founded chiefly on the considerable property bequeathed to her by Temple, and on the resemblance which she is said to have borne to him, and is corroborated by an article which professes to be written by one who knew Stella's mother towards the close of her life. According to this article, which appeared in the year 1757 in the "Gentleman's Magazine," [1] the relationship of Temple to Stella was universally recognized, and Temple informed her himself of "the history of her birth." Johnson is said to have been an unsuccessful merchant, who became master of a trading sloop which ran between England and Holland, and to have died in the latter country, and Stella's mother is represented as an accomplished woman, "the same among women that Sir William Temple was among men," and as being the divinity depicted by the poet Pomfret in "The Choice." It is difficult to believe that Swift's allusions in the Journal to Stella can be to the same person, or that Temple could have bracketed such a woman with his other servants when making his will.[2] "She was a person of a surprising genius," says the writer; "few women ever exceeded her in the extent of her reading; none in the charms of conversation. She had seen the world; her address and behaviour were truly polite, and whoever had the pleasure of conversing with her for a quarter of an hour was convinced that she had known a more genteel walk in life than her present situation confined her to. She was not so happy in her person as her mind; for she was low of stature, and rather fat and thick than well shaped; yet the imperfection of her shape was fully compensated by a set of fine features, and an excellent complexion, animated by eyes that perfectly described the brightness of her genius." Apart from the difficulty of reconciling this description with other allusions to Stella's mother, there are inaccuracies in the article which throw doubt on its authenticity, such as that Stella's migration to Ireland took place in the lifetime, and by the order, of Temple, and in the writer's belief, under the conduct of Swift, although he adds that he is not so confident of this, as that her mother parted from her as one whom she was never to see again.

When Swift saw Stella first is not certain. In the character of her, which he began to write on the night of her death, he says that he knew her from six years old, i.e., from the year 1687,[3] while eighteen months before her death in one letter he speaks of their being "perfect friends" for thirty-five years, i.e., from the year 1691, and in another he alludes to "the greatest friend-

---

[1] In the month of November (vol. xxvii, p. 487). The article is signed, C. M. P. G. N. S. T. N. S.

[2] *Supra*, vol. i, p. 22, n. 1.

[3] "Prose Works," xi, 127.

ship" that had existed between them for thirty-three years, *i.e.*, from the year 1693.[1] But it has always been assumed that Swift met Stella first when he went to reside with Temple in the spring of 1689. In the year 1687 he was, so far as is known, resident in Dublin as a student in Trinity College, and the later dates, as has been remarked in a footnote, denote probably the time when Stella's mind began to develop its attractive character, the second year, when she would have been twelve, being evidently the more correct one, as in the earlier year Swift was not residing with Temple.

Little is known of Stella's life at Moor Park. As the illustrations have shown,[2] a cottage in the demesne is now called by her name, and is said to have been inhabited by her mother, but it has been also said to have been occupied by Swift, and lines from Horace over one of the doors were fifty years ago pointed out as originally placed there by him:

> Plerumque gratae divitibus vices;
> Mundaeque parvo sub lare pauperum
> Coenae, sine aulaeis et ostro,
> Sollicitam explicuere frontem.[3]

From the Journal to Stella it is to be gathered that Swift, in addition to directing the books she should read and instructing her "in the principles of honour and virtue," taught her to write; and that she paid from time to time visits to London, and often passed such landmarks as Bagshot Heath and the inn with the sign of the Golden Farmer.[4] "She was sickly from her childhood until about the age of fifteen, but then grew into perfect health," says Swift,[5] "and was looked upon as one of the most beautiful, graceful, and agreeable young women in London, only a little too fat." The implication here seems to be that she had access to good society, to circles into which she could only have been introduced by the Temple family, but with the exception of a passing, perhaps ironical, reference to her acquaintance with Sir William Wyndham's wife, there is nothing in the Journal to Stella to show that such was the case. It is evident from the Journal, however, on the other hand, that she mixed much with the inhabitants of Farnham, and was acquainted with the vicar Savage, who afterwards displayed alarming leanings to Roman Catholicism, with Swift's friend Geree, and his sisters, one of whom was famed as a mantua maker, and their husbands who were in the Church, and with the dropsical Mrs. White and her old hang-dog husband.[6] If the writer in the "Gentleman's

---

[1] *Supra*, vol. iii, pp. 317, 322.
[2] *Supra*, vol. i, pp. 48, 112.
[3] " Notes and Queries," 2, ix, 9.
[4] " Prose Works," ii, 115, 188.
[5] *Ibid.*, xi, 127.
[6] *Ibid.*, vol. ii, *passim*.

Magazine" is to be believed she far exceeded then in her appearance and dress the rank and fortune of her mother, and was the only one of her mother's children allowed to reside with her at Moor Park, but such an idea is scouted by Deane Swift, who says that when Swift's sister visited Moor Park Stella was in the position of a servant,[1] and in bequeathing to her the lands of Morristown in the county of Wicklow, Temple describes her as "servant to my sister Giffard."[2]

The date of Stella's arrival in Ireland is left blank by Swift in his character of her, but the statement that she was about nineteen years old tends to show that she came to that country in 1700 or 1701. In referring a few months before her death to the triple bond of friendship that had lasted for thirty years, twenty-four of which were passed in Ireland,[3] Swift assigns her removal thither to the year 1703, which is hardly likely to have been correct. The first of his account-books, which have been preserved,[4] covers twelve months from 1 November, 1702, and discloses that the relations which became so familiar at a later time were then well established. The entries during the year 1703 include on 17 April: "advanced to MD for rent half year £5"; on 4 May "advanced to MD £2"; on 16 September "treat MD 2s. 8½d.";[5] and on 11 October "MD for coffee 1s. 9d." But it also reveals, what has not hitherto been noticed, that Swift gave MD an allowance of £50 a year. In the year 1702-3 it was paid by himself, quarterly, in four sums of £13, £12, £13, and £12, but subsequently the payments seem to have been sometimes made by his agent Parvisol, and blanks occur under the mystic symbols MD,[6] which invariably occupy a foremost place in his expenditure.

From the time of her arrival Stella appears to have resided principally in Dublin, where she became known to Swift's friends. "Her own lodgings, from before twenty years old," he says,[7] "were frequented by many persons of the graver sort who all respected her highly, upon her good sense, good manners, and conversation." One of her most frequent visitors at first was no doubt the hero of the famous proposal, William Tisdall, who filled then amongst Swift's intimates a position somewhat similar to that occupied subsequently by Sheridan, and, as an indication of her good abilities, Swift mentions that Primate Lindsay, Bishop Lloyd,

---

[1] "Essay," p. 89.

[2] Sieveking's "Sir W. Temple upon the Gardens of Epicurus," p. lxiv.

[3] *Supra*, vol. iii, p. 415.

[4] Forster Collection, Nos. 505-510.

[5] *I.e.*, half-a-crown British currency.

[6] The symbols more resemble MC than those which have been interpreted as MD in other places.

[7] "Prose Works," xi, 134.

Bishop Brown, Bishop Stearne, and Bishop Pullein were amongst those who sought her society. All these have come under notice as friends of Swift in the Correspondence, excepting Pullein, who was raised to the episcopal bench in the reign of William and Mary, and who may have made acquaintance with Stella through Jemmy Leigh,[1] to whom he was related by marriage.

Her conflict with burglars, which Swift says occurred when she was about twenty-four, no doubt took place while she was lodging in William Street, then an outskirt of the city,[2] and probably, as the circumstances were known to him, while the Duke of Ormond was resident in Dublin, *i.e.*, between 1703 and 1705. Of the occurrence Swift gives this account:[3] "She and her friend having removed their lodgings to a new house which stood solitary, a parcel of rogues, armed, attempted the house where there was only one boy. . . . Having been warned to apprehend some such attempt, she learned the management of a pistol; and the other women and servants being half dead with fear, she stole softly to her dining-room window, put on a black hood to prevent being seen, primed the pistol fresh, gently lifted up the sash, and taking her aim with the utmost presence of mind, discharged the pistol, loaden with the bullets, into the body of one villain, who stood the fairest mark. The fellow, mortally wounded, was carried off by the rest, and died the next morning, but his companions could not be found." The writer in the "Gentleman's Magazine" relates also the occurrence with considerable embroidery and animus to the Irish people. According to him "her noble air, her genteel appearance, and the visits of many persons of distinction" gave rise to a report that she was possessed of money and jewels of great value, and attracted "the notice of indigent villainy" as it could not fail to do in a country like Ireland. He goes on then to relate that on the night "destined to deprive the world of one of its most distinguished ornaments," since in Ireland "robbery and murder are terms synonymous," a burglar appeared at her bed-room window, to which he had climbed by a ladder while she was engaged at her devotions, and that instead of fainting or screaming, "the daughter of Sir William Temple," who knew "the cruel temper of the vulgar Irish" fetched a pistol from her closet and fired it "at the villain who immediately dropped from the ladder." Whether for greater security or not Stella appears to have removed soon after this episode to a place of greater security near St. Mary's Church, which was a more thickly populated part of Dublin.

Stella and her companion, Rebecca Dingley, doubtless went then, however, from time to time to the country, and stayed as

---

[1] *Supra*, vol. i, p. 43.   [2] *Supra*, vol. i, p. 41.
[3] "Prose Works," xi, 130.

they did at a later period either with friends or in lodgings. "O dear MD contrive to have some share of the country this spring," wrote Swift a few years later,[1] "go to Finglas, or Donnybrook, or Clogher, or Killala, or Louth." At Finglas and Clogher the Ashe fraternity reigned, at Donnybrook there were the Stoytes with their world of dinners and card-parties, at Killala Swift's friend Bishop Lloyd dominated the neighbourhood, and in the county of Louth there were the Leighs and the Tennisons. About the year 1707 the ladies ventured to cross the water, and paid the only visit to England that they are known to have made during their residence in Ireland. From Swift's letter to Archdeacon Walls in January 1707-8, it is evident that they had gone to England before Swift crossed to that country in November 1707 in the train of Lord Pembroke. "The ladies of St. Mary's are well," he writes, "and talk of going to Ireland in spring." If Deane Swift is not mistaken in his dates, it is possible that they had been in England for two years.[2] In April, as the reference to their dog, Pug, in Swift's letter to Stearne shows, they were still in London, but they must soon afterwards have returned to Ireland, for before November Swift had sent nine letters to MD and had received eight.[3]

During his residence in Ireland, from the summer of 1709 to the autumn of 1710, Swift saw much of Stella. In the Journal a year later he writes: "I am resolved when I come to keep no company but MD; you know I kept my resolution last time, and, except Mr. Addison, conversed with none but you and your club of Deans and Stoytes."[4] The second and third of his account-books, which cover two years from 1 November, 1708, confirms his assertion that such had been the case. Within a few weeks of his landing, on 6 July, money is noted as given to MD, and during the next twelve months "treat MD," and "coach MD," are not infrequent items. For at least a fortnight in the spring Stella and her companion were at Laracor, either in the vicarage with Swift, or in the cottage on the road thence to Trim which tradition says was their abode. Subsequently they appear to have gone elsewhere, possibly to Trim, and did not return home, i.e., to Dublin, until July.

Immediately after Swift's departure for London at the end of August 1710, Stella and her companion moved to his lodgings in Dublin, "at Mr. Curry's house over against the Ram in Capel Street," but five months later they returned to the lodgings close by, which had gained them the name of the St. Mary's ladies, at Mrs. de Caudres's house "over against St. Mary's Church near Capel Street." There they remained until Swift returned in the

---

[1] "Prose Works," ii, 169.
[3] *Supra*, vol. i, pp. 82, 119.
[2] *Supra*, vol. i, p. 71.
[4] "Prose Works," ii, 170.

summer of 1713 for his installation as Dean of St. Patrick's. What was the reason of their leaving his lodgings does not transpire. Although Swift believed that if they did not spend the money one way they would spend it another, and that it was not much matter, their occupation of his lodgings was an economy. " I compute you ought to save eight pounds by being in the others five months, and you have no more done it than eight thousand." The St. Mary establishment he regarded as the height of extravagance: "you'll be as poor as rats; that place will drain you with a vengeance." Possibly a desire for more gape-seed may have accounted for their preference of their old quarters, as Stella, who was apparently not a good church-goer, is pictured peeping out of her room "upon the folks as they come from church." [1]

Stella was not well when Swift left Ireland. "God Almighty bless poor Stella and her eyes and head. What shall we do to save them, poor dear life. . . . Would to Heaven I were this minute shaving your poor dear head either here or there." Her mother and he discussed her ailments, and agreed that exercise was the remedy. "Use exercise and walk; spend pattens and spare potions: wear out clogs and waste claret." But Stella relied on drugs and the advice of her medical friends, and expressed much anxiety about certain "palsy drops." [2] In the following spring she had some idea of going to Bath, and Swift urged her to do so if either the doctors, or her own fancy, gave reason for hope that the waters might be of benefit, and sent her money to defray the expenses. [3] But finally she decided to try a spa nearer home, and set out with Dingley for one at Wexford, where they stayed two months and spent thirty pounds. Swift, who had no faith in an Irish well, held the place, the company, the diversions, and the victuals up to ridicule, and prophesied that they would have to lie in sackcloth and straw, and to eat boiled chicken without parsley or butter, but the spring, which was a chalybeate one, was then in great repute, and was frequented by many leading Irish people. Archbishop King was amongst those who had tried its waters, and the ladies, who were accompanied by the wife of Proby, the great surgeon, met there the Bishop of Raphoe and a Fellow of Trinity College. During the following summer Stella drank waters even nearer home, at a place called Templeogue, five miles to the south of Dublin. This spring, which was also a chalybeate one, was apparently unknown then to Swift, but some years later became very popular as a fashionable

---

[1] "Prose Works," ii, 1, 108, 133, 143, 334.
[2] Ibid., pp. 35, 62, 125, 273.
[3] Ibid., p. 151.

resort, and boasted a journal of its own in which the gay doings of its visitors were recorded.[1]

In the January after Swift went to England Stella stayed on a visit at Donnybrook, and in the following one spent a fortnight with Thomas Ashe and his wife at their house near Finglas. During the autumn of the latter year she paid also, with Dingley, a long visit to Swift's cousin, Mrs. Swanton and her husband, on the coast about ten miles to the north of Dublin, in a peninsula known as Portrane, the place of which Pilkington subsequently became rector.[2] It was then a most deserted spot, marked only by a castle, in which the Swantons are said to have resided, and a church, and so remained until of recent years, when a great asylum for the mentally afflicted has been established there.[3]

Swift was constantly enjoining upon the ladies the necessity of frugality and of being good managers, and the items of their household expenses from November 1711 to March 1713, which are entered by Stella at the end of the third of his account-books, show that he had inspired her with his own extraordinary love of detail. The following are examples:

From Decr 22 to 29

—	Beef 1ˢ 6ᵈ, Pork 1ˢ 6ᵈ, A Fowle 8½ᵈ	.	0 3 8½
—	Butter 9ˢ, Washing 5ˢ 5ᵈ, Starch 5½ᵈ	.	0 14 10½
24	Sugar 11ᵈ, Wine 8ᵈ, Ale 3ᵈ, Coffee &c. 11ᵈ		0 2 9
26	Wine 4ᵈ, Bread 2ᵈ, Cream 1ᵈ, Mutton 7ᵈ .		0 1 2
28	A Pye 2ᵈ, Bread 8ᵈ, Milk 1ᵈ . . .		0 0 11

1 3 5

From Jan^r 23 to Feb^r 1 we were at Ballygall

Spent in that time	0 2 4
To Servants	0 6 6

0 8 10

---

[1] "Prose Works," ii, 202, 213, 238, 247, 372, and Rutty's "Mineral Waters of Ireland," pp. 143, 159.

[2] "Prose Works," ii, 108, 358, 382, 387, 398.

[3] See Miss Cobbe's article on "A Relic of Swift and Stella" (*supra*, vol. iii, p. 241). She was under the impression that the pickaxe was acquired by Stella while staying at Portrane.

From July 5 to 12

—	Beef 1ˢ 10ᵈ, Bread 6ᵈ, Bacon &c. 6ᵈ . . .	0	2	10
7	Mutton 1ˢ 6ᵈ, Gibbits 4ᵈ, Eggs 1ᵈ, Pepper 1ᵈ .	0	2	0
—	Flower 4ᵈ, Butter 2ᵈ, Roles 2ᵈ, Cockles 4ᵈ .	0	1	0
—	Roots 1ᵈ, Ale 8ᵈ, Baking 2ᵈ, Coffee 1ˢ . .	0	1	11
9	Starch 1ˢ 8ᵈ, Butter & Cream 1ˢ 4ᵈ . . .	0	3	0
10	Mutton 6ᵈ, Ale 3ᵈ, Coffee 6ᵈ, Lobster 7ᵈ . .	0	1	10

0 12 7

. . . .

We went to Portrain Augˢᵗ 20 and returned home Septʳ 9; spent while we were there

To Servants 0 11 0
To Margaret 0 3 11

0 14 11

. . . .

We went to Portrain the second time Septʳ 18 returned home Nov. 26 1712; spent in that time

To Servants 1 1 9
Spent and laid out by Margaret . . 0 16 1

1 17 10

. . . .

From Febʳ 28 to Mar. 7

—	Calf's Pluck & Bacon 8ᵈ	0	0	8
2	Mutton 8ᵈ, Bread 6ᵈ, Wine 1ˢ	0	2	2
3	Bacon &c. 6ᵈ, Roots 2ᵈ, Eggs 2ᵈ . . .	0	0	10
—	A Pullet 10ᵈ, Cakes 1ˢ 3ᵈ	0	2	1
6	Mutton 11ᵈ, Bread 6ᵈ, Wheat 3ᵈ . . .	0	1	8
—	Wine 1ˢ, Furs 1½ᵈ,[1] Coals 5ˢ 5ᵈ . . .	0	6	6½
—	Paid for Tea	2	2	0

2 15 11½

When Swift arrived in Ireland for his installation as Dean of St. Patrick's in the summer of 1713, it is doubtful whether Stella was in Dublin or at Trim, but she stayed evidently at the latter place while he was at Laracor. The fifth of his account-books covers that year, and between the day he left Dublin for Laracor, June 25, and July 18, the item "Dinner MD &c." occurs three times, the expenditure in the last two cases being 2s. 8d., and on the 21st there is "Dinner, wine, ale, &c. MD 6ˢ 6ᵈ." On his returning to Dublin for the christening of Walls's child she appears to have accompanied him, and was there when he crossed back to England.

[1] *I.e.*, furze.

Of the remaining years of Stella's life, the years of absorbing interest, little knowledge is to be gathered. First hand authorities are few, and the information imparted by them is scanty. As the Correspondence has shown, on Swift's return to England after his installation, Stella went again to Trim. She had an idea that country air would do her good, but Swift and Archdeacon Walls believed that she would be as well "where company was stirring." Swift declined to give advice himself, but thought that Walls ought to do so, and force "the black lady" to return to Dublin for Christmas. Whether Walls was successful or not there is nothing to show, but in the following March there is again a reference to the ladies "being not in town."[1] In the fateful year in which the supposed marriage ceremony is said to have taken place, the year 1716, Walls's house "over against the Hospital in Queen Street" was the Dublin residence of Stella and her companion. They appear to have gone to live with him and his wife about the time Swift returned from England in 1714, and to have spent the greater portion of the three succeeding years with them. The Christmas after the supposed marriage ceremony in the garden at Clogher was spent by the ladies with Bishop Stearne at Dromore, whither they were accompanied by Walls's wife, and where they expected Swift to join them.[2]

The sixth of Swift's account-books, which covers twelve months from 1 November, 1717, contains some interesting references to MD's dinners at the Deanery, but it must not be concluded that Swift and she were living at a distance from each other during all the intervals, as other entries show that was not the case:

Nov.	2	Dinner MD ..	2	0			MD, Grattan, Sheridan ..	7	8½
	9	Dinner MD, Walls, etc. ..	5	7	May	23	MD, bottling dinner ...	4	6
	16	Dinner MD ..	6	0		29	Dinner MD ..	5	0
	28	Dinner MD at home ...		5½	Aug.	30	Dinner MD, Sheridan ..	5	0
	29	Dinner MD ..	1	8	Sept.	5	Dinner MD, Eustace, Jervas . .	5	5½
	30	Birthday dinner, MD, etc. ..	10	6		20	Dinner MD, Grattan	4	9½
Jan.	15	Dinner, hogshead,[3] MD ..	5	11½	Oct.	1	Dinner MD, Grattan, etc. ..	3	10
	30	Dinner Raymond, MD, Prebendary Grattan. ..	11	9		4	Dinner MD, Grattan, Jacksons .	6	11
May	10	Dinner MD, Grattan, etc. ..	4	6		17	Dinner MD, Ric.	3	7
	17	Dinner Jervas,				23	Dinner MD, Grattan, Jacksons .	6	5

The money invested by Swift in South Sea stock belonged, no

---

[1] *Supra*, vol. ii, pp. 67, 69, 77, 94, 132.
[2] See Swift's letters to Walls, *supra*, vol. ii, pp. 256-368.
[3] *I.e.*, when one was broached.

doubt, in part to Stella,[1] and this was evidently not the only scheme by which he sought to increase her income. Two deeds, the contents of which have been communicated to "Notes and Queries"[2] by Dr. Stanley Lane-Poole, relate no doubt to investments in regard to which he came to her aid. By the first, which is dated 20 May, 1718, she assigned to him for a consideration of £200, a "house messuage or tenement, commonly called or known by the name of Talbot's Castle," in Trim, and by the second, which is dated 28 November, 1721, she assigned to him in consideration of a sum of £158 10s. 10d., "all those houses or tenements, with their backsides, stables, and gardens, late in the possession of one Hudson in St. Patrick Street, Dublin, with one moiety of the close or field near Cullenswood, in the county of Dublin, formerly in the possession of Thomas Gavan." The witnesses in both cases are Rebecca Dingley, "of the city of Dublin spinster," and David Bourne, "of Trim gentleman," and, as Dr. Lane-Poole is careful to point out, in both documents Stella is described as "spinster."[3]

The custom of sending verses to Stella on her birthday, the 13th of March, appears to have begun at the time Swift's "poetical muse" revived under the influence of Sheridan.[4] The first verses of the kind which are known were sent to her in the year 1718-9:

> Stella this day is thirty-four,
> (We shan't dispute a year or more;)
> However, Stella, be not troubled,
> Although thy size and years are doubled
> Since first I saw thee at sixteen,
> The brightest virgin on the green;
> So little is thy form declined,
> Made up so largely in thy mind.[5]

For 1719-20 no verses are forthcoming. It is possible that Swift was at the time too ill to write any,[6] and that the poems "To Stella visiting me in my sickness" and "To Stella who collected and transcribed his poems," which were written in that year,[7] were substituted. During the succeeding years, excepting that of 1725-6, the annual tribute did not fail and has been preserved.[8] On one occasion at least Stella attempted a reply, in the lines beginning:

> St. Patrick's Dean, your country's pride,
> My early and my only guide,

---

[1] *Supra*, vol. ii, p. 148.   [2] 8, ii, 302.
[3] Her name is spelled Johnston, but as the contents of the deeds are given from a copy the insertion of the "t" may have been a mistake of the transcriber.
[4] *Supra*, vol. iii, p. 75, n. 3.   [5] "Poetical Works," ii, 26.
[6] *Supra*, vol. iii, pp. 43, 53.   [7] "Poetical Works," ii, 28, 32.
[8] *Ibid.*, pp. 26, 37, 38, 45, 48, 51.

which were sent to him in 1721 on his birthday.[1] Her contributions to the "Elegy on Demar," a few lines asking the celestial powers to bestow on her mind what Time takes from her face, and her lines on Jealousy,[2] are her only other attempts at versification that have come down to us.

Notwithstanding Vanessa's shadow the ladies were then as much with Swift as they had ever been. In the verse letter to Sheridan in December 1719 they are introduced as partners in the amusements of Saul and David:

Mrs. Dingley and Mrs. Johnson say truly they don't care for your wife's company, though they like your wine, but they had rather have it in their own house to drink in quiet;

However they own it is very civil in Mrs. Sheridan to make the offer, and they cannot deny it,[3]

and a few months later Stella came to the Deanery, apparently for the first time, to nurse Swift in his sickness:

> How shall I act is not the case;
> But how would Brutus in my place?
> In such a case would Cato bleed?
> And how would Socrates proceed?[4]

The famous "answer to no letter" in April 1721 shows that the ladies, who appear to have been again inmates of Archdeacon Walls's house, often took then a frolic to the Deanery, and about the same time they appear to have gone with Swift on a visit to his friend the Rev. Thomas Wallis.[5] In the year 1722 Swift saw the ladies lamenting in spring the absence of Dan Jackson from their japan-board, and bid good-bye to them temporarily when they went to stay for Christmas with the Ludlows at Ardsallagh.[6]

Until that time Stella, although subject to occasional attacks of illness, appears to have enjoyed what may be considered good health, and was able to take an amount of riding exercise that would hardly have been possible for other than a fairly strong person. But in the month of February 1722-3 Swift drops a remark that tends to indicate that a change had come and that the illness of which she died had set in. "The ladies are as usually," he begins; but then seems forced to sound a lower note and adds: 'Mrs. Johnson eats an ounce a week which frights me from dining with her."[7] In such a condition she was ill prepared to hear two months later the confirmation of her fears as to a rival, and the whirl of gossip that succeeded Vanessa's death, and probably only

---

[1] "Poetical Works," ii, 35.   [2] *Ibid.*, i, 96; ii, 46.
[3] *Ibid.*, ii, 320.   [4] *Ibid.*, 32.
[5] *Supra*, vol. iii, pp. 79, 82.   [6] *Supra*, vol. iii, pp. 129, 147.
[7] *Supra*, vol. iii, p. 158.

STELLA'S COTTAGE NEAR LARACOR
From a photograph by Mr. Thomas J. Westropp, M.A. Dubl.

for Ford's kindness of heart and thought she would not have survived the blow. Whatever may have passed between them, no one can doubt that the old terms were resumed on Swift's return from his southern journey. The verses on "Stella at Wood Park" breathe tender affection on his part, and the verses addressed to her on her next birthday describe her "like an humble slave" attending on him when "tormented with incessant pains."[1]

Sheridan is said by Delany[2] to have visited Stella often while she was staying with Ford, and to have "used his utmost efforts to relieve, support and amuse her in this sad situation." From that time an intimate friendship between them is evident. The opening of the next year saw the ladies, Swift, and Sheridan together at Quilca,[3] and possibly other visits were made there before the long stay of six months in the year 1725. During it there are several references to her health, and in spite of bad days, Swift thought that some amendment was perceptible. But her strength no longer permitted the gallops that were customary in the past, and probably "the hitch in her horse's pace" was not the real cause of her finding "his gait too uneasy to bear."[4] Still Swift hoped her disease could be cured, and all the year was bent on her going to Montpelier, Bath, or Tunbridge.[5]

Soon after Swift went to England in March 1726, Stella, who was staying in the Deanery, became very ill, but would not allow Swift to be told. He seems, however, to have suspected the truth, and "feared the worst that was possible and doubted the accounts that were sent him." Early in July he learned from Sheridan and Worrall that her state was critical, and towards the end of the month that there was little hope. Swift believed that to see her die was more than he could bear, and hesitated to return, being only induced to do so finally by a letter of admonition from Sheridan.[6] The autumn was passed by Stella in the country, where she had the reviving companionship of Swift,[7] and under it she made what appears to have been an astonishing rally. When going to England the second time in the following April he was able to write cheerfully of her. "The ladies are now with me," he says, "they come to live at the Deanery for this summer."[8] But four months later the closing scenes began and Swift hourly expected "the most fatal news that could come to him." He appears then to have been very anxious to return and fretted because his own ailments and subsequently the elements delayed him.[9] Again his presence brought relief, but the improvement was only the

[1] " Poetical Works," ii, 40, 45.
[2] " Observations," p. 39.
[3] *Supra*, vol. iii, p. 187, n. 3.
[4] *Supra*, vol. iii, pp. 253, 258.
[5] *Supra*, vol. iii, p. 324.
[6] *Supra*, vol. iii, pp. 314-327.
[7] *Supra*, vol. iii, p. 355.
[8] *Supra*, vol. iii, p. 385.
[9] *Supra*, vol. iii, pp. 415-418.

flickering of the candle before it is extinguished, and on 28 January, 1727-8, Stella passed from him.

Beyond the fact that Swift composed three prayers for Stella in "her last sickness," nothing is known with certainty of their relations immediately before her death. One of the prayers, dated 17 October, was written on his return from London, and another, dated 6 November, a few weeks later.[1] According to Sheridan Stella adjured Swift on her death-bed to acknowledge her as his wife, and was deserted by him in her last hours,[2] and according to Sir Walter Scott he offered to acknowledge their marriage, but she replied it was too late.[3] The last conversation is said to have been overheard by Mrs. Whiteway, who had then no intercourse with Swift.[4]

Four weeks before her death, on 30 December, 1727, Stella made her will, which was evidently inspired by Swift.[5] The principal portion of her fortune was bequeathed for the endowment of a chaplaincy in Dr. Steevens's Hospital, of which her friend Proby had been the surgeon, but a life interest in it was left to her "dear mother Bridget Mose of Farnham in Surrey" and her "dear sister Ann Johnson alias Filby."[6] To Dingley she left her "little watch and chain and twenty guineas," and Swift's cousin, Mrs. Swanton, and a member of the Temple family, Mrs. Jane Temple, are also remembered. Provision for the apprenticing of a child, "who now lives with me and whom I keep on charity," is made, and there are bequests to her servants and to the poor of the parish in which she should die. To Swift she left her strong box and her papers whether in it or elsewhere. Sheridan, John Grattan, Nim Rochfort, and Francis Corbet, afterwards a successor of Swift in the deanery, were the executors.

A tablet, which is said to have been erected not long before the year 1780,[7] marks the place of her interment in St. Patrick's Cathedral. The inscription is as follows: "Underneath lie interred the mortal remains of Mrs. Hester Johnson, better known to the world by the name of Stella, under which she is celebrated in the writings of Dr. Jonathan Swift, Dean of this Cathedral. She was a person of extraordinary endowments and accomplishments in body, mind, and behaviour; justly admired and respected by all who knew her, on account of her many eminent virtues, as well as for her great natural and acquired perfections. She died January

---

[1] "Prose Works," iii, 312. [2] Sheridan's "Life," p. 361.
[3] Scott's "Life," p. 354. [4] Supra, p. 190.
[5] Wilde's "Closing Years," p. 97.
[6] From the Journal to Stella it would appear that Stella's mother did not marry Ralph Mose until after 1713; in the earlier part of the Journal her sister is mentioned as if still unmarried, but towards the end is referred to as the wife of Filby ("Prose Works," ii, 20, 431).
[7] Luckombe's "Tour through Ireland," p. 7.

the 27th 1727/8, in the 46th year of her age, and by her will bequeathed one thousand pounds towards the support of a chaplain to the hospital founded in this city by Doctor Steevens."

APPENDIX II

A CONNAUGHT TRIBUTE TO THE DRAPIER

SIR JOHN BROWNE TO GEORGE FAULKNER

Neale,[1] *February* 14, 1750.

SIR,[2]

I HAVE at last finished, what you have often heard me wish I might be able to do, a monument for the greatest genius of our age, the late Dean of St. Patrick's. The thing in itself is but a trifle; but it is more than I should ever have attempted, had I not with indignation seen a country honoured by the birth of so great a man, and so faithfully served by him all his life, so long and so shamefully negligent in erecting some monument of gratitude to his memory. Countries are not wise in such neglect; for they hurt themselves. Men of genius are encouraged to apply their talents to the service of their country, when they see in it gratitude to the memory of those who have deserved well of them. The ingenious Pere Castel told me at Paris, that he reckoned it the greatest misfortune to him that he was not born an Englishman; and, when he explained himself, it was only for this, that, after two hundred years, they had erected a monument to Shakespeare, and another to a modern, but to the greatest of them, Sir Isaac Newton.[3] Great souls are very disinterested in the affairs of life; they look for fame and immortality, scorning the mean paths of interest and lucre; and, surely, in an age so mercenary as ours, men should not be so sparing to give public marks of their gratitude to men of such virtue dead, however they may treat them living, since in so doing they bespeak, and almost insure to themselves, a succession of such useful persons in society. It was with this view that I have determined to throw in my mite.

In a fine lawn below my house, I have planted a hippodrome. It is a circular plantation, consisting of five walks; the central of which is a horse-course, and three rounds make exactly a mile.

---

[1] Near Ballinrobe in the county of Mayo; now the seat of Sir John Browne's descendant, Lord Kilmaine (*supra*, p. 24).

[2] First printed by Faulkner.

[3] This French mathematician, Louis Bertrand Castel, had published in 1743 a critical account of Newton's system.

All the lines are so laid out, that from the centre the six rows of trees appear but one, and form a hundred arches round the field; in the centre of which I have erected a mount, and placed a marble column on its proper pedestal, with all the decorations of the order; on the summit of which I have placed a Pegasus, just seeming to take flight to the Heavens, and, on the die of the pedestal I have engraved the following inscription, wrote by an ingenious friend:

IN MEMORIAM JONATHAN SWIFT, S. T. P. VIRI SINE PARI.

AONIDVM FONTES APERIS, DIVINE POETA,
ARTE NOVA: ÆTHEREAS PROPRIIS, VT PEGASVS, ALIS
SCANDE DOMOS: ÆTERNVM ADDET TVA FAMA COLVMNÆ
HVIC MEMORI DECVS. HIC, TANTI QVAM POSSVMVS VMBRAM
NOMINIS IN MENTEM, SACRO REVOCARE QVOTANNIS
LVDORVM RITV IVVAT; HIC TIBI PARVVS HONORVM
OFFERTVR CVMVLVS: LAVDVM QVO FINE TVARVM
COPIA CLAVDATVR QVI QVÆRIT, GENTIS IERNÆ
PECTORA SCRVTETVR, LATVMQVE INTERROGET ORBEM.
MDCCL.

I have also appointed a small fund for annual premiums to be distributed in the celebration of games at the monument yearly. The ceremony is to last three days, beginning the first of May yearly. On this day, young maids and men in the neighbourhood are to assemble in the hippodrome, with their garlands and chaplets of flowers, and to dance round the monument, singing the praises of this ingenious patriot, and strewing with flowers all the place; after which they are to dance for a prize: the best dancer among the maids is to be presented with a cap and ribbons, and, after the dance, the young men are to run for a hat and gloves.

The second day, there is to be a large market upon the ground; and the girl who produces the finest hank of yarn, and the most regular reel and count, is to have a guinea premium, and the person who buys the greatest quantity of yarn is to have a premium of two guineas.

The third day, the farmer who produces the best yearling calf of his own breed is to have two guineas premium; and he that produces the fairest colt or filly, of his own breed likewise, not over two years old, shall receive a premium of two guineas also. Thus the whole will not exceed ten pounds, and all these useful branches of our growth and manufacture will be encouraged, in remembering the patron who with so much care and tenderness recommended them to others, and cherished them himself. I am, dear Sir,

Your humble servant,

J. B.

APPENDIX III

A CHAPTER DINNER

March 16, 1715-6.[1]

	£	s.	d.
For coals		3	o
For lemons, chesnuts, oranges and walnuts .		5	o
For salmon		6	o
For cod, whitings, flounders and other fish .		5	5½
For lobsters		10	10
Calf's head		2	6
Meat for gravy			6
Calf's feet and palates . . .			10
A side of lamb		4	6
For butter		9	4
For teals, partridges, grouse and quails .		16	10
For bread		3	o
For cream			8
For charcoal		1	6
Sallett, by his bill		7	11
Oysters		3	4
Sirloin of beef		6	10
Flour		1	6
Mustard			2
Clean man			6
Eggs			6
Cheese			6
	£4	11	5½
Wine from Clackston		14	o
Nelson, the cook, bill . . .	1	10	o
May's bill for wine	1	5	10
Ale and beer		6	2
Wine by Nelson		3	o
Cook, wages		6	o
Washing the linen		1	6
	£8	17	11½

Endorsed—The Chapter Dinner 17 March 1715-6.

[1] Mason's "Hist. of St. Patrick's," p. 291.

APPENDIX IV

SWIFT'S CRITICISM ON DEAN JONES

The following endorsement appears on one of the deeds relating to the property of St. Patrick's Cathedral:[1]

A.D. 1584   A lease of Colemine, made by that rascal Dean Jones, and the knaves or fools his Chapter, to one John Allen, of 81 years to commence from the expiration of a lease of 81 years made in 1583. So here was a lease of 161 years of 253 acres in Saggart parish, within three miles of Dublin, for 2l. per annum. This would not expire till the year 1744, and the lands are now probably worth 150l. per annum, and so near Dublin, and could not then be worth less than 50l. per annum. How this lease was surrendered I cannot tell.

JONATHAN SWIFT.

January 31, 1714-5

APPENDIX V

KNIGHTLEY CHETWODE AND HIS FRIENDS

SOME light is thrown on Knightley Chetwode's life and associates in a number of letters addressed to Forster by his friend Mr. Edward Wilmot-Chetwode, and now preserved in the Forster Collection at South Kensington.[2] These letters, which bear dates half a century old, are written in the graceful easy style of a master in what was even then becoming a lost art, and in reading them one can easily understand Forster's being captivated by his correspondent's personality.[3] As the letters tell, Mr. Wilmot-Chetwode drew his knowledge of Swift's friend from an old and much prized chest of letters which contained a large miscellaneous correspondence of Knightley Chetwode, as well as the Swift and Marlborough[4] letters, and from his examination of its contents had come "to the silent conclusion, which he doubted might have

---

[1] Roscoe's "Works," ii, 853.   [2] Forster MSS., vol. xxxii, no. 110 *et seq.*
[3] *Supra*, vol. ii, p. 241, n. 2.   [4] *Supra*, vol. ii, p. 290, n. 2.

been wrongly founded on some latent stratum of soft feeling of relationship, either that old Knightley was something more than a common man, or else that amongst the private, even country, gentlemen of those days, there was more wit and learning, as well as more high feeling, current than is perhaps usually supposed to have existed in the back settlement of Ireland."[1] His source of information no longer exists, for an extract from the last letter which he appears to have sent Forster shows that the tradition as to the destruction of the Swift and Marlborough letters by damp is true, and that with them perished all the other correspondence. In that letter[2] he says: "Dean Swift's letters are, alas! gone. [My son writes that a great mistake was made in] our stowing away papers, etc., in a vault under my study there [*i.e.*, at Woodbrooke], and that during our years abroad the damp destroyed the papers in that vault. . . . He is still in Ireland, but he wrote to say that Swift's letters were absolutely illegible to him. I think that he will have their decayed remnants brought over, though I am afraid too certainly in a hopeless state. The only thing that remains seems to be to ask you to suggest what is best to be done with the copy which you providentially have got, and to thank God that so much is saved, but of course it will need your kind [help] to set it in the best way as to verification, etc. Our midnight toil was, I trust, complete enough to allow of this, but oh! what a task to impose upon my friend, and I fear without even my bearing a hand in the work, for I have been and still am very ill."

When Mr. Wilmot-Chetwode's correspondence with Forster opened, in the year 1855, he was living at Torquay, and was afraid that he would not be able to give him any useful information about "old Swift," because he was not in the congenial surroundings at "old Woodbrooke." He writes:[3] "Here I am in a lodging-house, away from my old library and my old books, and feeling like the schoolboy who could not dance one step in a new room because there was no *box* in it—an old box having stood in the room in which he learned to dance, and into the ways of which room he had got." However, he sent at last to Woodbrooke for the Swift letters, and a year later forwarded Forster a transcript of them, and of some of the copies of Chetwode's letters to Swift.[4] Forster called for more of the latter, and in response Mr. Wilmot-Chetwode sent him a transcript of a few more, and also of a letter to Knightley Chetwode from Peter Ludlow, and Knightley Chetwode's reply. As Mr. Wilmot-Chetwode observes, the correspondence with Peter Ludlow is "worth reading":

[1] 3 December 1856.   [2] 29 December 1871.
[3] 23 July 1855.   [4] 27 November 1856.

PETER LUDLOW TO KNIGHTLEY CHETWODE

April 16, 1715.

SIR,[1]

I WILL be judged by you now which of us two is the stranger sort of a man, I in happening once to keep my word in a trifle, or you for acknowledging it, and being grateful. To tell you the truth I have thought with great pleasure on our near neighbourhood,[2] but you set such an example that I am startled and think you had even better live where you are in the middle of a bog in a far country;[3] but if you will give me your promise to take pains with me to make me fit company for you, I will do all I can to get you near me. New Hall, I fear, we may throw our caps at, for Lord Meath is dead, and the late Lord Brabazon, who you say was so fond of that place, is now Lord Meath.[4] Upon the receipt of your letter I enquired for Jack Preston,[5] but he was in the country, and on second thoughts I do not know but it was well I missed him, considering what I told you of his lease. Gibson is my father's old friend, but since the management of that affair is not in his hands I do not know where to apply myself, for Jemmy Whitehead and I are two ever since I set the Hill of Tara, and as you observe, that would be a tedious way about. If you will give me any hint how to behave myself to Jack Preston, or to anyone else, I shall be glad to go about it, for my own sake, and not for yours I assure you.

I cannot imagine what reason you have to tell me I do not act fairly; what you complain of is that I am too happy by one half, and I can tell you the world strangely belies your lady, if you are not too happy; I wish my wife and she were often to meet. Let your rats enjoy themselves freely, for they have but a short time, poor creatures, to do it in, and little know, I warrant you, how near they are to their long home. I shall be down soon, but I bar your calling me in your next a ratcatcher, and now I talk of rats, poor Lord W[harto]n is dangerously ill, and so is Sun[derlan]d.[6] Lord Peterborough is forbade Court, and the Archbishop of Canterbury has deputed the Bishop of London for president of the Convocation; all this I suppose you heard before, but I do not

---

[1] See, for notice of Ludlow, *supra*, vol. ii, p. 365, n. 1.
[2] The reference is to Chetwode's change of residence in the county of Meath (*supra*, vol. ii, p. 273).
[3] *I.e.*, at Woodbrooke.   [4] *Supra*, vol. ii, p. 273, n. 1.
[5] His relative by marriage (*supra*, vol. ii, p. 365, n. 1).
[6] *Supra*, vol. ii, p. 278.

remember I ever told you, what I now assure you from a good hand, that I am, with great sincerity, Sir,

Your most faithful friend and obedient servant,

PETER LUDLOW.

Addressed—To Knightley Chetwode at Woodbrooke, near Portarlington.

KNIGHTLEY CHETWODE TO PETER LUDLOW

April 30, 1715.

ON my conscience I believe I must never write to Mr. Ludlow but I must begin with a complaint; but hold! I must first thank you for your kind letter which I received at Woodbrooke, you told me you would be down, as I remember, Passion week, and my passion for your coming made me believe you, and that belief made me ride like a courier to meet you at the sessions, and when I came to the sessions I met a parcel of Whigs, and these Whigs made a bear of me, and beat me for the diversion of the bystanders, and the devil a Ludlow or Ashe or any Tory to help me.[1] Well! for this want of charity one would almost swear you were a Whig. I heard Joney Anderson abused for the business at the Pace,[2] a Pratt for manners had his share to pay, and the glorious memory was drank too, and in short I was forced at last to offer to lay your parent, Preston,[3] a wager that the Lord Midleton[4] would allow me to be as good and as valuable a Whig as he was, which if he had understood as readily as I daresay you will, it is ten to one he would have been too angry to speak a word. Your tenant, Waller, was present, but either so surprised, so overpowered, or so pleased that the devil a word he said for me or my cause.

Well! but as to being your neighbour, for God sake and mine, try to get me New Hall. Mr. Henry, the attorney, has power: pray know if it can be had. I will thank you ever for doing this, but if I can get it, I will say a great many civil things to you. If you cannot succeed, then pray try Preston; he offered to sell me Lismullen, but would keep the park. I did not let him know my intentions, but I beg of you try what terms will be the lowest; a small number of acres, about fifty, would serve me. If I succeed in neither, I must go live in that same bog in a far country as you

---

[1] Chetwode had returned to the county of Meath, from Woodbrooke (*supra*, vol. ii, p. 275).

[2] A village in the county of Meath.

[3] *I.e.*, Ludlow's father-in-law.

[4] The Lord Chancellor, better known as Alan Brodrick.

say, and fatten through your means I will say, how justly it matters not, for this is not a world or a time either to do or say justly, but, however, as I would have you an honest exception to general rule of these times, leave off bantering your friends; let your genius stoop to a level with the country neighbours, and do not banter a poor country justice, *pro hac vice*, as you do in your letter.

I hear you sent down all your domestics in a horse-litter, or a glass which has occasionally represented them. I wish I could catch you at Ardsallagh or here, and instead of calling you a rat-catcher, I wish you would make me one; if you do not do it soon, they will catch me napping some night or other. Damn them by their perpetual noise; they think, I believe, they are Whigs, as Wharton is like Judas gone *ad locum proprium suum*, so I wish his relations, my rats, were with him. I hear you Tories have poisoned Wharton, and design to carry it on. Well! the Lord direct you, and so with my respects to your lady, I assure you with the best heart, as well as hand, I have, that I am with esteem and affection,

Your faithful friend and obedient servant.

I lay at Ashefield; I left Dick and Nancy in some sorrow for a very pretty child, which I left dead in that house.

In the same letter in which he sent the transcript of the Ludlow correspondence, Mr. Wilmot-Chetwode refers to a packet which had come to him from Woodbrooke with the Swift letters, and which contained letters received by Knightley Chetwode during "his exile in France and Holland in 1717 and 1718."[1] "Some of these are interesting," writes Mr. Wilmot-Chetwode, "and evidently from high hands, though generally secured by absence of signatures, often not written and as often torn off." In a later letter,[2] he mentions the existence also of "a curious old pocket-book which Knightley Chetwode had in his exile in the Low Countries and Paris, etc., with many curious notes about things and people in it, and a list of Englishmen in France, no doubt keeping out of the way like himself." Of the contents of the packet and the pocket-book all that reached Forster were the two following poems:

NERO THE SECOND[3]

Monstrum horrendum, etc.

As Nero laughing saw fierce fire consume
Europe's metropolis, imperial Rome,
So George unpitying grinn'd, and senseless sneer'd
When England's capital in flames appeared.

---

[1] *Supra*, vol. iii, p. 10, n. 5.   [2] 15 January 1859.
[3] There has been reference to the circulation of this poem in Dublin (*supra*, vol. ii, p. 285, n. 1).

Nor is the parallel to this confined,
If we compare their guilt of every kind,
Nero possess'd Britannicus's crown;
George has usurp'd our royal James's throne.
Nero deserted his Octavia's charms
To sate his lust in rank Poppaea's arms;
George in a public state of lewdness lives,
Immures his own, debauches others' wives.
Nero with thundering edicts soon began
To try the terror of his brutal reign;
George by his furious proclamation shows
A spirit prone to rage, averse to laws;
Nero in masks and revels spent the night; ⎫
George for the business of the crown unfit, ⎬
In plays and balls and banquets does delight. ⎭
Nero with horror of his crimes grew mad,
Scar'd by the ghosts of those whose blood he shed;
George conscious of his murders gloomy sits,
Worn by the spleen and hypochondric fits;
Nor all his sport can drown his inward care,
For Königsmark is always present there.
Such is our George and such we find his Court,
Where royal idiots with their train resort,
Where Marlborough rules and Ormond is cashier'd,
Where bullies swarm and ruffians are preferr'd,
Where Atheists, Turks and bawds the crown surround,
And a strange monster Ministry compound.
Oh! freeborn Britons, seeing a tyrant reigns,
Assert your liberty, shake off your chains;
Let us in justice rival ancient Rome, ⎫
Let Nero's vices meet with Nero's doom, ⎬
And quickly call King James from exile home. ⎭

[A SECOND BARABBAS]

Divinity and Justice, hand in hand,
Have this day left our poor unhappy land;
Ah! cursed Whigs 'twas you that drove them hence,
'Twas you who mock your God, and hate your Prince;
Bloodthirsty villains, there will come a day,
When you so just a debt, shall to the farthing pay.
The glory of this world to Whigs is given,
Whilst the poor Jacks by Tyburn go to Heaven;
Thus differing in their fate, as in their sense,
Are damn'd and favoured both by impenitence.
The Jews, though justly blamed for their offence,
Did Christ their God betray for thirty pence,
Yet Britons more for villainy renown'd,
Bid for their King an hundred thousand pound,
And in their choice, to be as like the Jews,
Abjur'd their God, and Barabbas did choose.

N.B.—Barabbas was a robber.

In the letter in which he enclosed these verses [1] Mr. Wilmot-Chetwode refers to "a very interesting correspondence" between

[1] 22 December 1856.

Knightley Chetwode and the second Duke of Chandos, which began while the Duke was Marquis of Carnarvon, and to a bundle of "admirably written" letters from William Phillips of Hammersmith between the years 1730 and 1737. He then goes on writing from Torquay: "There may be a few more letters at Woodbrooke, where his old library and his well marked and noted books seem to tell that Knightley was well versed in Latin and French, as well as old English authors, notwithstanding the wonder expressed in Swift's last bitter letter,[1] when alas! they quarrelled as to where he, a mere country squire, could have got hold of so much Latin and Divinity, which observation seems to have drawn forth a letter of the sarcastic power of his own pen against his great opponent. It was a cruel pity that such an interesting correspondence should have ended in such a way, but poor Knightley, I fear, must have been a little pugnacious. I find his apparently warm friend, the Duke of Chandos, in 1746, endeavouring to make up a quarrel between him and George Jeffreys,[2] whilst a curious old relic of his at Woodbrooke, a dagger, whose hilt is inscribed with the words, 'let the dead tell,' seems to imply that he did not go unarmed. However, he lived in troublous times, and seems to have had his share of tossing. He seems to have been a determined man, and having taken up the cause of what he considered loyalty to have stuck to it, as long as a rag of it remained nailed to the mast of his small bark, and thereby, I take it, to have lost the succession to his more lucky cousin's [3] English property which naturally should have come to him."

From Woodbrooke Mr. Wilmot-Chetwode added subsequently [4] a long list of persons with whom Knightley Chetwode had from time to time corresponded, including John Brownlow, Baron Charleville and Viscount Tyrconnel, whom Mrs. Delany refused to marry and described as "vastly rich, good-natured and silly"; James Caulfeild, third Viscount Charlemont, the father of the celebrated Earl of Charlemont, who was connected by marriage with the Ludlows; Major Josiah Champagne, the second Earl of Granard's son-in-law;[5] Charles Howe, of Greatworth, in Northamptonshire, the author of the "Devout Meditations"; William Wynne, serjeant-at-law and author of the "Life of Sir Leoline Jenkins"; Sir John Anstis, Garter King of Arms; and the Bishops of Peterborough and Worcester.

With many of these persons Knightley Chetwode was in correspondence regarding the claim of his family to the barony of

---

[1] *Supra*, p. 225.
[2] The versifier; who has been already mentioned in the capacity of agent to Bishop Hartstonge (*supra*, vol. ii, p. 422).
[3] The son of the Dean of Gloucester (*supra*, vol. ii, p. 290, n. 2).
[4] 14 and 15 January 1859. [5] *Supra*, vol. ii, p. 248.

Wahull, to which, on the death of his cousin, the only son of his uncle, the Dean of Gloucester, he became the heir. Writing to Forster in regard to it,[1] Mr. Wilmot-Chetwode says that the claim is said " to stand alone in its peculiarities," and that the barony is the senior in England, or "would contend the honour with one other house." After the breach with Swift, Knightley Chetwode's mind became entirely engrossed with the subject, and the following letter to Browne Willis, the ecclesiastical antiquary, concerning it is the last glimpse which we get of him:

KNIGHTLEY CHETWODE TO BROWNE WILLIS

St. James's, May 10, 1740.

SIR,[2]

THOUGH I have not the pleasure and advantage of being personally known to you, yet I endeavoured by Mr. Woodnoth's means and acquaintance with you, several times to see you formerly when I heard you were in this town, but was not so fortunate as I hoped and wished in those attempts. Since that time, in the course of my correspondence with my good Lords Bishops of Worcester and Peterborough, and others of my Lords the Bishops, to whom I have wrote about some information from registers, and other matters, in regard to the Barony of Wahull, which I claim as sole lineal heir to John de Wahull and Thomas de Wahull, summoned to Parliament by writ, temp. Edward 1st, and for which I have petitioned the present King, as Sir Richard Chetwode did King James 1st, my Lord Bishop of Peterborough is of opinion that as you are upon a history of Buckinghamshire, and that Sir Richard Chetwode was Lord of Chetwode, and his son Richard, who married Anne, the daughter and one of the co-heirs of Sir Valentine Knightley of Fawsley in Northamptonshire, lived there, as did Valentine Chetwode, my grandfather, and his eldest son, Knightley Chetwode, late Dean of Gloucester, was born at Chetwode, you have it in your power to do me many good offices, and to give me very friendly and material aid and assistance; and his Lordship has empowered and commissioned me to apply to you, and to make use of his name to you, as a gentleman whom he esteems his friend, and believes will on his account, as well as in regard to justice, do me all the favour in your power. I now therefore, Sir, do address myself to you, and request your friendship and favour to me.

That you may be informed of how far I have proceeded, and in what manner, I here enclose to you my petition to his Majesty, and with it a copy of the report made to King James 1st upon

---

[1] 3 December 1856.   [2] Brit. Mus. Addit. MSS., 5833, f. 42.

Sir Richard Chetwode's petition to that King; as also Mr. Serjeant Wynne's opinion upon it, and also his Majesty's order of reference to his Majesty's Attorney General, before whom it now lies, for him to report to the King upon it. It has, as you will observe, been referred to the Attorney General the 31st of last May; but through delays it was not lodged with the Attorney till July following, and when I thought myself ready to attend the Attorney General my own solicitor raised difficulties, which indeed he should have done several months sooner, if any he had. The difficulties started were, to prove my descent down from Sir Richard Chetwode to me, and that I was the sole heir to Sir Richard, and of consequence to John and Thomas, Lord Barons of Wahull. This put me to great trouble and expense, though a little surprising it may seem, and I have, however, at length accomplished it, by the help and assistance of my good Lords the Bishops, and their registers, and other worthy persons, whom I have applied to, in which the good Bishop of Worcester, Dr. Hough, has been most friendly and generous to me, and Dr. Clavering, present Bishop of Peterborough, and others of my Lords the Bishops have wrote to their clergy, and have sent, and delivered to me, the letters which they have received in answer, and with those letters, such extracts out of their registers, as they could meet with, relating to my family.

In the register at Chetwode Church, in your county, which I have had searched, I do not find any entry farther back than the baptism of Dr. Knightley Chetwode, late Dean of Gloucester, my father's eldest brother. The reason of it, as I am informed, is that there have been two leaves of Chetwode register cut out; but when, or by whom, I am quite uninformed. The greatest difficulty that I labour under at present is that Valentine Chetwode, my grandfather, had two elder brothers, by Sir Valentine Knightley's daughter, whom they put me upon proving dead, *sine prole*. To this the Bishop of Worcester says in his letters, that he conceives it a great hardship put upon me, to prove two minors dead, who have been so long reckoned amongst the dead, and from whom, none pretend to claim.

As you, Sir, in the opinion of all the world, are a gentleman of great learning and knowledge, and resident in Buckinghamshire, the county, which for so many ages, my ancestors resided in, I request your aid, and friendly assistance, in these matters, and that you will please to inform yourself as fully as you possibly can, of all that relates to me, my predecessors and family, and favour me with your opinion and advice, upon this whole matter: for the thing presses, and has lain a long time upon the *tapis*. I shall hope, good Sir, to hear from you fully, so soon as you have weighed and considered this affair, which is of so high import and

consequence to me, and my children. Your advice, aid and assistance, and favour to me herein will lay a most lasting obligation
upon me, and oblige me to embrace every occasion and opportunity to approve myself with cordial friendship, Sir,

Your sincere friend and humble servant, etc.,

KNIGHTLEY CHETWODE.

I enclose to you, in a cover, that you may know where to direct
to me, and I pray you to write to me so soon as you can. I pray
you to let me know how your history goes on; for I have some
things in my hands, which probably may be useful to you in the
progress of your undertaking.

Within the cover was written—For the Honble. Knightley Chetwode, Esqr., at George's Coffee House, in St. James's Street,
Westminster.

Addressed—To Browne Willis, Esq., at his house near Fenny Stratford, Bucks, these.

APPENDIX VI

SWIFT'S REPUTED BROTHER

Two inquiries have been made in "Notes and Queries"[1] as to the
following entry in the burial registers of the church of St. Andrew
in Northborough, Northamptonshire, which occurs under the
year 1737, "Thos. Swift Bro. to Dr. Jon. Swift Dean of St.
Patrick's Dublin Dec. 3d," but without eliciting any reply. All
that is known with absolute certainty as to the marriage of Swift's
parents and the birth of their children is that on 25 June, 1664,
James Margetson, Archbishop of Armagh, issued a licence for the
marriage of Jonathan Swift and Abigail Erick "of the city of
Dublin spinster,"[2] and that on 1 May, 1666, in St. Michan's
Church, Dublin, their daughter Jane was baptized.[3]

[1] 7, vi, 225; 8, iii, 447.
[2] Prerogative Grants in P.R.O., Ireland.
[3] *Supra*, vol. i, p. 8, n. 3.

APPENDIX VII

THE SUPPRESSED LETTER TO CHETWODE

To Ventoso

April 28, 1731.

SIR,[1]

YOUR letter has lain by me without acknowledging it longer than I intended, not for want of civility, but because I was wholly at a loss what to say, for, as your scheme of thinking, conversing, and living, differs in every point diametrically from mine, so I think myself the most improper person in the world to converse or correspond with you. You would be glad to be thought a proud man, and yet there is not a grain of pride in you, for you are pleased that people should know you have been acquainted with persons of great names and titles, whereby you confess, that you take it for an honour, which a proud man never does, and besides, you ran the hazard of not being believed. You went abroad, and strove to engage yourself in a desperate cause, very much to the damage of your fortune, and might have been to the danger of your life, if there had not been, as it were, a combination of some, who would not give credit to the account you gave of your transactions, and of others, who either really, or pretending, to believe you, have given you out as a dangerous person, of which last notion I once hinted something to you, because if what you repeated of yourself were true, it was necessary that you had either made your peace, or must have been prosecuted for high treason.

The reputation, if there be any, of having been acquainted with princes, and other great persons, arises from its being generally known to others, but never once mentioned by ourselves, if it can possibly be avoided. I say this perfectly for your service; because an universal opinion, among those who know or have heard of you, that you have always practised a direct contrary proceeding, has done you more hurt, than your natural understanding, left to itself, could ever have brought upon you. The world will never allow any man that character which he gives to himself, by openly confessing it to those with whom he converses. Wit, learning, valour, great acquaintance, the esteem of good men will be known, although we should endeavour to conceal them, however they may pass unrewarded, but, I doubt, our own

---

[1] First printed by Sheridan (*supra*, p. 224).

bare assertions, upon any of those points, will very little avail, except in tempting the hearers to judge directly contrary to what we advance. Therefore, at this season of your life, I should be glad you would act after the common custom of mankind, and have done with thoughts of courts, of ladies, of lords, of politics, and all dreams of being important in the world.

I am glad your country life has taught you Latin, of which you were altogether ignorant when I knew you first, and I am astonished how you came to recover it. Your new friend Horace will teach you many lessons agreeable to what I have said, for which I could refer to a dozen passages in a few minutes. I should be glad to see the house wholly swept of these cobwebs, and that you would take an oath, never to mention a prince or princess, a foreign or domestic lord, an intrigue of state or of love; but suit yourself to the climate and company where your prudence will be to pass the rest of your life. It is not a farthing matter to you what is doing in Europe, more than to every alderman who reads the news in a coffee-house.

If you could resolve to act thus, your understanding is good enough to qualify you for any conversation in this kingdom. Families will receive you without fear or restraint, nor watch to hear you talk in the grand style, laugh when you are gone, and tell it to all their acquaintance. It is a happiness that this quality may, by a man of sense, be as easily shaken off as it is acquired, especially when he has no proper claim to it; for you were not bred to be a man of business; you never were called to any employments at courts; but destined to be a private gentleman, to entertain yourself with country business and country acquaintance, or, at best, with books of amusement in your own language. It is an uncontrolled truth that no man ever made an ill figure who understood his own talents, nor a good one who mistook them. I am, etc.

APPENDIX VIII

THE "COUNTERFEIT" LETTER TO QUEEN CAROLINE

Dublin, *June* 22, 1731.

MADAM,[1]

I HAVE had the honour to tell your Majesty, on another occasion, that provinces labour under one mighty misfortune, which is in a great measure the cause of all the rest, and that is, that they

---

[1] From the original in the Forster Collection.

are for the most part far removed from the Prince's eye, and, of consequence, from the influence both of his wisdom and goodness. This is the case of Ireland beyond expression!

There is not one mortal here, who is not well satisfied of your Majesty's good intentions to all your people, and yet your subjects of this isle are so far from sharing the effects of your good dispositions, in any equitable degree; are so far from enjoying all the good to which they are entitled from your Majesty's most gracious inclinations, that they often find great difficulty how to enjoy even the relief of complaint.

To omit a thousand other instances, there is one person of Irish birth, eminent for genius and merit of many kinds, an honour to her country, and to her sex, I will be bold to say, not less so in her sphere than your Majesty in yours, and yet all talents and virtues have not yet been able to influence any one person about your Majesty, so far as to introduce her into your least notice. As I am your Majesty's most dutiful and loyal subject, it is a debt I owe your Majesty to acquaint you, that Mrs. Barber, the best female poet of this or perhaps of any age, is now in your Majesty's capital; known to Lady Hertford, Lady Torrington, Lady Walpole, etc., a woman whose genius is honoured by every man of genius in this kingdom, and either honoured or envied by every man of genius in England.

Your Majesty is justly reverenced for those great abilities with which God has blessed you, for your regard to learning, and your zeal for true religion. Complete your character, by your regard to persons of genius, especially those, who make the greatness of their talents, after your Majesty's example, subservient to the good of mankind and the glory of God, which is most remarkably Mrs. Barber's case and character.

Give me leave to tell you, Madam, that every subject of understanding and virtue, throughout your dominions, is appointed by Providence of your council, and this, Madam, is an open and an honest apology for this trouble; or, to speak more properly, for this dutiful information. It is your true interest that all your subjects should see that merit is regarded by you in one instance, or rather, that it is not disregarded in any instance. Let them daily bless God for every gift of wisdom and goodness bestowed upon you, and pray incessantly for the long continuance of them; as doth Your Majesty's most dutiful and loyal subject and servant,

JONATH. SWIFT.[1]

Endorsed by Swift—Counterfeit letter from me to the Queen sent to me by Mr. Pope, dated June 22, 1731; received July 19, 1731; given by the Countess of Suffolk.

---

[1] The signature is a very poor imitation of Swift's autograph.

APPENDIX IX

A LAMPOON ON THE REV. WILLIAM TISDALL

DEAR SIR,[1]
You desired me to finish some lines you wrote at Duns-haughlin:

> How can I finish what you have begun?
> Can fire to ripen fruit assist the sun?
> Should Raphael draw a virgin's blooming face,
> Exert his skill to give it every grace,
> And leave the rest to some Dutch heavy drone;
> Would you not rather see that face alone?
> Or should Praxiteles the marble take,
> A Venus' head and neck and shoulders make,
> And some rude hand attempt the rest from thence,
> Would you not think him void of common sense?
> These hints, I hope, will move you to excuse
> The first refusal of my humble muse,
> The task I must decline, and think it just
> Your piece continue as it is a bust.[2]

Being in a vein of writing epigrams, I send you the following piece upon Tisdall which I intend to send to all his acquaintance; for he goes from house to house to show his wit upon me, for which I think it reasonable he should have something to stare him in the face.

UPON WILLIAM TISDALL, D.D.

> When a Roman was dying, the next man of kin,
> Stood over him gaping to take his breath in.
> Were Tisdall the same way to blow out his breath
> Such a whiff to the living were much worse than death.
> Any man with a nose would much rather die,
> So would Jack, so would Dan, so would you, so would I.
> Without a reproach to the Doctor, I think,
> Whenever he dies, he must die with a stink.

---

[1] This fragment of a letter is printed by Sir Walter Scott ("Life," p. 74) from the original in Swift's handwriting, which was then in the possession of the Royal Dublin Society.

[2] Four lines are said to be erased, and there only remains:

> Since merit . . . show
> A golden charm . . . below. . . .

APPENDIX X

LETTERS FROM PILKINGTON TO WILLIAM BOWYER,
AND OTHER LETTERS RELATING TO THE
THIRD VOLUME OF THE MISCELLANY

The Rev. Matthew Pilkington to William Bowyer

November 9, 1731.

Sir,[1]

I have been much surprised at your long silence, and perhaps you have been affected in the same manner at mine. But as I hope always to preserve the friendship we have begun, I must acquaint you with the reasons of my conduct. I have the misfortune to live in a scene of great hurry, and between attending those who live in high stations who honour me with their friendship, and discharging the duties of my profession, I have scarce a moment disengaged, yet I constantly desired my friend Faulkner to write to you in my name, because I imagined it would save postage, and I thought it unreasonable to trouble you with my letters when I had no very urgent business to write to you upon, and had too many obligations to you to think of adding to your expense. But I cannot imagine what you can plead in your excuse for your neglect of writing to me, who am desirous to continue a constant correspondence; I shall be glad to hear you justify yourself.

Yesterday I saw a letter of yours to Mr. Faulkner, and on so distressful a subject that I very sensibly shared in your affliction.[2] I am naturally apt to pity the woes of my fellow creatures, but the wounds of my friend are my own. Here my office ought to be to administer comfort to you in so great a calamity, but I know how much easier it is to preach patience and resignation than to practise either. The strongest reason acts but feebly upon the heart that is loaded with grief, nor is the highest eloquence powerful enough to heal a wounded spirit. Time and a firm trust in Divine Providence, which undoubtedly orders all things for the best, are the only ministers of comfort in our misfortunes, and I

---

[1] Pilkington's letters were first printed by Nichols.
[2] The death of his wife.

hope your own virtue will enable you to bear this affliction with
the resolution of a Christian, though joined with all the tenderness
of a friend and the fondest esteem for the memory of that relation
you have lost.

I desired Mr. Faulkner, about six weeks ago, to return you my
thanks for your kindness in procuring me the books from Mr.
Giles's, which I received safe, and also the box of those writings
of mine, and I am extremely grieved to find that Faulkner neglected mentioning either. I had not known it only for your postscript wherein you desire to know whether I received them. I
would have wrote to you before this, if I had not believed that your
charge was paid; for Dr. Delany is, I believe, by this time in
London, and he wrote to me from Bath for directions where to
find you in London, that he might pay off his bill, and return you
his thanks for your kindness to us. Let me beg the favour of you
to acquaint Mr. Giles with this, because I would not for any consideration seem to forget my creditors, though in another country.
If Dr. Delany be not come to you, I desire you will inquire out his
lodgings; and I believe you may be informed either at Lord
Bolingbroke's or Mr. Percival's in Conduit Street. Tell him your
name whenever you go to wait upon him, and I assure you the
Doctor will be extremely friendly to you, and glad to see you, for
I have often talked to him of you.

I received ninety-four books[1] from you, but I believe you must
commit them to the charge of Mr. Faulkner, because I have no
opportunity of selling but bestowing them; for when any of my
friends are desirous to have one, and ask me where they are to be
had, I am always too generous or too bashful, which is a great
rarity among us Irish, to accept of payment for them, and by this
means I shall be under the necessity of giving all away, which
would be too expensive an article to me. Now what I think
would answer, would be to send what I have not bestowed to
Mr. Faulkner, and let him publish in his newspaper that he has
imported some of those books, and let him be accountable to you
for the sale. I wrote to you for thirty, which I expected to give
away, and I believe I have distributed so many. When I receive
your answer, I will give you a particular account, and remit you
the money for them the first opportunity. If I find Dr. Delany's
lodgings out from any friends here, or from his letters to me, I will
give you immediate notice. I should be glad to have any cata-
logues that were now selling in London, and if you could send
any of them, or any other little pamphlets, they may be directed
to the Lord Bishop of Killala, in Dublin, for me. I never received
either the " Monthly Chronicle " for March, nor the " Historia

---

[1] Copies of the London edition of Pilkington's Poems.

Literaria " for ditto; I believe it miscarried by being directed to
Faulkner; they were not for Dr. Delany, but for another gentleman in town; but I had forgot till the gentleman asked me for
them the other day. I shall be glad to hear from you soon,
and am

Your most sincere friend,

MATT. PILKINGTON.

There is one Green, a bookseller, lately come from London to
this town, who has imported a very curious collection of books,
but he has rated them so excessively dear, and seems to act so
haughtily in the sale of them, that I believe above three-fourths of
them will be sent back to-morrow to England again. I made the
Dean of St. Patrick's go with me there the first morning, but all
the books were too dear for either of us.

SAME TO SAME

February 5, 1732.

SIR,

I FIND you are resolved to lay me under so many obligations
to you, that, upon principles of gratitude, I must be always desirous to promote your interest to the utmost of my power. I
think you have nothing more left to do, but to make the experiment, by putting it in my way to return your favours. I sent
sixty-five books to Mr. Faulkner's, and hope, some time or other,
to have it in my power to make acknowledgments. I find
Mr. Faulkner sent you a little pamphlet of my writing, called
an Infallible Scheme to pay the Debts of this Nation. I have
the honour to see it mistaken for the Dean's, both in Dublin and
in your part of the world, but I am still diffident of it, whether it
will merit esteem or contempt. It was a sudden whim, and I was
tempted to send it into the world by the approbation which the
Dean, my wisest and best friend, expressed when he read it; if
you were concerned in the printing of it, I hope you will be no
sufferer. I am very much obliged to you for receiving the young
printer, whom I recommended to you, in so friendly a manner. If
I can, on this side of the water, be serviceable to any friend of
yours, command me.

I am much pleased to hear of your acquaintance with Dr. Delany,
who is the best of friends, and I do not doubt but your affection
for him will increase with your intimacy with him. I desire you
to present my service to him; and tell him that the Dean designs
to trouble him to buy a convenient microscope, that he may find
out both myself and my house with greater ease than he can at

present, because we are both so excessively small, that he can scarce discover either. I hope to hear soon from you, although it be Parliament time, and you hurried with business; and shall always be

Your sincere friend and servant,
MATT. PILKINGTON.

SAME TO SAME

Dublin, *August* 17, 1732.

SIR,

I RECEIVED your last letter with the note to Mr. North. I am extremely obliged to you for the favour of such a present, and shall be glad to have an opportunity to express my gratitude to you.

I would send with this letter two or three of those papers which I design for your volume, but the Dean is reading them over to try if there be any alteration requisite in any of them. I showed him your note to Mr. North, and I believe he was at least as much pleased as the person who was to receive it. We have thoughts of preparing a preface to your edition in the name of the editor. Let me know whether I shall send the pamphlets by post, and whether you have the Journal of a Dublin Lady, the Ballad on the English Dean, and Rochfort's Journal, because you shall have the copies sent to you and the property effectually secured. I mentioned your request to the Dean, and I shall get you the right of printing the Proposal for Eating Children. I mentioned the alteration of the titles; and he thinks it will be most proper to give them both the Irish and English titles; for instance, the Soldier and the Scholar, or Hamilton's Bawn, etc. I have some hope of being able to send all these in about a week or fortnight's time, and shall venture to send them by post, though it will be expensive. The Dean says he thinks the assignment as full as it is possible for him to write, but that he will comply with any alterations we think proper. I shall expect to hear from you as soon as possible, because I have some schemes to transact which probably I shall acquaint you with in my next letter. I am, Sir,

Your most obliged servant,
MATT. PILKINGTON.

SAME TO SAME

August 28, 1732.

SIR,

I HAVE sent you some of the pamphlets I promised, in as large a parcel as I could venture. The Dean has, with his own hand, made some alterations in some of them. I will by next post, or next but one, send you another pamphlet at least, and a new assignment from the Dean. He received a letter from Mr. Pope and Mr. Motte, but neither have been of the least disadvantage to my request. I cannot say but I am proud of his friendship to me.

I desire that you will insist upon your right by the assignment I formerly sent, and let Mr. Motte show you anything under the Dean's hand which will invalidate it! Our affair is a point where the Dean's honour is concerned, and that very consideration may convince you that your interests will be secured. You shall hear from me more particularly in a post or two.

I send you a catalogue of some of those pieces which you are entitled to print, and if you would add any of the Intelligencers, I can inform you which are the Dean's, and which not.

A catalogue of pieces which you are empowered to print by the Dean's assignment:—the Barrack; an Ode to Ireland, from Horace; a Libel on Dr. Delany and Lord Carteret; to Dr. Delany, on the Libels against him; O'Rourke; the Dressing-room; the Defence of it; the Journal at Rochfort's; the Thorn; City Cries; Project, Bishops' Lands; On Bishops' Leases; Arguments against repealing the Test Act; Considerations on the Bishops' Bills; Vindication of Lord Carteret; Proposal for Eating Children; Poem on the English Dean; Journal of a Dublin Lady.

ALEXANDER POPE TO BENJAMIN MOTTE

August 16, 1732.

SIR,[1]

HAD I had the least thought you would have now desired what you before so deliberately refused, I would certainly have preferred you to any other bookseller. All I could now do was to speak to Mr. Gilliver, as you requested, to give you the share you would have in the property, and to set aside my obligation and covenant with him so far to gratify the Dean and yourself. You cannot object, I think, with any reason to the terms which he pays, and which at the first word he agreed to. I am, Sir,

Your friend and servant,

ALEXANDER POPE.

To Mr. Motte.

[1] First printed by Nichols.

ALEXANDER POPE TO THE REV. MATTHEW PILKINGTON

[*November*, 1732.]

SIR,[1]

SINCE I mentioned to you the pretensions of Mr. Bowyer, the printer, in order to be clear in my intentions of doing justice to him, as well as in those intentions he appealed to, namely the Dean's in that paper he signed, I find by a long letter he sent to Gilliver that he departs from that foot he first put it up upon, and does not seem to leave the matter to the Dean and me at all. His words to me in his letter, which caused me to apply to the Dean, were that he would readily submit to have his claim bounded within such limits as he and I should prescribe. In compliance to his pretension I writ; the Dean answered no man had any title from him more than Curll. Nevertheless I writ again that Bowyer had something under his hand. He answered, his intention was nothing of a perpetuity, but a leave only to reprint [to] Mr. Faulkner and him, with promise not to molest them by any interest of his as to such pieces as were imputed to him. He declares he had no thoughts of giving them a perpetuity, but a permission to the former end only; "however Faulkner and Bowyer may have contrived to turn those papers into a property." These are his words.

I have done what Bowyer desired, and it is plain if he would be guided by the Dean's intentions here they are. But I find he is a true bookseller, and therefore shall leave it to himself and Gilliver. If there be a legal title, I presume he will not leave it in any wise to oblige us; and if not, I will not presume to determine what I do not know, nor to meddle, if he rejects me as an arbitrator. But I understand by you that he has no right to the Scheme for paying the Debts, nor to the Intelligencers, in the latter of which Dr. Sheridan only has a right by a prior gift of the Dean's. Mr. Bowyer also puts these into his catalogue, and two pieces into the bargain, which are not the Dean's. It is a very comprehensive assignment, this he speaks of, which claims not only what is owned, but what is not owned, nay what is not his. He represented to me that it would be a hardship to print in our collection what the Dean might not care to own, and at the same time print them in his name.

Upon the whole, it is plain I was deceived in thinking Mr. Bowyer so civil and candid to the Dean and to me. When I suggested the best way he could take to please him, by separating the ludicrous things as the present collection, and leaving to him to

---

[1] From a copy in the Forster Collection.

print the serious or political, his reply was, he thought I could not persuade him that half was more than the whole; yet this is a great truth as authors well know, though booksellers do not. He also went so far as to ask what authority I had from the Dean that was prior to his assignment. When the authority was subsisting from the time he and I published the three volumes of our Miscellanies, and in the preface to them he may see, this other volume then intended by the Dean as well as myself. Since he has no other sense of my complying with his plea than to suppose he is arguing with me instead of Gilliver, pray assure him I will not take upon me to limit his pretensions or to enlarge them, but leave the matter between the booksellers as they can agree it, and that the only reason that made me offer any opinion about it, was his pretending to have his claim bounded by the Dean and me.

If his assignment be plain and legal, it is not I that will obstruct, or can obstruct, or intend to obstruct it. So there it rests. Only, let Mr. Bowyer know he has, by the modest manner in which he first proposed it, given me more trouble than I find he thanks me for. I am, Sir,

Your affectionate servant,
A. POPE.

MR. CLARKE TO WILLIAM BOWYER[1]

December 16, 1732.

I HOPE the great affairs about property in Irish wit are in a fair way of being amicably adjusted and that Mr. Pope and you are to divide the interest of it. It is awkward dealing with a man who stands foremost in his profession, and at such a distance from the rest of them, especially if he be a wit and critic. He then imagines himself absolute in his own province and that everything he meddles with belongs to it, disputing with him is touching his prerogative, and the way to fall under his resentment. Have you come off safe from the dangerous controversy, or is Mr. Pope less assuming since he has drawn off such a quantity of spleen with the Dunciad?

SAME TO SAME

May 5, 1733.

I WISH you joy of the peaceful situation you seem to be in at present, and hope your disputes are finished to your satisfaction. I have heard that ladies of the first rank begin to espouse your side of the question and fall upon your powerful adversary; that

---

[1] Nichols's "Literary Anecdotes of the Eighteenth Century," vol. ii, p. 10.

Lady Betty Germain particularly has written a most severe satire upon him. I have not seen it, but wonder you should take no notice that the fair sex are not at all in his interest. For my part I generally prefer peace before victory and your letters confirm me in these sentiments. You talk of the dispute with more candour than either the victors or the vanquished are used to do. But whatever are the terms of your accommodation, I like the issue of it extremely as it gives you leisure to talk of it with your friends in the country.

CHISWICK PRESS: CHARLES WHITTINGHAM AND CO.
TOOKS COURT, CHANCERY LANE, LONDON.

		DATE DUE	